Scoring Strategies for the TOEFL® iBT A Complete Guide

by

Bruce Stirling

Second Edition

Strategies and test samples by Bruce Stirling.
Graphics and layout design by Bruce Stirling.
Audio written and produced by Bruce Stirling.
Sound engineer Jon Conine.

Editors
Gretchen Anderson, Yosra Ben Chikh Brahim, Kateryna Kucher, Patricia Stirling, Martina Sulakova, Cora Van Laer.

Audio Talent
Gretchen Anderson, Jon Conine, Jennie Farnell, Bill and Liz Foster, Ami Kothari, Bruce Stirling, Patricia Stirling.

ISBN: 1-889057-84-3

ISBN: 978-1-889057-84-2

Published by *Nova Press*
9058 Lloyd Place
Los Angeles, CA USA 90069
1-800-949-6175
info@novapress.net
www.novapress.net

Contents

Scoring Strategies: *A New Approach*

Start with the Independent Essay

All TOEFL students want to know one thing: How can I get the highest possible TOEFL iBT score? Answer: Start by learning how to write a proficient independent essay. That is where this textbook begins. Why start with the independent essay? Because it is the best way and the fastest way to learn argument strategies. By learning how to write an independent essay, you will acquire the argument strategies you need for TOEFL iBT success.

Why Argument Strategies?

Argument strategies are critical for TOEFL iBT success. Why? Because they are the TOEFL iBT's main testing tool and because: 1) the English-speaking university system is based on the classical Greek method of teaching; 2) the classical Greek method of teaching is based on argument development and analysis. At English-speaking universities and colleges, students read essays (written arguments), write essays (written arguments), listen to lectures (verbal arguments), and express opinions (verbal arguments). The TOEFL iBT will test you in these four areas. By doing so, the TOEFL iBT recreates the English-speaking university experience, the foundation of which is argument development and analysis. That means to get the highest possible TOEFL iBT score, *you must understand those argument strategies used in English-speaking colleges and universities*. This textbook will teach you those argument strategies using the scoring strategy called *rhetorical analysis*.

Rhetorical Analysis

To get the highest possible TOEFL iBT score, you must also understand the iBT's testing method. You will learn that method by analyzing sample arguments at the start of each test section. By rhetorically analyzing sample arguments, you will:

- learn how the TOEFL iBT recycles opinion-based and fact-based arguments for testing purposes in all four test sections: reading, listening, speaking, writing;
- learn how to analyze, develop and deliver opinion-based and fact-based arguments using college-level rhetorical strategies;
- learn how most of the prompts and questions on the TOEFL iBT test your knowledge of college-level arguments;
- learn how to maximize scoring when practicing and on test day by combining your ability to analyze arguments with your ability to analyze argument-based questions;

- learn how to analyze your responses and identify those sections of the TOEFL iBT you need to focus on to maximize scoring when practicing and on test day;
- acquire the confidence you need to maximize your score on test day.

By rhetorically analyzing sample arguments and argument-based questions, you will learn how the scoring strategies in one section of the TOEFL iBT can be applied to the other three sections, and vice versa. This strategy is called *strategy recycling.*

Strategy Recycling

The TOEFL iBT is a game—a very challenging game—but a game all the same. Like all games, the TOEFL iBT uses tools to measure (test) your ability to play the game. Those testing tools are opinion-based and fact-based arguments. These two argument types do not change from task to task. For example, an opinion-based reading passage uses the same rhetorical strategies as an opinion-based lecture. The same holds true for fact-based arguments. In other words, the TOEFL iBT recycles the same two argument types for testing purposes. That means the scoring strategies you learn for both argument types *can be applied to any argument in any test section.* This process of recycling scoring strategies from one test section to the next will reduce the time it takes you to learn new strategies. More importantly, by recycling scoring strategies, you will realize that the TOEFL iBT is, like all games, predictable. Because it is predictable, you will know which tasks and questions to expect and how to analyze them with greater confidence and proficiency. This, in turn, will maximize your score on test day.

The R symbol means recycle. When you see it, it means you are recycling scoring strategies from previous sections.

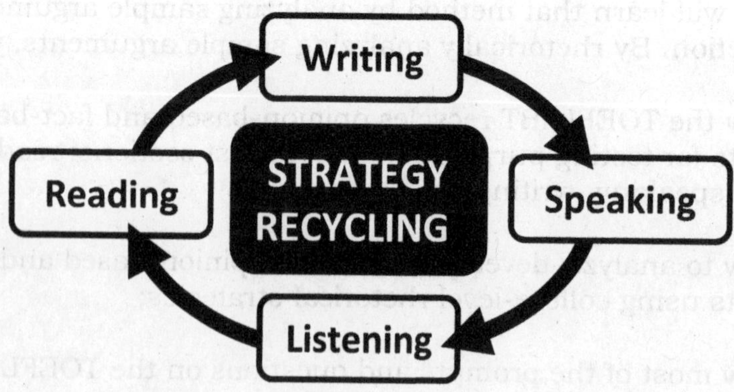

Your TOEFL iBT Range Score

When practicing, it is not possible to recreate test-center conditions thus it is not possible to calculate a final, accurate, single-number TOEFL iBT score. However, it is possible to calculate a range score. That is what this textbook will give you. This is how it works: 1) at the end of each section, you will do a section test; 2) you will total your section scores for a score out of 120 points; 3) your score will be the mid-point of a ten-point range. For example, the test-taker below scored 80/120 with 80 the mid-point of a ten-point range. This range score predicts that this test-taker will score in the 75-85 range on test day.

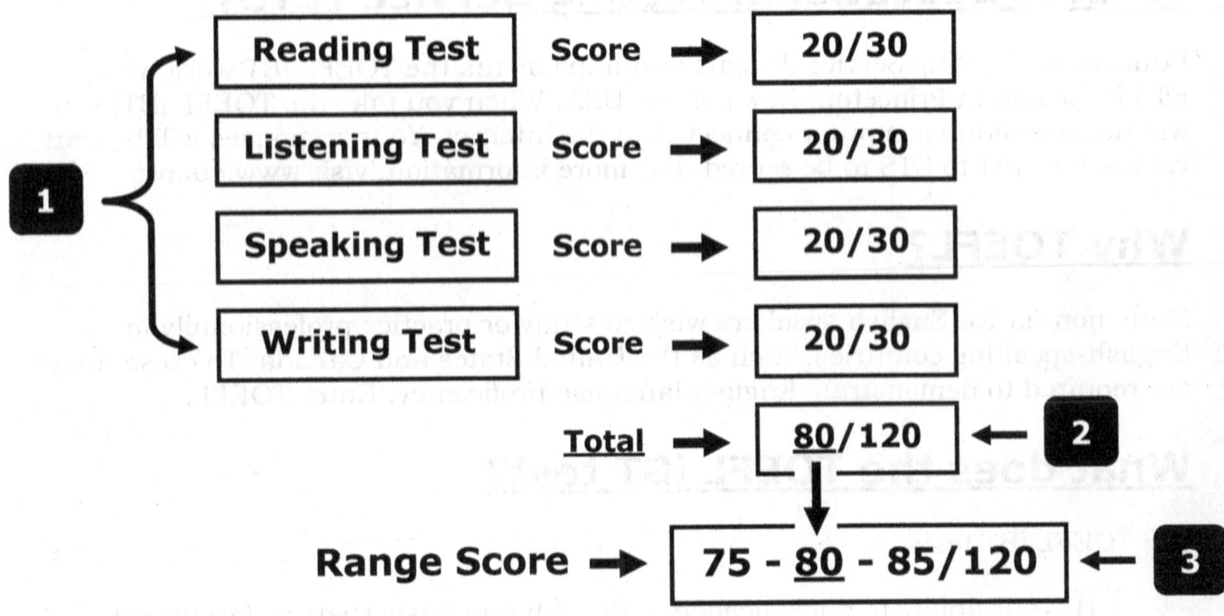

Also...

- ✓ This textbook uses a graphics-based teaching method. Classroom experience proves that students acquire scoring strategies faster and more proficiently through visualization. The visual learning method in this textbook is called *argument mapping.*
- ✓ This textbook provides easy-to-understand scoring rubrics for the speaking and writing sections (pages 694-706). These user-friendly rubrics will help you identify which areas you must revise to maximize scoring when practicing and on test day.
- ✓ This textbook includes real TOEFL questions from real TOEFL students.

Q *Q is a student question about the TOEFL iBT.*

A *A is the answer to that question.*

TOEFL® iBT Facts

What is the TOEFL iBT?

The TOEFL iBT is an English-language proficiency test. TOEFL means *test of English as a foreign language*. iBT means *internet-based test*.

What is Educational Testing Service (ETS)?

Educational Testing Service designs and implements the TOEFL iBT worldwide. ETS is located in Princeton, New Jersey, USA. When you take the TOEFL iBT, you will use a desktop computer connected to the internet. Your responses will be sent via the internet to ETS to be scored. For more information, visit www.ets.org.

Why TOEFL?

Many non native English speakers wish to study or practice professionally in English-speaking countries, such as the United States and Canada. To do so, they are required to demonstrate English-language proficiency. Enter TOEFL.

What does the TOEFL iBT test?

The TOEFL iBT tests:

1) your ability to apply academic English and basic rhetoric (argument strategies) across four skill sets: reading, listening, speaking, writing;

2) your ability to learn new material (arguments) at the academic English level, then answer questions about that material in a timed environment.

What are the topics?

The topics used for testing are those found in first and second year university life science and humanities courses, such as biology, economics, art, geology, zoology, literature, and history. The TOEFL iBT does not test applied sciences, such as physics and mathematics, nor does it test current events.

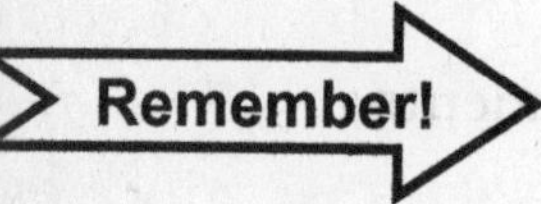

You do not need to study life sciences and the humanities before you take the TOEFL iBT. The TOEFL iBT will teach you all you need to know to answer questions specific to the task. In this way, the TOEFL iBT is "a learning test."

The following chart illustrates how the TOEFL iBT measures English-language proficiency, and why argument strategies are essential for TOEFL iBT success.

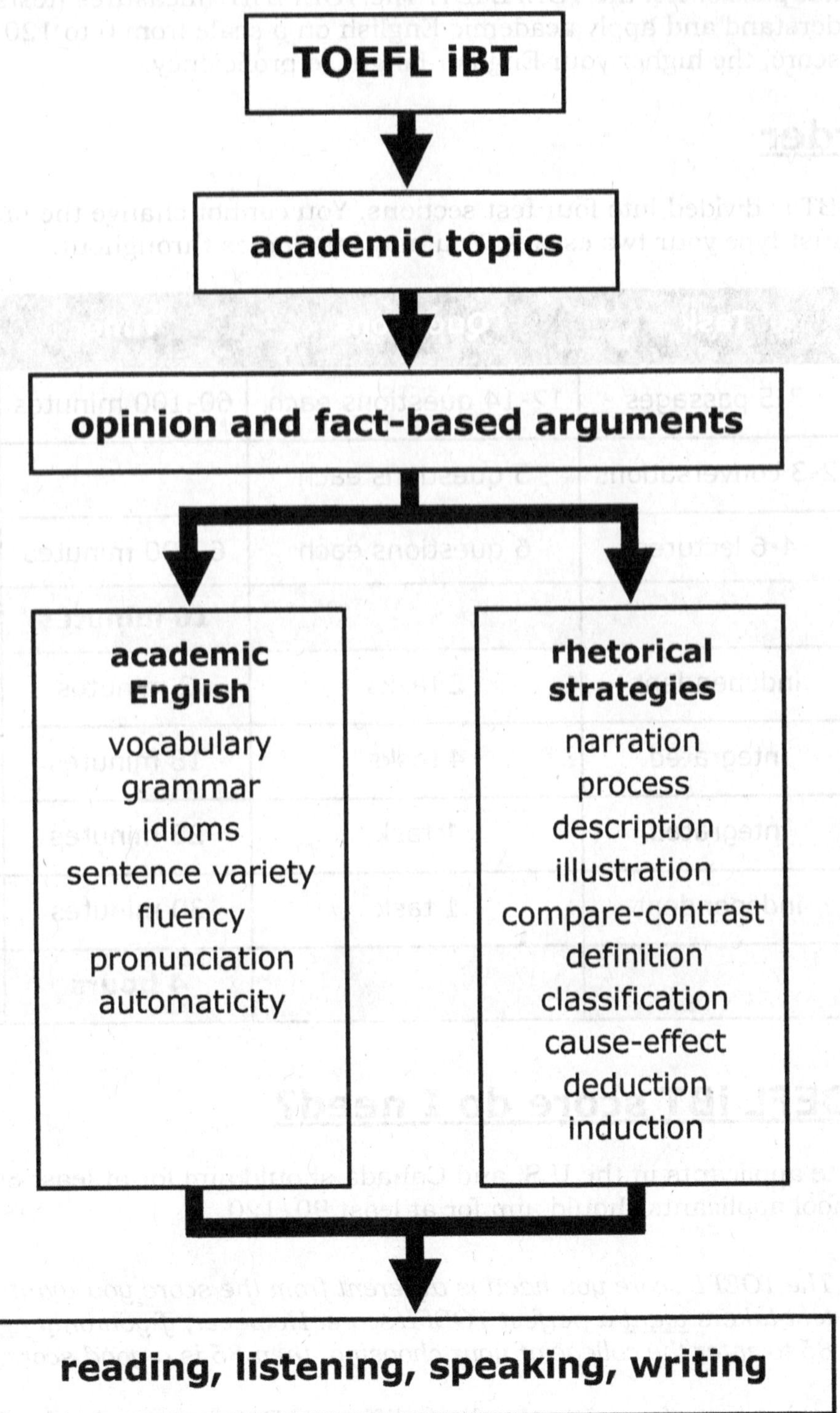

Can I fail the TOEFL iBT?

No. You cannot pass or fail the TOEFL iBT. The TOEFL iBT measures (tests) your ability to understand and apply academic English on a scale from 0 to 120. The higher your score, the higher your English-language proficiency.

Task Order

The TOEFL iBT is divided into four test sections. You cannot change the task order. You must type your two essays. You may take notes throughout.

Section	Task	Questions	Time	Score
Reading	3-5 passages	12-14 questions each	60-100 minutes	30/30
Listening	2-3 conversations	5 questions each		
	4-6 lectures	6 questions each	60-90 minutes	30/30
BREAK			**10 minutes**	
Speaking	independent	2 tasks	2 minutes	
	integrated	4 tasks	18 minutes	30/30
Writing	integrated	1 task	23 minutes	
	independent	1 task	30 minutes	30/30
TOTAL			**4 hours**	**120/120**

What TOEFL iBT score do I need?

Undergraduate applicants in the U.S. and Canada should aim for at least 80/120. Graduate school applicants should aim for at least 90/120.

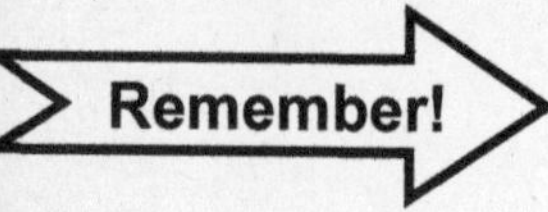

The TOEFL score you need is different from the score you want. All test-takers <u>want</u> a perfect TOEFL score. However, if you only <u>need</u> 85 to enter the college of your choosing, then 85 is a good score.

The TOEFL requirements for each school are different. Before you take the TOEFL iBT, contact the school of your choosing and find out their TOEFL requirements. Professional license applicants should consult their licensing agencies for TOEFL requirements.

The TOEFL PBT and CBT

The TOEFL PBT (paper-based test) is the original TOEFL test. It was replaced by the CBT (computer-based test), which was replaced by the iBT (internet-based test). The CBT has been discontinued. The PBT is still offered at select locations. Visit www.ets.org for PBT test locations. See the chart below for score comparisons.

TOEFL iBT	TOEFL PBT	TOEFL CBT
120	677	300
110	637	270
100	600-603	250
90	577	233
80	550	213
70	523	193
60	497	170

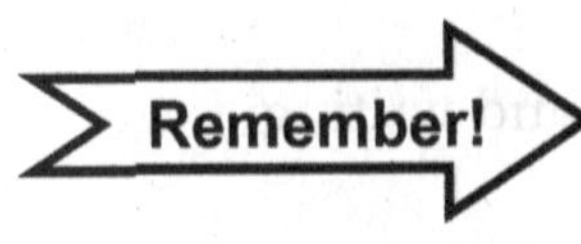

If you are applying for undergraduate or graduate school in the United States or Canada, do not take the PBT. American and Canadian schools want to know if you can communicate verbally at the academic level. The iBT tests speaking proficiency at the academic level. The PBT does not test speaking.

Do not take the PBT simply because you have heard it is easier than the iBT. The TOEFL test you take will depend on the requirements of the school/agency to which you are applying.

How important is TOEFL in the admissions process?

Your TOEFL iBT score is only one part of your university/college application. You will also be required to write a personal essay, submit your official grades, and provide letters of recommendation. You might also be interviewed. Most U.S. and Canadian universities and colleges base admittance on your application as a whole. If you are applying as an undergraduate in the United States, you must also submit an SAT score.

What is the SAT?

SAT means *Scholastic Aptitude Test.* American high school students take the SAT upon graduation. The SAT tests knowledge of high-school reading, writing, and math. A foreign-born student applying as an undergraduate to a U.S. university or college is required to submit an SAT score. Visit www.ets.org for more about the SAT.

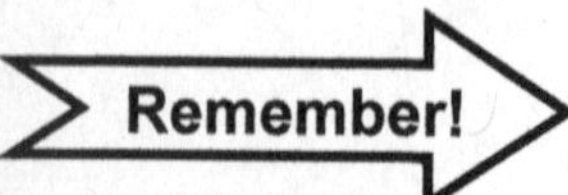

Ask those schools to which you are applying for their SAT requirements, and for any other test requirements.

How long is my TOEFL iBT score good for?

Your TOEFL iBT score is good for two years. You cannot renew your score. You must retake the test.

How do I register for the TOEFL iBT?

You can register for TOEFL online or by phone. In the United States, the busiest registration times are at the end of each school semester when TOEFL courses end and TOEFL students are ready to take the test. The TOEFL test is very popular. Register early. For registration information, visit www.ets.org.

How should I prepare for the TOEFL iBT?

1. Take advanced ESL classes to practice reading, listening, speaking, and writing at the college academic level.

2. Take a TOEFL iBT class. By doing so, you will meet test-takers with similar goals and interests. Chances are you will meet someone who has already taken the TOEFL iBT. Learn from his/her experiences.

3. Improve your typing. Classroom experience indicates that a majority of TOEFL students are not proficient typists. Poor typing can reduce your writing score.

4. Read. For advanced English speakers, reading English material is the best way to acquire an academic-level vocabulary.

5. Do not take the TOEFL iBT without preparation. Many test-takers have taken the TOEFL iBT without preparation only to realize the TOEFL iBT was much harder than they had expected.

6. Visit Educational Testing Service's web site (www.ets.org). Everything you need to know about TOEFL is there. While at www.ets.org, take "the TOEFL iBT test tour." Also, do the "free TOEFL iBT test samples" and read "TOEFL iBT Test Tips." By doing so, you will familiarize yourself with the TOEFL iBT.

7. Understand that the TOEFL iBT is an academic English-language proficiency test that uses arguments as its main testing tool. Look at the following chart.

Section	Tasks	Argument Type Used For Testing
Reading	3-5 passages	The passages are excerpts of opinion-based and fact-based arguments from university texts.
Listening	2-3 conversations	The conversations are opinion-based and fact-based arguments.
Listening	4-6 lectures	The lectures are fact-based verbal arguments.
Speaking	2 independent	These tasks are opinion-based arguments.
Speaking	4 integrated	These tasks are fact-based arguments. Some combine both fact-based and opinion-based arguments.
Writing	integrated essay	This task combines two opinion-based arguments and one fact-based argument.
Writing	independent essay	This task is an opinion-based argument.

As the chart on the previous page illustrates, the TOEFL iBT uses both written and verbal arguments to test your ability to learn and apply academic English. In short, the TOEFL iBT is all arguments. Therefore, to get the highest possible TOEFL iBT score, you must know argument strategies, specifically:

- how to analyze and summarize opinion-based and fact-based written arguments (reading section);
- how to analyze and summarize opinion-based and fact-based verbal arguments (listening section);
- how to develop, deliver, and summarize opinion-based and fact-based verbal arguments (speaking section);
- how to develop, deliver, and summarize opinion-based and fact-based written arguments (writing section).

This textbook will teach you how to do all that - and more.

Q *What about grammar and vocabulary? Are they important?*

A *Proficient grammar and a good vocabulary are critical for TOEFL iBT success. However, grammar and vocabulary are both integral parts of argument development and are rated as such, as you will learn.*

Q *Do I need to learn any special computer skills before I take the test?*

A *No. The TOEFL iBT is user-friendly. You will use a mouse, a keyboard, and a headset with an attached microphone. If you have any questions, the test center manager will help you.*

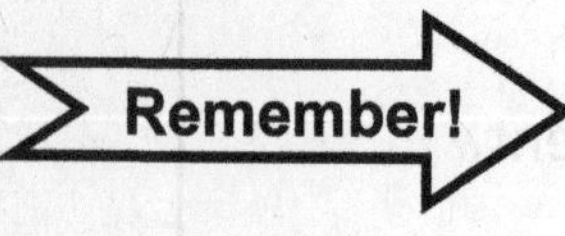

Visit www.ets.org and watch the video "Welcome to the TOEFL iBT Testing Site" (http://www.ets.org/s/toefl/flash/15571_toefl_prometric.html). This excellent video tells you what to expect and what to do, step-by-step, on test day at the test center.

Q *Does ETS reuse old TOEFL tests?*

A *No. ETS does not recycle old iBT or PBT tests. The test you take will be new and will not be used again.*

Argument Strategies

This section will introduce you to argument strategies essential for TOEFL iBT success.

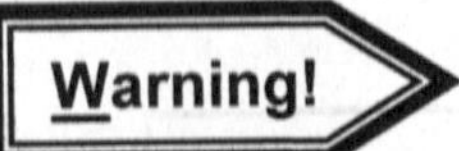

Do not skip this section. The strategies in this textbook are all based on the strategies in this section.

What is an Argument?

An argument is the process of presenting an opinion for the purpose of persuading an audience. For the TOEFL iBT, this argument type is called an *opinion-based argument*. An opinion-based argument can be either verbal or written. An argument can also inform an audience by presenting facts. For the TOEFL iBT, this argument type is called a *fact-based argument*. A fact-based argument can be either verbal or written.

Proficiency = Coherence

An argument that successfully persuades or informs, or does both, demonstrates *coherence*. Coherence means the argument is clear and logical because it demonstrates *proficiency*. For the TOEFL iBT, proficiency means *skill and knowledge* of the English language at the academic level.

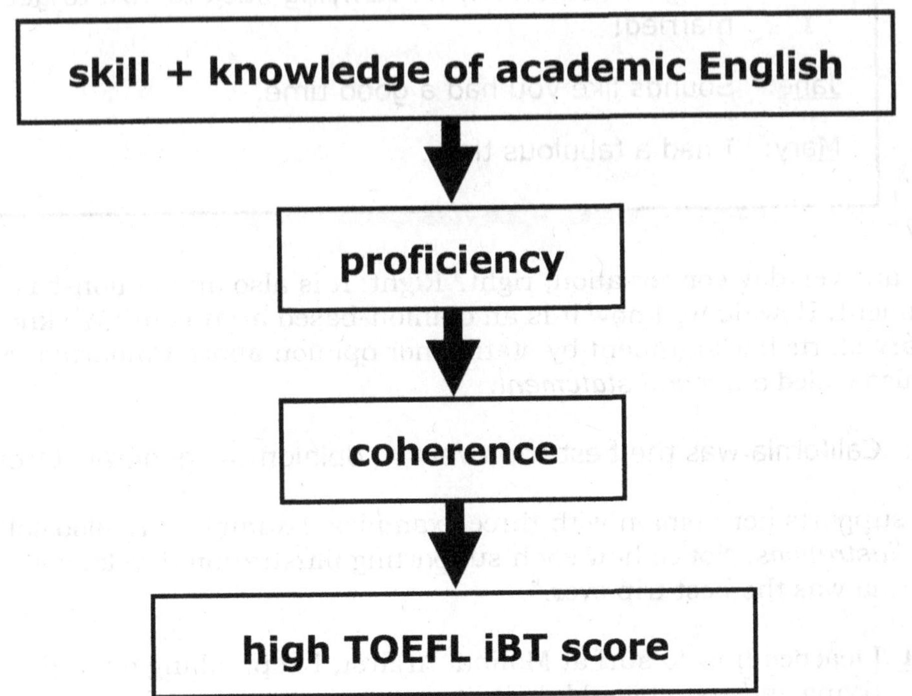

A coherent argument starts with a clear method of organization. There are two ways to organize an argument when speaking and when writing: deduction and induction. Let's start with an opinion-based verbal argument and deduction.

Opinion-Based Argument: *Deduction*

An opinion-based, verbal argument states an opinion, then supports it. Read the following dialogue.

Jane: Hi, Mary. How was California?

Mary: California was the best trip ever. I learned how to surf at Malibu. At first, I kept falling off, but I kept trying and soon I could do it. It was great. And the sights.

Jane: Tell me.

Mary: I visited Hollywood first, Disneyland next, and Catalina Island last. There is so much to see and do. I was exhausted. Did I tell you about Jack?

Jane: Jack?

Mary: I met him at Venice Beach. He's a movie producer. He's so handsome. As a matter of fact, we're having dinner tonight. Tomorrow, we're flying back to L.A. to get married!

Jane: Sounds like you had a good time.

Mary: I had a fabulous time.

This is just an everyday conversation, right? Right. It is also an opinion-based, verbal argument. How do we know it is an opinion-based argument? We know because Mary starts her argument by stating her opinion about California. An opinion is also called a *general statement*.

Mary: California was the best trip ever = opinion = general statement

Next, Mary supports her opinion with three examples. Examples are also called *supporting illustrations*. Notice how each supporting illustration develops a reason why "California was the best trip ever."

example #1 I learned how to surf at Malibu. At first, I kept falling off, but I kept trying and soon I could do it. It was great.

example #2 And the sights. I visited Hollywood first, Disneyland next, and Catalina Island last. There is so much to see and do. I was exhausted.

example #3 Did I tell you about Jack? I met him at Venice Beach. He's a movie producer. He's so handsome. As a matter of fact, we're having dinner tonight. Tomorrow, we're flying back to L.A. to get married!

In the end, Mary makes a conclusion based on her opinion and her examples. A conclusion is also called a *general statement.*

Mary: I had a fabulous time = conclusion = general statement

Where did Mary have "a fabulous time"? In California, of course.

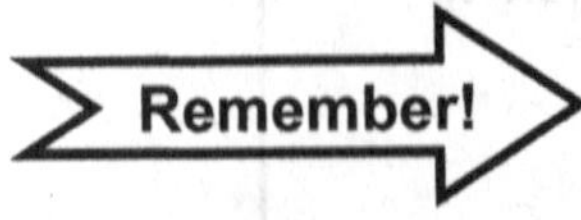
Remember!

When a speaker or a writer makes a conclusion based on his/her opinion and supporting illustrations, he/she is using deduction as the method of organizing his/her opinion-based argument.

By mapping out Mary's dialogue, we can see how she uses deduction as a method of organizing her opinion-based, verbal argument. Note how the opinion and conclusion are called *general.* Note also how the examples are called *specific.*

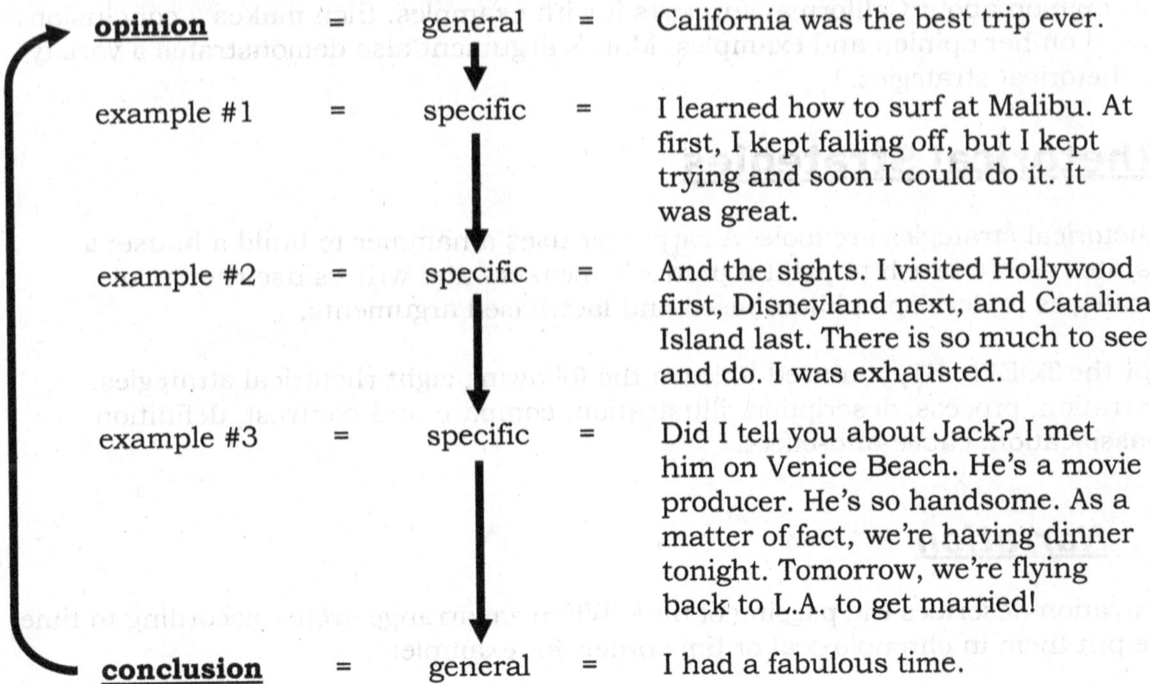
opinion = general = California was the best trip ever.
example #1 = specific = I learned how to surf at Malibu. At first, I kept falling off, but I kept trying and soon I could do it. It was great.
example #2 = specific = And the sights. I visited Hollywood first, Disneyland next, and Catalina Island last. There is so much to see and do. I was exhausted.
example #3 = specific = Did I tell you about Jack? I met him on Venice Beach. He's a movie producer. He's so handsome. As a matter of fact, we're having dinner tonight. Tomorrow, we're flying back to L.A. to get married!
conclusion = general = I had a fabulous time.

Note how Mary's **conclusion** confirms her **opinion**, and takes us right back to the start. This closed or formal structure tells us that Mary is using deduction as a method of organizing her opinion-based argument.

By adding **transitions** (connecting words), we can change Mary's opinion-based, verbal argument into an opinion-based, written argument.

California was the best trip ever.

For example, I learned how to surf at Malibu. At first, I kept falling off, but I kept trying and soon I could do it. It was great.

And the sights. I visited Hollywood first, Disneyland next, and Catalina Island last. There is so much to see and do. I was exhausted.

Also, did I tell you about Jack? I met him at Venice Beach. He's a movie producer. He's so handsome. As a matter of fact, we're having dinner tonight. Tomorrow, we're flying back to L.A. to get married!

In conclusion, I had a fabulous time.

TOEFL calls this opinion-based, written argument an *independent essay*. Yes, this independent essay is short and simple; nevertheless, it demonstrates coherence. Why? Because it starts with a clear method of organization in which Mary states her opinion about California, supports it with examples, then makes a conclusion based on her opinion and examples. Mary's argument also demonstrates a variety of rhetorical strategies.

Rhetorical Strategies

Rhetorical strategies are tools. A carpenter uses a hammer to build a house; a painter uses a brush to paint a portrait; speakers and writers use rhetorical strategies to develop opinion-based and fact-based arguments.

For the TOEFL iBT, you need to learn the following eight rhetorical strategies: narration, process, description, illustration, compare-and-contrast, definition, classification, cause-and-effect.

1. *Narration*

Narration describes the passing of time. When we arrange events according to time, we put them in chronological or time order, for example:

a. Yesterday, Jane got up at seven o'clock and took a shower. After that she had breakfast, then rode the bus to work. When she got to work, she checked her email, then discussed the new business plan with her colleagues.

b. Every Monday after class, Eduardo goes to the gym and practices karate for three hours. When he is finished, he goes shopping, then takes the bus home.

2. *Process*

Process means putting events in sequential or step-by-step order. In the following examples, notice how each step-by-step process also describes the passing of time.

a. When making tea, first boil water. Next, put a tea bag into a cup. When the water is boiling, pour the water into the cup. Finally, add milk and sugar as you prefer.

b. *Titanic* hit an iceberg, broke in two, then sank.

3. *Description*

Description creates pictures of people, places and things using adjectives and adverbs. Description appeals to the senses: smell, sight, taste, hearing, and touch.

a. Jon, the bass player in the band, is wearing a black leather jacket, faded jeans and red cowboy boots.

b. The old man lived alone in an old house high on a rugged cliff overlooking a stormy sea.

4. *Illustration*

Illustration means example or supporting illustration, for example:

a. There are many places to go for a honeymoon. For example, many newlyweds go to Hawaii.

b. When you visit Manhattan, I suggest you visit Times Square and Central Park.

5. *Compare-and-Contrast*

Compare-and-contrast describes the differences and similarities between two or more objects, people, or ideas. Compare-and-contrast also describes differences in opinion, for example:

a. Joan tried the apple pie and decided the cherry pie was sweeter.

b. Fisal believes that all high school students should wear school uniforms; however, Mohamed believes that students should have the right to choose what they want to wear.

6. *Definition*

A definition is a detailed description of a person, place, object, or idea. The purpose of a definition is to give meaning, for example:

a. The dodo was a flightless bird native to New Zealand.

b. The TOEFL iBT is an English-language proficiency test developed and implemented by Educational Testing Service (ETS).

7. *Classification*

To classify means to put people, things, or ideas into sub groups under a main topic, for example:

a. There are three kinds of wine: red, white and rosé.

b. TOEFL, TOEIC and IELTS are English-language proficiency tests.

8. *Cause-and-Effect*

Cause-and-effect means action and result. We use cause-and-effect to describe an action and the results, or consequences, of that action, for example:

a. Cora studied hard and got a high TOEFL score.

b. Global warming is melting the ice at the South Pole.

More about Cause-and-Effect

Of the eight-above rhetorical strategies, the most important one for the TOEFL iBT is cause-and-effect. Why? Because reasons are created by cause-and-effect relationships. Reason identification and application is an integral part of the TOEFL iBT testing method. The reading and listening sections contain a variety of reason-based questions. For the writing and speaking tasks, you must identify and apply reasons when developing, delivering, and summarizing opinion-based and fact-based arguments.

What is a Reason?

A reason is the cause or the effect in a cause-and-effect relationship. Look at the following example. Note how the *cause* is the reason in the first example.

Question: Why did Eva get a high TOEFL score? What was the reason?

Answer: She studied hard (cause).

Look at another example. Note how the *effect* is the reason.

Man: Why should I study for the TOEFL test?

Woman: You should study (cause) because you will get a higher score (effect).

Man: A higher score (effect)? That's a good reason to study for TOEFL.

One way to state a reason is by using an *adverb clause of reason*. An adverb clause of reason begins with a subordinating conjunction, such as ***because***, ***since***, or ***owing to the fact that***, for example:

1. Anna exercises ***because*** *it is a great way to reduce stress.*

2. Veronica needs to buy a car ***since*** *she is always late for work.*

3. ***Owing to the fact that*** it is raining, Renata did not go jogging.

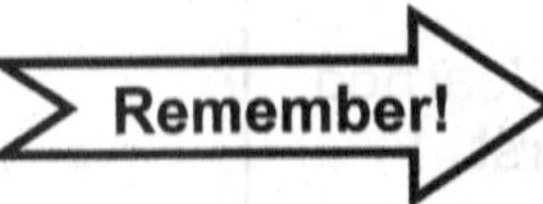

We will return to reason identification and application using cause-and-effect throughout this textbook.

Now go back to Mary's argument on page 25. Look at the rhetorical strategies she uses to develop her examples. These, in turn, support her opinion and conclusion.

illustration

places to visit: Malibu Beach, Hollywood, Disneyland, Catalina Island, Venice Beach.
things to do: surfing, sightseeing, meeting guys (Jack).

description

surfing at Malibu: "It was great."
after sightseeing: "I was exhausted."
Jack: "He's so handsome."
Jack: "He's a movie producer."

process

surfing: "At first, I kept falling off, but I kept trying and soon I could do it."
sightseeing: I visited Hollywood first, Disneyland next, and Catalina Island last.

cause-effect

surfing: "At first, I kept falling off (effect), but I kept trying (cause) and soon I could do it (effect)."
Jack: "I met him at Venice Beach." Go to Venice Beach and meet Jack (cause), fall in love (effect) and get married (effect).
Mary: She goes to California (cause) and her life changes completely (effect).
Jack: He visits Venice Beach (cause) and his life changes too (effect).

Opinion-Based Argument: *Induction*

Induction is another way to organize an opinion-based argument, be it verbal or written. Look at the following examples. Note how the deductive response begins with an opinion. In contrast, the inductive response develops three examples first, then ends with a conclusion (opinion) based on the examples.

Deduction

California was the best trip ever.

I learned how to surf at Malibu. At first, I kept falling off, but I kept trying and soon I could do it. It was great.

And the sights. I visited Hollywood first, Disneyland next, and Catalina Island last. There is so much to see and do. I was exhausted.

Did I tell you about Jack? I met him on Venice Beach. He's a movie producer. He's so handsome. As a matter of fact, we're having dinner tonight. Tomorrow, we're flying back to L.A. to get married!

I had a fabulous time.

Induction

When I was in California, I learned how to surf at Malibu. At first, I kept falling off, but I kept trying, and soon I could do it. It was great.

And the sights. I visited Hollywood first, Disneyland next, and Catalina Island last. There is so much to see and do. I was exhausted.

Did I tell you about Jack? I met him at Venice Beach. He's a movie producer. He's so handsome. As a matter of fact, we're having dinner tonight. Tomorrow, we're flying back to L.A. to get married!

I had a fabulous time in California.

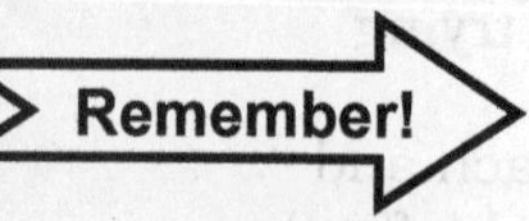

When a speaker or a writer starts an opinion-based argument with examples—then makes a conclusion based on those examples—he/she is using induction as the method of organizing his/her argument.

Q *Which is better, deduction or induction?*

A *Neither. They are simply two ways to organize an opinion-based argument when writing or when speaking.*

Developing an Opinion

The most important part of an opinion-based argument is the opinion. The opinion signals the start of the argument. An opinion is also called a *general statement* or *thesis*.

Is the opinion also the main topic?

No. Look at the two sentences below.

A. I think California was the best trip ever.

B. I think California was the worst trip ever.

In sentence A, the writer will write about California. California, therefore, is the main topic (also called the main idea or main subject). The writer's opinion is "*...was the best trip ever.*" In sentence B, the speaker will speak about California. Once again, California is the main topic. However, the speaker's opinion is "*...was the worst trip ever.*" As you can see, the main topic (California) is the same in both sentences. However, the writer and the speaker express different opinions about California (best trip vs. worst trip).

Q

How do I know if a sentence is an opinion or not?

By asking these five questions.

1. Is it a grammatically-complete sentence?
2. Is it arguable?
3. Is it supportable?
4. Is it a question or not?
5. Does it express a main topic and a controlling idea?

Go back to Mary's argument on page 25. Mary said, "California was the best trip ever." That's her opinion. But how do we know it is an opinion without guessing? By asking the five questions.

1. Is it a grammatically-complete sentence?

Yes. The sentence "California was the best trip ever" is a grammatically complete sentence. It has a subject, a verb, and a tense.

2. Is it arguable?

Yes. Mary has obviously considered her other vacations and concluded that California was the best compared to the rest. Where were her other vacations? We do not know. They are implied (suggested).

3. Is it supportable?

Yes. Mary supports her opinion with three examples: 1) learning how to surf at Malibu; 2) going sightseeing; 3) meeting Jack.

4. Is it a question or not?

Mary's opinion is not a question.

An opinion is never a question.

5. Does it express a main topic and a controlling idea?

An opinion consists of two parts: the main topic and the controlling idea. Look at the following opinion.

Personally, I think that all cars should be hybrids.

In this opinion, the main topic is all cars. To find the controlling idea, simply ask, "What about them (all cars)?" Answer: S*hould be hybrids* = the controlling idea.

Look at the next opinion.

I believe that downloading music off the web and not paying for it is a crime.

In this opinion, the main topic is downloading music off the web. To find the controlling idea, ask, "What about it (downloading music off the web)?" Answer: *Not paying for it (downloaded music) is a crime* = the controlling idea.

Next, look at Mary's opinion.

California was the best trip ever.

California is the main topic. What about it (California)? Answer: *Was the best trip ever* = the controlling idea.

Does Mary's opinion state a main topic and a controlling idea? Answer: Yes.

Based on the five questions, is the sentence "California was the best trip ever" an opinion? Answer: Yes.

What is not an Opinion?

Follow these four rules.

1. An opinion is not a statement of fact.

a. *Alaska is a big state.*

This is not an opinion. It is a fact therefore not arguable.

b. *Californian red wine is the best in the world.*

This is an opinion. It is a complete sentence, arguable, supportable, is not a question, and expresses a main topic and a controlling idea.

2. An opinion is not a question.

a. *Is progress always good?*

This is not an opinion. This is a question. An opinion is never a question.

b. *I believe that global warming is the number one threat in the world today.*

This is an opinion. It is a complete sentence, arguable, supportable, is not a question, and expresses a main topic and a controlling idea.

3. An opinion is not a sentence fragment.

a. *Cairo: the most beautiful city in Africa.*

This is not an opinion. It is not a complete sentence. It is a sentence fragment. It is missing the verb "is."

b. *Vancouver, British Columbia is the most beautiful city in the world.*

This is an opinion. It is a complete sentence, arguable, supportable, is not a question, and expresses a main topic and a controlling idea.

4. An opinion does not simply announce the topic you will argue.

a. *In this essay, I will talk about the qualities of a good boss.*

This is not an opinion. The test-taker is simply announcing (telling the reader or listener) what he/she will write/speak about.

b. *Personally, I think that teenagers must finish high school before they can get a driver's license.*

This is an opinion. It is a complete sentence, arguable, supportable, is not a question, and expresses a main topic and a controlling idea.

Fact-Based Argument: *Deduction*

The TOEFL iBT also uses verbal and written fact-based arguments for testing. A fact-based argument does not state an opinion. Instead, a fact-based argument begins by stating a general truth or *premise*. Read the following example.

> Rice is classified according to grain size.
>
> First is long-grain rice. An example is Basmati. It is long and slender, and low in starch. When cooked, it becomes light and fluffy with the grains separating.
>
> Next is medium-grain rice. An example is Calrose. This type of rice is three times as long as it is wide and has more starch than long-grain rice. When cooked, medium-grain rice tends to stick together.
>
> Finally, there is short-grain rice. An example is Arborio. It has the highest starch level. It is kernel-shaped and becomes very moist and tender when cooked.
>
> As illustrated, rice is classified according to grain size.

Note how this fact-based argument uses deduction as the method of organization. However, instead of starting with an opinion, it starts with a premise. A premise is also called a *general statement*.

Rice is classified according to grain size = premise = general statement

Note how this premise is supported by three examples. Note also how each supporting illustration develops and supports the fact (the premise) that "Rice is classified according to grain size."

example #1 First is long-grain rice. An example is Basmati. It is long and slender, and low in starch. When cooked, it becomes light and fluffy with the grains separating.

example #2 Next is medium-grain rice. An example is Calrose. This type of rice is three times as long as it is wide and has more starch than long-grain rice. When cooked, medium-grain rice tends to stick together.

example #3 Finally, there is short-grain rice. An example is Arborio. It has the highest starch level. It is kernel-shaped and becomes very moist and tender when cooked.

Finally, the speaker or writer makes a conclusion based on the premise supported by the three examples. Note that the conclusion is simply the restated premise.

conclusion = As illustrated, rice is classified according to grain size.

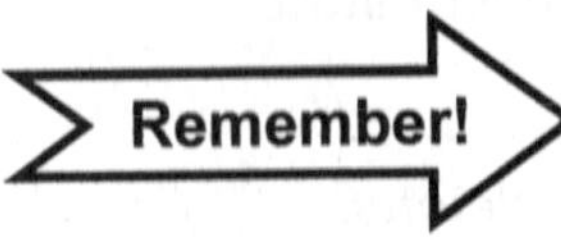
Remember!

When a speaker or a writer makes a conclusion based on the premise and the supporting examples, he/she is using deduction as the method of organizing his/her fact-based argument.

By mapping out this fact-based argument, we can see how the writer or speaker is using deduction as the method of organizing his/her argument.

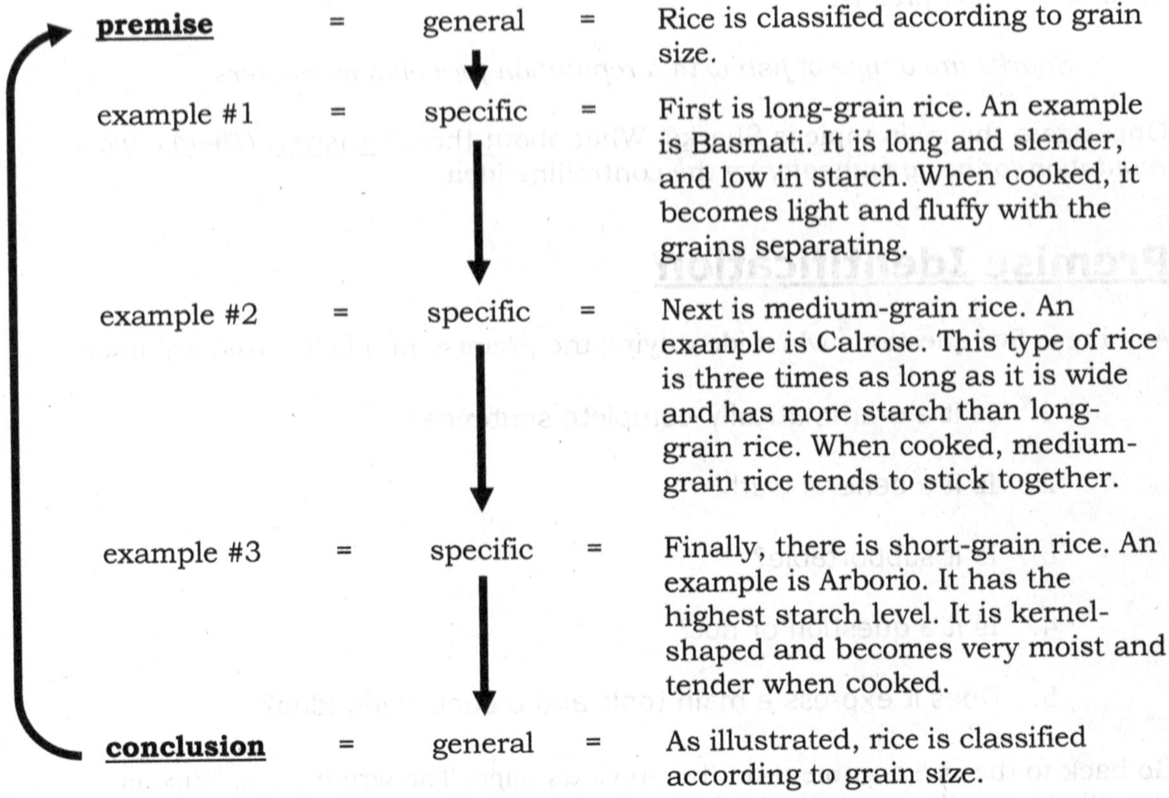
premise = general = Rice is classified according to grain size.
example #1 = specific = First is long-grain rice. An example is Basmati. It is long and slender, and low in starch. When cooked, it becomes light and fluffy with the grains separating.
example #2 = specific = Next is medium-grain rice. An example is Calrose. This type of rice is three times as long as it is wide and has more starch than long-grain rice. When cooked, medium-grain rice tends to stick together.
example #3 = specific = Finally, there is short-grain rice. An example is Arborio. It has the highest starch level. It is kernel-shaped and becomes very moist and tender when cooked.
conclusion = general = As illustrated, rice is classified according to grain size.

In this example, note how the **conclusion** restates the **premise**, and takes us right back to the start. This closed or formal structure means the speaker or writer is using deduction as the method of organizing his/her fact-based argument.

Developing a Premise

For the TOEFL iBT, each fact-based reading passage, lecture, dialogue, and speaking and writing prompt will have a premise. Some premises are stated directly. Others are implied (not directly written or spoken). The premise will state the main topic and the controlling idea. Look at the following examples.

Sharks are a type of fish with streamlined bodies and cartilage skeletons.

In this premise, the main topic is Sharks. To find the controlling idea, ask, "What about them (sharks)? Answer: *Are a type of fish with streamlined bodies and cartilage skeletons* = the controlling idea.

Look at the next premise.

Sharks are a type of fish with a reputation for being maneaters.

Once again the main topic is Sharks. What about them? Answer*: (They) have a reputation for being maneaters* = the controlling idea.

Premise Identification

Ask these five questions when identifying the premise in a fact-based argument.

1. Is it a grammatically-complete sentence?
2. Is it a general truth?
3. Is it supportable?
4. Is it a question or not?
5. Does it express a main topic and a controlling idea?

Go back to the rice argument on the previous page. The writer says, "Rice is classified according to grain size." That is the premise, the general truth. But how do we know it is a premise without guessing? By asking these five questions.

1. Is it a grammatically-complete sentence?

Yes. The sentence "Rice is classified according to grain size" is a grammatically complete sentence. It has a subject, a verb, and a tense.

2. Is it a general truth?

Yes. Scientists, chefs, and farmers worldwide all agree it is true: *Rice is classified according to grain size.*

3. Is it supportable?

Yes. The writer supports the premise with three examples: 1) long-grain Basmati rice; 2) medium-grain Calrose rice; 3) short-grain Arborio rice.

4. Is it a question or not?

The premise "Rice is classified according to grain size" is not a question. A premise is never a question.

5. Does it express a main topic and a controlling idea?

A premise consists of two parts: the main idea and the controlling idea. Look at the following premise.

Rice is classified according to grain size.

In this premise, the main topic is Rice. To find the controlling idea, ask, "What about it (rice)?" Answer: *Can be classified according to grain size* = the controlling idea..

Does this premise express a main idea and a controlling idea? Answer: Yes.

Based on the five questions is the sentence "Rice is classified according to grain size" a premise? Answer: Yes.

What is not a Premise?

Follow these four rules.

1. A premise is not an opinion.

a. *Alaska is the greatest state in the United States.*

This is not a premise. It is someone's opinion therefore arguable.

b. *Alaska has a resource-based economy.*

This is a premise. It is a complete sentence, a general truth, supportable, not a question, and it expresses a main topic and a controlling idea.

2. A premise is not a question.

a. *Are hurricanes a naturally occurring phenomena?*

This is not a premise. This is a question. A premise is never a question.

b. *A hurricane is a naturally occurring phenomena.*

This is a premise. It is a complete sentence, a general truth, supportable, not a question, and it expresses a main topic and a controlling idea.

3. A premise is not a sentence fragment.

a. *Google: a web-based search engine.*

This is not a premise. It is not a complete sentence. It is a sentence fragment. It is missing the verb "is."

b. *Google is a popular web-based search engine.*

This is a premise. It is a complete sentence, a general truth, supportable, not a question, and it expresses a main topic and a controlling idea.

4. A premise does not simply announce the topic you will argue.

a. *In this essay, I will talk about English-language proficiency tests.*

This is not a premise. The writer (or speaker) is simply announcing (telling the reader or listener) what he/she will write/speak about.

b. *The TOEFL iBT tests English-language proficiency at the academic level.*

This is a premise. It is a complete sentence, a general truth, supportable, not a question, and it expresses a main topic and a controlling idea.

Fact-Based Argument: *Induction*

Induction is another way of organizing a fact-based argument, be it verbal or written. Look at the following examples. Note how the deductive response begins with a premise. In contrast, the inductive response develops three examples first, then ends with a conclusion (premise) based on the examples.

Deduction

Rice is classified according to grain size.

First is long-grain rice. An example is Basmati. It is long and slender, and low in starch. When cooked, it becomes light and fluffy with the grains separating.

Next is medium-grain rice. An example is Calrose. This type of rice is three times as long as it is wide and has more starch than long-grain rice. When cooked, medium-grain rice tends to stick together.

Finally, there is short-grain rice. An example is Arborio. It has the highest starch level. It is kernel-shaped and becomes very moist and tender when cooked.

As illustrated, rice is classified according to grain size.

Induction

An example of a long-grain rice is Basmati. It is long and slender, and low in starch. When cooked, it becomes light and fluffy with the grains separating.

Next is medium-grain rice. An example is Calrose. This type of rice is three times as long as it is wide and has more starch than long-grain rice. When cooked, medium-grain rice tends to stick together.

Finally, there is short-grain rice. An example is Arborio. It has the highest starch level. It is kernel-shaped and becomes very moist and tender when cooked.

As illustrated, rice is classified according to grain size.

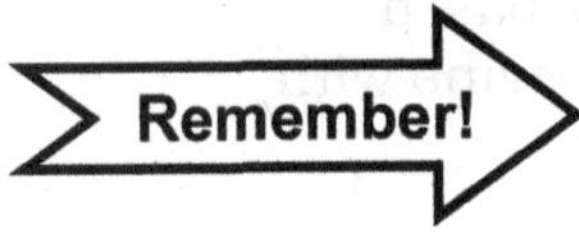

When a writer or a speaker starts a fact-based argument with examples—then makes a conclusion based on those examples—he/she is using induction as the method of organizing his/her argument.

This fact-based argument also demonstrates a variety of rhetorical strategies.

classification	Rice is classified according to grain size: long, medium, short.
illustration	rice examples: long grain (Basmati); medium grain (Calrose); short grain (Arborio).
description	rice: long grain; medium grain; short grain long grain: long and slender; low in starch; light and fluffy when cooked. medium grain rice: three times as long as it is wide; more starch than long grain; sticky when cooked. short grain rice: highest starch level; kernel-shaped; moist and tender when cooked.
cause-effect	long grain: When cooked (cause), it becomes light and fluffy (effect) with the grains separating (effect). medium grain: When cooked (cause), medium grain rice tends to stick together (effect). short grain: It...becomes very moist and tender (effect) when cooked (cause).

Argument Mapping

ETS, the company that designs the TOEFL iBT, says that the TOEFL iBT is "an integrated test." Integrated, according to ETS's definition, means testing four skill sets (reading, listening, speaking, writing) by combining them in various tasks.

The word "integrated" also has a rhetorical definition, one upon which the strategies in this textbook are based. As you know, each of the four test sections tests a different skill. Yet the testing method in each section is rhetorically the same. That testing method is based on arguments, either opinion-based or fact-based. Because the TOEFL iBT's testing method is rhetorically consistent across the four test sections, it is an integrated testing system, one that is also, by nature of its repeating design, predictable. Because the TOEFL's iBT testing method is rhetorically integrated, and therefore predictable, the arguments ETS uses for testing purposes on the TOEFL iBT can be mapped out using the strategy called *argument mapping*.

Argument mapping is a graphics-based scoring strategy designed to help test-takers visualize (map out) the structure of all the opinion-based and fact-based arguments on the TOEFL iBT. An understanding of argument mapping begins with the paragraph map G+TiC. Translated, G+TiC means:

General statement + **T**ransition + **i**llustration + **C**onclusion

G+TiC describes the three-parts of a paragraph.

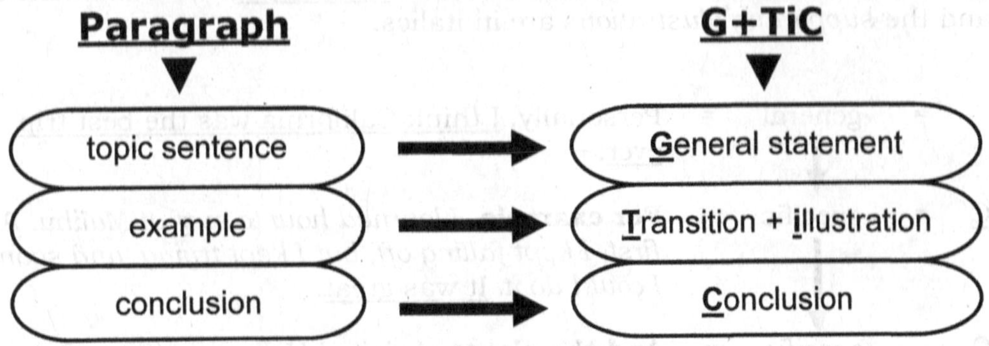

By adding two more body paragraphs (2TiC) and a conclusion (C = restated opinion or premise), G+TiC expands to the argument map G+3TiC=C.

G+3TiC=C

G+3TiC=C maps out a three-part, opinion-based argument and a three-part, fact-based argument, both of which use deduction as the method of organization.

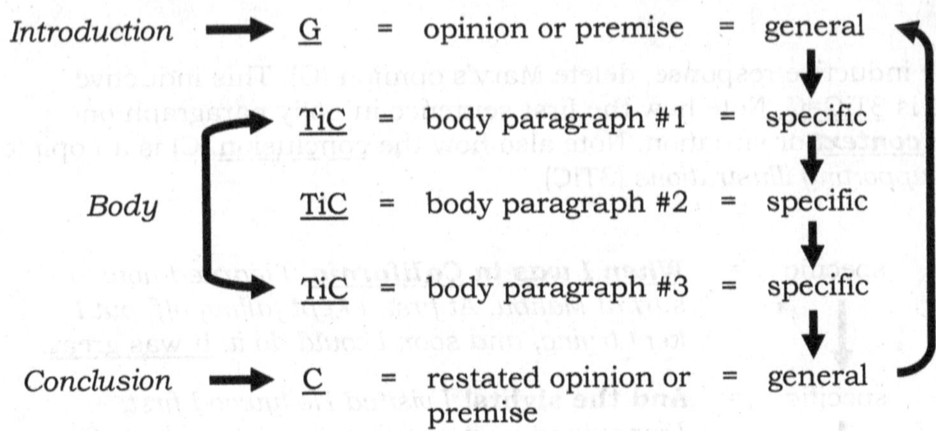

Q *Why three body paragraphs (3TiC)?*

A *G+3TiC=C is based on the five-paragraph essay. The five-paragraph essay consists of an introduction, three body paragraphs, and a conclusion. The five-paragraph essay is the foundation essay taught in American high schools. American high school students learn the five-paragraph essay and continue to apply it, and expand upon it, at community college and at university.*

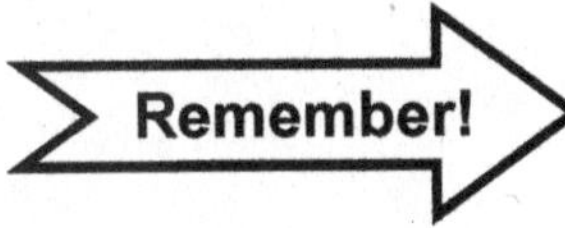

Because the five-paragraph essay is the rhetorical foundation of the American educational system, you are expected to know it when taking the TOEFL iBT, an American-designed test.

Let's map out Mary's deductive, opinion-based argument about California using G+3TiC=C. The opinion (G) and conclusions (C) are underlined, the transitions are in **bold**, and the *supporting illustrations* are in italics.

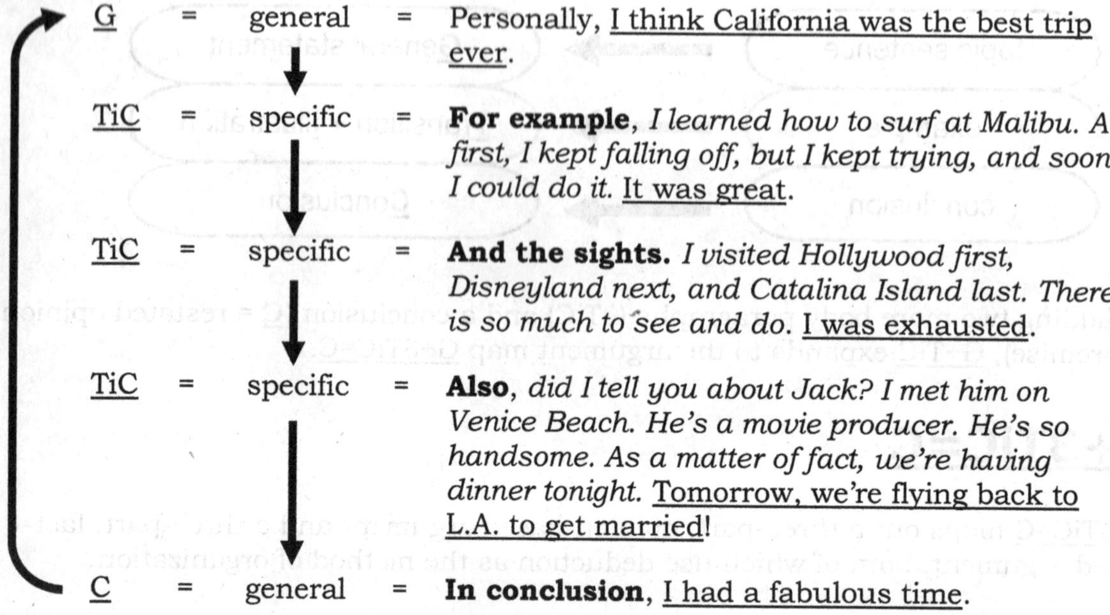

G	=	general	=	Personally, I think California was the best trip ever.
TiC	=	specific	=	**For example**, *I learned how to surf at Malibu. At first, I kept falling off, but I kept trying, and soon I could do it.* It was great.
TiC	=	specific	=	**And the sights.** *I visited Hollywood first, Disneyland next, and Catalina Island last. There is so much to see and do.* I was exhausted.
TiC	=	specific	=	**Also**, *did I tell you about Jack? I met him on Venice Beach. He's a movie producer. He's so handsome. As a matter of fact, we're having dinner tonight.* Tomorrow, we're flying back to L.A. to get married!
C	=	general	=	**In conclusion**, I had a fabulous time.

To map out the inductive response, delete Mary's opinion (G). This inductive argument map is 3TiC=C. Note how the first sentence in body paragraph one introduces the ***context*** or situation. Note also how the conclusion (C) is an opinion based on the *supporting illustrations* (3TiC).

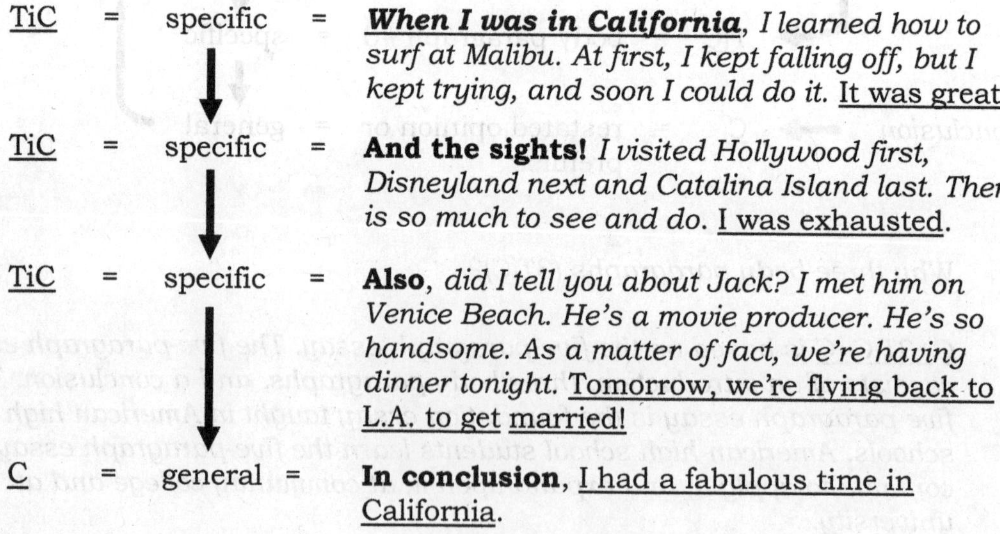

TiC	=	specific	=	***When I was in California***, *I learned how to surf at Malibu. At first, I kept falling off, but I kept trying, and soon I could do it.* It was great.
TiC	=	specific	=	**And the sights!** *I visited Hollywood first, Disneyland next and Catalina Island last. There is so much to see and do.* I was exhausted.
TiC	=	specific	=	**Also**, *did I tell you about Jack? I met him on Venice Beach. He's a movie producer. He's so handsome. As a matter of fact, we're having dinner tonight.* Tomorrow, we're flying back to L.A. to get married!
C	=	general	=	**In conclusion**, I had a fabulous time in California.

Next, let's map out the deductive, fact-based argument about rice using G+3TiC=C. The premise and conclusions are underlined, the transitions are in **bold**, the *illustrations* are in italics. Note that the general statement (G) is a premise.

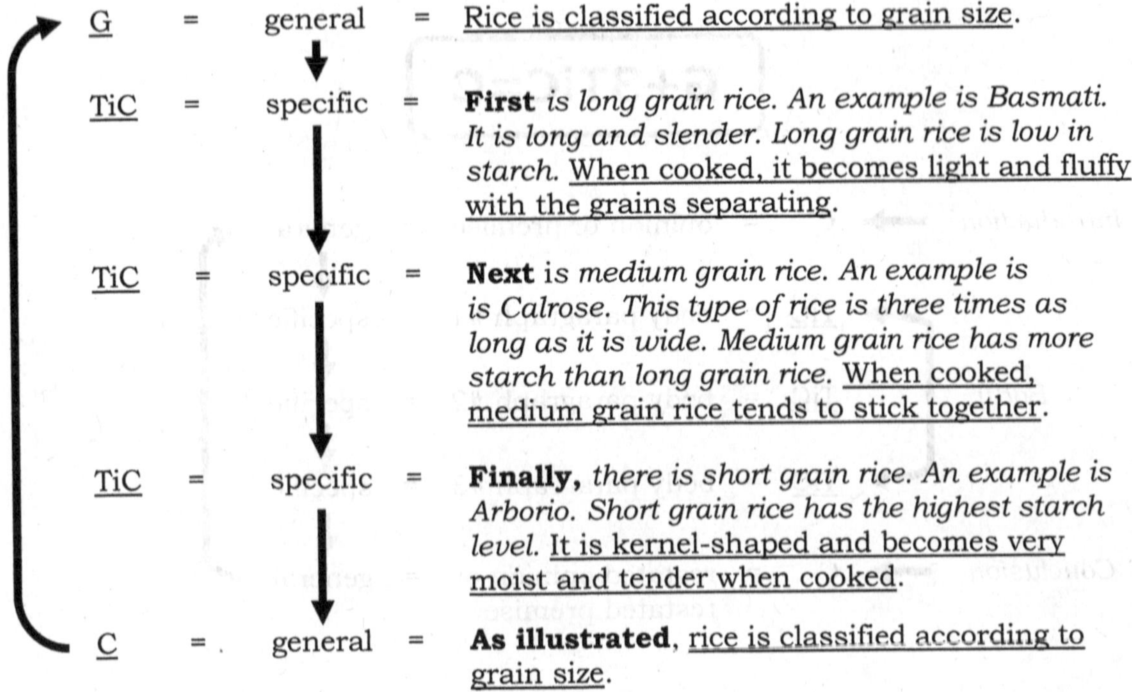

G = general = Rice is classified according to grain size.
TiC = specific = First is long grain rice. An example is Basmati. It is long and slender. Long grain rice is low in starch. When cooked, it becomes light and fluffy with the grains separating.
TiC = specific = Next is medium grain rice. An example is is Calrose. This type of rice is three times as long as it is wide. Medium grain rice has more starch than long grain rice. When cooked, medium grain rice tends to stick together.
TiC = specific = Finally, there is short grain rice. An example is Arborio. Short grain rice has the highest starch level. It is kernel-shaped and becomes very moist and tender when cooked.
C = general = As illustrated, rice is classified according to grain size.

To map out the inductive response (3TiC=C), start with an example. Note how the conclusion (C) is a premise based on the *supporting illustrations* (3TiC).

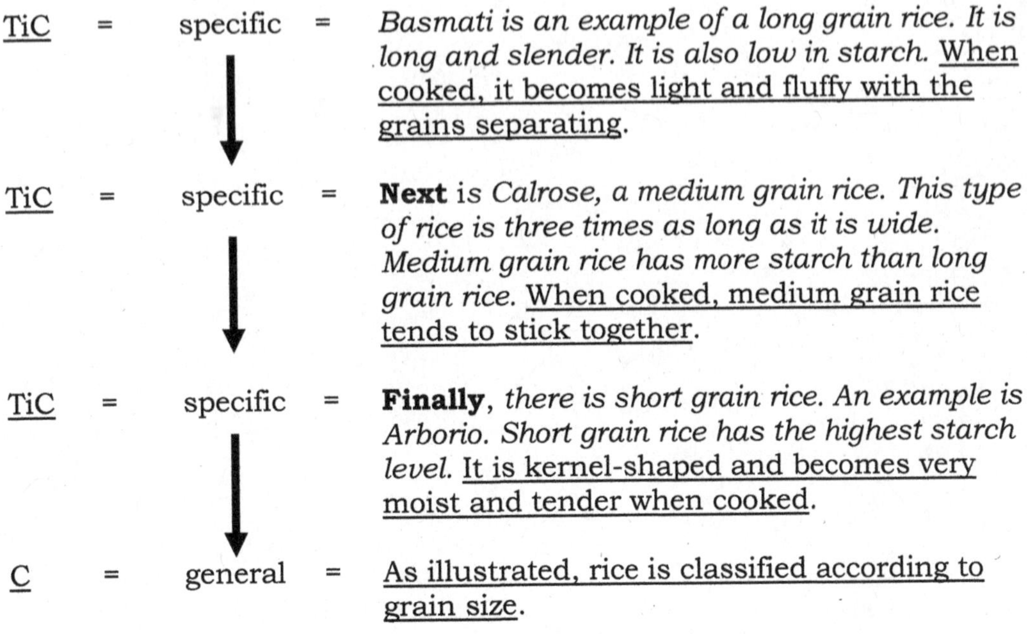

TiC = specific = Basmati is an example of a long grain rice. It is long and slender. It is also low in starch. When cooked, it becomes light and fluffy with the grains separating.
TiC = specific = Next is Calrose, a medium grain rice. This type of rice is three times as long as it is wide. Medium grain rice has more starch than long grain rice. When cooked, medium grain rice tends to stick together.
TiC = specific = Finally, there is short grain rice. An example is Arborio. Short grain rice has the highest starch level. It is kernel-shaped and becomes very moist and tender when cooked.
C = general = As illustrated, rice is classified according to grain size.

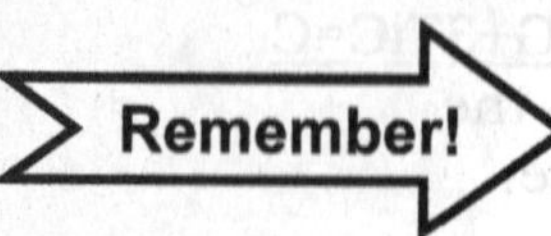

Memorize G+3TiC=C. You will use this argument map when analyzing and learning scoring strategies for each TOEFL iBT task.

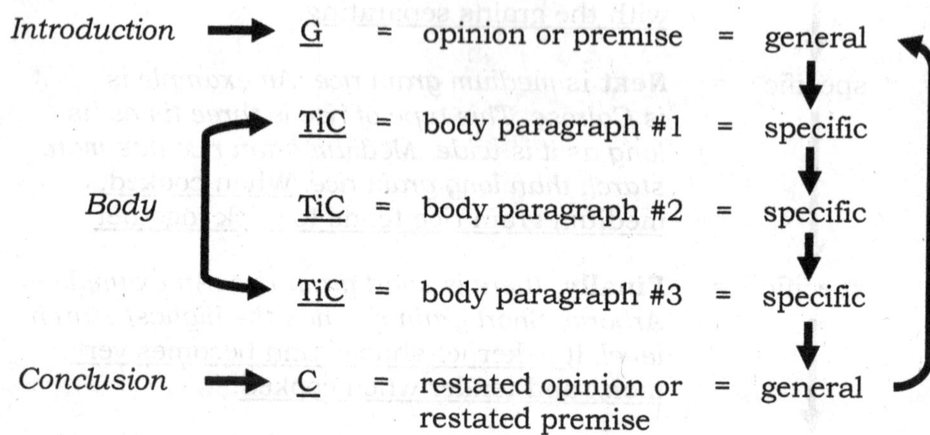

Writing Section

The writing section is the last section on the TOEFL iBT.

Reading | **Listening** | **Speaking** | **Writing**

There are two writing tasks: the integrated writing task and the independent writing task. You will have approximately 53 minutes to complete both tasks. You cannot change the task order. You must type both essays.

TASK	TIME
1. Integrated Writing Task	23 minutes
2. Independent Writing Task	30 minutes

The integrated writing task measures your ability to write a fact-based argument. This task also measures your ability to integrate five skill sets: reading, listening, note taking, summarizing, and writing objectively. The independent writing task measures your ability to write an opinion-based argument. This task also measures your ability to write subjectively using your personal experience to develop and support your opinion.

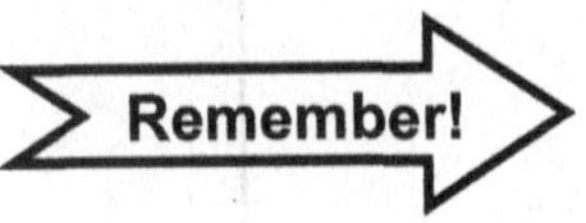

On the official TOEFL iBT, you will write the integrated essay first. However, in this textbook, you will study the independent essay first, then the integrated essay. In order to write a proficient integrated essay, you must first learn how to write a proficient independent essay. By learning how to write an independent essay and an integrated essay, you will start to acquire the foundational argument strategies essential for TOEFL iBT success (see page 13 "Start with the Independent Essay").

Typing: *An Essential TOEFL Strategy*

To maximize your writing score, you must know how to write both fact-based and opinion-based arguments. You must also be able to type proficiently under a time pressure. Proficient typing = fewer mistakes = a higher writing score = a higher TOEFL iBT score.

How proficiently can you type? Take the test on the next page.

Typing Test

Directions: You have one minute to type the 60-word passage below. If you make one mistake, you can type 59 wpm (60 words – 1 mistake = 59 words per minute), two mistakes, 58 wpm, etc. Note: A letter not capitalized is a mistake. A comma in the wrong place is a mistake. A missing comma is a mistake.

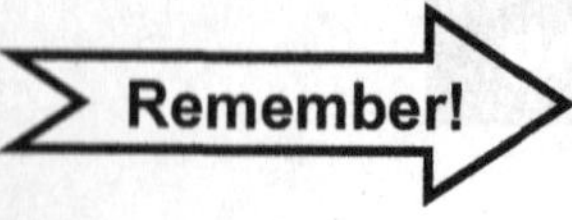

You will use a standard keyboard on test day. A standard keyboard is not touch sensitive like a laptop keyboard. If you are using a laptop computer, I highly recommend that you buy a standard keyboard. Buy one and plug it into your laptop via the USB port. By practicing with a standard keyboard, you will be test-ready.

Typing Test

You have 60 seconds to type the following 60-word passage.

> Topical unity means you focus on one topic from start to finish. If you suddenly introduce a new and unrelated topic, you are changing topics. For example, you are writing about pizza when you suddenly change to TOEFL. This obvious change in topic direction is called a topic digression. This will result in a lack of topical unity and coherence.

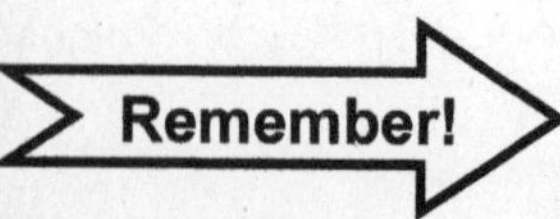

If you type less than 30 words-per-minute, you need typing practice. If you need typing practice, see 500 Words, Phrases and Idioms for the TOEFL iBT plus Typing Strategies by Bruce Stirling.

Independent Writing Task

The independent writing task (independent essay) is the last task on the TOEFL iBT. This task measures your ability to write (construct) an opinion-based argument using your personal experience. The task description follows.

TASK	TIME
Read the prompt. Write an independent essay.	30 minutes

Prompt Types

There are two prompt types: paired-choice and single-question. A paired-choice prompt gives you a choice between two opposing positions, for example:

> Prompt We need zoos. Do you agree or disagree? Why? Give examples and reasons to develop your opinion.

> Prompt Do you prefer to use a laptop or a desktop computer? Why? Give examples and reasons to support your argument.

A single-question prompt asks a question, for example:

> Prompt How would you make the world a better place? Give examples and reasons to support and develop your position.

> Prompt Which person has been the greatest influence in your life? Give examples and reasons to support and develop your opinion.

Typing Your Essay

When you type your independent essay on test day, you will use a basic word processing program. All the functions you need (cut, paste, undo) will be visible on screen. There is no spell checker or grammar checker. When you are finished, your essay will be sent via the internet to ETS to be scored.

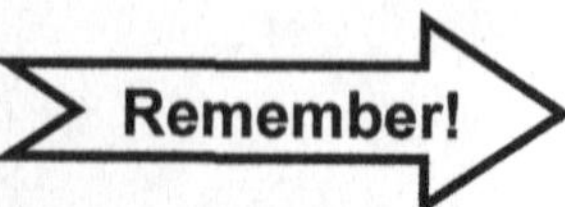

You cannot use your own pen and paper to take notes. Note paper and pencils will be supplied. At the end of the test, you must submit your notes to the site manager. Your notes will be destroyed.

Task Screen

The task screen for the independent essay is divided into four panels. The top panel tells you the section you are in and the question number. You will also see a task clock, a help button, and a navigation button. The two left panels contain the directions and the prompt. You will type your essay in the right panel.

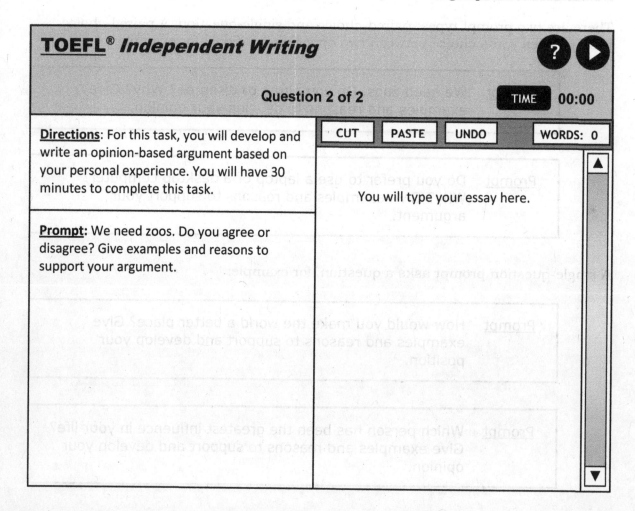

TOEFL® *Independent Writing*

Question 2 of 2

TIME 00:00

CUT PASTE UNDO WORDS: 0

Directions: For this task, you will develop and write an opinion-based argument based on your personal experience. You will have 30 minutes to complete this task.

Prompt: We need zoos. Do you agree or disagree? Give examples and reasons to support your argument.

You will type your essay here.

OPDUL=C: *Thinking like a Writing Rater*

To get the highest possible independent essay score, you must give the writing raters what they are trained to measure. They are trained to measure (rate) your writing proficiency against a set of rubrics or rules. Those rules are defined by OPDUL=C.

OPDUL=C (Op-dull-see) is an argument analyzer that rates coherence using proficiency as a measure. Proficiency means your ability to demonstrate skill and knowledge specific to **O**rganization, **P**rogression, **D**evelopment, **U**nity and **L**anguage Use. For example, if your independent essay demonstrates proficiency in all areas of OPDUL, then your essay will demonstrate **C**oherence. This will result in a higher independent essay score.

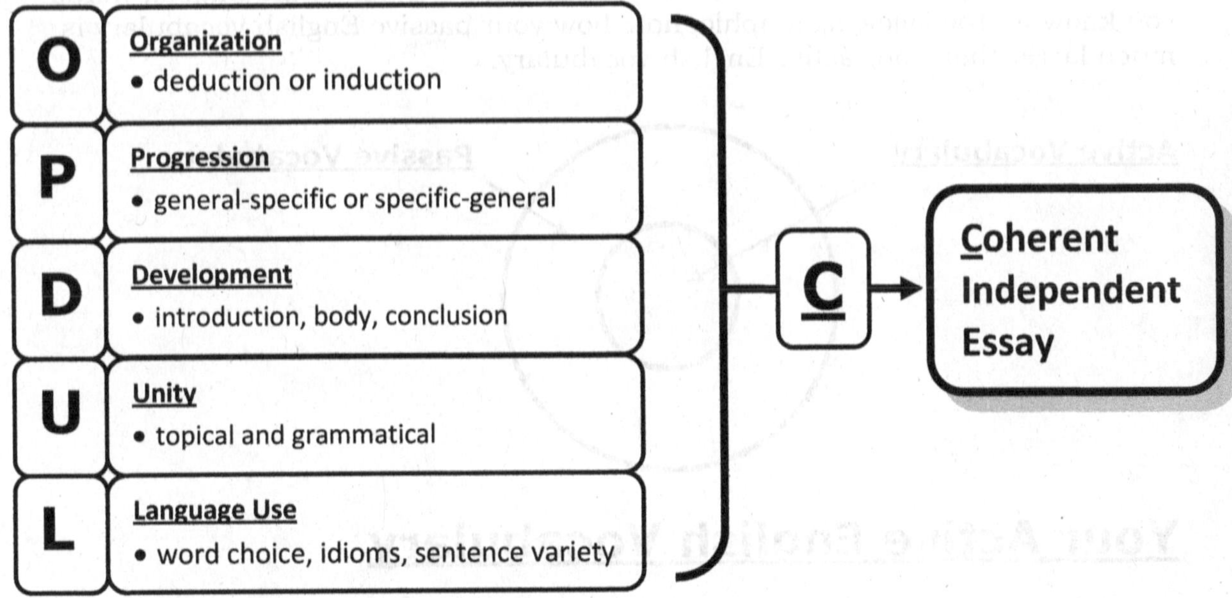

G+3TiC=C and OPDUL=C

You can demonstrate OPDUL=C by using G+3TiC=C.

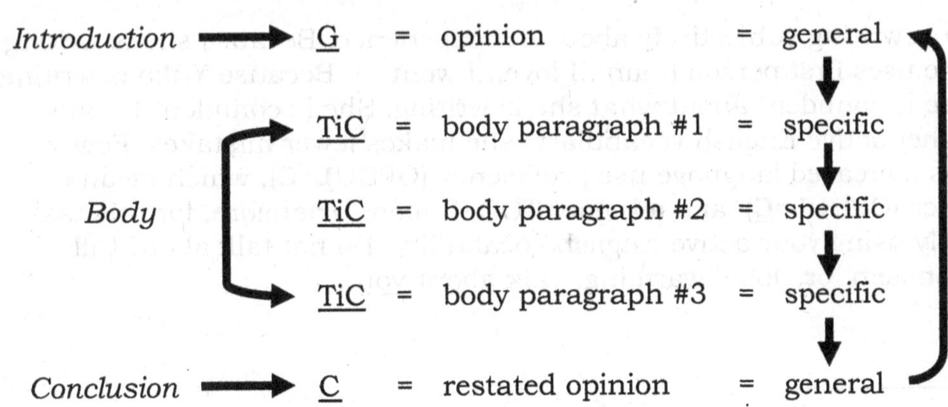

Basic Independent Essays

To get a high independent essay score[1], you must demonstrate OPDUL=C. That is what you will practice in this section using G+3TiC=C. Later, you will learn how to develop a basic independent essay into an advanced independent essay. When writing an independent essay, you will write subjectively using your personal experience. You will describe your experience using your active English vocabulary.

Active vs. Passive English Vocabulary

You have two English vocabularies: active and passive. They are part of language use (OPDU**L**=C). Combined, these two vocabularies contain all the English words you know. In the following graphic, note how your passive English vocabulary is much larger than your active English vocabulary.

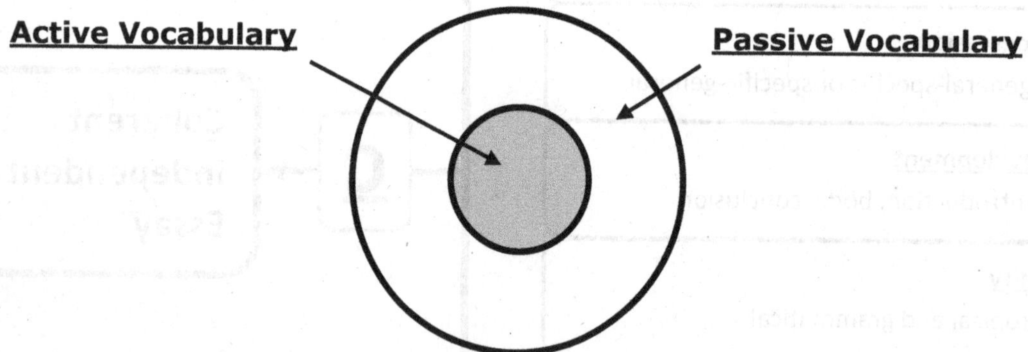

Your Active English Vocabulary

Your active English vocabulary consists of English words you use every day. These words are about you and your personal experience, for example:

> "My name is Yuko. I am a software engineer from Tokyo, Japan. In my free time, I love to travel and take photos. Last year I went to Bali, Indonesia and took lots of photos. Next year I will go to Paris and London."

Note how Yuko is writing subjectively about her experience. Because she is writing subjectively, she uses first person (I am...I love...I went...). Because Yuko is writing subjectively, she is confident about what she is writing. She is confident because when she uses her active English vocabulary, she makes fewer mistakes. Fewer mistakes means increased language use proficiency (OPDU**L**=C), which means greater coherence (OPDUL=**C**), and a higher TOEFL score. Therefore, for this task, write subjectively using your active English vocabulary. Do not talk about Bill Gates, Albert Einstein, or global warming. Talk about you.

[1] Throughout this text the words score, rate and rating are synonymous.

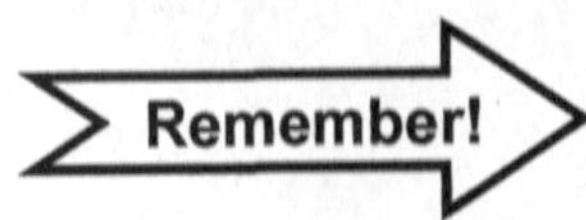

The writing raters do not care about your opinion. They only want to know if you can develop and write an opinion-based argument in 30 minutes. Do so using G+3TiC=C and OPDUL=C.

Your Passive English Vocabulary

Your passive English vocabulary consists of English words you do not use regularly. Idioms are a good example. The English idioms you use regularly are part of your active vocabulary. However, like most non native English speakers, you probably know more idioms than you use thus they are not part of your active vocabulary. Because you do not use some idioms regularly, you do not use them proficiently. Because you do not use them proficiently, you make more language use errors (OPDU**L**=C) = a lower level of coherence (OPDUL=**C**) = a lower score.

Technical words (jargon) are also part of your passive vocabulary. For example, you know hard drive, keyboard, and mouse. But what about these computer terms: frontside bus, PCIe slot, and motherboard. Maybe you have heard of them, maybe not. If you are not 100% sure, do not use them.

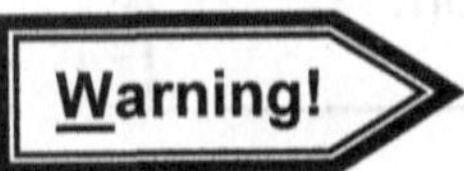

TOEFL is not the place to experiment with new English words, especially idioms. If you do not use an idiom regularly, do not use it.

An understanding of TOEFL's testing method for this task begins with a rhetorical analysis of basic independent essays starting with agree-disagree prompts.

Agree-Disagree Prompts

Agree-disagree prompts give you a choice between a pair of *opposing positions* specific to a topic. You must choose one position and argue in support of it.

Prompt	We need zoos. Do you *agree or disagree*? Why? Give examples and reasons to develop your opinion.

Avoid double arguments. Choose one side of the argument (single argument) and develop it, for example:

	Prompt:	We need zoos. Do you agree or disagree?
X	Double Argument:	Sometimes I think that we needs zoos, and sometimes I think that we don't need zoos.
√	Single Argument:	Personally, I think that we needs zoos.

Q *Why is a single argument best?*

A *If you try to develop a double argument, you will run out of time. Because you will run out of time, you will not be able to develop both arguments. This will result in a lack of topic development (OPDUL=C) and a lower score.*

1. Agree-Disagree: *Step-by-Step*

When answering an agree-disagree prompt, write subjectively using G+3TiC=C and follow these six steps. You have 30 minutes.

Step #1 **Carefully read the prompt; formulate an opinion.**

> Prompt We need zoos. Do you agree or disagree? Why? Give examples and reasons to support your opinion.

Step #2 **Make a G+3TiC=C note map; include transitions (T).**

> G =
>
> TiC = for example
>
> TiC = another example
>
> TiC = finally
>
> C = for those reasons

Q *What about the writing strategy that says, "Take five minutes to pre-write, twenty minutes to write, and five minutes to revise"?*

A *If that strategy works for you, great. However, many test-takers do not follow this strategy. Instead, they jump right in and start writing. These same test-takers often become frustrated because they have trouble organizing their ideas. However, by using G+3TiC=C, you will know exactly where to start writing, what to write, how to write it and why, without getting lost.*

Next, answer the prompt question ("Do you agree or disagree?"). State your *opinion* (G = general statement), then restate it in the conclusion (C).

G = agree *I think that we need zoos*

TiC = for example

TiC = another example

TiC = also

C = for those reasons *I think that we need zoos*

Q *Do I have to repeat "I agree" in my conclusion?*

A *No. By the time the raters reach your conclusion, your position (whether you agree or disagree) should be clear.*

Next, develop *supporting illustrations* (TiC). Do not worry about spelling or grammar at this point. Just think of *examples*. Remember to write subjectively. By doing so, you will be answering that part of the prompt that says "give [personal] examples."

G = agree I think that we need zoos

Ti = for example *when 12 went to zoo, on TV lions very small but so big at zoo!!*
C =

Ti = another example *my family goes to zoo + picnic*
C =

Ti = also *zoos good for animals like pandas*
C =

C = for those reasons I think that we need zoos

Next, answer that part of the prompt that says "give reasons." Give reasons by stating a **cause**-and-*effect* relationship beside each C (Ti**C**). C is the concluding sentence in each body paragraph. Remember: Each **cause**-and-*effect* relationship is a reason why you (the test-taker) think zoos are important.

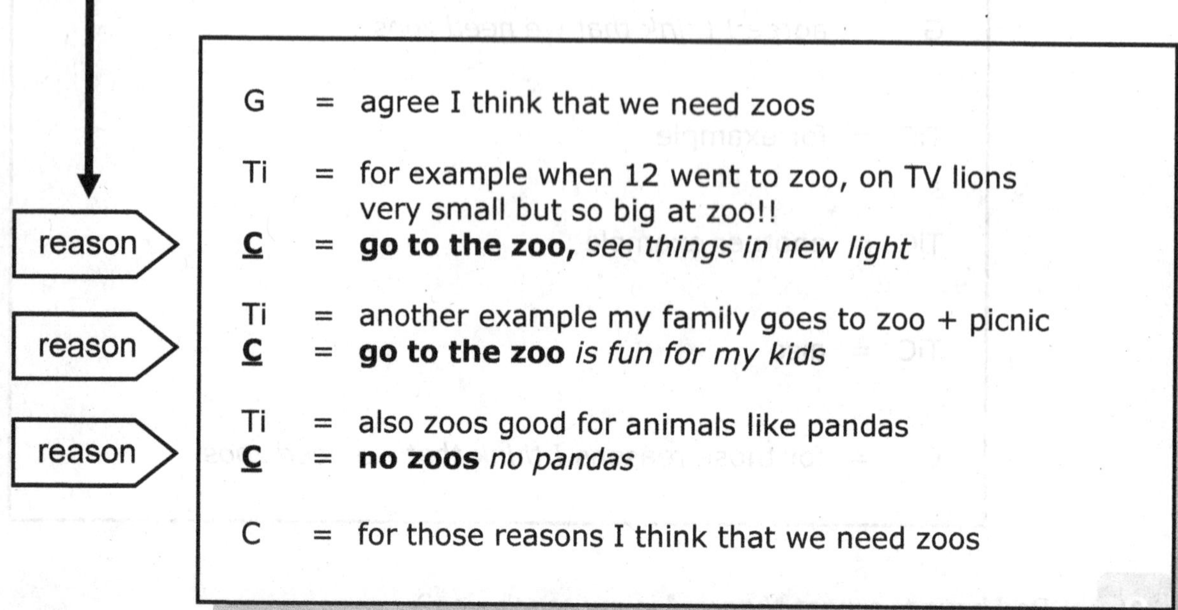
G = agree I think that we need zoos
Ti = for example when 12 went to zoo, on TV lions very small but so big at zoo!!
reason
C = go to the zoo, see things in new light
Ti = another example my family goes to zoo + picnic
reason
C = go to the zoo is fun for my kids
Ti = also zoos good for animals like pandas
reason
C = no zoos no pandas
C = for those reasons I think that we need zoos

Step #3 **Type a first draft. Do not include the note map.**

Note: There are mistakes in this first draft. Can you identify them? See the corrections in Step #5.

Personally, I agree. I think that we need zoos.

For example, when I was 12, my teacher took us to the zoo. I have never seen wild animals before. I just read about them on books or on the TV. But seeing them in real life was amazing, especially the lion. On the Tv, they look small, but seeing them so close they are really big. By going to the zoo, I definitely saw a new hole in the light.

Now I have a family and we went to the zoo at summer. My wife makes a picnick and we spend all days there. My kids love taking pictures and learning all about the animals, specially the gorillas. This is good for my children be outside. Best of all, they can leave the internet and the TV at home.

Also, zoos look after extinct animals like pandas. I saw two in the Washington DC zoo. Zoo take care of animals like pandas.

For those reasons, I think that we need zoos.

You now have a first draft. It looks coherent. But how do you know it is coherent without guessing? Moreover, how can you revise your first draft when practicing and on test day to maximize scoring? By checking your first draft for coherence using the argument analyzer OPDUL=C.

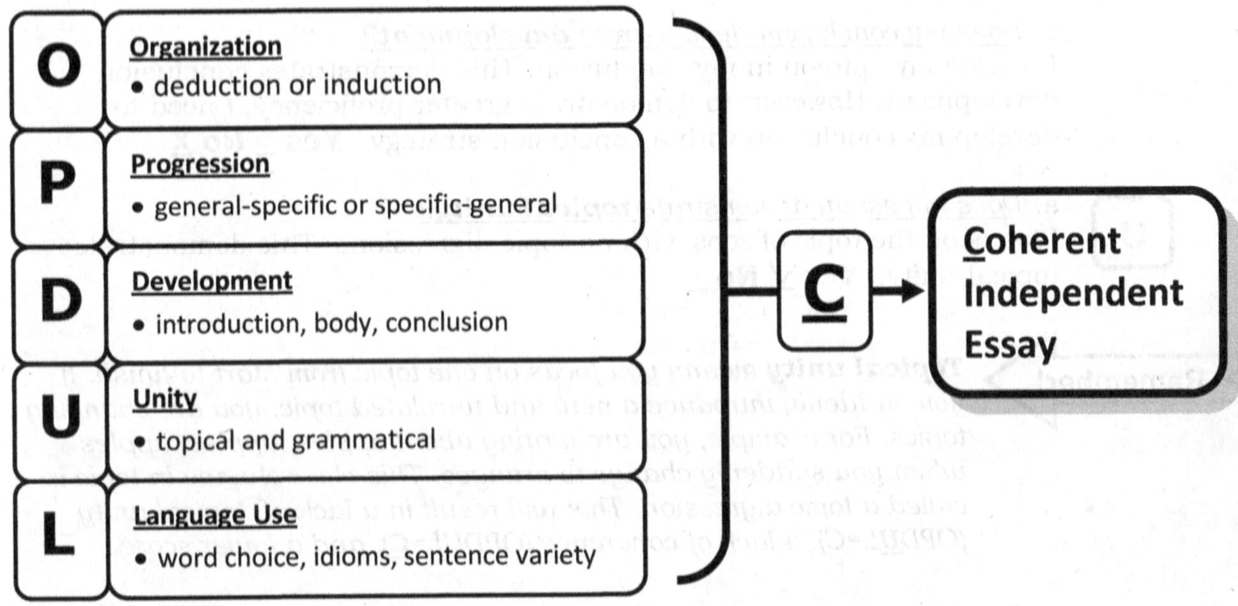

Step #4 **Check your first draft for Coherence using OPDUL=C.**

You are the writer. Check the first draft of the zoo essay (Step #3) for Coherence using OPDUL=C. Start with Organization and ask yourself "yes-no" questions.

O *Does my essay demonstrate* ***organization****?*
I'm using deduction as a method of organization. This demonstrates organization. **Yes √ No _**

P *Does my essay demonstrate* ***progression****?*
Because I'm using deduction, the ideas progress from general to specific. This demonstrates progression. **Yes √ No _**

D a. *Does my introduction demonstrate* ***development***.
I say, "I think that we need zoos." That is my opinion. It is a grammatically complete sentence, it is arguable, it is supportable, it is not a question, and it expresses a main topic and a controlling idea. However, to get a higher score, I need to develop my introduction with a hook. **Yes _ No X**

b. *Do my body paragraphs demonstrate **development**?*
Body paragraphs #1 and #2 each develop an example that supports my opinion and conclusion. This demonstrates body paragraph development. However, body paragraph #3 lacks development. To get a higher score, I need to develop body paragraph #3. **Yes _ No X**

c. *Does my conclusion demonstrate **development**?*
I restate my opinion in my conclusion. This demonstrates conclusion development. However, to demonstrate greater proficiency, I need to develop my conclusion with a conclusion strategy. **Yes _ No X**

U

a. *Does my essay demonstrate **topical unity**?*
I focus on the topic of zoos with no topic digressions. This demonstrates topical unity. **Yes √ No _**

Remember!

***Topical unity** means you focus on one topic from start to finish. If you suddenly introduce a new and unrelated topic, you are changing topics. For example, you are writing about apples, apples, apples when you suddenly change to oranges. This clear change in topic is called a topic digression. This will result in a lack of topical unity (OPDUL=C), a lack of coherence (OPDUL=C), and a lower score.*

b. *Does my essay demonstrate **grammatical unity**?*
The transitions are all correct. This demonstrates grammatical unity.
Yes √ No _

L

*Does my essay demonstrate **proficient language use**?*
I need to be more proficient with word choice, idiom usage, and grammar usage, especially in body paragraph #3. Combined, this will demonstrate greater language use proficiency. **Yes _ No X**

C

*Does my essay (argument) demonstrate **coherence**?*
Because of proficient Organization, Progression and Unity, my first draft demonstrates Coherence. Even though there are problems with Development and Language Use, my position is clear: "I think that we need zoos." **Yes √ No _**

According to the *Independent Essay Rating Guide* on page 695, this first draft will score in the 2.5-3.5 range. If you (the writer) want a higher score, you must revise those parts of OPDUL=C that received an **X**. By doing so, you will demonstrate greater proficiency and coherence. You will also receive a higher score. The **X's** are your revision checklist.

Revision Checklist: *What do I need to revise?*

1. I need to start my essay with a hook. The purpose of a hook is "to hook" the reader's attention in the first sentence. A hook will demonstrate greater introduction development (OP**D**UL=C).

   Note: You will learn hooks and other advanced introduction strategies later on in this chapter.

2. I need to end my essay with a conclusion strategy. This will demonstrate greater conclusion development (OP**D**UL=C).

   Note: You will learn advanced conclusion strategies later on in this chapter.

3. I need to correct any word choice, grammar, and idiom issues. This will demonstrate more proficient language use (OPDU**L**=C).

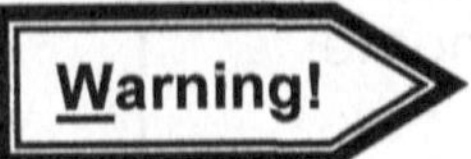

Do not use an idiom if you are not 100% sure of its meaning and in which context it is used. An idiom used incorrectly (out of context) will stick out like a sore thumb, for example:

By going to the zoo, I definitely saw a new hole in the light.

should be...

By going to the zoo, I definitely saw things in a whole new light.

4. I need to develop the panda topic in body paragraph #3. This will demonstrate greater topic development (OP**D**UL=C).

*Lack of topic development (OP**D**UL=C), especially in the body paragraphs, is a big reason why independent essays score low.*

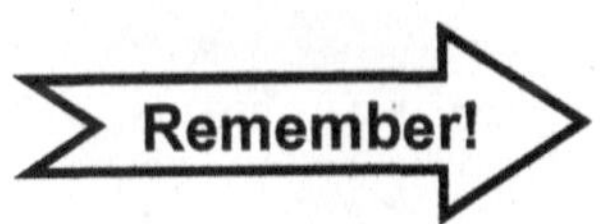

*If you want a high independent essay score, your body paragraphs must be well-developed. Well-developed means you have a clear supporting illustration (T**i**C) in each body paragraph, and you show a cause-and-effect relationship (reason) in your concluding sentence (Ti**C**).*

Why is body paragraph development so important?

A

Body paragraph development is important because developing examples is the hardest part of the independent essay. Why is it the hardest part? Because body paragraph development will test your automaticity. Automaticity means your ability to develop ideas quickly and proficiently under a time pressure. Well-developed body paragraphs will demonstrate automaticity, proficiency, and coherence. That is what the raters look for.

Step #5 Revise your first draft using your revision checklist.

Personally, I agree. I think that we need zoos.

For example, when I was 12, my teacher took us to the zoo in Berlin. I had never seen wild animals before. I had just read about them in books and seen them on the TV. But seeing them in real life was amazing, especially the lions. On TV, they looked so small, but seeing them live they were really big. By going to the zoo, I definitely saw things in a whole new light.

Now I have a family and we always go to the zoo every summer. My wife makes a picnic and we spend all day there. My kids love taking pictures and learning all about the animals, especially the gorillas. Being outside is good for my children. Best of all, they can leave the internet and the TV at home.

Also, zoos look after endangered animals like pandas. I saw two in the Washington DC zoo last year and they had a baby. If there were no zoos, the pandas would disappear because we are taking their land away. However, in a zoo the pandas are safe. It is not perfect, but without zoos there might not be any pandas left.

For those reasons, I think that we need zoos.

Step #6 Submit your essay.

After you have revised your essay, submit it.

Make sure you have made all the necessary revisions before you submit your essay. Once you submit your essay, you cannot get it back.

Mapped out, you can see how G+3TiC=C gives the writing raters what they are trained to look for: an independent essay that demonstrates OPDUL=C. The opinion (G) and the conclusions (C) are underlined, the transitions (T) are in **bold**, and the supporting illustrations (i) are in *italics*.

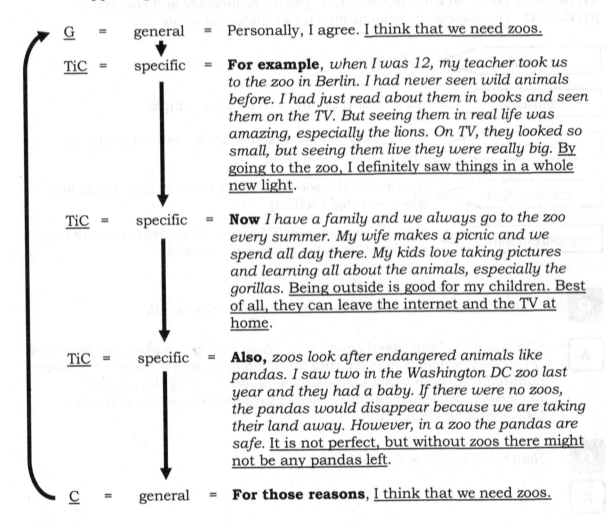

G = general = Personally, I agree. I think that we need zoos.

TiC = specific = **For example**, *when I was 12, my teacher took us to the zoo in Berlin. I had never seen wild animals before. I had just read about them in books and seen them on the TV. But seeing them in real life was amazing, especially the lions. On TV, they looked so small, but seeing them live they were really big.* By going to the zoo, I definitely saw things in a whole new light.

TiC = specific = **Now** *I have a family and we always go to the zoo every summer. My wife makes a picnic and we spend all day there. My kids love taking pictures and learning all about the animals, especially the gorillas.* Being outside is good for my children. Best of all, they can leave the internet and the TV at home.

TiC = specific = **Also,** *zoos look after endangered animals like pandas. I saw two in the Washington DC zoo last year and they had a baby. If there were no zoos, the pandas would disappear because we are taking their land away. However, in a zoo the pandas are safe.* It is not perfect, but without zoos there might not be any pandas left.

C = general = **For those reasons**, I think that we need zoos.

TASK: Rate the zoo essay above using the *Independent Essay Rating Guide* on page 695. Compare your score to the score on page 789.

Q *What if I can only think of two body paragraphs (G+2TiC=C)?*

A *There is no rule that says you must have three body paragraphs. If you can write an independent essay that demonstrates OPDUL=C using G+2TiC=C, great. Go for it.*

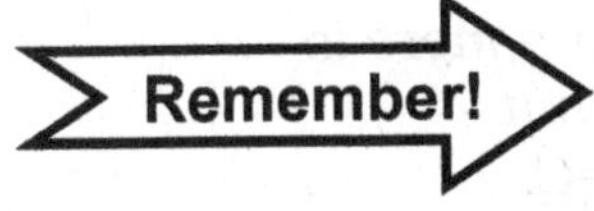

*If you write your independent essay using G+2TiC=C, make sure both body paragraphs are well developed. A lack of body paragraph development (OP**D**UL=C) will result in a lower score.*

Rhetorical Strategies

Rhetorical strategies demonstrate topic development (OP**D**UL=C) and language use (OPDU**L**=C). These, in turn, demonstrate greater proficiency and coherence (OPDUL=**C**). The zoo essay demonstrates these rhetorical strategies.

illustration	the student, family, and panda example
narration	the student, family, and panda example
description	on TV, they [lions] looked so small, but seeing them live they were really big
cause-effect	by going to the zoo (action), I definitely saw things in a whole new light (effect)
compare-contrast	lions in book and on TV are small vs. real lions are big; pandas in zoos vs. pandas in the wild

Q *How long should my independent essay be? Is there a rule?*

A *ETS has no "official" word-length rule. There is only this guideline from ETS: "[A]n effective [independent] essay will usually contain a minimum of three hundred words; however, test-takers may write more if they wish." Remember: "Effective" means proficient. Demonstrate proficiency using G+3TiC=C and OPDUL=C.*

Q *How many words is the zoo essay?*

A *213.*

The Word Counter

When you write your independent essay, you will see a word counter on your computer screen. Ignore it. You are not counting words. You are writing an independent essay that demonstrates OPDUL=C, not aiming for "a minimum of three hundred words."

*A long essay does not always mean a coherent ("effective") argument. On the contrary, a long essay often means a lack of coherence (OPDUL=**C**). Some test-takers simply type and type, thinking more is better. Wrong. Your job is to write an independent essay that proficiently demonstrates OPDUL=C. Do so using G+3TiC=C.*

2. Agree-Disagree: *Step-by-Step*

Let's map out another agree-disagree essay. Remember to use G+3TiC=C and the six steps to demonstrate OPDUL=C in your essay. Remember to write subjectively.

Step #1 **Carefully read the prompt; formulate an opinion.**

Prompt: Television is a good influence on children. Do you agree or disagree? Why? Develop your opinion using examples and reasons.

Step #2 **Make a note map; state your opinion (G); restate it in your conclusion (C); develop examples (3TiC).**

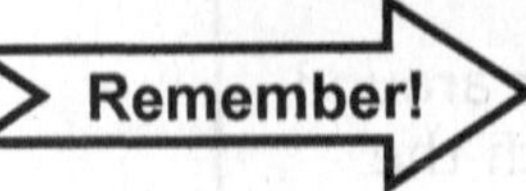

*Give reasons by stating a **cause**-and-effect relationship beside each C (TiC). Each **cause**-and-effect relationship is a reason why TV is a bad influence on children.*

G = disagree - TV is a bad influence

Ti = for example boy next door watches Power Rangers
C = **power rangers teach him** *bad behavior*

Ti = another example my brother, he watches TV and eats junk food
C = **junk food + TV** *not healthy for brother*

Ti = finally Britney wants TV all the time
C = **TV** *like an addiction for Britney*

C = for those reasons TV bad influence

Step #3 **Type a first draft. Do <u>not</u> include the note map.**

<u>Note</u>: There are mistakes in this first draft. Can you identify them? See the corrections in Step #5.

> Personally, I with the statement. I believe that TV is a bad influence on our children.
>
> For example, my neighbor boy he is started kicking and punching his little sister. I told him to stop, but he didn't. He says he was a Power Ranger. He even kicked me. I told his mom and she said Power Rangers has been his favorite TV shows, but she never stopped him from kicking people.
>
> On the other hand is my eight-year brother. He love the TV. When he watch, he eat a lot of junk food like chips and choclates. He also drinks Coca Colas alot. All that stuff has so much sugar. My brother he used to be skinny but because he never exercise is definitely get fat and so young.
>
> Finally is Britney little girl I babysats. When I drive her around, like going shopping in the car she always want to watch the DVD. I say let's talk but she scream and wants the DVD. Then she gets home and watch even more the TV. This is her addiction. Her mother says no but this little girl all she do is scream for TV more.
>
> For those reason, I believe that the TV is a bad influence four our children.

Step #4 **Check your first draft for <u>C</u>oherence using <u>OPDUL=C</u>.**

O <u>*Does my essay demonstrate **organization**?*</u>
I use deduction as a method of organization. This demonstrates organization. **Yes √ No _**

P <u>*Does my essay demonstrate **progression**?*</u>
Because I am using deduction, the ideas progress from general to specific. This demonstrates progression. **Yes √ No _**

D a. <u>*Does my introduction demonstrate **development**?*</u>
I say, "I believe that TV is a bad influence on our children." That is my opinion. It is a grammatically complete sentence, it is arguable, it is supportable, it is not a question, and it expresses a main topic and a controlling idea. This demonstrates introduction development for a basic response. **Yes √ No _**

b. *Do my body paragraphs demonstrate* ***development****?*
Each body paragraph develops a specific personal example that supports and develops my opinion and conclusion. However, each body paragraph does not have a concluding sentence (Ti**C**) which states a cause-and-effect reason. This demonstrates a lack of body paragraph development.
Yes _ No X

c. *Does my conclusion demonstrate* ***development****?*
I restate my opinion in the conclusion. This demonstrates conclusion development for a basic response. **Yes √ No _**

U

a. *Does my essay demonstrate topical unity?*
I focus on the topic of television being a bad influence on children with no topical digressions. This demonstrates topical unity. **Yes √ No _**

b. *Does my essay demonstrate* ***grammatical unity****?*
The transitions are correct. This demonstrates grammatical unity.
Yes √ No _

L

Does my essay demonstrate proficient ***language use****?*
I use only basic words and sentences. I don't use any idioms. Also, there are many basic errors in word choice and verb tense. This demonstrates a lack of proficient language use. **Yes _ No X**

C

Does my essay (argument) demonstrate ***coherence****?*
Because of proficient Organization, Progression and Unity, my first draft is Coherent. Even though there are problems with Development and Language Use, my position is clear: "Television is a bad influence on our children." **Yes √ No _**

According to the *Independent Essay Rating Guide* on page 695, this first draft will score in the 2.5-3.5 range. If you (the writer) want a higher score, you must revise those parts of OPDUL=C that received an **X**. By doing so, your essay will demonstrate greater proficiency and coherence, and receive a higher score.

Revision Checklist: *What do I need to revise?*

1. In the TV essay, each body paragraph needs a concluding sentence (Ti**C**). In each concluding sentence, I need to state a reason using a cause-and-effect relationship. This will demonstrate greater topic development (OP**D**UL=C).

2. I also need to correct the spelling and grammar errors, and use idioms and more sentence variety. This will demonstrate more proficient language use (OPDU**L**=C).

Step #5 Revise your first draft using your revision checklist.

Note the revised conclusions at the end of each body paragraph and the cause-and-effect relationship.

I disagree with the statement. Personally, I believe that TV is a bad influence on our children.

For example, my neighbor's boy started kicking and punching his little sister. I told him to stop, but he didn't. He said he was a Power Ranger like on TV. He even kicked me. I told his mom and she said Power Rangers is his favorite TV show, but she never stopped him from kicking people. She thought it was funny. Not me. This little boy was a nice kid, but watching Power Rangers has definitely taught him things he should not do.

Another example is my little brother. He is eight and loves to watch TV. When he watches TV, he eats a lot of junk food like chips and chocolate and Coca Cola. That stuff has so much sugar. My brother used to be skinny but now he is definitely a couch potato. My parents tell him to exercise but he never does. All he does is eat junk food and watch TV. Watching TV this way is definitely not good for his health because now he is diabetic.

Finally, there is Britney, the little girl I babysit. When I drive her around, like when going shopping, she always wants to watch DVDs. I say let's talk but she screams and just wants to watch a DVD. Then at home she watches more TV. Her mother says no, but all Britney does is scream for the TV. It's like an addiction. Right now, her parents cannot control her any more. This is not good.

For those reasons, I believe that TV is a bad influence on our children.

Words: 278

Step #6 Submit your essay.

After you have revised your essay, submit it.

Mapped out, you can see how G+3TiC=C gives the writing raters what they are trained to look for: an independent essay that demonstrates OPDUL=C. The opinion (G) and the conclusions (C) are underlined, the transitions (T) are in **bold**, and the supporting illustrations (i) are in *italics*.

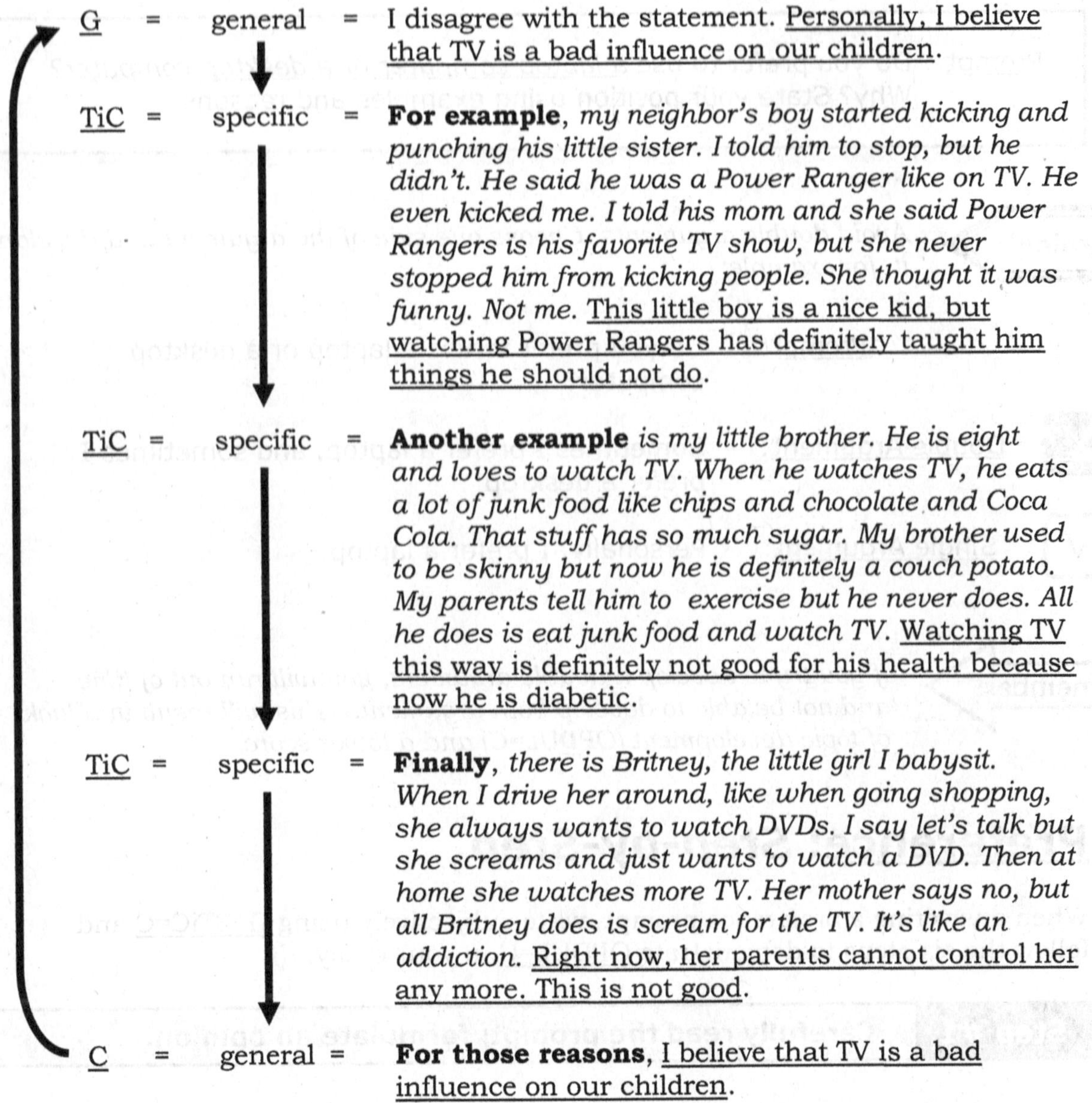

G	=	general	=	I disagree with the statement. Personally, I believe that TV is a bad influence on our children.
TiC	=	specific	=	**For example**, *my neighbor's boy started kicking and punching his little sister. I told him to stop, but he didn't. He said he was a Power Ranger like on TV. He even kicked me. I told his mom and she said Power Rangers is his favorite TV show, but she never stopped him from kicking people. She thought it was funny. Not me.* This little boy is a nice kid, but watching Power Rangers has definitely taught him things he should not do.
TiC	=	specific	=	**Another example** *is my little brother. He is eight and loves to watch TV. When he watches TV, he eats a lot of junk food like chips and chocolate and Coca Cola. That stuff has so much sugar. My brother used to be skinny but now he is definitely a couch potato. My parents tell him to exercise but he never does. All he does is eat junk food and watch TV.* Watching TV this way is definitely not good for his health because now he is diabetic.
TiC	=	specific	=	**Finally**, *there is Britney, the little girl I babysit. When I drive her around, like when going shopping, she always wants to watch DVDs. I say let's talk but she screams and just wants to watch a DVD. Then at home she watches more TV. Her mother says no, but all Britney does is scream for the TV. It's like an addiction.* Right now, her parents cannot control her any more. This is not good.
C	=	general	=	**For those reasons**, I believe that TV is a bad influence on our children.

TASK: Check this essay for coherence using the *Independent Essay Proficiency Checklist* on page 694, then rate it using the *Independent Essay Rating Guide* on page 695. Compare your score to the score on page 789.

Preference Prompts

Preference prompts give you a choice between a pair of opposing positions specific to a topic. You must choose one position and argue in support of it, for example:

Prompt	Do you prefer to use *a laptop computer or a desktop computer*? Why? State your position using examples and reasons.

Avoid double arguments. Choose one side of the argument and develop it, for example:

	Prompt:	Do you prefer to use a laptop or a desktop computer?
X	Double Argument:	Sometimes I prefer a laptop, and sometimes I prefer a desktop.
√	Single Argument:	Personally, I prefer a laptop.

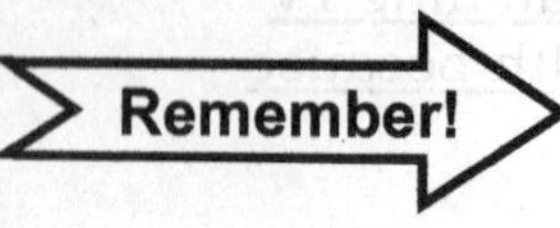

*If you try to develop a double argument, you will run out of time and not be able to develop both arguments. This will result in a lack of topic development (OP**D**UL=C) and a lower score.*

Preference: *Step-by-Step*

When answering a preference prompt, write subjectively using G+3TiC=C and follow the six steps to demonstrate OPDUL=C in your essay.

Step #1	Carefully read the prompt; formulate an opinion.

Prompt	Do you prefer to use a laptop computer or a desktop computer? Why? State your position using examples and reasons.

Step #2 **Make a note map; state your opinion (G); restate it in your conclusion (C); develop examples (3TiC).**

G = prefer laptop

Ti = for example I'm a student, need a laptop for notes
C = laptop good and fast for taking notes in class

Ti = in addition my roommate plays loud music – I can take my laptop to library and do homework
C = laptop is light, easy to carry

Ti = moreover prices are cheap, good laptop under $600, fast with lots of memory

C = buy laptop save $$$

Step #3 **Type a first draft. Do not include the note map.**

Note: There are mistakes in this first draft. Can you identify them? See the corrections in Step #6.

I definitely prefer laptop computers to a desktops.

For example, am student and need a laptop for my classes. If I don't have laptop I will take notes by my pen and that is really slow and my handwriteing is really bad. But with my laptop my notes is clear. This saves my time. I could not do this with a desktop. It's too big and not light to carry. As you can see, a laptop is the best for notes taking in class.

In addition, I can take my laptops everywhere to study. This is good because sometime my roommate, he has his loud musik. If he plays loud musik, I cannot do the homework so I go the library or to a Starbuck. There I connect to the internet and do my homework. Because my laptop is small, I can do these things and not hear the loud music.

Moreover, a few year ago, a laptops were very expensive but now you can get a really fast Sony for cheaper than a desktop. This is good because I can save my money and I need this money for other stuff because I'm a student.

In the final analysis, I definitely prefer a laptop.

Step #4 **Check your first draft for Coherence using OPDUL=C.**

Note: This test-taker has checked his first draft for coherence using OPDUL=C and has moved on to step #5.

Step #5 **Revise your first draft using your revision checklist.**

Note: This test-taker has revised his essay according to his revision checklist and moved on to step #6.

Step #6 **Submit your essay.**

TASK: Check this essay for coherence using the *Independent Essay Proficiency Checklist* on page 694, then rate it using the *Independent Essay Rating Guide* on page 695. Compare your proficiency checklist and your rating to those on page 789.

Personally, I prefer a laptop to a desktop.

For example, I'm a university student and I need a laptop for my classes. If I didn't have a laptop, I'd have to take notes by hand, and that would be really slow. Also, my handwriting is really bad, but with my laptop I can quickly take notes. This saves me a lot of time. I couldn't take notes with a desktop. It is too big and not made for carrying. As you can see, a laptop is definitely best for note taking in class.

In addition, I can take my laptop anywhere to study. This is good because sometimes my roommate plays really loud music. When he plays his music, I can't do any homework so I go to the library or to Starbucks. There I can connect to the internet and do my homework. Because my laptop is small and portable, I can do these things. Best of all, I don't have to listen to my roommate's music.

Moreover, a few years ago laptops were very expensive but now you can get a really fast laptop with lots of memory, like my Sony, for cheaper than a desktop. This is good because I can save money. With this money, I can buy other school things like books.

In the final analysis, I definitely prefer a laptop.

Words: 225

Compare-Contrast Prompts

Compare-and-contrast prompts ask you to argue the opposite sides of a topic, for example:

> Prompt — What do you think a friend might *like and not like* about the place you call home? Why? Develop your position using examples and reasons.

Q *There are many things my friend might like and dislike about my hometown. I could write forever! What should I do?*

A *Keep it simple. Change G+3TiC=C to G+2TiC=C. Develop one positive example in body paragraph one and one negative example in body paragraph two. By doing so, you will compare and contrast both sides of the topic.*

1. Compare-and-Contrast: *Step-by-Step*

When answering a compare-and-contrast prompt, use G+2TiC=C and the six steps to demonstrate OPDUL=C in your essay.

Step #1 — **Carefully read the prompt; formulate an opinion.**

> Prompt — What do you think a friend might like and not like about the place you call home? Why? Develop your position using examples and reasons.

Step #2 **Make a note map; state your opinion (G); restate it in your conclusion (C); develop examples (2TiC).**

Note **<u>However</u>** connecting the body paragraphs. **<u>However</u>** is a transition of contrast.

G = my friend will like some things and not like some things

Ti = <u>for example</u> food is delicious and cheap
C = friend will like this

Ti = **<u>However</u>** New Delhi is very hot and very humid
C = friend will not like this

C = <u>for those reasons</u> friend will like some things and not like some things

Step #3 **Type a first draft. Do <u>not</u> include the note map.**

There are some things my friend will like and won't like about the place I call my home, New Delhi in India.

For example, the delicious food. There are many kinds of food. Also, there are a lot of restaurants and the prices are very reasonable for tourists. My friend will like this.

However, New Delhi is very hot and very humid. My friend will not like this.

For those reasons, there are some things my friend will like and won't like about the place I call my home, New Delhi in India.

Step #4 **Check your first draft for <u>C</u>oherence using <u>OPDUL=C</u>.**

<u>Note</u>: This test-taker has checked his first draft for coherence using <u>OPDUL=C</u> and has moved on to step #5.

Step #5 **Revise your first draft using your revision checklist.**

Note: This test-taker has revised his essay according to his revision checklist and moved on to step #6.

Step #6 **Submit your essay.**

According to OPDUL=C, what is the main problem with this essay?

> There are some things my friend will like and won't like about the place I call my home, New Delhi in India.
>
> For example, the delicious food. There are many kinds of food. Also, there are a lot of restaurants and the prices are very reasonable for tourists. My friend will like this.
>
> However, New Delhi is very hot and very humid. My friend will not like this.
>
> For those reasons, there are some things my friend will like and won't like about the place I call my home, New Delhi in India.
>
> Words: 93

The main problem with this essay is that it lacks body paragraph development (OP**D**UL=C). This essay looks like Map A. It should look like Map B. Map B is an independent essay that demonstrates well-developed body paragraphs.

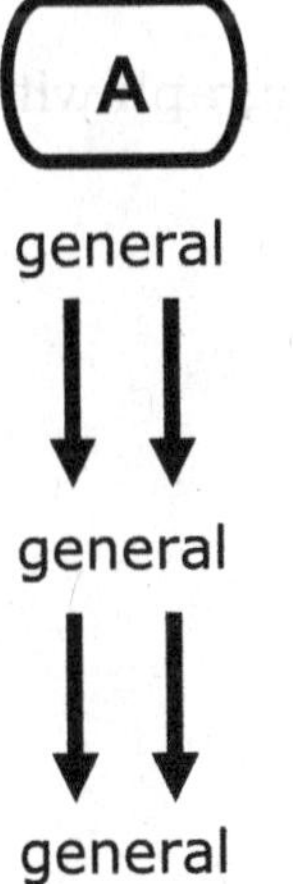

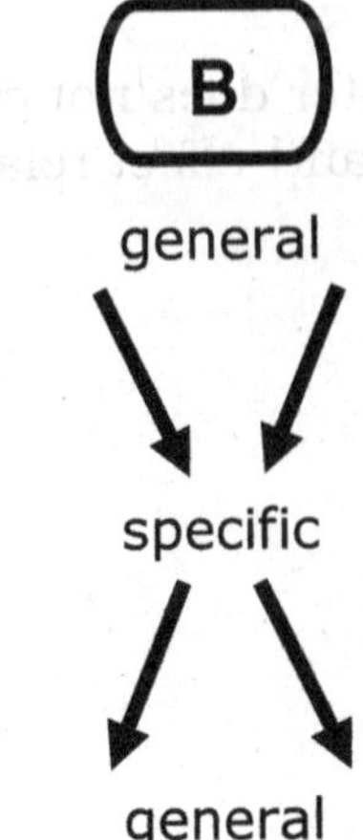

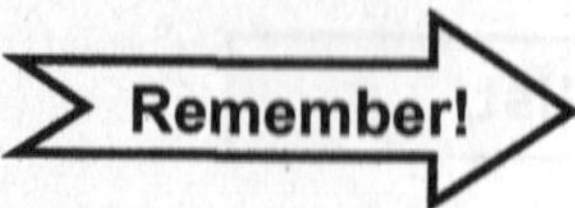

*Well developed means you have a clear supporting illustration (T**i**C) in each body paragraph, and you show a reason based on a cause-and-effect relationship in your concluding sentence (Ti**C**).*

Fixing a Lack of Body Paragraph Development

You can fix a lack of body paragraph development two ways.

1) For each body paragraph, use one specific personal experience example. Then, using the rhetorical strategy of narration, develop the example subjectively, like you are telling a personal story to a friend. Use description and illustration for names, places, dates, prices, etc. The raters will look for these details. More details = greater body paragraph development (OP**D**UL=C) = greater coherence (OPDUL=**C**) = a higher score.

2) Write a concluding sentence (Ti**C**). The conclusion will be based on your illustration. State the conclusion using a cause-and-effect relationship. This, in turn, will create a reason to support your opinion.

Go back to the New Delhi essay. Look at body paragraph one.

> For example, the delicious food. There are many kinds of food. Also, there are a lot of restaurants and the prices are very reasonable for tourists. My friend will like this.

Body paragraph one lacks development because:

1) the writer does not develop a personal experience example writing subjectively, and;

2) the writer does not conclude the paragraph with a reason based on a cause-and-effect relationship.

Look at the same paragraph revised. Note the details and the **cause**-and-*effect* relationship in the concluding sentence (Ti**C**) giving the reason why the friend will like New Delhi.

> For example, the food is very delicious in New Delhi. When I am hungry, I go to Sheshraj's, the best restaurant in New Delhi. It is a family restaurant and they have been doing a good business for many years. The prices are very reasonable and you get a lot of food. The lamb curry is excellent as is the aloo gobi. For a good meal, my friend can spend maybe one American dollar. **Eating at this excellent restaurant** *will give my friend a real New Delhi experience*.

Next, look at body paragraph two. It too demonstrates a lack of development.

> However, New Delhi is very hot and very humid. My friend will not like this.

Look at paragraph two revised. Note the reason in the concluding sentence (Ti**C**) based on a **cause**-and-*effect* relationship. Note also that there are two concluding sentences.

> However, the weather in the summer months of July and August can be extreme. Temperatures can reach 120 degrees Fahrenheit or higher. Last summer, I remember the temperature reached 123 degrees. If my friend is not careful, he can get too much sun and feel very weak and ill. Also, it rains very much and is very humid. As you can see, **visiting New Delhi in summer** *might not be a good time for my friend.* **This might give him some difficulty** and *test his patience*.

Look at the revised essay. Note that the test-taker is using G+2TiC=C.

> There are some things my friend will like and won't like about the place I call my home, New Delhi in India.
>
> For example, the food is very delicious in New Delhi. When I am hungry, I go to Sheshraj's, the best restaurant in New Delhi. It is a family restaurant and they have been doing a good business for many years. The prices are very reasonable and you get a lot of food. The lamb curry is excellent as is the aloo gobi. For a good meal, my friend can spend maybe one American dollar. Eating at this excellent restaurant will give my friend a real New Delhi experience.
>
> However, the weather in the summer months of July and August can be extreme. Temperatures can reach 100 degrees Fahrenheit or higher. Last summer, I remember the temperature reached 123 degrees. If my friend is not careful, he can get too much sun and feel very weak and ill. Also, it rains very much and is very humid. As you can see, visiting New Delhi in summer might not be a good time for my friend. This might give him some difficulty and test his patience.
>
> In conclusion, there are some things my friend will like and won't like about the place I call my home, New Delhi, India.
>
> Words: 219

TASK: Check this essay for coherence using the *Independent Essay Proficiency Checklist* on page 694, then rate it using the *Independent Essay Rating Guide* on page 695. Compare your proficiency checklist and your rating to those on page 789.

2. Compare-and-Contrast: *Step-by-Step*

Let's map out another compare-and-contrast essay. Remember to use G+2TiC=C and the six steps to demonstrate OPDUL=C in your essay.

Step #1 **Carefully read the prompt; formulate an opinion.**

> Prompt — Eating out has both positive and negative aspects. What are they? Why? Develop your argument using examples and reasons.

Step #2 | **Make a note map; state your opinion (G); restate it in your conclusion (C); develop examples (2TiC).**

Note **<u>However</u>** connecting the body paragraphs. **<u>However</u>** is a transition of contrast.

G = positive point: eating out is fast; negative = *$$$*

Ti = <u>for example</u> people love to eat out, pizza, Chinese, Thai
C = people like this a lot

Ti = **<u>However</u>** eating out is *$$$*
C = eating out you can't save *$$$*

C = <u>in conclusion</u> eating out has good and bad points.

Step #3 | **Type a first draft.**

Personally, I think eating out has good and bad aspects.

For example, people love to go to restaurants. There are many restaurants in my town such as pizza, Chinese and Thai restaurants. This is good for people because they can go and have different food every night.

However, eating out is very expensive. Who has money these days? The economy is not so good, so people stay home because restaurants are expensive.

In conclusion, eating out has good and bad points.

Step #4 | **Check your first draft for <u>C</u>oherence using <u>OPDUL=C</u>.**

<u>Note</u>: This test-taker has checked her first draft for coherence using <u>OPDUL=C</u> and has moved on to step #5.

Step #5 **Revise your first draft using your revision checklist.**

Note: This test-taker has revised her essay according to her revision checklist and moved on to step #6.

Step #6 **Submit your essay.**

What is the problem with this submitted essay?

> Personally, I think eating out has both good and bad points people should think about.
>
> For example, people really love to go to restaurants. There are many restaurants in my hometown, such as pizza, Chinese and Thai restaurants. This is very good for people, especially when they are very busy at work. They can go to have a different meal every night and not worry about dishes.
>
> However, to eat out can be very expensive. Who has money these days to go to restaurants? The economy is not so good, so people stay home and cook. This is what people do.
>
> In conclusion, eating out has many good and bad points for people to consider.
>
> Words: 115

The problem with this essay is that the test-taker is not writing subjectively. Instead, she is writing *objectively.* When you write objectively, you are writing about other people and their experiences. In the above essay, who are these "people who love to go to restaurants"? We don't know. This demonstrates a lack of topic development (OP**D**UL=C) and coherence (OPDUL=**C**).

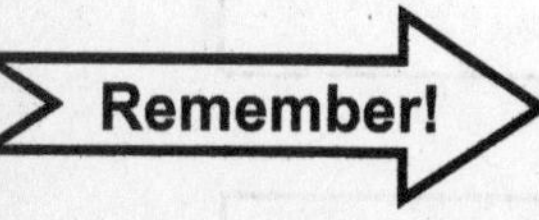

*Write subjectively. Write about yourself. Also, be specific. Include as many details as possible. Details = greater topic development (OP**D**UL=C) = greater coherence (OPDUL=**C**) = a higher score.*

Look at the revised essay. Note how the test-taker is writing subjectively. The test-taker is now the main topic.

> Personally, I think eating out has both good and bad points people should think about.
>
> For example, I love to eat out. My favorite is Thai. There is a great Thai restaurant near my apartment. It is called The Bangkok. The service there is very fast and the food is always excellent, especially the pad Thai and the curry shrimp. I can eat a good meal at The Bangkok for about twenty dollars. This is good for me because I am single and sometimes I work late, so I just go to this restaurant and eat a lot. Best of all, I don't have to wash the dishes, which I really hate to do.
>
> However, to eat out can be very expensive. If I eat at The Bangkok every night for a week, I can spend $140 or more. If I drink alcohol, like a beer, it is even more expensive. For me, $140 is a lot of money. And that is eating at a cheap restaurant. If I go to a more expensive restaurant, like a sushi restaurant, I can spend a lot of money fast. This is something I must watch. Eating out is fun and convenient, but if I am not careful it can be very expensive.
>
> In conclusion, eating out has good and bad points.
>
> Words: 219

TASK: Check this essay for coherence using the *Independent Essay Proficiency Checklist* on page 694, then rate it using the *Independent Essay Rating Guide* on page 695. Compare your proficiency checklist and your rating to those on page 790.

Advantage-Disadvantage Prompts

Advantage-disadvantage prompts, like compare-contrast prompts, ask you to argue by comparing and contrasting the opposing sides of a topic, for example:

Prompt	What are the *advantages and disadvantages* of owning a car? State your opinion using illustrations and reasons.

Q *There are many advantages and disadvantages of owning a car. I could write forever! What should I do?*

A *Keep it simple. Change G+3TiC=C to G+2TiC=C. Develop one advantage in body paragraph one and one disadvantage in body paragraph two.*

Advantage-Disadvantage: *Step-by-Step*

When answering an advantage-disadvantage prompt, use G+2TiC=C and the six steps to demonstrate OPDUL=C in your essay. Remember to write subjectively.

Step #1	Carefully read the prompt; formulate an opinion.

Prompt	What are the advantages and disadvantages of owning a car? State your opinion using examples and reasons.

Step #2	**Make a note map; state your opinion (G); restate it in your conclusion (C); develop examples (2TiC).**

Note **in contrast** connecting the body paragraphs. **In contrast** is a transition of contrast.

G	=	there are advantages + disadvantages to own a car
Ti	=	for example I took the bus to work but the bus it is very slow, always late for work = not good so I bought a car
C	=	my car = not late for work = big advantage for me
Ti	=	**in contrast** a car uses gas, oil and insurance I must make budget
C	=	having a car is expensive for me
C	=	to sum up a car has advantages + disadvantages

Step #3	**Type a first draft. Do not include the note map.**

Note: There are mistakes in this first draft. Can you identify them? See the corrections in Step #6.

Personally, I think there is the advantages and disadvantages to be own the car.

For example, I have a Honda care. Every time I drives to work. Before I have to take the bus. The bus it take a long time. Sometimes the bus misses me and I am late for work. Then I saved my money and bought a Honda care. Now I am always on time and my boss he no get angry no more for being so late owning a Honda care is big advantage.

Also, owning a car can be so much expensive I drive to work every time so I use a lots of the gasoline. Which costs a lot of money these days. In one week I spend more than $100 on the gas. Insurance and repairs also expensive tire too. That means I have to spend less dollars on other things like the food and the cloths this is a big disadvantage two so I am to think about buying the motorcycle Suzuki 750cc. Wow, is so fast. You can't belief.

To sum, better to be owning a motorcyle.

Step #4 **Check your first draft for Coherence using OPDUL=C.**

Note: This test-taker has checked his first draft for coherence using OPDUL=C and has moved on to step #5.

Step #5 **Revise your first draft using your revision checklist.**

Note: This test-taker has revised his essay according to his revision checklist and moved on to step #6.

Step #6 **Submit your essay.**

TASK: Check this essay for coherence using the *Independent Essay Proficiency Checklist* on page 694, then rate it using the *Independent Essay Rating Guide* on page 695. Compare your proficiency checklist and your rating to those on page 790.

Note: There are mistakes in this final essay. Can you identify them?

Personally, I think there is the advantages and disadvantages to be own the car.

For example, I have a Honda care. Every time I drives to work. Before I have to take the bus. The bus takes a long time. Sometimes the bus misses me and I am late for work. Then I saved my money and bought a Honda care. Now I am always on time and my boss he no get angry no more for being so late so owning a Honda car is big advantage so you should buy a Honda car to.

Also owning a car can be so much expensive I drive to work every time so I use a lots of the gasoline so I am to think about buying the motorcycle Suzuki 750cc, wow, is so fast. You can't belief. Another one is the Harley Davision but is so expensive to. But so nice on weekends I can drive in the country and leave city. This is what I want to do with friends they have motorcyle and ride all the times.

To sum, better to be owning a motorcyle.

Words: 187

Advantage Prompts

Advantage prompts ask you to argue the *positive side* of a topic. The positive side states the advantages, for example:

> Prompt What are the *advantages* of telecommuting? State your argument using examples and reasons.

When answering an advantage prompt, use G+3TiC=C and the six steps to demonstrate OPDUL=C in your essay. Remember to write subjectively.

Step #1	**Carefully read the prompt; formulate an opinion.**
Step #2	**Make a note map; state your opinion (G); restate it in your conclusion (C); develop examples (3TiC).**
Step #3	**Type a first draft. Do not include the note map.**

Note: There are mistakes in this first draft. Can you identify them? See the corrections in Step #6.

> From my experience, I can definately say that their are many advantages to working from your home.
>
> For example, at work I have a small cubicle. It's really noisy because of people always talking and using the copi machines. Also, people are always stopping and saying hello to me. This is not good because it waists a lot of time. It also makes it hard for me to finish my work. But at home, nobody bothers me and I finish my work without interruption. This is a big advantage of telecomuting.
>
> Also, when I do go to work, I must get early and drive. It takes an hour. Offen the traffic is bad. When there is an accident, I get to work late. That means I have to stay late to finish my assignments. Plus gas is expensive, especially since I have an SUV. But if I work at home, I don't have to worry about traffic and I can save money on gas. Those are definately advantages.
>
> For those reasons, I believe there are advantages to working from home.

Step #4 **Check your first draft for Coherence using OPDUL=C.**

Note: This test-taker has checked her first draft for coherence using OPDUL=C and has moved on to step #5.

Step #5 **Revise your first draft using your revision checklist.**

Note: This test-taker has revised her essay according to her revision checklist and moved on to step #6.

Step #6 **Submit your essay.**

TASK: Check this essay for coherence using the *Independent Essay Proficiency Checklist* on page 694, then rate it using the *Independent Essay Rating Guide* on page 695. Compare your proficiency checklist and your rating to those on page 791.

From my experience, I can definitely say that there are many advantages to working from your home.

For example, at work I have a small cubicle in a big office. It's really noisy because people are always talking and using the copy machines. Also, people are always stopping and saying hello to me. This is not good because it wastes a lot of time. It also makes it hard for me to finish my work. But at home, nobody bothers me and I finish my work without interruption. This is a big advantage of telecommuting.

Also, when I do go to work, I must get up early and drive. It takes an hour. Often the traffic is bad. When there is an accident, I get to work late. That means I have to stay late to finish my assignments. Plus gas is expensive, especially since I have an SUV. But if I work at home, I don't have to worry about traffic, and I can save money on gas. Those are definitely advantages.

Finally, my children are very small, only seven and eight. Every morning I drop them off at day care. But when I work at home, I can look after them. This saves me money and time. Also, I can see my children more often, and this makes us all very happy. This is the best advantage of telecommuting, killing two birds with one stone.

For those reasons, I believe there are advantages to working from home.

Words: 249

Disadvantage Prompts

Disadvantage prompts ask you to argue the *negative side* of a topic. The negative side states the disadvantages. When answering a disadvantage prompt, use G+3TiC=C and the six steps to demonstrate OPDUL=C in your essay.

Step #1 **Carefully read the prompt; formulate an opinion.**

Prompt What are the *disadvantages* of getting a university degree online? Develop your argument using illustrations and reasons.

Note: This test-taker has completed steps #2 to #5.

Step #6 **Submit your essay.**

TASK: Check this essay for coherence using the *Independent Essay Proficiency Checklist* on page 694, then rate it using the *Independent Essay Rating Guide* on page 695. Compare your proficiency checklist and your rating to those on page 791.

It goes without saying that there are disadvantages to getting a university degree on the internet.

For example, I enrolled in an online university course last year. I wanted an MBA. I thought I would have lots of time to fit it into my schedule, especially on the weekends. But I soon learned it was not that easy. On the weekends, I did not want to study. I just wanted to rest and be with my family all the time. That is what I did. As a result, I did not finish the course.

Another problem is the reputation of the school. My friend was about to finish an online course. He had been studying for two years when the school just disappeared and took his money.

What else? Oh, yeah. If you like talking to professors, go to a regular university. Online, you only talk to professors by email and not all the time. Some people prefer this, but not me.

For those reasons, you can see that getting a university degree on the internet has many disadvantages.

Words: 179

Reason Prompts

Reason prompts are single-question prompts. The question in the prompt will often begin with *Why*. If the question starts with *Who, Where, When, How*, or *If* , why will follow, for example: What is your favorite movie? Why?

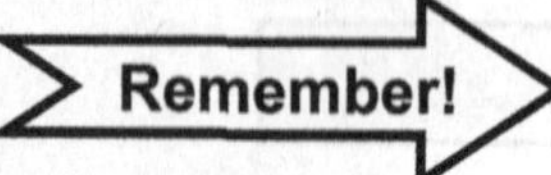

Reasons come from cause-and-effect relationships, for example:

Man: Why should I study for the TOEFL test?

Woman: You should study (cause) because you will get a higher score (effect).

Man: A higher score (effect)? That's a good reason to study for the TOEFL test (cause).

1. Reason: *Step-by-Step*

When answering a reason prompt, use G+3TiC=C and the six steps to demonstrate OPDUL=C in your essay. Remember to write subjectively.

Step #1 **Carefully read the prompt; formulate an opinion.**

Prompt Which technology in the past fifty years has changed your life the most? Why? Develop your position using examples and reasons.

Step #2 **Make a note map; state your opinion (G); restate it in your conclusion (C); develop examples (3TiC).**

G = internet changed my life most

Ti = first use email and Skype every day
C = friends and family feel closer

Ti = second good for research + other information
C = internet research saves time

Ti = third meet scientists round the world
C = internet a good way to share ideas + save money

C = for the aforementioned reasons internet changed my life most

Step #3 **Type a first draft.**

Note: There are mistakes in this first draft. Can you identify them? See the corrections in Step #6.

> Personally, I think internet change my world most.
>
> First, I from China. I now working in US. That mean my family and friend back in Beijing is very far away. Yet by using internet, I can talk to them as much as I want using email and IM. Best is Skype. Skype I can see their faces and they see mind. Before internet, people have to send letter. That take so long. But internet change all that. Internet make communication fast and easy for me and my family. It like magic.
>
> Also, internet good for researching. I am researching laser for testing weather. I develop a new way to measure nitrogen in cloud. To research my idea, I always use internet. It is good for finding article and research paper that can help me with my research paper. If I did not have internet, I have to go to library. That take a lot of time and much travel and cost too much. But with internet, all I do is google and I get information fast and easy. This is really a big change for research.
>
> Third is people I meet. When I have question about my work, I email other scientist I know in the world. With email we can talk about our work and share idea. Before the internet, scientist must travel or talk by phone. Both very expensive. Now instead we talk every day by email or IM for a cheap price.
>
> For the aforementioned reason, internet change my life most.

Step #4 **Check your first draft for Coherence using OPDUL=C.**

Note: This test-taker has checked his first draft for coherence using OPDUL=C and has moved on to step #5.

Step #5 **Revise your first draft using your revision checklist.**

Note: This test-taker has revised his essay according to his revision checklist and moved on to step #6.

Step #6 **Submit your essay.**

TASK: Check this essay for coherence using the *Independent Essay Proficiency Checklist* on page 694, then rate it using the *Independent Essay Rating Guide* on page 695. Compare your proficiency checklist and your rating to those on page 792.

Personally, I believe that the internet has changed my life the most.

First, I am from China. I am now working in the US. That means my family and friends back in Beijing are very far away. Yet by using internet, I can talk to them as much as I want using email and IM. The best way is Skype. With Skype, I can see my parents' faces and they can see mine. Before the internet, people had to send letters. That took so long. But the internet has changed all that. The internet makes communication fast and easy for me and my family. It's like magic.

Also, the internet is good for researching. Right now, I'm researching lasers for testing weather. I'm developing a new way to measure nitrogen in clouds. To research my idea, I always use the internet. It's good for finding articles and papers that can help me with my research. If I didn't have the internet, I would have to go to the library. That would take a lot of time and much travel, and cost a lot. But with the internet, all I have to do is google and I can get the information fast and easy. This is really a big change for research scientists like myself.

Third is the people I can meet. When I have question about my work, I can email other scientists I know around the world. With email, we can chat about our work and share ideas. Before the internet, scientists had to travel or talk by phone. Both were very expensive. Now we can talk every day by email or by IM for a low cost.

For the aforementioned reasons, the internet has changed my life the most.

Words: 291

2. Reason: *Step-by-Step*

Let's map out another reason essay using G+3TiC=C and the six steps to demonstrate OPDUL=C in your essay. Remember to write subjectively.

Step #1 **Carefully read the prompt; formulate an opinion.**

Prompt Why do people travel? Use examples and reasons to support your argument.

Note: This test-taker has completed steps #2 to #5.

Step #6 **Submit your essay.**

TASK: Check this essay for coherence using the *Independent Essay Proficiency Checklist* on page 694, then rate it using the *Independent Essay Rating Guide* on page 695. Compare your proficiency checklist and your rating to those on page 792.

Note: There are mistakes in this essay. Can you identify them?

Personally, I think people travel because they like to learn new stuff.

For example, I went to Manhattan last year. I visited many famous places like Radio City Hall. The most place was the Ground Zero. Ground Zero has been the World Trade Center was. Now it is nothing but big whole. On TV it no look so big. But seeing it for real, wow! So big. Amazing!

Also, I love to shopping. When I travel, I always go to big department stores because they always have sell. When I went to Manhattan I went to Macy because they was having this big sell. I bought so many things, such a handbag and stuffs. I saved lots of money. Definately, you can save money going to sells.

And you can meets lots of friends when you travels.

For though reason, I think traveling is definitely a learned experience.

Words: 148

3. <u>Reason</u>: *Step-by-Step*

Let's map out another reason essay using <u>G+3TiC=C</u> and the six steps to demonstrate <u>OPDUL=C</u> in your essay.

Step #1 **Carefully read the prompt; formulate an opinion.**

<u>Prompt</u> If you could change the world, what would you do? Why? Give illustrations and reasons to support your argument.

<u>Note</u>: This test-taker has completed steps #2 to #5.

Step #6 **Submit your essay.**

<u>TASK</u>: Check this essay for coherence using the *Independent Essay Proficiency Checklist* on page 694, then rate it using the *Independent Essay Rating Guide* on page 695. Compare your proficiency checklist and your rating to those on page 793.

<u>Note</u>: There are mistakes in this essay. Can you identify them?

If I can, I will stop all the pollutes in world this day. First, I no more the pollute from cars. This pollute is CO2. This stop green gazes. Next, I will no more the plastic bottle. These day everywhere you look is water bottle. This is a big problem. You can find this bottle everywhere. Finally, noisey pollution. I live in Roma. Is so noisey pollute I can no sleep. Now I work and live in Manhattan and is still same noisey pollution. For that reasons, I stop the pollutes.

Words: 91

4. Reason: *Step-by-Step*

Let's map out another reason essay using G+3TiC=C and the six steps to demonstrate OPDUL=C in your essay. Remember to write subjectively.

Step #1 **Carefully read the prompt; formulate an opinion.**

Prompt How has technology made our lives better? Why? Develop your argument using examples and reasons.

Step #2 **Make a note map; state your opinion (G); restate it in your conclusion (C); develop examples (3TiC).**

G =

Ti = example sister
C

Ti = also typewriter
C

Ti = finally car
C

C =

Step #3 **Type a first draft. Do not include the note map.**

Note: This test-taker is using induction as a method of organizing her argument.

Note: There are mistakes in the first draft on the next page. Can you identify them? See the corrections in Step #6.

My sister had brest cancer ten year ago. She was able to have it treated with chemotherapy. Chemo are very powerful cancer drugs. My sister is alive because of this drugs. This medical technology definately made my sister's life better.

At high school never had computers. We had just only old fashioned typewriters. When I was tying, I made lots of mistake, so always I had to go back and start over again. But now with computers, typing is fast and so easy. If I make a mistake, all I to do is back space or cut and delete. Using a computer has made my live better, especially now writing this TOEFL essay.

Finally, I can say that the car has made a big chance in my life. Before I had to always go everywhere by the bus. I hated it. It took up so much of my time. Also when I went to work, I have to get up early and sometimes the bus was late an never came. The bus was a nightmare for me. But then I got a car and no longer did I need the bus. Owning a car has definately made my life better.

For the aforementioned, you can see how technology has definately changed my life and many others for the better.

Step #4 **Check your first draft for <u>C</u>oherence using <u>OPDUL=C</u>.**

<u>Note</u>: This test-taker has checked her first draft for coherence using <u>OPDUL=C</u> and has moved on to step #5.

Step #5 **Revise your first draft using your revision checklist.**

<u>Note</u>: This test-taker has revised her essay according to her revision checklist and moved on to step #6.

Step #6 **Submit your essay.**

<u>TASK:</u> Check the essay on the next page for coherence using the *Independent Essay Proficiency Checklist* on page 694, then rate it using the *Independent Essay Rating Guide* on page 695. Compare your proficiency checklist and your rating to those on page 793.

When my sister was told she had breast cancer, she was able to have it treated with special drugs called chemotherapy. "Chemo" is very powerful medicine. My sister had to take it by IV every day for six weeks. It made her really sick but without chemo, my sister might not be here today. She had cancer ten years ago and today she is happy with a good job and a big family. As you can see, medical technology such as chemotherapy has made my sister's life better.

Another example is when I was in high school. When I was learning how to type, we never had computers. We just had old fashioned typewriters. They were really hard to use because the keys were so heavy. Also, when I was typing, I made lots of mistake, so I had to go back and start again. But now with computers, typing is fast and easy. If I make a mistake, I can back space or cut and delete. Using a computer has definitely made my life better, especially now writing this TOEFL essay.

Finally, I can say that the car has really made a big difference in my life. Before I bought a car, I commuted by bus. I hated it. It took up so much time. Also, when I went to work, I had to get up early and sometimes the bus was late or never came. What a hassle! In a nutshell, the bus was a nightmare. But then I got a car, and suddenly the bus was history. Now I can go anywhere, anytime. I can't live without my car. Owning one has really made my life better.

For the aforementioned reasons, you can see how and why technology has had a positive impact on my life and other lives as well.

Words: 304

Quality Prompts

Quality prompts ask you to argue in support of the qualities of a person, place, or thing. Qualities are *positive aspects or characteristics*, for example:

> Prompt What are the *qualities of a good* university? Develop your position using illustrations and reasons.

Quality: *Step-by-Step*

When answering a quality prompt, use G+3TiC=C and the six steps to demonstrate OPDUL=C in your essay. Remember to write subjectively.

Step #1 **Carefully read the prompt; formulate an opinion.**

> Prompt What are the qualities of a good university? Develop your position using illustrations and reasons.

Step #2 **Make a note map; state your opinion (G); restate it in your conclusion (C); develop examples (3TiC).**

G	=	good qualities = Shelton University, it has good teachers, courses + location
Ti	=	for example Shelton U., excellent ESL teachers have lots of experience, helpful, nice too
C	=	teachers help me improve my English quickly
Ti	=	moreover lots of courses; grammar, business
C	=	business English helped me get a job
Ti	=	in addition good location, subway close to school
C	=	take subway to school saves time, very convenient
C	=	for those reasons good qualities = excellent teachers, courses and location, like Shelton U.

Step #3 Type a first draft. Do <u>not</u> include the note map.

<u>Note</u>: There are mistakes in this first draft. Can you identify them? See the corrections in Step #6.

> A good university should have many qualitys.
>
> For example, I study ESL at the Shelton University. The teachers have lots of experience. This is good because they explain things very well and I can learn fast.
>
> Moreover, at Shelton University there is lots of great coarses. I can take grammar or writing coarses. There is a coarse for every level. So far the best coarse for me was the English for Business. In that class Professor Morrison taught me how to write a resume and a cover letter. Because of this, I now have a part time job as a translator.
>
> In addition, Shelton University is a good location. It's right at downtown and very close to the subway estation. It takes me five minutes from estation to school. This is very convenient. Best of all, I don't have to drive my car and find a place to park, which is expensive too.
>
> For those reasons, I believe that Sheldon University has many good qualities.

Step #4 Check your first draft for <u>C</u>oherence using <u>OPDUL=C</u>.

<u>Note</u>: This test-taker has checked his first draft for coherence using <u>OPDUL=C</u> and has moved on to step #5.

Step #5 Revise your first draft using your revision checklist.

<u>Note</u>: This test-taker has revised his essay according to his revision checklist and moved on to step #6.

Step #6	Submit your essay.

TASK: Check this essay for coherence using the *Independent Essay Proficiency Checklist* on page 694, then rate it using the *Independent Essay Rating Guide* on page 695. Compare your proficiency checklist and your rating to those on page 794.

Personally, I contend that a good university should have many qualities.

For example, I study ESL at Shelton University. The teachers there have lots of teaching experience. Also, many of them taught English in foreign countries. This is good because the teachers at Shelton University can understand my situation in America and teach me words and idioms I can use when shopping or at the bank, like "credit" and "debit." This really makes living in America easier for me.

Also, at Shelton University there are lots of great ESL courses. I can take grammar or writing, or speaking courses. There is a course for every level. For me, the best course was English for Business. In that class, Professor Morrison showed me how to write a resume and a cover letter. Because of this, I now have a part time job as a Spanish-English translator.

Finally, Shelton University has a good location. It's right downtown and very close to the subway station. It takes me just five minutes from the station to school. This is very convenient. Best of all, I don't have to drive my car and find a parking place, which is always a pain.

Those, I believe, are the qualities of a good school, like my school, Shelton University.

Words: 212

Common Essay Problems

Avoid these common essay problems on test day.

Shell Introductions

A shell introduction is a false introduction. A shell introduction begins with a sentence or a passage the test-taker has memorized from a book, for example:

> It goes without saying that if power rests in the hands of the minority, the majority will have no recourse but to rise up and reclaim what is rightfully theirs in a fashion that would do their forebears proud, for if no action is to be taken, tyranny will prevail, and Lady Democracy will have been banished into the endless night—forever.

Next, read the same sentence followed by the test-taker's *opinion*.

> It goes without saying that if power rests in the hands of the minority, the majority will have no recourse but to rise up and reclaim what is rightfully theirs in a fashion that would do their forebears proud, for if no action is to be taken, tyranny will prevail, and Lady Democracy will have been banished into the endless night—forever. *I am agree. Progress is good.*

Why is this a shell introduction? Because the first sentence was obviously written by a native English speaker. Moreover, the first sentence is grammatically a complex sentence demonstrating advanced language use. In contrast, the opinion is a simple sentence written by a non native English-speaking writer. Compared to the first sentence, the opinion demonstrates a serious lack of language use and a basic grammatical error: *I agree* not *I am agree*. It is like *apples, apples, apples*, then suddenly *oranges*.

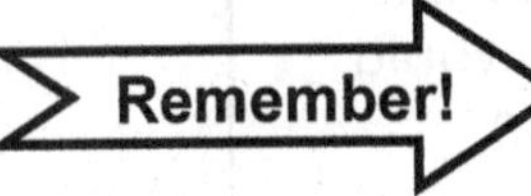

Avoid shell introductions. The raters know this trick.

Serial Topic Listing

Look at the following body paragraph. Can you identify the problem?

> A new sports arena in my hometown will create new jobs for young people. A new sports arena will also help increase taxes. In addition, a new sports arena will bring more people to my hometown. Best of all, a new sports arena will help create other businesses that will support the sports arena, such as hotels and restaurants. Finally, a new sports arena will reduce unemployment. As you can see, a new sports arena is a good idea.

This paragraph is grammatically perfect. However, note how each sentence introduces a new topic. We can put these topics in a list.

A new sports arena in my hometown will:

1. create new jobs for young people
2. increase taxes
3. bring more people
4. create support-businesses
5. reduce unemployment

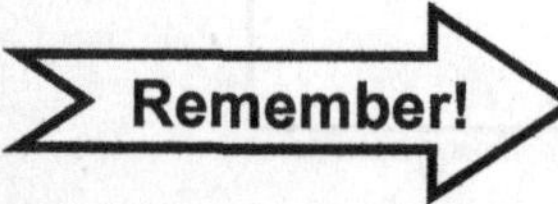

Avoid serial topic listing. Focus instead on one top topic per paragraph and develop it, for example:

> A new sports arena in my hometown will create new jobs for young people. In my hometown, when young people graduate from high school and college, they leave right away and go to the big cities. In the cities, there are more jobs and a better future. However, if we had a new sports arena, the young people would stay because there would be new jobs. There would be jobs like construction and catering, as well other jobs like hotels and restaurants. This would be good because more new jobs would mean the young people would have a reason to stay and develop the economy of my hometown.

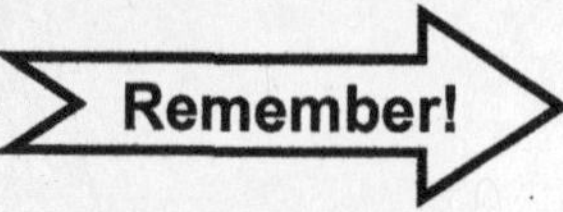

A lack of topic development—especially in the body paragraphs—is a big reason why test-takers score low on the independent essay.

Topic Redundancy

Look at the following paragraph. Can you identify the problem?

> A new sports arena in my hometown will create new jobs for young people. In my hometown, young people need jobs because jobs are good for young people. Jobs are good because they give work to young people who need jobs. I am young and I need a job so new jobs are good for young people like me. New jobs will help not only young people but all people. So new jobs are good for everyone, old and young. I support the new sports arena and new jobs.

This is an example of topic redundancy. Topic redundancy means *repeating the same topic*. In this example, the topic of jobs is repeated, over and over. The result is a lack of topic development (OP**D**UL=C). This will result in a lack of language use (OPDU**L**=C) and a lack of coherence (OPDUL=**C**). Avoid topic redundancy by developing one topic per body paragraph.

Topic Development = Language Use

A well-developed paragraph (1) will focus on one example. As you develop the example, you will use vocabulary and grammar specific to the example. This will test your ability to use your active and passive vocabularies, and your knowledge of grammar. As you can see, language use is a direct result of topic development. If an example is not developed (2), the paragraph will lack topic development and language use (OP**D**U**L**=C). This will result in a lower score.

> **1 ➔** A new sports arena in my hometown will create new jobs for young people. In my hometown, when young people graduate from high school and college, they leave right away and go to the big cities. In the cities, there are more jobs and a better future. However, if we had a new sports arena, the young people would stay because there would be new jobs. There would be jobs like construction and catering, as well other jobs like hotels and restaurants. This would be good because more new jobs would mean the young people would have a reason to stay and develop the economy of my hometown.

> **2 ➔** A new sports arena in my hometown will create new jobs for young people. A new sports arena will also help increase taxes. In addition, a new sports arena will bring more people to my home-town. Best of all, a new sports arena will help create other businesses that will support the sports arena, such as hotels and restaurants. Finally, a new sports arena will reduce unemployment. As you can see, a new sports arena is a good idea.

Writing Practice

Using G+3TiC=C or G+2TiC=C and the six steps, write a basic independent essay that demonstrates OPDUL=C for each of the following prompts you have studied. If you need help, go back and look at the sample responses. Check each essay for coherence using the *Independent Essay Proficiency Checklist* on page 694, then rate each essay using the *Independent Essay Rating Guide* on page 695. By doing so, you will memorize G+3TiC=C and OPDUL=C. You will also be ready to learn advanced strategies to maximize scoring.

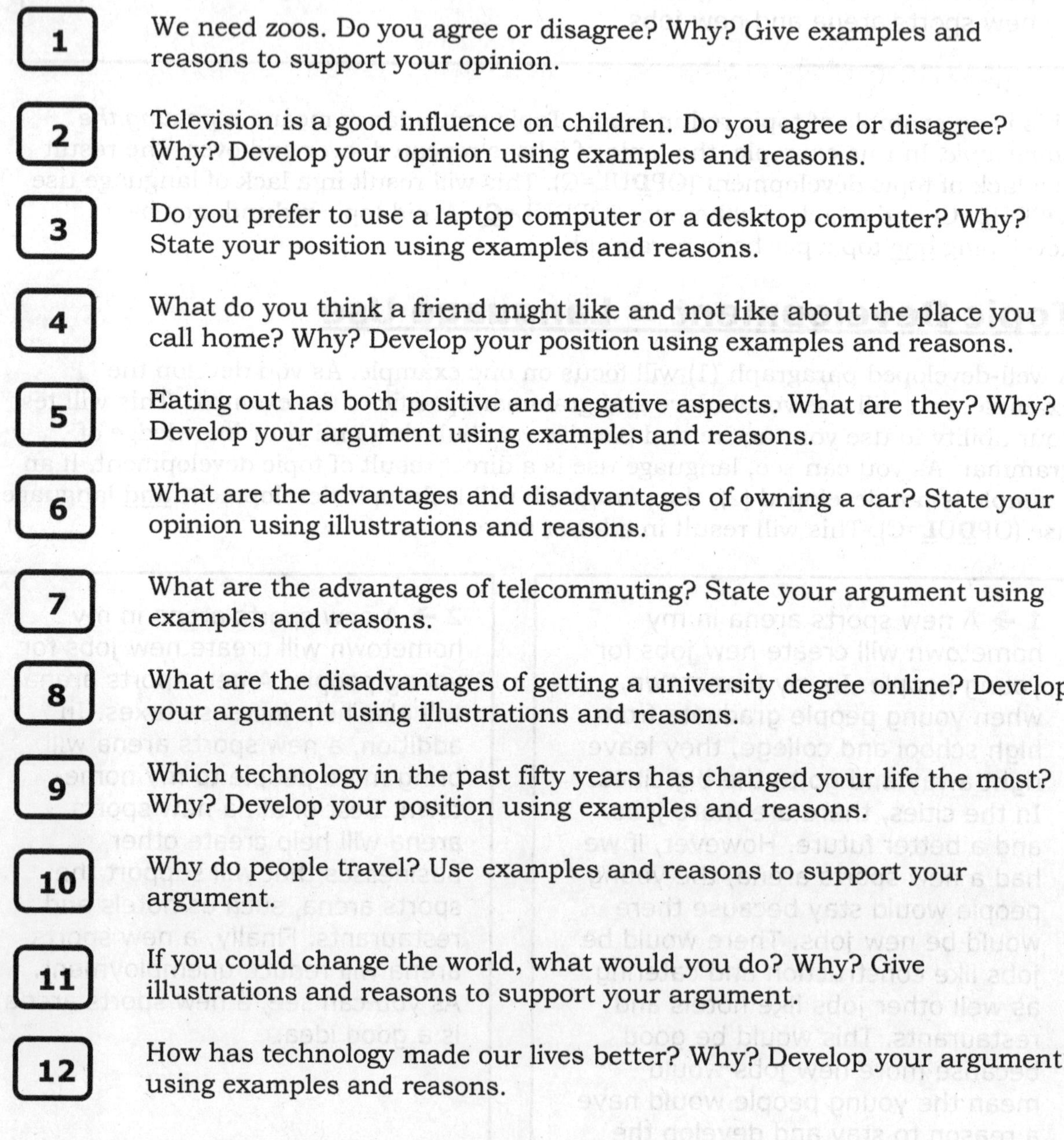

1 We need zoos. Do you agree or disagree? Why? Give examples and reasons to support your opinion.

2 Television is a good influence on children. Do you agree or disagree? Why? Develop your opinion using examples and reasons.

3 Do you prefer to use a laptop computer or a desktop computer? Why? State your position using examples and reasons.

4 What do you think a friend might like and not like about the place you call home? Why? Develop your position using examples and reasons.

5 Eating out has both positive and negative aspects. What are they? Why? Develop your argument using examples and reasons.

6 What are the advantages and disadvantages of owning a car? State your opinion using illustrations and reasons.

7 What are the advantages of telecommuting? State your argument using examples and reasons.

8 What are the disadvantages of getting a university degree online? Develop your argument using illustrations and reasons.

9 Which technology in the past fifty years has changed your life the most? Why? Develop your position using examples and reasons.

10 Why do people travel? Use examples and reasons to support your argument.

11 If you could change the world, what would you do? Why? Give illustrations and reasons to support your argument.

12 How has technology made our lives better? Why? Develop your argument using examples and reasons.

Advanced Introduction Strategies

To maximize scoring, apply the following advanced introduction strategies to develop a basic independent essay into an advanced independent essay.

Simple Hooks

The purpose of a hook is to capture or hook the reader's attention in the very first sentence of your essay. For the independent essay, there are two types of hook: simple and complex. A simple hook uses the information in the prompt. In the following examples, notice how the *hook* comes first, followed by the **transition** and the opinion. Combined, they form the general introduction of your essay, G.

introduction (G) = *hook* + **transition** + opinion

a. *Or-Question Hook*

For this hook, start with an *or question*. Next, write a **transition**, then answer the question. The answer is your opinion, for example:

G *Do we need zoos or not?* **From my point of view**, I believe that we need zoos.

b. *Restate-the-Prompt Hook*

For this hook, first *restate (paraphrase) the prompt*. Next, write a **transition**, then state your opinion, for example:

G *The question is whether we need zoos or not.* **As far as I am concerned**, I assert that we need zoos.

c. *Pro-Con Hook*

For this hook, *state the pro (positive) side and the con (negative) side of the topic*. Next, write a **transition**, then state your opinion, for example:

G *Some people think that we don't need zoos while others think that we do.* **Personally speaking**, I posit that we need zoos.

d. ***General Fact + Or-Question Hook***

For this hook, start with a *general fact.* Next, *ask an or-question about that fact including both the pro and the con sides of the argument.* Next, write a **transition**, then answer the question. The answer is your opinion, for example:

> G *Zoos are popular all over the world. Yet do we need them or not?* **In my estimation**, I believe that we need zoos.

Complex Hooks

A complex hook uses information from researched sources, information you bring to the test. Look at the following complex hooks.

a. ***Statistic Hook***

A statistic hook uses numbers (data) to capture reader attention, for example:

> *According to Educational Testing Services, for the year ending 2009, the average worldwide TOEFL iBT score was 79/120.*

b. ***Definition Hook***

A definition begins an essay by giving a dictionary-like definition, for example:

> *Telecommuting, or e-commuting, is a work arrangement in which an employee works at home and is connected to his or her office by means of a telecommunications link.*

c. ***Shocking-Statistic Hook***

A shocking-statistic hook is often stated as a question, for example:

> *Did you know that next year, six million people will die from smoking cigarettes? That's equal to forty-seven passenger planes crashing every day for a year.*

d. ***Famous-Quote Hook***

When using a famous-quote hook, make sure you state the quote exactly (verbatim) using the correct punctuation and quotation marks, for example:

> *Thomas Edison once said, "Genius is one percent inspiration and ninety-nine percent perspiration."*

e. ***Idiom Hook***

When using an idiom hook, make sure you state the idiom verbatim, for example:

Correct: *My mother always said, "The early bird catches the worm."*

Incorrect: *My mother always said, "The morning bird catches the worm."*

f. ***Anecdote Hook***

An anecdote is a very short story used to introduce the main topic of your essay. An anecdote can be either humorous or serious, for example:

I have been speaking English for twenty years, but I still have a hard time pronouncing some words. Take yesterday for example. I asked a waitress for a "bowel." She looked at me like I was crazy until my American friend said "bowl."

Last year, my friend Juan took an online MBA course. It cost a lot of money, but he enrolled anyway because he could finish in six months. The day after he started studying, the school suddenly closed and Juan lost all his money.

g. ***Provocative Hook***

When using a provocative hook, make sure you can support what you are claiming.

Did you know that women are more intelligent than men?

Warning! *Complex hooks will test your language use proficiency (OPDU**L**=C). If you are confident of your writing ability—and the information you bring to the test—start your essay with a complex hook, for example:*

> A report in *Pediatrics* states that by age sixteen, teenagers who watch TV shows with a high degree of sexual content are twice as likely to have babies out of wedlock than those teens who watch TV with a low degree of sexual content. This evidence proves that television is indeed having a negative influence on the youth of America. It also supports my belief that parents are failing to monitor their children's viewing habits.

The first part of this introduction is a complex hook, specifically a statistic.

hook ➧ A report in *Pediatrics* states that by age sixteen teenagers who watch TV shows with a high degree of sexual content are twice as likely to have babies out of wedlock than those teens who watch TV with a low degree of sexual content.

Next comes *the transition.*

transition ➧ *This evidence proves that television is indeed having a negative influence on the youth of America.*

The transition is followed by the test-taker's opinion.

opinion ➧ *It also* supports my belief that parents are failing to monitor their children's viewing habits.

Notice how the transitions "*This evidence*" and "*It also*" connect the three parts of this introduction, grammatically and topically (OPD**U**L=C). This, in turn, demonstrates coherence (OPDUL=**C**).

Hooks: *Avoid this Problem!*

Look at the following introduction. Can you identify the problem?

> Did you know that every hour three animal species become extinct? Personally, I think that all governments should ban the logging of old growth forests.

This introduction demonstrates a common problem test-takers make when starting their independent essays with a hook: *No transition between the hook and the opinion.*

Look at the same introduction mapped out. Because there is no transition between the hook and the opinion, this introduction demonstrates a lack of organization, development, progression, unity, and language use (**OPDUL**=C). The result is a lack of coherence (OPDUL=**C**).

hook ➧ Did you know that every hour three animal species become extinct?

transition ➧ **?**

opinion ➧ Personally, I think that all governments should invest more in green technology.

Sometimes there is a transition. However, the transition is not topically or grammatically connected to the hook or the opinion, for example:

hook ➧ Did you know that more people are telecommuting these days?

transition ➧ This is a new kind of technology.

opinion ➧ Personally, I think that there are advantages to working from home.

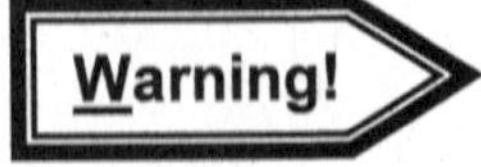
Warning!

A good hook is hard to write. If you are not confident using hooks, do not waste time trying to write one on test day. Instead, state your opinion, then concentrate on developing each body paragraph (3TiC).

Inverted-Pyramid Introduction

Why is a hook an effective advanced strategy? Because your introduction (hook + transition + opinion) will look like an inverted (upside down) pyramid in which the ideas progress from general to specific.

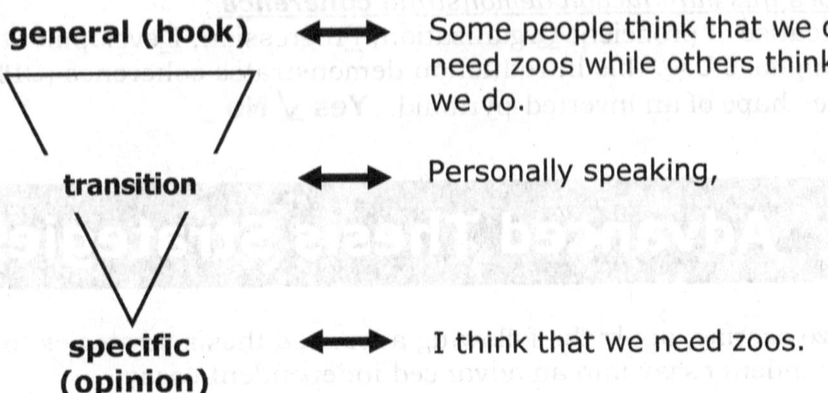
general (hook)
Some people think that we do not need zoos while others think that we do.
transition
Personally speaking,
specific (opinion)
I think that we need zoos.

The writing raters will look for an inverted-pyramid introduction. An inverted-pyramid introduction demonstrates OPDUL=C.

O *Does this introduction demonstrate **organization**?*
The test-taker is using an inverted pyramid that includes a hook, a transition and the test-taker's opinion. This demonstrates organization. **Yes √ No _**

P *Does this introduction demonstrate **progression**?*
The hook is a general statement. It is connected to the opinion by the transition "Personally speaking." This demonstrates progression from general (hook) to specific (opinion). **Yes √ No _**

D

*Does this introduction demonstrate **development**?*
The hook introduces the general topic of zoos and whether we need them or not. The test-taker's opinion focuses on the topic by specifically stating, "I think that we need zoos." The test-taker's opinion is arguable, supportable, a complete sentence and not a question. Combined, this demonstrates introduction development. **Yes √ No _**

U

a. *Does this introduction demonstrate **topical unity**?*
The topic of zoos in the hook and in the opinion are the same. This demonstrates topical unity. **Yes √ No _**

b. *Does this introduction demonstrate **grammatical unity**?*
The transition, "Personally speaking," connects the hook and the opinion, and is grammatically correct. All other grammar is correct. This demonstrates grammatical unity. **Yes √ No _**

L

*Does this introduction demonstrate proficient **language use**?*
The sentence, "Some people think that we do not need zoos while others think that we do" is a complex sentence. This demonstrates proficient language use. **Yes √ No _**

C

*Does this introduction demonstrate **coherence**?*
Because of proficient Organization, Progression, Development, Unity and Language Use, this introduction demonstrates coherence (OPDUL=**C**) in the shape of an inverted-pyramid. **Yes √ No _**

Advanced Thesis Strategies

To maximize scoring, apply the following advanced thesis strategies to develop a basic independent essay into an advanced independent essay.

Predictor Thesis

Read the following theses.

Thesis #1 ➧ Personally, I think that we need zoos.

Thesis #2 ➧ Personally, I think that we need zoos because they are educational, they are fun for families, and they look after endangered animals.

Thesis #1 is a general thesis. In contrast, thesis #2 is *a predictor thesis*. To predict means *to identify in advance*. Notice how thesis #2 is predicting three topics, one for each body paragraph. The topic predicted in body paragraph one is *They (zoos) are educational*; the topic predicted in body paragraph two is *They (zoos) are fun for families*; the topic predicted in body paragraph three is *They (zoos) look after endangered animals.*

Writing a Predictor Thesis

A predictor thesis is a complex sentence. A complex sentence has two parts: independent clause and dependent clause. An independent clause has a subject and a verb. Together, they form a complete idea. In a predictor thesis, the independent clause states your opinion about the **topic** in the prompt. The independent clause connects to the dependent clause with a conjunction. The dependent clause contains the predictors. The predictors are reasons. You will develop each reason using an example in each body paragraph. The reasons, in turn, will support your opinion and conclusion.

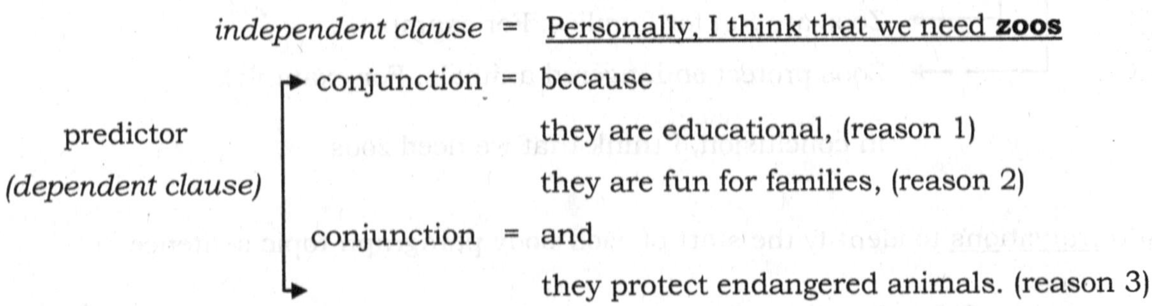

independent clause = Personally, I think that we need **zoos**
conjunction = because
predictor
(dependent clause)
they are educational, (reason 1)
they are fun for families, (reason 2)
conjunction = and
they protect endangered animals. (reason 3)

Look at the following predictor thesis. Note how each predictor becomes a topic sentence in each body paragraph. The topic sentence is the first sentence. Note also how **they** becomes the topic identifier **Zoos** in each body paragraph topic sentence (**T**iC).

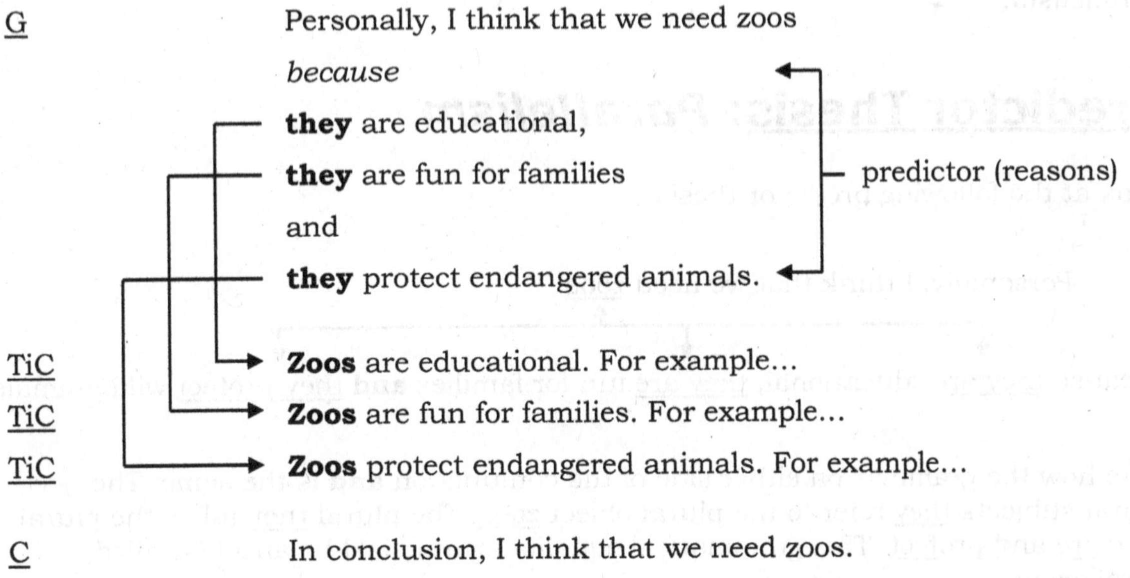

G
Personally, I think that we need zoos
because
they are educational,
they are fun for families
and
they protect endangered animals.
predictor (reasons)
TiC
Zoos are educational. For example...
TiC
Zoos are fun for families. For example...
TiC
Zoos protect endangered animals. For example...
C
In conclusion, I think that we need zoos.

To shorten the predictor, delete the subject and verb in the *second* and *third* predictors.

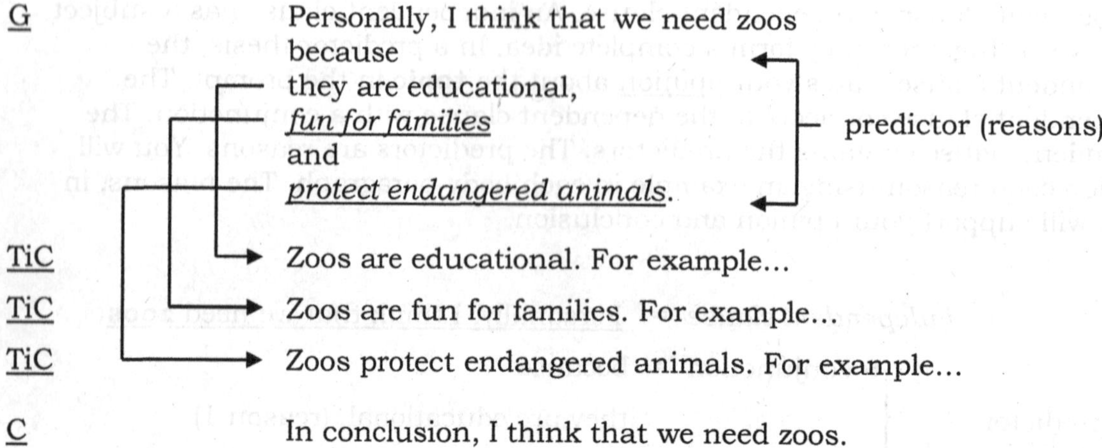
G
Personally, I think that we need zoos
because
they are educational,
fun for families
and
protect endangered animals.
predictor (reasons)
TiC
Zoos are educational. For example...
TiC
Zoos are fun for families. For example...
TiC
Zoos protect endangered animals. For example...
C
In conclusion, I think that we need zoos.

Add transitions to identify the start of each body paragraph topic sentence.

TiC First, zoos are educational. For example...

TiC Also, zoos are fun for families. For example...

TiC Moreover, zoos protect endangered animals. For example...

A predictor thesis demonstrates organization, progression, development, and unity (**OPDU**L=C). It also demonstrates proficient language use (OPDU**L**=C), specifically parallelism.

Predictor Thesis: *Parallelism*

Look at the following predictor thesis.

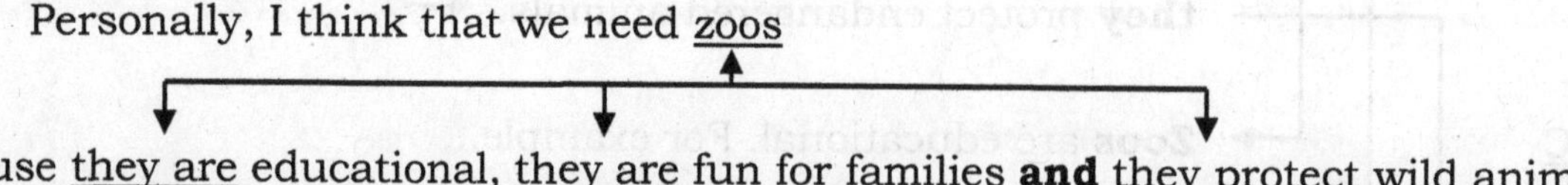
Personally, I think that we need zoos
because they are educational, they are fun for families **and** they protect wild animals.

Note how the grammar on either side of the conjunction **and** is the same. The plural subjects they refer to the plural object zoos. The plural they takes the plural verb are and protect. This grammatical equality (syntactical balance) is called parallelism.

In the next example, note how the grammatical balance is incorrect. When the balance is incorrect, there is *a lack of parallelism.*

Personally, I think that we need zoos

because they is educational, they be fun for families **and** they protects wild animals.

Because this predictor thesis lacks parallelism, it demonstrates a lack of grammatical unity (OPDU**L**=C). This will result in a lack of coherence (OPDUL=**C**) and a lower score.

Gerund Predictor Thesis

Another way to develop your introduction is to use a gerund predictor thesis. Look at the predictor thesis below. Note that it is two sentences.

> Personally, I believe that the internet is a dangerous place. Using the internet increases the risk of identity theft and the risk of downloading viruses.

The first sentence is a general thesis. It identifies the **topic** and the test-taker's opinion about the topic.

> Personally, I believe that the **internet** is a dangerous place.

The second sentence is the predictor. Notice how it begins with a **gerund phrase**. A gerund is an ing noun (Using) followed by an object (the internet). Together, they form the subject. The *verbs and their objects* are the predictors joined by the conjunction and.

> **Using the internet** *increases the risk of identify theft* and *increases the risk of downloading viruses.*

In the following example, note how the grammar on either side of the conjunction **and** is parallel. This demonstrates grammatical unity (OPD**U**L=C) and coherence (OPDUL=**C**).

> From my perspective, I assert that exercising is good for you. Exercising keeps *you happy* **and** keeps *you healthy*.

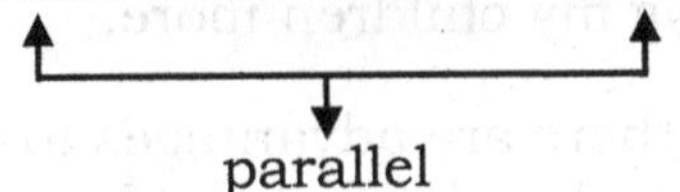

In the following example, notice how the predictor is not parallel after the gerund *Exercising*. This demonstrates a lack of grammatical unity (OPD**U**L=C) and a lack of coherence (OPDUL=**C**).

> From my perspective, I assert that exercising is good for you. *Exercising* keeps *you happy* **and** to keep *you healthy*.

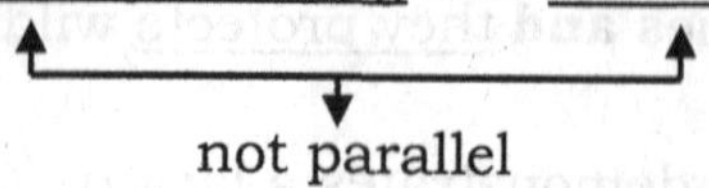

To make this predictor parallel, change *to keep* to *keeps*.

Predictor Thesis: *Using Synonyms*

Look at the following predictor thesis.

> Personally, I think that there are many advantages to working from home such as privacy, cost and seeing my children more.

To demonstrate language use, replace "Personally" with a synonymous phrase, for example:

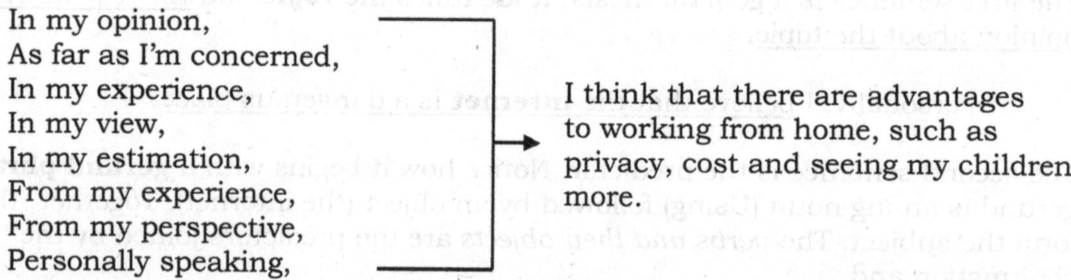

In my opinion,
As far as I'm concerned,
In my experience,
In my view,
In my estimation,
From my experience,
From my perspective,
Personally speaking,
I think that there are advantages to working from home, such as privacy, cost and seeing my children more.

Next, look at the main verb think followed by that.

> Personally, I think that there are many advantages to working from home such as privacy, cost and seeing my children more.

Replace think that with a synonymous phrase. This will demonstrate language use (OPDU**L**=C).

1. In my opinion, I claim that there are advantages to working from home, such as privacy, cost and seeing my children more.

2. As far as I'm concerned, I assert that there are advantages to working from home, for example privacy, cost and seeing my children more.

3. In my experience, I feel that there are advantages to working from home, including privacy, convenience and less stress.

4. In my view, I posit that there are advantages to working from home, namely privacy, cost and spending more time with my children.

5. From my perspective, I contend that there are advantages to working from home, specifically privacy, cost and seeing my children more.

6. Personally speaking, I believe that there are advantages to working from home, including privacy, cost and seeing my children more.

7. In my estimation, I conclude that there are advantages to working from home, such as privacy, cost and seeing my children more.

8. In my opinion, I postulate that there are advantages to working from home, including privacy, convenience and seeing my children more.

9. Personally speaking, I reason that there are advantages to working from home, specifically privacy, cost and less stress.

10. From my perspective, I think that there are advantages to working from home, for example privacy, cost and spending more time with my children.

1. Predictor Thesis: *When to Write*

You can write a predictor thesis when you map out and develop ideas in Step #2.

Step #2	Make a note map; state your opinion (G); restate it in your conclusion (C); develop examples (3TiC).

When developing a predictor thesis this way, first identify the question in the prompt. Next, choose a position to argue. If you agree, ask yourself "Why?" In this case, "Why do we needs zoos?"

> Prompt We need zoos. Do you agree or disagree? Why? Give examples and reasons to develop your opinion.

Next, answer the question "Why do we need zoos?" three times. Each answer will be a body paragraph topic that will support your opinion and conclusion. Each answer will also be one of your **three predictors** (reasons).

After each predictor, write for example. Restate the predictors in your conclusion (for restating predictors in your conclusion, see *Conclusion Strategies*, page 116).

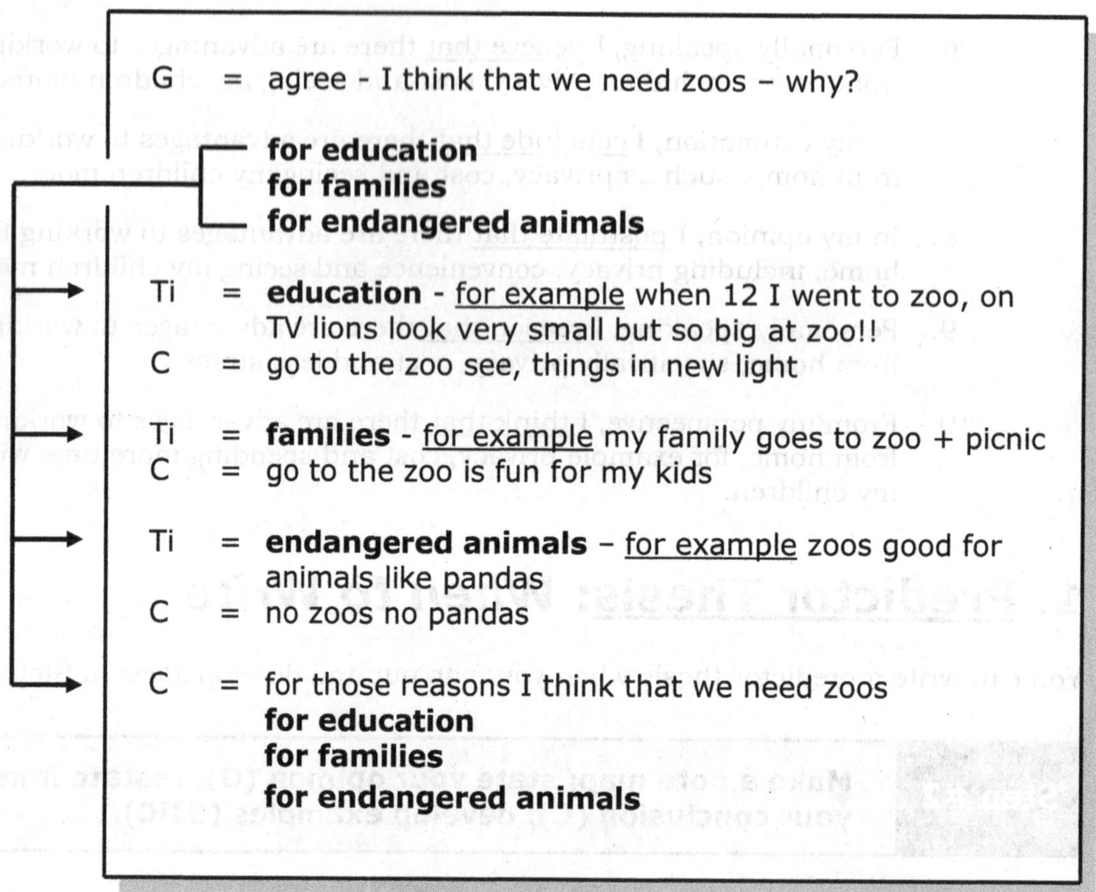

G = agree - I think that we need zoos – why?
for education
for families
for endangered animals
Ti = **education** - for example when 12 I went to zoo, on TV lions look very small but so big at zoo!!
C = go to the zoo see, things in new light
Ti = **families** - for example my family goes to zoo + picnic
C = go to the zoo is fun for my kids
Ti = **endangered animals** – for example zoos good for animals like pandas
C = no zoos no pandas
C = for those reasons I think that we need zoos
for education
for families
for endangered animals

When you are finished mapping out your essay, complete it by following the remaining four steps.

Step #3 **Type a first draft.**

Step #4 **Check your first draft for Coherence using OPDUL=C.**

Step #5 **Revise your first draft using your revision checklist.**

Step #6 **Submit your essay.**

2. Predictor Thesis: *When to Write*

You can also write a predictor thesis when you are revising your first draft. First map out, then write a basic independent essay up to Step #5.

Step #1 **Read the prompt; formulate an opinion.**

Step #2 **Make a note map; state your opinion (G); restate it in your conclusion (C); develop examples (3TiC).**

Step #3 **Type a first draft.**

Step #4 **Check your first draft for Coherence using OPDUL=C.**

Step #5 **Revise your first draft using your revision checklist.**

First Draft

Personally, I agree. I think that we need zoos.

For example, when I was 12, my teacher took us to the zoo in Berlin. I had never seen wild animals before. I had just read about them in books and seen them on the TV. But seeing them in real life was amazing, especially the lions. On TV, they looked so small, but seeing them alive they were really big. By going to the zoo, I definitely saw things in a whole new light.

Now I have a family and we always go to the zoo every summer. My wife makes a picnic and we spend all day there. My kids love taking pictures and learning all about the animals, especially the gorillas. Being outside is good for my children. Best of all, they can leave the internet and the TV at home.

Also, zoos look after endangered animals like pandas. I saw two in the Washington DC zoo last year and they had a baby. If there were no zoos, the pandas would disappear because we are taking their land away. However, in a zoo the pandas are safe. It is not perfect, but without zoos there might not be any pandas left.

For those reasons, I think that we need zoos.

When you finish Step #5, you can: a) submit your essay if you have run out of time, or; b) if you have time, add a predictor thesis.

If you have time—and you want to add a predictor thesis—first identify the main topic in each body paragraph. In this essay, the main topic in body paragraph one is <u>education</u>; the main topic in body paragraph two is <u>families</u>; the main topic in body paragraph three is <u>endangered animals</u>. Next, combine the main topics and make a predictor thesis.

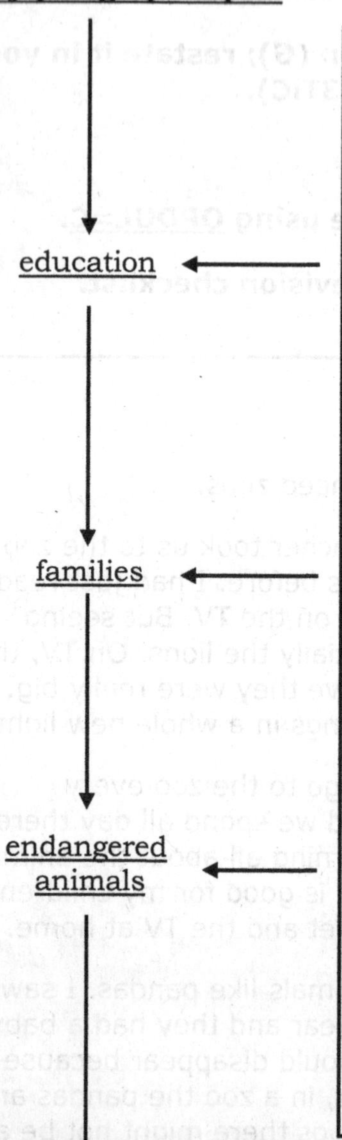

Personally, I agree. I think that we need zoos.

For example, when I was 12, my teacher took us to the zoo in Berlin. I had never seen wild animals before. I had just read about them in books and seen them on the TV. But seeing them in real life was amazing, especially the lions. On TV, they looked so small, but seeing them alive they were really big. By going to the zoo, I definitely saw things in a whole new light.

Now I have a family and we always go to the zoo every summer. My wife makes a picnic and we spend all day there. My kids love taking pictures and learning all about the animals, especially the gorillas. Being outside is good for my children. Best of all, they can leave the internet and the TV at home.

Also, zoos look after endangered animals like pandas. I saw two in the Washington DC zoo last year and they had a baby. If there were no zoos, the pandas would disappear because we are taking their land away. However, in a zoo the pandas are safe. It is not perfect, but without zoos there might not be any pandas left.

For those reasons, I think that we need zoos.

<u>make a predictor thesis</u>

Personally, I agree. I think that we need zoos because they are educational, they are fun for families and they protect endangered animals.

Next: 1) add your predictor thesis to your introduction; 2) write a topic sentence for each body paragraph; 3) restate your predictor thesis in your conclusion.

1) Personally, I agree. I think that we need zoos because they are educational, they are fun for families and they protect endangered animals.

2) Zoos are educational. For example, when I was 12, my teacher took us to the zoo in Berlin. I had never seen wild animals before. I had just read about them in books and seen them on the TV. But seeing them in real life was amazing, especially the lions. On TV, they looked so small, but seeing them alive they were really big. By going to the zoo, I definitely saw things in a whole new light.

2) Zoos are also fun for families. For example, I have a family and we always go to the zoo every summer. My wife makes a picnic and we spend all day there. My kids love taking pictures and learning all about the animals, especially the gorillas. Being outside is good for my children. Best of all, they can leave the internet and the TV at home.

2) Finally, zoos protect endangered animals. For example, I saw two pandas in the Washington DC zoo last year and they had a baby. If there were no zoos, the pandas would disappear because we are taking their land away. However, in a zoo the pandas are safe. It is not perfect, but without zoos there might not be any pandas left.

3) For those reasons, I believe that we need zoos because they are educational, they are fun for families and they protect endangered animals.

Words: 251

Step #6 **Submit your essay.**

Advanced Conclusion Strategies

To maximize scoring, apply the following advanced conclusion strategies to develop a basic independent essay into an advanced independent essay.

a. *Suggestion*

For this strategy, start with a **transition**, restate your opinion, then end with a *suggestion.*

C **In sum**, I assert that television is a bad influence on our children. *Instead of watching so much television, parents should make their kids read a book, or make them go outside and play.*

C **As I have illustrated**, I believe that we need zoos. *If you want to have fun and learn something new, you should go to a zoo.*

b. *Suggestion + Prediction*

For this strategy, start with a **transition**, restate your opinion, then end with a *suggestion and a prediction.* Notice how the *prediction* contains the auxiliary verb "will" to describe a future action.

C **In the final analysis**, I contend that television is a bad influence on our children. *They should spend at least one hour a day playing outside. It will make them happier and healthier.*

C **In the end**, I posit that it is better to save the money that you make. *The best thing you can do is put your money in the bank. In a few years, that money will help you buy a new car or help you go to university.*

c. *Warning + Prediction*

For this strategy, start with a **transition**, restate your opinion, then end with *a warning that contains a prediction of future events.*

C **It goes without saying that** television is a bad influence on our children. *It is creating a lot of fat and lazy kids who will develop serious health problems when they are adults.*

C **As far as I'm concerned**, I believe that a new factory in my home town is not a good idea. *It will create a lot of pollution and destroy our beautiful neighborhoods with more traffic.*

d. ***Rhetorical Question***

For this strategy, start with a **transition**, restate your opinion, then end with *a rhetorical question.* A rhetorical question will make your reader think about your argument after your essay has ended.

C **Suffice it to say**, I think that a new factory in my home town is not a good idea. *How would you like a big smelly factory in your backyard?*

C **In my estimation**, I believe that telecommuting has many advantages. *Don't you wish you could just fall out of bed and go to work in your pajamas?*

e. ***Call-To-Action***

For this strategy, start with a **transition**, restate your opinion, then end with *a call-to-action.* Call-to-action means to tell people to do something (take action) with an emphatic (strong) voice.

C **In sum**, I conclude that television is a bad influence on our children. *Parents, turn off the TV now!*

C **Finally**, I assert that a new airport will be good for our town. *Support the new airport! Invest in our future!*

f. ***Call-To-Action + Rhetorical Question***

For this strategy, start with a **transition**, restate your opinion, *give a call-to-action,* then end with *a rhetorical question.*

C **In closing**, I believe that television is a bad influence on our children. *Parents, turn off the TV now! Do you really want unhealthy kids who are violent too?*

C **When all is said and done**, I contend that a new airport will be good for our town. *Support the new airport! Don't you want to create jobs?*

You can also state the *rhetorical question* first, then end with a call-to-action.

C **In closing**, I conclude that television is a bad influence on our children. *Do you really want unhealthy kids who are violent too?* Parents, turn off the TV now!

C **When all is said and done**, I contend that a new airport will be good for our town. *Don't you want to create jobs?* Support the new airport!

g. Suggestion + Prediction + Rhetorical Question

For this strategy, start with a **transition**, restate your opinion, make *a suggestion and a prediction*, then end with a rhetorical question.

C **In the final analysis**, I conclude that television is a bad influence on our children. *If you are a parent, tell your kids to turn the TV off and read or go outside and play. Doing so will definitely make your kids happier and healthier. Isn't that how you want your kids to grow up?*

C **All in all**, I contend that the internet is a dangerous place. *If you do not want to lose your money and your personal identification, you should always use spyware software when you surf the internet. Spyware software will protect you from internet criminals. Better safe than sorry, right?*

h. Predictor Thesis Restated in Your Conclusion

To develop your conclusion, restate your predictor thesis in your conclusion. After you restate your *predictor thesis*, add a conclusion strategy.

C **In sum,** *I assert that we need zoos because they are educational, fun for families and protect endangered animals.* Visit a zoo. You will definitely have a good time and learn something new.

C **For those reasons,** *I posit that exercising reduces stress, makes me healthier and helps me sleep better.* If you want a happier and healthier life, you too should exercise every day.

i. Predictor Conclusion + Synonyms

Look at the following predictor thesis restated in the conclusion.

C In conclusion, I believe that there are many advantages to working from home, such as privacy, cost and seeing my children more.

To demonstrate language use, replace the transition "In conclusion" with a synonymous phrase, for example:

In the end,
As I have illustrated,
As the aforementioned examples show,
To sum up,
Indeed,
When all is said and done,
All things considered,

→ I believe that there are many advantages to working from home, such as privacy, convenience and freedom.

Pyramid Conclusion

Why is an advanced conclusion an effective strategy? Because your conclusion will look like a pyramid in which the ideas progress from specific to general.

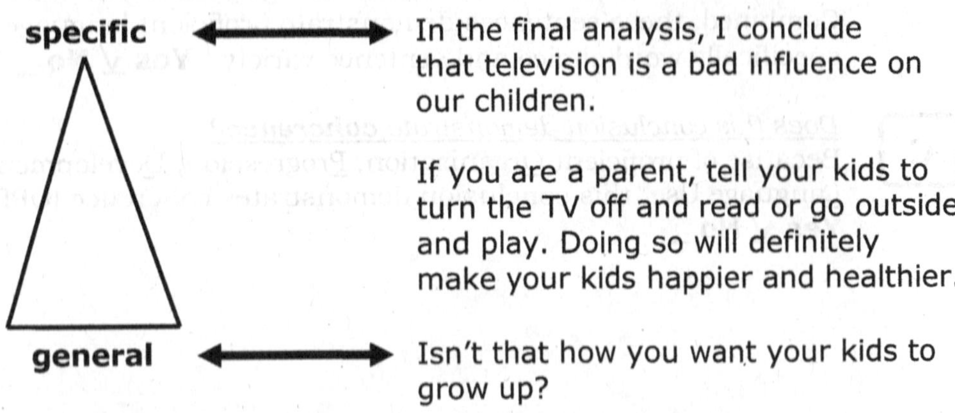
specific
In the final analysis, I conclude that television is a bad influence on our children.
If you are a parent, tell your kids to turn the TV off and read or go outside and play. Doing so will definitely make your kids happier and healthier.
general
Isn't that how you want your kids to grow up?

The writing raters will look for a pyramid conclusion. A pyramid conclusion demonstrates OPDUL=C.

O *Does this conclusion demonstrate* ***organization****?*
The test-taker is using a pyramid structure starting with the restated opinion (specific) followed by a suggestion, a prediction and a rhetorical question (general). This demonstrates organization. **Yes √ No _**

P *Does this conclusion demonstrate* ***progression****?*
The ideas move from the specific restating of the test-taker's opinion to the stating of a general suggestion, prediction and rhetorical question. This demonstrates progression. **Yes √ No _**

D *Does this conclusion demonstrate* ***development****?*
The conclusion restates the test-taker's opinion while the suggestion, prediction and rhetorical question offer general solutions to the problem of television being a bad influence. This demonstrates development.
Yes √ No

U a. *Does this conclusion demonstrate* ***topical unity****?*
The topic of television in the restated opinion and the topic in the suggestion, prediction and rhetorical question (TV) are the same. This demonstrates topical unity. **Yes √ No _**

b. *Does this conclusion demonstrate* ***grammatical unity****?*
There are no errors in grammar. This demonstrates grammatical unity.
Yes √ No _

L *Does this conclusion demonstrate proficient **language use**?*
This conclusion uses a variety of sentence types including a conditional (*If you are a parent, you should tell your kids to turn the TV off and do something else, like read or go out and play and meet new friends*), the future tense (*Doing so will definitely make your kids happier and healthier*) and a rhetorical question (*Isn't that how you want your kids to grow up?*) Combined, these sentences demonstrate proficient language use, specifically word choice and sentence variety. **Yes √ No _**

C *Does this conclusion demonstrate **coherence**?*
Because of proficient Organization, Progression, Development, Unity and Language Use, this conclusion demonstrates coherence (OPDUL=**C**).
Yes √ No _

Advanced Independent Essays

The following essays demonstrate how advanced scoring strategies turn a basic independent essay into an advanced independent essay. Check the rating for each essay on page 794.

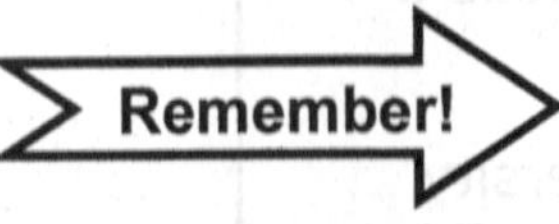

ETS says: "[A]n effective [independent] essay will usually contain a minimum of three hundred words."

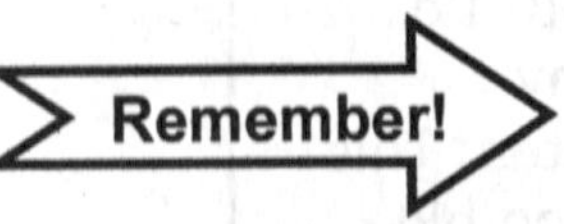

Demonstrate <u>OPDUL=C</u> first, then count words.

Agree-Disagree Essay

Do we or don't we need zoos? Personally, I agree with the statement. I think that we need zoos. We need zoos because they are educational, they are fun for families and they protect endangered animals.

Zoos are educational. For example, when I was 12, my teacher took us to the zoo in Berlin. I had never seen wild animals before. I had just read about them in books and seen them on the TV. But seeing them in real life was amazing, especially the lions. On TV, they looked so small, but seeing them alive they were really big. By going to the zoo, I definitely saw things in a whole new light.

Zoos are also fun for families. For example, I have a family and we always go to the zoo every summer. My wife makes a picnic and we spend all day there. My kids love taking pictures and learning all about the animals, especially the gorillas. Being outside is good for my children. Best of all, they can leave the internet and the TV at home.

Finally, zoos protect endangered animals. For example, I saw two pandas in the Washington DC zoo last year and they had a baby. If there were no zoos, the pandas would disappear because we are taking their land away. However, in a zoo the pandas are safe. It is not perfect, but without zoos there might not be any pandas left.

For those reasons, I believe that we need zoos because they are educational, they are fun for families and they protect endangered animals. If you want to have fun and learn something new, you should go to a zoo.

Words: 280

Preference Essay

Today, people have a big choice between laptop computers and desktop computers. So which do I prefer? Personally, I prefer a laptop because a laptop is great for taking notes in class, portable and affordable.

A laptop is great for taking notes in class. For example, I'm a university student and I need a laptop for my classes. If I didn't have a laptop, I'd have to take notes by hand, and that would be really slow. Also, my handwriting is really bad, but with my laptop I can quickly take notes. This saves me a lot of time. I couldn't take notes with a desktop. It is too big and not made for carrying. As you can see, a laptop is definitely best for taking notes in class.

Also, a laptop is portable. For example, I can take my laptop anywhere to study. This is good because sometimes my roommate plays really loud music. This drives me nuts. When he plays his music, I can't do any homework, so I go the library or Starbucks. There I can do my homework and connect to the internet with Wi-Fi. Because my laptop is portable, I can do these things. Best of all, I don't have to listen to my roommate's music.

In addition, a laptop is affordable. For example, a few years ago laptops, like my Sony Vaio, were very expensive but now you can get a really fast laptop with lots of memory for cheaper than a desktop. This is good because I can save money. With this money, I can buy other school things like books.

In the final analysis, I definitely prefer a laptop because it is great for taking notes in class, portable and affordable. What more do I need?

Words: 294

Compare-Contrast Essay

What will my friend like and not like when visiting the place I call home, New Delhi, India? Personally speaking, I contend that my friend will like the food however he will not be crazy about the summer temperatures or the crowds.

My friend will like the delicious food in New Delhi. When I am hungry, I go to Sheshraj's, the best restaurant in New Delhi. The prices are very reasonable and you get a lot of food. The lamb curry is excellent as is the aloo gobi. For a good meal, my friend can spend maybe one American dollar. Eating at Sheshraj's will definitely give my friend a real New Delhi experience that is both affordable and delicious.

However, my friend will not like summer in New Delhi. The temperature can reach 120F plus the humidity is high as well. This makes New Delhi uncomfortable in the summer. Unlike America, air conditioning is not found everywhere in New Delhi. This is most evident on the trains and buses. With the high temperatures and the high humidity, this can make traveling difficult. Because of these factors, my friend may want to avoid visiting New Delhi in the summer.

As mentioned, New Delhi is crowded. My friend might not like this because he comes from a small town in Connecticut, so he does not feel the pressure of big city life. Also, he does not see any poverty because Connecticut is wealthy unlike parts of New Delhi which are extremely poor. This might be a big shock for my friend since he is not used to such cultural extremes.

As illustrated, there are many reasons why my friend will like and won't like New Delhi. However, this should not stop him from visiting. I guarantee he will have a wonderful time.

Words: 300

Advantage-Disadvantage Essay

The question is what are the advantages and disadvantages of owning a car. From my experience, I can safely say that an advantage of owning a car is freedom and a disadvantage is the cost.

A big advantage of owning a car is freedom. For example, I have a Honda. With my car, I can go anywhere I want. Before I bought a car, however, I had to take the bus everywhere. Sometimes the bus was late, so I got to work late. My boss didn't like that. But since I bought a car, I've never been late for work. Also, I can go for a drive in the country or go shopping and I don't have to worry about bus schedules or money for tickets. This is a big advantage of owning a car.

In contrast, owning a car can be very expensive. For example, I drive to work every day. The distance is fifty miles from my house to my office. That means I use a lot of gasoline. In a week, I can spend more than $75.00 on gas. If the price of gas is higher, I spend more. Insurance and repairs can also be expensive. Tires and parking too. As a result, I have to budget my money and spend less on clothes and video games, and other things I like. This is definitely a disadvantage.

As I have illustrated, I think that there are advantages and disadvantages to owning a car. Should you buy a car? Yes. It's a no-brainer. Go for it. Buy a car and be free! Just watch your money!

Words: 269

Advantage Essay

What is telecommuting? Telecommuting means you can work from home while being connected to your office by the internet. Personally, I prefer to work from home. Working from home has many advantages, such as more privacy, less stress and seeing my children more.

First, telecommuting gives me more privacy. For example, at work I have a cubicle. It's really noisy because people are always talking and using the copy machine. Also, people are always stopping and saying hello to me. This is not good because it wastes a lot of time. It also makes it hard for me to finish my work. But if I work from home, nobody bothers me and I finish my work without interruption. This is an advantage of telecommuting.

Also, with telecommuting there is less stress. When I go to work, I must get up early and drive. It takes an hour and the traffic is always bad. If there is an accident, I get to work late. That means I have to stay late to finish my assignments. But if I work from home, I don't have to worry about getting up early or about traffic or being late for work. This is another big advantage of telecommuting.

Finally, working from home lets me see my children more. My children are very young, only seven and eight. I drop them off at day care when I go to work but when I work from home, I can look after them. This really saves me money. Also, I can spend more time with my children. This makes us all very happy. This is the best advantage of telecommuting.

Suffice it to say, telecommuting has a myriad of advantages. Don't you wish you could just fall out of bed and go to work in your pajamas?

Words: 300

Disadvantage Essay

Last year, I wanted to get an MBA, so I took an online course. I thought I'd have time to do all the work; however, I soon realized that I didn't have enough time. I couldn't study during the week because I was too busy at work. On the weekends, I didn't want to study either. I just wanted to be with my family and relax. As a result, I didn't do any homework and I didn't finish the course. Obviously, if you have no time like me, an online course is not a good way to get a university degree.

Also, if you are going to take an online course, you must be careful about the school's reputation. For example, my friend Maria had a job interview at this company and they asked about her diploma she got online. They thought it was fake because they'd never heard of her school before. This made Maria feel two inches small because she'd worked so hard to get her degree. Unfortunately, she didn't get the job.

Something like this also happened to my friend Hiroshi. He's really good with computers, so he took an IT course because he wanted a computer job. The course cost him a lot of money, but he took it anyway because he could finish in six months and get a job. However, the day after he started studying, the school suddenly closed and Hiroshi lost all his money. Now, he has no school, no money and no job.

As you can see, studying online is like gambling. Does this mean you should not take an e-course? No. Just look before you leap!

Words: 276

Reason Essay

Because I'm a scientist, I use many technologies. However, I can honestly say that the technology that has changed my life the most is the internet. Using the internet makes communication fast and easy, is good for research and it saves me money.

First, the internet makes communication fast and easy. For example, I'm from China and I'm now working in the United States. That means my family and friends back in Beijing are very far away. Yet by using the internet, I can talk to them as much as I want. The best way is Skype. Using Skype, I can see their faces and they can see mine. Before the internet, people like my parents had to send letters. That took so long. But the internet has changed all that. The internet makes communication fast and easy for me and my family. It's like magic. Best of all, I don't get homesick.

Next, the internet is good for research. I'm a research physicist developing lasers for weather testing. To research my ideas, I always use the internet. It's good for finding articles and the latest research papers that can help me with my research. If I didn't have the internet, I'd have to go to libraries. But with the internet, all I have to do is search with Google and I have the information right at my fingertips.

Finally, the internet saves me money. When I have questions about my work, I can email scientists all over the world for answers. This saves money because I don't have to travel. Also, scientists can contact me and ask questions. For example, last week a scientist from Norway emailed me and asked about my work. Before the internet, he would have had to have flown or called long distance. This is very expensive. But now scientists can save time and money using the internet.

In sum, the internet has changed my life the most. Using the internet is fast and easy, is great for research and it saves me money. Can you imagine a world without the internet?

Words: 347

Quality Essay

What are the qualities of a good university? Personally, I posit that a good university should have many qualities, such as excellent teachers, lots of good courses and a convenient location.

A good university should have excellent teachers. For example, I study ESL at Shelton University. The teachers there have lots of teaching experience. Also, many of them have taught English in foreign countries. This is good because the teachers at Shelton University can understand my situation in America. In other words, the teachers can see life through my eyes and know that learning a new language is not easy, especially when living in a new culture.

Moreover, a good university should have a variety of courses. For example, at Shelton University there are lots of great ESL courses. I can take grammar, idioms and composition. I can even take TOEFL! For me, the best course was English for Business. In that class, Professor Morrison showed me how to write a resume and a cover letter. Because of this, I now have a part time job as a Spanish-English translator.

Furthermore, a good university should have a convenient location. Shelton University has a great location. It's right downtown and very close to the subway station. It takes me just five minutes from the station to school. This is so convenient. Best of all, I don't have to drive my car and find a parking place, which is always a hassle.

As the aforementioned examples have illustrated, a good university should have many qualities, such as excellent teachers, lots of great courses and a convenient location. If you want to study ESL in America, you should check out Shelton University. You won't be disappointed.

Words: 283

Emergency Independent Essay

What if you can't write an independent essay? What if you blank out? What should you do? Follow these five steps and write an emergency independent essay.

When writing an emergency independent essay, use induction and 2TiC=C (two body paragraphs and a conclusion), and follow the six steps.

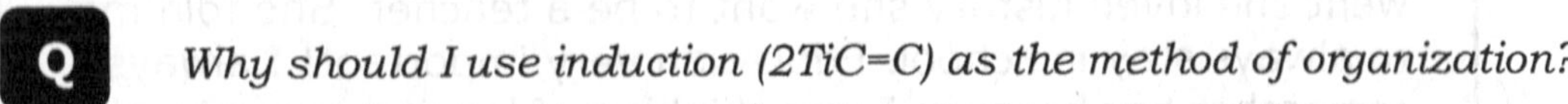

Q *Why should I use induction (2TiC=C) as the method of organization?*

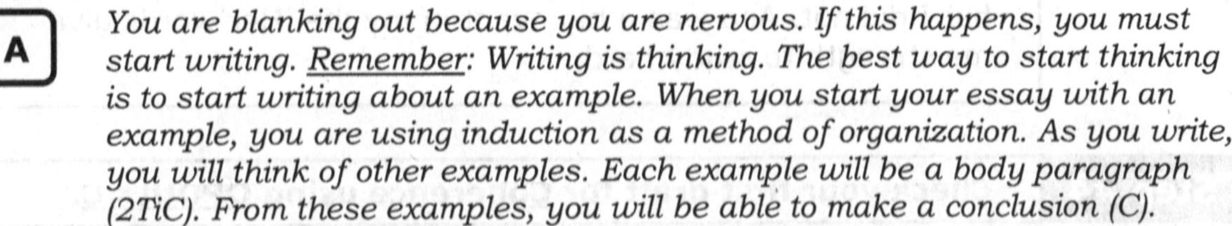

A *You are blanking out because you are nervous. If this happens, you must start writing. Remember: Writing is thinking. The best way to start thinking is to start writing about an example. When you start your essay with an example, you are using induction as a method of organization. As you write, you will think of other examples. Each example will be a body paragraph (2TiC). From these examples, you will be able to make a conclusion (C).*

Emergency Response: *Step-by-Step*

Let's work through an emergency independent essay using 3TiC=C and the six steps to demonstrate OPDUL=C in your essay. Remember to write subjectively.

Step #1 **Carefully read the prompt.**

> Prompt What event changed your life? Why? Give examples and reasons to explain your position.

Next, go directly to step #3 and start writing.

Step #3 **Type a first draft.**

Start by developing one personal example. Use narration and description. Write like you are telling a story to a friend.

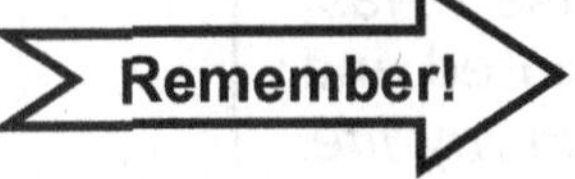

Don't worry about mistakes. Just write.

Note: There are mistakes in the first draft on the next page. Can you identify them? See the corrections in Step #5.

> When I was in university I always see an old woman. She was homeless she live on the street she had a dog and some box. She live on the corner. I saw her in good weather and bad. When he see me she always wave and say hello. Always she smile. I thought was strange. But I talk to her and she was a nice. her name was Ana. She never ask for money or nothin. She just talk about life. Ana, she tell me something I never forget. She say she wished she could go to school. she never went she loved history she want to be a teacher. She told me to always stay in school. Education very important! I always remember her because I was thinking of leaving my university but I did not. Ana was a big event in my life. Her words give me strength to study hard

Step #4 **Check your first draft for Coherence using OPDUL=C.**

Step #5 **Revise your first draft using your revision checklist.**

When you revise your first draft, make sure you: 1) establish *the context* (time and place) in the first sentence; 2) have **transitions** connecting the body paragraphs; 3) state your *opinion* in the end.

> *When I was a university student in Peru*, I always saw an old homeless woman. All she had was a dog and some boxes. I saw her in good weather and bad. When she saw me, she always waved and said hello. I thought she was strange, always so happy, so I avoided her. But then one day I talked to her and she was really nice. Her name was Ana. She never asked for money or anything. She just wanted to talk and be friends.
>
> **One day** Ana told me something I have never forgotten. She said she really wanted to go to university when she was young. She said she always loved history. Unfortunately, she came from a poor family and had no chance to go to school. She told me to stay in school. Education, she said, is very important.
>
> **In sum**, I will always remember what Ana said because I was thinking of leaving my university. But I didn't. I graduated and got a good job. *As you can see, Ana was a big event in my life. Her wisdom gave me strength to continue my studies and be who I am today.*
>
> Words: 197

Step #6 **Submit your essay.**

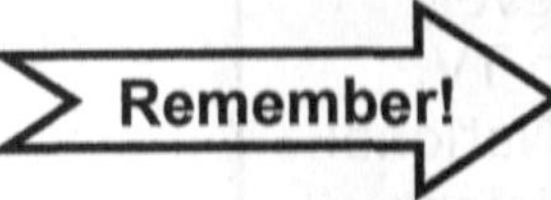

If you blank out, do not stop writing. Writing is thinking. The more you write, the more you will think. The more you think, the more ideas will come to you.

Contrarian Response

What if you think the prompt is strange, does not make sense, or is not asking the right question? What should you do? Write a contrarian essay. Read the following prompt, then read the contrarian response.

Step #1 **Carefully read the prompt; formulate an opinion.**

Prompt   Television is bad for children. Do you agree or disagree? Why? Use examples and reasons to support your argument.

Next, complete steps 2, 3, 4 and 5.

Step #6 **Submit your essay.**

The question asks whether television is bad for children. Personally, I don't agree or disagree. The fact is television is neither good nor bad for children. Television is just an electronic device that delivers information. The real problem is those parents who do not control what their children watch on television.

For example, my friend Pierre lets his kids watch TV all the time. Whenever I go over to his house, his kids are always watching violent movies like Terminator and Die Hard. When Pierre tells them to do their homework or go outside and play, his kids just yell and fight, and Pierre does nothing to stop them. His kids want to watch garbage all day, so he lets them watch garbage all day. Pierre is a great guy but as you can see, the TV is controlling him. As a result, his kids are out of control.

(continued on the next page)

> In contrast, my friend Carla lets her kids watch only two hours of TV every night. Before her kids can watch TV, however, they must do their homework. Then, when they watch TV, Carla tells her kids which shows they can watch, like National Geographic, and which shows they can't watch, like violent movies. This way Carla controls the TV. By doing so, she makes sure that television is a good influence on her kids.
>
> As illustrated, television is neither good nor bad for children. The question should be about parents, and how well they control the TV.
>
> Word: 247

In this contrarian essay, the test-taker is arguing that the prompt is asking the wrong question. The test-taker develops and supports that argument with examples, then concludes by suggesting what the question should be.

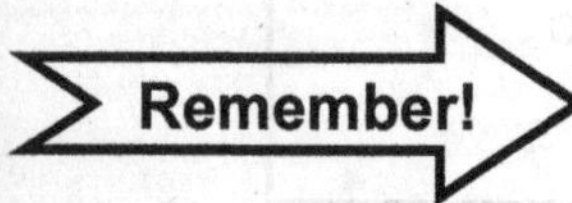

Make sure your contrarian essay is serious. Avoid this type of response.

> What a stupid question!!! TV is not good or bad. It's the parents. They are the problem. Like my friend Pierre. His kids watch TV all the time and they are monsters. But Carla's kids are angels cuz she let's them watch only two hours of TV every night. And good TV. Not bad.

As you can see, the above response is not serious. This will result in a lack of coherence (OPDUL=**C**) and a lower score.

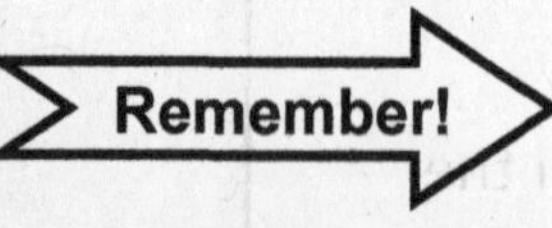

Make sure your contrarian essay is a serious argument. Even if you think the prompt is asking the wrong question, you must still demonstrate OPDUL=C.

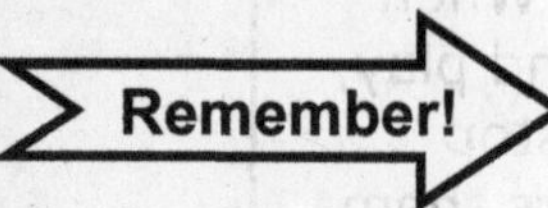

The writing raters do not care about your opinion. They simply want to know if you can construct a coherent independent essay in 30 minutes.

Writing Practice

For each prompt, write an independent essay demonstrating OPDUL=C using either G+3TiC=C or G+2TiC=C and the six steps. You have 30 minutes. Check your essays for coherence using the *Independent Essay Proficiency Checklist* on page 694, then rate each essay using the *Independent Essay Rating Guide* on page 695.

1. Before an important exam, do you think it is better to prepare for a long time or only for a few days? Give examples and reasons to support your argument.

2. What are the advantages and disadvantages of living in a foreign country? Give illustrations and reasons to develop your opinion.

3. Which teacher has had the greatest influence on your life? Why? Give examples and reasons to support and develop your opinion.

4. Some prefer to stay home while on vacation while others prefer to travel. Which do you prefer? Why? Give examples and reasons to support your position.

5. Many people leave their home country. Why? Give illustrations and reasons to support your argument.

6. What is your idea of the perfect neighborhood? Support your opinion with examples and reasons.

7. When is the best time to go on a vacation? Support your argument using examples and reasons.

8. Is it better to buy a product when you want it at the regular price or wait for the product when it is on sale? Use examples and reasons to argue your position.

9. In America, customers can return a purchased item for a full refund within thirty days. Do you agree or disagree with this policy? Develop your position with illustrations and reasons.

10. University education should be free. Do you agree or disagree? Why? Use examples and reasons to develop your argument.

11. Compare and contrast the advantages and disadvantages of using a cell phone. Give illustrations and reasons to support your opinion.

12. Do you agree or disagree? Every student should travel or work for a year before going to university or college. Support your argument using examples and reasons.

Integrated Writing Task

The integrated writing task is the first writing task in the writing section. For this task, you will do either the argument counter-argument or the show-support task. Both are objective writing tasks. Both measure your ability to integrate three skill sets: reading, listening, and writing.

Argument Counter-Argument Task

For this task, you will summarize two opinion-based arguments: one in a short reading, the other in a short lecture. In your essay, you will illustrate how the opinion in the lecture argues against the opinion in the reading.

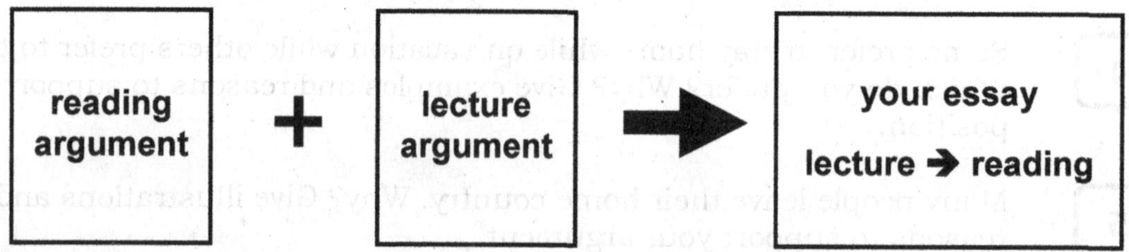

Show-Support Task

For this task, you will read a fact-based passage. Next, you will listen to a fact-based lecture on the same topic as in the reading. In your essay, you will illustrate how the information in the lecture supports the topic in the reading.

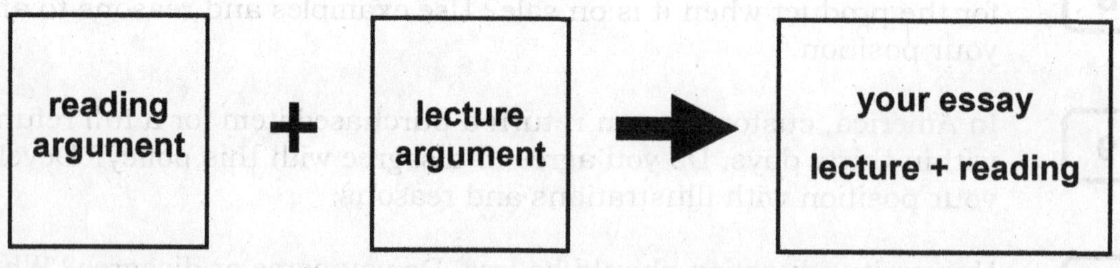

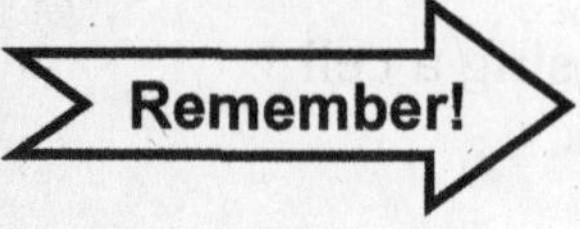

On test day, expect the argument counter-argument task. TOEFL uses this task type more often. For this task, you will write an argument counter-argument integrated essay.

Argument Counter-Argument Essay

This task measures your ability to summarize two opinion-based arguments: one in a short reading passage, the other in a short lecture. In your essay, you will illustrate how the opinion in the lecture argues against the opinion in the reading. The task order follows.

TASK	TIME
1. Read a short academic passage.	3 minutes
2. Listen to a short lecture on the same topic as in the reading.	2-3 minutes
3. Read the prompt. Write an essay that integrates points in the lecture and points in the reading.	20 minutes

The Prompt

The prompt for this task is as follows.

> <u>Prompt</u> Summarize the points made in the lecture and show how they cast doubt on the points made in the reading.

This task measures your ability to:

✓ **take notes** as you read and listen;

✓ **summarize** the main points in the reading and in the lecture;

✓ **synthesize** the main points in the reading and in the lecture;

✓ **paraphrase** the main points in the reading and in the lecture;

✓ **demonstrate** how the lecture "casts doubt on" the reading.

You can write an integrated essay using G+3TiC=C. By doing so, your integrated essay will demonstrate OPDUL=C.

Note the ***additions*** ** to OPDUL=C for the integrated essay.

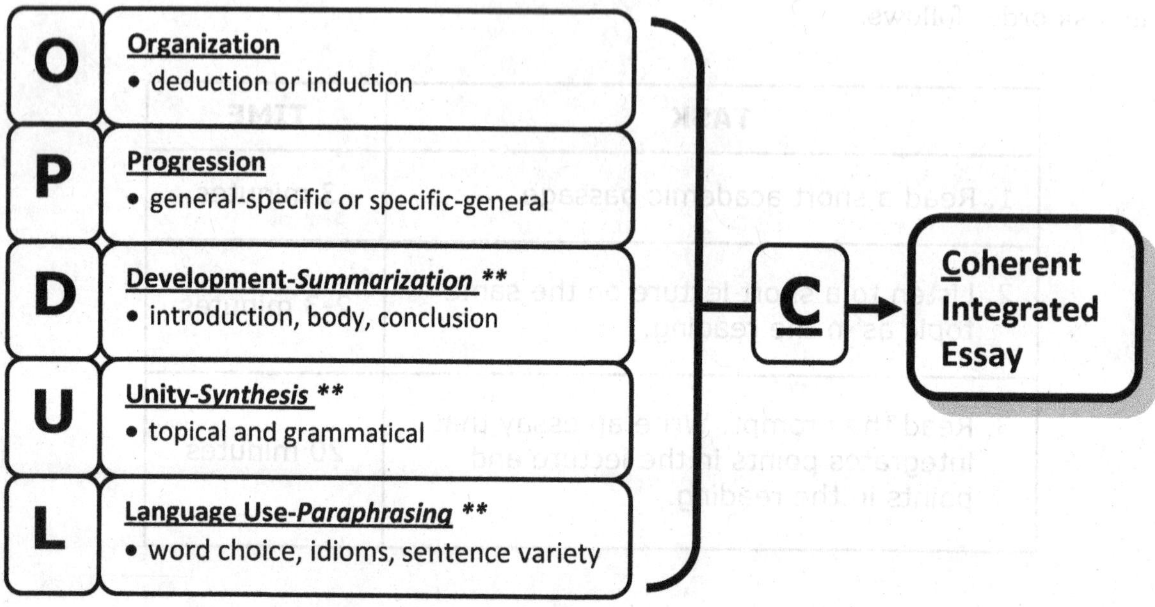

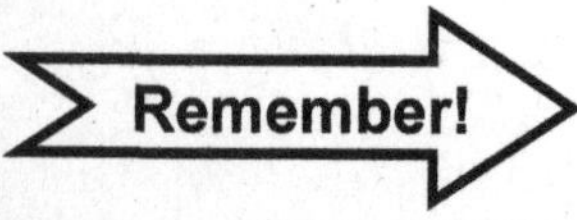

By using G+3TiC=C, you will give the writing raters what they are trained to look for: an integrated essay that demonstrates OPDUL=C.

TOEFL's Testing Method

An understanding of TOEFL's testing method for this task begins with a rhetorical analysis of a test sample. This analysis will help you take effective notes and maximize scoring. First, read a short academic passage. Note: The passage below has been simplified for teaching purposes.

> Personally, I believe that oil companies are a vital part of the American economy.
>
> First, oil companies create thousands of jobs. They need geologists to find new oil reserves and engineers to bring them to market. Economists predict this segment of the job market will continue to grow.
>
> In addition, oil companies pay taxes that build roads and bridges. Last year, big oil paid over $100 billion dollars in tax revenue. America needs this money to maintain its infrastructure.
>
> Finally, the products oil companies make are the life-blood of many industries. Oil is vital for the transportation and plastics industries. These segments of the economy would disappear without oil.
>
> In sum, oil companies are critical to America's health and well being.

In the passage, the author *argues for oil companies*. Next, listen to a lecture on the same topic. Note: The lecture has been simplified for teaching purposes.

> On the contrary, oil companies do more harm than good.
>
> For starters, big oil eliminates jobs to increase profits. Last year, oil companies reduced their work force by 25% while profits were up 50% percent. This trend does not appear to be changing.
>
> Also, oil companies avoid paying taxes by moving overseas. One company, Hamilton, moved to Dubai to reduce its U.S. corporate tax rate. How does this help our roads and bridges?
>
> Worse, petroleum products are the number one cause of global warming. Every day cars pour billions of tons of CO2 into the atmosphere. CO2 has been directly linked to the greenhouse effect.
>
> The evidence is clear. Oil companies do more harm than good.

In the sample lecture, the lecturer *argues against oil companies*. Mapped out, the argument in the reading and the counter argument in the lecture look like this.

Reading (argument)			**Lecture** (counter argument)		
G	=	opinion	G	=	opinion
TiC	=	example	TiC	=	example
TiC	=	example	TiC	=	example
TiC	=	example	TiC	=	example
C	=	conclusion	C	=	conclusion

Where have you seen this structure before? Answer: The independent essay. As you can see, for this task, the reading and the lecture are two opposing, opinion-based arguments (one written, one verbal) connected by topic.

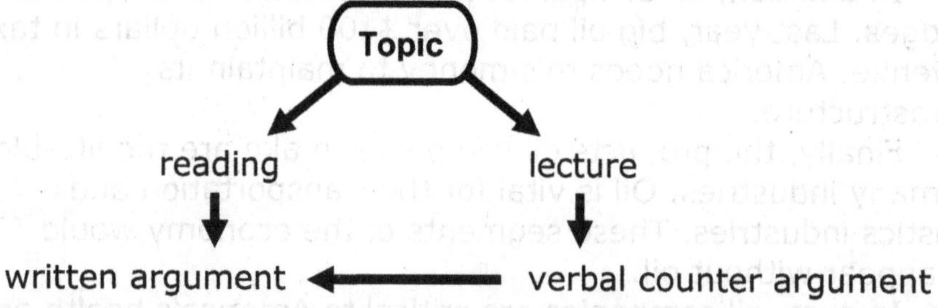

Sometimes the reading will state the pro (positive) position and the lecture will state the anti or con (negative) position, and vice versa.

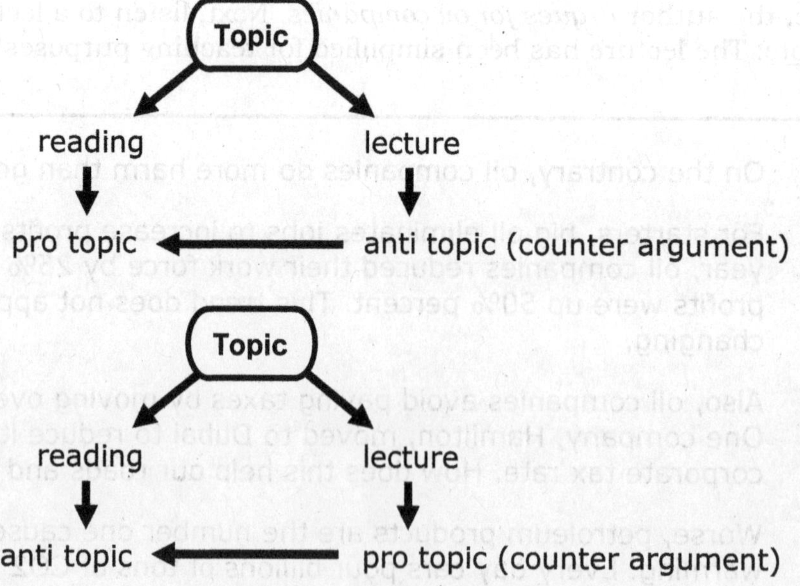

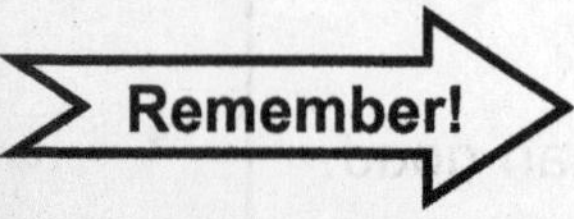

The lecture always argues against (counter argues) the reading. The reading never counter argues the lecture. This testing method does not change. It is therefore predictable.

Now that you understand TOEFL's testing method, let's work through an argument counter-argument integrated essay, step-by-step.

1. Argument-Counter Argument: *Step-by-Step*

When writing an argument counter-argument integrated essay, use G+3TiC=C and follow these six steps to demonstrate OPDUL=C in your essay. You have 20 minutes. You may take notes.

Step #1 Make an G+3TiC=C note map; summarize the reading.

The integrated essay is the first task in the writing section. Before you write your integrated essay, you will see and hear the directions for the writing section. Do not dismiss them. Use this time to make a note map. Write G+3TiC=C twice on note paper. Put **Reading** above the left map and **Lecture** above the right map. Put *point-by-point transitions* under **Reading**. Because each point in the lecture will counter argue each point in the reading, put transitions of contrast under **Lecture**.

Reading	**Lecture**
G	G however
Ti *first* C	Ti however C
Ti *next* C	Ti however C
Ti *finally* C	Ti however C
C *In sum*	C however

Read the Passage

When the writing directions end, the reading passage will appear on your computer screen. You will have 3 minutes to read it.

Read the following passage. Read it from start to finish to understand the author's argument, and the position he/she supports (pro or con).

> Music. We all love it. In fact, I'm listening to music right now, music I downloaded off the internet without paying for it. That's right. I didn't pay a nickel. Not one red cent. And for that, many would call me a criminal. Well, go right ahead. As far as I'm concerned, downloading music off the internet without paying for it is not a crime. Why not?
>
> Let's start with a little history. The internet was originally invented to be a source of free information benefiting all. Downloading music off the internet without paying for it is a perfect example of this democratic ideal in action. In this light, I am not criminal. I am simply exercising my democratic right to move freely in the vast new democracy called cyberspace.
>
> Now if you're like me, you love to share music with your friends by downloading it from their computers. This is not stealing music. Hardly. My friends and I are simply sharing songs. In fact, I share music with people all over the world, people I don't know and will never meet. This process is called P2P or peer-to-peer file sharing. Now think: Is sharing something you love a crime? I don't think so.
>
> Finally, and this point I really want to stress: What I do in the privacy of my home is nobody's business but my own. Period. I don't need the government telling me what I can or can't do with my computer. The United States is a democracy not a dictatorship.
>
> To sum up, just because I refuse to pay for downloaded music does not make me a felon. The real criminals are those in government and business determined to deny music-loving individuals their right to freedom and privacy.

Clearly, this author is pro downloading music off the internet without paying for it.

Next, on your note paper, summarize each part of the author's argument starting with the opinion.

Summarize the Opinion (G)

To locate the author's opinion, check the introduction first. As you read, look for signal words such as the following. They will identify the start of the author's opinion.

> *Personally, I believe that...I feel that...I think that...In my experience...From my perspective...In my estimation...It goes without saying that...As far as I am concerned...I posit that...I contend that...I reason that...I postulate that...*

If the author's opinion is not in the introduction, check the conclusion. As you read, look for transition signal words such as the following. They will identify the start of the author's restated opinion in the conclusion.

> *In sum...In conclusion...To sum up...As you have seen...In the end...All in all...To restate...As illustrated...In closing...In the final analysis...It goes without saying that...Indeed...*

In the sample passage, the author's opinion is *"As far as I'm concerned, downloading music off the internet without paying for it is not a crime."* How do we know this is the author's opinion? Because it is: 1) arguable; 2) supportable; 3) a complete sentence; 4) not a question; 5) has a main topic and a controlling idea, and; 6) it is restated in the conclusion ("To sum up, just because I refuse to pay for downloaded music does not make me a felon.")

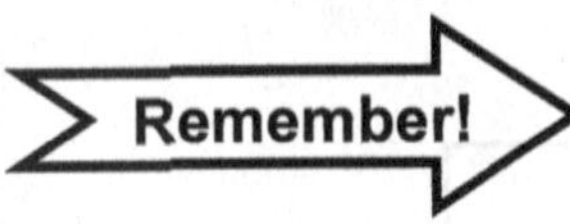

Not all opinions begin with signal words. Look at following opinions.

A. As far as I'm concerned, downloading music off the internet without paying for it is not a crime.

B. Downloading music off the internet without paying for it is not a crime.

Note how opinion A starts with the signal words "As far as I'm concerned...". In contrast, opinion B does not start with signals words. However, both A and B are the same opinion. The difference is style: author A chose to use signal words to identify himself in his opinion using "I'm", whereas author B chose not to.

Next, identify the main point in the introduction. The main point is the author's opinion. **The author's opinion** is identified by the signal phrase <u>As far as I'm concerned</u>. The author's opinion is the beginning of his argument.

> Music. We all love it. In fact, I'm listening to music right now, music I downloaded off the internet without paying for it. That's right. I didn't pay a nickel. Not one red cent. And for that, many would call me a criminal. Well, go right ahead. **<u>As far as I'm concerned</u>, downloading music off the internet without paying for it is not a crime**. Why not?

Next, summarize the author's opinion beside G under Reading on your note map. Use the ***third-person singular*** and ***the present tense*** (*He says...She says...It says...*) Don't worry about grammar and spelling. Just write. Also, make sure you identify the **cause**-and-*effect* relationship.

> Reading
>
> G reading says **downloading music off web without paying** *is not a crime*

Summarize the Body (3TiC)

In the reading, the author begins his argument by stating his opinion. That means he is using deduction as a method of organization. It also means that his supporting illustrations (body paragraphs) will come right after his opinion. How can you identify each body paragraph? Look for transition signal words, such as:

> *First...First off...For starters...Let's start with...Let me begin by saying... Also...Moreover...In addition...Next...Now...Furthermore...Not only that but...On top of that...Finally...*

Transition signal words will identify the start of each body paragraph.

> Music. We all love it. In fact, I'm listening to music right now, music I downloaded off the internet without paying for it. That's right. I didn't pay a nickel. Not one red cent. And for that, many would call me a criminal. Well, go right ahead. As far as I'm concerned, downloading music off the internet without paying for it is not a crime. Why not?
>
> **Let's start with** a little history. The internet was originally invented to be a source of free information benefiting all. Downloading music off the internet without paying for it is a perfect example of this democratic ideal in action. In this light, I am not criminal. I am simply exercising my democratic right to move freely in the vast new democracy called cyberspace.
>
> **Now** if you're like me, you love to share music with your friends by downloading it from their computers. This is not stealing music. Hardly. My friends and I are simply sharing songs. In fact, I share music with people all over the world, people I don't know and will never meet. This process is called P2P or peer-to-peer file sharing. Now think: Is sharing something that you love a crime? I don't think so.
>
> (continued on the next page)

> **Finally**, and this point I really want to stress: What I do in the privacy of my home is nobody's business but my own. Period. I don't need the government telling me what I can or can't do with my computer. The United States is a democracy not a dictatorship.
>
> To sum up, just because I refuse to pay for downloaded music does not make me a felon. The real criminals are those in government and business determined to deny music-loving individuals their right to freedom and privacy.

Some body paragraphs do not start with a transitional signal word. In this case, use formatting to identify the start of each paragraph. Look at the following passage. Note how the first sentence of each body paragraph is indented. This formatting style signals the start of a new body paragraph *when there are no transitional signal words*.

indent

> If you're like me, you love to share music with your friends by downloading it from their computers. This is not stealing music. Hardly. My friends and I are simply sharing songs. In fact, I share music with people all over the world, people I don't know and will never meet. This process is called P2P or peer-to-peer file sharing. Now think: Is sharing something that you love a crime? I don't think so.

indent

> I really want to stress this point: what I do in the privacy of my home is nobody's business but my own. Period. I don't need the government telling...

Body paragraphs can also be separated by a space.

> If you're like me, you love to share music with your friends by downloading it from their computers. This is not stealing music. Hardly. My friends and I are simply sharing songs. In fact, I share music with people all over the world, people I don't know and will never meet. This process is called P2P or peer-to-peer file sharing. Now think: Is sharing something that you love a crime? I don't think so.

space

> I really want to stress this point: what I do in the privacy of my home is nobody's business but my own. Period. I don't need the government telling me...

After you identify the body paragraphs, summarize them as follows:

1. Write Objectively

When you write, write objectively using the ***third-person singular*** and ***the present tense*** (*He says...She says...The reading says...It says...*) Do not worry about grammar and spelling at this point. Just write.

Ti	first ***reading says*** internet is a democracy; downloading music example of internet democracy
C	because ***internet is*** democracy ***music is*** free
Ti	next ***friends just sharing*** music example P2P
C	sharing love for music not stealing, not a crime
Ti	finally ***author talks*** about privacy, example his home
C	***what he does*** in home no business of government or music companies

2. Identify the Topic in each Body Paragraph (TiC)

Summarize ***the topic*** of each body paragraph after the transition (T). Next, identify the supporting illustration (i) and summarize it.

Ti	first reading says ***internet is a democracy***; downloading music example of internet democracy
C	because internet is democracy *music is free*
Ti	next friends just ***sharing music*** example P2P
C	sharing love for music *not stealing, not a crime*
Ti	finally author talks about ***privacy***, example his home
C	what he does in home *no business of government or music companies*

3. Identify the Cause-and-Effect Relationship

The **cause**-and-*effect* relationship in each body paragraph is the reason (main point) that supports the author's opinion. Write each reason beside C.

Ti first reading says internet is a democracy; downloading music example of internet democracy
C **because internet is democracy,** *music is free*

Ti next friends just sharing music example P2P
C **sharing love for music** *not stealing, not a crime*

Ti finally author talks about privacy, example his home
C **what he does in home** *no business of government or music companies*

4. Summarize the Conclusion (C)

Often the author will restate his/her opinion in the conclusion. Opinions in the conclusion are restated using synonyms.

opinion →

Music. We all love it. In fact, I'm listening to music right now, music I downloaded off the internet without paying for it. That's right. I didn't pay a nickel. Not one red cent. And for that, many would call me a criminal. Well, go right ahead. **As far as I'm concerned, downloading music off the internet without paying for it is not a crime.** Why not?

body paragraphs

restated opinion →

To sum up, just because I refuse to pay for downloaded music does not make me a felon. The real criminals are those in government and business determined to deny music-loving individuals their right to freedom and privacy.

Next, summarize the main point in the conclusion. The main point is the author's restated opinion expressed in a **cause**-and-*effect* relationship. Write it beside <u>C</u>.
Use third-person singular and the present tense.

<u>C</u>	in sum author says *not a felon* **if he doesn't pay, government and music companies deny freedom and privacy,** *they are the criminals,* US democracy not dictatorship

You now have a complete note map summarizing the main points in the reading.

<u>Reading</u>

<u>G</u>	reading says downloading music off web without paying is not a crime
<u>Ti</u>	first reading says internet is a democracy; downloading music is example of internet democracy
<u>C</u>	because internet is democracy, music is free
<u>Ti</u>	next friends just sharing music, example P2P
<u>C</u>	sharing love for music is not stealing, not a crime
<u>Ti</u>	finally author talks about privacy, example his home
<u>C</u>	what he does at home is no business of government or music companies
<u>C</u>	in sum author says he is not a felon if he doesn't pay, govt and music companies deny freedom and privacy, they are the criminals, US democracy not dictatorship

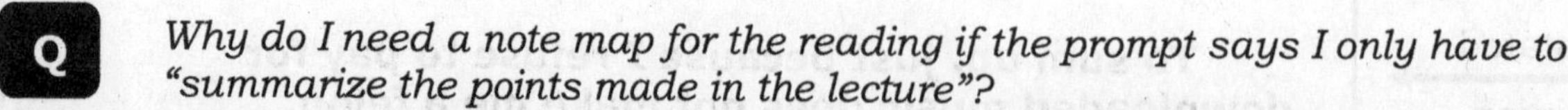

Q *Why do I need a note map for the reading if the prompt says I only have to "summarize the points made in the lecture"?*

A *For three reasons.*

1) You must demonstrate to the writing raters that you understand the argument in the reading.

2) In your essay, you will demonstrate how each point in the lecture counter argues each point in the reading.

*3) Greater development (OP**<u>D</u>**UL=C) = greater coherence (OPDUL=**<u>C</u>**) = a higher score.*

Step #2 **Listen to the lecture.**

When the reading time is up, the passage will leave your computer screen. It will be replaced by the lecture. The lecture will last 2-3 minutes. You cannot replay the lecture. You will hear it only once. That means you must take good notes. An important part of taking good lecture notes is being able to predict the counter-argument in the lecture.

Predicting the Counter-Argument

The author in the sample reading argues that it is not a crime to download music and not pay for it. In contrast, the lecturer will always argue the opposite (counter argue). She will say that *it is a crime not to pay for downloaded music.* I call this the black-and-white rule.

The Black-and-White Rule

The black-and-white rule is simple. If the reading says "Black," the lecture will say the opposite, "White." If the reading says "White," the lecture will say "Black." Being able to predict the counter-argument this way will help you anticipate the main points in the lecture and take notes quickly and proficiently.

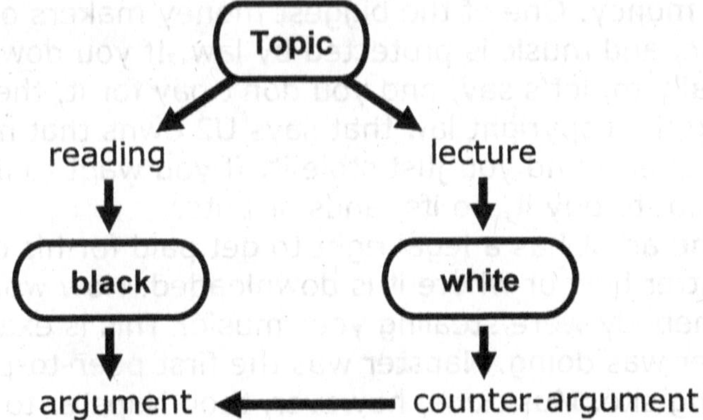

Listening Strategies

For many test-takers, the hardest part of the integrated writing task is the lecture. Why? Because: 1) you hear the lecture only once, and; 2) there are a lot of new words. What should you do to take effective notes as you listen? Do the following.

1. Look at the Lecture side of your note map.
2. Anticipate the counter argument using the black-and-white rule.
3. Listen for signals words that identify the opinion.
4. Listen for the cause-and-effect relationship in the opinion.

5. Listen for transition signal words that identify each body paragraph, its topic and supporting illustration.
6. Listen for the cause-and-effect relationship in each body paragraph.
7. Listen for transition signal words that identify the conclusion.
8. Listen for the cause-and-effect relationship in the conclusion.

As you identify the main points in the lecture, note them under Lecture on your note map. For practice, read the following lecture as you listen to it.

Internet Piracy

It happens every second of every day all over the world. One click and that new song—the one you didn't pay for—is on your iPod. You may think it's legal. After all, downloading music is fast and easy, right? Think again. It goes without saying that downloading music off the web without paying for it is a crime.

I know. I know. Some will argue that "It's my democratic right to download music without paying for it." Nonsense. The internet might have started out with the intention of being a democracy but believe me, those days are long gone. The internet these days is about two things: information and money. Big money. One of the biggest money makers on the web is music, and music is protected by law. If you download U2's latest album, let's say, and you don't pay for it, then you are breaking the copyright law that says U2 owns that music. It is their property and you just stole it. If you want to listen to U2, you've got to buy it, no ifs, ands or buts.

Also, the artist has a legal right to get paid for his or her work no matter how or where it is downloaded. How would you like it if somebody were stealing your music? This is exactly what Napster was doing. Napster was the first peer-to-peer music sharing site. Musicians, however, took Napster to court for not paying royalties, money owed each time a song was downloaded via Napster. Napster argued that it was just helping friends share music. The courts disagreed. Napster paid a big fine and is now a pay site.

Moreover, illegally downloading music off the web is not a privacy issue. If you break the law by illegally downloading music, you are a criminal. I'm sorry, but you can't have it both ways. You can't break the law and hide behind the privacy issue. The law is clear. Criminals have no right to privacy. Period.

It bears repeating that downloading music without paying for it is a crime no matter what anyone says about "the freedom of cyberspace." Just because downloading music is fast and easy doesn't mean you have the right to steal it.

Look at the finished note map for the lecture. Note the **cause**-and-*effect* relationships within each part of G+3TiC=C. Note also that the test-taker writes using third-person singular and the present tense.

Lecture

G however lecture says **downloading music without paying** *is a crime!*

Ti however lecture says web is not democracy, all info and money, example U2
C **not pay for U2?** *break copyright law*
want new U2? you must pay

Ti however lecture says musicians have right to get paid example Napster
C **Napster said P2P sharing** *okay, no crime*
court disagreed, if artist makes music *court says musicians should get paid*
napster now pay site

Ti however lecture says it is not a privacy issue
C **download without paying** means *you are a criminal*
criminals have *no right to privacy*
you can't have your cake *and eat it too*

C however lecture says that **downloading music and not paying is easy** *but still a crime*

Q *Do I have to repeat "however" at the start of each body paragraph?*

A *No. When you write a first draft, use synonyms to demonstrate language use-paraphrasing. However, when taking notes, use one transition of contrast, such as however, to save time.*

Next, look at the two note maps side by side. Look at the arrows. Notice how the lecture counter-argues the reading *point-by-point* even in rough note form.

READING		**LECTURE**
G reading says downloading music off web without paying is not a crime	←	G however lecture says downloading music without paying is a crime
Ti first reading says internet is a democracy; downloading music is example of internet democracy C because internet is democracy music is free	←	Ti however lecture says web is not democracy, all info and money example U2 C not pay for U2? break copyright law want new U2? you must pay
Ti next friends just sharing music, example P2P C sharing love for music is not stealing, not a crime	←	Ti however lecture says musicians have right to get paid, example Napster C Napster said P2P sharing okay, no crime court disagreed, if artist makes music court says musicians should get get paid, napster now pay site
Ti finally author talks about privacy, example his home C what he does at home is no business of govt or music companies	←	Ti however lecture says not a privacy issue C download without paying means you are a criminal, criminals have no right to privacy, you can't have your cake and eat it too
C in sum author says he is not a felon if he doesn't pay, government and record companies deny freedom and privacy, they are criminals, US democracy not dictatorship	←	C however lecture says that downloading music and not paying is easy but still a crime

Step #3 **Read the prompt; write a first draft.**

When the lecture ends, the reading passage will return to your computer screen. The directions and the prompt will also appear on your screen.

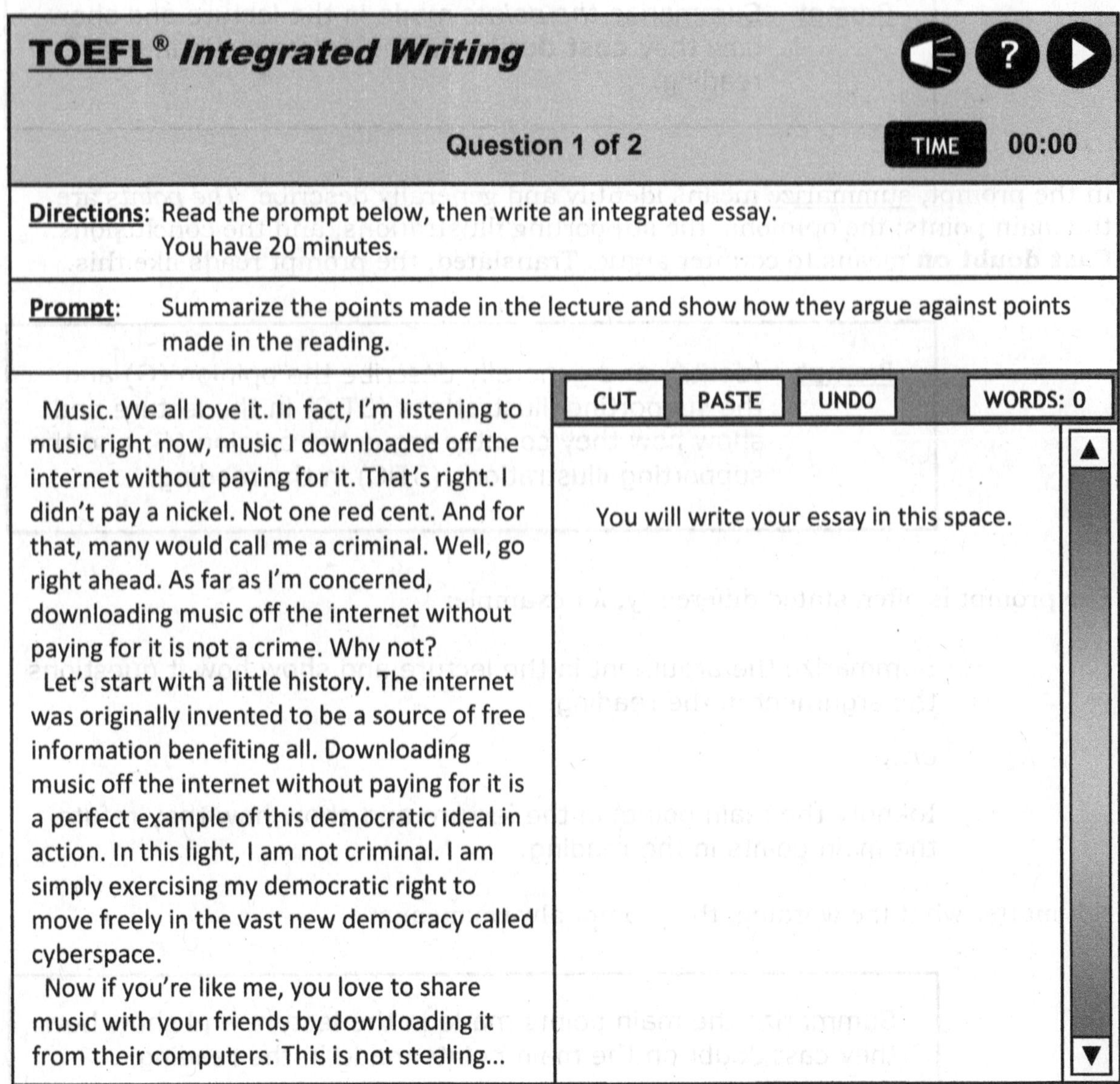
TOEFL® Integrated Writing
?
Question 1 of 2
TIME
00:00
Directions: Read the prompt below, then write an integrated essay. You have 20 minutes.
Prompt: Summarize the points made in the lecture and show how they argue against points made in the reading.
Music. We all love it. In fact, I'm listening to music right now, music I downloaded off the internet without paying for it. That's right. I didn't pay a nickel. Not one red cent. And for that, many would call me a criminal. Well, go right ahead. As far as I'm concerned, downloading music off the internet without paying for it is not a crime. Why not?
Let's start with a little history. The internet was originally invented to be a source of free information benefiting all. Downloading music off the internet without paying for it is a perfect example of this democratic ideal in action. In this light, I am not criminal. I am simply exercising my democratic right to move freely in the vast new democracy called cyberspace.
Now if you're like me, you love to share music with your friends by downloading it from their computers. This is not stealing...
CUT
PASTE
UNDO
WORDS: 0
You will write your essay in this space.

The Prompt

Look at the prompt for this task.

> Prompt   Summarize *the points* made in the lecture and show how they **cast doubt on** *the points* made in the reading.

In the prompt, summarize means identify and generally describe. *The points* are the main points: the opinions, the supporting illustrations, and the conclusions. **Cast doubt on** means to counter argue. Translated, the prompt reads like this.

> Prompt   Identify and generally describe the opinion (G) and the supporting illustrations (3TiC) in the lecture and show how they counter argue the opinion (G) and the supporting illustrations (3TiC) in the reading.

The prompt is often stated differently, for example:

Summarize the argument in the lecture and show how it questions the argument in the reading.

or...

Identify the main points in the lecture and show how they refute the main points in the reading.

Not matter what the wording, the prompt always means:

> Summarize the main points made in the lecture and show how they cast doubt on the main points made in the reading.

Organization: *Point-by-Point Style*

One way to organize an integrated essay is by using point-by-point style. Look at the following sample. Note how the opinion of the lecturer (G) comes first. It is followed by the opinion of the author in the reading. Next, each supporting illustration in the lecture (TiC) argues successively (*point-by-point*) against each supporting illustration in the reading. Note also how the transitional phrases (*This argues against...This point refutes...This opposes...*) connect each contrasting point throughout.

point

The lecture says that downloading music without paying for it is a crime. **This argues against** the reading which says it's not a crime.

point

First, the lecture states that copyright laws protect music. If you don't pay for U2's latest album, you're breaking the law. **This point refutes** the reading which says that the internet is a source of free info and that downloading music without paying is an example of democracy in action.

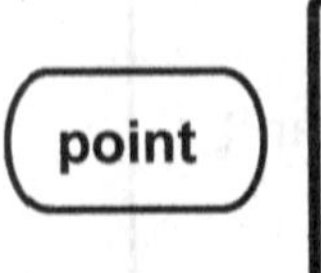

Next, the lecture claims that musicians should get paid. For example Napster, a P2P site, didn't pay musicians. Napster said file sharing wasn't a crime. The court disagreed and fined Napster for not paying. **This argues against** the reading that says downloading music from a friend's computer is not stealing but simply sharing things you love.

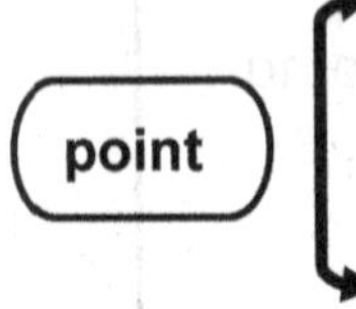

Also, the lecture says if you steal music, you're a thief and have no right to privacy. The law is black and white. **This opposes** the reading which says that the government and record companies have no right telling people what they can or can't do in their homes.

In conclusion, the lecture asserts that ripping music off the web is a crime. **This argues against** the reading which states that downloading music off the internet without paying for it isn't a crime.

Words: 213

Should I start by summarizing the lecture or the reading?

The order in which you summarize does not matter nor does it affect scoring. You just have to demonstrate OPDUL=C in an integrated essay. Look at the example on the next page.

In this sample, the reading is summarized first. Note how the lecture points are introduced by **transitions of contrast**.

> The reading says that downloading music off the internet without paying for it is not a crime. **However**, the lecturer believes it's a crime.
>
> First, the reading states that the internet was invented to be a source of free information. Downloading music without paying for it is an example of this democratic ideal. **In contrast**, the lecturer states that copyright laws protect music. If you don't pay for U2's latest album, you're breaking the law.
>
> Next, the reading says that downloading music from a friend's computer is not stealing but file sharing, which is not a crime. **However**, the lecturer says that musicians should get paid. For example, Napster, a P2P site, didn't pay musicians. Napster said file sharing wasn't a crime. The court disagreed and fined Napster for not paying.
>
> Finally, the author says that what he does in the privacy of his home is no business of the government. **In contrast**, the lecturer believes that if you steal music, you're a thief and have no right to privacy. The law is black and white. You can't have your cake and eat it too.
>
> In sum, the reading states that downloading music off the internet without paying for it isn't a crime. The criminals are the government and record companies trying to take away people's freedom. **However**, the lecturer asserts that ripping music off the web is a crime.
>
> Words: 221

Q *In this essay, the test-taker does not paraphrase the reading. Do I have to paraphrase the reading?*

A *Yes. You must paraphrase the main points in the reading. Paraphrasing the reading and the lecture demonstrates language-use paraphrasing (OPDUL=C). This will result in a higher score.*

Warning! *Do not copy the reading passage word-for-word. The raters know this trick. Also, do not summarize only the reading. The raters want to know if you can integrate (synthesize-combine) the argument in the reading and the counter-argument in the lecture.*

Organization: *Block-Style*

Block style is another way to organize an integrated essay. In the following example, notice how the reading is summarized first followed by the lecture. If you use block style, use *step-by-step transitions* and a **transition of contrast** to connect the reading and the lecture.

reading block

The reading says that downloading music off the internet without paying for it is not a crime.
First, the reading says the internet was invented to be a source of free information. Downloading music without paying for it is an example of democracy in action.
Next, the reading states that downloading music from a friend's computer is file sharing, which isn't a crime.
Finally, the author says that what he does in the privacy of his home is no business of the government.
In sum, the reading states that downloading music off the internet without paying for it is not a crime. The real criminals are the government and the record companies trying to take away people's freedom.

lecture block

However, the lecturer believes that not paying for downloaded music is a crime.
First, the lecturer states that copyright laws protect music. If you don't pay for U2's latest album, you're breaking the law.
Next, the lecturer says that musicians should get paid. For example, Napster, a P2P site, didn't pay musicians. Napster said that file sharing wasn't a crime. The court disagreed and fined Napster for not paying.
Finally, the lecturer believes that if you steal music, you're a thief and have no privacy. The law is black and white.
In conclusion, the lecturer asserts that ripping music off the web is a crime.

Words: 223

Which method of organization is best, point-by-point or block style?

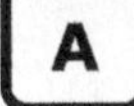

Neither. They are simply two ways to organize an integrated essay.

Only by practicing will you know which method of organization you prefer: point-by-point or block style.

Step #4 **Check your first draft for Coherence using OPDUL=C.**

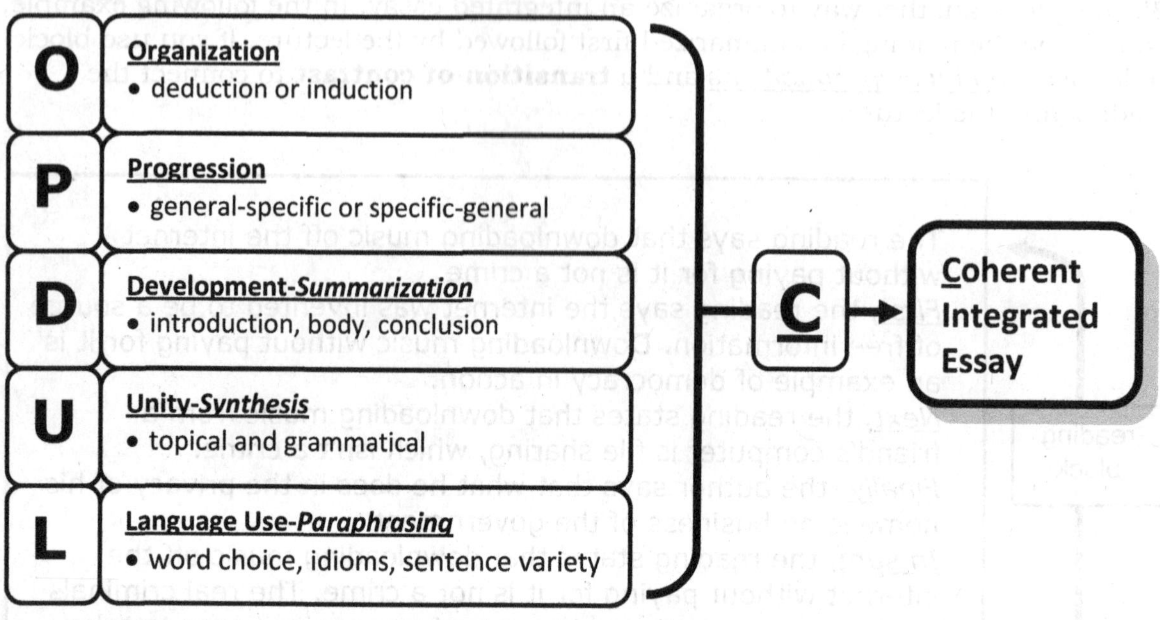

TASK: Go back to page 151 and check the point-by-point internet music essay for coherence using OPDUL=C above.

O *Does this essay demonstrate **organization**?*
The writer demonstrates organization by using deduction and point-by-point style. **Yes √ No _**

P *Does this essay demonstrate **progression**?*
Because the writer is using deduction and point-by-point style, the points in the lecture and in the reading progress in parallel from general to specific. This demonstrates progression. **Yes √ No _**

D a. *Do the introductions demonstrate **development-summarization**?*
The writer has proficiently summarized the main point (the opinion) in the the lecture and in the reading with no points left out. This demonstrates introduction development-summarization. **Yes √ No _**

b. *Do the bodies demonstrate **development-summarization**?*
The writer has proficiently summarized the main points (the supporting illustrations) in the body paragraphs of the lecture and the reading with no points left out. This demonstrates body development-summarization. **Yes √ No _**

c. *Do the conclusions demonstrate* ***development-summarization****?*
The writer has proficiently summarized the main point (the restated opinion in the conclusion) in the lecture and in the reading with no points left out. This demonstrates conclusion development-summarization.
Yes √ No _

U

a. *Does this essay demonstrate* ***topical unity-synthesis****?*
Using deduction and point-by-point style, the writer demonstrates how each point in the lecture and in the reading is topically united. Because of topical unity, each point in the lecture "casts doubt on" each corresponding point in the reading. There are no topical digressions. This demonstrates topical unity-synthesis. **Yes √ No _**

b. *Does this essay demonstrate* ***grammatical unity-synthesis****?*
There are no mistakes in syntax, word choice or spelling. The transitions of contrast connecting each point are correct. This demonstrates grammatical unity-synthesis. **Yes √ No _**

L

Does this essay demonstrate proficient ***language use-paraphrasing****?*
The writer has paraphrased the lecture but not the reading. This demonstrates a lack of proficient language-use paraphrasing. **Yes _ No X**

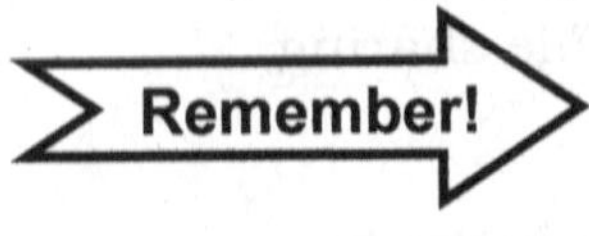

*As of this writing, paraphrasing—as a discrete writing task—is not described in ETS's official Integrated Writing Rubrics[2], thus it is not rated. However, you should paraphrase the reading and the lecture. Paraphrasing demonstrates language-use (OPDU**L**=C).*

C

Does this essay demonstrate ***coherence****?*
Because of Organization, Progression, Development-summarization and Unity-synthesis, the writer has proficiently "summarized the points in the lecture" and shown how they "cast doubt on the points in the reading." However, to get a higher score, the writer needs to paraphrase the reading passage. **Yes _ No X**

Revision Checklist: *What do I need to revise?*

1. Paraphrase the reading passage. This will demonstrate greater language use-paraphrasing (OPDU**L**=C).

[2] See the official ETS *Integrated Writing Rubrics*, page 47 in TOEFL® iBT Tips
http://www.ets.org/Media/Tests/

Step #5 **Revise your first draft using your revision checklist.**

Paraphrasing

To paraphrase means to restate using synonyms. When you paraphrase, write objectively. Use third-person singular and the present tense, for example:

1. original The author of the reading states that downloading music off the internet without paying for it is not a crime.

paraphrase The reading says that it is not a crime to download music off the web and not pay for it.

2. original First, the reading says that the internet was originally invented to be a source of free information. Downloading music without paying for it is an example of this democratic ideal in action.

paraphrase First, the reading states that the internet is a democracy. Therefore, everything on the internet is free, including music.

3. original Next, the reading states that downloading music from a friend's computer is not stealing. It is peer-to-peer file sharing. File sharing, he says, is not a crime.

paraphrase Next, the reading claims that P2P file sharing isn't a crime. You're simply sharing what you love: music.

4. original Finally, the author says that what he does in the privacy of his own home is no business of the government or the record companies. The US is a democracy not a dictatorship.

paraphrase Finally, the author of the reading believes that this is a privacy issue. Record companies and the government can't tell him what he can or can't do.

5. original In sum, the reading states that downloading music off the internet without paying for it is not a crime. The real criminals are the government and record companies trying to take away people's freedom and privacy.

paraphrase In conclusion, the reading claims that downloading internet music without paying for it isn't a crime. The true criminals are the government and the music industry taking away people's right to freedom and privacy.

Step #6 Submit your essay.

Look at the submitted essay. Note the space between each point. This makes it easier for the raters to read and rate.

The reading says that it is not a crime to download music off the web and not pay for it.
However, the lecturer believes it's a crime.

First, the reading states that the internet is a democracy. Therefore, everything on the internet is free, including music.
In contrast, the lecturer states that copyright laws protect music. If you don't pay for U2's latest album, you're breaking the law.

Next, the reading claims that P2P file sharing isn't a crime. You're simply sharing what you love: music.
However, the lecturer says that musicians should get paid. For example, Napster, a P2P site, didn't pay musicians. Napster said file sharing wasn't a crime. The court disagreed and fined Napster for not paying.

Finally, the author of the reading believes that this is a privacy issue. Record companies and the government can't tell him what to do.
In contrast, the lecturer believes that if you steal music, you are a thief therefore you have no privacy. The law is black and white. You can't have your cake and eat it too.

In conclusion, the reading claims that downloading internet music without paying for it isn't a crime. The true criminals are the government and the music industry taking away his right to freedom and privacy.
However, the lecturer asserts that ripping music off the web is a crime.

Words: 225

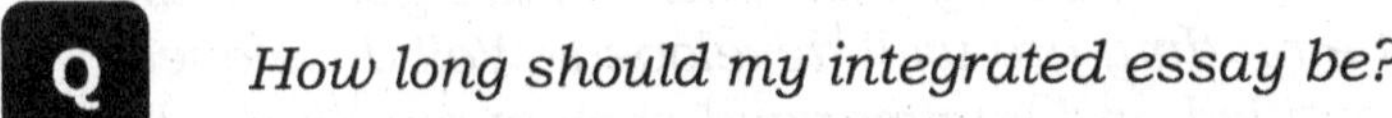

Q *How long should my integrated essay be?*

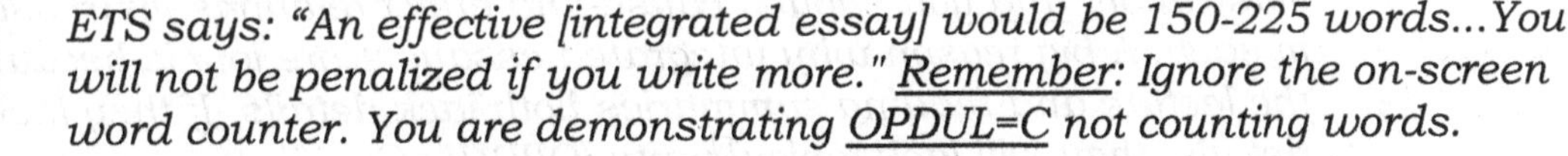

A *ETS says: "An effective [integrated essay] would be 150-225 words...You will not be penalized if you write more." Remember: Ignore the on-screen word counter. You are demonstrating OPDUL=C not counting words.*

Mapped out, you can see how G+3TiC=C gives the writing raters what they are trained to look for: an integrated essay that demonstrates OPDUL=C. The summarized opinions (G) and conclusions (C) are underlined, the transitions (T) are in **bold**, and the summarized supporting illustrations (i) are in *italics*.

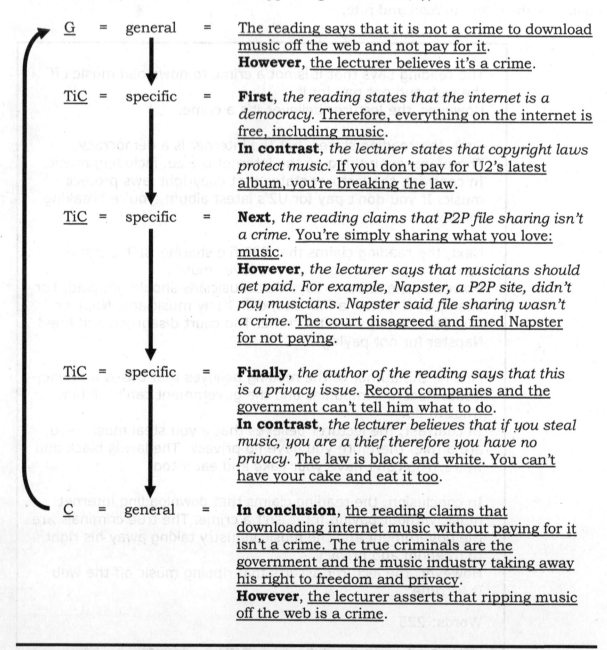

G	=	general	=	The reading says that it is not a crime to download music off the web and not pay for it. **However**, the lecturer believes it's a crime.
TiC	=	specific	=	**First**, *the reading states that the internet is a democracy*. Therefore, everything on the internet is free, including music. **In contrast**, *the lecturer states that copyright laws protect music.* If you don't pay for U2's latest album, you're breaking the law.
TiC	=	specific	=	**Next**, *the reading claims that P2P file sharing isn't a crime.* You're simply sharing what you love: music. **However**, *the lecturer says that musicians should get paid. For example, Napster, a P2P site, didn't pay musicians. Napster said file sharing wasn't a crime.* The court disagreed and fined Napster for not paying.
TiC	=	specific	=	**Finally**, *the author of the reading says that this is a privacy issue.* Record companies and the government can't tell him what to do. **In contrast**, *the lecturer believes that if you steal music, you are a thief therefore you have no privacy.* The law is black and white. You can't have your cake and eat it too.
C	=	general	=	**In conclusion**, the reading claims that downloading internet music without paying for it isn't a crime. The true criminals are the government and the music industry taking away his right to freedom and privacy. **However**, the lecturer asserts that ripping music off the web is a crime.

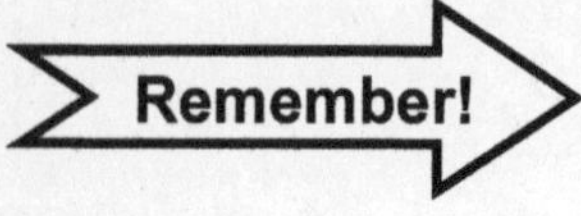

If you want a high integrated essay score, make sure your summary of the lecture and the reading are well developed. Well developed means you have identified and summarized each supporting illustration, and you show a cause-and-effect relationship (reason) in each. A big reason why integrated essays score low is because the lecture and reading summaries both lack details. If they lack details, they will lack topical unity (OPDUL=C).

2. Argument Counter-Argument: *Step-by-Step*

Let's work through another argument counter-argument integrated essay. Use G+3TiC=C and the six steps to demonstrate OPDUL=C in your essay.

Step #1	Make an G+3TiC=C note map; summarize the reading.

READING	LECTURE
G	G however
Ti *first* C	Ti however C
Ti *next* C	Ti however C
Ti *finally* C	Ti however C
C *In sum*	C however

Read the Passage

When the writing instructions end, the reading passage will appear on your computer screen. You will have 3 minutes to read and summarize it.

Read the passage on the next page.

Teleconferencing

In this article, I will take a closer look at teleconferencing. For starters, perhaps the greatest benefit of teleconferencing is convenience. No longer do business people have to fly around the world to meet face-to-face with customers or colleagues. Now they can simply dial into a conference line or click open a web cam and they're ready to do business. Not only that, but with teleconferencing you can schedule meetings all day long from the comfort of your office or home. Never has there been a more convenient way to do business.

Another big advantage is the savings. These days, with the average business class airline ticket costing well over four thousand dollars—not to mention the cost of hotels, meals and transportation—the cost saving advantages of teleconferencing are enormous. According to *Economy Magazine,* the average blue chip company saved over $40 million last year by cutting back on travel costs. Now ask yourself: What's better, spending time and money getting from point A to point B—and feeling exhausted in the process—or simply picking up the phone and using same-time email? The choice is obvious.

Teleconferencing also allows business people from a wide variety of cultures to come together to solve time-sensitive problems. For example, if you're working towards a deadline, and you don't have a solution to your problem, one of your colleagues in Brazil or Spain might have the solution you are looking for. By sharing experiences, business people can, via teleconferencing, offer insights and solutions to problems by simply picking up the phone or turning on a web cam.

Summarize the Opinion (G)

In this reading passage, note how the author does not state an opinion at the start or in the conclusion. There are simply three body paragraphs.

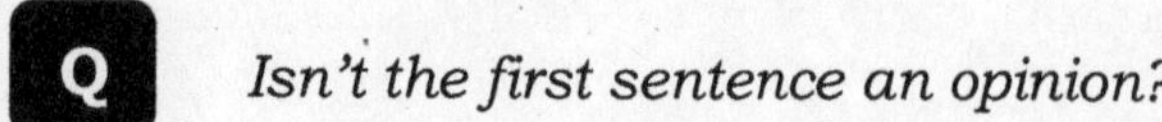

Q *Isn't the first sentence an opinion?*

A *No. The author is simply announcing the topic he/she will talk about, specifically teleconferencing. This is a fact therefore not arguable. Remember: The reading passage does not always state a direct opinion in the introduction or in the conclusion (a direct opinion is stated in writing). Often, the opinion-conclusion is implied (not direct-not written), as it is in this passage.*

Q *What if there is no opinion in the introduction or in the conclusion? How do I know what the author's opinion is?*

A *You can identify the author's opinion by adding facts together, then making a conclusion from those facts. This is called inferring. Look at the following graphic. Note how the author describes one advantage of teleconferencing in each body paragraph.*

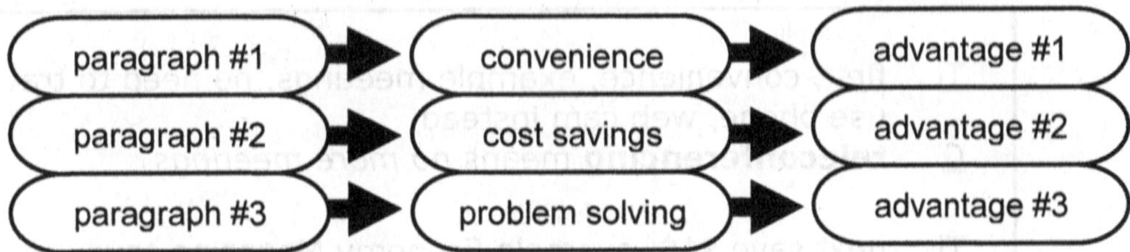

By adding up the advantages (facts), you can infer (conclude) what the author's opinion is.

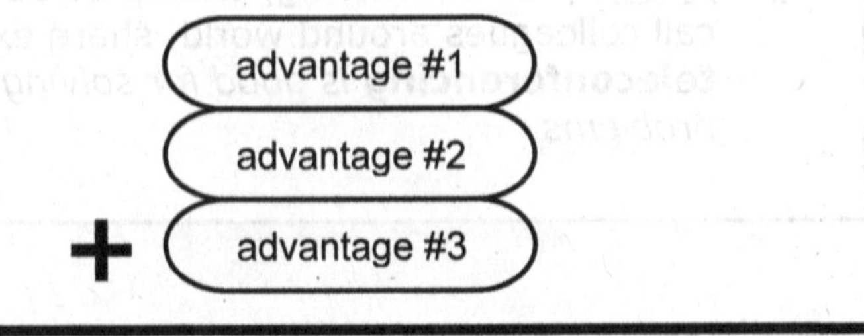

the author believes teleconferencing has advantages

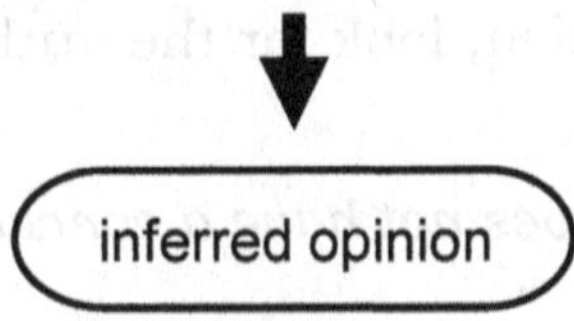

After you infer the author's opinion, summarize it beside G under **Reading**. Write it as a **cause**-and-*effect* relationship.

READING

G the reading says **teleconferencing** *has advantages*

Summarize the Body (3TiC)

When summarizing the body, start with signal words. They identify the start of each body paragraph. Next summarize the body paragraph. Remember to state the **cause**-and-*effect* relationship in the concluding sentences of each of your body paragraphs (Ti**C**).

Ti first, convenience, example meetings, no need to travel use phone, web cam instead
C **teleconferencing** means *no more meetings*

Ti next save $$$, example Economy Magazine says companies saved $40 million in travel costs
C **teleconferencing** means *you can save $$$*

Ti finally, problem solving, example you have a problem, call colleagues around world, share experience/solutions
C **teleconferencing** *is good for solving time-sensitive problems*

Summarize the Conclusion (C)

When summarizing the conclusion, look for the author's restated opinion.

Q *This reading passage does not have a conclusion. What should I do?*

A *Simply restate the author's inferred opinion.*

C the reading says teleconferencing has advantages

You now have a complete note map for the reading passage.

Reading

G the reading says teleconferencing has advantages

Ti first, convenience, example meetings, no need to travel use phone, web cam instead
C teleconferencing means no more meetings

Ti next savings, example Economy Magazine says companies saved $40 million travel costs
C teleconferencing means you can save $$$

Ti finally, problem solving, example you have a problem, call colleagues around world, share experience/solutions
C teleconferencing is good for solving time sensitive problems

C the reading says teleconferencing has advantages

Step #2 **Listen to the lecture; summarize it.**

When the reading time is up, the reading passage will leave your screen. It will be replaced by the lecture. As you listen:

1. Look at the Lecture side of your note map.
2. Anticipate the counter argument using the black-and-white rule.
3. Listen for signal words that identify the opinion, the body paragraphs and the conclusion. Note the cause-and-effect relationship in each.

TASK: Take notes as you listen to a lecture on teleconferencing.

LECTURE

Audio Track #3

G

Ti however

C

Ti however

C

Ti however

C

C in sum

➔ Audio script: page 709

Step #3 Read the prompt; write a first draft.

When the lecture ends, it will leave your computer screen. The reading passage will return. You will also see the prompt.

> Prompt Summarize the points made in the lecture and show how they cast doubt on the points made in the reading.

TASK: Using the reading notes already illustrated and your lecture notes, write a first draft using either point-by-point or block style. Type your essay. Don't time yourself. Just write. Replay the lecture as needed for practice.

Step #4 Check your first draft for Coherence using OPDUL=C.

Check your first draft for coherence using the *Integrated Essay Proficiency Checklist* on page 697.

Step #5 Revise your first draft using your revision checklist.

Step #6 Submit your essay.

TASK: Rate your teleconferencing essay using the *Integrated Essay Rating Guide* on page 698.

Three Common Problems

Check the following integrated essay using OPDUL=C. What problems can you identify?

> He argues that zoos are a bad investment.
> In addition, she claims that zoos have value.
>
> First, he says that zoos are a waste of money. They use money that could help poor neighborhoods.
> Moreover, she argues against this.
>
> Next, he claims that zoos are not good for animals. He uses many clear examples, such as small cages.
> Also, she argues that he is totally wrong about that.
>
> Finally, he contends that zoos take up valuable land.
>
> In addition, she gets really angry about that.
>
> In sum, he argues that zoos are a waste of money.
> In conclusion, she disagrees.

According to OPDUL=C, this essay demonstrates:

1. A lack of language-use paraphrasing (OPDU**L**=C), specifically a lack of word choice.
2. A lack of unity-synthesis (OPD**U**L=C), specifically a lack of topical unity.
3. A lack of development-summarization (OP**D**UL=C) of the introductions, the bodies, and the conclusions.

Combined, these three problem areas result in a lack of coherence (OPDUL=**C**). Let's analyze each so you can avoid these mistakes on test day.

1. Lack of Language-Use Paraphrasing

Look at the sample essay once again. Note **he** and **she**. Because he and she are not identified, we do not know who represents the reading and who represents the lecture. The result is a lack of language-use paraphrasing, specifically a lack of word choice (OPDU**L**=C), and a lack of topical unity-synthesis (OPD**U**L=C).

> **He** argues that zoos are a bad investment.
> In addition, **she** claims that zoos have value.
>
> First, **he** says that zoos are a waste of money. They use money that could help poor neighborhoods.
> Moreover, **she** argues against this.
>
> Next, **he** claims that zoos are not good for animals. **He** uses many clear examples, such as small cages.
> Also, **she** argues that **he** is totally wrong about that.
>
> Finally, **he** contends that zoos take up valuable land.
> In addition, **she** gets really angry about that.
>
> In sum, **he** argues that zoos are a waste money.
> In conclusion, **she** disagrees.

Look at how **he** and **she** have been replaced by identifying nouns: the reading and the lecturer. These changes identify the source of each argument and create greater coherence.

> The reading argues that zoos are a bad investment.
> In addition, the lecturer claims that zoos have value.
>
> First, the reading says that zoos are a waste of money. They use money that could help poor neighborhoods.
> Moreover, the lecturer argues against this.
>
> Next, the reading claims that zoos are not good for animals.
> The reading uses many clear examples, such as small cages.
> Also, the professor in the lecture argues that the reading is totally wrong about that.
>
> Finally, the reading contends that zoos take up valuable land.
> In addition, the lecturer gets really angry about that.
>
> In sum, the reading argues that zoos are a waste money.
> In conclusion, the lecturer disagrees.

2. Lack of Unity-Synthesis

Note the **transitions** in the sample essay below. They are transitions of addition (adding information). They should be transitions of contrast. This demonstrates a lack of proficient language use-paraphrasing, specifically word choice (OPDU**L**=C), and a lack of unity-synthesis, both grammatical and topical (OPD**U**L=C).

> The reading argues that zoos are a bad investment. **In addition**, the lecturer claims that zoos have value.
>
> First, the reading says that zoos are a waste of money. They use money that could help poor neighborhoods. **Moreover**, the lecturer argues against this.
>
> Next, the reading claims that zoos are not good for animals. The reading uses many clear examples, such as small cages. **Also**, the professor in the lecture argues that the reading is totally wrong about that.
>
> Finally, the reading contends that zoos take up valuable land. **In addition**, the lecturer gets really angry about that.
>
> In sum, the reading argues that zoos are a waste of money. **In conclusion**, the lecturer disagrees.

Look at the same essay with **transitions of contrast**. These transitions demonstrate unity-synthesis and language use-paraphrasing (OPD**UL**=C).

> The reading argues that zoos are a bad investment. **However**, the lecturer claims that zoos have value.
>
> First, the reading says that zoos are a waste of money. They use money that could help poor neighborhoods. **Conversely**, the lecture argues against this.
>
> Next, the reading claims that zoos are not good for animals. The reading uses many clear examples, such as small cages. **On the contrary**, the professor in the lecture argues that the reading is totally wrong about that.
>
> Finally, the reading contends that zoos take up valuable land. **In contrast**, the lecturer gets really angry about that.
>
> In sum, the reading argues that zoos are a waste of money. **Countering that**, the lecturer disagrees.

3. Lack of Development-Summarization

When summarizing the main points in the reading and in the lecture, make sure that you identify and describe the **cause**-and-*effect* relationship in the opinions, the body paragraphs and the conclusions. The **cause**-and-*effect* relationships are the reasons each arguer gives to defend his or her position.

> The reading argues that **zoos** *are a bad investment.* However, the lecturer claims that **zoos** *have value.*
>
> First, the reading says that **zoos use money** *that could help poor neighborhoods*. For example, in Washington DC, **the zoo got more tax money than the public schools**. *As a result, many schools closed but the zoo got a new elephant exhibit*. Conversely, the lecturer argues that the money for the elephant exhibit was donations. She also says that the *Washington DC school problem* is **due to bad government not a lack of tax money.**
>
> Next, the reading claims that **zoos** *are not good for animals* like the panda. It **cannot breed in captivity**. The reading says *the panda would do better in the wild.*
> On the contrary, the professor in the lecture argues that the **panda's habitat** *is disappearing*. **Returning pandas to the wild** *is not an option.*
>
> Finally, the reading contends that **zoos take up valuable land** *that could be used to build houses*. **This** *would create jobs*.
> In contrast, the lecturer argues that **building houses** *is a short-term solution to job creation*. **Building zoos** *would create permanent jobs.*
>
> In sum, the reading argues that **zoos** *are not a good investment.*
> Countering that, the lecturer claims that **we need zoos** *to save wild animals from extinction*. **Building zoos** *is how we can invest in the environment.*
>
> Words: 225

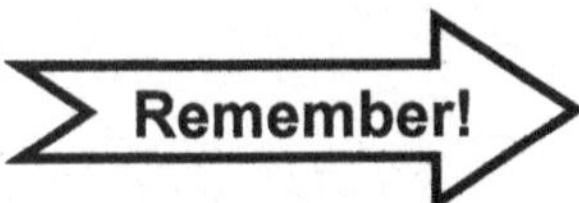

*Lack of development-summarization (OP**D**UL=C), especially of the lecture body paragraphs, is a big reason why integrated essays receive a low score.*

Mapped out, you can see how G+3TiC=C gives the writing raters what they are trained to look for: an integrated essay that demonstrates OPDUL=C. The summarized opinions (G) and conclusions (C) are underlined, the transitions (T) are in **bold**, and the summarized supporting illustrations (i) are in *italics*.

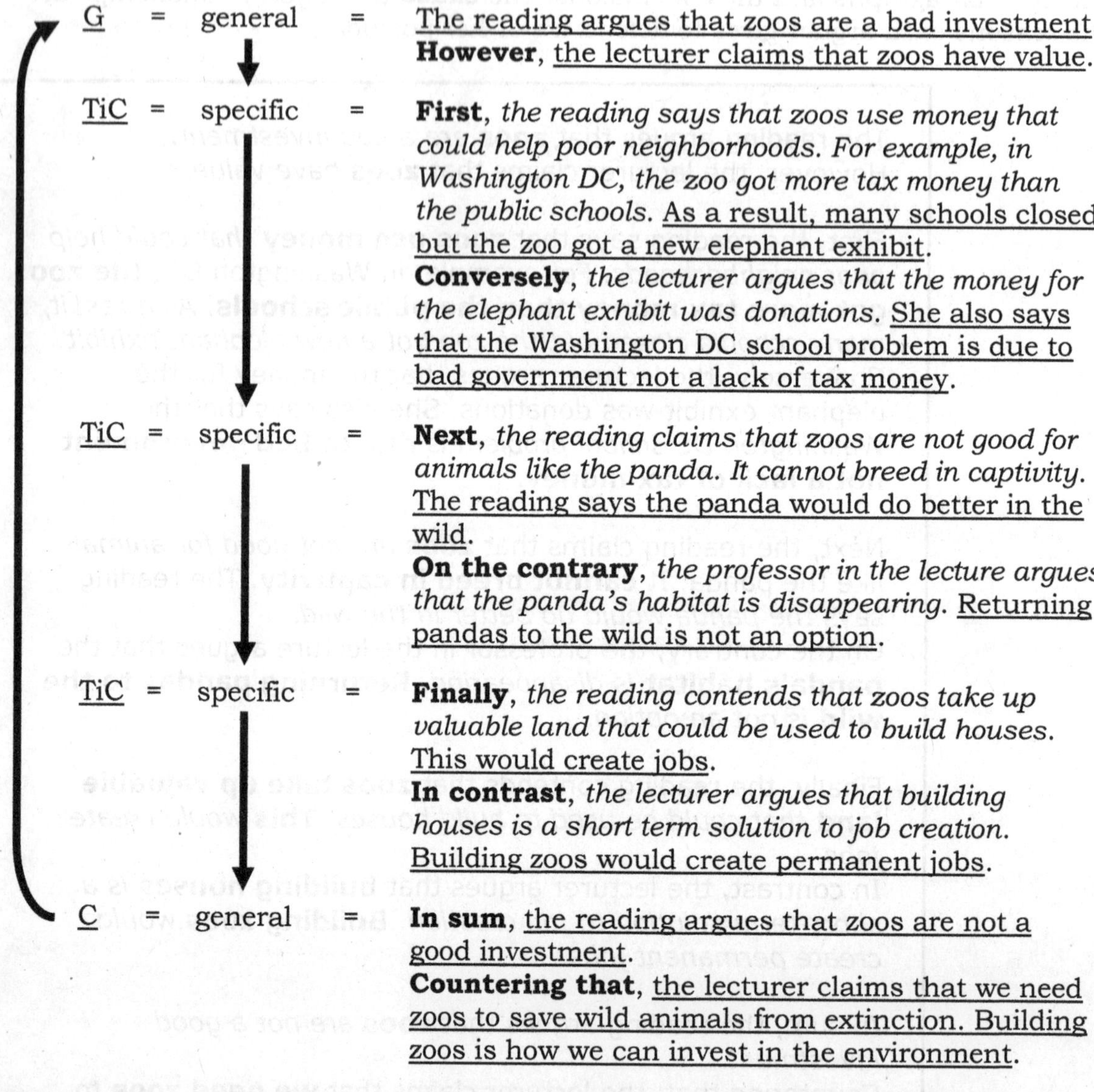
G = general = The reading argues that zoos are a bad investment. **However**, the lecturer claims that zoos have value.
TiC = specific = **First**, *the reading says that zoos use money that could help poor neighborhoods. For example, in Washington DC, the zoo got more tax money than the public schools.* As a result, many schools closed but the zoo got a new elephant exhibit. **Conversely**, *the lecturer argues that the money for the elephant exhibit was donations.* She also says that the Washington DC school problem is due to bad government not a lack of tax money.
TiC = specific = **Next**, *the reading claims that zoos are not good for animals like the panda. It cannot breed in captivity.* The reading says the panda would do better in the wild. **On the contrary**, *the professor in the lecture argues that the panda's habitat is disappearing.* Returning pandas to the wild is not an option.
TiC = specific = **Finally**, *the reading contends that zoos take up valuable land that could be used to build houses.* This would create jobs. **In contrast**, *the lecturer argues that building houses is a short term solution to job creation.* Building zoos would create permanent jobs.
C = general = **In sum**, the reading argues that zoos are not a good investment. **Countering that**, the lecturer claims that we need zoos to save wild animals from extinction. Building zoos is how we can invest in the environment.

TASK: Rate the zoo essay above using the *Integrated Essay Rating Guide* on page 698. Compare your rating to the one on page 795.

Writing Practice

For each of the following tasks, use G+3TiC=C and the six steps to demonstrate OPDUL=C in your argument counter-argument integrated essay. Check each for proficiency using the *Integrated Essay Proficiency Checklist* on page 697. Rate each using the *Integrated Essay Rating Guide* on page 698.

Task #1 - Audio Track #4

Directions: Read the following passage. You have 3 minutes.

Global Warming

Are humans responsible for global warming? This is a contentious issue. But let's be clear: The increase in CO2 in the atmosphere is not a result of man's burning of fossil fuels. To the contrary, the increase in CO2 specifically, and greenhouse gases generally, is a direct result of the Earth naturally warming itself. Where then, you might ask, is all that CO2 coming from if not from man? It is coming from carbon sinks. Simply put, a carbon sink is a place where carbon dioxide is naturally stored. The largest carbon sinks are the Arctic tundra and the oceans. As the Earth warms, carbon sinks release CO2. To state otherwise is to ignore the fact that over the past 250,000 years, periods of global warming were a direct result of large amounts of CO2 being naturally released from carbon sinks.

In this debate, computer modeling is held up as evidence that global warming is a man-made phenomena. Let's put this issue to rest as well. Yes, computers are capable of immense calculations. However, when it comes to predicting future climate patterns, computers fail repeatedly. Case in point: Computers cannot accurately measure the global mean ocean surface temperature, or GMST. If scientists agree that measuring the GMST is the best indicator of climate change, and since we can't measure it, how can anyone state with any degree of certainty that man is responsible for global warming? Simple. They can't.

The last point I want to make concerns water vapor. Water vapor is a naturally occurring greenhouse gas. Not only that but it is also the most abundant greenhouse gas. Concentrations of water vapor are natural events caused by storms and are driven globally by the movement of ocean currents. According to one study, water vapor in the stratosphere increased the global warming rate in the 1990's by 30%. The conclusion? Why blame man when it is obvious that global warming is a natural phenomena we are just beginning to understand.

(This task continues on the next page.)

Directions: Now listen to a lecture on the same topic.

Now get ready to write your response.

Prompt Summarize the points made in the lecture and show how they cast doubt on the points made in the reading.

Writing Time: 20 minutes

audio script page 709

Task #2 - Audio Track #5

Directions: Read the following passage. You have 3 minutes.

America and Oil

Whenever an oil spill occurs, environmentalists are quick to remind us that we need to move away from a petroleum-based economy. Yet what environmentalists fail to realize is that the petroleum industry is an integral part of the American way of life.

Let's start with a few statistics. According the *American Petroleum Institute*, in the year ending 2010, over 9.2 million people worked in the American oil industry, doing everything from designing software to finding new oil reserves to transporting food to offshore oil rigs. Those 9.2 million jobs added over one-trillion dollars to the U.S. economy in the form of taxes, taxes that helped build and maintain America's infrastructure. It doesn't take a rocket scientist to realize that a move away from oil would spell the end of the American way of life as we now know it.

If you are still not convinced that oil is the life-blood of the American economy, take a look around you. Those plastic bottles used for water? The natural gas we use for cooking and heating? That wrapper or box your Big Mac comes in? Let's face it. We are surrounded by oil-based products. Without them, our lives would be less convenient. And if there is one thing Americans love, it is convenience.

Finally, there is the political imperative. There is no denying that the majority of the world's oil is controlled by foreign governments not always friendly to the United States. As a result, we need to secure a safe and reliable source of petroleum. That source is in our own backyard. Less than twenty miles off our coasts is the oil that will free us from the vagaries of foreign governments. By exploiting that oil reserve, we will be investing in America's security and economic future.

In closing, consider this: By the time you are finished reading this paragraph, the U.S. will have used over 8,000 barrels of oil. That's about 340,000 gallons. Contrary to what environmentalists might argue, turning off the oil tap is easier said than done.

(This task continues on the next page.)

Directions: Now listen to a lecture on the same topic.

Now get ready to write your response.

Prompt	Summarize the points made in the lecture and show how they cast doubt on the points made in the reading.

Writing Time: 20 minutes

audio script page 710

Task #3 - Audio Track #6

Directions: Read the following passage. You have 3 minutes.

Computer Games

In the year ending 2008, 97% of U.S. children between the ages of twelve and seventeen had played computer games. In that same year, six of the top ten selling games were rated "mature" due to violent content. Is it any wonder then that computer games (herein all electronic games) are having a detrimental effect on our children's behavior?

For starters, computer games teach children as young as four that violence is the preferred way of solving problems. This idea is reinforced by the design of violent computer games, one that is premised on a problem-solution scenario in which a hero fights to get from A to Z. To survive, the hero must kill as a means of protection and as a means of advancing (read: winning). Such a scenario teaches adolescents and teens that in order to reach a goal safely, violence is an essential part of the process. The more a child kills, the more this notion is reinforced. Reaching the end of the game only confirms the fact that violence is a panacea for any and all problems, be they emotional or physical. Shootings at schools are evidence of this false precept in action.

Even more alarming is the fact that video games teach a false sense of reality. This trend is none more evident than in military recruiting centers in shopping malls. These high-tech centers are magnets for boys who spend hours freely killing enemies from virtual helicopters armed with virtual machine guns. The boys are so captivated, so thrilled by the virtual experience that they feel immortal and free from the crueler realities of war. Imbued with this false sense of romance, the recruiters make their pitch. Now I ask you. Is that any way to recruit soldiers? By fooling them into believing that war is just another virtual experience in which only the bad guys die?

Finally, computer games denigrate women. Suffice it to say, the women in such games have no redeeming value. They are there to either support the hero in his violent quest or to act as wallpaper. When they do act, their violent behavior runs contrary to woman as the symbol of life, not the taker of it. If anyone tries to tell you that such women are role models, then they need to take a good hard look at themselves in the mirror.

(This task continues on the next page.)

Directions: Now listen to a lecture on the same topic.

Now get ready to write your response.

Prompt	Summarize the points made in the lecture and show how they cast doubt on the points made in the reading.

Writing Time: 20 minutes

audio script page 710

Task #4 - Audio Track #7

Directions: Read the following passage. You have 3 minutes.

Standardized Testing

A hot-button issue in education these days continues to be standardized testing. Simply put, a standardized test measures the general knowledge of a particular student group. The SAT, taken nation-wide by graduating high school seniors, is perhaps the most well-known standardized test in the U.S. Standardized tests, such as the SAT, do indeed have their detractors; however, as an experienced educator, I support standardized testing for both high school and middle school students.

One of the greatest benefits of standardized testing is the statistics afforded to administrators. These statistics provide invaluable insight into a school's academic performance. Administrators can then compare their school's performance to other schools within the same district and within the same state. The end result is that administrators can accurately assess the efficacy of the educational system at the local, state, and national level. By doing so, administrators know which schools are performing below average and can take the appropriate action to improve those scores.

Teachers also benefit from standardized testing. For example, if students in a particular middle school are scoring consistently low in math, their teachers can spend more class time on math. By targeting low-scoring subjects, teachers can make better use of class time. In short, standardized testing helps teachers plan their curriculum with a particular focus on maximizing standardized test scores.

Finally, standardized testing not only measures student performance but teacher performance as well. High school students who score consistently high on the SAT, for example, obviously have results-driven teachers. Conversely, if high school students score consistently low on the SAT, a teacher review is warranted. More often than not, low standardized test scores are directly traceable to a lack of teacher performance. Armed with the information, administrators can replace teachers as needed.

(This task continues on the next page.)

Directions: Now listen to a lecture on the same topic.

Now get ready to write your response.

Prompt	Summarize the points made in the lecture and show how they cast doubt on the points made in the reading.

Writing Time: 20 minutes

audio script page 711

Task #5 - Audio Track #8

Directions: Read the following passage. You have 3 minutes.

Organic Food

Organic food is very trendy these days. Everywhere you go, people are jumping on the organic bandwagon. I used to be organic. I did. But I kicked the habit. Believe me, I'd bought all the arguments, like the one that says that organic food is priced the same as non organic. Right. Let me give you an example of just how wrong that argument is. At my local grocery store, a small box of organic strawberries costs four dollars. Four dollars for maybe twelve strawberries! I can buy twice that many non organic strawberries for half that price. The fact is organic fruits and vegetables are a good forty to fifty percent more expensive than non organic. Imagine trying to feed a family of four at those prices. You'd have to take out a bank loan every time you went shopping.

Another thing about organic is that it's not always easy to get. At my local grocery store, I can buy organic fruit and vegetables no problem, but not organic rice or grains like barley and wheat. If I want organic rice, I have to drive ten miles across town through heavy traffic to a health food store that doesn't take credit cards. Then I have drive all the way back home. All that for five pounds of rice. Believe me, it's easier just to grab a bag of good old non organic rice at my local grocery store.

And what about taste? Does my family even know the difference between organic and non organic? No. A good example is organic milk. I used to buy it all the time but I stopped because it was more expensive than non organic. Did my husband and kids miss the organic milk? Did they suddenly notice a taste change from organic to non organic milk? Not at all. Food for thought next time you wander through the organic section of your local grocery store.

(This task continues on the next page.)

Directions: Now listen to a lecture on the same topic.

Now get ready to write your response.

Prompt Summarize the points made in the lecture and show how they cast doubt on the points made in the reading.

Writing Time: 20 minutes

audio script page 712

Show-Support Integrated Essay

On test day, expect to write an argument counter-argument essay. However, you must be prepared to write a show-support integrated essay. For this task, you will have 3 minutes to read a fact-based, academic passage. Next, you will listen to a short, fact-based lecture on the same topic as in the reading. In your essay, you will demonstrate how the facts in the lecture "add to and support" (develop) the topic in the reading.

Prompt	Summarize the points made in the lecture and show how they add to and support the information in the reading.

This task measures your ability to:

- ✓ **take notes** as you read and listen;
- ✓ **summarize** the main points in the reading and in the lecture;
- ✓ **synthesize** the main points in the reading and in the lecture;
- ✓ **paraphrase** the main points in the reading and in the lecture;
- ✓ **demonstrate** how the lecture adds to and supports the reading.

TOEFL's Testing Method

Understanding TOEFL's testing method for this task is the first step in writing a show-support integrated essay that demonstrates OPDUL=C. Start by reading the passage on the next page. You have three minutes.

Animal Behavior

Animal behavior can be classified according to the time of day an animal is active. Animals, such as horses, elephants and most birds, are said to be diurnal because they are active during the day and rest at night. Humans by far are the largest segment of this group. The majority of us work during the day and sleep at night. Those animals that are active at dawn and dusk are said to be crepuscular. Beetles, skunks and rabbits fall into this category. The third group are those animals that sleep during the day and are active at night. They are called nocturnal. A good example is the bat. Bats have highly developed eyesight and hearing, and an excellent sense of smell. This helps them avoid predators and locate food. Being nocturnal also helps them avoid high temperatures during the day, especially in deserts where temperatures can reach well over one hundred degrees. Also, because it is cooler at night, bats and other nocturnal animals use less energy. This, in turn, means they retain more body water essential for survival.

Note how the reading is a general introduction to animal behavior. Note also that there is no opinion; however, there is *a premise* in the first or topic sentence: *"Animal behavior can be classified according to the time of day an animal is active."* This premise has a main topic (animal behavior) and a controlling idea. What about animal behavior? "It can be classified according to the time of day an animal is active" = the controlling idea.

Next, read as you listen to a lecture on the same topic. As you read, listen for supporting illustrations (3TiC) to support the topic of classifying animal behavior.

Good afternoon. In this lecture, we'll focus on a common nocturnal animal, the bat. There are two types of bat: micro bats, or true bats, and mega bats, also called fruit bats. Let's start with mega bats. Size wise, mega bats are from two to sixteen inches in length. Mega bats have extremely sensitive sight and smell. This helps them locate the flowers and fruit upon which they feed. It is while eating that mega bats play an important role in the distribution of plants. Like bees, mega bats serve as pollinators. When they lick nectar or eat flowers, their bodies become covered in pollen which they, in turn, carry to other trees and plants thereby acting as pollinators. In fact, many of the fruits and vegetables on our tables, such as bananas and peaches, would not be there if mega bats did not pollinate plants and trees.

(continued on the next page)

> Next are micro bats. As the name implies, micro bats are quite small, about the size of a mouse. To find food, micro bats use echolocation, high frequency sounds they bounce off insects. The most common micro bat is the vesper or evening bat. Like mega bats, micro bats play an important role in the environment. The average vesper bat, for example, can eat one thousand mosquitoes in one night. By doing so, they control the mosquito population.

In this lecture, two examples of a nocturnal animal are developed: mega bats and micro bats. These examples "add to and support" (develop) the premise in the reading: *Animal behavior can be classified according to the time of day an animal is active.*

The structure of the reading and the lecture combined can be mapped out using G+2TiC=C. Therefore, use G+2TiC=C when constructing an essay for this example.

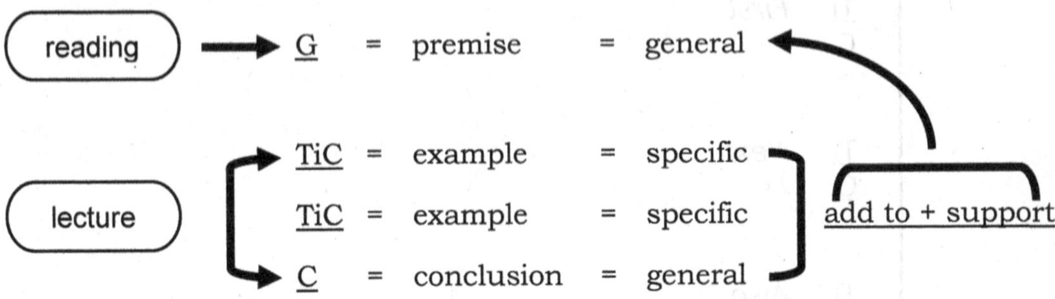

Q *Are there always two lecture examples?*

A *No. Sometimes there is one well-developed example (1TiC). Sometimes there are two examples (2TiC). Sometimes there are three examples (3TiC). Be prepared for three examples.*

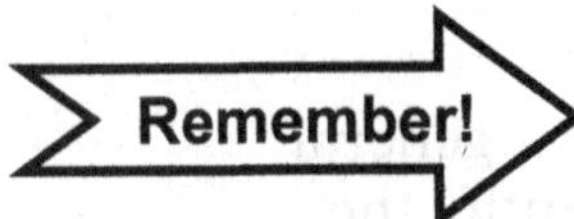

The lecture (specific) always adds to and supports the reading (general).

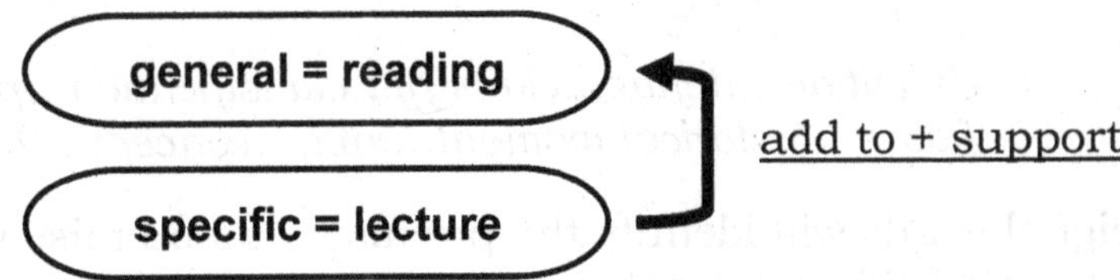

Show Support: *Step-by-Step*

When writing a show-support integrated essay, use G+3TiC=C and the six steps to demonstrate OPDUL=C in your essay.

Step #1	**Make a G+3TiC=C note map; include transitions of addition.**

Because the reading is a general description of the main topic, summarize it first. Because the lecture will "add to and support" the reading with specific examples, use *transitions of addition* in the lecture.

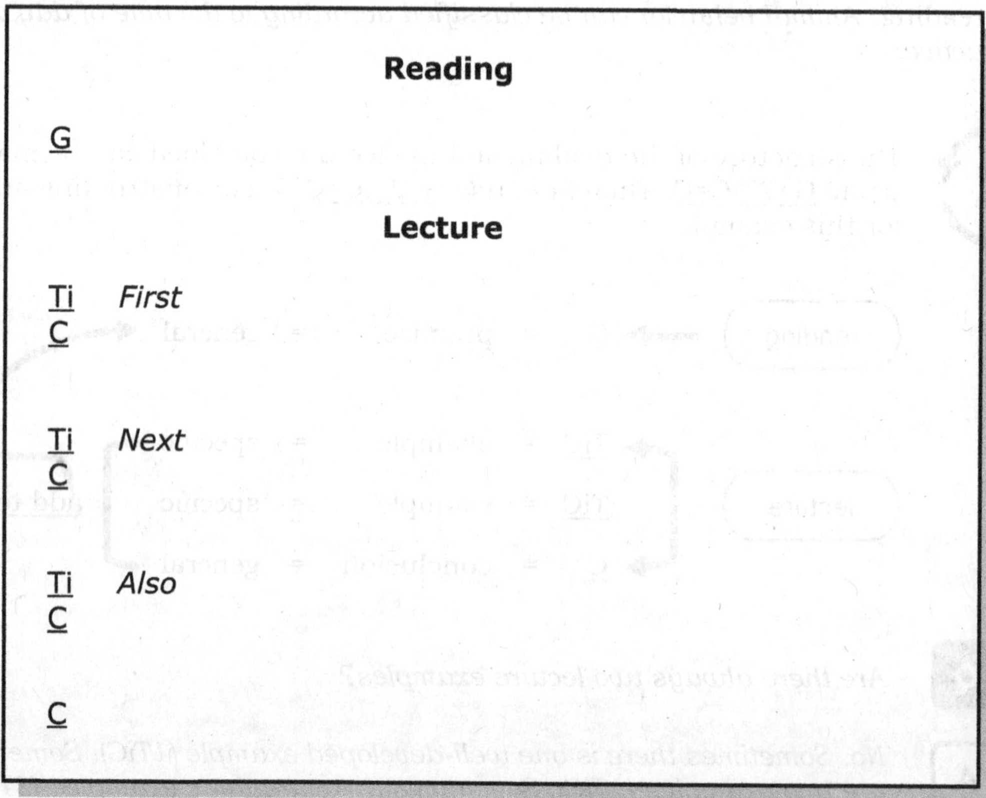

Reading
G
Lecture
Ti First
C
Ti Next
C
Ti Also
C
C

Read the Passage

You will have 3 minutes to read the passage. Read it twice. Read first for a general understanding. As you read a second time, look for signal words that identify the premise. Remember: The premise is the main topic and the controlling idea.

> *definition...define...classify...classification...process...historical figure...historical moment...idea...concept...theory...design...*

These signal words will identify the premise. The premise will contain the main topic, a topic TOEFL will teach you about.

TOEFL-as-Teacher

Many of the integrated writing topics will be new to you. Therefore, TOEFL will teach you about them. TOEFL teaches you by starting with a premise, then develops it with supporting illustrations. This way the TOEFL iBT is both a teaching test and a learning test.

For this task, the premise will introduce the main topic by using a definition or a description of a person, place, or thing (see page 299 *Identifying the Premise*). The premise might also be defined by a process, a concept, a natural phenomena, a social or psychological theory, or an historical moment. The premise might also be a classification, as is the one in sample passage below. Note how the premise is stated in the first sentence. Note also how the *controlling idea* is identified by the signal words "**can be classified** *according to the time of day an animal is active*."

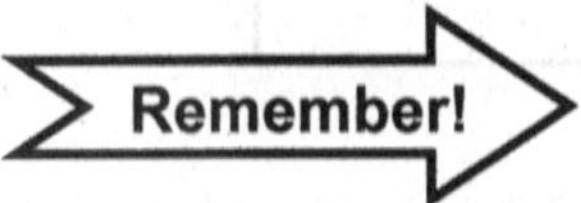

Because the reading passage is short, the premise will often be in the topic (first) sentence.

Animal behavior **can be classified** *according to the time of day an animal is active*. Animals, such as horses, elephants and most birds, are said to be diurnal because they are active during the day and rest at night. Humans by far are the largest segment of this group. The majority of us work during the day and sleep at night. Those animals that are active at dawn and dusk are said to be crepuscular. Beetles, skunks and rabbits fall into this category. The third group are those animals that sleep during the day and are active at night. They are called nocturnal. A good example is the bat. Bats have highly developed eyesight and hearing, and an excellent sense of smell. This helps them avoid predators and locate food. Being nocturnal also helps them avoid high temperatures during the day, especially in deserts where temperatures can reach well over one hundred degrees. Also, because it is cooler at night, bats and other nocturnal animals use less energy. This, in turn, means they retain more body water essential for survival.

As you read the passage, summarize it under Reading on your note map. To summarize means to identify and generally describe the main points. In the reading, the main points are the premise and *a general description of the premise.*

Reading

G classifies animal behavior according to time of day

day is diurnal – eat during day, sleep at night, humans horses, elephants
twilight is crepuscular – active dawn and dusk, beetles, rabbits, skunks

night is nocturnal – sleep during day, active at night

Warning!

The reading passage will contain a lot of information. Most of it is distractor (details that are not important in your summary). Your job is to identify and summarize the premise only. Do not summarize every sentence. You will waste time. Remember: You only have 20 minutes.

Step #2 Listen to the lecture.

When the reading time is up, the passage will leave your screen. It will be replaced by the lecture. The lecture will be 2-3 minutes long. As you listen to the sample lecture (audio track #9), look at the lecture notes below. Note how each example of a bat is developed. Note also the **cause**-and-*effect* relationship in the concluding sentence of each body paragraph (C). Note also how the conclusion (C) *restates the task described in the prompt* (see the prompt on the next page).

Lecture

Ti First mega bats, 2 - 16 inches
good eyesight and smell, helps bat find food
food is flowers and fruit
C like bees **mega bats pollinate plants/trees peaches, bananas** = *good for environment*

Ti Next micro bats, very small size of mouse
use echolocation to find food (insects)
C **micro bats eat 1,000 mosquitoes a night** = *good for controlling mosquitoes*

C *These examples add to and support the reading*

Step #3 Read the prompt; write a first draft.

When the lecture ends, the reading passage will return to your computer screen. The prompt will also appear.

> Prompt Summarize the points made in the lecture and show how they add to and support the information in the reading.

When writing a first draft, summarize the reading first, then the lecture. Do so using block style as the method of organization.

reading

The reading classifies animal behavior three ways: diurnal, crepuscular and nocturnal. Diurnal animals are active during the day and sleep at night. Crepuscular animals are active at dawn and dusk. Nocturnal animals hunt at night and rest during the day. An example of a nocturnal animal is the bat.

lecture

The lecture develops the example of the bat. First, there are mega bats or fruit bats. They live in Africa, Asia and Oceania and eat fruit and flowers which they locate by smell and with their excellent eyesight. As they eat, seeds from the fruit fall to the forest floor and new trees grow. This is good for the environment because new trees replace the old ones. Mega bats also pollinate. When they eat a flower, their bodies get covered with pollen which they carry to other flowers. The lecture says without mega bats pollinating, we would have no peaches or bananas.

Next the lecture talks about micro bats or small bats. Micro bats use echolocation to find insects to eat. Like mega bats, micro bats are also good for the environment. In one night, a micro bat called the vesper bat can eat approximately 1,000 mosquitoes. By doing so, they control the mosquito population.

These examples add to and support the reading.

Words: 212

Q *How long should my show-support integrated essay be?*

A *ETS says: "An effective [integrated essay] would be 150-225 words."*
Remember: "Effective" means your essay demonstrates OPDUL=C.

Step #4	**Check your first draft for Coherence using OPDUL=C.**

O

Does this essay demonstrate ***organization****?*
This essay has a premise, a body and a conclusion. This demonstrates block-style organization. **Yes √ No _**

P

Does this essay demonstrate ***progression****?*
The writer develops the premise followed by supporting illustrations in the body. After the body, there is a conclusion stating how the main points in the lecture "add to and support the reading." This demonstrates progression (general-specific). **Yes √ No _**

D

a. *Does the introduction demonstrate* ***development-summarization****?*
The writer identifies and summarizes the premise in the reading with no points left out. This demonstrates introduction development-summarization. **Yes √ No _**

b. *Does the body demonstrate* ***development-summarization****?*
The writer identifies and summarizes the supporting illustrations in the lecture with no points left out. This demonstrates body development-summarization. **Yes √ No _**

c. *Does the conclusion demonstrate* ***development-summarization****?*
The conclusion states how the main points in the lecture add to and support the general topic in the reading. This demonstrates conclusion development-summarization. **Yes √ No _**

U

a. *Does this essay demonstrate* ***topical unity-synthesis****?*
The writer focuses on how animals are classified by behavior with no topical digressions. This demonstrates topical unity-synthesis.
Yes √ No _

b. *Does this essay demonstrate* ***grammatical unity-synthesis****?*
There are no mistakes in syntax. The transitions are correct. These elements combined demonstrate grammatical unity-synthesis.
Yes √ No _

L

Does this essay demonstrate proficient ***language use-paraphrasing****?*
There are no mistakes in word choice or spelling. The writer paraphrases the reading and the lecture. This demonstrates proficient language use-paraphrasing. **Yes √ No _**

C

Does this essay demonstrate ***coherence****?*
Because of Organization, Progression, Development-summarization, Unity-synthesis and Language Use-paraphrasing, this essay proficiently demonstrates how the main points in the lecture "add to and support the reading." This demonstrates coherence (OPDUL=C). **Yes √ No _**

Step #5 **Revise your first draft using your revision checklist.**

Step #6 **Submit your essay.**

The reading classifies animal behavior three ways: diurnal, crepuscular and nocturnal. Diurnal animals are active during the day and sleep at night. Crepuscular animals are active at dawn and dusk. Nocturnal animals hunt at night and rest during the day. An example of a nocturnal animal is the bat.

The lecture develops the example of the bat. First, there are mega bats or fruit bats. They live in Africa, Asia and Oceania and eat fruit and flowers which they locate by smell and with their excellent eyesight. As they eat, seeds from the fruit fall to the forest floor and new trees grow. This is good for the environment because new trees replace the old ones. Mega bats also pollinate. When they eat a flower, their bodies get covered with pollen which they carry to other flowers. The lecture says without mega bats pollinating, we would have no peaches or bananas.

Next the lecture talks about micro bats or small bats. Micro bats use echolocation to find insects to eat. Like mega bats, micro bats are also good for the environment. In one night, a micro bat called the vesper bat can eat approximately 1,000 mosquitoes. By doing so, they control the mosquito population.

These examples add to and support the reading.

Words: 212

TASK: Rate the show-support essay above using the *Integrated Essay Rating Guide* on page 698. Compare your rating to the one on page 795.

Writing Practice

For each of the following tasks, use G+3TiC=C and the six steps to demonstrate OPDUL=C in a show-support integrated essay. Check each for proficiency using the *Integrated Essay Proficiency Checklist* on page 697, then rate each using the *Integrated Essay Rating Guide* on page 698.

Task #1 - Audio Track #10

Directions: Read the following passage. You have three minutes.

Brown-Headed Cowbird

Brown-headed cowbirds are native to North America. Cowbirds, as they are more commonly called, reside in the southern United States in winter. Come spring, they migrate as far north as Canada to breed. Size wise, they are about eight inches long from the tip of the beak to the end of the tail. The males have chocolate-brown heads and black, iridescent bodies while females are grey. Their heavy beaks give them a finch-like appearance. However, the cowbird is not a finch. It is a brood-parasitic icterid. Icterids are small to medium-sized passerine birds, passerine meaning to perch. Icterids include New World blackbirds, such as Bobolinks, meadowlarks, and grackles. Before European settlers arrived in North America, the cowbird followed the buffalo across the Great Plains, eating the insects stirred up by the passing herds. In this way, cowbirds were nomadic, always on the move in search of food, much like the buffalo themselves. However, with the clearing of the land and the introduction of grazing animals, cowbirds found a ready food source: the insects stirred up by domesticated, non nomadic animals, such as cows and sheep. As a result, the cowbird became a permanent resident in agricultural areas. Today, cowbirds are a common sight at backyard birdfeeders, arriving in early spring and staying till late September when they head south for winter.

(This task continues on the next page.)

Directions: Now listen to a lecture on the same topic.

Now get ready to write your response.

Prompt	Summarize the points made in the lecture and show how they add to and support the information in the reading.

Writing Time: 20 minutes

audio script page 713

Task #2 - Audio Track #11

Directions: Read the following passage. You have three minutes.

Demography

The science of demography is the statistical study of human populations. More specifically, demography studies human population and how it impacts man and his environment. Demography helps us understand current population trends, such as the movement of immigrants to new lands and the reasons for those moves. Demography also tracks land use trends by asking why a certain population is located in a specific area. Is it due to a dependable food source, the availability of jobs, or the influence of war? Demography also provides insight into the past. By studying the population characteristics of a past civilization, for example, demographers can get a clearer picture of that society's social fabric. When studying past population trends, demographers focus on a variety of factors that impacted those trends, such how labor shortages due to disease affected crop yields. Demographers also gather data pertaining to the fertility and mortality rates. This statistical information is not only valuable to demographers, but also to historians and anthropologists, and to any number of scientists seeking a clearer window into the past. In fact, demographers would argue that everything is connected in some way to demography. For example, the eradication of disease and technological innovation are both clearly linked to changes in the human population.

(This task continues on the next page.)

Directions: Now listen to a lecture on the same topic.

Now get ready to write your response.

Prompt	Summarize the points made in the lecture and show how they add to and support the information in the reading.

Writing Time: 20 minutes

audio script page 713

Emergency Integrated Essay

What if you can't write an integrated essay? What if you blank out? What should you do? Write an emergency integrated essay.

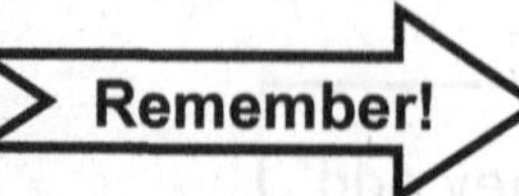

The emergency integrated essay is for the argument counter-argument essay only. Expect to write an argument counter-argument essay on test day.

1. Emergency Integrated Essay: *Step-by-Step*

When writing an emergency integrated essay, use G+3TiC=C and follow the six steps to demonstrate OPDUL=C in your essay.

Step #1 **Make a G+3TiC=C note map; include transitions.**

Make a note map using block style. Next, read the passage twice. Under Reading, summarize the author's opinion, the supporting illustrations and the conclusion. Note the **transition of contrast** under Lecture.

Reading		Lecture	
G		G	**however**
Ti	first	Ti	first
C		C	
Ti	next	Ti	next
C		C	
Ti	finally	Ti	finally
C		C	

Step #2 **Listen to the lecture.**

1. Predict the counter argument using the black-and-white rule.
2. On your note map under **Lecture**, summarize the lecturer's opinion, supporting illustrations and conclusion.

Step #3 Read the prompt; write a first draft.

When the lecture ends, the reading passage will return to your screen. The prompt will also appear.

<u>Prompt</u> Summarize the points made in the lecture and show how they cast doubt on the points made in the reading.

Using your notes, summarize as much of the reading and the lecture as you can using block style. If your lecture notes are incomplete, use the black-and-white rule to summarize the lecture. Start by looking at each reading point, then state the opposite in the corresponding lecture point.

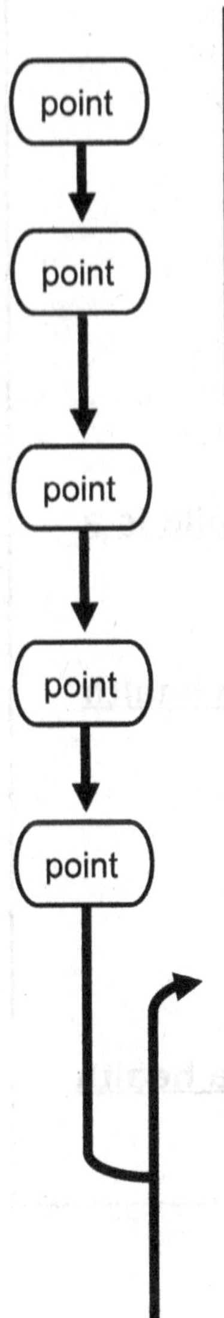

The reading argues that milk is a health risk and we should not drink it.

First, the reading says that cows are injected with a hormone called rBGH. rBGH forces cows to produce far more milk than is naturally possible. rBGH stays in the milk and enters your body. The author says just imagine how much rBGH you've been consuming over the years.

Next, the reading states that a study in England says that children with attention-deficit-hyperactivity disorder (ADHD) are allergic to milk. This allergy increases hyper activity and attention problems in children with ADHD.

Finally, the reading claims that for older women, drinking milk does not decrease bone loss or fractures. In fact, drinking milk actually reduces calcium absorption making bones more fragile in older women.

For those reasons, the reading argues that milk is a health risk.

However

First...

Next...

Finally...

In sum...

Using the black-and-white rule, state the opposite of the **reading opinion** and the opposite of the **reading conclusion** in your lecture summary.

reading

(G) The reading argues that **milk is a health risk** and we should not drink it.

First, the reading says that cows are injected with a hormone called rBGH. rBGH forces cows to produce far more milk than is naturally possible. rBGH stays in the milk and enters your body. The authors says just imagine how much rBGH you've been consuming over the years.

Next, the reading states that a study in England says that children with attention-deficit/hyperactivity disorder (ADHD) are allergic to milk. This allergy increases hyper activity and attention problems in children with ADHD.

Finally, the reading claims that for older women, drinking milk does not decrease bone loss or fractures. In fact, drinking milk actually reduces calcium absorption making bones more fragile in older women.

(C) For those reasons, the reading argues that **milk is a health risk.**

lecture

(G) However, the lecture says that **milk is not a health risk.**

First

Next

Finally

(C) In sum, the lecture argues that **milk is not a health risk.**

Next, look at each supporting illustration (3TiC) in the reading. Using the black-and-white rule, state the opposite point in your lecture summary.

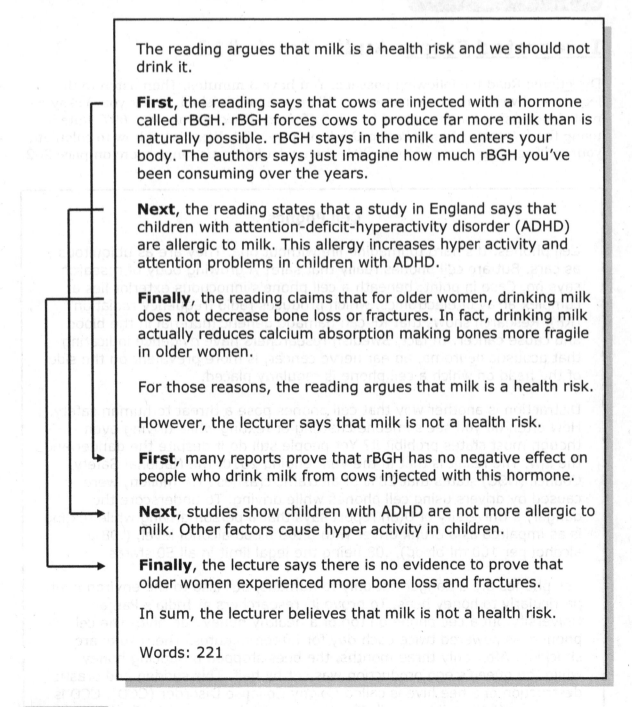

The reading argues that milk is a health risk and we should not drink it.

First, the reading says that cows are injected with a hormone called rBGH. rBGH forces cows to produce far more milk than is naturally possible. rBGH stays in the milk and enters your body. The authors says just imagine how much rBGH you've been consuming over the years.

Next, the reading states that a study in England says that children with attention-deficit-hyperactivity disorder (ADHD) are allergic to milk. This allergy increases hyper activity and attention problems in children with ADHD.

Finally, the reading claims that for older women, drinking milk does not decrease bone loss or fractures. In fact, drinking milk actually reduces calcium absorption making bones more fragile in older women.

For those reasons, the reading argues that milk is a health risk.

However, the lecturer says that milk is not a health risk.

First, many reports prove that rBGH has no negative effect on people who drink milk from cows injected with this hormone.

Next, studies show children with ADHD are not more allergic to milk. Other factors cause hyper activity in children.

Finally, the lecture says there is no evidence to prove that older women experienced more bone loss and fractures.

In sum, the lecturer believes that milk is not a health risk.

Words: 221

Step #4 **Check your first draft for Coherence using OPDUL=C.**

Step #5 **Revise your first draft using your revision checklist.**

Step #6 **Submit your essay.**

Writing Test

Integrated Essay: Audio Track #12

Directions: Read the following passage. You have 3 minutes. Then listen to the lecture and write an integrated essay. When you are finished, check your essay for proficiency using the *Integrated Essay Proficiency Checklist* on page 697. Rate it using the *Integrated Essay Rating Guide* on page 698. Next, learn how to calculate your writing range score on page 201, then calculate your range score on page 202.

Cell Phones

Cell phones. It's hard to imagine life without one. They are as ubiquitous as cars. But are cell phones really that safe? A growing body of research says no. Case in point: beneath a cell phone's innocuous exterior lies a complex array of electronics, which produces radio frequency radiation (RF). Research shows that RF can damage genetic material in the blood and cause cancer. In fact, Swedish researchers have evidence indicating that acoustic neuroma, an ear nerve cancer, is more prevalent on the side of the head on which a cell phone is regularly placed.

Distraction is another way that cell phones pose a threat to human safety. How often do you see someone chatting or texting while driving even though most states prohibit it? Yet people still do it despite the danger and the law. The result is that in the year ending 2010, the National Safety Council (NSC) states that 28% of all traffic crashes (1.6 million) were caused by drivers using cell phones while driving. To underscore the danger, a University of Utah report says that a person driving while texting is as impaired as a drunk driver with a .08 blood alcohol level, (.08 g alcohol per 100 ml blood), .08 being the legal limit in all 50 states.

Cell phones are a danger not only to humans, but also to the environment, particularly to honey bees. To prove it, researchers at India's Panjab University put a cell phone on top of a healthy honey bee hive. The cell phone was powered twice each day for fifteen minutes. The results are shocking. After only three months, the bees stopped producing honey while the queen's egg production was cut by half. This sudden and drastic destruction of a bee hive is called Colony Collapse Disorder (CCD). CCD is happening in the wild as well. If action is not taken soon, the British Bee Keepers Association (BBKA) predicts that the honey bee will disappear from Britain by 2018.

(This task continues on the next page.)

Directions: Now listen to a lecture on the same topic.

Now get ready to write your response.

Prompt	Summarize the points made in the lecture and show how they cast doubt on the points made in the reading.

Writing Time: 20 minutes

audio script page 714

Independent Essay

Directions: Read the following prompt, then write an independent essay. When you are finished, check your essay for proficiency using the *Independent Essay Proficiency Checklist* on page 694. Rate it using the *Independent Essay Rating Guide* on page 695. Next, learn how to calculate your writing range score on page 201, then calculate your range score on page 202.

Prompt Honesty is the best policy. Do you agree or disagree? Why? Use examples and reasons to support your argument.

Writing Time: 30 minutes

Calculate Your Writing Range Score

After you complete the writing test, follow these steps when calculating your writing range score.

1. Identify the range score of your integrated essay (task #1) using the *Integrated Essay Proficiency Checklist* and the *Integrated Essay Rating Guide* (pages 694-699).

   for example your range score = 2.5 - 3.5 / 5

2. Identify the range score of your independent essay (task #2) using the *Independent Essay Proficiency Checklist* and the *Independent Essay Rating Guide.*

   for example your range score = 4.0 - 5.0 / 5

3. Total the scores, then divide by 2 tasks to find your average writing range score.

   task #1 2.5 - 3.5
   task #2 4.0 - 5.0
   total 6.5 - 8.5 / 2 = 3.25 - 4.25 / 5 → average range score

4. Convert your range score (3.25 - 4.25) rating to a writing section range score.

Rating	Section Score
5.0	30
4.75	29
4.5	28
4.25	**27**
4.0	**25**
3.75	**24**
3.5	**22**
3.25	**21**
3.0	20
2.75	18
2.5	17
2.25	15
2.0	14
1.75	12

The approximate writing section range score for this test-taker is 21-27 with a mid-range score of 24. On test day, this test-taker will likely score in this range. Remember: These are approximate scores. On test day, conditions can vary.

Calculate Your Writing Section Range Score

Integrated Essay Range Score = / 5

Independent Essay Range Score = / 5

total = / 10

Divide the total by 2 = / 5 = your rating

Convert your rating to a writing section range score.

Rating ⟶	Writing Section Range Score
5.0	30
4.75	29
4.5	28
4.25	27
4.0	25
3.75	24
3.5	22
3.25	21
3.0	20
2.75	18
2.5	17
2.25	15
2.0	14
1.75	12

Writing Section Range Score = ______

➔ **Record the mid-point* of your writing section range score on page 707.**

* For example, if the averaged range of your two scores is 4.0 - 5.0, then your mid-point, writing section range score is 28/30.

How ETS Calculates Your Writing Score

ETS says that both your essays will be rated by 2 to 4 certified raters on a scale from 0 to 5. The average of their scores will be your final writing section score.[3] For example, the three raters below have rated your independent essay. ETS then averages the three scores to find your independent essay score.

Rater 1 = 4.0/5
Rater 2 = 3.5/5
Rater 3 = 4.5/5

average = 12/15

12 / 3 raters = 4/5 = your independent essay score

Your integrated essay will be scored the same way. ETS will then average your two writing scores for a writing section score out of 30.

Integrated Writing Task = 4/5
Independent Writing Task = 4/5

total = 8/10

8 / 2 tasks = 4/5 = your averaged writing score

Your averaged writing section score (4) will then be converted to writing section range score out of 30 total points.

4 = 25/30

Your final writing score (25/30) will appear with your other section scores under your photograph on your official *TOEFL Internet-Based Test Examine Score Report.*

---

[3] TOEFL® iBT Tips: How to Prepare for the TOEFL® iBT , Page 26; Educational Testing Service, 2008

Notes

Speaking Section

The speaking section is the third section on the TOEFL iBT.

Reading **Listening** **Speaking** **Writing**

The speaking section will last approximately 20 minutes. For this section, there are six tasks. The independent tasks measure your ability to deliver opinion-based, verbal arguments based on personal experience. The integrated tasks measure your ability to deliver fact-based, verbal arguments integrating three language skills: reading, listening, speaking. The task order follows.

TASK DESCRIPTION	PREPARATION TIME	SPEAKING TIME
1. Independent Speaking - *speak only*	15 seconds	45 seconds
2. Independent Speaking - *speak only*	15 seconds	45 seconds
3. Integrated Speaking - *read, listen, speak*	30 seconds	60 seconds
4. Integrated Speaking - *read, listen, speak*	30 seconds	60 seconds
5. Integrated Speaking - *listen, speak*	20 seconds	60 seconds
6. Integrated Speaking - *listen, speak*	20 seconds	60 seconds

Sound Check

For this section, you will wear a headset with a microphone. Before testing begins, you will do a sound check to make sure the headset and microphone are working properly.

Task #1 - Independent Speaking

This task measures your ability to use your personal experience to develop and deliver a verbal, opinion-based argument. Your response will be based on a question in a prompt. The task order follows.

TASK	TIME
1. Read the prompt. 2. Prepare your response.	15 seconds
3. Deliver your response.	45 seconds

Single-Question Prompt

For this task, you will answer a single-question prompt, for example:

> Prompt Which technology has changed your life the most? Develop your opinion using examples and reasons.

Where have you seen single-question prompts before? Answer: The independent essay. In fact, independent speaking task #1 is really just a mini independent essay. However, instead of developing your argument in writing, you will develop it in 15 seconds, then deliver it verbally in 45 seconds.

G+TiC=C

Because your response will be a mini verbal independent essay, you can develop and deliver your response by changing G+3TiC=C to G+TiC=C, wherein G (general statement) is your opinion.

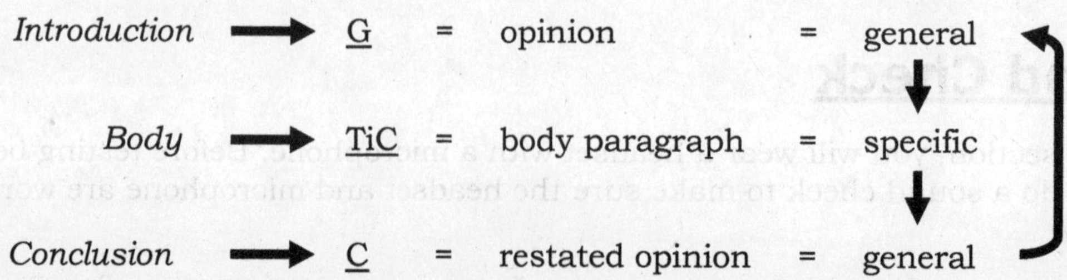

Independent Essay → **Speaking Task #1**

	Independent Essay		Speaking Task #1
G	**Because I'm a scientist, I use many technologies. However, I can honestly say that the technology that has changed my life the most is the internet.** Using the internet makes communication fast and easy, is good for research and it saves me money.	G	Because I'm a scientist, I use many technologies. However, I can honestly say that the technology that has changed my life the most is the internet.
TiC	First, the internet makes communication fast and easy. **For example, I'm from China and I'm now working in the United States. That means my family and friends back in Beijing are very far away. Yet by using the internet, I can talk to them as much as I want. The best way is Skype. Using Skype, I can see their faces and they can see mine. Before the internet, people like my parents had to send letters. That took so long. But the internet has changed all that. The internet makes communication fast and easy for me and my family. It's like magic. Best of all, I don't get homesick.**	TiC	For example, I'm from China and I'm now working in the United States. That means my family and friends back in Beijing are very far away. Yet by using the internet, I can talk to them as much as I want. The best way is Skype. Using Skype, I can see their faces and they can see mine. Before the internet, people like my parents had to send letters. That took so long. But the internet has changed all that. The internet makes communication fast and easy for me and my family. It's like magic. Best of all, I don't get homesick.
TiC	Next, the internet is good for research. I'm a research physicist developing lasers for weather testing. To research my ideas, I always use the internet. It's good for finding articles and the latest research papers that can help me with my research. If I didn't have the internet I'd have to go to libraries. But with the internet, all I have to do is search with Google and I have the information right at my fingertips.		
TiC	Finally, the internet saves me money. When I have questions about my work, I can email scientists all over the world for answers. This saves money because I don't have to travel. Also, scientists can contact me and ask questions. For example, last week a scientist from Norway emailed me and asked about my work. Before the internet, he would have had to have flown or called long distance. This is very expensive. But now we can save time and money using the internet.		
C	**In sum, the internet has changed my life the most.** Using the internet is fast and easy, is great for research and it saves me money. Can you imagine a world without the internet?	C	In sum, the internet has changed my life the most.

As you can see on the previous page, G+TiC=C will help you give the speaking raters what they are trained to listen for: a short, opinion-based, verbal argument that demonstrates OPDUL=C.

OPDUL=C

Note the changes to OPDUL=C under Language Use. For this task, the raters will also rate your ****Delivery***.

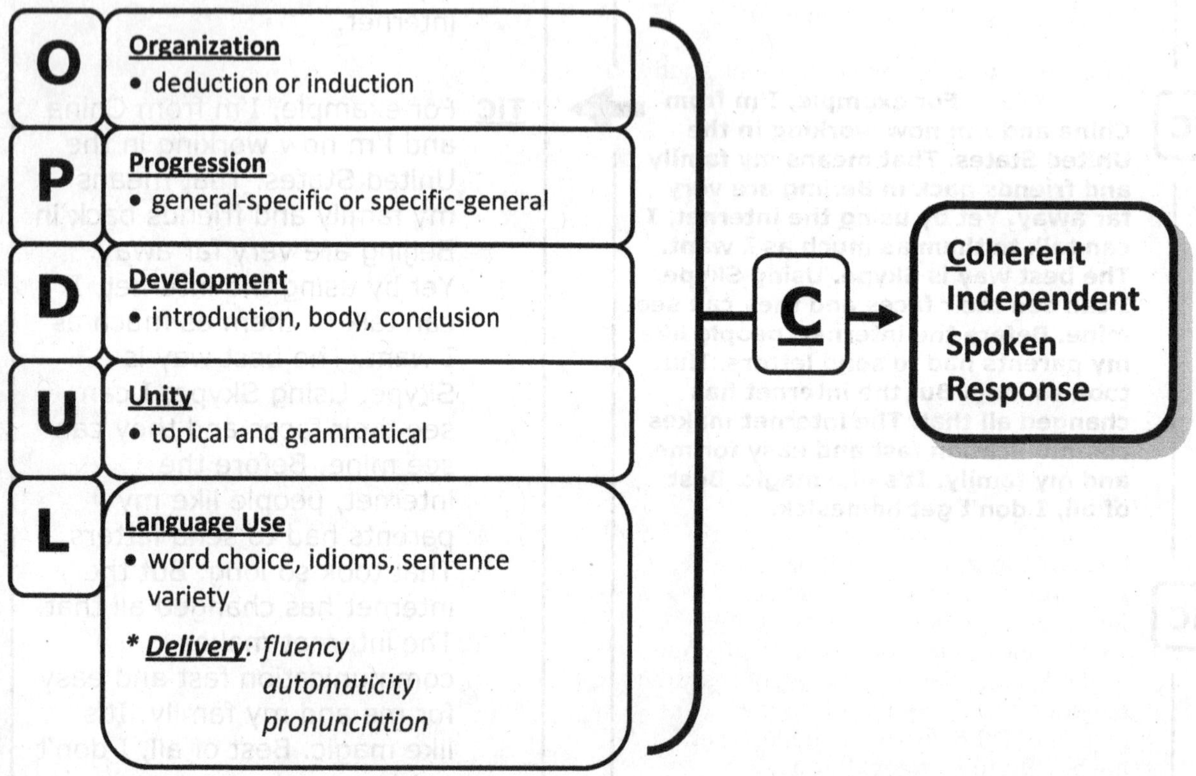

Delivery

When you speak, the raters will measure the proficiency of your delivery in these three areas: fluency, automaticity, and pronunciation.

Fluency — Fluency means how easily (naturally) you speak. Do you speak smoothly and confidently, or do you hesitate and speak in fragments?

Automaticity — Automaticity means how fast you think and speak. Do you pause to translate, or do you think and speak automatically without pausing to translate?

Pronunciation — Pronunciation means how proficiently you produce the sound of English words. Do you stress the right syllables with accurate intonation and volume, or not?

Speaking Subjectively

For this task, the raters will measure your ability to speak subjectively. Speaking subjectively means speaking about you and your life experience using your active English vocabulary (see page 50), for example:

> "Hi, my name is Carla. I'm an architect from Buenos Aries, Argentina. Last year, I graduated from university. Now, I'm interning for an architect in Barcelona, Spain. I have been so busy, but I love it. It's like a dream come true. Next year, I will return to Argentina and start my own business."

Notice how Carla is speaking about herself using first-person singular (*I am... I graduated...I have been...I will return...*). Because Carla is speaking subjectively using her active vocabulary, she is confident about what she is saying. She is confident because when she talks about herself, she makes fewer mistakes even when using idioms (*"It's like a dream come true!"*).

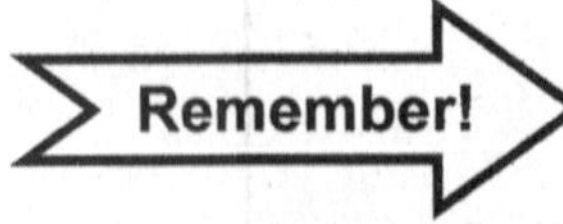

*Fewer mistakes = greater language use proficiency (OPDU**L**=C) = greater coherence (OPDUL=**C**) = a higher speaking score = a higher iBT score.*

Basic Response

When delivering a basic response for this task, you must be able to organize your opinion-based argument quickly and proficiently while speaking subjectively. In this section, you will learn these basic but essential speaking strategies. Later on in this chapter, you will learn how to develop a basic response into an advanced response to maximize scoring.

1. Basic Response: *Step-by-Step*

Before you begin independent speaking task #1, you will hear the directions for the speaking section. The directions will last approximately two minutes. Do not dismiss them. As you listen to the directions, make a G+TiC=C note map.

Step #1 | **Make a G+TiC=C note map; include transitions.**

G = personally
TiC = for example
C = for those reasons

Step #2 **Read the prompt.**

When the speaking directions end, the prompt will appear on your screen. A narrator will read it. You will also see the preparation and response time clocks.

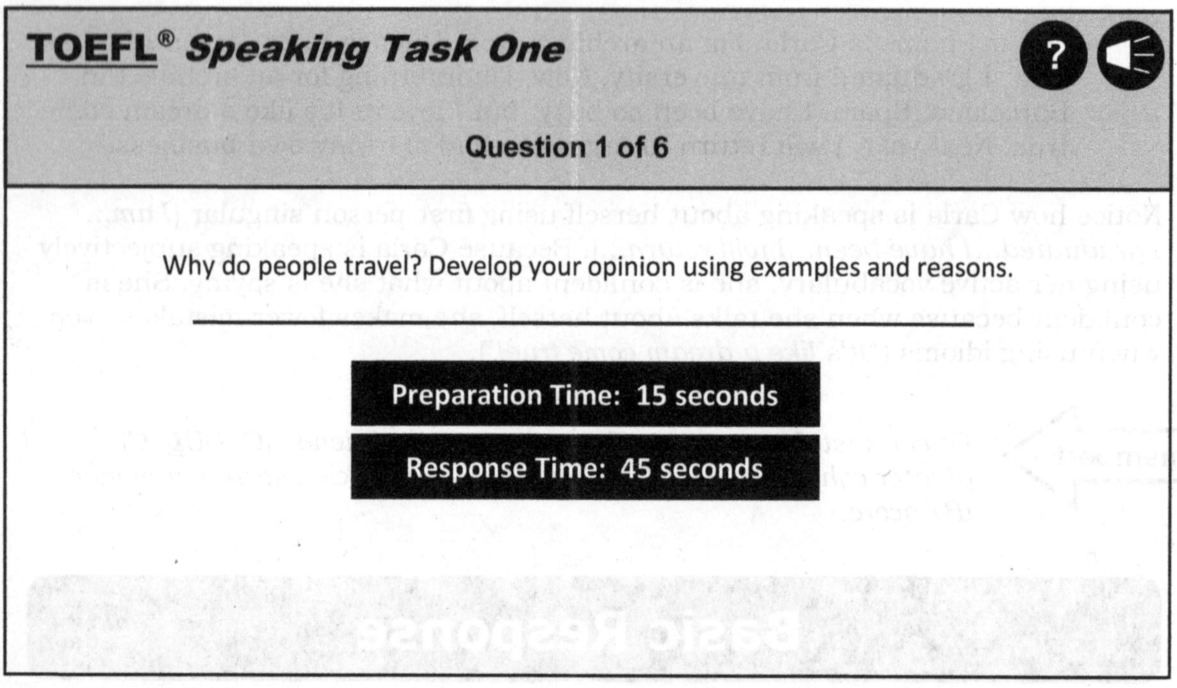

TOEFL® Speaking Task One
?
Question 1 of 6
Why do people travel? Develop your opinion using examples and reasons.
Preparation Time: 15 seconds
Response Time: 45 seconds

Step #3 **Develop ideas (15 seconds).**

When the narrator stops, the preparation clock will start. You will have 15 seconds to prepare your response. The preparation clock will count down (15, 14, 13...). On your note map, jot down *your opinion* and *one example.*

G	=	personally *travel to learn*
TiC	=	for example *Manhattan*
C	=	for those reasons

Step #4 **Speak (45 seconds).**

When the preparation clock reaches zero, you will hear a "Beep!" At this point, the response clock will starting counting down (45, 44, 43...) Look at your note map. It is your guide. Start speaking subjectively. State your opinion, then your supporting illustration. End with your conclusion.

In the following sample response, note how the opinion (G) is restated in the conclusion (C). By restating your opinion in your conclusion, you will know exactly what to say at the end and you will save time.

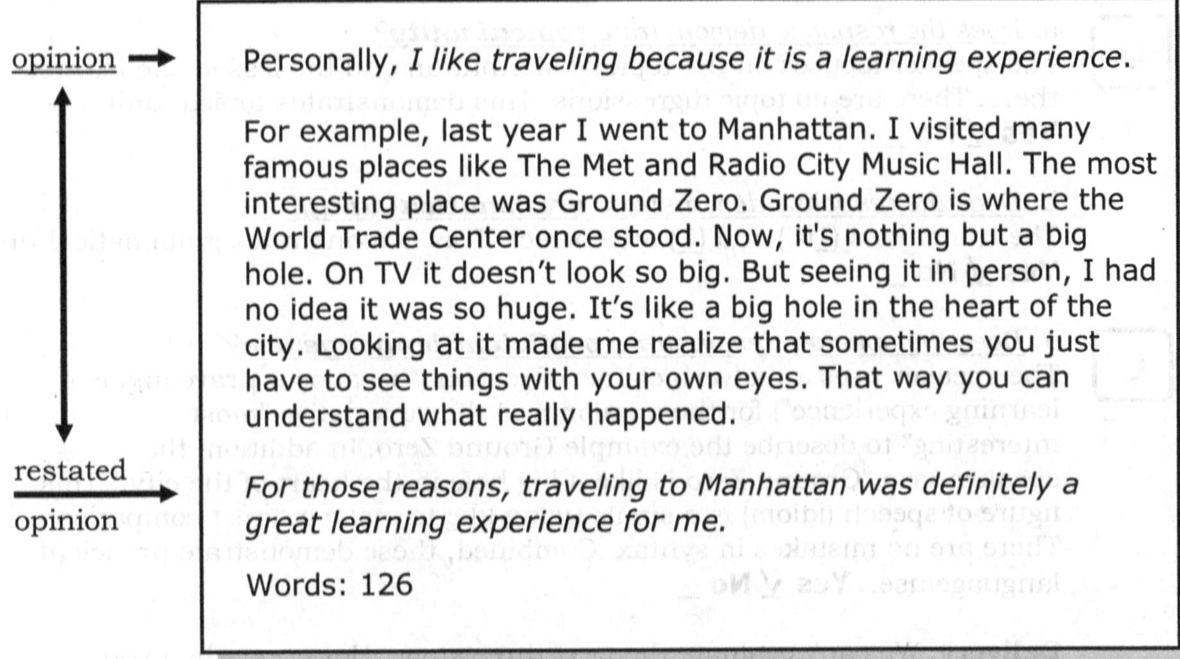

opinion →

Personally, *I like traveling because it is a learning experience.* For example, last year I went to Manhattan. I visited many famous places like The Met and Radio City Music Hall. The most interesting place was Ground Zero. Ground Zero is where the World Trade Center once stood. Now, it's nothing but a big hole. On TV it doesn't look so big. But seeing it in person, I had no idea it was so huge. It's like a big hole in the heart of the city. Looking at it made me realize that sometimes you just have to see things with your own eyes. That way you can understand what really happened.

restated opinion →

For those reasons, traveling to Manhattan was definitely a great learning experience for me.

Words: 126

Next, check this response for Coherence using OPDUL=C. Remember to ask "yes-no" questions starting with Organization.

O *Does the response demonstrate* ***organization****?*
The speaker uses deduction as a method of organization. This demonstrates organization. **Yes √ No _**

P *Does the response demonstrate* ***progression****?*
Because the speaker uses deduction, the ideas progress from general to specific. This demonstrates progression. **Yes √ No _**

D a. *Does the introduction demonstrate* ***development****?*
The speaker says, "Personally, I like traveling because it is a learning experience." This is an opinion. It is arguable, supportable, a complete sentence and not a question. This demonstrates introduction development.
Yes √ No _

b. *Does the body demonstrate* ***development****?*
The speaker uses the supporting illustration of Manhattan and develops it to describe the lesson learned from visiting Ground Zero. This demonstrates body development. **Yes √ No _**

c. *Does the conclusion demonstrate **development**?*
The speaker restates her opinion in the conclusion. This demonstrates conclusion development.
Yes √ No _

U

a. *Does the response demonstrate **topical unity**?*
The speaker focuses on the topic of Manhattan and the lesson she learned there. There are no topic digressions. This demonstrates topical unity.
Yes √ No _

b. *Does the response demonstrate **grammatical unity**?*
The transitions (TiC) and (C) are correct. This demonstrates grammatical unity.
Yes √ No _

L

a. *Does the speaker demonstrate **proficient language use**?*
The speaker uses an adverb clause of reason ("because it [traveling] is a learning experience") for the opinion and the superlative "most interesting" to describe the example Ground Zero. In addition, the speaker says "Ground Zero is like a big hole in the heart of the city." This figure of speech (idiom) is a simile using like to make a direct comparison. There are no mistakes in syntax. Combined, these demonstrate proficient language use. **Yes √ No _**

Delivery: We can't evaluate the next three steps. However, when you practice in class, or with a recording device, ask these three questions.

a. *Is the speaker's fluency proficient?* Yes — No —

b. *Does the speaker demonstrate automaticity?* Yes — No —

c. *Is the speaker's pronunciation proficient?* Yes No —

Note: For this response, the speaker's delivery was proficient.

C

*Does the response (argument) demonstrate **coherence**?*
Because the speaker has proficiently demonstrated Organization, Progression, Development, Unity and Language Use, the response is coherent (OPDUL=**C**). The speaker's argument is clear: "Traveling to Manhattan was definitely a great learning experience." **Yes √ No _**

Mapped out, you can see how G+TiC=C gives the speaking raters what they are trained to listen for: a short, opinion-based, verbal argument that demonstrates OPDUL=C. The opinion (G) and the conclusions (C) are underlined, the transitions (T) are in **bold**, and the supporting illustration (i) is in *italics*.

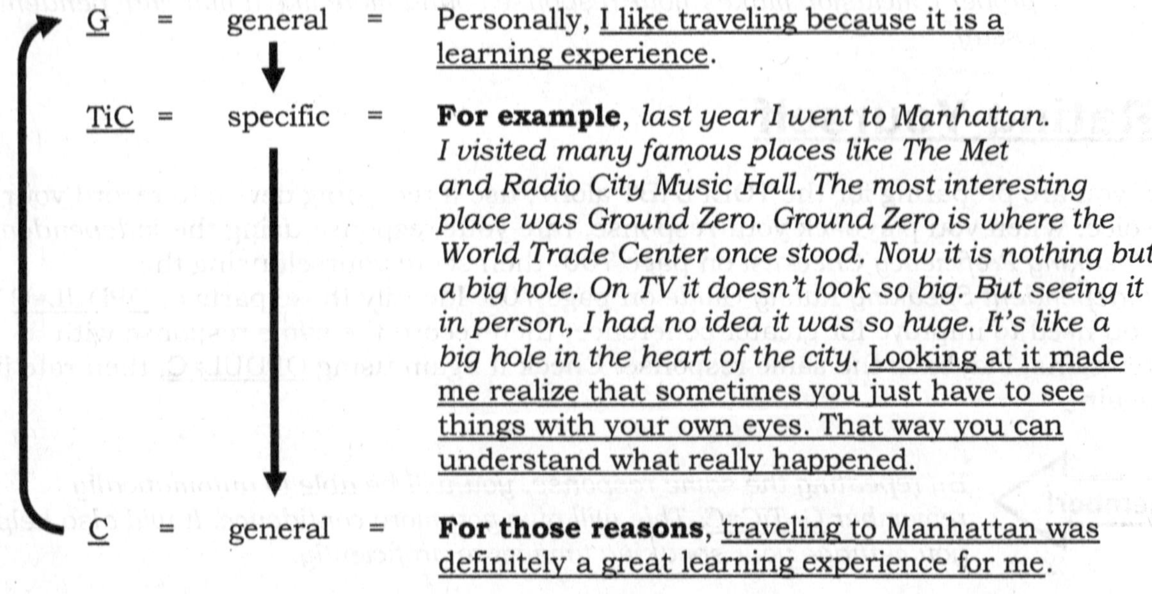

G = general = Personally, I like traveling because it is a learning experience.
TiC = specific = For example, last year I went to Manhattan. I visited many famous places like The Met and Radio City Music Hall. The most interesting place was Ground Zero. Ground Zero is where the World Trade Center once stood. Now it is nothing but a big hole. On TV it doesn't look so big. But seeing it in person, I had no idea it was so huge. It's like a big hole in the heart of the city. Looking at it made me realize that sometimes you just have to see things with your own eyes. That way you can understand what really happened.
C = general = For those reasons, traveling to Manhattan was definitely a great learning experience for me.

In the example above (and below), note how the concluding sentences in the paragraph (TiC) each state a **cause**-and-*effect* relationship.

> **Looking at it** *made me realize that sometimes you just have to see things with your own eyes.* **That way** *you can understand what really happened.*

Cause-and-effect relationships are the **reasons** stated in the prompt.

Prompt	Why do people travel? Develop your opinion using examples and **reasons**.

Note also how the conclusion (C) states a **cause**-and-*effect* relationship, and restates the opinion.

> For those reasons, **traveling to Manhattan** *was definitely a great learning experience for me.*

Q *Do I have to state a conclusion (C) after the paragraph conclusion (Ti<u>C</u>)?*

A *Yes. The conclusion (C) completes the deductive map. The signal phrase (For those reasons...) tells the raters that this is the end of your response. Also, a proper conclusion makes your response sound more like a mini independent essay.*

Rating Yourself

If you are preparing for the TOEFL iBT alone, use a recording device to record your voice. When you playback your response, rate your response using the *Independent Speaking Proficiency Checklist* on page 700, then score yourself using the *Independent Speaking Rating Guide* on page 701. Identify those parts of <u>OPDUL=C</u> you need to improve for greater coherence, then record the same response with revisions. Playback the same response. Check it again using <u>OPDUL=C</u>, then rate it again.

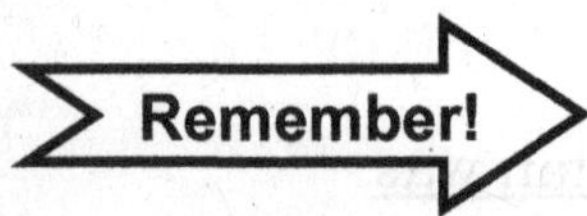

By repeating the same response, you will be able to automatically remember <u>G+TiC=C</u>. This will give you more confidence. It will also help you manage your speaking time more proficiently.

Rating in a Class

When preparing for the TOEFL iBT in a TOEFL class, ask your instructor and classmates to check your response for coherence using the *Independent Speaking Proficiency Checklist*, then rate your response using the *Independent Speaking Rating Guide*. Repeat the same response until you proficiently demonstrate <u>OPDUL=C</u>.

<u>TASK:</u> Rate the response about traveling-and-learning on the previous page using the *Independent Speaking Rating Guide* 701. Compare your rating to the one on page 796. <u>Note</u>: For this response, the speaker's delivery was proficient.

Q *Do I have to use all 45 seconds? Is there some rule?*

A *No. There is no official rule that says you have to speak for all 45 seconds.*

*A response that uses all 45 seconds does not always mean a coherent response. On the contrary, such a response might suggest a lack of coherence (OPDUL=**<u>C</u>**). Some test-takers simply speak and speak, thinking more is better. Wrong. Your job is to deliver a response that proficiently demonstrates <u>OPDUL=C</u>. Do so using <u>G+TiC=C</u>.*

How Long Should My Response Be?

Everyone speaks at a different pace. However, using G+TiC=C and speaking at a natural pace, you will able to deliver a response that demonstrates OPDUL=C in 45 seconds. The following map illustrates approximate time divisions for each step of G+TiC=C.

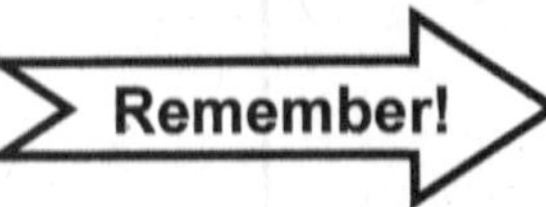

You are reading this example. On test day, you will pause and hesitate when you speak and thus use more time.

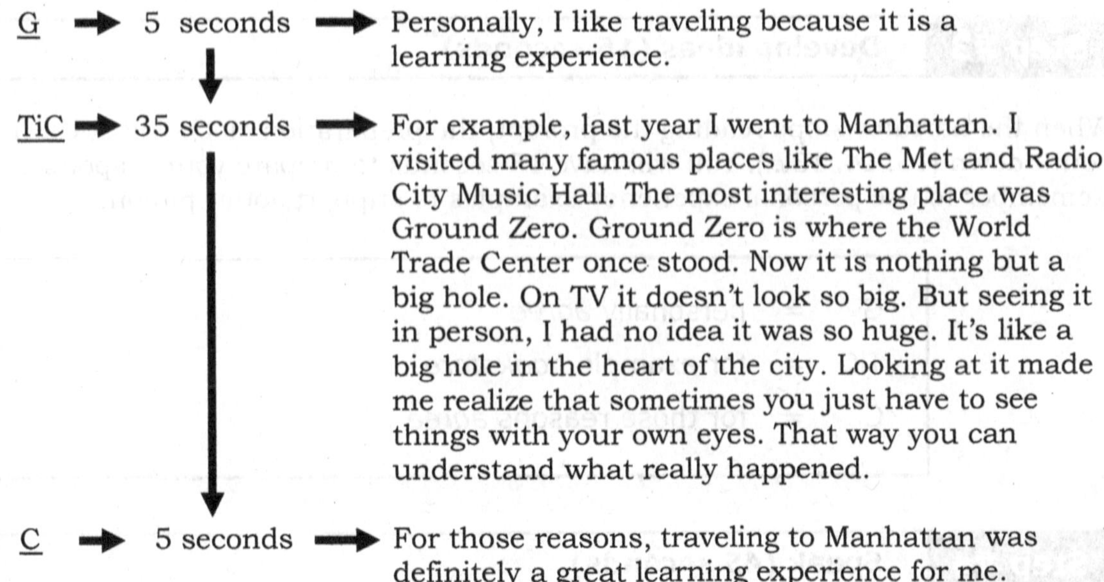

G → 5 seconds → Personally, I like traveling because it is a learning experience.

TiC → 35 seconds → For example, last year I went to Manhattan. I visited many famous places like The Met and Radio City Music Hall. The most interesting place was Ground Zero. Ground Zero is where the World Trade Center once stood. Now it is nothing but a big hole. On TV it doesn't look so big. But seeing it in person, I had no idea it was so huge. It's like a big hole in the heart of the city. Looking at it made me realize that sometimes you just have to see things with your own eyes. That way you can understand what really happened.

C → 5 seconds → For those reasons, traveling to Manhattan was definitely a great learning experience for me.

TASK: For speaking practice, read the sample responses in this chapter out loud. Remember to time yourself.

2. Basic Response: *Step-by-Step*

Let's map out another single-question response. Remember to use G+TiC=C and the four steps to demonstrate OPDUL=C in your argument.

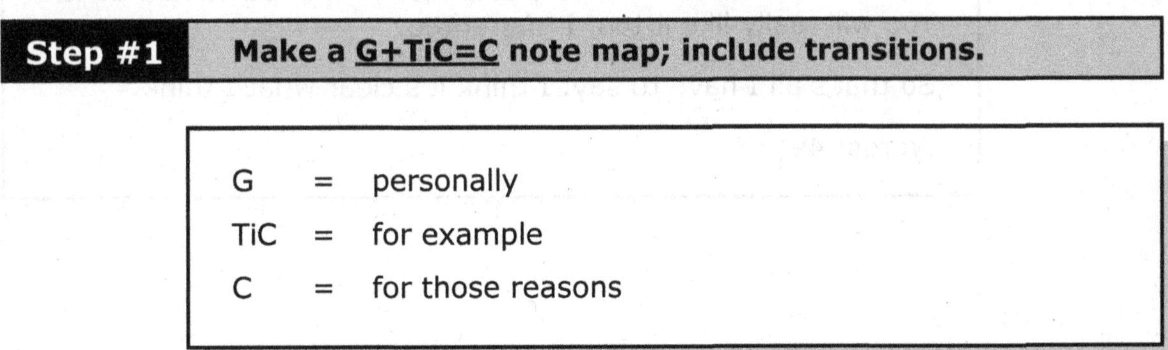

Step #1 **Make a G+TiC=C note map; include transitions.**

G = personally

TiC = for example

C = for those reasons

Step #2 **Read the prompt.**

When the speaking directions end, the prompt will appear on screen. A narrator will read it.

Prompt: Should teenagers work during high school? Why? Give illustrations and reasons to develop your argument.

Step #3 **Develop ideas (15 seconds).**

When the narrator stops reading the prompt, the preparation clock will start. It will count down (15, 14, 13...). You will have 15 seconds to prepare your response. Remember to use personal experience examples to support your opinion.

G	=	personally *agree*
TiC	=	for example *bookstore*
C	=	for those reasons *agree*

Step #4 **Speak (45 seconds).**

When the preparation clock reaches zero, you will hear a "Beep!" Look at your note map. Start speaking. State your opinion first, then your example. End with your conclusion.

I agree.

For example, when I was a high school student, I had a job at a bookstore. It was, you know, fun. You should do it. You will really like it too. I guarantee.

So that's all I have to say. I think it's clear what I think.

Words: 49

Check this response for coherence using <u>OPDUL=C</u>.

O <u>*Does the response demonstrate **organization**?*</u>
The speaker uses neither deduction nor induction. This demonstrates a lack of organization. **Yes _ No <u>X</u>**

P <u>*Does the response demonstrate **progression**?*</u>
Because the speaker does not use a method of organization, the ideas do not progress. This demonstrates a lack of progression. **Yes _ No <u>X</u>**

D a. <u>*Does the introduction demonstrate **development**?*</u>
The speaker says, "I agree." But with what? This is not an opinion. It is a fact. It is not arguable. This demonstrates a lack of introduction development. **Yes _ No <u>X</u>**

b. <u>*Does the body demonstrate **development**?*</u>
The speaker does not develop a specific example. This demonstrates a lack of body development. **Yes _ No <u>X</u>**

c. <u>*Does the conclusion demonstrate **development**?*</u>
The speaker does not restate his opinion at the end. This demonstrates a lack of conclusion development. **Yes _ No <u>X</u>**

U a. <u>*Does the response demonstrate **topical unity**?*</u>
The speaker focuses on the topic of working in high school. This demonstrates topical unity. **Yes <u>√</u> No _**

b. <u>*Does the response demonstrate **grammatical unity**?*</u>
The transitions (<u>T</u>i<u>C</u>) and (<u>C</u>) are correct. This demonstrates grammatical unity. **Yes <u>√</u> No _**

L a. <u>*Does the speaker demonstrate **proficient language use**?*</u>
There are no mistakes in syntax; however, the speaker uses only simple sentences. There are no idioms. There is no advanced vocabulary. This demonstrates a lack of language use. **Yes _ No <u>X</u>**

<u>Delivery</u>: We can't evaluate the next three steps. However, when you practice in class, or with a recording device, ask these three questions.

a. <u>*Is the speaker's fluency proficient?*</u> Yes __ No __

b. <u>*Does the speaker demonstrate automaticity?*</u> Yes __ No __

c. <u>*Is the speaker's pronunciation proficient?*</u> Yes __ No __

<u>Note</u>: For this response, the speaker's delivery was proficient.

C

Does the response demonstrate ***coherence****?*
The speaker does not demonstrate a method of organization. Because there is no method of organization, the ideas do not progress or develop. Because the ideas do not progress or develop, there is a lack of language use. The result is a serious lack of coherence (OPDUL=**C**).
Yes _ No X

According to the *Independent Speaking Rating Guide* on page 701, this response will score in the 1.5-2.0 range. If you (the speaker) want a higher score, you must revise those parts of OPDUL=C that received an **X**. The **X's** are your revision checklist. By identifying problem areas, you can focus on revising them when you practice. This, in turn, will make you test-ready.

Now read the revised response.

Personally, I think that high school students should work while going to school.

For example, when I was a high school student, I had a job at an English bookstore in Budapest, Hungary. I worked every Saturday and Sunday, and sometimes at night during the week. I loved it because I was always meeting foreigners who spoke English. By helping them find books, I was able to practice my English. It was great because at school, I only learned grammar from books, but at the bookstore I was learning conversational English. Not only that but I made money for myself. This helped me because I didn't always have to ask my parents for money for books and other things. As you can see, by working at the bookstore I killed two birds with one stone.

In conclusion, I believe that all high school students should work part-time during high school.

Words: 150

TASK: Rate this response using the *Independent Speaking Rating Guide* on page 701. Compare your rating to the one on page 796. Note: For this response, the speaker's delivery was proficient.

Rhetorical Strategies

Rhetorical strategies demonstrate topic development (OP**D**UL=C) and language use (OPDU**L**=C). These, in turn, demonstrate coherence (OPDUL=**C**). The previous response demonstrates a variety of rhetorical strategies, including:

illustration	the writer working in a bookstore in Budapest, Hungary;
narration	the writer's personal story of working in a bookstore;
description	English bookstore...worked every Saturday and Sunday and sometimes at night...I loved it;
cause-effect	- work at the bookstore (cause) make money (effect); - work at the bookstore (cause) "kill two birds with one stone" (effect); - work at bookstore (cause) learn conversational English (effect); - work at the bookstore (cause) no longer depend on parents for money (effect);
compare-contrast	learn English grammar at high school vs. learn conversational English at the bookstore.

3. Basic Response: *Step-by-Step*

Let's map out another single-question response. Remember to use G+TiC=C and the four steps to demonstrate OPDUL=C in your argument.

Step #1 **Make a G+TiC=C note map; include transitions.**

G = personally
TiC = for example
C = for those reasons

Step #2 **Read the prompt.**

Prompt People are living longer. Why? Develop your position using examples and reasons.

Step #3 **Develop ideas (15 seconds).**

G	=	personally *better care*
TiC	=	for example *grandfather*
C	=	for those reasons *better care*

Step #4 **Speak (45 seconds).**

Personally, I contend that people are living longer because they are taking better care of themselves.

For example, my grandfather is eighty. When he was younger, he used to smoke and drink a lot. Also, he never ate very well. Then, when he was fifty, he had heart attack. He was in the hospital for a long time. The doctor told him he should stop smoking and drinking, and start eating better. That's what my grandfather did. Now, he doesn't drink or smoke anymore. Also, he eats lots of healthy food like salads and fish, and he exercises every day. As a result, he feels much better than before and has lots more energy.

By changing his lifestyle, my grandfather is definitely going to live longer because he is taking better care of himself.

Words: 134

TASK: Check this response for coherence using the *Independent Speaking Proficiency Checklist* on page 700, then rate it using the *Independent Speaking Rating Guide* on page 701. Compare your rating to the one on page 796. Note: For this response, the speaker's delivery was proficient.

Q *Do I always have to say "For example" when I start to give my example?*

A *No. "For example" is simply there to remind you that you need a transition after you state your opinion. Remember: A transition is a signal word (or phrase) that tells the raters you are moving from general to specific.*

The following are synonymous phrases for "for example." Remember: You can use these examples in your independent essay as well.

> Personally, I contend that people are living longer because they are taking better care of themselves.
>
> For example, my grandfather...
> A good example is my grandfather...
> An excellent example is my grandfather...
> A good illustration is my eighty-year-old grandfather...
> An illustration to support my opinion is my grandfather...
> My grandfather, who is eighty, is an excellent illustration.

Four Common Speaking Problems

Read the following prompt and the response.

> Prompt In your view, what was the greatest invention of the twentieth century? Why? Give examples and reasons to support your argument.

> Personally, I believe that the greatest invention of the twentieth century was women developing and winning many special rights they never had before from countries that didn't care about them, and I believe this is a good thing for all women.
>
> For example, women were very successful. They did a lot of very important things that changed their lives. They won many rights they never had before.
>
> Women winning rights was the greatest invention of the twentieth century because it helped them so much.
>
> Words: 84

This response demonstrates four common speaking problems you should avoid on test day.

1. Overstated Opinion

Read the speaker's opinion once again.

> Personally, I believe that the greatest invention of the twentieth century was women developing and winning many special rights they never had before from countries that didn't care about them and I believe this is a good thing for all women.

This test-taker is overstating her opinion. To overstate means to say too much. Avoid overstating your opinion by delivering it in one concise sentence, for example:

> Personally, I believe that the greatest invention of the twentieth century was women winning many rights.

2. Lack of Topic Development

Read the supporting illustration from the same response.

> For example, women were very successful. They did a lot of very important things that changed their lives. They won many rights they never had before.

In this body paragraph, does the test-taker develop a specific personal example to support her opinion? Is there a cause-and-effect relationship providing a reason? No. Because there is a lack of topic development (OP**D**UL=C), there is a lack of coherence (OPDUL=**C**). This will result in a lower score.

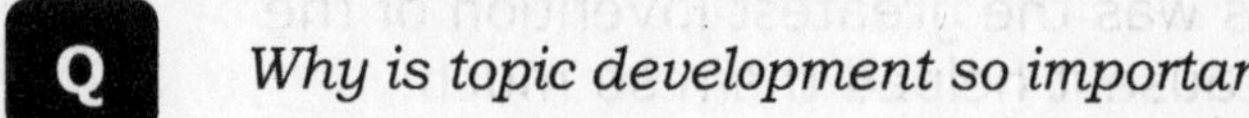

Q *Why is topic development so important?*

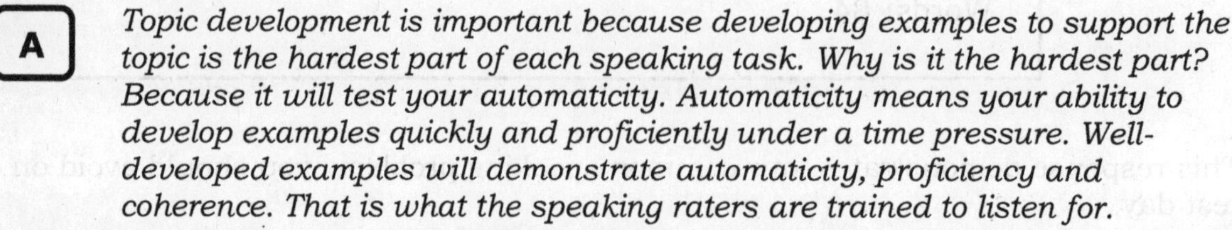

A *Topic development is important because developing examples to support the topic is the hardest part of each speaking task. Why is it the hardest part? Because it will test your automaticity. Automaticity means your ability to develop examples quickly and proficiently under a time pressure. Well-developed examples will demonstrate automaticity, proficiency and coherence. That is what the speaking raters are trained to listen for.*

Look at the following maps. The supporting example in Map A lacks development. In contrast, Map B has a supporting example that is well developed. If you want a high score, your response should look like Map B.

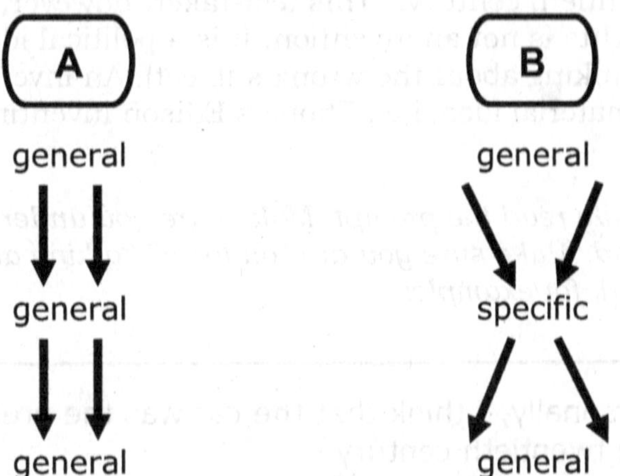

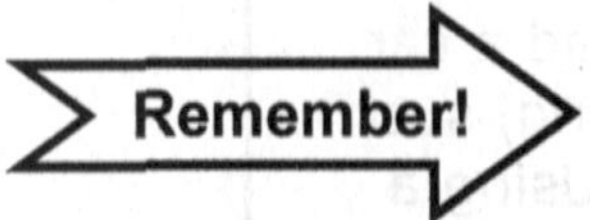

Lack of topic development, especially in the body paragraph(s), is a big reason why test-takers score low on independent speaking task #1.

3. <u>Lack of Subjectivity</u>

Why was this test-taker unable to develop a supporting example for women's rights? Because she was trying to speak objectively using her passive English vocabulary. In her own language, she knew what she wanted to say objectively, but she couldn't translate her passive English into her active English in 45 seconds. In the end, she became frustrated and lost focus. As a result, she hesitated too much. This demonstrated a lack of proficient language use (OPDU**<u>L</u>**=C), specifically the delivery areas of fluency and automaticity. The result was a lack of coherence (OPDUL=**<u>C</u>**).

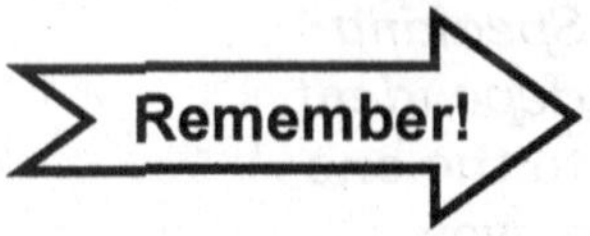

Avoid "big" topics. Don't talk about Einstein or Bill Gates. Talk subjectively using your active English vocabulary. Talk about <u>you</u>.

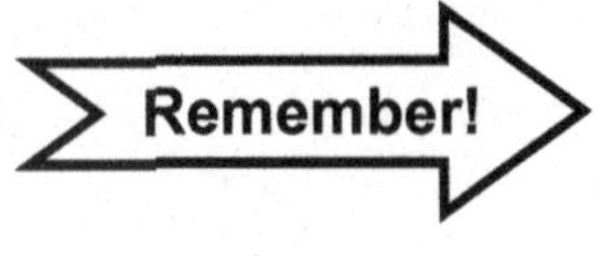

*When you speak subjectively, you are using your active English vocabulary. When you use your active English vocabulary, you are more confident. Because you are more confident, you make fewer mistakes. Fewer mistakes = increased language use proficiency (OPDU**<u>L</u>**=C) = greater coherence (OPDUL=**<u>C</u>**) = a higher speaking score = a high final score.*

4. Off-Topic Response

Read the prompt once again. Note that the topic in the prompt is "the greatest invention of the twentieth century." This test-taker, however, talks about "women's rights." Women's rights is not an invention. It is a political idea. The speaker is therefore off topic (talking about the wrong subject). An invention, in this context, means an original material idea, i.e., Thomas Edison inventing the phonograph.

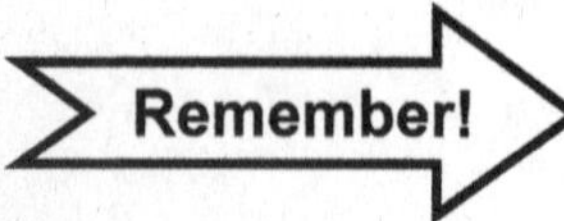

Carefully read the prompt. Make sure you understand it before you respond. Make sure you are "on topic" (talking about the topic in the prompt), for example:

> Personally, I think that the car was the greatest invention of the twentieth century.
>
> For example, I am from Turkey. I remember my mother and father telling me how they had a horse before they had a car. The horse was very important because it did everything, such as work in the fields and take vegetables to market. Using a horse, though, was very slow. Everything took so much time. But then my father bought a car and everything changed completely. He could go places more quickly and he could take more vegetables to market. Best of all, he took my mother to the hospital to have me.
>
> In conclusion, I think that for me and my family, the greatest invention of the twentieth century was the car.
>
> Words: 128

TASK: Check this response for coherence using the *Independent Speaking Proficiency Checklist* on page 700, then rate it using the *Independent Speaking Rating Guide* on page 701. Compare your rating to the one on page 796. Note: For this response, the speaker's delivery was proficient.

Help! – *My Response is Too Long!*

The following are reasons why your response is longer than 45 seconds.

Reason #1 Your opinion is too long.

Solution
1. Make your opinion shorter.
2. State your opinion in one concise sentence.
3. State your opinion in 5 seconds or less.
4. Speak faster; try not to hesitate.

Reason #2 When the clock starts, you are not speaking right away. As a result, you are losing valuable seconds at the start.

Solution Start speaking right after the beep. Remember: *The speaking tasks come up fast. Be ready for them*

Reason #3 You are being too careful. When you are too careful, you slow down to pronounce correctly. When you slow down, you waste time. You also decrease fluency and automaticity.

Solution
1. Speak at a natural pace.
2. Record your voice, then play it back. You will know if you are speaking too slowly. If so, speak faster.

Reason #4 You are pausing or hesitating too much. Record your voice and play it back. You will soon know if you are pausing or hesitating too much. Pausing and hesitating waste time. Pausing and hesitating will also decrease fluency and automaticity.

Solution
1. Avoid pauses; try not to hesitate.
2. Practice reading sample responses until you speak confidently and at the right speed.
3. Ask a native speaker to demonstrate the right speed.

Reason #5 You are pausing and/or hesitating too much because you have not memorized G+TiC=C.

Solution
1. Memorize G+TiC=C.
2. Practice reading sample responses using G+TiC=C.

Reason #6 Your supporting illustration (TiC) contains too much information.

Solution
1. Do not include information that is not important or off topic.
2. Develop one example only (G+TiC=C). Remember*: One well-developed example is better than two examples that lack development.*

Reason #7 Your conclusion is too long.

Solution
1. State your conclusion in five seconds or less.
2. Simply repeat your opinion.

Reason #8 The clock makes you so nervous you can't speak.

Solution
1. Do not time yourself when you practice. Just speak. When you are more confident, time yourself.

Help! – *My Response is Too Short!*

The following are reasons why your response is too short.

Reason #1 You are nervous. When you are nervous, you speak too fast and finish too soon.

Solution
1. Record your voice and play it back. You will soon know if you are speaking too fast. If so, slow down.

Reason #2 Your supporting illustration is too short. If your example is too short, it will lack development.

Solution
1. Include more details when you develop your supporting example. Identify all place names and people names. Remember: *Be specific. If you studied mechanical engineering at Tsinghua University in China from 2000 to 2003, say, "I studied mechanical engineering at Tsinghua University in China from 2000 to 2003."*

Reason #3 You speak, then suddenly stop because you are shy, afraid, or feel stupid.

Solution
1. Practice reading into a recording device. Read an English magazine article or a book while recording. This will help you develop confidence speaking into a microphone.
2. Take an ESL class to develop your speaking skills and your confidence.
3. Practice. Practice. Practice.

Reason #4 You are not confident using G+TiC=C.

Solution
1. Practice developing and delivering responses until you have memorized G+TiC=C and you can remember it automatically without notes.

Reason #5 You blank out.

Solution

1. You are trying too hard and/or are too nervous. Try to relax. When you practice speaking, don't time yourself. Just speak until you are confident. When you are more confident, then time yourself.
2. Forget about trying to demonstrate OPDUL=C. Just speak. The more you speak, the more confident you will become.

Clean Start

A clean start means you start speaking with no hesitation. You state your opinion clearly and succinctly, then progress to your supporting illustration, for example:

G = Personally, I think that students should have part-time jobs while in high school.

TiC = For example, when I was a high school student, I had a job at an English bookstore in Budapest, Hungary. My job was to put books on the shelves and help customers.

Rough Start

A rough start means you are using conversational (non academic, non formal) English, or you are looking for focus. This will result in a lack of coherence (OPDUL=**C**), for example:

G = Yo. S'up? I think it's good. You know, working in high school. Dawg should do it. Make some money. Cool.

TiC = A good example? There are lots. Really.

Clean End

A clean end means you clearly and succinctly restate your opinion and stop. Resist the temptation to say more or to correct yourself, for example:

C = For those reasons, working in a bookstore in high school really helped me to become more independent and responsible.

Rough End

A rough end means you are speaking conversationally and/or have lost focus. This will result in a lack of coherence (OPDUL=**C**), for example:

C = Working was, you know, fun. Everybody should do it. That's all. No. Actually, I hated it. Money causes nothing but problems. Is this microphone on?

Advanced Speaking Strategies

To maximize scoring, apply the following advanced strategies to develop a basic, opinion-based verbal argument into an advanced, opinion-based, verbal argument.

G+2TiC=C

One way to develop a basic response into an advanced response is by adding a second body paragraph. Do so by changing G+TiC=C to G+2TiC=C.

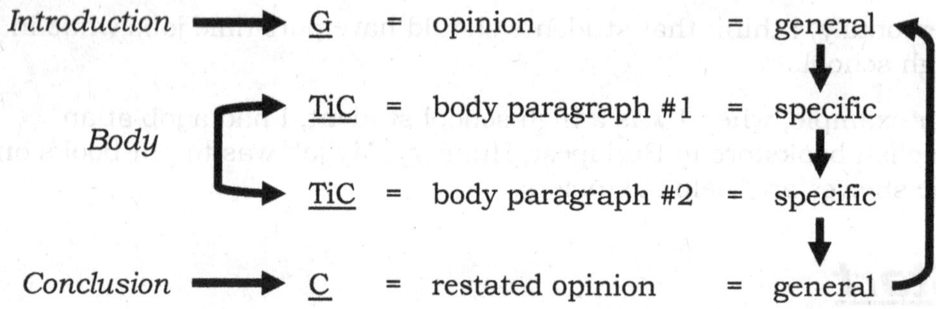

A second body paragraph will result in greater topic development (OP**D**UL=C). For example, read the following prompt.

Prompt	Which person has been the greatest influence in your life? Why? Give examples and reasons to support and develop your opinion.

Now read the sample response on the next page.

Personally, I believe that my mother has been the biggest influence in my life.

For example, I am now in America working as an au pair. An au pair is like a babysitter who lives with an American family. I am doing this for a year in Stamford, Connecticut. At first I didn't want to come to America and leave all my friends in Estonia, but my mother said it would be a great experience and a great way to develop my English. She was right. Living with an American family has been a wonderful experience and my English is so much better.

Also, my mother is my inspiration. When I was growing up, she was a high school teacher. This was strange because all my friends' mothers were housewives. But my mother wanted to work. She always told me to just follow my heart. I remember these words whenever I have problems in America, and they give me strength.

For those reasons, my mother has been the biggest influence in my life.

Words: 173

Q *Which is better? G+TiC=C or G+2TiC=C?*

A *If you can demonstrate OPDUL=C using G+TiC=C, good. G+2TiC=C? Great. If you try to develop three examples (G+3TiC=C), remember to watch the clock. You only have 45 seconds speaking time.*

Q *What if I keep running out of time when practicing using G+2TiC=C?*

A *Develop only one example using G+TiC=C.*

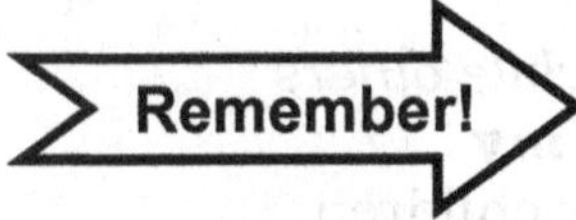

One well-developed example is better than two or three examples that lack development.

Advanced Introduction Strategies

To maximize scoring, apply the following advanced introduction strategies to develop a basic, opinion-based verbal argument into an advanced, opinion-based verbal argument.

These strategies can also be applied to the independent essay.

Simple Hooks

A simple hook uses the information in the prompt. In the following examples, note how the *hook* comes first, followed by the **transition** and the opinion. Combined, they form the introduction (G) of your response.

introduction (G) = *hook* + **transition** + opinion

a. *Or-Question Hook*

For this hook, start with an *or question.* Next, give a **transition**, then answer the question. The answer is your opinion, for example:

G *Is surfing the internet dangerous or not?* **From my point of view**, I believe that surfing the net is not dangerous.

b. *Restate-the-Prompt Hook*

For this hook, first *restate the prompt.* Next, give a **transition**, then state your opinion, for example:

G *The question is whether fast food is good or bad for children.* **As far as I'm concerned**, I think fast food is bad for children.

c. *Pro-Con Hook*

For this hook, state *the pro (positive) side* and *the con (negative) side of the argument.* Next, give a **transition**, then state your opinion, for example:

G *Some think that homeschooling is best for children while others argue that children should go to a regular school.* **In my estimation**, I believe that homeschooling is best for children.

d. ***General Fact + Question Hook***

For this hook, start with a *general fact*. Next, ask an *or question*. Write a **transition**, then answer the question. The answer is your opinion, for example:

> G *Children all over the world watch a lot of television every day. Is it good or bad for them?* **Personally**, I think it is bad for them.

Complex Hooks

A complex hook uses information from researched sources, information you bring to the test. For complex hook strategies you can use to develop your introduction for this speaking task, see *Complex Hooks* for the Independent Essay.

Warning!

Watch the clock. Hooks can use up a lot of time.

Inverted-Pyramid Introduction

Why is a hook an effective strategy? Because your introduction (hook + transition + opinion) will look like an inverted (upside down) pyramid in which the ideas progress from general to specific.

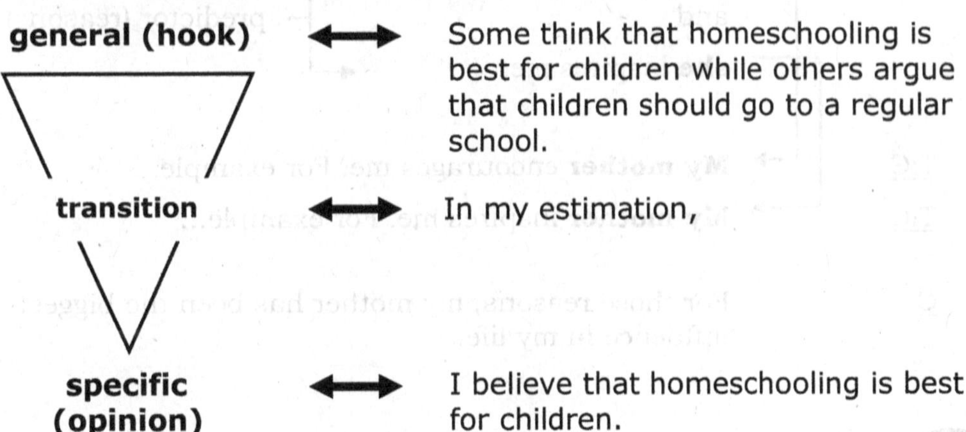
general (hook)
Some think that homeschooling is best for children while others argue that children should go to a regular school.
transition
In my estimation,
specific (opinion)
I believe that homeschooling is best for children.

Remember!

The speaking raters will listen for an inverted-pyramid introduction. An inverted-pyramid introduction demonstrates OPDUL=C.

Predictor Thesis

To maximize scoring, start your response with a predictor thesis.

opinion = Personally, I believe that my mother has been the biggest influence in my life

predictor
- conjunction = because
- she encourages me (reason #1)
- conjunction = and
- she inspires me (reason #2).

Look at the following predictor thesis. Note how each predictor becomes a topic sentence in each body paragraph. Notice also how **she** becomes the topic identifier **My mother** in each body paragraph topic sentence (**T**iC).

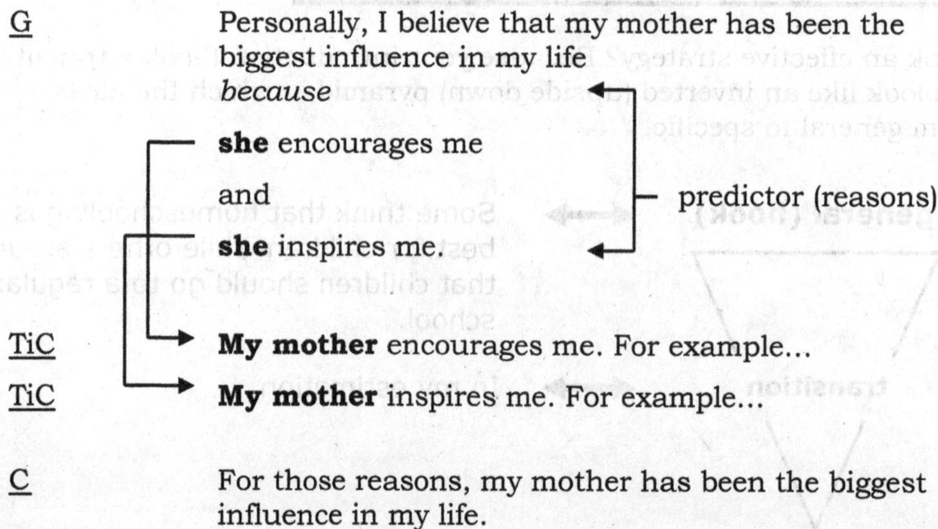

G
Personally, I believe that my mother has been the biggest influence in my life
because
she encourages me
and
she inspires me.
predictor (reasons)
TiC
My mother encourages me. For example...
TiC
My mother inspires me. For example...
C
For those reasons, my mother has been the biggest influence in my life.

Predictor strategies can also be applied to the independent essay.

Predictor Thesis: ***Using Synonyms***

Look at the following predictor thesis.

> Personally, I think that customers should be allowed to return purchased items for a full refund within thirty days.

To demonstrate language use (OPDU**L**=C), replace "Personally" with a synonymous phrase, for example:

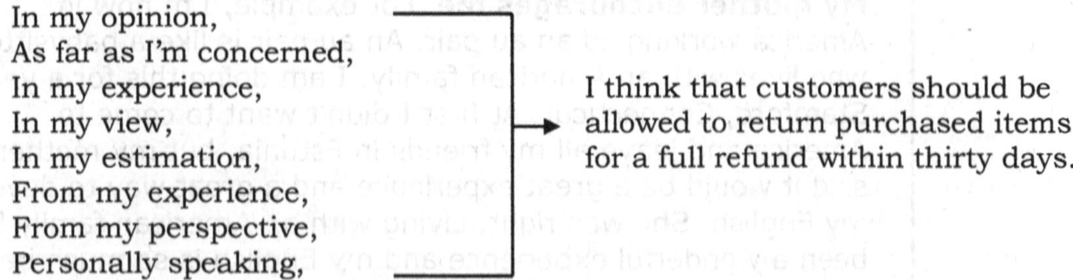

In my opinion,
As far as I'm concerned,
In my experience,
In my view,
In my estimation,
From my experience,
From my perspective,
Personally speaking,
I think that customers should be allowed to return purchased items for a full refund within thirty days.

Next, look at the main verb think followed by that.

> Personally, I think that customers should be allowed to return purchased items for a full refund within thirty days.

Replace think that with a synonymous phrase. This will demonstrate language use (OPDU**L**=C).

1. In my experience, I feel that customers should be allowed to return purchased items for a full refund within thirty days.

2. In my view, I posit that customers should be allowed to return purchased items for a full refund within thirty days.

3. From my perspective, I contend that customers should be allowed to return purchased items for a full refund within thirty days.

4. Personally speaking, I believe that customers should be allowed to return purchased items for a full refund within thirty days.

5. In my estimation, I postulate that customers should be allowed to return purchased items for a full refund within thirty days.

6. From my perspective, I reason that customers should be allowed to return purchased items for a full refund within thirty days.

Look at the following response with a predictor thesis. Note how the **predictors** topically unite with each body paragraph **topic sentence**. This demonstrates organization, progression, development, unity and language use (**OPDUL**=C). This, in turn, demonstrates coherence (OPDUL=**C**).

> Personally speaking, I believe that my mother has been the biggest influence in my life because **she encourages** and **inspires me**.
>
> **My mother encourages me**. For example, I'm now in America working as an au pair. An au pair is like a babysitter who lives with an American family. I am doing this for a year in Stamford, Connecticut. At first I didn't want to come to America and leave all my friends in Estonia, but my mother said it would be a great experience and a great way to develop my English. She was right. Living with an American family has been a wonderful experience and my English is so much better.
>
> **Also, my mother inspires me**. When I was growing up, she was a high school teacher. This was strange because all my friends' mothers were housewives. But my mother wanted to work. She always told me to just follow my heart. I remember these words whenever I have problems in America, and they give me strength.
>
> For those reasons, I believe that my mother has been the biggest influence in my life.
>
> Words: 185

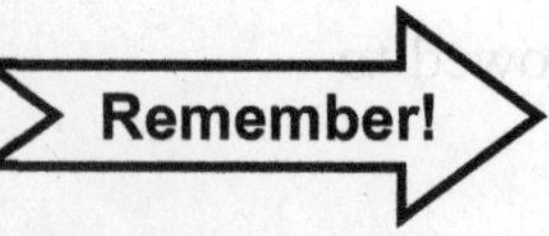

Only by practicing will you know if you can develop and deliver a spoken response that starts with a predictor thesis.

Watch the clock. A predictor thesis can use up a lot of time.

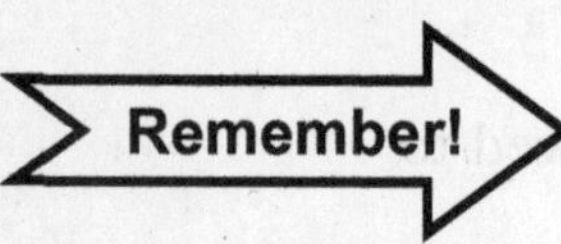

A predictor thesis is an excellent advanced speaking strategy; however, if your body paragraphs are not well developed, a predictor thesis will not substantially increase your score. A predictor thesis and well-developed body paragraphs will substantially increase your score.

The Rhetorical Why

Asking yourself why rhetorically is an effective way to develop your opinion and start your argument. It is also a good way to start speaking, especially if you are nervous. Look at the following examples. Note how the speaker asks herself why, then answers her own question.

> Personally, I believe that my mother has been the biggest influence in my life. **Why** has my mother been the biggest influence in my life? Because she encourages and inspires me.

> In my opinion, exercising is good for you. **Why** is exercising good for you? Because it reduces stress and helps you sleep.

In the above examples, note how the rhetorical why is followed by the predictor. Note also how the predictor begins with *Because*. *Because* signals the start of the speaker's argument.

Often the rhetorical why is reduced to **Why** only, as in the following examples.

> Personally, I believe that my mother has been the biggest influence in my life. **Why?** Because she encourages and inspires me.

> In my opinion, exercising is good for you. **Why?** Because it reduces stress and helps you sleep.

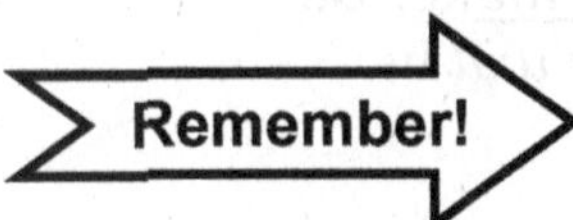

By only asking why, you will save time. Use that time to develop your supporting illustrations.

The rhetorical why can also be applied to the independent essay.

Advanced Conclusion Strategies

To maximize scoring, apply the following advanced conclusion strategies to develop a basic, opinion-based verbal argument into an advanced, opinion-based verbal argument.

These strategies can also be applied to the independent essay.

a. *Suggestion*

For this strategy, start with a **transition**, restate your opinion, then end with a *suggestion.*

C **In sum**, I assert that video games are a bad influence on kids. *Instead of playing video games, I think that parents should make their kids go outside and play.*

C **As I have illustrated**, video games are a bad influence on kids. *If you want healthy kids, I suggest that you turn off the computer for a few hours every day and make your kids go outside and play.*

b. *Suggestion + Prediction*

For this strategy, start with a **transition**, restate your opinion, then end with a *suggestion and a prediction.* Notice how the *prediction* contains the auxiliary verb "will" to describe a future action.

C **In the final analysis**, I contend that playing sports is good for children. *They should try and play a winter sport like hockey and a summer sport like soccer or baseball. It will teach them how to socialize and be team players.*

C **In the end**, I think that it's better to spend the money you make. *Be like me and spend all the money you earn. By doing so, you will be happy and never worry about tomorrow.*

c. *Warning + Prediction*

For this strategy, start with a **transition**, restate your opinion, then end with *a warning that contains a prediction of future of events.*

C **It goes without saying that** global warming is a serious problem. *The ice at the North Pole is melting so fast that soon there will be no more ice, just water.*

C **As far as I'm concerned**, I believe that a new factory in my home town is a good idea. *It will create a lot of new jobs and provide more tax money, money the town can use to build new roads and bridges.*

d. *Rhetorical Question*

For this strategy, start with a **transition**, restate your opinion, then end with *a rhetorical question.* A rhetorical question makes your reader think about your argument after your response has ended.

C **Suffice it to say**, I think that a new factory in my hometown is a good idea. *Yes, there will be some pollution, but aren't jobs more important?*

C **In my estimation**, I believe that homeschooling is not good for children. *Do you really want your kids to miss the fun of going to school every day?*

e. *Call-To-Action*

For this strategy, start with a **transition**, restate your opinion, then end with *a call-to-action.* Call-to-action means you are telling people to do something (take action) with an emphatic (strong) voice.

C **In sum**, I conclude that video games are a bad influence on kids. *Parents, turn off the computer. Now!*

C **Finally**, I believe that recycling is a good way to help the planet. *Don't throw paper and plastic away. Recycle!*

f. *Call-To-Action + Rhetorical Question*

For this strategy, start with a **transition**, restate your opinion, *give a call-to-action,* then end with *a rhetorical question.*

C **In closing**, I believe that video games are a bad influence on kids. *Parents, turn off the computer! Do you really want violent kids?*

C **When all is said and done**, I contend that recycling is important. *Save the planet! Can you imagine a world full of garbage?*

You can also ask *a rhetorical question* first, then end with a call-to-action.

C **In closing**, I conclude that video games are not good for children. *Do you really want violent kids? Parents, turn off the computer. Now!*

C **When all is said and done**, I assert that computers are important for fun and for learning. *Can you imagine a world without computers? Be happy. Be productive. Buy a computer!*

g. ***Suggestion + Prediction + Rhetorical Question***

For this strategy, start with a **transition**, restate your opinion, make *a suggestion and a prediction*, then end with *a rhetorical question.*

C **In the final analysis**, I conclude that video games are a bad influence on kids. *If you are a parent, tell your kids to turn the computer off and go outside. Doing so will make your kids happier and healthier. Isn't that how you want your kids to grow up?*

C **All in all**, I believe that the internet is great for research. *If you need information fast, just log on to the internet. You can google whatever you're looking for and you will find it fast. What more could you ask for?*

h. ***Predictor Thesis Restated in Your Conclusion***

To develop your conclusion, restate your predictor thesis in your conclusion. After you restate your *predictor thesis*, add a conclusion strategy.

C It goes without saying that my mother has been the biggest influence in my life because she encourages and inspires me. I hope that when I have a daughter, I can encourage and inspire her.

i. ***Predictor Conclusion + Synonyms***

Look the following predictor thesis restated in the conclusion.

C In conclusion, my mother has been the biggest influence in my life because she encourages and inspires me. I hope that when I have a daughter, I can encourage and inspire her too.

To demonstrate language use, replace the transition In conclusion with a synonymous phrase, for example:

In the end,
As I have illustrated,
As the aforementioned example shows,
To sum up,
Indeed,
When all is said and done,
All things considered,

→ my mother has been the biggest influence in my life because she encourages and inspires me. I hope that when I have a daughter, I can encourage and inspire her too.

Pyramid Conclusion

Why is an advanced conclusion an effective speaking strategy? Because your conclusion will look like a pyramid in which the ideas progress from specific to general.

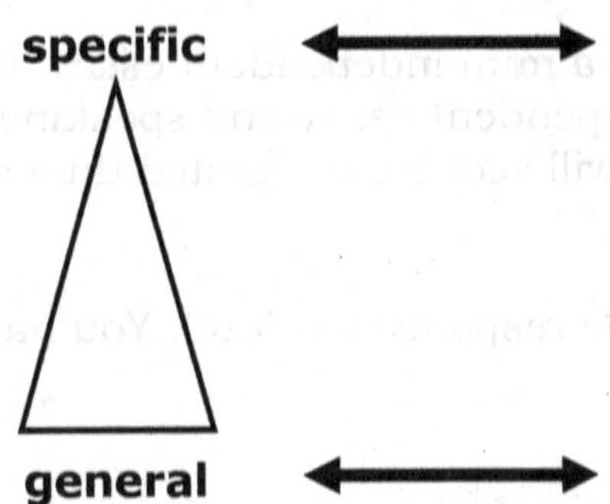

All in all, I believe that the internet is great for research.

If you need information fast, just log on to the internet. You can google whatever you're looking for and you will find it fast. What more could you ask for?

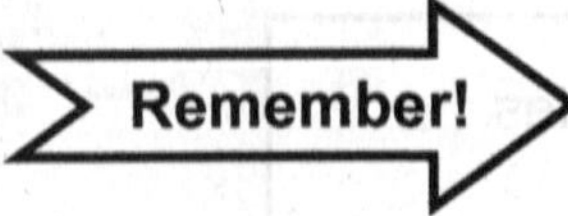

The speaking raters will listen for a pyramid conclusion. A pyramid conclusion demonstrates OPDUL=C.

Advanced Responses

The following samples demonstrate how advanced strategies can turn a basic, opinion-based verbal argument into an advanced, opinion-based verbal argument.

Note how each sample is also a mini independent essay. In other words, scoring strategies for the independent essay and speaking task #1 (and for speaking task #2, as you will see) are integrated thus can be recycled.

TASK: For practice, read each sample response out loud. You have 45 seconds for each.

Sample #1

Prompt Why do people travel? Develop your opinion using examples and reasons.

People travel for many reasons. Some travel for fun. Others travel to learn about new cultures. From my experience, I like traveling because it's a learning experience.

For example, last year I went to Manhattan. I visited many famous places like The Met and Radio City Music Hall. The most interesting place was Ground Zero. Ground Zero is where the World Trade Center once stood. Now, it's nothing but a big hole. On TV it doesn't look so big. But seeing it in person, I had no idea it was so huge. It's like a big hole in the heart of the city. Looking at it made me realize that sometimes you just have to see things with your own eyes. That way you can understand what really happened.

It goes without saying that traveling to Manhattan was a great learning experience for me. If you want to learn about a new culture, you should travel. Go for it! You'll have a great time.

Words: 164

Sample #2

Prompt Should teenagers work during high school? Why? Give illustrations and reasons to develop your argument.

The question is should teenagers work during high school. Personally, I think that all students should work while going to high school.

For example, when I was a high school student, I had a job at an English bookstore in Budapest, Hungary. I worked every Saturday and Sunday, and sometimes at night during the week. I loved it because I was always meeting foreigners who spoke English. By helping them find books, I was able to practice my English. It was great because at school, I only learned grammar from books, but at the bookstore I was learning conversational English. Not only that but I made money for myself. This helped me because I didn't always have to ask my parents for money for books and other things. As you can see, by working at the bookstore I killed two birds with one stone.

To sum up, I believe that all high school students should work part-time during high school. It's a great experience that will open many new doors. Isn't that what life's all about?

Words: 176

Sample #3

Prompt In your view, what was the greatest invention of the twentieth century? Why? Give examples and reasons to support your argument.

There were so many inventions in the last century, such as the airplane and the microprocessor. Yet in my opinion, I can honestly say that the car was the greatest invention in the twentieth century. Why? Let me explain.

I am from Turkey. I remember my mother and father telling me how they had a horse before they had a car. The horse was very important because it did everything, such as work in the fields and take vegetables to market. Using a horse, though, was very slow. Everything took so much time. But then my father bought a car and everything changed completely. Like day and night. Suddenly, my father could go places more quickly and he could take more vegetables to market. Best of all, he took my mother to the hospital to have me.

In conclusion, I think that for me and my family, the greatest invention of the twentieth century was the car. No car. No me.

Words: 161

Sample #4

Prompt These days people are living longer. Why? Develop your position using examples and reasons.

Why are people living longer these days? Personally, I contend that people are living longer because they are taking better care of themselves.

A good example is my grandfather. When he was younger, he used to smoke and drink a lot. Also, he never ate very well. Then when he was fifty, he had heart attack. He was in the hospital for a long time. The doctor told him he should stop smoking and drinking, and start eating better. That's what my grandfather did. Now, he doesn't drink or smoke anymore. Also, he eats lots of healthy food like salads and fish, and he exercises every day. As a result, he feels much better than before and has lots more energy.

As you can see, by changing his lifestyle, my grandfather is definitely going to live longer because he is taking better care of himself. If you want to live longer, you should take care of yourself too.

Words: 158

Sample #5

Prompt Which person has been the greatest influence in your life? Why? Give examples and reasons to support and develop your opinion.

A lot of people have influenced my life. However, it goes without saying that my mother has been the biggest influence in my life because she encourages and inspires me.

My mother encourages me. For example, I'm now in America working as an au pair. An au pair is like a babysitter who lives with an American family. I'm doing this for a year in Stamford, Connecticut. At first I didn't want to come to America and leave all my friends in Estonia, but my mother said it would be a great experience and a great way to develop my English. She was right. Living with an American family has been a wonderful experience and my English is so much better.

Also, my mother inspires me. When I was growing up, my mother was a high school teacher. This was strange because all my friends' mothers were housewives. But my mother wanted to work. She always told me to just follow your heart. I remember these words whenever I have problems in America, and they give me strength.

As you can see, my mother has been the biggest influence in my life because she encourages and inspires me. I hope that when I have a daughter, I can encourage and inspire her.

Words: 210

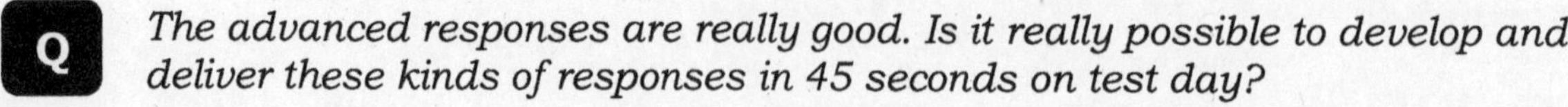

The advanced responses are really good. Is it really possible to develop and deliver these kinds of responses in 45 seconds on test day?

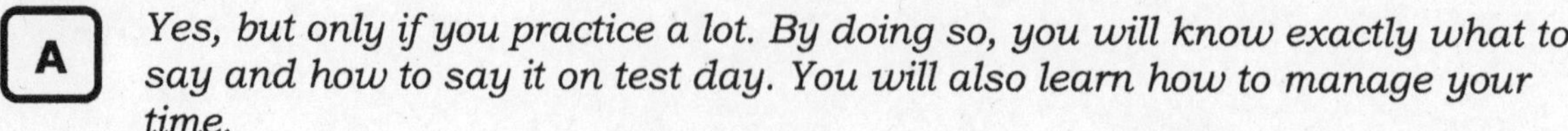

Yes, but only if you practice a lot. By doing so, you will know exactly what to say and how to say it on test day. You will also learn how to manage your time.

The TOEFL iBT is an English-language proficiency test and a time-management test.

Emergency Response

What if you can't develop a response for this task? What if you blank out? What should you do? Follow these four steps and deliver an emergency response.

Step #1 **Make a G+TiC=C note map; include transitions.**

Step #2 **Read the prompt.**

Make sure you understand the prompt before you respond. Make sure you are "on topic" (talking about the topic in the prompt) not "off topic" (talking about a different topic).

Prompt Can a pet change a person's behavior? Explain your position using supporting illustrations and reasons.

Step #3 **Develop ideas (15 seconds).**

Step #4 **Speak (45 seconds).**

If you blank out, do not try and state your opinion. Instead, tell a personal story. When you tell a personal story, use the inductive map, TiC=C. Look at the following example using induction as the method of organization. Note how the response progresses from specific (TiC; the story of the test-taker's brother) to a conclusion (C) about the benefits of pets for autistic children.

My younger brother has autism and for a long time he never talked to anybody. Also, he would get angry really easily for reasons nobody could understand. Then one day the doctor told my parents that they should get a dog. We never had a dog or any pets before, but my parents really wanted to make my brother happy, so we got a dog and called him Happy. Well, I'm telling you, it was amazing. My brother loves Happy. Before my brother was always quiet and angry, but with Happy, my brother always talks and smiles. The change was amazing. Now, my brother and Happy are just like best friends.

(continued on the next page)

As you can see, a pet can really change a someone's life. If you have a brother or sister with the autism, I recommend that you to get a dog or a cat. It will make them smile like you've never seen before.

Words: 154

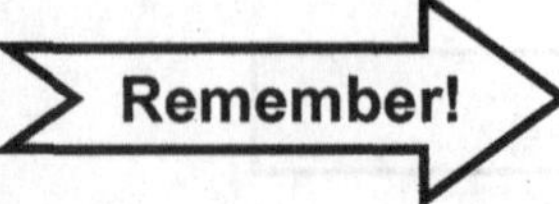

We all love to tell stories. Use this innate human ability to develop an emergency response for independent speaking tasks #1 and #2, and for the independent essay.

Contrarian Response

What if you think the question in the prompt is strange, doesn't make sense, or is not asking the right question? How can you respond? In this case, develop a contrarian response. Read the following prompt, then read the contrarian response.

Prompt How has technology made the world a better place? Develop your argument using examples and reasons.

Has technology made the world a better place? No. Technology has not made the world a better place. This is only what people in rich countries believe.

For example, here in America people think that everybody is the same all over the world. Everybody has a car and a laptop, and a cell phone. But this is not true. Why not? Because two-thirds of the people in the world, over 3 billion people, make less than one American dollar a day. Moreover, these same people have no education. Because they have no education, they don't have good jobs, or the money to buy computers and iPods. Most are lucky if they eat one meal a day. Come to my country, and you will see that this is true.

In conclusion, technology has not made the world a better place. If anything, technology has simply drawn a clearer line between the majority poor and the minority rich.

Words: 156

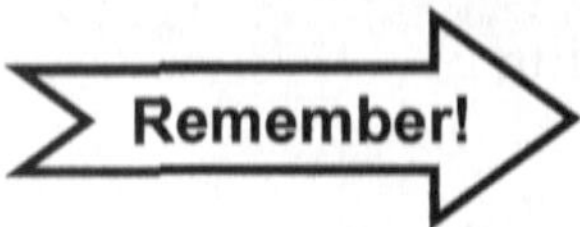

Make sure your contrarian response is a serious argument. Even if you think that the prompt is asking the wrong question, you must still demonstrate OPDUL=C.

Speaking Practice

Using G+TiC=C or G+2TiC=C and the four steps, develop and deliver a response that demonstrates OPDUL=C for each of the following prompts you have studied. If you have trouble, go back and look at the sample responses for help. Use a recording device and check each response for coherence using the *Independent Speaking Proficiency Checklist* on page 700. Rate each response using the *Independent Speaking Rating Guide* on page 701.

1 Why do people travel? Develop your opinion using examples and reasons.

2 Should teenagers work during high school? Why? Give illustrations and reasons to develop your argument.

3 Which technology in the past fifty years has changed your life the most? Why? Develop your position using examples and reasons.

4 In your view, what was the greatest invention of the twentieth century? Why? Give examples and reasons to support your argument.

5 These days people are living longer. Why? Develop your position using examples and reasons.

6 Which person has been the greatest influence in your life? Why? Give examples and reasons to support and develop your opinion.

7 Can a pet change a person's behavior? Explain your position using supporting illustrations and reasons.

More Speaking Practice

Using G+TiC=C or G+2TiC=C and the four steps, develop and deliver a response for each of the following prompts. Use a recording device and check each response for coherence using the *Independent Speaking Proficiency Checklist* on page 700. Rate each response using the *Independent Speaking Rating Guide* on page 701.

1 Many people leave their home country. Why? Give examples and reasons to support your argument.

2 What is your idea of the perfect neighborhood? Why? Support your position with illustrations and reasons.

3 Why is a car important in daily life? Develop your response using examples and reasons.

4 When is the best time to go on a vacation? Why? Support your argument using examples and reasons.

5 Why do some people never get married? Use examples and reasons to develop your argument.

6 If you won the lottery, what would you do? Why? Develop your response using examples and reasons.

7 Why do people listen to music? Give examples and reasons to support your argument.

8 What is the number one problem facing the world today? Why? Support your position with illustrations and reasons.

9 How do you measure success? Why? Use examples and reasons to develop your position.

10 Which area of English do you need to improve? Why? Develop your response using examples and reasons.

Task #2 - Independent Speaking

Speaking task #2, like speaking task #1, measures your ability to use your personal experience to develop and deliver a verbal, opinion-based argument. Your response will be based on a question in a prompt. The task order follows.

TASK	TIME
1. Read the prompt. 2. Prepare your response.	15 seconds
3. Deliver your response.	45 seconds

Paired-Choice Prompt

For this task, you will answer a paired-choice prompt, for example:

> Prompt Exercising reduces stress. Do you agree or disagree? Develop your opinion using examples and reasons.

Where have you seen paired-choice prompts before? Answer: The independent essay. In fact, independent speaking task #2—like independent speaking task #1—is really just a mini independent essay. However, instead of developing your argument in writing, you will develop it in 15 seconds, then deliver it verbally in 45 seconds.

G+TiC=C

Because your response will be a mini verbal independent essay, you can develop and deliver your response by changing G+3TiC=C to G+TiC=C, wherein G (general statement) is your opinion.

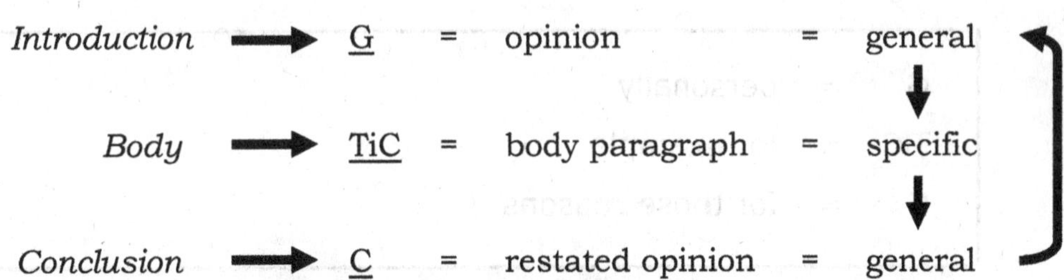

G+TiC=C will help you give the speaking raters what they are trained to listen for: a short, opinion-based, verbal argument that demonstrates OPDUL=C.

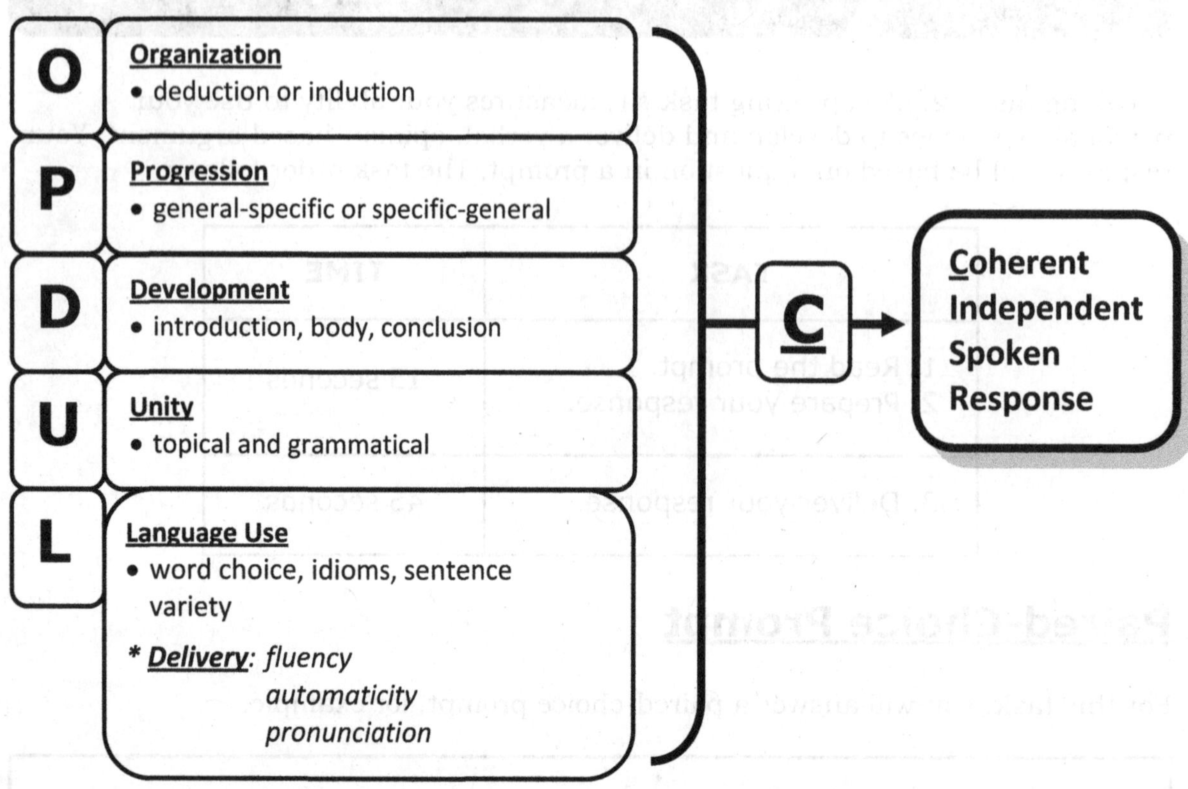

As you learn the following strategies, note how each prompt can also be used to write an independent essay. In other words, independent essay prompts and independent speaking prompts are interchangeable thus can be recycled. That means the scoring strategies for the independent essay and the independent speaking tasks are also interchangeable thus can be recycled.

1. Agree-Disagree Prompt: *Step-by-Step*

When answering an agree-disagree prompt, speak subjectively using G+TiC=C and follow the four steps to demonstrate OPDUL=C in your argument.

Step #1 **Make a G+TiC=C note map; include transitions.**

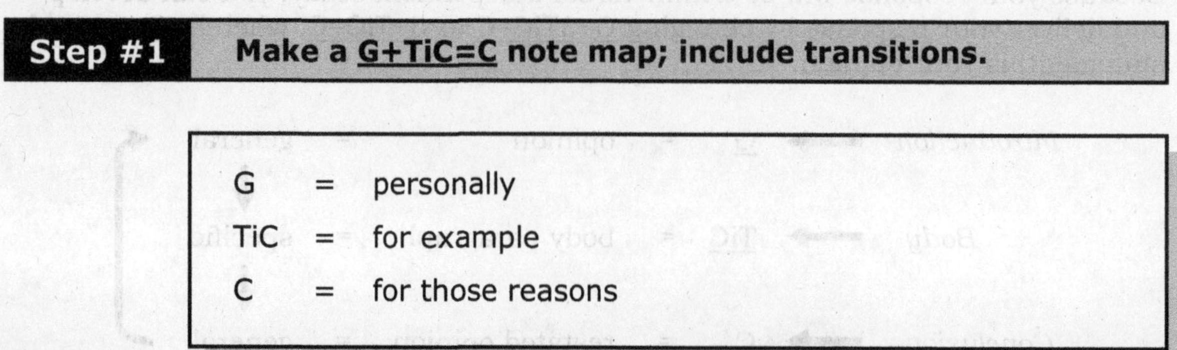

G = personally
TiC = for example
C = for those reasons

Step #2 Read the prompt.

The prompt will appear on your screen. A narrator will read it.

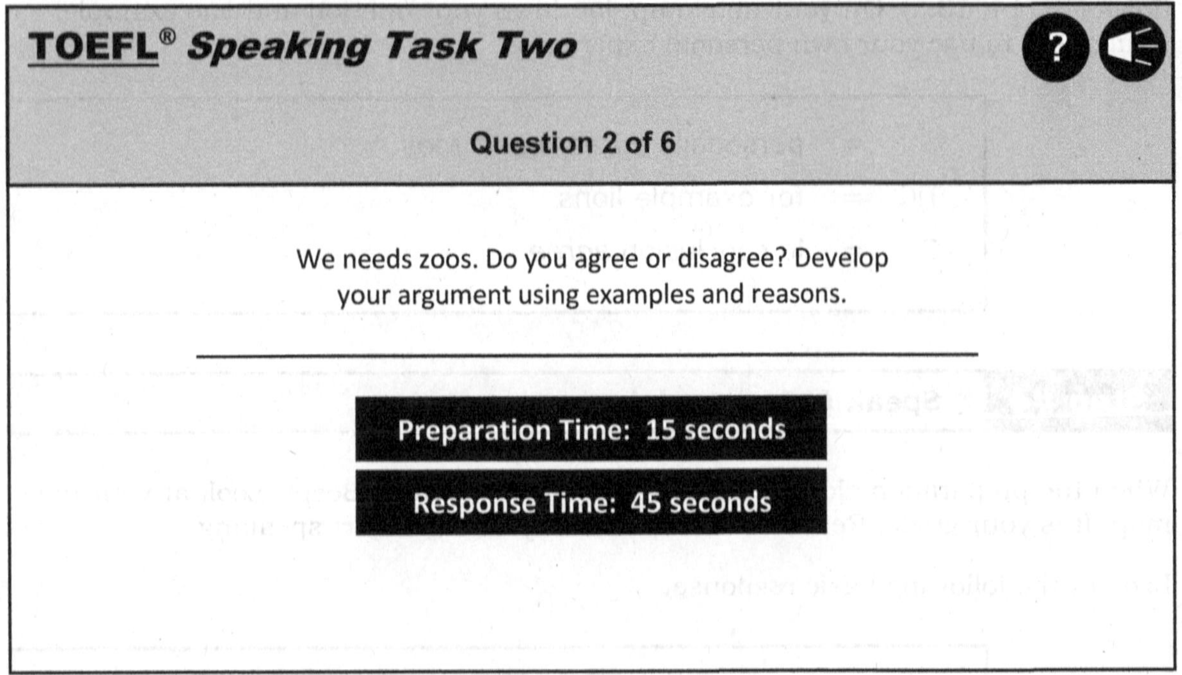

TOEFL® Speaking Task Two
?
Question 2 of 6
We needs zoos. Do you agree or disagree? Develop your argument using examples and reasons.
Preparation Time: 15 seconds
Response Time: 45 seconds

Avoid double arguments. Double arguments are identified by "or" or "prefer" in paired-choice prompts. Choose one side of the argument and develop it, for example:

Prompt: We need zoos. Do agree or disagree?

X Double Argument: Sometimes I think that we need zoos, and sometimes I think that we don't need zoos.

√ Single Argument: Personally, I think that we need zoos.

Remember!

You only have 45 seconds speaking time. If you try to develop a double argument, you will run out of time and not be able to develop both arguments. This will result in a lack of topic development (OPDUL=C) and a lower score.

Step #3 **Develop ideas (15 seconds).**

When the narrator stops speaking, the preparation clock will start running. You will have 15 seconds to develop your response. The preparation clock will count down (15, 14, 13...). On your note map, jot down your opinion and one example. Remember to use your own personal experience.

G	=	personally *agree, need zoos*
TiC	=	for example lions
C	=	in conclusion *agree*

Step #4 **Speak (45 seconds).**

When the preparation clock reaches zero, you will hear a "Beep!" Look at your note map. It is your guide. Remember to speak subjectively. Start speaking.

Look at the following basic response.

> Personally, I agree. I think that we need zoos.
>
> For example, when I was 12, my teacher took us to the zoo in Berlin. I had never seen wild animals before. I had just read about them in books and seen them on the TV. But seeing them in real life was amazing, especially the lions. On TV, they looked so small, but seeing them alive they were really big. By going to the zoo, I definitely saw things in a whole new light.
>
> In sum, I think that we need zoos.

To develop this basic response, add another body paragraph (G+2TiC=C).

> Personally, I agree. I think that we need zoos. Why?
>
> For example, when I was 12, my teacher took us to the zoo in Berlin. I had never seen wild animals before. I had just read about them in books and seen them on the TV. But seeing them in real life was amazing, especially the lions. On TV, they looked so small, but seeing them alive they were really big. By going to the zoo, I definitely saw things in a whole new light.
>
> Now I have a family and we always go to the zoo every summer. My wife makes a picnic and we spend all day there. My kids love taking pictures and learning all about the animals, especially the gorillas. Being outside is good for my children. Best of all, they can leave the internet and the TV at home.
>
> For those reasons, I think that we need zoos.

To develop this response, add a **predictor** after Why, then *restate the predictor thesis in the conclusion.*

> From my point of view, I agree. I believe that we need zoos. Why? **Because zoos are educational and fun for families**.
>
> **Zoos are educational**. For example, when I was 12, my teacher took us to the zoo in Berlin. I had never seen wild animals before. I had just read about them in books and seen them on the TV. But seeing them in real life was amazing, especially the lions. On TV, they looked so small, but seeing them alive they were really big. By going to the zoo, I definitely saw things in a whole new light.
>
> **Zoos are also good for families**. For example, now I have a family and we always go to the zoo every summer. My wife makes a picnic and we spend all day there. My kids love taking pictures and learning all about the animals, especially the gorillas. Being outside is good for my children. Best of all, they can leave the internet and the TV at home.
>
> For those reasons, I contend that we need zoos. *Zoos are educational and fun for families*.
>
> Words: 183

2. Agree-Disagree Prompt: *Step-by-Step*

Let's map out another agree-disagree response using G+2TiC=C. Remember to follow the four steps to demonstrate OPDUL=C in your argument. Speak subjectively.

Step #1 **Make a G+2TiC=C note map; include transitions.**

G	=	personally
TiC	=	for example
TiC	=	next
C	=	for those reasons

Step #2 **Read the prompt.**

Prompt: Exercising reduces stress. Do you agree or disagree? Develop your opinion using examples and reasons.

Step #3 **Develop ideas (15 seconds).**

When the narrator stops speaking, the preparation clock will appear on your screen. You will have 15 seconds to develop your response. The clock will count down (15, 14, 13...). On your note map, jot down ideas.

G	=	personally *agree*
TiC	=	for example *me*
TiC	=	next *girlfriend*
C	=	in sum *agree*

Step #4 **Speak (45 seconds).**

When the preparation clock reaches zero, you will hear a "Beep!" Look at your note map. It is your guide. Start speaking.

> The prompt asks whether exercising reduces stress or not. Personally, I posit that exercising does reduce stress. Why? For these reasons.
>
> First, after class I run up and down a big hill near my university. The distance is ten miles. It is definitely hard work, but I love it. If I don't run every day, I have a hard time sleeping. After I run, I feel stress free. Best of all, I sleep like a log.
>
> Next is my girlfriend. She loves to exercise too. After a hard day of work, she hits the gym near our house and does yoga and pilates. She says it is a great way to relieve the pressures of being a new lawyer in a big law firm.
>
> In sum, exercising definitely reduces stress. If you want to stay happy and healthy, you should exercise every day.
>
> Words: 143

Mapped out, you can see how G+2TiC=C gives the speaking raters what they are trained to look for: a verbal, opinion-based argument that demonstrates OPDUL=C. The opinion (G) and the conclusions (C) are underlined, the transitions (T) are in **bold**, and the supporting illustrations (i) are in *italics*.

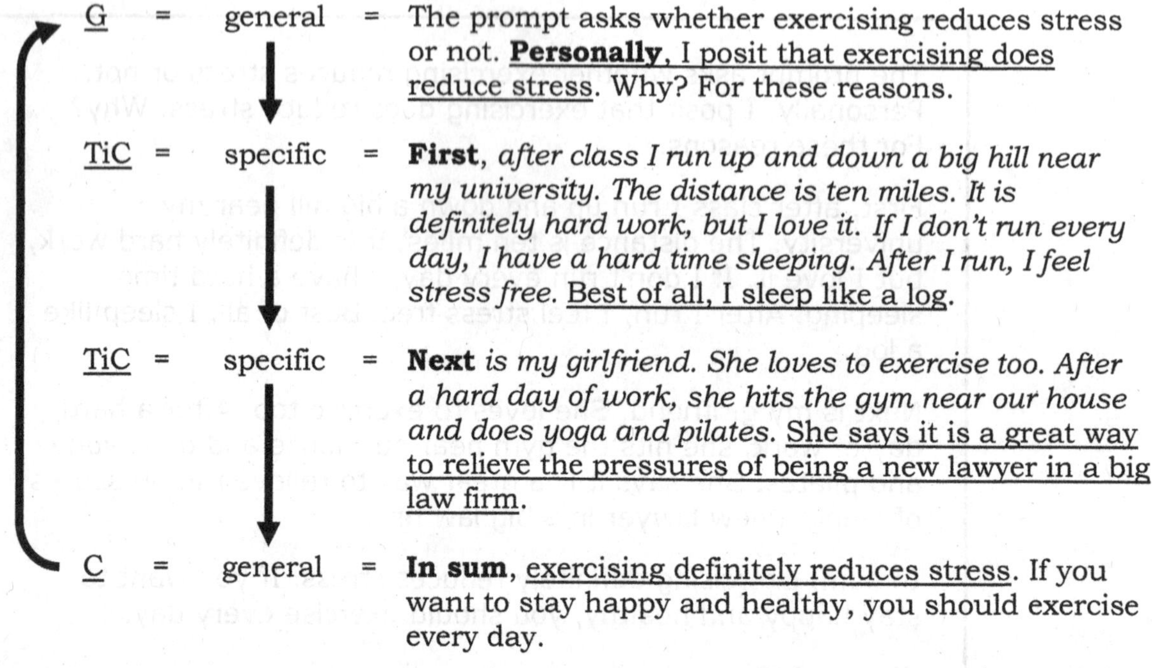

G	=	general	=	The prompt asks whether exercising reduces stress or not. **Personally**, I posit that exercising does reduce stress. Why? For these reasons.
TiC	=	specific	=	**First**, *after class I run up and down a big hill near my university. The distance is ten miles. It is definitely hard work, but I love it. If I don't run every day, I have a hard time sleeping. After I run, I feel stress free.* Best of all, I sleep like a log.
TiC	=	specific	=	**Next** *is my girlfriend. She loves to exercise too. After a hard day of work, she hits the gym near our house and does yoga and pilates.* She says it is a great way to relieve the pressures of being a new lawyer in a big law firm.
C	=	general	=	**In sum**, exercising definitely reduces stress. If you want to stay happy and healthy, you should exercise every day.

TASK: Check this response for coherence using the *Independent Speaking Proficiency Checklist* on page 700. Rate it using the *Independent Speaking Rating Guide* on page 701. Compare your rating to the one on page 797. Note: For this response, the speaker's delivery was proficient.

3. Support-Don't Support Prompt: *Step-by-Step*

When answering a support-don't support prompt, use G+TiC=C and the four steps to demonstrate OPDUL=C in your argument.

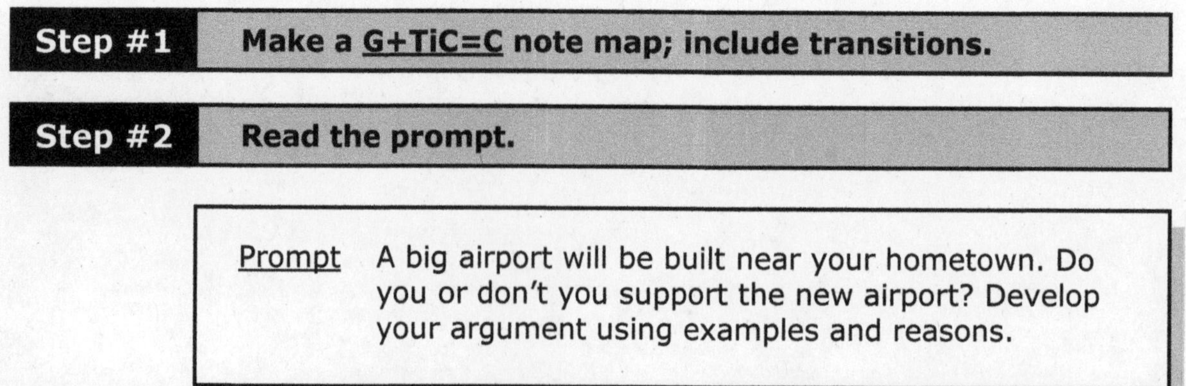

Step #1 **Make a G+TiC=C note map; include transitions.**

Step #2 **Read the prompt.**

Prompt A big airport will be built near your hometown. Do you or don't you support the new airport? Develop your argument using examples and reasons.

Step #3 **Develop ideas (15 seconds).**

G = from my perspective *support*

TiC = example *jobs*

C = for the aforementioned reasons - *support*

Step #4 **Speak (45 seconds).**

From my perspective, I support a new airport near my hometown. Why? Because we need jobs.

I live in Osnabrueck, Germany. Osnabrueck is a small city with many tourist attractions. The businesses we have, however, are small and don't offer many jobs to young people, so the young people always move away to big cities like Berlin and Frankfurt. But if we got a new airport, we could have many jobs for young people. If they got jobs, they could stay and help develop the economy of Osnabrueck. Also, the airport will attract other new businesses, and that is good for creating jobs too.

For the aforementioned reasons, I support the new airport. A new airport will be good for Osnabrueck. If we don't accept it, some other town will and Osnabrueck will lose jobs and young people.

Words: 138

TASK: Check this response for coherence using the *Independent Speaking Proficiency Checklist* on page 700. Rate it using the *Independent Speaking Rating Guide* on page 701. Compare your rating to the one on page 797. Note: For this response, the speaker's delivery was proficient.

Rhetorical Strategies

By using G+TiC=C or G+2TiC=C, your response will demonstrate a variety of rhetorical strategies. Rhetorical strategies demonstrate topic development (OP**D**UL=C) and proficient language use (OPDU**L**=C). Topic development and proficient language use = greater coherence (OPDUL=**C**) = a higher score.

The airport response demonstrates a variety of rhetorical strategies, including:

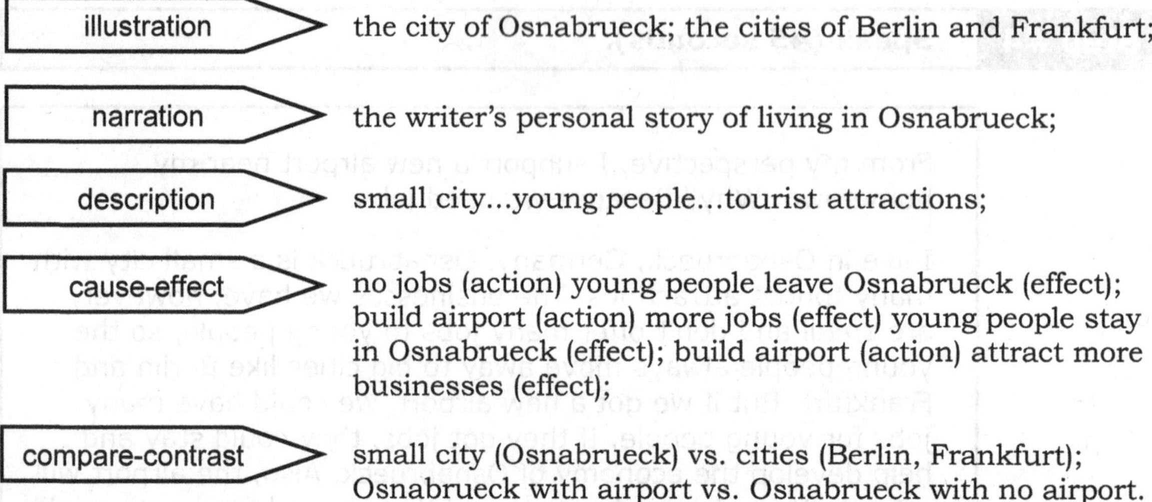

illustration → the city of Osnabrueck; the cities of Berlin and Frankfurt;

narration → the writer's personal story of living in Osnabrueck;

description → small city...young people...tourist attractions;

cause-effect → no jobs (action) young people leave Osnabrueck (effect); build airport (action) more jobs (effect) young people stay in Osnabrueck (effect); build airport (action) attract more businesses (effect);

compare-contrast → small city (Osnabrueck) vs. cities (Berlin, Frankfurt); Osnabrueck with airport vs. Osnabrueck with no airport.

4. Preference Prompt: *Step-by-Step*

When answering a preference prompt, use G+TiC=C and the four steps to demonstrate OPDUL=C in your argument.

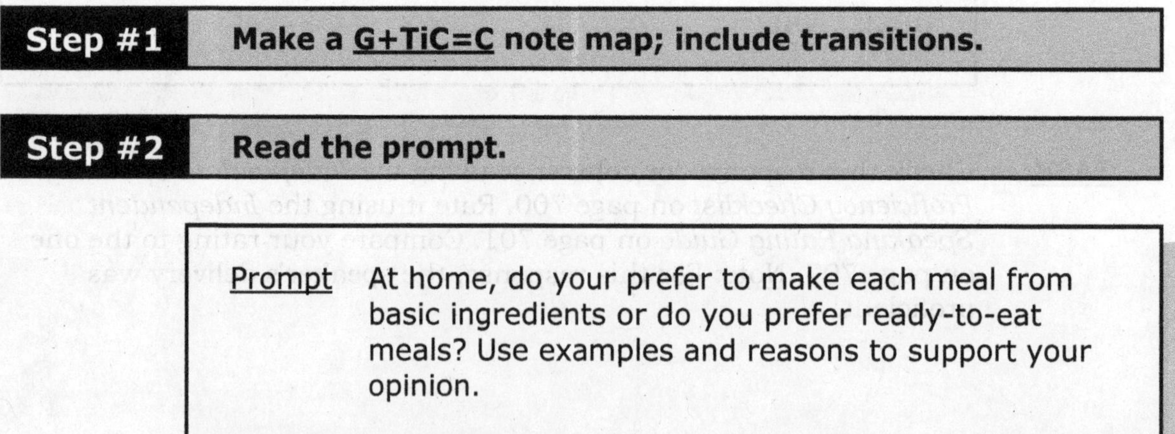

Step #1 **Make a G+TiC=C note map; include transitions.**

Step #2 **Read the prompt.**

Prompt At home, do your prefer to make each meal from basic ingredients or do you prefer ready-to-eat meals? Use examples and reasons to support your opinion.

Step #3 **Develop ideas (15 seconds).**

G	=	prefer ready-to-eat
TiC	=	for example after work
C	=	to sum up prefer ready-to-eat

Step #4 **Speak (45 seconds).**

From my experience, I prefer ready-to-eat meals. Why? Because they are fast and easy for me to prepare.

When I get up in the morning, I don't have time to make breakfast from basic ingredients like bacon and eggs. I have to get ready and leave my house early so I can get to work on time. I usually eat some yogurt and a banana. Sometimes I buy a bagel on the way to work. After work, I'm too tired to make dinner from basic ingredients, so I just put some spaghetti or a chicken dinner into the microwave and I can have a hot meal quickly. You pay more for ready-to-eat meals, but I don't mind. Besides, I hate cooking and washing dishes.

To sum up, I prefer to eat ready-to-eat meals.

Words: 133

<u>**TASK:**</u> Check this response for coherence using the *Independent Speaking Proficiency Checklist* on page 700. Rate it using the *Independent Speaking Rating Guide* on page 701. Compare your rating to the one on page 797. <u>Note</u>: For this response, the speaker's delivery was proficient.

5. Argument Counter-Argument: *Step-by-Step*

A second type of preference prompt is the argument counter-argument prompt Follow these steps to demonstrate OPDUL=C in your argument. For more on argument counter-arguments, see the *Integrated Essay*.

Step #1	**Make a G+TiC=C note map; include transitions.**

Step #2	**Read the prompt.**

Prompt Some prefer to shop online while others prefer to shop at stores. Discuss both options, then state your preference. Use illustrations and reasons to develop your position.

Step #3	**Develop ideas (15 seconds).**

Step #4	**Speak (45 seconds).**

Note the transition **However**. This transition of contrast connects the two arguments: the argument that supports online shopping vs. the speaker's *counter argument* (the preference for shopping at the mall).

Some people prefer to shop at a mall while others prefer to shop online. Personally, I prefer to shop at a mall.

These days the internet makes everything so easy, especially shopping. You can find a big selection and lots of really good prices online, and you don't even have to leave your home.

However, *I prefer to go to a mall, especially for shoes. When I buy shoes, I need to try them on. If I buy them online, I never know how they will fit. This is a hassle because if they don't fit, it takes a lot of time to return them and get my money back. But if I buy shoes at a mall, and they don't fit, I can exchange them or get the right size right away. This is much more convenient.*

For those reasons, I definitely prefer to shop at a mall.

Words: 149

TASK: Check the response on the previous page for coherence using the *Independent Speaking Proficiency Checklist* on page 700. Rate it using the *Independent Speaking Rating Guide* on page 701. Compare your rating to the one on page 797. Note: For this response, the speaker's delivery was proficient.

6. Advantage-Disadvantage: *Step-by-Step*

When answering an advantage-disadvantage prompt, use G+2TiC=C. Develop an advantage in body paragraph one and a disadvantage in body paragraph two, or vice versa.

Step #1 **Make an G+2TiC=C note map; include transitions.**

G	=	personally
TiC	=	advantage
TiC	=	disadvantage
C	=	in sum

Step #2 **Read the prompt.**

Prompt What are the advantages and disadvantages of home schooling? Use illustrations and reasons to develop your argument.

Step #3 **Develop ideas (15 seconds).**

G	=	personally *good + bad*
TiC	=	advantage *sarah*
TiC	=	disadvantage *sarah*
C	=	in sum *good + bad*

Step #4 **Speak (45 seconds).**

Note how body paragraph one develops a *disadvantage* of homeschooling while body paragraph two develops an *advantage*. Note as well how **However** connects the two opposing arguments.

Personally, I think there are advantages and disadvantages to homeschooling.

For example, my friend Sarah studied at home with her mom. Sarah was really smart but she never knew how to talk to people. She never went to parties or a had a boyfriend. All she did was study with her mom. That is one big disadvantage of home schooling. You don't have many friends.

However, by studying all the time, Sarah got really good grades. She is now going to Harvard. She wants to be a doctor. To be a doctor, you must study very hard. That is one big advantage of studying at home. You can study with no distractions like sports or band practice.

For those reasons, there are advantages and disadvantages to homeschooling. Personally, I think you need a balance between making friends and studying.

Words: 139

<u>**TASK:**</u> Check this response for coherence using the *Independent Speaking Proficiency Checklist* on page 700. Rate it using the *Independent Speaking Rating Guide* on page 701. Compare your rating to the one on page 797. <u>Note</u>: For this response, the speaker's delivery was proficient.

Refer to independent speaking task #1 for how you can maximize scoring by recycling the following strategies when answering a paired-choice prompt.

- *Advanced Introduction Strategies, page 230*
- *Advanced Conclusion Strategies, page 236*
- *Emergency Response, page 245*
- *Contrarian Response, page 246*

Refer to independent speaking task #1 for these strategies.

- *How Long Should My Response Be? page 215*
- *Four Common Speaking Problems page 221*
- *Help! – My Response is Too Long! page 225*
- *Help! – My Response is Too Short! page 226*

Speaking Practice

Using G+TiC=C or G+2TiC=C and the four steps, develop and deliver a response that demonstrates OPDUL=C for each of the following prompts you have studied. If you have trouble, go back and look at the sample responses for help. Use a recording device and check each response for coherence using the *Independent Speaking Proficiency Checklist* on page 700. Rate each response using the *Independent Speaking Rating Guide* on page 701.

1. We need zoos. Do you agree or disagree? Why? Give examples and reasons to support your opinion.

2. Exercising reduces stress. Do you agree or disagree? Develop your opinion using examples and reasons.

3. A big airport will be built near your hometown. Do you or don't you support the new airport? Develop your argument using illustrations and reasons.

4. At home, do your prefer to make each meal from basic ingredients or do you prefer ready-to-eat meals? Use examples and reasons to support your opinion.

5. Some prefer to shop online while others prefer to shop at stores. Discuss both options, then state your preference. Use illustrations and reasons to develop your position.

6. What are the advantages and disadvantages of home schooling? Use illustrations and reasons to develop your argument.

More Speaking Practice

Using G+TiC=C or G+2TiC=C and the four steps, develop and deliver a response for each of the following prompts. Use a recording device and check each response for coherence using the *Independent Speaking Proficiency Checklist* on page 700. Rate each response using the *Independent Speaking Rating Guide* on page 701.

1 Do you think it is better to give a gift or receive a gift? Give examples and reasons to support your opinion.

2 Education should be free. Do you agree or disagree? Give illustrations and reasons to support your answer.

3 What are the advantages and disadvantages of text messaging? Support your argument with examples and reasons.

4 Which would you prefer a boat, a car, or a house? Why? Develop your position with illustrations and reasons.

5 Do you agree or disagree? Watching a movie at home is better than going to the movie theatre. Support your argument with examples and reasons.

6 Before an important exam, do you think it is better to prepare for a long time or only for a few days? Give examples and reasons to support your argument.

7 What are the advantages and disadvantages of living in a foreign country? Give illustrations and reasons to develop your opinion.

8 Some prefer to stay home while on vacation while others prefer to travel. Which do you prefer? Why? Give examples and reasons to support your position.

9 What are the advantages and disadvantages of airplane travel? Give examples and reasons to support your argument.

10 Is it better to buy a product when you want it at the regular price or wait for the product when it is on sale? Use examples and reasons to argue your position.

11 In America, customers can return a purchased item for a full refund within thirty days. Do you agree or disagree with this policy? Develop your position with illustrations and reasons.

12 Do you agree or disagree? Every student should travel or work for a year being going to university or college. Support your argument using examples and reasons.

Task #3 - Integrated Speaking

Read + Listen + Speak

This task measures your ability to integrate three skills: reading, listening, speaking. You will integrate these skills while summarizing a university announcement and a student's opinion of the announcement. Your summary will be based on a question in a prompt. The prompt will appear after the dialogue. The task order is below.

TASK	TIME
1. Read a short announcement.	45 seconds
2. Listen to a dialogue on the same topic as in the reading.	60-90 seconds
3. Read the prompt. 4. Prepare your response.	30 seconds
5. Deliver your response.	60 seconds

This task also measures your ability to:

- ✓ **take notes** as you read and listen;
- ✓ **summarize** the main points in the reading and in the dialogue;
- ✓ **synthesize** the main points in the reading and in the dialogue;
- ✓ **paraphrase** the main points in the reading and in the dialogue.

You can develop and deliver a response for this task by recycling G+3TiC=C. G+3TiC=C will help you take notes and give the speaking raters what they are trained to listen for: a fact-based argument that summarizes the announcement and the student's opinion regarding the announcement. By doing so, your response will demonstrate OPDUL=C.

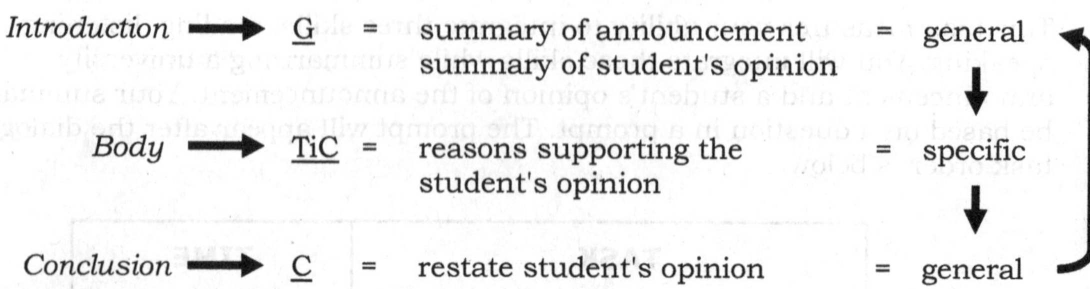

Note in OPDUL=C below how *summarization* is part of Development, *synthesis* is part of Unity and *paraphrasing* is part of Language Use

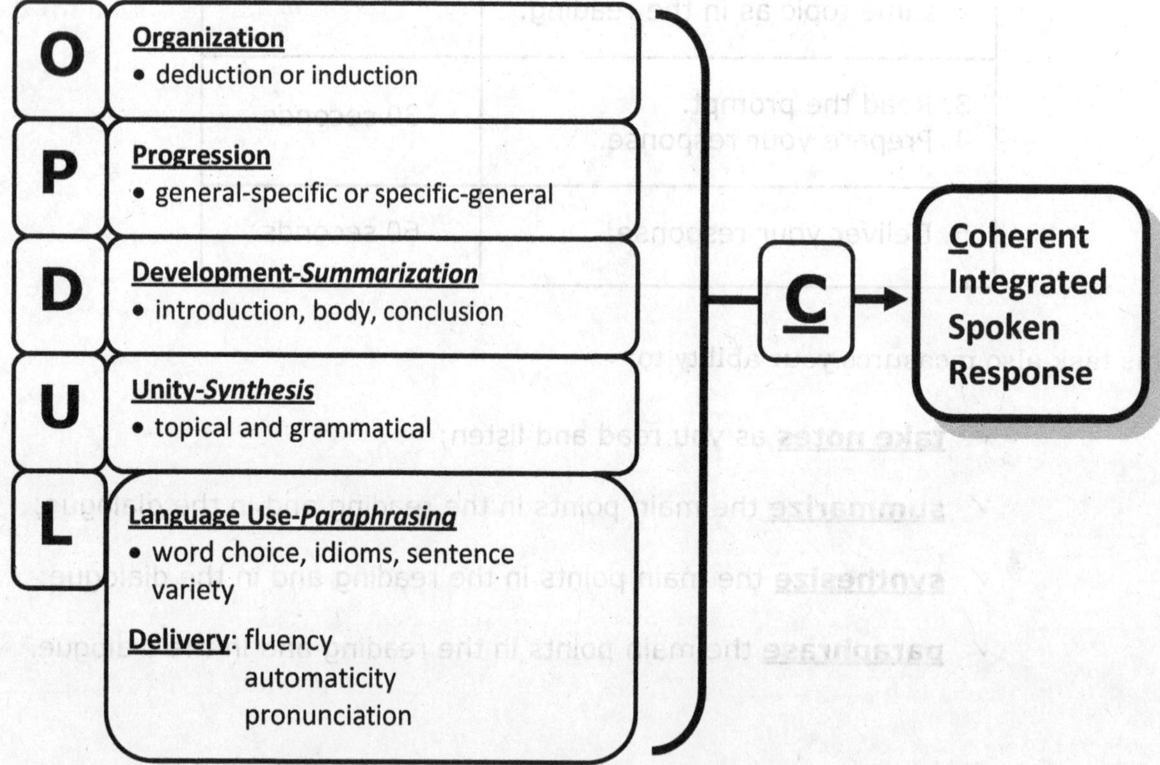

TOEFL's Testing Method

Understanding TOEFL's testing method is the first step in delivering a coherent integrated response. First, you will read a short university announcement. The announcement might be a new university policy.

Next, you will listen to a dialogue in which two students (a man and a woman) argue about the new policy. One student will argue in support of the new policy while the other student will argue against the new policy.

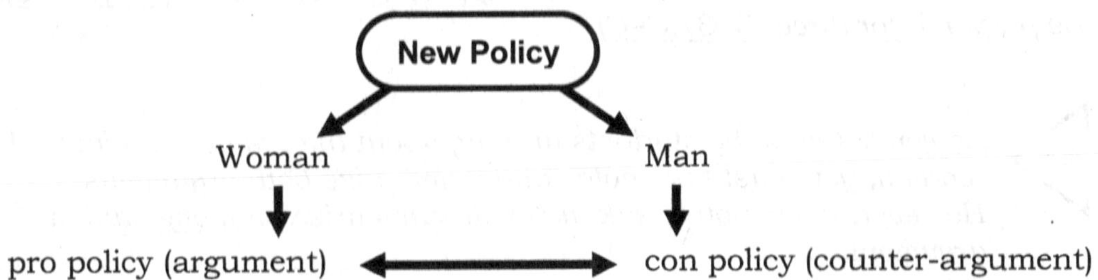

This method of testing is called *argument counter-argument*. The TOEFL iBT uses this same testing method for the argument counter-argument integrated essay.

Because TOEFL recycles the same testing method for this task, you can summarize both student arguments, then map out your response using G+3TiC=C.

Look at the following map. For this example, the reading announces that university parking fees are going up 20%. The woman tells the man that the fee increase is *a good idea*. That is her opinion, the start of her argument. The man replies by saying that fee increase is *a bad idea*. That is his opinion, the start of his counter argument. Next, the woman will defend her opinion by giving her first *pro reason* (TiC). The man will counter the woman's first reason with his first *con reason* (TiC). The two students will ping-pong (argue counter-argue) like this until the end.

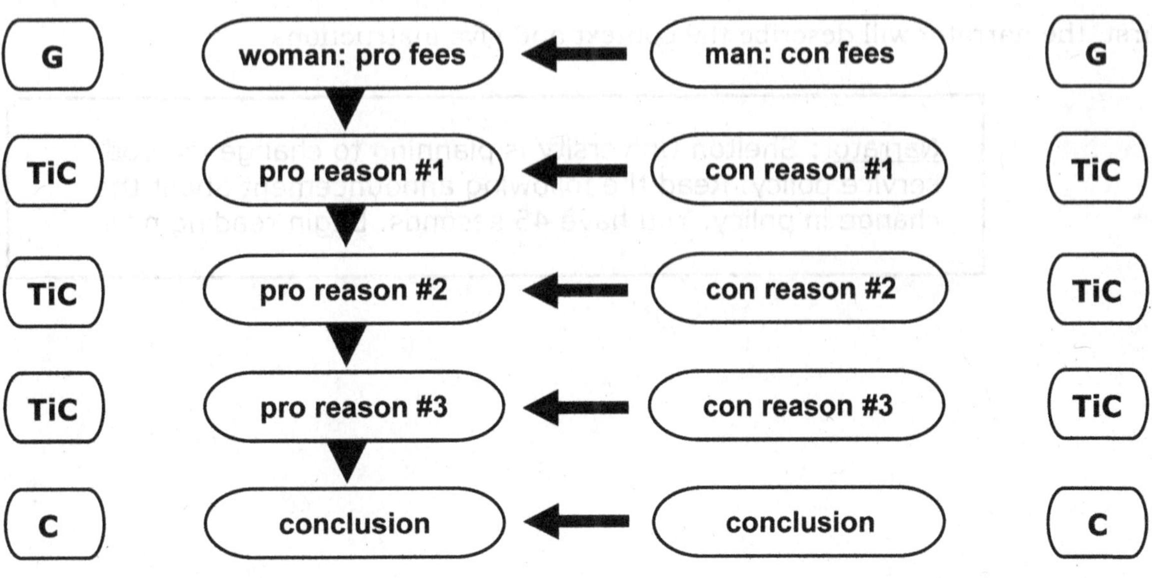

Note that the two arguments above are two opposing, verbal independent essays (G+3TiC=C) connected by topic. Once again, the TOEFL iBT is recycling opinion-based arguments for testing purposes.

Q *Does each student always give three supporting illustrations to support their argument?*

A *No. Sometimes a student will give two supporting illustrations (G+2TiC=C). Be prepared for three (G+3TiC=C).*

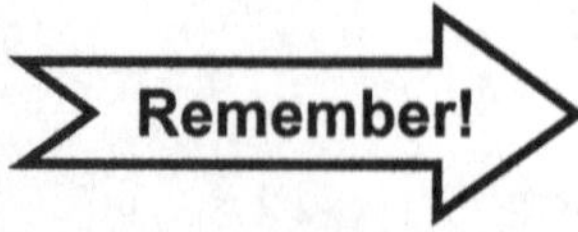

As you listen to the students arguing about the announcement in the reading, you must take notes and summarize both arguments. However, when you speak, you will summarize only one student argument.

Q *How will I know which student argument to summarize?*

A *After you read the announcement and listen to the dialogue, the prompt will appear on your screen. The prompt will tell you which student argument to summarize.*

Developing a Response: *Step-by-Step*

When developing and delivering a response for this task, use G+3TiC=C and the following five steps to demonstrate OPDUL=C in your summary.

Step #1	Make a note map; read and summarize the reading.

First, the narrator will describe the context and give instructions.

> Narrator: Shelton University is planning to change its food service policy. Read the following announcement about the change in policy. You have 45 seconds. Begin reading now.

As you listen to the narrator, make a note map using G+3TiC=C. Put **Reading** at the top. Under **Reading**, put **Man** and **Woman**. Because time is limited, number each body paragraph. For G (general statement), use O for opinion.

READING

MAN	**WOMAN**
O	O
1	1
2	2
3	3
C	C

When the narrator finishes speaking, the reading clock will appear on your screen. You will have 45 seconds to read the passage. The clock will countdown (45, 44, 42...). Read the sample passage below.

TOEFL® *Speaking Task Three*

Question 3 of 6

Announcement from the President

Starting next semester, all food sold at Shelton University will be organic. This will include all food prepared and served in the main cafeteria, as well as snacks bought in vending machines throughout campus. This policy also includes beverages as well, both hot and cold. When possible, the university will contract local growers to provide fresh organic produce. Student meal tickets will continue to be honored. The university is implementing this policy in order to regulate the sugar and fat content in student diets. This change in policy reflects health awareness programs being implemented at other colleges and universities across the nation.

As you read, summarize the passage under **Reading** on your note map. The first point to summarize is the main topic in the **topic sentence**. Next, summarize those points that support the main topic. Those points are the reasons why the new policy is being introduced.

READING

main topic → - new policy at Shelton U., next semester, all food organic

reasons → - create health awareness

→ - control sugar and fat in student diets

Step #2 **Listen to the dialogue; summarize both arguments.**

When the reading ends, it will be replaced by the dialogue. It will last 60-90 seconds. On the next page, read as you listen as two students argue about the new food policy announced in Step #1. As you listen to the dialogue, summarize each argument under **Man** and **Woman** on your note map.

<u>Narrator</u>: Directions. Now listen as two students discuss the announcement.

<u>Man</u>: Hi, Wendy.

<u>Woman</u>: Hey, Tom. Have you heard about the new organic food policy?

<u>Man</u>: Yeah. What a great idea. It's about time the school did something to improve the food around here.

<u>Woman</u>: If you ask me, I think the new policy is all wrong.

<u>Man</u>: Why?

<u>Woman</u>: Because organic food is way more expensive. In some cases, at least fifty per cent more. Add that to labor costs, you know, money to pay the cafeteria staff, and I'm going to be paying a lot more for my coffee and the milk I put in it. I hate to think what a salad will cost. Organic may be cheaper in the future, but right now it's for people with money not poor students like me.

<u>Man</u>: But think of all the health benefits. You'll be eating food that doesn't have any chemicals or antibiotics in it. Not only that but all that good organic food will be lower in fat and calories. I mean, that's got to be good, right?

<u>Woman</u>: Don't be fooled. A hamburger is a hamburger whether the meat is organic or not. Both will have the same amount of fat and calories. The only difference is the organic hamburger has no pesticides or antibiotics in it.

<u>Man</u>: Well, I still think it's a good idea. By offering organic food, we'll be eating a lot better. Even the snacks in the vending machines will be organic. It's definitely the wave of the future. Best of all, we'll be helping local farmers.

<u>Woman</u> What I don't like is the university telling us what we can and can't eat. Not everybody wants to eat organic, you know. If I want to eat non organic, that's my choice. Sorry, but the school should not be in the health care business.

Next, look at both arguments summarized in note form. Note the **transitions of addition** (first, next, finally) at the start of each body paragraph (**T**iC).

READING

- new policy at Shelton U., all food organic next semester
- create health awareness
- control sugar and fat in student diets

	MAN		WOMAN
O	supports policy	O	against policy
1	**first** thinks it is a good idea improve university food	1	**first** organic 50% more expensive she is poor and will pay more
2	**next** organic means less fat + fewer calories good for students' health	2	**next** organic does not mean fat + calorie-free can get fat eating organic
3	**finally** students will eat better wave of the future help farmers	3	**finally** school should not tell students what to eat no choice = no freedom
C	for those reasons supports policy	C	for those reasons against policy

Do not summarize the entire reading passage, only the main points. If your summary of the reading is too long, you will run out of time summarizing the student argument. This will result in a lack of development-summarization (OPDUL=C) and a lower score.

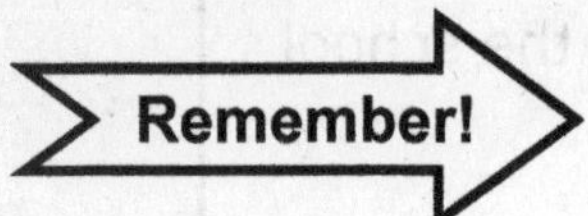

When the 45 seconds are up, the reading passage will leave your screen. The reading passage will not return. Therefore, you must summarize it at this step.

Step #3 **Read the prompt.**

When the dialogue ends, it will leave your screen. You cannot replay it. The dialogue will be replaced by the prompt. The narrator will read it.

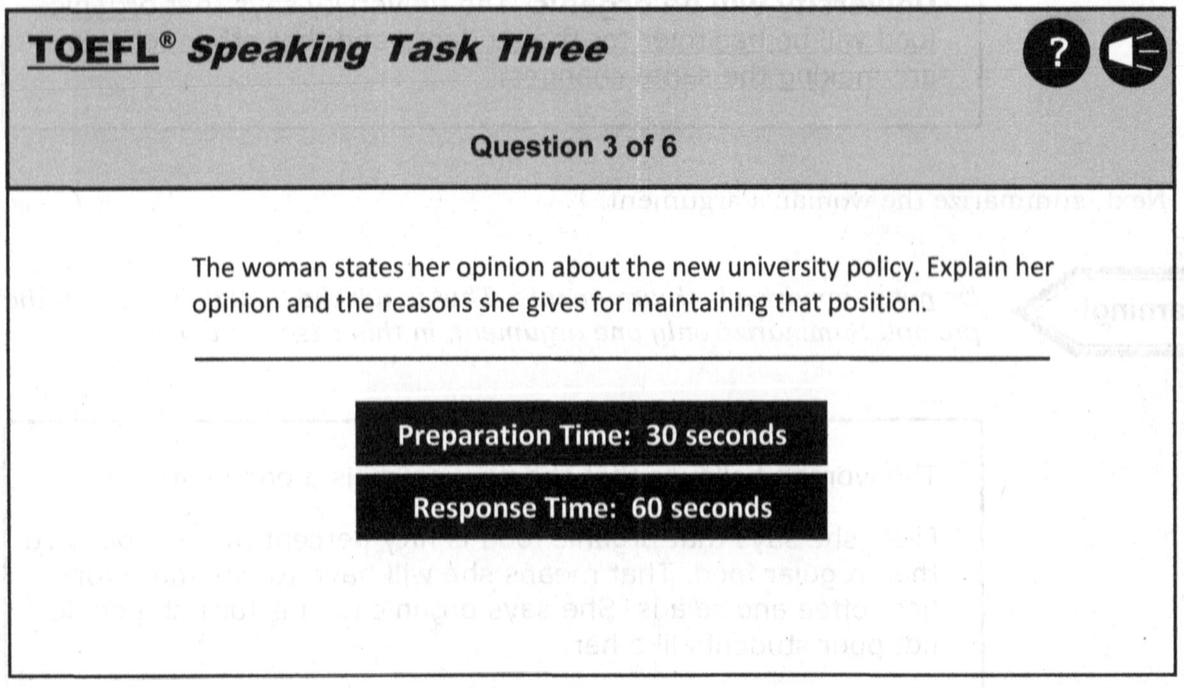

TOEFL® Speaking Task Three
Question 3 of 6
The woman states her opinion about the new university policy. Explain her opinion and the reasons she gives for maintaining that position.
Preparation Time: 30 seconds
Response Time: 60 seconds

Step #4 **Prepare your response (30 seconds).**

When the narrator stops reading the prompt, the preparation clock will count down (30, 29, 28...). You will have 30 seconds to prepare your response. Look at your map and begin to organize your ideas using G+3TiC=C.

Step #5 **Speak (60 seconds).**

When the preparation clock reaches zero, you will hear a "Beep!" Look at your note map. Start speaking. You will have 60 seconds. Start by summarizing the context. Use the present tense and speak objectively (*He says...She says...They are...*), for example:

context	Two students are discussing the new organic food policy at Shelton University.

Next, summarize the reading passage. First, identify the **new policy** (the main topic) and the reasons for the new policy.

> **Starting next semester, all the food at Shelton University will be organic**. The university says that organic food will be healthier for the students and that other schools are making the same changes.

Next, summarize the woman's argument.

Do not summarize both arguments. That is not the task described in the prompt. Summarize only one argument, in this case the woman's.

> The woman believes that the new policy is a bad idea.
>
> First, she says that organic food is fifty percent more expensive than regular food. That means she will have to pay more for her coffee and salads. She says organic food is for rich people, not poor students like her.
>
> Next, she says that organic food does not mean healthy food. For example, she says a regular hamburger and an organic hamburger have the same calories and fat. Organic food, she says, is not healthier.
>
> Finally, she doesn't want the university telling her what she should eat. The university is taking away her freedom to choose. If she wants to eat regular food, that is her choice.
>
> For those reasons, the woman is against the new food policy.

Mapped out, the structure of the sample response reads as follows.

context →	Two students are discussing the new organic food policy at Shelton University.
summary of the reading →	Starting next semester, all the food at Shelton University will be organic. The university says that organic food will be healthier for the students and that other schools are making the same changes.
summary of the woman's argument	The woman argues that the new policy is a bad idea. First, she says that organic food is fifty percent more expensive than regular food. That means she will have to pay more for her coffee and salads. She says organic food is for rich people, not poor students like her. Next, she says that organic food does not mean healthier food. For example, she says a regular hamburger and an organic hamburger have the same calories and fat. Organic food, she says, is not healthier. Finally, she doesn't want the university telling her what she should eat. The university is taking away her freedom to choose. If she wants to eat regular food, that is her choice. For those reasons, the woman is against the new food policy.
	Words: 174

Mapped out, you can see how G+3TiC=C gives the speaking raters what they are trained to listen for: an integrated response that objectively summarizes the announcement and the student's opinion of the announcement. By doing so, this response demonstrates OPDUL=C. The general context (G) and the woman's summarized opinion (G) and conclusions (C) are underlined, the transitions (T) are in **bold**, and the summarized supporting illustrations (i) are in *italics*.

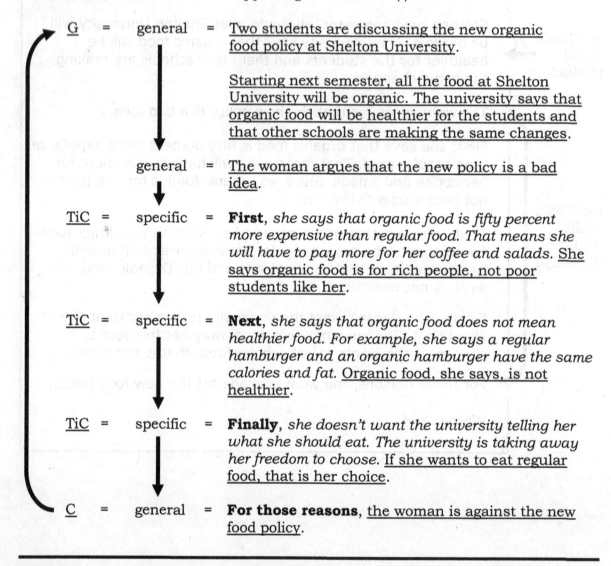

G	=	general	=	Two students are discussing the new organic food policy at Shelton University. Starting next semester, all the food at Shelton University will be organic. The university says that organic food will be healthier for the students and that other schools are making the same changes.
		general	=	The woman argues that the new policy is a bad idea.
TiC	=	specific	=	**First**, *she says that organic food is fifty percent more expensive than regular food. That means she will have to pay more for her coffee and salads.* She says organic food is for rich people, not poor students like her.
TiC	=	specific	=	**Next**, *she says that organic food does not mean healthier food. For example, she says a regular hamburger and an organic hamburger have the same calories and fat.* Organic food, she says, is not healthier.
TiC	=	specific	=	**Finally**, *she doesn't want the university telling her what she should eat. The university is taking away her freedom to choose.* If she wants to eat regular food, that is her choice.
C	=	general	=	**For those reasons**, the woman is against the new food policy.

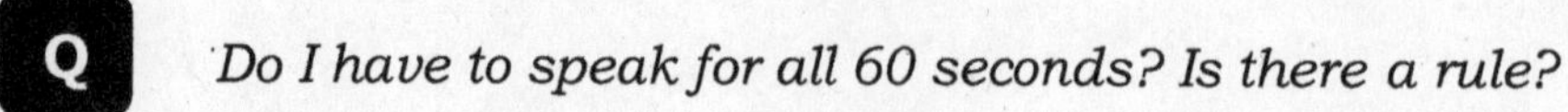

Q *Do I have to speak for all 60 seconds? Is there a rule?*

A *No. There is no rule that says you must speak continuously for 60 seconds.*

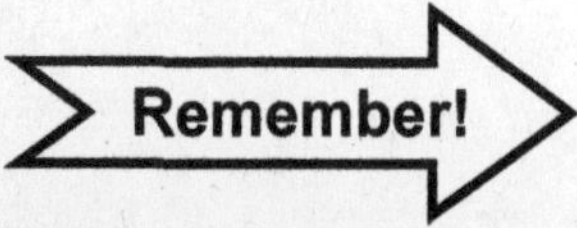

You are demonstrating OPDUL=C. If you have demonstrated OPDUL=C in 50 seconds, great. Just sit there and wait for the next task. While waiting, make a note map for speaking task four.

How Long Should My Response Be?

Using G+3TiC=C, and speaking at a normal pace, you should be able to deliver a response that demonstrates OPDUL=C in 60 seconds. The following map illustrates approximate time divisions for each step of this task.

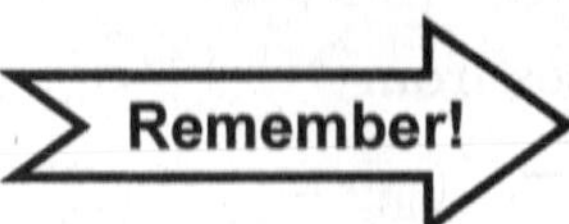

You are reading this example. On test day, you will pause and hesitate when you speak and thus use more time.

G → 5 seconds → Two students are discussing the new organic food policy at Shelton University.

10 seconds → Starting next semester, all the food at Shelton University will be organic. The university says that organic food will be healthier for the students and that other schools are making the same changes

40 seconds

The woman argues that the new policy is a bad idea.

TiC — First, she says that organic food is fifty percent more expensive than regular food. That means she will have to pay more for her coffee and salads. She says organic food is for rich people, not poor students like her.

TiC — Next, she says that organic food does not mean healthier food. For example, she says a regular hamburger and an organic hamburger have the same calories and fat. Organic food, she says, is not healthier.

TiC — Finally, she doesn't want the university telling her what she should eat. The university is taking away her freedom to choose. If she wants to eat regular food, that is her choice.

C → 5 seconds → For those reasons, the woman is against the new food policy.

Next, check the sample response for OPDUL=C using the proficiency checklist.

O *Does the response demonstrate **organization**?*
The speaker uses deduction as a method of organizing her argument. This demonstrates organization. **Yes √ No**

P *Does the response demonstrate **progression**?*
Because the speaker is using deduction, the response progresses from general to specific. This demonstrates progression. **Yes √ No _**

D a. *Does the introduction demonstrate **development-summarization**?*
The speaker has summarized the main points in the reading and the main points in the woman's argument with no points left out. This demonstrates introduction development-summarization. **Yes √ No _**

b. *Does the body demonstrate **development-summarization**?*
The speaker has summarized the main points (3TiC) in the woman's argument with no points left out. This demonstrates body development-summarization. **Yes √ No _**

c. *Does the conclusion demonstrate **development-summarization**?*
The speaker restates the woman's opinion in the conclusion. This demonstrates conclusion development-summarization. **Yes √ No _**

U a. *Does the response demonstrate **topical unity-synthesis**?*
The speaker focuses on the new policy and why the woman argues against it. There are no topical digressions. This demonstrates topical unity-synthesis. **Yes √ No _**

b. *Does the response demonstrate **grammatical unity-synthesis**?*
The transitions of addition are correct. The connection between the reading summary and the woman's argument is also clear. This demonstrate grammatical unity-synthesis. **Yes √ No _**

L *Does the response demonstrate proficient **language use-paraphrasing**?*
The speaker objectively paraphrases the main points in the reading and the main points in the woman's argument. There are no errors in syntax. This demonstrates proficient language-use paraphrasing. **Yes √ No _**

Delivery: We can't evaluate the next three steps. However, when you practice in class, or with a recording device, ask these three questions.

a. *Is the speaker's fluency proficient?* Yes _ No _

b. *Does the speaker demonstrate automaticity?* Yes _ No _

c. *Is the speaker's pronunciation proficient?* Yes _ No _

Note: For this response, the speaker's delivery was proficient.

Does the response demonstrate ***coherence****?*
Because of Organization, Progression, Development-summarization, Unity-synthesis and Language Use-paraphrasing, the test-taker has proficiently summarized the points in the reading and the woman's argument, and has shown how the woman opposes the new policy. This demonstrates coherence. (OPDUL=**C**). **Yes √ No _**

Note: When you practice speaking, use a recording device or get your classmates and instructor to help you with your revision checklist. After you identify areas that lack coherence, repeat the same response until the coherence level increases.

TASK: Rate the response on page 276 using the *Integrated Speaking Rating Guide* on page 704. Compare your rating to the one on page 797. Note: For this response, the speaker's delivery was proficient.

Five Common Speaking Problems

Avoid these problem areas when delivering your response.

1. *Lack of Reading Passage Development-Summarization*

When summarizing the reading passage, make sure you identify the main topic and the reasons why the university is introducing the new policy.

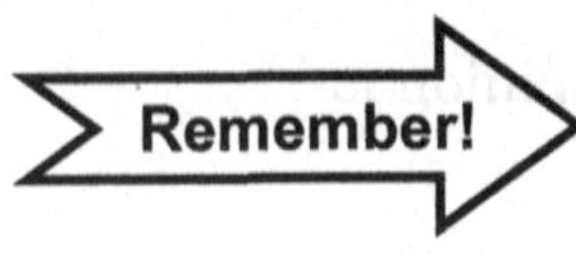

*A lack of reading passage development-summarization (OP**D**UL=C) will result in a lack of topical unity-synthesis (OPD**U**L=C) between the reading passage and the student's argument. This will result in a lack of coherence (OPDUL=**C**) and a lower score.*

2. *Lack of Body Paragraph Development-Summarization*

When summarizing the student's argument, make sure you summarize each supporting illustration (3TiC). Also, make sure you identify the cause-and-effect relationship in each body paragraph. They are the reasons that support the student's opinion.

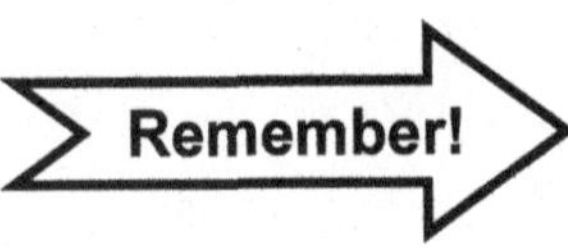

*A lack of body paragraph development-summarization (OP**D**UL=C), particularly the summarization of cause-and-effect reasons, is a big reason why test-takers score low on integrated speaking task three.*

3. ***Summarizing Both Student Arguments***

Carefully read the prompt. Make sure you identify which student's argument you must summarize. Do not summarize both arguments. Summarizing the second student argument will be off topic. This will demonstrate a lack of topical unity-synthesis (OPD**U**L=C). This, in turn, will result in a lack of coherence (OPDUL=**C**) and a lower score.

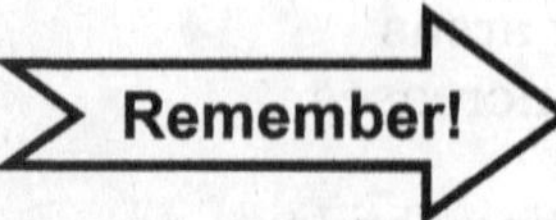

Make sure you summarize the right argument.

4. ***Mixing Verb Tenses***

When you summarize, use a consistent verb tense. If you start off using the present tense (*The student says that...The student argues that...*), do not change to the past tense (*The student said that...The student argued that...*).

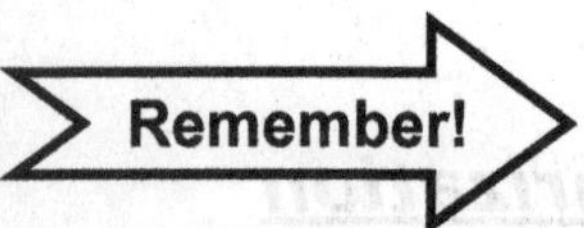

*Mixing verb tenses demonstrates a lack of unity-synthesis (OPD**U**L=C), specifically a lack of grammatical unity. This will result in a lack of coherence (OPDUL=**C**) and a lower score.*

5. ***Stating Your Opinion***

For this task, do not state your opinion. This is an objective task. Your opinion is subjective.

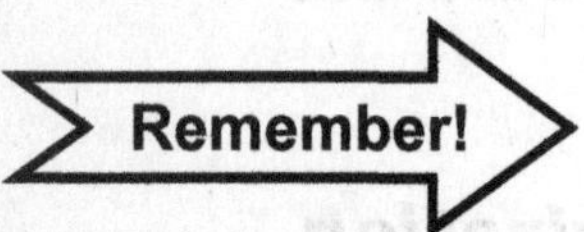

*Stating your opinion will demonstrate a lack of unity-synthesis (OPD**U**L=C), specifically a lack of topical unity. This will result in a lack of coherence (OPDUL=**C**) and a lower score.*

Help! – *My Response is Too Long!*

The following are reasons why your response is longer than 60 seconds.

Reason #1 Your summary of the reading is too long.

Solution
1. Make your summary shorter.
2. Do not include details (dates, scores, costs, etc).
3. Summarize the reading in 10 seconds or less.
4. Speak faster; try not to hesitate.

Reason #2 When the clock starts, you are not speaking right away. That means you are losing valuable seconds at the start.

Solution

1. Start speaking right after the beep. Remember: *The speaking tasks come up fast. Be ready for them.*

Reason #3 You are being too careful. When you are too careful, you slow down to pronounce correctly. When you slow down, you waste time. You also decrease fluency and automaticity.

Solution

1. Speak at a normal pace.
2. Record your voice, then play it back. You will know if you are speaking too slowly. If so, speak faster.

Reason #4 You are pausing or hesitating too much. Record your voice and play it back. You will soon know if you are pausing or hesitating too much. Pausing and hesitating waste time. Pausing and hesitating will also decrease fluency and automaticity.

Solution

1. Avoid pauses; try not to hesitate.
2. Practice reading sample responses.
3. Ask a native speaker to demonstrate the right speed.

Reason #5 You are pausing or hesitating too much because you did not summarize the student's argument using G+3TiC=C.

Solution

1. Memorize G+3TiC=C.
2. Practice summarizing student arguments using sample responses.

Reason #6 Your summary of the student's supporting illustrations (3TiC) contains too much information.

Solution

1. Identify the topic in each body paragraph and the reason stated by the cause-and-effect relationship.
2. Do not include details (dates, scores, costs, etc).

Reason #7 Your conclusion is too long.

Solution

1. State the conclusion in one sentence.
2. State the conclusion in 5 seconds or less.
3. Simply repeat the student's opinion.

Reason #8 The clock makes you so nervous you blank out.

Solution

1. Do not time yourself when you practice. Just speak. When you are more confident, time yourself.

Help! – *My Response is Too Short!*

The following are reasons why your response is too short.

Reason #1 You are nervous. When you are nervous, you speak too fast and finish too soon.

Solution

1. Record your voice and play it back. You will soon know if you are speaking too fast. If so, slow down.
2. Do not time yourself. Just speak at a regular speed.

Reason #2 Your summary of the student's supporting illustrations (3TiC) is too short.

Solution

1. Make sure you have identified the topic in each supporting example.
2. Make sure you have identified the cause-and-effect relationship in each example.
3. Make sure you have summarized all supporting examples.

Reason #3 You speak, then suddenly stop because you are shy, afraid, or feel stupid.

Solution

1. Practice reading into a recording device. Read an English magazine article or a book while recording. This will help you develop confidence speaking into a microphone.
2. Take an ESL class to develop your speaking skills and confidence.
3. Practice. Practice. Practice.

Reason #4 You are not confident using G+3TiC=C.

Solution

1. Practice developing and delivering responses until you have memorized G+3TiC=C, and you remember it automatically without notes.
2. Practice. Practice. Practice.

Reason #5 You blank out.

Solution

1. You are trying too hard or are too nervous. Try to relax. When you practice speaking, don't time yourself. Just speak until you are confident. When you are more confident, then time yourself.
2. Forget about trying to demonstrate OPDUL=C. Just speak. The more you speak, the more confident you will become.

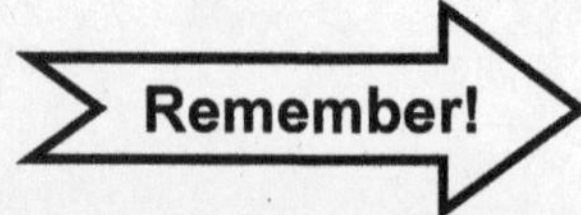

Start clean, end clean.

Emergency Response

What if you can't deliver a response for this task? What if you blank out? What should you do? Follow these four steps and deliver an emergency response.

Step #1 **Make a G+3TiC=C note map.**

Step #2 **Read and summarize the passage (45 seconds).**

Some test-takers blank out when they read the passage. If this happens, focus on the first and second sentences. These are the most important sentences. Sentence one is usually the topic sentence. If not, sentence two will be the topic sentence.

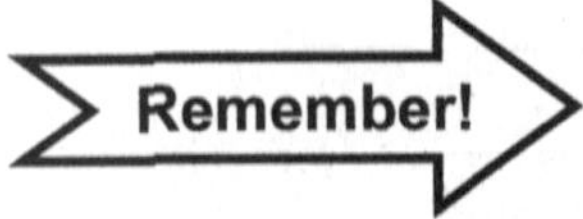

If you can remember only one point from the reading passage, make sure it is the main point. The main point is the topic sentence. The topic sentence will describe the new policy.

Step #3 **Listen to the dialogue; summarize the two arguments.**

Some test-takers blank out when they listen to the dialogue. If this happens, try to remember what each student said at the very start. For example, if the man starts by saying, "What a great policy!", you know he supports the new policy. If the woman says, "I don't believe it!", you know she does not support the policy.

Because the dialogue is short (60-90 seconds), each student will state his/her opinion about the new policy in the first few lines of dialogue. Be ready for them. Each opinion will signal the start of each argument.

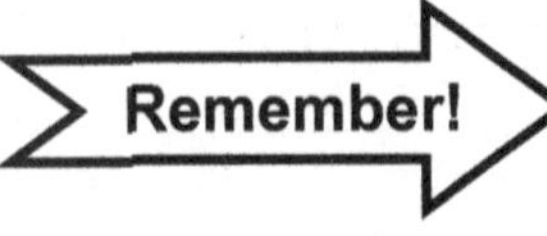

Tone (the emotion in a speaker's voice) is a sign that will tell you what each student thinks. For example, if one student says, "What a stupid policy!", this sentence will be expressed using a negative tone. Conversely, "What a good idea!" will be expressed using a positive tone. Tone is one way of identifying a speaker's opinion.

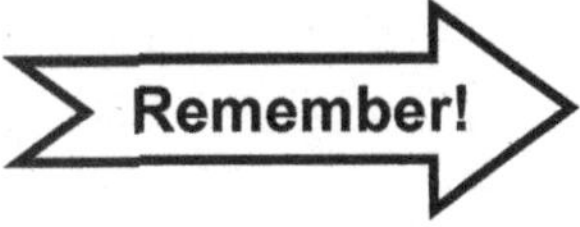

Carefully read the prompt. Make sure you understand the prompt before you respond. Make sure you are summarizing the correct argument. Do not summarize both arguments.

Step #4 **Speak (60 seconds).**

When you speak, state the context first. Next, briefly describe the policy. If you can't remember the reason(s) for the policy, move on. Try and summarize the student's opinion about the announcement. Look at your notes. If you have notes for the wrong student (the argument *you don't have to summarize*), use the black-and-white rule. Try and state the opposite of what is in your notes.

Notes

Speaking Practice

Using G+3TiC=C and the four steps, develop and deliver a response for each of the following tasks. Use a recording device so you can play back your responses and check them for coherence using the *Integrated Speaking Proficiency Checklist* on page 703. After you check your responses for coherence, rate them using the *Integrated Speaking Rating Guide* on page 704.

Task #1

Directions: Darien College is changing its textbook policy. Read about the policy change in the following announcement. You have 45 seconds.

Announcement from the Dean

In order to reduce the school's carbon footprint, and to reduce the spiraling cost of pulp-based text books, the campus bookstore will go digital starting next semester. Students will have two e-text buying options. Using a computer terminal at the bookstore, students can purchase e-texts with a credit card, then download their purchase to a storage device. Students will also be able to download e-texts via the school website. The move to digital texts will result in greater savings for students when purchasing required texts. Please note: Due to the policy change, campus bookstores will no longer be offering buy-backs. If you have any questions, please contact the Dean's office.

Directions: Now listen as two students discuss the announcement.

(This task continues on the next page.)

<u>Prompt</u> The man gives his opinion about the new policy. State his position and explain the reasons he gives for holding that opinion.

<u>Preparation Time</u>: 30 seconds **<u>Speaking Time</u>: 60 seconds**

audio script page 715

Task #2

Directions: Wilton University is introducing a new policy. Read about the new policy in the following announcement. You have 45 seconds.

Announcement from the Dean

Starting next semester, Wilton University will introduce a new dress code policy. This policy pertains to students, faculty and support staff. Starting next semester, the wearing of shorts will no longer be permitted inside campus buildings. Also, tank tops, and any other top that does not completely cover the mid section down to the belt, will be prohibited. Sandals and other open-toed shoes will also be prohibited, as will the wearing of hats and caps. Those individuals not in accordance with the new policy will be asked to leave the school and return properly attired. Excessive jewelry will also be prohibited. If you have any questions, please go to the Dean's office.

Directions: Now listen as two students discuss the announcement.

Audio Track #15

(This task continues on the next page.)

<u>Prompt</u> The woman expresses her opinion about the announcement. State her opinion and explain the reasons she gives for holding that opinion.

<u>Preparation Time</u>: 30 seconds **<u>Speaking Time</u>: 60 seconds**

audio script page 716

Task #3

Directions: Read the following announcement from the student government at Greenwich College. You have 45 seconds.

Announcement from Student Government

Recently the student body submitted ideas for a new mascot. Your ideas were then voted on. The final two choices for the new school mascot are a bear and a chicken. When voting, please keep in mind that a mascot should symbolize the strengths and traditions of our three-hundred-year-old institution. Please remember as well that the mascot's image will appear on a variety of media, including school uniforms, the school web-site, school stationery, and school clothing. Voting will occur next Monday in the Student Government office, room 310. Each student will get one vote. The results are final. If you have any questions, please contact the Mascot Committee, room 310. Don't forget to vote!

Directions: Now listen as two students discuss the announcement.

Audio Track #16

(This task continues on the next page.)

<u>Prompt</u> The woman expresses her opinion about the announcement. State her opinion and explain the reasons she gives for holding that opinion.

<u>Preparation Time</u>: 30 seconds **<u>Speaking Time</u>: 60 seconds**

audio script page 716

Directions: Stamford College is introducing a new policy. Read about the new policy in the following announcement. You have 45 seconds.

Announcement from the Dean

Starting immediately, students will no longer be able to bring pets to campus and/or keep pets in the dormitories. This policy includes all possible nature of pet, including, but not limited to, cats, dogs, fish, birds, reptiles, monkeys, and ferrets. Exclusions to this policy are seeing-eye dogs and those animals brought on to campus for safety and security reasons, or for teaching purposes. Those wishing to bring an animal on to campus must fill out a permission form. If a student is found to be keeping a pet, the student will be asked to relinquish the animal. If the student does not comply, the animal in question will be taken away by the proper authority. If you have questions concerning this policy, please contact the Dean's office.

Directions: Now listen as two students discuss the announcement.

Audio Track #17

(This task continues on the next page.)

Prompt	The man gives his opinion about the new policy. State his position and explain the reasons he gives for holding that opinion.

Preparation Time: 30 seconds **Speaking Time: 60 seconds**

audio script page 717

Task #5

Directions: Old Lovell College has a new president. Read the announcement about the new president. You have 45 seconds.

Announcement from the President

It is with great honor and pleasure that Old Lovell College announces the appointment of its new president, William Alfred Liddell the Third. Mr. Liddell brings to his new position a wealth of academic and private sector experience. Prior to joining Old Lovell College, Mr. Liddell was Dean of Saint Lionel's, one of New England's most prestigious preparatory schools. Prior to Saint Lionel's, Mr. Liddell was CEO of Riley, Richards and Levine, a leader in real estate development. He was also CEO of Links, Inc., a developer of golf courses and theme parks. Please join me in welcoming Mr. Liddell as the sixty-third Dean of Old Lovell College. Mr. Liddell's formal welcoming will be held in Ross Lindsey Hall. For more information, please contact the President's office.

Directions: Now listen as two students discuss the announcement.

Audio Track #18

(This task continues on the next page.)

<u>Prompt</u> The woman expresses her opinion about the announcement. State her opinion and explain the reasons she gives for holding that opinion.

<u>Preparation Time</u>: 30 seconds **<u>Speaking Time</u>: 60 seconds**

audio script page 718

Task #4 - Integrated Speaking

Read + Listen + Speak

This task measures your ability to integrate three skills: reading, listening, speaking. You will integrate these skills while summarizing how a fact-based lecture supports a fact-based reading passage. Your summary will be based on a question in a prompt. The prompt will appear after the lecture. The task order follows.

TASK	TIME
1. Read a short academic passage.	45 seconds
2. Listen to a lecture on the same topic as in the reading.	60-90 seconds
3. Read the prompt. 4. Prepare your response.	30 seconds
5. Deliver your response.	60 seconds

This task also measures your ability to:

- ✓ **take notes** as you read and listen;
- ✓ **summarize** the main points in the reading and in the lecture;
- ✓ **synthesize** the main points in the reading and in the lecture;
- ✓ **paraphrase** the main points in the reading and in the lecture.

You can develop and deliver a response for this task by recycling G+3TiC=C. G+3TiC=C will help you take notes and give the speaking raters what they are trained to listen for: a fact-based argument that illustrates how the lecture supports the reading. By doing so, your response will demonstrate OPDUL=C.

TOEFL's Testing Method

Understanding TOEFL's testing method for this task is the first step in delivering a coherent integrated response. Begin by reading the sample passage. You have 45 seconds.

Animal behavior can be classified according to the time of day an animal is active. Animals, such as horses, elephants and most birds, are said to be diurnal because they are active during the day and rest at night. Those animals active at dawn and dusk are said to be crepuscular. Beetles, skunks and rabbits fall into this category. The third group are those animals that sleep during the day and are active at night. They are called nocturnal. A good example is the bat. Bats have highly developed eyesight, hearing and smell. This helps them avoid predators and locate food. Being nocturnal also helps them avoid high temperatures during the day, especially in deserts where temperatures can reach well over one hundred degrees Fahrenheit.

Next, read along as you listen to a sample lecture on the same topic.

Good afternoon. In this lecture, we'll focus on a common nocturnal animal, the bat. There are two types of bat: micro bats, or true bats, and mega bats, also called fruit bats. Let's start with mega bats. Size wise, mega bats are from two to sixteen inches in length. Mega bats have extremely sensitive sight and smell. This helps them locate the flowers and fruit upon which they feed. It is while eating that mega bats play an important role in the distribution of plants. Like bees, mega bats serve as pollinators. When they lick nectar or eat flowers, their bodies become covered in pollen which they, in turn, carry to other trees and plants thereby acting as pollinators. In fact, many of the fruits and vegetables on our tables, such as bananas and peaches, would not be there if mega bats did not pollinate plants and trees.

Next are micro bats. As the name implies, micro bats are quite small, about the size of a mouse. To find food, micro bats use echolocation, high frequency sounds they bounce off insects. The most common micro bat is the vesper or evening bat. Like mega bats, micro bats play an important role in the environment. The average vesper bat, for example, can eat one thousand mosquitoes in one night. By doing so, they control the mosquito population.

In the lecture, the professor develops two examples of a nocturnal animal: the mega bat and the micro bat. These examples add to and support (develop) the premise in the reading: *"Animal behavior can be classified according to the time of day an animal is active."*

Mapped out, you can see how the reading and the lecture are organized. Note how G is the premise, a general truth that introduces the main topic.

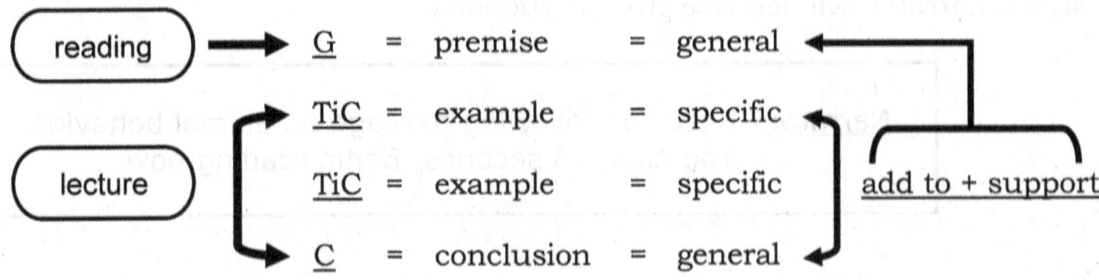

R TOEFL uses this testing method (demonstrating topic integration between the reading and the lecture) for the show-support integrated essay.

Q *Are there always two lecture examples (2TiC) to support the reading?*

A *No. Sometimes there is only one example (TiC). Sometimes there are two examples (2TiC). Sometimes three (3TiC). Be prepared for three examples.*

Developing a Response: ***Step-by-Step***

When developing and delivering a response for this task, use G+3TiC=C and the following five steps to demonstrate OPDUL=C in your response.

Step #1	**Make a note map; read and summarize the reading.**

First, the narrator will describe give instructions.

> Narrator: Read the following passage on animal behavior.
> You have 45 seconds. Begin reading now.

As you listen to the narrator, make a note map. Put **Reading** at the top. Under **Reading** put **Lecture**. Because time is limited, number each body paragraph. Remember that G = general statement = premise.

READING

G

LECTURE

1

2

3

C

When the narrator finishes speaking, the preparation clock will start to countdown (45, 44, 43...). Start reading. As you read, look for signal words such as:

> *definition...define...classify...classification...process...historical figure...historical moment...idea...concept...theory...design...*

These signal words will help you identify the premise.

TOEFL® *Speaking Task Four*

Question 4 of 6

Animal Behavior

Animal behavior can be classified according to the time of day an animal is active. Animals, such as horses, elephants and most birds, are said to be diurnal because they are active during the day and rest at night. Those animals active at dawn and dusk are said to be crepuscular. Beetles, skunks and rabbits fall into this category. The third group are those animals that sleep during the day and are active at night. They are called nocturnal. A good example is the bat. Bats have highly developed eyesight, hearing and smell. This helps them avoid predators and locate food. Being nocturnal also helps them avoid high temperatures during the day, especially in deserts where temperatures can reach well over one hundred degrees Fahrenheit.

Identifying the Premise

The premise is the main topic plus the controlling idea. The main topic and the controlling idea are usually stated in the topic (first) sentence. The premise will be expressed using a rhetorical strategy. For example, a date in the premise will signal the rhetorical strategy of narration. Narration, in turn, will signal the start of a general description of an historical person or event, often including predictors, for example:

> In America, the 1920's was a period of great innovation in music, literature, and the visual arts.

In this premise, *America in the 1920's* is the main topic. What about it? Controlling idea = *was a period of great innovation in music, literature, and the visual arts.* For this particular prompt, you will read and hear about music, literature, and the visual arts specific to America in the 1920's.

The premise might also employ the rhetorical strategy of process...

Making microprocessors is a complicated process.

In this premise, *Making microprocessors* is the main topic. What about it? Controlling idea = *is a complicated process.* For this prompt, you will read and hear about the process of making microprocessors.

Or description...

J. D. Salinger, an eccentric recluse, penned *The Catcher in the Rye*, a seminal, coming-of-age novel which introduced a new literary character: the rebellious teenager.

In this premise, *J. D. Salinger* is the main topic. What about him? Controlling idea = *introduced a new literary character. the rebellious teenager.* For this prompt, you will read and hear about *The Catcher and the Rye* and how it *introduced a new literary character. the rebellious teenage.*

Or cause-and-effect...

Nicotine in cigarettes is more addictive than heroin.

In this premise, *Nicotine in cigarettes* is the main topic. What about it? Controlling idea = *is more addictive than heroin.* For this prompt, you will read and hear about how smoking cigarettes (cause) is more addictive than heroin (effect).

Or definition...

Estrogen is a hormone found in both men and women.

In this premise, *Estrogen* is the main topic. What about it? Controlling idea = *is found in both men and women.* For this prompt, you will read and hear about estrogen in men and women.

Or illustration...

Louis Comfort Tiffany, an American artist and designer, is best known for his stained glass.

In this premise, *Louis Comfort Tiffany* is the main topic. What about him? Controlling idea = *is best known for his stained glass.* For this prompt, you will read and hear about Louis Comfort Tiffany's achievements in stained glass.

Or classification...

Animal behavior can be classified according to the time of day an animal is active.

In this premise, *Animal behavior* is the main topic. What about it? Controlling idea = *can be classified according to the time of day an animal is active.* For this prompt, you will read and hear about animal activity according to the time of day.

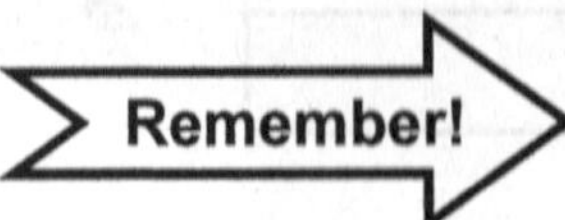

The premise will be introduced in the reading and will be supported and developed by an example or examples in the lecture.

Next, read the sample passage once again. Note how the **premise** is stated in the topic (first) sentence and is identified by the signal words **can be classified** followed by *a description of the classifying process.*

> **Animal behavior can be classified according to the time of day an animal is active.** *Animals, such as horses, elephants and most birds, are said to be diurnal because they are active during the day and rest at night. Those animals active at dawn and dusk are said to be crepuscular. Beetles, skunks and rabbits fall into this category. The third group are those animals that sleep during the day and are active at night. They are called nocturnal.* A good example is the bat. Bats have highly developed eyesight, hearing and smell. This helps them avoid predators and locate food. Being nocturnal also helps them avoid high temperatures during the day, especially in deserts where temperatures can reach well over one hundred degrees Fahrenheit.

Next, summarize the **Reading** on your note map. Summarize the main points. In the sample reading, the main points are the **premise** and a *general description of each animal classification.*

> **READING**
>
> G **animal behavior classified according to time of day**
>
> *day is diurnal – eat during day, sleep at night, humans horses, elephants*
> *twilight is crepuscular – active dawn and dusk, beetles, rabbits, skunks*
> *night is nocturnal – sleep during day, active at night*

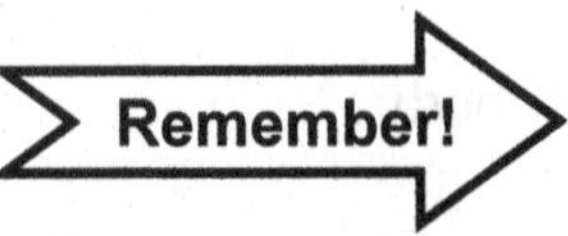

Do not summarize every sentence in the reading. You will waste time. You only have 45 seconds.

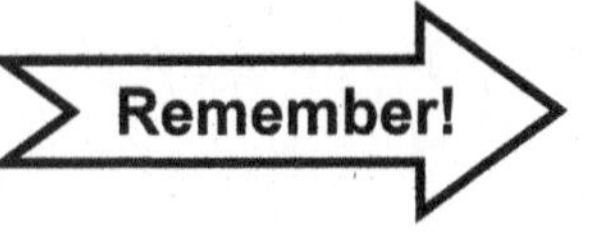

The reading passage will not return after you read it. That means you must summarize it at this point.

Step #2 Listen to the lecture; summarize it.

When the reading ends, you will hear the lecture. It will last 60-90 seconds.

Read along as you listen to the sample lecture. As you listen, summarize the main points of the lecture under **LECTURE** on your note map.

Directions: Now listen to a lecture on animal behavior.

Good afternoon. In this lecture, we'll focus on a common nocturnal animal, the bat. There are two types of bat: micro bats, or true bats, and mega bats, also called fruit bats. Let's start with mega bats. Size wise, mega bats are from two to sixteen inches in length. Mega bats have extremely sensitive sight and smell. This helps them locate the flowers and fruit upon which they feed. It is while eating that mega bats play an important role in the distribution of plants. Like bees, mega bats serve as pollinators. When they lick nectar or eat flowers, their bodies become covered in pollen which they, in turn, carry to other trees and plants thereby acting as pollinators. In fact, many of the fruits and vegetables on our tables, such as bananas and peaches, would not be there if mega bats did not pollinate plants and trees. Next are micro bats. As the name implies, micro bats are quite small, about the size of a mouse. To find food, micro bats use echolocation, high frequency sounds they bounce off insects. The most common micro bat is the vesper or evening bat. Like mega bats, micro bats play an important role in the environment. The average vesper bat, for example, can eat one thousand mosquitoes in one night. By doing so, they control the mosquito population.

Next, look at the lecture notes on the next page.

Note the **cause**-and-*effect* relationship in the concluding sentence of each body paragraph (Ti**C**).

LECTURE

1 first mega bats, 2 - 16 inches
good eyesight and smell, helps bat find food = flowers and fruit
like bees **mega bats pollinate plants + tree** *good for environment, we get peaches, bananas*

2 next micro bats, size of mouse
use echolocation to find food = insects
micro bats eat 1,000 mosquitoes a night *good for controlling mosquitoes*

3 also

C These examples add to and support the reading

Step #3 **Read the prompt.**

When the lecture ends, it will leave your screen. You cannot replay it. The lecture will be replaced by the prompt. The narrator will read it.

Prompt The reading illustrates how animal behavior is classified. Show how the information in the lecture supports and develops this classification.

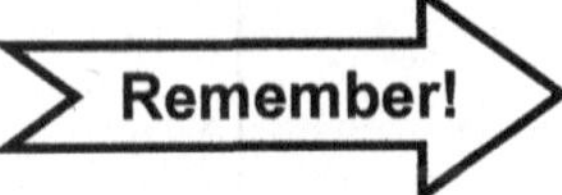

The prompt for this task can be phrased various ways, for example:

Prompt The reading and the lecture focus on the classification of animal behavior. Describe how the reading and the lecture define and develop this idea.

Prompt According to the reading, animals are classified by their behavior. How do the examples in the lecture develop and illustrate this point?

Prompt How does the lecture support and illustrate the classification of bats?

Translated, the previous four prompts all mean:

Prompt	Summarize the points made in the lecture and show how they add to and support the information in the reading.

Step #4 **Prepare your response (30 seconds).**

When the narrator stops reading the prompt, the preparation clock will count down (30, 29, 28...). You will have 30 seconds to prepare your response. Look at your note map and begin to organize your ideas using G+3TiC=C.

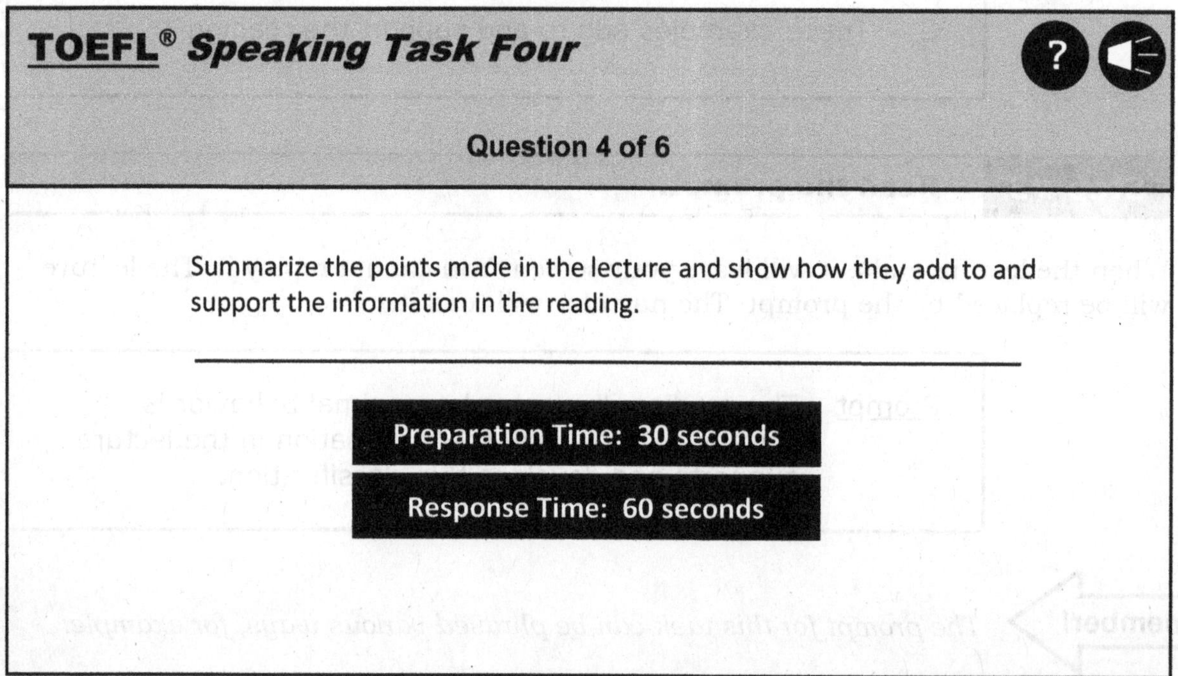
TOEFL® Speaking Task Four
?
Question 4 of 6
Summarize the points made in the lecture and show how they add to and support the information in the reading.
Preparation Time: 30 seconds
Response Time: 60 seconds

Step #5 **Speak (60 seconds).**

When the preparation clock reaches zero, you will hear a "Beep!" Look at your note map. Start speaking. Start by summarizing the reading followed by the lecture.

reading summary → The reading classifies animal behavior three ways. Diurnal animals are active during the day and sleep at night. Crepuscular animals are active at dawn and dusk. Nocturnal animals hunt at night and rest during the day. An example of a nocturnal animal is the bat.

transition → The lecture says there are two kinds of bat: mega bats and micro bats.

lecture summary

→ First are mega bats. They eat fruit and flowers they find by smell. As they eat, seeds fall to the forest floor. This is good for the environment because new trees grow. Mega bats also pollinate. When they eat, their bodies get covered with pollen which they carry to other flowers. The lecture says without mega bats pollinating, we would not have peaches or bananas.

→ Next are micro bats. They use echolocation to find insects. Micro bats are also good for the environment. A micro bat can eat 1,000 mosquitoes a night. This controls mosquitoes and is good for the environment.

conclusion → These examples illustrate how bats are classified.

Q *This response has two lecture examples. How many examples can I expect in the lecture on test day?*

A *It depends on how ETS designs the task. You can expect one well-developed example (G+TiC=C) or two examples (G+2TiC=C) or three examples (G+3TiC=C). Be prepared for three examples (G+3TiC=C).*

Do I have to summarize the reading first? Is there a rule?

There is no rule that says you must summarize the reading first. You can use induction as the method of organization and summarize the lecture first, for example:

lecture summary →

The lecture talks about mega bats. They eat fruit and flowers they find by smell. As they eat, seeds fall to the forest floor. This is good for the environment because new trees grow. Mega bats also pollinate. When they eat, their bodies get covered with pollen which they carry to other flowers. The lecture says without mega bats pollinating, we would not have peaches or bananas.

Next are micro bats. They use echolocation to find insects. Micro bats are also good for the environment. A micro bat can eat 1,000 mosquitoes a night. This controls mosquitoes and is good for the environment.

reading summary →

According to the reading, bats are nocturnal. This means they are active at night and sleep during the day. In contrast, diurnal animals are active during the day and sleep at night while crepuscular animals are active at dawn and dusk.

conclusion →

That is how the lecture supports the reading.

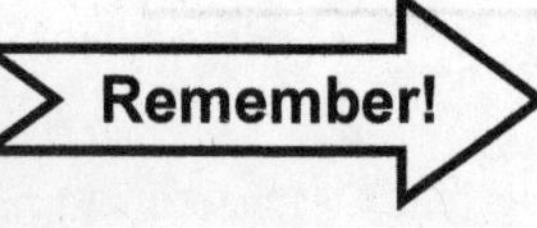

There is no right or wrong way to summarize this task or any other integrated task. Just make sure each summary, be it verbal or written, answers the prompt and demonstrates OPDUL=C specific to the task.

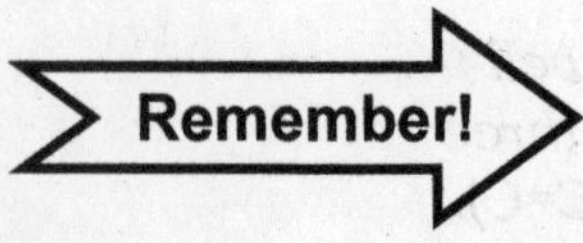

If you blank out at the start of this task, and can remember only the examples, then start with them. By doing so, you will start speaking. As you speak, you might remember information in the reading.

Mapped out, you can see how G+2TiC=C gives the speaking raters what they are trained to listen for: an integrated, fact-based argument that demonstrates OPDUL=C. The summary of the reading-premise (G) and the conclusions (C) are underlined, the transitions (T) are in **bold**, and the summarized supporting illustrations (i) are in *italics*.

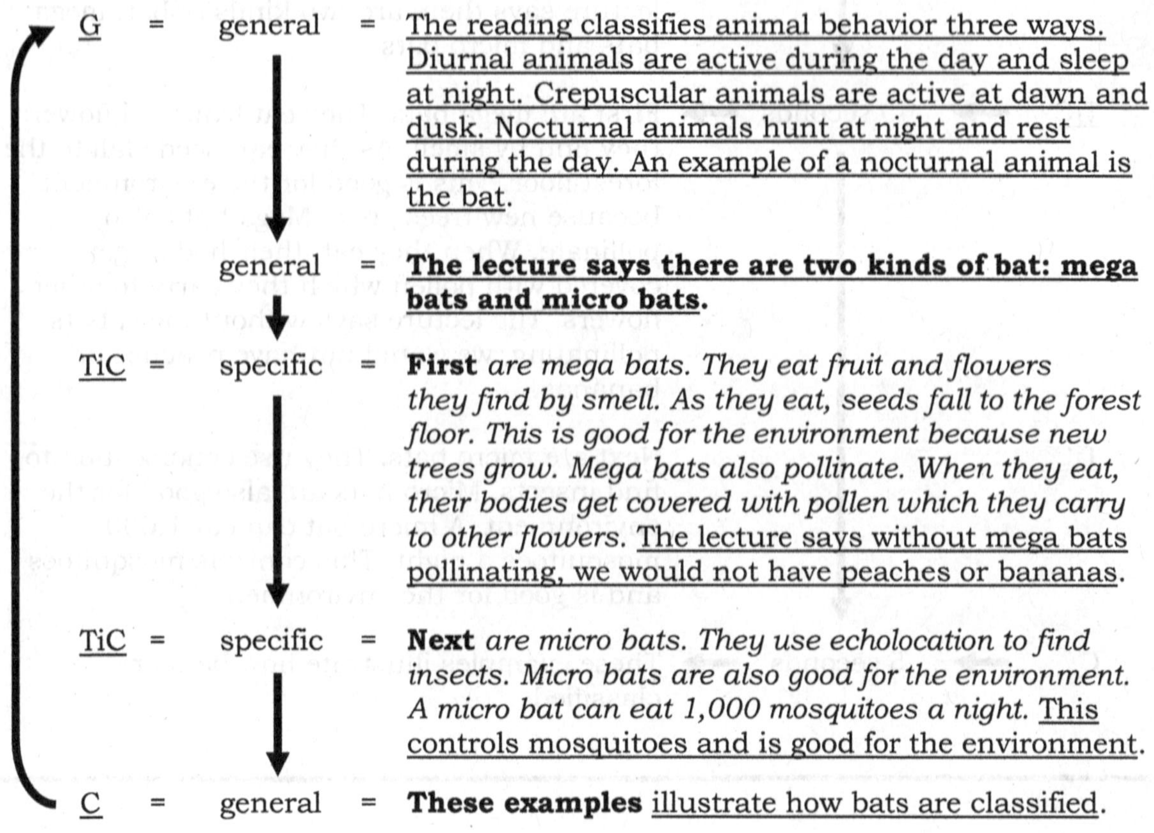
G = general = The reading classifies animal behavior three ways. Diurnal animals are active during the day and sleep at night. Crepuscular animals are active at dawn and dusk. Nocturnal animals hunt at night and rest during the day. An example of a nocturnal animal is the bat.
general = The lecture says there are two kinds of bat: mega bats and micro bats.
TiC = specific = First are mega bats. They eat fruit and flowers they find by smell. As they eat, seeds fall to the forest floor. This is good for the environment because new trees grow. Mega bats also pollinate. When they eat, their bodies get covered with pollen which they carry to other flowers. The lecture says without mega bats pollinating, we would not have peaches or bananas.
TiC = specific = Next are micro bats. They use echolocation to find insects. Micro bats are also good for the environment. A micro bat can eat 1,000 mosquitoes a night. This controls mosquitoes and is good for the environment.
C = general = These examples illustrate how bats are classified.

How Long Should My Response Be?

Using G+2TiC=C or G+3TiC=C, and speaking at a normal pace, you should be able to deliver a response that demonstrates OPDUL=C in 60 seconds. The following map illustrates approximate time divisions for each step of this task.

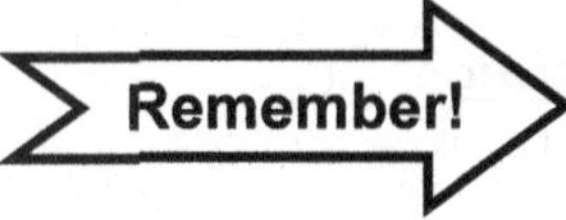
Remember!

You are reading the example on the next page. On test day, you will pause and hesitate when you speak and thus use more time.

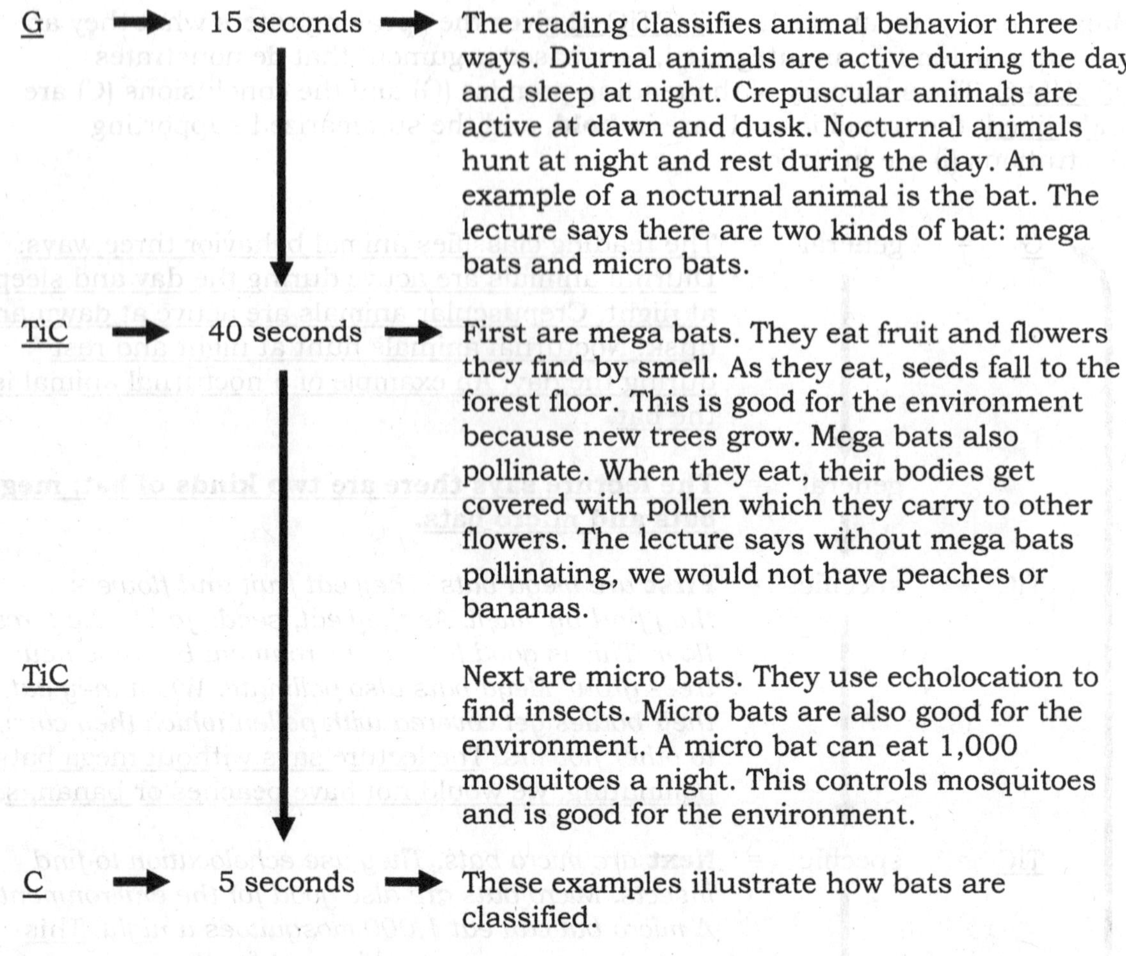

G →	15 seconds →	The reading classifies animal behavior three ways. Diurnal animals are active during the day and sleep at night. Crepuscular animals are active at dawn and dusk. Nocturnal animals hunt at night and rest during the day. An example of a nocturnal animal is the bat. The lecture says there are two kinds of bat: mega bats and micro bats.
TiC →	40 seconds →	First are mega bats. They eat fruit and flowers they find by smell. As they eat, seeds fall to the forest floor. This is good for the environment because new trees grow. Mega bats also pollinate. When they eat, their bodies get covered with pollen which they carry to other flowers. The lecture says without mega bats pollinating, we would not have peaches or bananas.
TiC		Next are micro bats. They use echolocation to find insects. Micro bats are also good for the environment. A micro bat can eat 1,000 mosquitoes a night. This controls mosquitoes and is good for the environment.
C →	5 seconds →	These examples illustrate how bats are classified.

Check the sample response for coherence using OPDUL=C.

O *Does the response demonstrate* ***organization****?*
The speaker uses deduction as the method of organizing how the lecture supports and develops the topic of the reading: classifying animal behavior. This demonstrates organization. **Yes √ No _**

P *Does the response demonstrate* ***progression****?*
Because the speaker is using deduction, the response progresses from general to specific. This demonstrates progression. **Yes √ No _**

D a. *Does the introduction demonstrate* ***development-summarization****?*
The speaker has summarized the main points in the reading with no points left out. This demonstrates introduction development-summarization. **Yes √ No _**

b. *Does the body demonstrate* ***development-summarization****?*
The speaker has summarized the main points in the lecture with no points left out. This demonstrates body development-summarization. **Yes √ No _**

c. *Does the conclusion demonstrate* ***development-summarization****?*
The speaker concludes by summarizing how the lecture supports and develops the topic in the reading: classifying animal behavior. This demonstrates conclusion development-summarization. **Yes √ No _**

U

a. *Does the response demonstrate* ***topical unity-synthesis****?*
The speaker demonstrates how the two bat examples in the lecture support and develop the topic in the reading: classifying animal behavior. There are no topic digressions. This demonstrates topical unity-synthesis. **Yes √ No _**

b. *Does the response demonstrate* ***grammatical unity-synthesis****?*
The transition (*"The lecture says there are two kinds of bats: mega bats and micro bats."*) between the lecture and the reading is clear and correct, and unites the reading and the lecture. The transitions within the lecture summary are also clear and correct. This demonstrates grammatical unity-synthesis. **Yes √ No _**

L

Does the response demonstrate ***proficient language-use paraphrasing****?*
The speaker paraphrases the main points in the reading and in the lecture. There are no errors in syntax or word choice. The speaker also demonstrates sentence variety, for example a complex sentence with an adverb clause of reason: *This is good for the environment because new trees replace the old ones*. The speaker also uses a complex sentence with an adverb clause of time: *When they eat a flower, their bodies get covered with pollen which they carry to other flowers*. This demonstrates language-use paraphrasing. **Yes √ No _**

Delivery: We can't evaluate the next three steps. However, when you practice in class, or with a recording device, ask these three questions.

a. *Is the speaker's fluency proficient?* Yes _ No _

b. *Does the speaker demonstrate automaticity?* Yes _ No _

c. *Is the speaker's pronunciation proficient?* Yes _ No _

Note: For this response, the speaker's delivery was proficient.

C

Does the response demonstrate ***coherence****?*
Because of Organization, Progression, Development-summarization, Unity-synthesis and Language-use paraphrasing, the speaker has proficiently demonstrated how the points in the lecture support and develop the topic in the reading: classifying animal behavior. This demonstrates coherence. **Yes √ No _**

Note: When you practice, use a recording device or get your class and instructor to help you with your revision checklist. After you identify areas that lack coherence, repeat the same response until the coherence level increases.

TASK: Rate the response on page 307 using the *Integrated Speaking Rating Guide* on page 704. Compare your rating to the one on page 797. Note: For this response, the speaker's delivery was proficient.

Four Common Speaking Problems

Avoid these problem areas when delivering a response for this task.

1. *Lack of Reading Passage Development-Summarization*

When you summarize the reading passage, make sure you identify the premise and accurately summarize it.

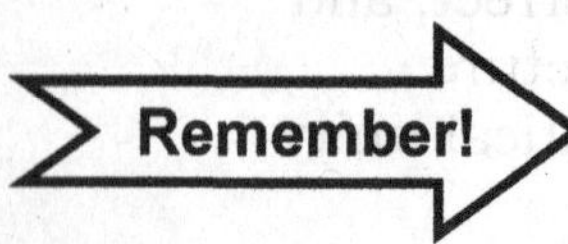

*A lack of reading passage development-summarization will result in a lack of unity-synthesis, specfically a lack of topical unity between the reading and the lecture (OPD**U**L=C). This will result in a lack of coherence (OPDUL=**C**) and a lower score.*

2. *Lack of Body Paragraph Development-Summarization*

When you summarize the lecture, make sure you identify each supporting example (TiC). Identify the cause-and-effect relationships as well. The cause-and-effect relationships are the reasons that support and develop each example which, in turn, "add to and support" the topic in the reading.

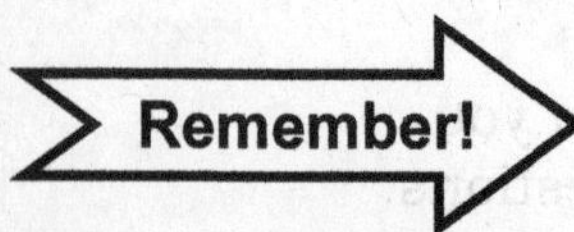

*A lack of body paragraph development-summarization (OP**D**UL=C) is a big reason why test-takers score low on integrated speaking task four.*

3. *Mixing Verb Tenses*

When you summarize, use a consistent verb tense. If you start off using the present tense (*The reading says that...The lecture states that...*), do not change to the past tense (*The reading said that...The lecture stated that...*). Be consistent.

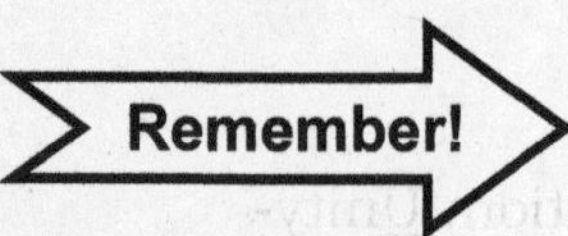

*Mixing verb tenses will demonstrate a lack of unity-synthesis, specifically a lack of grammatical unity (OPD**U**L=C). This will result in a lack of coherence (OPDUL=**C**) and a lower score.*

4. ***Stating Your Opinion***

For this task, do not state your opinion. This is an objective task. Your opinion is subjective. Stating your opinion will demonstrate a lack of unity-synthesis, specifically a lack of topical unity (OPD**U**L=C). This will result in a lack of coherence (OPDUL=**C**) and a lower score.

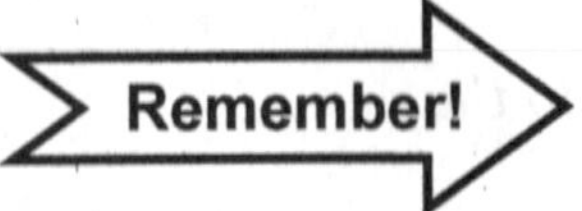

Refer to speaking task #3 for these topic areas.

- *Help! – My Response is Too Long!, page 280*
- *Help! – My Response is Too Short!, page 282*

Emergency Response

What if you can't deliver a response for this task? What if you blank out? What should you do? Follow these three steps and deliver an emergency response.

Step #1	Make a note map; summarize the reading (45 seconds).

Some test-takers blank out when they read the passage. If this happens, read the passage once again. Focus on the first sentence. It is the topic sentence. It will contain the premise. If the premise is not in the first sentence, then it will be in the second sentence.

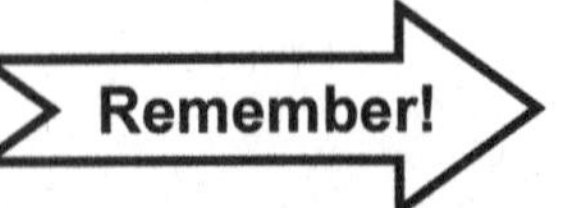

If you can remember only one point from the reading passage, make sure it is the premise. It will be developed by examples in the lecture.

Step #2	Listen to the lecture; summarize it.

Some test-takers blank out when they listen to the lecture. If this happens, try and remember the supporting examples. They will be *nouns or noun phrases* identified by transitions of addition: i.e., "For example, *the mega bat...*" or "A good example is *the polar bear.*" Topic nouns in the lecture are topically related to the premise in the reading. If you can remember the topic nouns in the lecture, there is a chance you will be able to develop at least one of them to demonstrate how it adds to and supports the premise in the reading.

Step #3 **Speak (60 seconds).**

If you remember the lecture more than the reading, summarize the lecture first. There is no rule that says you must summarize the reading first. As you summarize the lecture, there is a chance you will remember the main topic in the reading.

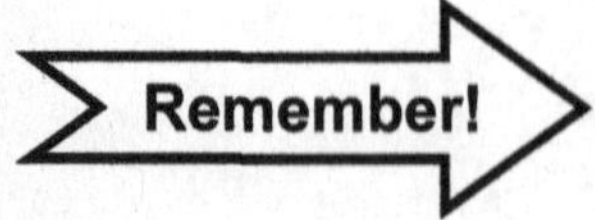

If you summarize the lecture first, make sure you connect it to the main topic in the reading with a transition.

Speaking Practice

Using G+2TiC=C or G+3TiC=C and the five steps, develop and deliver a response for each of the following tasks. Use a recording device so you can play back your responses and check them for coherence using the *Integrated Speaking Proficiency Checklist* on page 703. Rate each response using the *Integrated Speaking Rating Guide* on page 704.

Task #1

Directions: Read the following passage about bestsellers. You have 45 seconds.

Bestsellers

The term bestseller describes a book that is popular because it sells well, hence the term bestseller. Bestsellers can be both fiction and non fiction. The most famous bestseller list in America is *The New York Times* bestseller list. A book that makes it onto this list is not only popular but, with the added prestige of making *The New York Times* bestseller list, will also sell well. Publishing a bestseller is the aim of most, if not all, publishers. A bestseller guarantees a revenue stream not only in the form of increased publishing but also, for novels especially, the chance that Hollywood will come knocking. Yet just because a book makes *The New York Times* bestseller list does not mean that the book is of the highest literary quality. On the contrary, many of the books on *The New York Times* bestseller list are aimed at a general audience more interested in being entertained than edified.

Directions: Now listen to a lecture on the same topic.

___

___

___

___

(This task continues on the next page.)

<u>Prompt</u> How do the reading and the lecture add to our understanding of the term bestseller in a contemporary and in an historical sense?

<u>Preparation Time</u>: 30 seconds **<u>Speaking Time</u>: 60 seconds**

audio script page 719

Directions: Read the following passage about refining. You have 45 seconds.

Refining

Refining is an industrial process whereby crude oil—raw, unprocessed oil taken directly from the ground—is refined into usable petroleum products such as gasoline, diesel fuel, asphalt, heating oil, and liquefied natural gas. This process occurs at a chemical plant called a refinery. Refineries are a mass of snaking pipes and massive metal towers connecting various parts of the refining process. Refineries are often located beside a body of water, such as a river or ocean. Such proximity expedites the off-loading of crude oil transported by ships, such as supertankers. Crude oil is black or dark brown, and consists of naturally occurring hydrocarbons and other organic compounds. It is toxic and highly flammable. It is found deep beneath the Earth's surface and is extracted by drilling wells, many of which extend for a mile or more. With the increasing demand for oil, oil companies are now drilling offshore in areas once thought too dangerous for oil operations.

Directions: Now listen to a lecture on the same topic.

Audio Track #20

(This task continues on the next page.)

Prompt Refining is a complex and dangerous process. Using information from the reading and lecture, describe this process.

Preparation Time: 30 seconds **Speaking Time: 60 seconds**

audio script page 719

Task #3

Directions: Read the following passage on brown-headed cowbirds. You have 45 seconds.

Brown-Headed Cowbird

Brown-headed cowbirds are native to North America. Size wise, they are about eight inches long from the tip of the beak to the end of the tail. The cowbird is a brood-parasitic icterid. Icterids are small to medium-sized passerine birds, passerine meaning to perch. Before European settlers arrived in North America, the cowbird followed the buffalo across the Great Plains, eating the insects stirred up by the passing herds. In this way, cowbirds were nomadic, always on the move in search of food, much like the buffalo. However, with the clearing of land and the introduction of grazing animals, cowbirds found a ready food source: the insects stirred up by domesticated animals, such as cows and sheep. As a result, the cowbird became a permanent resident in agricultural areas. Today, cowbirds are a common sight at backyard birdfeeders, arriving in early spring and staying till late September when they head south for winter.

Directions: Now listen to a lecture on the same topic.

(This task continues on the next page.)

Prompt	The brown-headed cowbird is a brood parasite. How do the reading and lecture define and develop this classification?

Preparation Time: 30 seconds **Speaking Time: 60 seconds**

audio script page 720

Directions: Read the following passage on seamounts. You have 45 seconds.

Seamounts

Seamounts are undersea mountains rising off the ocean floor. Seamounts range in height from 1,000 meters to over 4,000 meters. Worldwide, there are approximately 100,000 seamounts, most of which have not been charted. Approximately half of the world's seamounts are found in the Pacific Ocean. Because seamounts are so big, they affect the flow of ocean currents. Currents flowing up from the ocean floor bring life-sustaining nutrients into the photosynthetic zone, a place where sunlight and carbon dioxide are converted into food energy for plants and other organisms. As a result, seamounts have great biodiversity. Moreover, because of the nutrient rich waters around seamounts, a great variety of plants and fish make seamounts their home. Some of these fish are endemic species, fish that are found only around seamounts. Such biodiversity, in turn, attracts larger fish, such as sharks and tuna, as well as marine mammals, such as seals. It also attracts commercial fishing.

Directions: Now listen to a lecture on the same topic.

Audio Track #22

(This task continues on the next page.)

Prompt Seamounts are under threat. Why? Using information from the reading and the lecture, illustrate the threat and the reason for it.

Preparation Time: 30 seconds **Speaking Time: 60 seconds**

audio script page 720

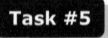

Directions: Read the following passage on Robert E. Lee. You have 45 seconds.

Robert E. Lee

The American Civil War was fought between the northern and the southern states from 1861 to 1865. It started when the South withdrew from the Union. The South accused the federal government of being a dictatorship intent on denying the southern states the right to set their own laws, particularly in regard to the right to own slaves. The first shot of the Civil War was fired at the supply ship *Star of the West* on January 10, 1861 when it was trying to resupply the Union Fort Sumter in Charleston harbor, South Carolina. The last shot of the war, however, is in dispute. Some think it was fired by a rebel soldier on May 6, 1865 in White Sulphur Springs, North Carolina while others contend that it was fired by the *CSS Shenandoah*, a southern ship firing upon Union whalers in Alaska on June 28, 1865. Historians, however, agree that the war ended when the south's most celebrated general, Robert E. Lee, surrendered to General U.S. Grant on April 9, 1865 at Appomattox Courthouse, Virginia.

Directions: Now listen to a lecture on the same topic.

Audio Track #23

(This task continues on the next page.)

<u>Prompt</u> Using information from the reading and the lecture, illustrate the historical significance of Robert E. Lee.

<u>Preparation Time</u>: 30 seconds **<u>Speaking Time</u>: 60 seconds**

audio script page 721

Task #5 - Integrated Speaking

Listen + Speak

This task measures your ability to integrate two skills: listening and speaking. You will integrate these skills while summarizing a dialogue in which two solutions are suggested to solve a problem. You will also state your opinion about which solution you prefer and why. Your summary and opinion will be based on a question in a prompt. The prompt will appear after the dialogue. The task order follows.

TASK	TIME
1. Listen to a short dialogue.	60-90 seconds
2. Read the prompt. 3. Prepare your response.	20 seconds
4. Deliver your response.	60 seconds

This task also measures your ability to:

- ✓ **take notes** as you listen to the dialogue;
- ✓ **summarize** the main points in the dialogue;
- ✓ **synthesize** your opinion with the main points in the dialogue;
- ✓ **paraphrase** the main points in the dialogue.

You can develop and deliver a response for this task by recycling G+2TiC=C and G+TiC=C. These maps will help you take notes and give the speaking raters what they are trained to listen for: an integrated response that summarizes the problem and the two solutions, and your argument for which solution you think is best and why. By doing so, your response will demonstrate OPDUL=C.

TOEFL's Testing Method

Understanding TOEFL's testing method for this task is the first step in delivering a coherent integrated response. Begin by listening to the sample dialogue on the next page.

Audio Track #24

Man: Hi, Betty. What's wrong?

Woman: Well, there's good news and bad.

Man: Okay, so what's the good news?

Woman: I got accepted into Harvard law.

Man: Congratulations! That's fantastic.

Woman: Thanks. Now for the bad news. Harvard is not cheap. I nearly died when I saw the tuition.

Man: Yeah, but it's Harvard. Ivy League.

Woman: I know. I want to go, but I can't afford it. I already have four years worth of undergrad loans at this school. If I do three years of Harvard law, I'll be even more in debt. I'm not sure what to do.

Man: What about applying for a scholarship? How are your grades?

Woman: I'm at the top of my class.

Man: There you go. You'd have a really good chance of getting a scholarship. Some scholarships pay all your tuition. If you don't get a full scholarship, you should at least get something for books. I got a scholarship here, and boy did I save a bundle.

Woman: Applying for a scholarship is definitely an option. I'll have to check it out.

Man: You could also take time off and work for a year or two, you know, postpone admittance. That way you could save money for tuition. You might not be able to pay off the full cost, but you could at least pay off some of it. That way you'd owe less in the long run.

Woman: Yeah. Obviously, I have to make a decision.

Problem-Solution

In the dialogue above, the woman has a problem: She was accepted by Harvard law, but the tuition is too high for her. The man, in turn, suggests two solutions to the woman's problem. This testing method is called *problem-solution*.

Mapped out, TOEFL's problem-solution testing method looks like this.

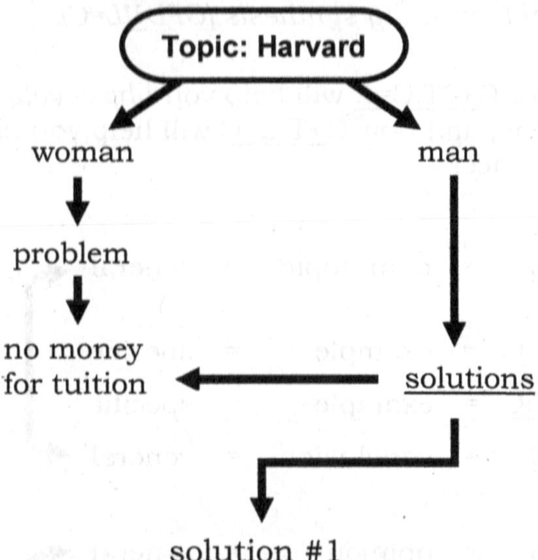

solution #1

try and get a scholarship to pay for the tuition

solution #2

take time off; work for money to pay for the tuition

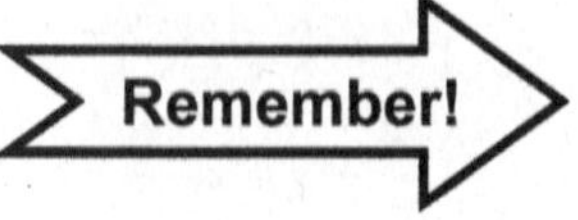

Two solutions will be suggested. Not one or three. Two.

Next, look at the prompt. Note that it is a three-task prompt. First, you must summarize the woman's problem, then you must **summarize the two solutions**. Finally, you must *state which solution you prefer and why.*

> Prompt The students discuss **two solutions** to the woman's problem. Describe the problem, then *state which solution you prefer and why.*

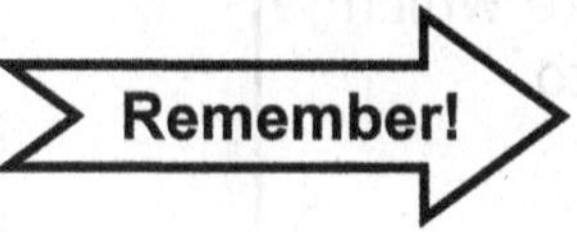

1) When you summarize the problem and the solutions, summarize them objectively using third person and the present tense (*The woman says that...The man recommends that...*).

2) When you state your solution preference (your opinion), speak subjectively in the present tense (*I believe that...I think that...*).

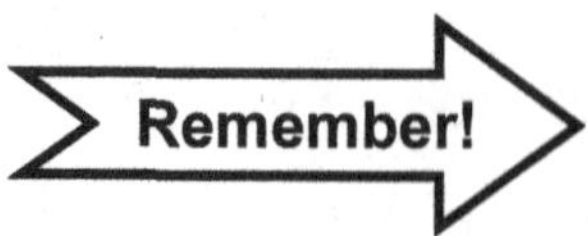

*When stating which solution you think is best, use your own experience for support. This will demonstrate development-summarization (OP**D**UL=C) and topic-unity synthesis (OPD**U**L=C).*

Mapped out, you can see how G+2TiC=C will help you *objectively* summarize the problem and the two solutions, and how G+TiC=C will help you *subjectively* state your opinion (solution preference).

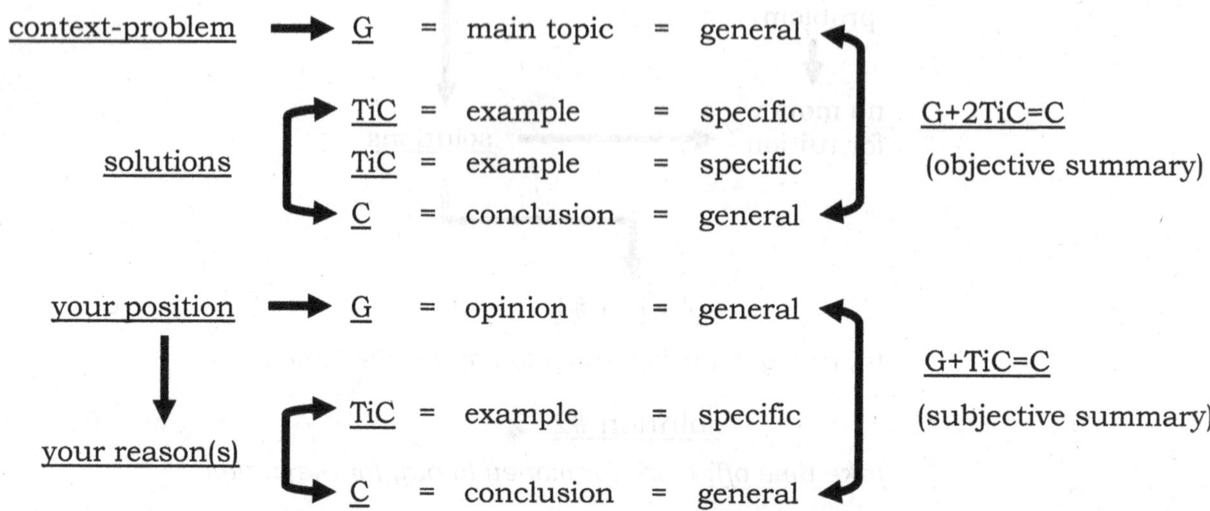

Developing a Response: *Step-by-Step*

When developing and delivering a response for this task, use G+2TiC=C and G+TiC=C, and the following five steps to demonstrate OPDUL=C in your response.

Step #1	Make a Problem-Solution-Opinion note map.

First, the narrator will give instructions.

Narrator	For this task, you will listen to a dialogue between a student and a professor. After you listen to the dialogue, you will summarize the problem and the two solutions, then state which solution you prefer and why. You will have 20 seconds to prepare your response and 60 seconds to speak.

A two-student dialogue is the most common prompt. Variations are a student and a professor, and a student and a campus employee. Even if the characters change, the problem-solution-opinion testing method remains the same.

As the narrator gives instructions, make a note map. On a page, write **Problem**, **Solutions**, and **My Opinion** across the top. Under **Solutions**, map out G+2TiC=C using 1 and 2 for the two solutions. Under **My Opinion**, map out G+TiC=C with G = your Opinion.

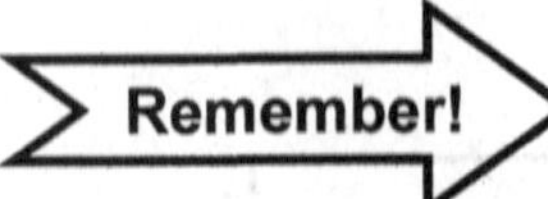

*Use transitions of addition to connect each body paragraph when you summarize the **Solutions**.*

PROBLEM	SOLUTIONS	MY OPINION
	G	O
	1 *first*	1
	2 *second*	C
	C	

Step #2 **Listen to the dialogue; summarize it (60-90 seconds).**

When the narrator is finished giving instructions, you will hear the dialogue.

Read as you listen to a sample dialogue.

Audio Track #25

Student: Professor Morrison?

Professor: Hi, Sue. Come in. What's up?

Student: I just wanted to remind you of the meeting tonight in Anderson Hall.

Professor: Meeting? What meeting?

Student: The Environmental Club meeting. You said you'd come and give a talk about winning the National Science Prize.

Professor: Tonight? Oh, no. I promised the Biology Club I'd speak to them tonight in Farnell Hall.

Student: I see. But we're expecting a big crowd. We've been advertising it all month. We even sold tickets to raise money. I guess I'll just have to refund them.

Professor: Look, maybe we can work something out. You know, I could always record my talk to the Biology Club, then email you the file. That way you could present my talk to your group at your convenience.

Student: Yeah. That would work.

Professor: Also, I'm part of a lecture tomorrow night over at Gethin-Jones Hall. The topic is ethics and nano engineering. You have to buy tickets, but since I'm speaking, I'm sure I can get you and your group in free. I'd be willing to stay after and answer questions about the prize. What do you think?

Student: That's a possibility too. Let me talk to my group first and see what they say.

When taking notes, first identify the context. The context introduces the speakers and the **main topic**. The *problem* will come right after the context.

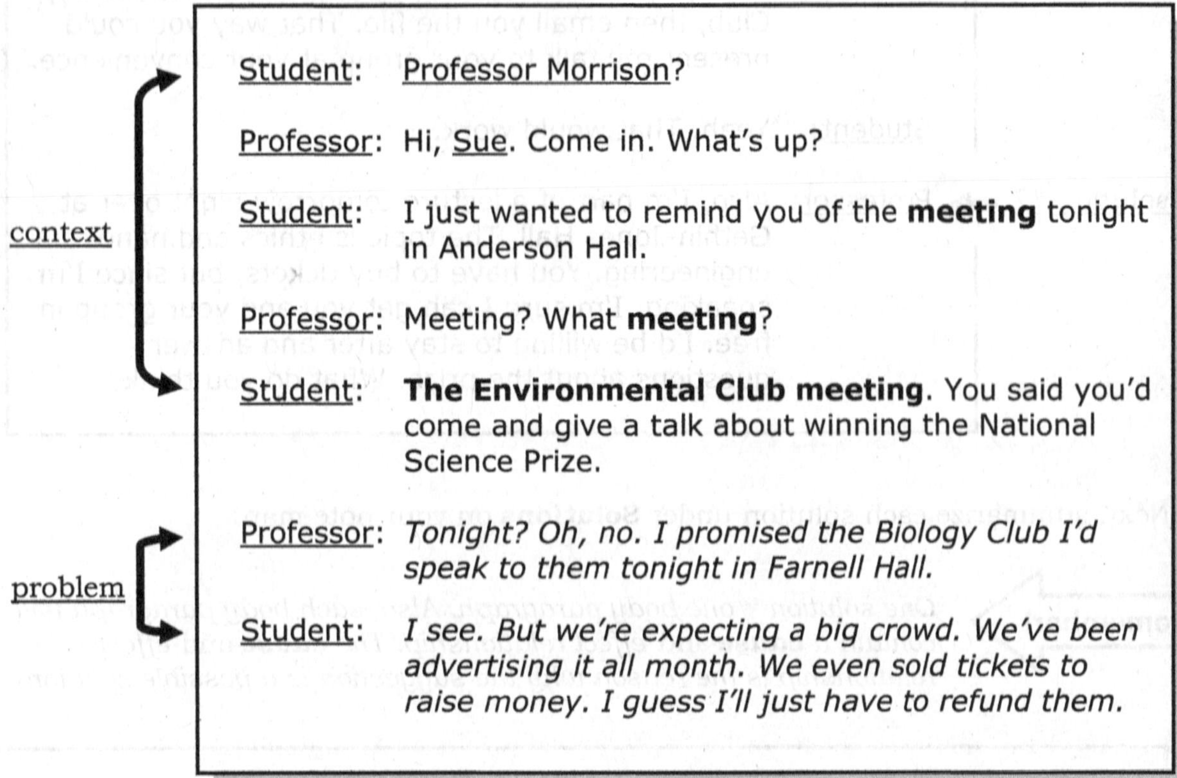

context

Student: Professor Morrison?

Professor: Hi, Sue. Come in. What's up?

Student: I just wanted to remind you of the **meeting** tonight in Anderson Hall.

Professor: Meeting? What **meeting**?

Student: **The Environmental Club meeting**. You said you'd come and give a talk about winning the National Science Prize.

problem

Professor: *Tonight? Oh, no. I promised the Biology Club I'd speak to them tonight in Farnell Hall.*

Student: *I see. But we're expecting a big crowd. We've been advertising it all month. We even sold tickets to raise money. I guess I'll just have to refund them.*

On your note map, summarize the context and the problem under **Problem.**

	PROBLEM	**SOLUTIONS**
context →	student reminds professor about talking to the environmental club	G 1 *first*
problem →	professor forgot about meeting; he will talk to biology club instead	2 *second* C

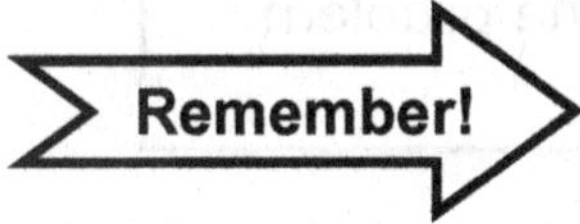

Your summary of the two solutions will come right after your summary of the context-problem.

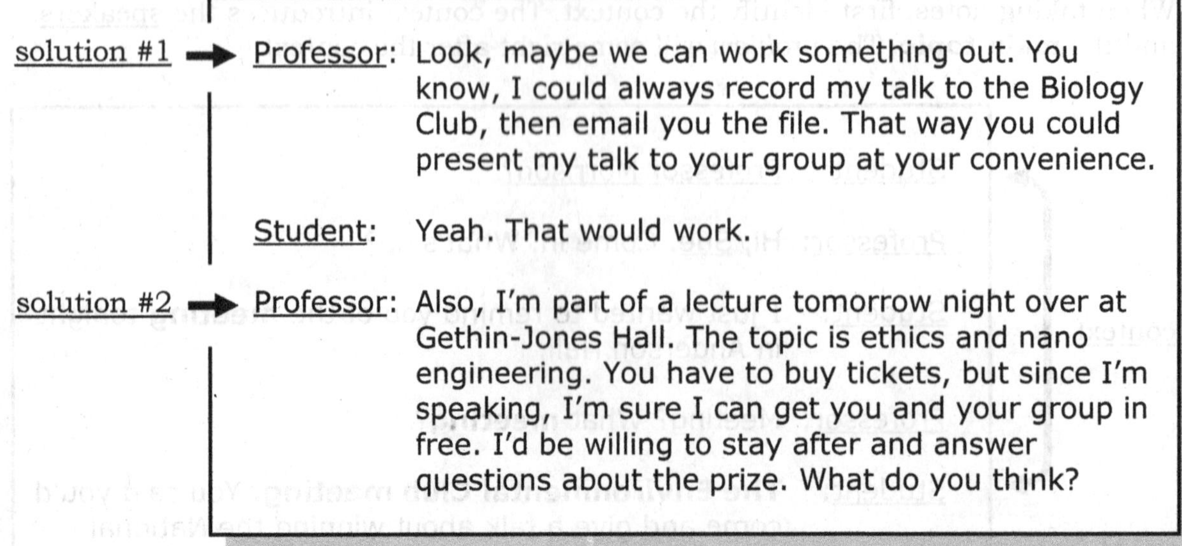
solution #1 → Professor: Look, maybe we can work something out. You know, I could always record my talk to the Biology Club, then email you the file. That way you could present my talk to your group at your convenience.

Student: Yeah. That would work.

solution #2 → Professor: Also, I'm part of a lecture tomorrow night over at Gethin-Jones Hall. The topic is ethics and nano engineering. You have to buy tickets, but since I'm speaking, I'm sure I can get you and your group in free. I'd be willing to stay after and answer questions about the prize. What do you think?

Next, summarize each solution under **Solutions** on your note map.

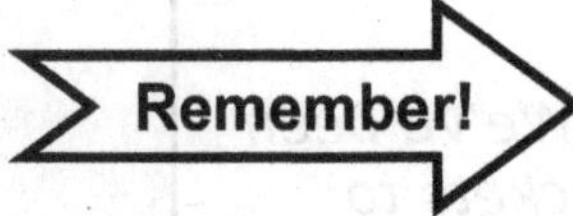

One solution = one body paragraph. Also, each body paragraph will contain a ***cause****-and-effect relationship. The* ***cause****-and-effect relationship is the reason why the suggestion is a possible solution.*

PROBLEM		**SOLUTIONS**
student reminds professor about talking to the environmental club	G	
however professor forgot meeting; he will talk to biology club instead	1	first professor could record his talk to bio club then email it to student **student could present professor's recorded talk to her club** *at her convenience*
	2	second professor is part of a lecture tomorrow night; he can get student free tickets and talk to her club after about his prize **that way** *he can keep promise*
	C	those are the solutions to the problem.

Step #3 **Read the prompt.**

After you listen to the dialogue, the prompt will appear on your screen. The narrator will read the prompt.

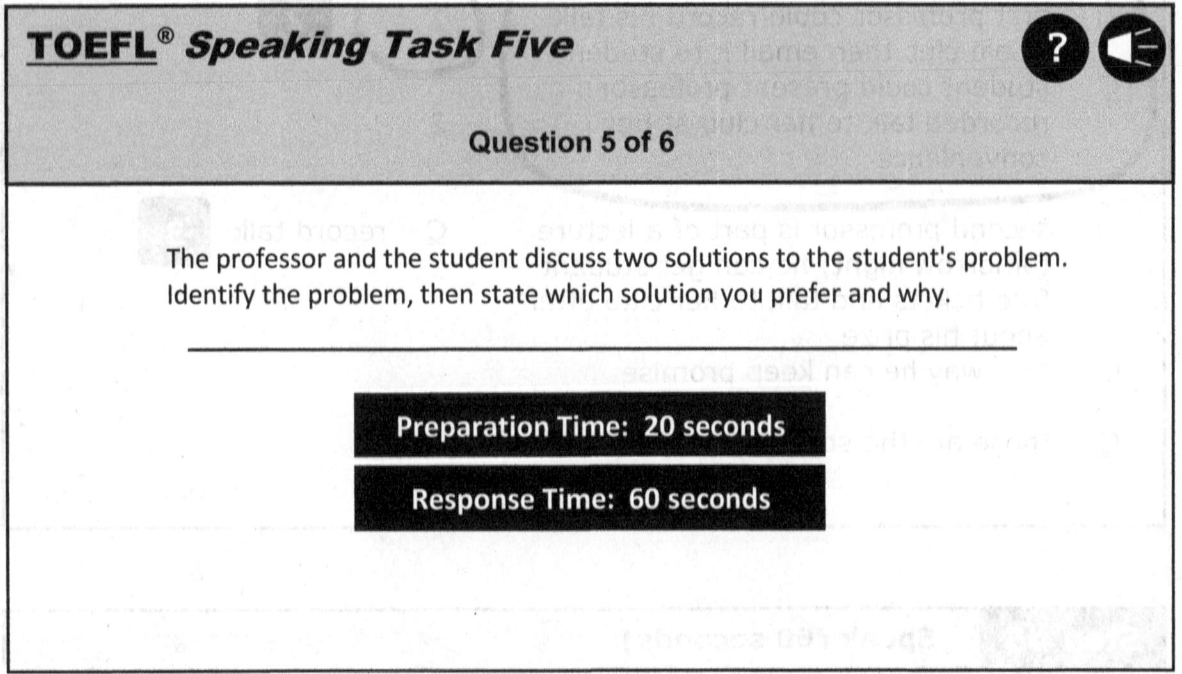

TOEFL® Speaking Task Five
?
Question 5 of 6
The professor and the student discuss two solutions to the student's problem.
Identify the problem, then state which solution you prefer and why.
Preparation Time: 20 seconds
Response Time: 60 seconds

Step #4 **Speak (60 seconds).**

When the narrator stops speaking, the preparation clock will start (20, 19, 18...). You will have 20 seconds to prepare your response.

On your note map under **My Opinion** (see next page), 1) state your Opinion; 2) circle the solution you prefer; 3) repeat your opinion in your conclusion.

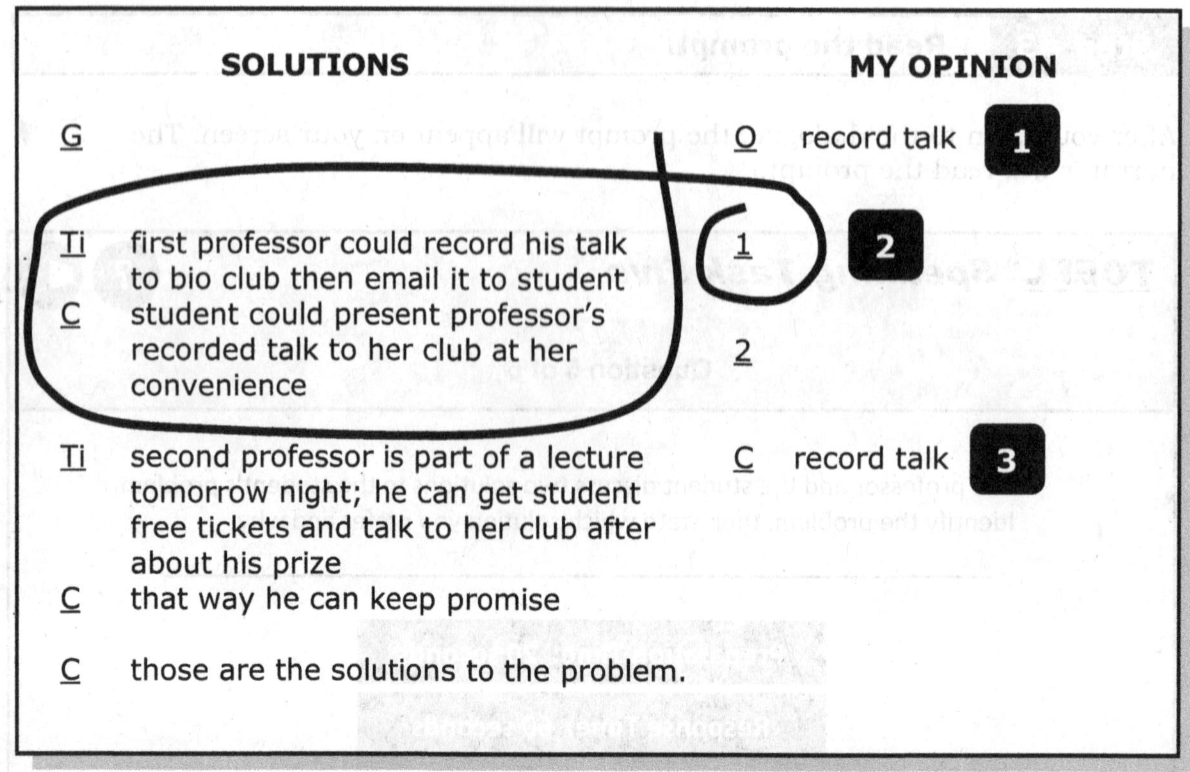

	SOLUTIONS		MY OPINION	
G		O	record talk	1
Ti	first professor could record his talk to bio club then email it to student	1		2
C	student could present professor's recorded talk to her club at her convenience	2		
Ti	second professor is part of a lecture tomorrow night; he can get student free tickets and talk to her club after about his prize	C	record talk	3
C	that way he can keep promise			
C	those are the solutions to the problem.			

Step #5 **Speak (60 seconds).**

When the preparation clock reaches zero, you will hear a "Beep!" Look at your note map. Start speaking. You will have 60 seconds. Start by summarizing the context and the problem.

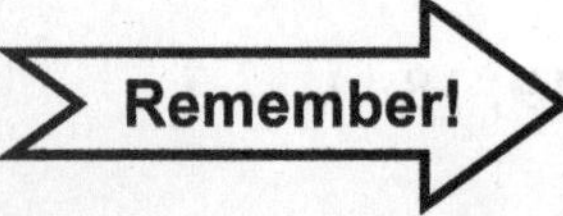

When summarizing the context and the problem, speak objectively using third person and the present tense, for example:

> In the dialogue, a student from the Environmental Club reminds her professor that he is supposed to talk to her club about his prize. The student is expecting a big crowd. However, there is a problem. The professor forgot about the meeting and is talking to the Biology Club instead.

Next, identify and summarize the two solutions. Continue to speak objectively.

> The professor offers two solutions to the student's problem.
>
> First, he suggests that he can record his talk to the Biology Club, then email it to the Environmental Club. That way the Environmental Club can watch his talk whenever they want.
>
> Second, he suggests that the Environmental Club can see his lecture tomorrow night. The professor offers free tickets and says he will stay and talk to the club after about his prize. That way he can keep his promise.
>
> Those are the two solutions to the student's problem.

Next, state your opinion using G+TiC=C. When you state your position, identify and describe which solution you prefer and why.

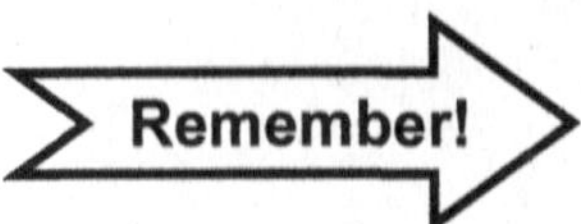

When you give your opinion, speak subjectively using first person and the present tense, for example:

> Personally, I think that the professor should record his talk, then email it to the Environmental Club.
>
> By doing so, the Environmental Club can watch the recording whenever they want.
>
> Also, because the talk is recorded, the Environmental Club can watch it many times.
>
> For those reasons, recording the talk is definitely the best solution.

Note how this speaker has given two reasons (2TiC) to support his solution preference.

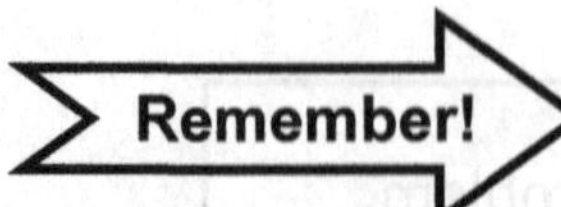

Use your own experience to support your solution preference, for example:

Personally, I think that the professor should record his talk, then email it to the Environmental Club.

By doing so, the Environmental Club can watch the recording whenever they want. This is what I did when a professor of mine missed some classes. To stay on schedule, the professor recorded her lectures, then emailed them to all her students. It was great because I could watch the lectures as much as I wanted. By doing so, I got more out of them.

For those reasons, recording the talk is definitely the best solution.

Mapped out, you can see how G+2TiC=C and G+TiC=C give the speaking raters what they are trained to listen for: an integrated response that summarizes the problem and the two solutions, and states the speaker's solution preference. This, in turn, demonstrates OPDUL=C. The context-problem and opinions (G) and the conclusions (C) are underlined, the transitions (T) are in **bold**, and the summarized supporting illustrations (i) are in *italics*.

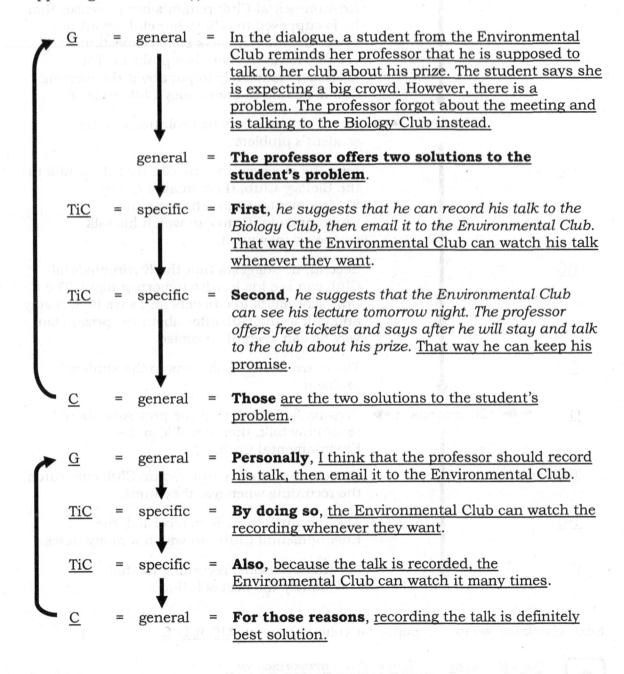

G	=	general	=	In the dialogue, a student from the Environmental Club reminds her professor that he is supposed to talk to her club about his prize. The student says she is expecting a big crowd. However, there is a problem. The professor forgot about the meeting and is talking to the Biology Club instead.
		general	=	**The professor offers two solutions to the student's problem**.
TiC	=	specific	=	**First**, *he suggests that he can record his talk to the Biology Club, then email it to the Environmental Club.* That way the Environmental Club can watch his talk whenever they want.
TiC	=	specific	=	**Second**, *he suggests that the Environmental Club can see his lecture tomorrow night. The professor offers free tickets and says after he will stay and talk to the club about his prize.* That way he can keep his promise.
C	=	general	=	**Those** are the two solutions to the student's problem.

G	=	general	=	**Personally**, I think that the professor should record his talk, then email it to the Environmental Club.
TiC	=	specific	=	**By doing so**, the Environmental Club can watch the recording whenever they want.
TiC	=	specific	=	**Also**, because the talk is recorded, the Environmental Club can watch it many times.
C	=	general	=	**For those reasons**, recording the talk is definitely best solution.

Watch the clock. For this task, there is a lot of information to squeeze into 60 seconds.

How Long Should My Response Be?

The following map illustrates approximate time divisions for each step of this task.

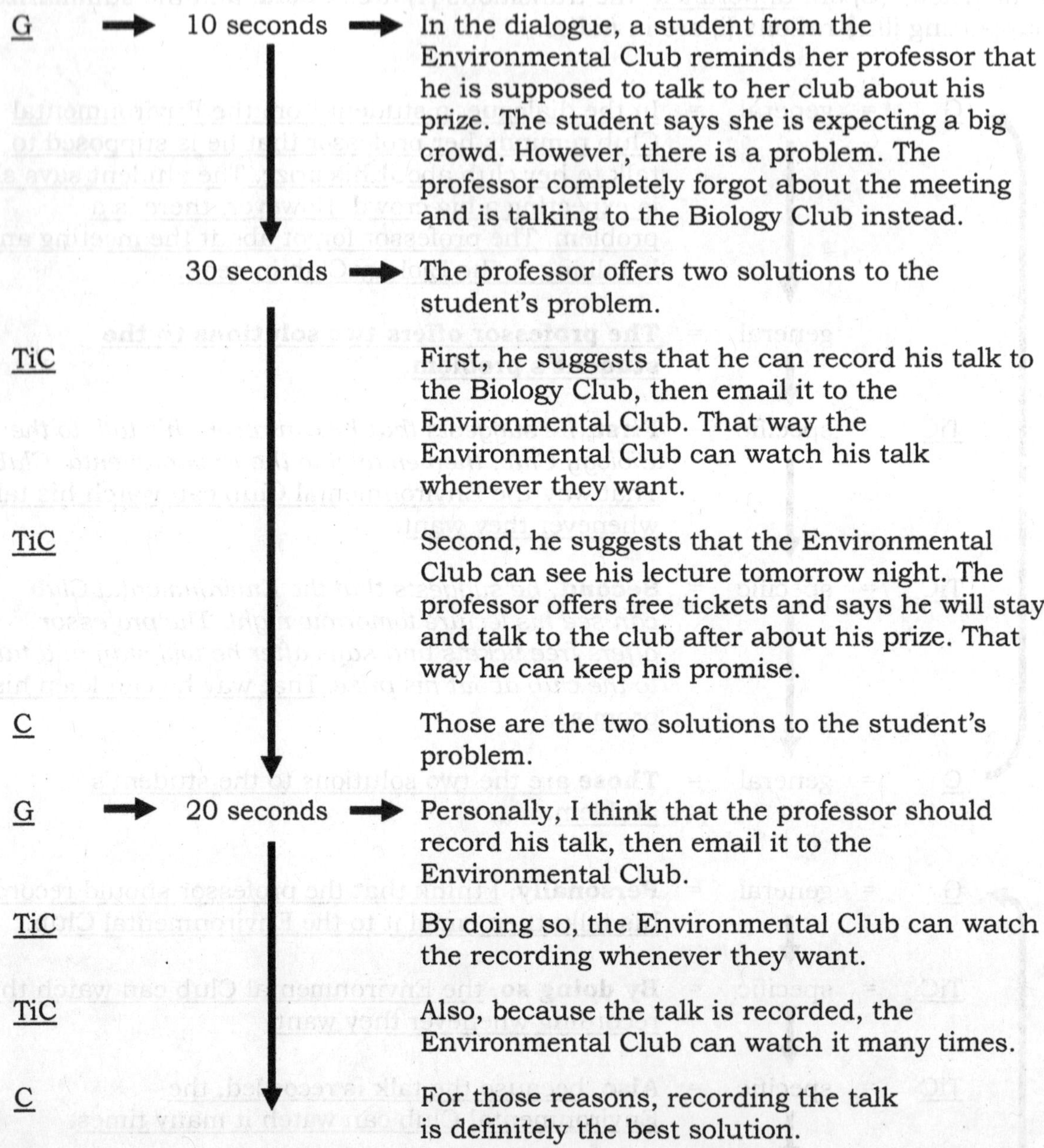

G → 10 seconds → In the dialogue, a student from the Environmental Club reminds her professor that he is supposed to talk to her club about his prize. The student says she is expecting a big crowd. However, there is a problem. The professor completely forgot about the meeting and is talking to the Biology Club instead.

30 seconds → The professor offers two solutions to the student's problem.

TiC — First, he suggests that he can record his talk to the Biology Club, then email it to the Environmental Club. That way the Environmental Club can watch his talk whenever they want.

TiC — Second, he suggests that the Environmental Club can see his lecture tomorrow night. The professor offers free tickets and says he will stay and talk to the club after about his prize. That way he can keep his promise.

C — Those are the two solutions to the student's problem.

G → 20 seconds → Personally, I think that the professor should record his talk, then email it to the Environmental Club.

TiC — By doing so, the Environmental Club can watch the recording whenever they want.

TiC — Also, because the talk is recorded, the Environmental Club can watch it many times.

C — For those reasons, recording the talk is definitely the best solution.

Next, check the sample response for coherence using OPDUL=C.

O — *Does the response demonstrate **organization**?*
The speaker uses deduction as the method of organizing his summary of the context-problem and the solutions suggested. Also, the speaker uses deduction as the method of organizing his opinion and the reasons for why he thinks the recording solution is best. This demonstrates organization.
Yes √ No _

P

*Does the response demonstrate **progression**?*
Because the speaker uses deduction for the summary of the dialogue and for his opinion, both his objective summary and his subjective opinion progress from general to specific. This demonstrates progression.
Yes √ No _

D

a. *Does the introduction demonstrate **development-summarization**?*
The speaker has summarized the main points in the dialogue with no points left out. Also, the speaker has stated his opinion regarding which solution he thinks is best. The speaker's opinion is arguable, supportable, a complete sentence, expresses one idea, and is not a question. This demonstrates introduction development-summarization. **Yes √ No _**

b. *Does the body demonstrate **development-summarization**?*
The speaker has summarized the main points in the dialogue with no points left out. Also, the speaker has developed his opinion with reasons explaining why he thinks recording the talk is the best solution. This demonstrates development-summarization. **Yes √ No _**

c. *Does the conclusion demonstrate **development-summarization**?*
The speaker concludes the dialogue summary with a conclusion summary. In his argument, the speaker restates his opinion in his conclusion. This demonstrates conclusion development-summarization. **Yes √ No _**

U

a. *Does the response demonstrate **topical unity-synthesis**?*
The speaker demonstrates how his summary of the problem-solutions and his argument are topically united. He does so by focusing on which solution he thinks is best from the two suggested solutions in his dialogue summary. There are no topic digressions. This demonstrates topical unity-synthesis. **Yes √ No _**

b. *Does the response demonstrate **grammatical unity-synthesis**?*
The topic-sentence transition between the dialogue summary and the speaker's argument is correct. The transitions within both the dialogue summary and the speaker's argument are also correct. This demonstrates grammatical unity-synthesis. **Yes √ No _**

L

*Does the response demonstrate **proficient language-use paraphrasing**?*
The speaker paraphrases the main points in the dialogue using third-person singular and the present tense. There are no errors in syntax or word choice. This demonstrates proficient language-use paraphrasing.
Yes √ No _

Delivery: We can't evaluate the next three steps. However, when you practice in class, or with a recording device, ask these three questions.

a. *Is the speaker's fluency proficient?* Yes __ No __

b. *Does the speaker demonstrate automaticity?* Yes __ No __

c. *Is the speaker's pronunciation proficient?* Yes __ No __

Note: For this response, the speaker's delivery was proficient.

C *Does the response demonstrate* ***coherence****?*
Because of Organization, Progression, Development-summarization, Unity synthesis and Language-use paraphrasing, the speaker has proficiently identified and summarized the problem in the dialogue and the solutions. The speaker has also stated which solution he thinks is best and why. This demonstrates coherence. **Yes √ No _**

Note: When practicing, use a recording device or get your class and instructor to help you with your OPDUL=C revision checklist. After you identify areas that lack coherence, repeat the same response until the coherence level increases.

TASK: Rate the response on page 335 using the *Integrated Speaking Rating Guide* on page 704. Compare your rating to the one on page 797. Note: For this response, the speaker's delivery was proficient.

Contrarian Response

What if you think the suggested solutions are not good enough? What if you have a better solution? Can you state it? Yes. Look at the following contrarian response.

> Personally, I think that the professor's solutions are not good enough.
>
> The Environmental Club will be disappointed because he did not bother to check his schedule. If students do not check their schedules, they can get into a lot of trouble. The best solution is for the professor to reschedule his talk with the Environmental Club.
>
> By rescheduling his talk, the professor will keep his promise and set a good example.

In the above response, the speaker is arguing against the suggested solutions. More importantly, the speaker offers a new solution.

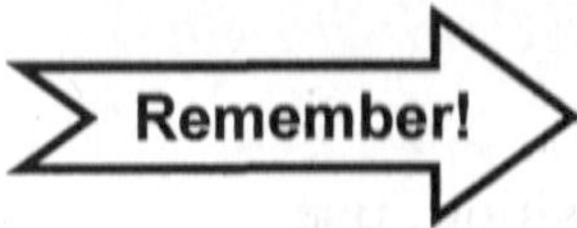

Make sure your contrarian solution is serious. Avoid this type of response.

> I can't believe the professor BROKE HIS PROMISE!!! That's not very nice. And he's a professor?! Personally, I would have absolutely no respect for him after that! If bought a ticket, I would be VERY MAD!!!

As you can see, the above response is not serious. The speaker is not arguing. The speaker is simply complaining and FLAMING. Worse, the speaker *does not offer a solution to the problem.* This will result in a lack of coherence (OPDUL=**C**) and a lower score.

Three Common Speaking Problems

Avoid these problem areas when delivering a response for this task.

1. *Lack of Context-Problem Development-Summarization*

When summarizing the dialogue, make sure you accurately summarize the context and the problem.

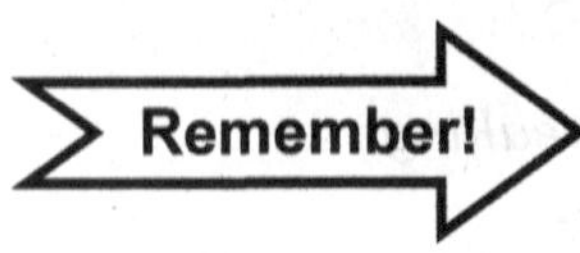

*A lack of context-problem development-summarization (OP**D**UL=C), will result in a lack of unity-synthesis (OPD**U**L=C), specifically a lack of topical unity between the dialogue and your argument stating which solution you think is best. This will result in a lack of coherence (OPDUL=**C**) and a lower score.*

2. *Lack of Solution Development-Summarization*

When summarizing the dialogue, identify and summarize both solutions to the problem. Also, make sure you identify the cause-and-effect relationship in each solution. The cause-and-effect relationships are the reasons that support and develop each solution. This in turn, will help you develop your argument in which you state which solution you think is best and why.

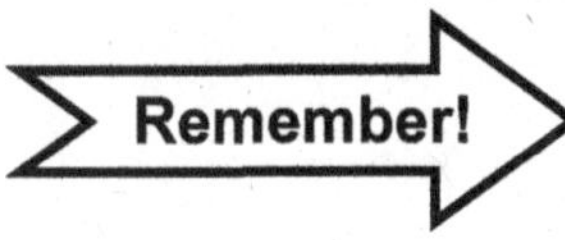

*A lack of solution development-summarization (OP**D**UL=C) is a big reason why test-takers score low on integrated speaking task five.*

3. ***Mixing Verb Tenses***

When you summarize the problem and the solutions, then state your position, use a consistent verb tense. If you start off using the present tense (*The problem is...*), do not change to the past tense (*Personally, I think that the best solution was...*) Be consistent.

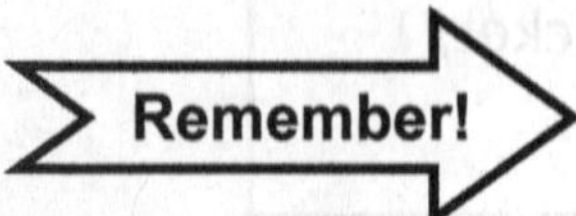

Mixing verb tenses will demonstrate a lack of unity-synthesis (OPDUL=C), specifically a lack of grammatical unity. This will result in a lack of coherence (OPDUL=C) and a lower score.

Help! – *My Response is Too Long!*

The following are reasons why your response is longer than 60 seconds.

Reason #1 Your summary of the context-problem is too long.

Solution

1. Make your summary shorter.
2. Avoid details like dates, places, costs, etc.
3. Summarize the context-problem in 15 seconds or less.
4. Speak faster; try not to hesitate.

Reason #2 When the clock starts, you are not speaking right away. That means you are losing valuable seconds at the start.

Solution

1. Start speaking right after the beep. Remember: *The speaking tasks come up fast. Be ready for them*

Reason #3 You are being too careful. When you are too careful, you slow down to pronounce correctly. When you slow down, you waste time. You also decrease fluency and automaticity.

Solution

1. Speak at a normal pace.
2. Record your voice, then play it back. You will know if you are speaking too slowly. If so, speak faster.

Reason #4 You are pausing or hesitating too much. Record your voice and play it back. You will soon know if you are pausing or hesitating too much. Pausing and hesitating waste time. Pausing and hesitating will also decrease fluency and automaticity.

Solution

1. Avoid pauses; try not to hesitate.
2. Practice reading sample responses.
3. Ask a native speaker to demonstrate the right speed.

Reason #5 You are pausing or hesitating too much because you did not summarize problem and the solutions using G+2TiC=C.

Solution
1. Practice summarizing sample dialogues using G+2TiC=C.
2. Practice one response over and over until you are confident summarizing the problem and the solutions using G+2TiC=C.

Reason #6 Your summary of the two solutions contains too much information.

Solution
1. Summarize only the topic in each solution and the cause-and-effect relationship.
2. Reduce the number of specific details (dates, costs, ages, etc).

Reason #7 You are summarizing each solution, then explaining why it is not a good idea.

Solution
1. Do not analyze each solution in detail. This will waste time. Also, it is not part of the task.
2. Summarize each solution only.
3. State your argument (solution preference) at the end.

Reason #8 Your summary of the dialogue conclusion is too long.

Solution
1. State the conclusion in one sentence.
2. State the conclusion in 5 seconds or less.

Reason #9 Your solution preference (G+TiC=C) is too long.

Solution
1. Reduce the number of details in your argument.
2. Develop only one solution preference.
3. State your argument in 20 seconds or less.

Reason #10 The clock makes you so nervous you blank out.

Solution
1. Do not time yourself when you practice. Just speak. When you are more confident, time yourself.

Help! – *My Response is Too Short!*

Listed below are reasons why your response is too short.

Reason #1 You are nervous. When you are nervous, you speak too fast and finish too soon.

Solution
1. Record your voice and play it back. You will soon know if you are speaking too fast. If so, slow down.
2. Do not time yourself. Just speak at a regular speed.

Reason #2 You speak, then suddenly stop because you are shy, afraid, or feel stupid.

Solution
1. Practice reading into a recording device. Read an English magazine article or a book while recording. This will help you develop confidence speaking into a microphone.
2. Take an ESL class to develop your speaking skills and confidence.
3. Practice. Practice. Practice.

Reason #3 You are not confident using G+2TiC=C.

Solution
1. Practice developing and delivering one response until you have memorized G+2TiC=C and can remember it automatically without notes.
2. Practice. Practice. Practice.

Reason #4 You blank out.

Solution
1. You are trying too hard or are too nervous. Try to relax. When you practice speaking, don't time yourself. Just speak until you are confident. When you are more confident, then time yourself.
2. Don't worry about fluency, automaticity and pronunciation. Just speak. The more you speak, the more confident you will become.

Reason #5 Your summary of the context-problem is too short.

Solution
1. Make sure you have accurately identified the context and the problem.

Reason #6 Your summary of the two solutions is too short.

Solution
1. Make sure you have accurately summarized each solution.
2. Make sure you have accurately summarized the cause-and-effect relationship in each solution.

Reason #7 Your solution-preference argument (G+TiC=C) is too short.

Solution
1. Identify which solution you think is best.
2. Develop your argument with a cause-and-effect reason.
3. Use a personal example to support your position.

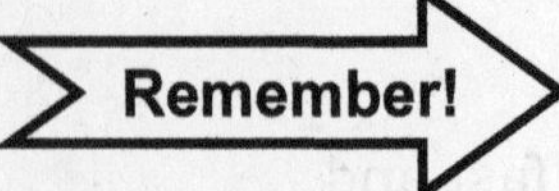

Start clean, end clean.

Emergency Response

What if you can't develop and deliver a response for this task? What if you blank out? What should you do? Follow these two steps and deliver an emergency response.

Step #1 **Identify the problem; summarize the problem.**

After you listen to the dialogue, look at your note map. Try and identify the problem. The problem is the most important part of this task. If you can identify the problem, you might remember the two solutions.

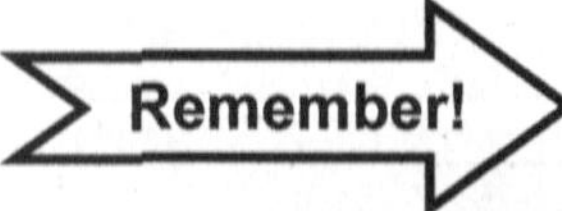

If you can remember only one point from the dialogue, make sure it is the problem.

Step #2 **Suggest solutions to the problem.**

If you can remember the problem but not the solutions, then offer your own solutions to the problem. There is a chance they might be similar to the two solutions suggested.

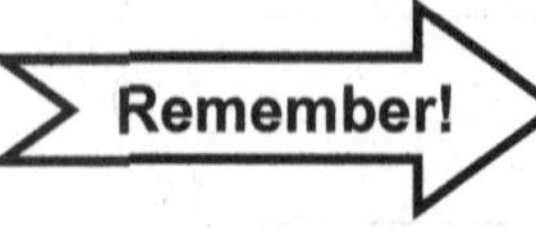

Don't stop talking. The more you talk, the more you think. The more you think, the more you might remember the problem and the solutions.

Speaking Practice

Using G+2TiC=C and G+TiC=C and the five steps, develop and deliver a response for each of the following tasks. Use a recording device so you can play back your response and check it for coherence using the *Integrated Speaking Proficiency Checklist* on page 703. After you check your response for coherence, rate it using the *Integrated Speaking Rating Guide* on page 704.

Task #1

Audio Track #26

Directions: Listen to a conversation between two students.

Prompt The students discuss two solutions to the woman's problem. Identify the problem and the solutions, then state which solution you think is best and why.

Preparation Time: 20 seconds **Speaking Time: 60 seconds**

audio script page 722

Task #2

Directions: Listen to a conversation between two students.

Audio Track #27

<u>Prompt</u> The students discuss two solutions to the man's problem. Identify the problem and the solutions, then state which solution you think is best and why.

<u>Preparation Time</u>: 20 seconds **<u>Speaking Time</u>: 60 seconds**

audio script page 723

Task #3

Audio Track #28

Directions: Listen to a conversation between two students.

Prompt The students discuss two solutions to the woman's problem. Identify the problem and the solutions, then state which solution you think is best and why.

Preparation Time: 20 seconds **Speaking Time: 60 seconds**

audio script page 723

Task #4

Audio Track #29

Directions: Listen to a conversation between two students.

Prompt The students discuss two solutions to the man's problem. Identify the problem and the solutions, then state which solution you think is best and why.

Preparation Time: 20 seconds **Speaking Time: 60 seconds**

audio script page 724

Task #5

Audio Track #30

Directions: Listen to a conversation between two students.

Prompt The students discuss two solutions to the woman's problem. Identify the problem and the solutions, then state which solution you think is best and why.

Preparation Time: 20 seconds **Speaking Time: 60 seconds**

audio script page 724

Task #6 - Integrated Speaking

Listen + Speak

This task measures your ability to integrate two skills: listening and speaking. You will integrate these two skills while summarizing a fact-based lecture. Your summary will answer a question in a prompt. The prompt will appear after the lecture. The task order follows.

TASK	TIME
1. Listen to a short lecture.	60-90 seconds
2. Read the prompt. 3. Prepare your response.	20 seconds
4. Deliver your response.	60 seconds

This task also measures your ability to:

- ✓ **take notes** as you listen to the lecture;
- ✓ **summarize** the main points in the lecture;
- ✓ **paraphrase** the main points in the lecture.

You can develop and deliver a response for this task using G+3TiC=C. This map will help you take notes and give the speaking raters what they are trained to listen for: an integrated response that demonstrates OPDUL=C.

TOEFL's Testing Method

For this task, TOEFL uses the same testing method it uses for speaking task four. For speaking task four, you read a short academic passage. The passage provides a general topic introduction. That topic is developed with examples in a lecture. You then integrate the reading (general) and the lecture (specific) in your response. TOEFL recycles this same testing method for this task. However, for this task, the topic (general) and the examples (specific) are combined in the lecture, as the maps on the next page illustrate.

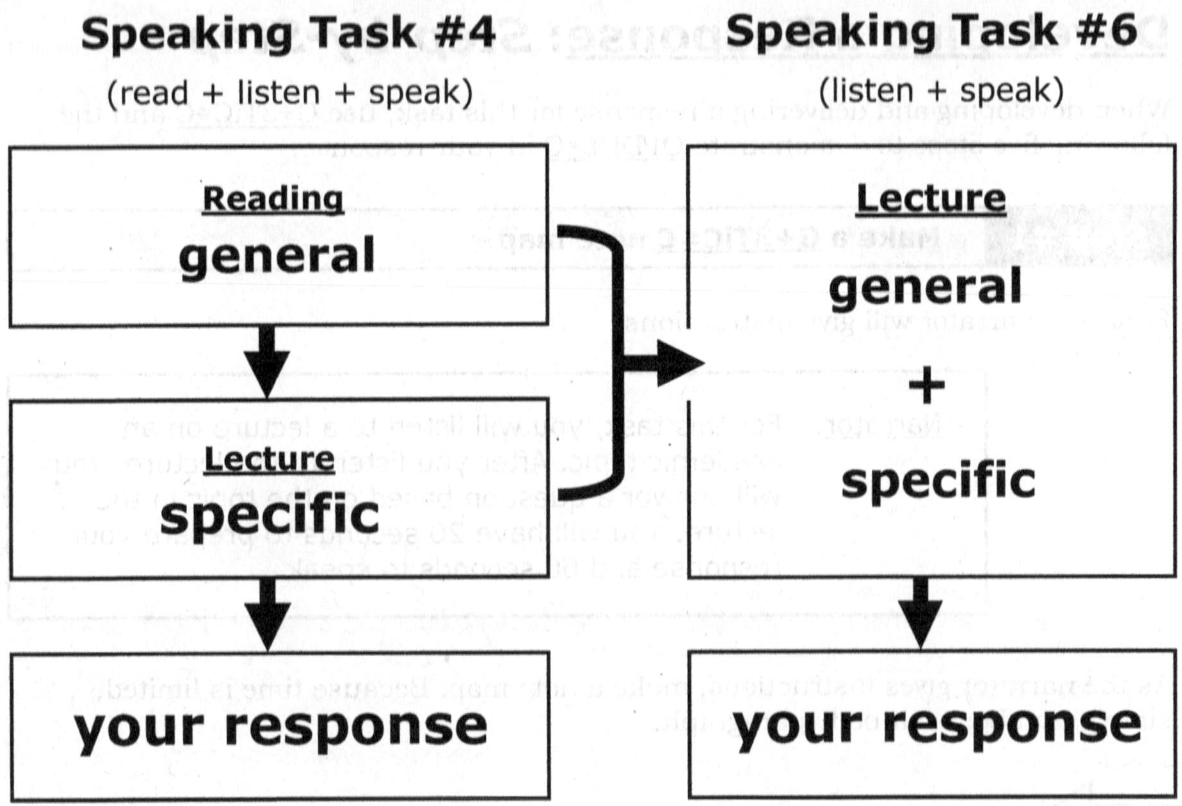

The TOEFL iBT recycles the same testing methods throughout the speaking and writing sections. Because TOEFL recycles the same testing methods, they are predictable. Because they are predictable, you can apply G+3TiC=C and its variations (G+TiC=C, G+2TiC=C, 2TiC=C, 3TiC=C) to all speaking and writing tasks. By doing so, you will demonstrate OPDUL=C in all eight constructive tasks. This, in turn, will result in higher speaking and writing sections scores, and a higher TOEFL iBT score.

For this task, use G+3TiC=C to develop and deliver your response. Because the lecture is a fact-based argument, it will start with premise (topic + controlling idea).

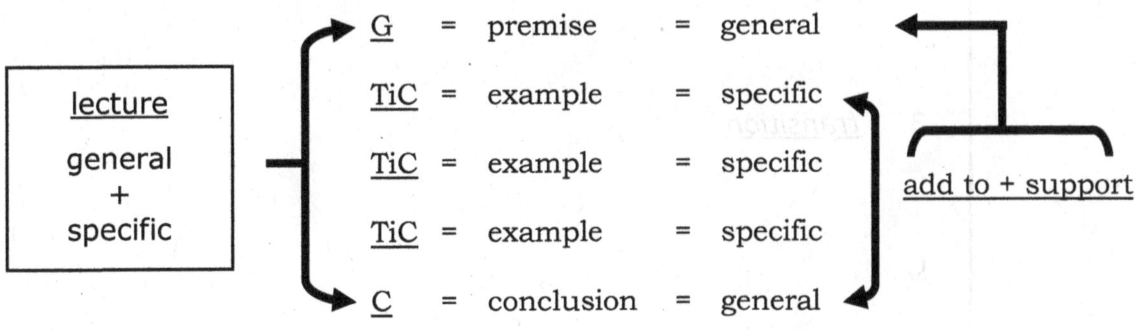

Developing a Response: *Step-by-Step*

When developing and delivering a response for this task, use G+3TiC=C and the following five steps to demonstrate OPDUL=C in your response.

Step #1 **Make a G+3TiC=C note map.**

First, the narrator will give instructions.

Narrator: For this task, you will listen to a lecture on an academic topic. After you listen to the lecture, you will answer a question based on the topic in the lecture. You will have 20 seconds to prepare your response and 60 seconds to speak.

As the narrator gives instructions, make a note map. Because time is limited, simply number each body paragraph.

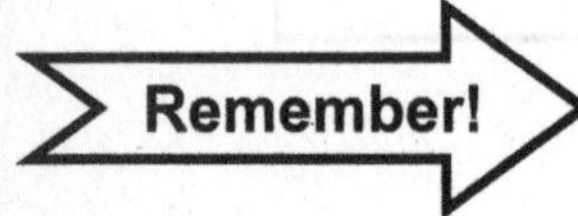

The transitions connecting the body paragraphs will depend upon the lecture topic.

G

1 *transition*

2 *transition*

3 *transition*

C

Step #2 **Listen to the lecture.**

When the narrator is finished giving instructions, you will hear the lecture.

Read along as you listen to a sample lecture.

Animal behavior can be classified according to the time of day an animal is active. Animals, such as horses, elephants and most birds, are said to be diurnal because they are active during the day and rest at night. Those animals active at dawn and dusk are said to be crepuscular. Beetles, skunks and rabbits fall into this category. The third group are those animals that sleep during the day and are active at night. They are called nocturnal. A good example is the bat. Bats have highly developed eyesight, hearing and smell. This helps them avoid predators and locate food. Being nocturnal also helps them avoid high temperatures during the day, especially in deserts where temperatures can reach well over one hundred degrees Fahrenheit. There are two types of bat: micro bats, or true bats, and mega bats, also called fruit bats. Let's start with mega bats.

Size wise, mega bats range from two to sixteen inches in length. Mega bats have extremely sensitive sight and smell. This helps them locate the flowers and fruit upon which they feed. It is while eating that mega bats play an important role in the distribution of plants. Like bees, mega bats serve as pollinators. When they lick nectar or eat flowers, their bodies become covered in pollen which they, in turn, carry to other trees and plants thereby acting as pollinators. In fact, many of the fruits and vegetables on our tables, such as bananas and peaches, would not be there if mega bats did not pollinate plants and trees.

Next are micro bats. As the name implies, micro bats are quite small, about the size of a mouse. To find food, micro bats use echolocation, high frequency sounds they bounce off insects. The most common micro bat is the vesper or evening bat. Like mega bats, micro bats play an important role in the environment. The average vesper bat, for example, can eat one thousand mosquitoes in one night. By doing so, they control the mosquito population.

Identifying the Premise

Identifying and summarizing the premise is the first task. The premise will be stated in the topic sentence.

The premise will be the first or second sentence. Be ready for it. If you miss the premise, the rest of the lecture will be difficult to comprehend.

As you know from previous tasks, the premise will be expressed using a rhetorical strategy. A date in the premise will signal the rhetorical strategy of narration, for example:

In 1793, Eli Whitney invented the cotton gin and revolutionized the cotton industry in the American south.

The premise might employ the rhetorical strategy of process...

Extracting DNA from old bones is a complicated and time-consuming process. First, you must...

Or description...

Pangea was a supercontinent that existed during the Mesozoic and the Paleozoic eras approximately 250 million years ago.

Or cause-and-effect...

Exercising is an excellent way to reduces stress.

Or compare-and-contrast...

In the mid-nineteenth century, two diametrically opposite art movements emerged: Impressionism in France and the Pre-Raphaelite Brotherhood in England.

Or definition...

Revolution 1.0 and 2.0 refer to the Tunisian and Egyptian revolutions of 2011, popular uprisings that used social media to spread their messages.

The premise might also employ the rhetorical strategy of **classification**, as does the premise in the topic sentence in the sample lecture.

> **Animal behavior can be classified according to the time of day an animal is active**. Animals, such as horses, elephants and most birds, are said to be diurnal because...

After you identify the premise, summarize. To summarize identify and generally describe the **premise** and, for this sample, *each animal classification.*

> G **animal behavior classified according to time of day**
>
> *day is diurnal – eat during day, sleep at night, humans horses, elephants*
> *twilight is crepuscular – active dawn and dusk, beetles, rabbits, skunks*
> *night is nocturnal – sleep during day, active at night*

General to Specific

The premise (general) will be followed by supporting illustrations (specific) identified by **transitional signal words**. It there are no transitional signal words, look for new topic nouns.

> Animal behavior can be classified according to the time of day an animal is active. Animals, such as horses, elephants and most birds, are said to be diurnal because they are active during the day and rest at night. Those animals active at dawn and dusk are said to be crepuscular. Beetles, skunks and rabbits fall into this category. The third group are those animals that sleep during the day and are active at night. They are called nocturnal. A good example is the bat. Bats have highly developed eyesight, hearing and smell. This helps them avoid predators and locate food. Being nocturnal also helps them avoid high temperatures during the day, especially in deserts where temperatures can reach well over one hundred degrees Fahrenheit.
>
> transition → **There are two types of bat: micro bats, or true bats, and mega bats, also called fruit bats. Let's start with mega bats.**
>
> Size wise, mega bats range from two to sixteen inches in length. Mega bats have extremely sensitive sight and smell. This helps them locate the flowers and fruit upon which they feed. It is while eating that mega bats play a important role in the distribution of plants. Like bees, mega bats serve as pollinators. When they lick nectar or eat flowers, their bodies become covered in pollen which they, in turn, carry to other trees and plants thereby acting as pollinators. In fact, many of the fruits and vegetables on our tables, such as bananas and peaches, would not be there if mega bats did not pollinate plants and trees.
>
> (continued on the next page)

Next are micro bats. As the name implies, micro bats are quite small, about the size of a mouse. To find food, micro bats use echolocation, high frequency sounds they bounce off insects. The most common micro bat is the vesper or evening bat. Like mega bats, micro bats play an important role in the environment. The average vesper bat, for example, can eat one thousand mosquitoes in one night. By doing so, they control the mosquito population.

In this lecture, note how the general (nocturnal animal) transitions into the specific (the bat), which is classified into two specific sub groups. The sub groups are the supporting illustrations (2TiC). They, in turn, develop the topic (nocturnal animal). This demonstrates organization (**O**PDUL=C), progression (O**P**DUL=C), topical unity-synthesis (OPD**U**L=C), and coherence (OPDUL=**C**).

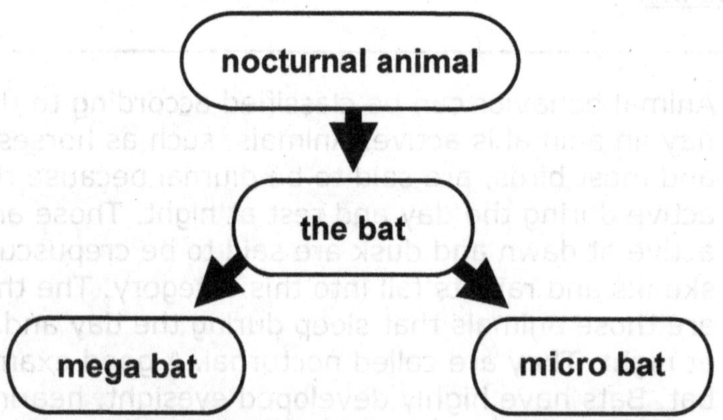

Next, summarize the supporting illustrations and the conclusion. Note the *transitions of addition* (**T**iC) and the **cause**-and-*effect* relationship (Ti**C**) in each body paragraph.

1 *first* mega bats, 2 - 16 inches
good eyesight and smell, helps bat find food = flowers and fruit
like bees **mega bats pollinate plants + tree** *good for environment, we get peaches, bananas*

2 *next* micro bats, size of mouse
use echolocation to find food = insects
micro bats eat 1,000 mosquitoes a night *good for controlling mosquitoes*

3 also

C These examples add to and support the reading

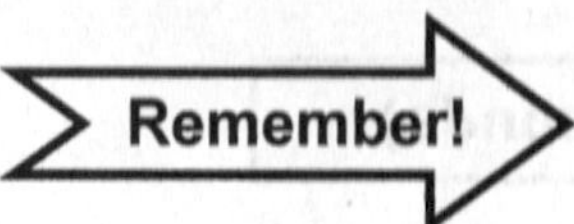

The number of supporting illustrations (TiC) depends on how ETS designs the task. There might be one, two, or three supporting illustrations. Be prepared for three (G+3TiC=C).

Transitions

The transitions that connect the body paragraphs (**T**iC) are determined by the rhetorical strategy in the premise. For example, the premise might use the rhetorical strategy of description and process.

> *Early in his career, Picasso moved through three stylistic periods: Blue, Rose, and African.*

In this lecture, each of Picasso's artistic periods will be developed in a separate body paragraph. The transitions (**T**iC) connecting the body paragraphs will be steps: *First, the Blue Period...Next Rose...Finally, African*...etc.

The premise might also use compare-and-contrast, for example:

> *British and German castles represent two distinct styles of medieval architecture.*

In this lecture, the two castle types will be developed in separate body paragraphs connected by a transition(s) of contrast: *British castles are...However, German castles were*...etc.

The premise might also be defined by cause-and-effect.

> *The psychologist Abraham Maslow believed that humans are motivated by unsatisfied needs.*

In this lecture, the topic sentence of each body paragraph might be a cause-and-effect relationship, for example: *When humans are hungry, they eat. This behavior is typical of...* or *Humans also take action when they feel an emotional attraction.*

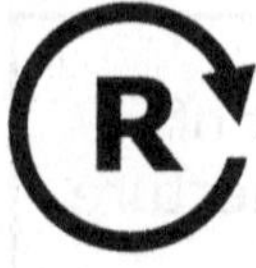

TOEFL will teach you about the topic in the lecture. To do so, TOEFL starts with a general topic introduction (G = premise) supported by specific supporting illustrations (2TiC or 3TiC). (For more, see TOEFL as Teacher, page 185).

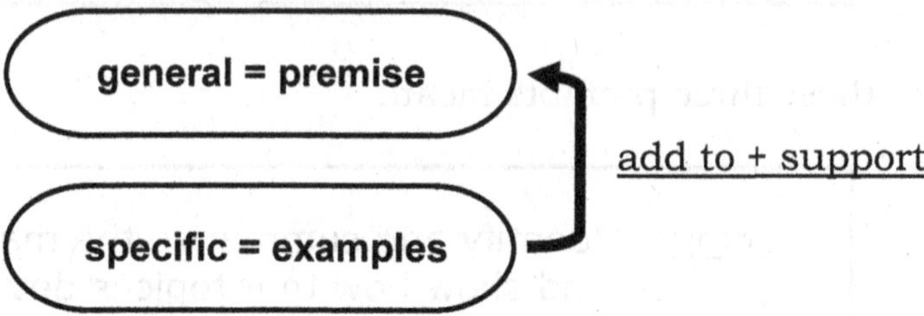

Step #3 **Read the prompt; prepare your response (20 seconds).**

When the lecture ends, it will leave your screen. You cannot replay it. The lecture will be replaced by the prompt. The narrator will read it.

TOEFL® *Speaking Task Six*

Question 6 of 6

The lecture illustrates how animal behavior is classified. Show how the information in the lecture supports this classification.

Preparation Time: 20 seconds

Response Time: 60 seconds

Remember! *The prompt for this task can be phrased different ways, for example:*

Prompt — Summarize the main points in the lecture and show how bats are an important part of the environment.

Prompt — According to the lecture, bats are a critical part of the environment. How do the examples in the lecture develop and illustrate this point?

Translated, these three prompts mean:

Prompt — Identify and summarize the main topic in the lecture and show how that topic is developed and supported by specific examples.

Step #4 **Prepare your response (20 seconds).**

After the narrator reads the prompt, you will have 20 seconds to prepare your response. The preparation clock will countdown (20, 19, 18...).

Step #5 **Speak (60 seconds).**

When the preparation clock reaches zero, you will hear a "Beep!" Look at your note map. Start speaking. Remember to speak objectively.

Prompt	Summarize the main points in the lecture and show how bats are an important part of the environment.

general summary →	The lecture classifies animal behavior three ways. Diurnal animals are active during the day and sleep at night. Crepuscular animals are active at dawn and dusk. Nocturnal animals hunt at night and rest during the day. An example of a nocturnal animal is the bat.
transition →	The lecture says there are two kinds of bats: mega bats and micro bats.
specific summary →	First are mega bats. They eat fruit and flowers. As they eat, seeds fall to the forest floor. This is good for the environment because new trees grow. Mega bats also pollinate. When they eat, their bodies get covered with pollen which they carry to other flowers. The lecture says without mega bats pollinating, we would not have peaches or bananas.
specific summary →	Next are micro bats. They use echolocation to find insects. A micro bat can eat 1,000 mosquitoes a night. This controls mosquitoes and is good for the environment.
conclusion →	These examples illustrate how bats are an important part of the environment.

Note in the above response that there are two supporting illustrations (2TiC): mega bats and micro bats.

Mapped out, you can see how G+2TiC=C gives the speaking raters what they are trained to listen for: an integrated, fact-based argument that demonstrates OPDUL=C. The summarized premise (G) and the conclusions (C) are underlined, the transitions (T) are in **bold**, and the summarized supporting illustrations (i) are in *italics*.

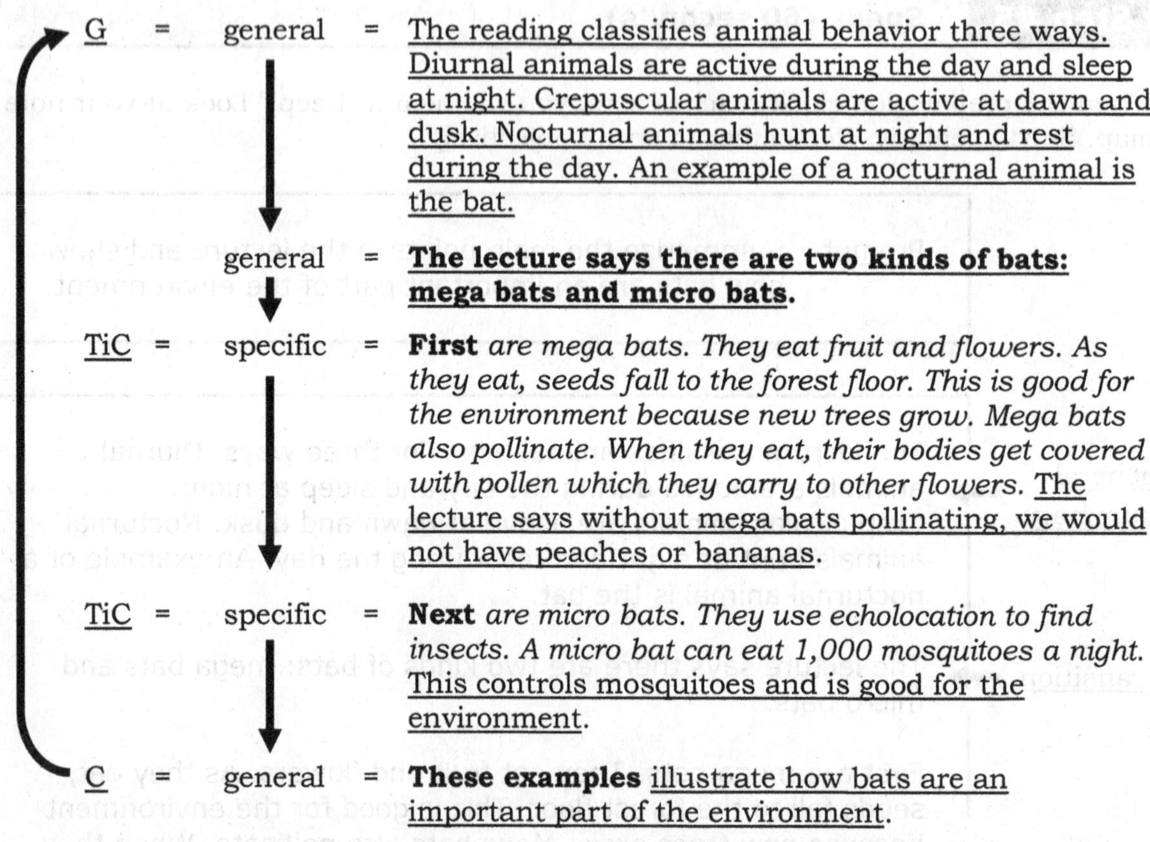
G = general = The reading classifies animal behavior three ways. Diurnal animals are active during the day and sleep at night. Crepuscular animals are active at dawn and dusk. Nocturnal animals hunt at night and rest during the day. An example of a nocturnal animal is the bat.
general = **The lecture says there are two kinds of bats: mega bats and micro bats.**
TiC = specific = **First** *are mega bats. They eat fruit and flowers. As they eat, seeds fall to the forest floor. This is good for the environment because new trees grow. Mega bats also pollinate. When they eat, their bodies get covered with pollen which they carry to other flowers.* The lecture says without mega bats pollinating, we would not have peaches or bananas.
TiC = specific = **Next** *are micro bats. They use echolocation to find insects. A micro bat can eat 1,000 mosquitoes a night.* This controls mosquitoes and is good for the environment.
C = general = **These examples** illustrate how bats are an important part of the environment.

How Long Should My Response Be?

The following map illustrates approximate time divisions for each step of this task. Remember: You are reading this example. On test day, you will pause and hesitate when you speak thus use more time.

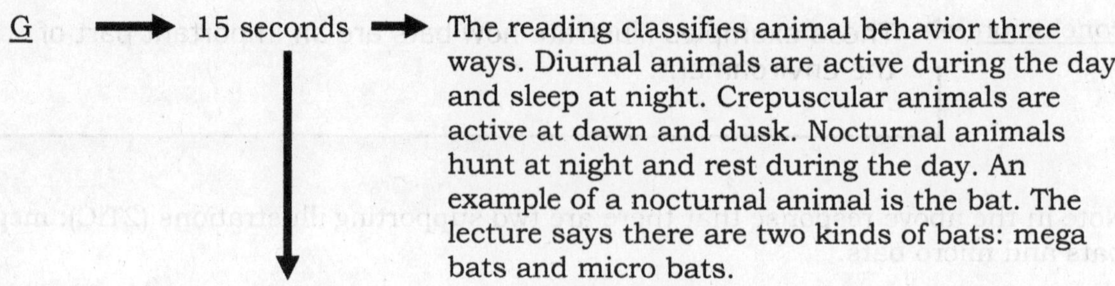
G → 15 seconds → The reading classifies animal behavior three ways. Diurnal animals are active during the day and sleep at night. Crepuscular animals are active at dawn and dusk. Nocturnal animals hunt at night and rest during the day. An example of a nocturnal animal is the bat. The lecture says there are two kinds of bats: mega bats and micro bats.

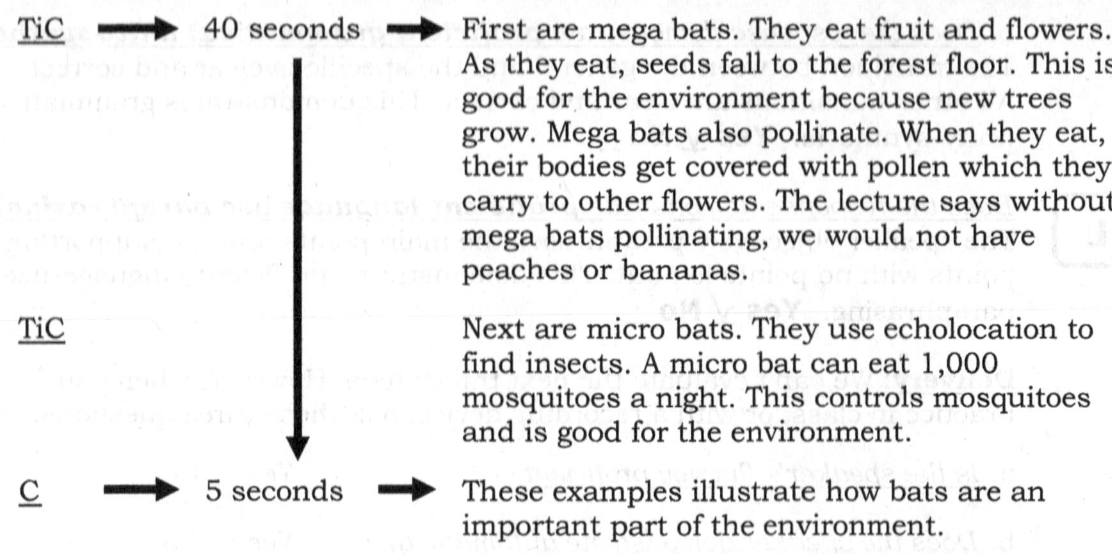
TiC
40 seconds
First are mega bats. They eat fruit and flowers. As they eat, seeds fall to the forest floor. This is good for the environment because new trees grow. Mega bats also pollinate. When they eat, their bodies get covered with pollen which they carry to other flowers. The lecture says without mega bats pollinating, we would not have peaches or bananas.
TiC
Next are micro bats. They use echolocation to find insects. A micro bat can eat 1,000 mosquitoes a night. This controls mosquitoes and is good for the environment.
C
5 seconds
These examples illustrate how bats are an important part of the environment.

Next, check the sample response for OPDUL=C.

O *Does the response demonstrate **organization**?*
The speaker uses deduction as a method of summarizing the main points in the lecture. This demonstrates organization. **Yes √ No _**

P *Does the response demonstrate **progression**?*
Because the speaker is using deduction, the response progresses from general to specific. This demonstrates progression. **Yes √ No _**

D a. *Does the introduction demonstrate **development-summarization**?*
The speaker has summarized the general classification of animal behavior, and under which classifications bats fall. This demonstrates introduction development-summarization. **Yes √ No _**

b. *Does the body demonstrate **development-summarization**?*
The speaker has summarized two specific types of bat and illustrated how they are good for the environment. This demonstrates body development-summarization. **Yes √ No _**

c. *Does the conclusion demonstrate **development-summarization**?*
The speaker concludes by summarizing how bats are good for the environment. **Yes √ No _**

U a. *Does the response demonstrate **topical unity-synthesis**?*
The speaker focuses on animal classification in general with two bat examples to develop this classification. There are no topic digressions. This demonstrates topical unity-synthesis. **Yes √ No _**

b. *Does the response demonstrate* ***proficient grammatical unity-synthesis****?*
The transition between the general and the specific is clear and correct. All other transitions are clear and correct. This demonstrates grammatical unity-synthesis. **Yes √ No _**

L *Does the response demonstrate* ***proficient language-use paraphrasing****?*
The speaker objectively paraphrases the main points and the supporting points with no points left out. This demonstrates proficient language-use paraphrasing. **Yes √ No _**

Delivery: We can't evaluate the next three steps. However, when you practice in class, or with a recording device, ask these three questions.

a. *Is the speaker's fluency proficient?* Yes __ No __

b. *Does the speaker demonstrate automaticity?* Yes __ No __

c. *Is the speaker's pronunciation proficient?* Yes __ No __

Note: For this response, the speaker's delivery was proficient.

C *Does the response demonstrate* ***coherence****?*
Because of Organization, Progression, Development-summarization, Unity-synthesis and Language-use paraphrasing, the speaker has proficiently summarized the main points in the lecture and demonstrated "how bats are a critical part of the environment." This demonstrates coherence.
Yes √ No _

Note: When you practice, use a recording device or get your class and instructor to help you with your revision checklist. After you identify areas that lack coherence, repeat the same response until the coherence level increases.

TASK: Rate the response on page 364 using the *Integrated Speaking Rating Guide* on page 704. Compare your rating to the one on page 797. Note: For this response, the speaker's delivery was proficient.

Three Common Speaking Problems

Avoid these problem areas when delivering a response for this task.

1. *Lack of General Development-Summarization*

When summarizing the lecture, make sure you identify the main topic and how it is developed either by definition, process, classification, narration, description, compare-and-contrast, or cause-and-effect.

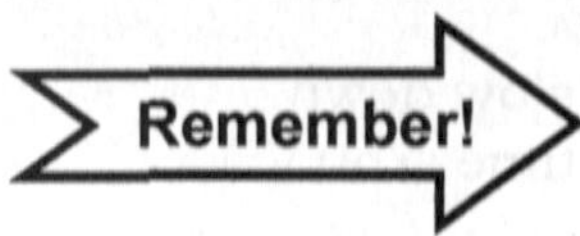

*A lack of general development-summarization (OP**D**UL=C) will result in a lack of unity-synthesis (OPD**U**L=C), specifically a lack of topical unity between the general (G) and the specific (3TiC). This will result in a lack of coherence (OPDUL=**C**) and a lower score.*

2. *Lack of Specific Development-Summarization*

When summarizing the lecture, make sure you identify the correct number of supporting illustrations (TiC, 2TiC, 3TiC). Also, make sure you identify the cause-and-effect relationship in each. The cause-and-effect relationships are the reasons that support and develop each example which, in turn, "add to and support" the general topic.

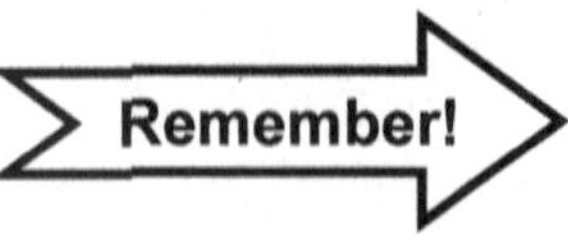

*A lack of specific development-summarization (OP**D**UL=C) will result in a lack of unity-synthesis (OPD**U**L=C), specifically a lack of topical unity between the general (G) and the specific (2TiC, 3TiC). This will result in a lack of coherence (OPDUL=**C**) and a lower score.*

3. *Mixing Verb Tenses*

When you summarize the lecture, use a consistent verb tense. If you start off using the present tense (*The lecture says that...*), do not change to the past tense (*The lecture said that...*)

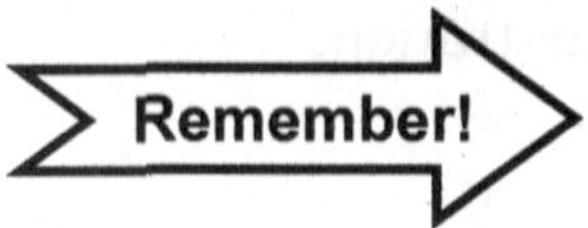

*Mixing verb tenses demonstrates a lack of unity-synthesis, specifically a lack of grammatical unity (OPD**U**L=C). This will result in a lack of coherence (OPDUL=**C**) and a lower score.*

Help! – *My Response is Too Long!*

The following are reasons why your response is longer than 60 seconds.

Reason #1 Your summary of the general topic is too long.

Solution
1. Make your summary shorter.
2. Avoid details like dates, places, costs, etc.
3. Speak faster; try not to hesitate.

Reason #2 When the clock starts, you are not speaking right away. That means you are losing valuable seconds at the start.

Solution
1. Start speaking right after the beep. Remember: *The speaking tasks come up fast. Be ready for them.*

Reason #3 You are being too careful. When you are too careful, you slow down to pronounce correctly. When you slow down, you waste time. You also decrease fluency and automaticity.

Solution
1. Speak at a normal pace.
2. Record your voice, then play it back. You will know if you are speaking too slowly. If so, speak faster.

Reason #4 You are pausing or hesitating too much. Record your voice and play it back. You will soon know if you are pausing or hesitating too much. Pausing and hesitating waste time. Pausing and hesitating will also decrease fluency and automaticity.

Solution
1. Avoid pauses; try not to hesitate.
2. Practice reading the sample responses.
3. Ask a native speaker to demonstrate the right speed.

Reason #5 You are pausing or hesitating too much because you did not summarize the lecture using G+3TiC=C.

Solution
1. Memorize G+3TiC=C.
2. Practice one response over and over until you are confident summarizing the lecture using G+3TiC=C.

Reason #6 Your summary of the lecture contains too much information.

Solution
1. Summarize only the main topic in each supporting illustration.
2. Reduce the number of details (dates, costs, ages, etc).

Reason #7 The conclusion is too long.

Solution
1. State the conclusion in one sentence.
2. State the conclusion in 5 seconds or less.

Reason #8 The clock makes you nervous so you blank out.

Solution
1. Do not time yourself when you practice. Just speak. When you are more confident, time yourself.

Help! – *My Response is Too Short!*

The following are reasons why your response is too short.

Reason #1 You are nervous. When you are nervous, you speak too fast and finish too soon.

Solution
1. Record your voice and play it back. You will soon know if you are speaking too fast. If so, slow down.
2. Do not time yourself. Just speak at a regular speed.

Reason #2 Your summary of the lecture is too short.

Solution
1. Make sure you have identified the main topic in the general introduction.
2. Make sure you have identified the each supporting illustration in the body.

Reason #3 You speak, then suddenly stop because you are shy, afraid, or feel stupid.

Solution
1. Practice reading into a recording device. Read an English magazine article or a book while recording. This will help you develop confidence speaking into a microphone.
2. Take an ESL class to develop your speaking skills and confidence.
3. Practice. Practice. Practice.

Reason #4 You are not confident using G+3TiC=C.

Solution
1. Practice developing and delivering one response until you have memorized G+3TiC=C and can remember it automatically without notes.
2. Practice. Practice. Practice.

Reason #5 You blank out.

Solution
1. You are trying too hard or are too nervous. Try to relax. When you practice speaking, don't time yourself. Just speak until you are confident. When you are more confident, then time yourself.
2. Don't worry about fluency, automaticity and pronunciation. Just speak. The more you speak, the more confident you will become.

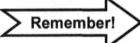

Start clean, end clean.

Emergency Response

What if you can't deliver a response for this task? What if you blank out? What should you do? Follow these two steps and deliver an emergency response.

Step #1 **Identify the main topic (20 seconds).**

After you listen to the lecture, look at your note map. Try and identify the main topic. The main topic is the most important part of this task. If you can identify the main topic, you might be able to remember the premise and the supporting illustrations.

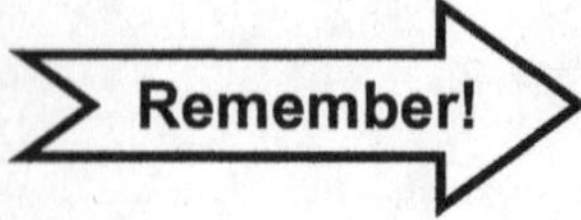

If you can remember only one point from the lecture, make sure it is the main topic.

Step #2 **Speak (60 seconds).**

If you can only remember the main topic—and not the supporting illustrations—then develop the main topic only.

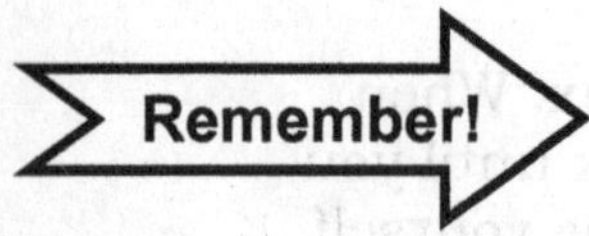

Don't stop talking. The more you talk, the more you think. The more you think, the more you might remember the main topic and the supporting illustrations.

Speaking Practice

Using G+2TiC=C or G+3TiC=C and the five steps, develop and deliver a response for each of the following tasks. Use a recording device so you can play back your responses and check them for coherence using the *Integrated Speaking Proficiency Checklist* on page 703. Rate each response using the *Integrated Speaking Rating Guide* on page 704.

Task #1

Directions: Listen to a lecture in a biology class.

Prompt According to the lecture, how did Charles Darwin revolutionize agricultural science?

Preparation Time: 20 seconds **Speaking Time: 60 seconds**

audio script page 726

Task #2

Directions: Listen to a lecture in a women's studies class.

<u>Prompt</u> The lecture talks about hormone replacement therapy (HRT). Summarize the recent history of HRT usage in the United States and its impact on women's health.

<u>Preparation Time</u>: 20 seconds **<u>Speaking Time</u>: 60 seconds**

audio script page 726

Task #3

Directions: Listen to a lecture in a sociology class.

Audio Track #34

Prompt How does the lecture define and develop the concept of white-collar crime?

Preparation Time: 20 seconds **Speaking Time: 60 seconds**

audio script page 727

Task #4

Directions: Listen to a lecture in an astronomy class.

Audio Track #35

Prompt According to the lecture, what are the origins of space junk and why is it a problem?

Preparation Time: 20 seconds **Speaking Time: 60 seconds**

audio script page 727

Task #5

Audio Track #36

Directions: Listen to a lecture in a marine biology class.

Prompt What does the lecture teach us about sharks?

Preparation Time: 20 seconds **Speaking Time: 60 seconds**

audio script page 728

Speaking Test

Directions: Complete each of the following tasks, then rate yourself using the rating guides, pages 700-706. Keep track of each score on page 392. When you are finished the speaking test, learn how to calculate your speaking section range score on page 391, then calculate your speaking range score on page 392.

Independent Speaking: Task #1

Prompt Why do people take photographs? Give examples and reasons to support your argument.

Preparation Time: 15 seconds **Speaking Time: 45 seconds**

Independent Speaking: Task #2

Prompt Do you prefer reading traditional, paper-based books or from a computer screen? Why? Give examples and reasons to support your position.

Preparation Time: 15 seconds **Speaking Time: 45 seconds**

Integrated Speaking: Task #3

Directions: Shelton University is introducing a new computer policy. Read about the new policy. You have 45 seconds.

Announcement from the Dean

Starting next semester, students at Shelton University will not be allowed to use laptop computers during class time. Any student using a laptop computer during class time will be asked to turn it off or leave the room. This policy is in response to complaints saying that increased laptop usage during class time is noisy and distracting. Laptop usage will be permitted in all main campus areas, including libraries and food service areas. If you have any questions regarding this policy, please feel free to contact the Dean. Office hours are Monday-Friday 9 to 5pm.

Directions: Now listen as two students discuss the announcement.

Audio Track #37

(This task continues on the next page.)

<u>Prompt</u> The woman expresses her opinion about the new policy. State her opinion and explain the reasons she gives for maintaining that position.

<u>Preparation Time</u>: 30 seconds **<u>Speaking Time</u>: 60 seconds**

audio script page 728

Integrated Speaking: Task #4

Directions: Read the following passage on the Green Revolution. You have 45 seconds.

The Green Revolution

The Green Revolution of the 1960's had one goal: to eliminate famine worldwide. It did so by introducing the concept of industrialized agriculture. Prior to the Green Revolution, farming in less developed nations had changed little since man first planted seeds. Crop yields were unpredictable, insects uncontrollable, and disease impossible to fight. At the same time, the world's population was skyrocketing with famine threatening the lives of millions. To feed the world, agronomist engineers, like American Norman Ernest Borlaug, developed high-yielding cereal grains that were also disease resistant. At the same time, scientists developed synthetic fertilizers and pesticides. The result was the Green Revolution, a global revolution in which technology took control of the agricultural process. The results were immediate. Countries like Mexico were soon net exporters of wheat while in Pakistan and India, wheat yields doubled between 1965 and 1970.

Directions: Now listen to a lecture on the same topic.

Audio Track #38

(This task continues on the next page.)

<u>Prompt</u> What is the Green Revolution and what are its short and long term effects?

<u>Preparation Time</u>: 30 seconds **<u>Speaking Time</u>: 60 seconds**

audio script page 729

Integrated Speaking: Task #5

Audio Track #39

Directions: Listen to a conversation between a student and a professor.

Prompt The professor offers two solutions to the student's problem. Identify the problem and the solutions, then state which solution you think is best and why.

Preparation Time: 20 seconds **Speaking Time: 60 seconds**

audio script page 729

Integrated Speaking: Task #6

Audio Track #40

Directions: Listen to a lecture in a composition class.

(This task continues on the next page.)

<u>Prompt</u> According to the lecture, what are Aristotle's three appeals? Use examples to support your summary.

<u>Preparation Time</u>: 20 seconds **<u>Speaking Time</u>: 60 seconds**

audio script page 730

1. Calculate Your Speaking Range Score

After you complete the speaking test, follow these steps when calculating your speaking range score.

1. Identify the range score of each independent task using the *Independent Speaking Proficiency Checklist* and the *Independent Speaking Rating Guide.*

    for example your task #1 range score = 2.5 - 3.0 / 4
    for example your task #2 range score = 2.5 - 3.0 / 4

2. Identify the range score of each integrated task using the *Integrated Speaking Proficiency Checklist* and the *Integrated Speaking Rating Guide.*

    for example your task #3 range score = 2.5 - 3.0 / 4
    for example your task #4 range score = 2.5 - 3.0 / 4
    for example your task #5 range score = 2.5 - 3.0 / 4
    for example your task #6 range score = 2.5 - 3.0 / 4

3. Total the scores, then divide by 6 tasks to find your average speaking range score.

task #1	2.5 - 3.0
task #2	2.5 - 3.0
task #3	2.5 - 3.0
task #4	2.5 - 3.0
task #5	2.5 - 3.0
task #6	2.5 - 3.0
total	15.0 - 18.0

15.0 / 6 = 2.5   18.0 / 6 = 3.0 ➔ **2.5 - 3.0 / 4** = average range score

5. Convert your average range score (2.5 - 3.0) to a speaking section range score.

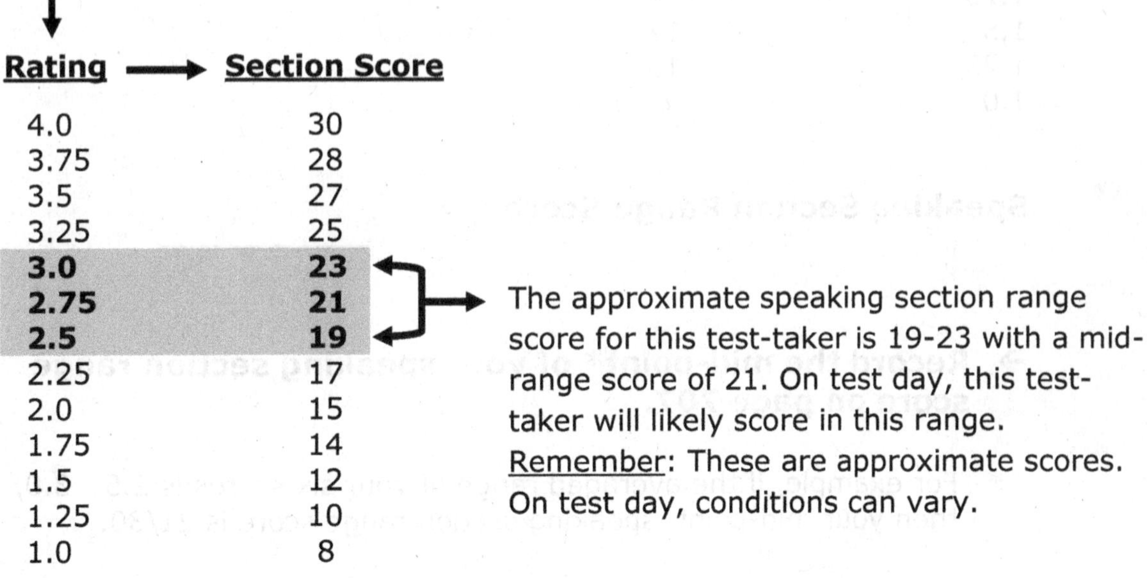

Rating	Section Score
4.0	30
3.75	28
3.5	27
3.25	25
3.0	**23**
2.75	**21**
2.5	**19**
2.25	17
2.0	15
1.75	14
1.5	12
1.25	10
1.0	8

The approximate speaking section range score for this test-taker is 19-23 with a mid-range score of 21. On test day, this test-taker will likely score in this range. Remember: These are approximate scores. On test day, conditions can vary.

2. Calculate Your Speaking Section Range Score

Speaking Task #1 = / 4

Speaking Task #2 = / 4

Speaking Task #3 = / 4

Speaking Task #4 = / 4

Speaking Task #5 = / 4

Speaking Task #6 = / 4

total = / 24

Divide the total by 6 = / 4 = your rating

Convert your rating to a speaking section range score.

Rating →	Speaking Section Range Score
4.0	30
3.75	28
3.5	27
3.25	25
3.0	23
2.75	21
2.5	19
2.25	17
2.0	15
1.75	14
1.5	12
1.25	10
1.0	8

Speaking Section Range Score = ________

➔ **Record the mid-point* of your speaking section range score on page 707.**

* For example, if the averaged range of your six scores is 2.5 - 3.0, then your mid-point, speaking section range score is 21/30.

Calculating Your Official Speaking Score

According to ETS, each spoken response will be scored by 3 to 6 different certified raters. The response for each task is rated on a scale from 0 to 4. The average of all six ratings is averaged to a scaled score of 0 to 30.[4] For example, three raters have scored your independent speaking task #1. The average of their three scores is your score for speaking task #1.

Rater 1 = 4.0/4

Rater 2 = 4.0/4

Rater 3 = 4.0/4

average = 12/12

12 / 3 raters = 4/4 = your score for task #1

ETS will do the same for all six speaking tasks. The average of your six speaking scores will be your speaking section score.

Speaking Task 1 = 4.0/4

Speaking Task 2 = 3.0/4

Speaking Task 3 = 4.0/4

Speaking Task 4 = 3.0/4

Speaking Task 5 = 4.0/4

Speaking Task 6 = 3.0/4

total = 21/24

21 / 6 tasks = 3.5/4 = your averaged speaking score

ETS will convert your averaged speaking score (3.5) into a final speaking section score out of 30.

3.5 = 27/30 = your speaking section score

Your final speaking score (27/30) will appear with your other section scores under your photograph on your official *TOEFL Internet-Based Test Examine Score Report.*

---

[4] TOEFL® iBT Tips, How to Prepare for the TOEFL iBT® , Page 26, Educational Testing Services, 2008

Notes

Listening Section

The listening section is the second section on the TOEFL iBT.

Reading | **Listening** | Speaking | Writing

The listening section will last between 60-90 minutes. This section measures your ability to understand "authentic speech patterns" used in academic (formal) and non academic (informal) situations. Authentic speech patterns include hesitations, digressions, self-corrections, repetitions, false starts, and idioms.

Prompt Types

The TOEFL iBT measures listening proficiency using conversation and lecture prompts. The conversations and lectures will be either opinion-based or fact-based arguments. You cannot change the task order. You must also answer the questions in order. You cannot jump to question four, then go back to question one, etc. You can take notes.

PROMPT	NUMBER	LENGTH	QUESTIONS
Conversations	2-3	2-3 minutes each	5
Lectures	4-6	4-6 minutes each	6

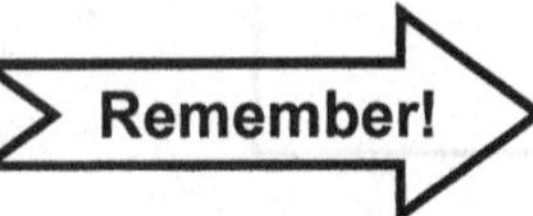

A lecture is a three-part, verbal argument. A conversation is also a three-part, verbal argument.

You have already studied opinion-based and fact-based arguments in the writing and speaking sections. You will recycle those strategies when learning listening strategies. By recycling speaking and writing argument strategies, you will continue to see how the TOEFL iBT uses opinion-based and fact-based arguments for testing English language proficiency in the listening section. You will also see how the TOEFL iBT's testing methodology is predictable due to its repeating design.

Sound Check

Before you begin the listening section, you will do a sound check. Follow the on-screen directions. Adjust the headset and volume as needed. If you are having problems, immediately alert the site manager.

Directions

The directions for the listening section are below. Because the listening directions do not change, skip over them on test day and go directly to the first task.

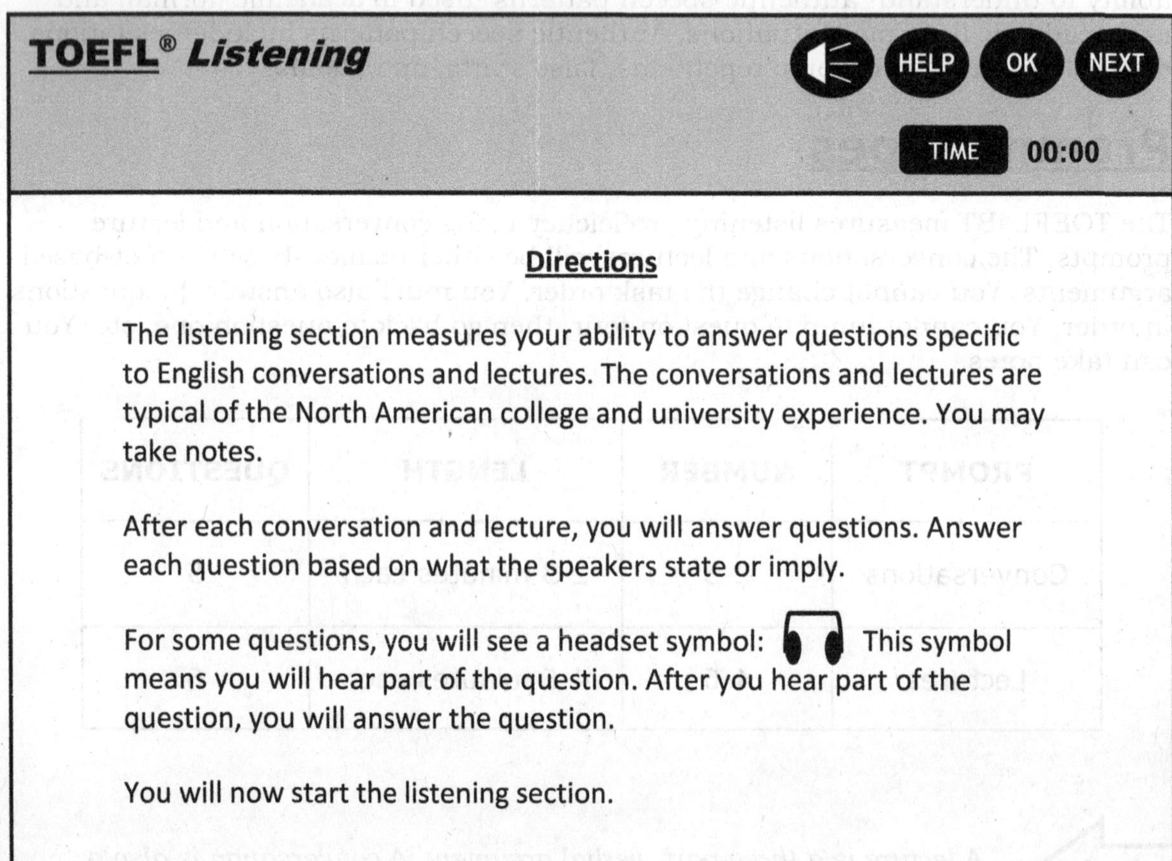

TOEFL® Listening
HELP
OK
NEXT
TIME
00:00
Directions
The listening section measures your ability to answer questions specific to English conversations and lectures. The conversations and lectures are typical of the North American college and university experience. You may take notes.
After each conversation and lecture, you will answer questions. Answer each question based on what the speakers state or imply.
For some questions, you will see a headset symbol: This symbol means you will hear part of the question. After you hear part of the question, you will answer the question.
You will now start the listening section.

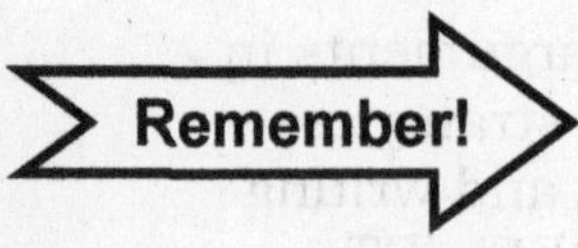

The clock will not run when you listen to a conversation or a lecture. The clock will run only when you answer questions. That means you control how much time you need to answer each question.

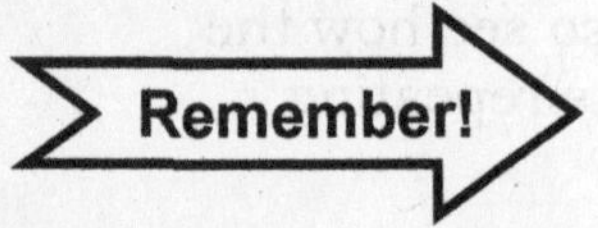

If you do not know an answer, guess. You will not lose points for a wrong answer, so answer everything. <u>Never</u> leave a question unanswered.

Conversation Prompts

There are two conversation prompt types: office hours and service encounters. Both prompt types are based on real-life campus situations. The speakers will speak naturally using authentic speech patterns.

Office Hours

For this prompt type, a student will talk to a professor in his or her office. The student and the professor will formally discuss an academic topic. Common topics are methods of research, a student's request for a project extension, a student's request for help with homework, and a student's attendance record.

Service Encounters

For this prompt type, a student will talk to a campus employee, such as a librarian, an admissions officer, or IT support. The student and the employee will informally discuss a campus-related topic. Common topics are how to use the library for research, arranging housing, parking problems, and applying for scholarships.

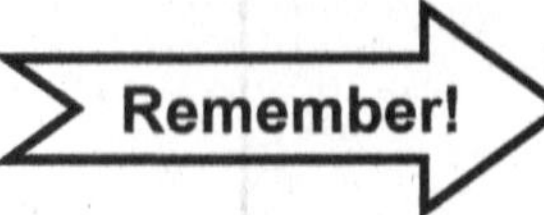

You cannot replay the conversations or the questions, so be prepared to take notes. The test center will supply paper and pencils.

Office-Hours Conversations

An analysis of this prompt type begins by listening to a test sample.

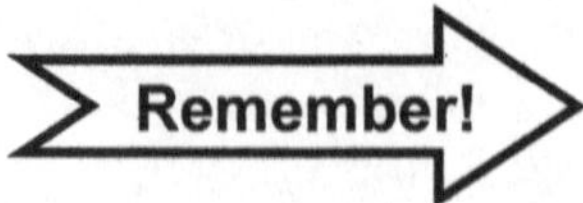
Remember!

When answering questions, do not look for perfect answers. There are no perfect answers on the TOEFL iBT. Instead, look for the closest possible answer.

Sample: Office-Hours Conversation
Audio
Track
#41

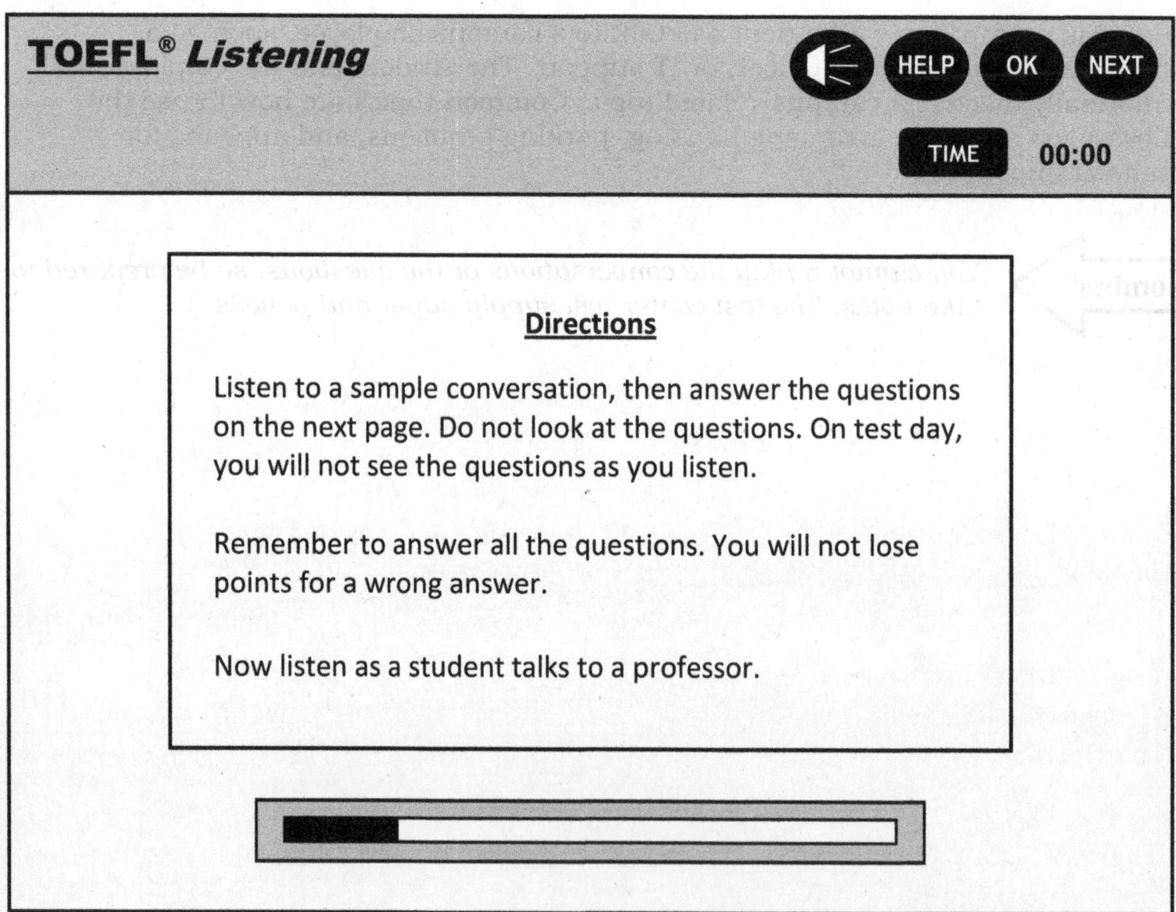
TOEFL® Listening
HELP
OK
NEXT
TIME
00:00
Directions
Listen to a sample conversation, then answer the questions on the next page. Do not look at the questions. On test day, you will not see the questions as you listen.
Remember to answer all the questions. You will not lose points for a wrong answer.
Now listen as a student talks to a professor.

Questions

Directions: Now get ready to answer the questions. Answer each question based on what is stated or implied in the conversation.

#1

What are the student and the professor mainly discussing?

A) the student's opinion
B) the student's essay about illegal drugs
C) the student's attendance record
D) the student's most recent grade

#2

Why does the student visit the professor?

A) to learn how to write better essays
B) to find out why she got a low grade on her essay
C) to discuss the pros and cons of the marijuana debate
D) to ask for an extension

#3

In which areas does the student's essay need revising? Select two. This is a 1-point question.

A) the developer
B) the body
C) the thesis
D) the sentence variety

#4

What does the professor think about short essays?

A) One focused page is best.
B) Short essays always get high grades.
C) A focused, short essay is best.
D) A short essay never has an opinion.

#5

Listen again to part of the conversation, then answer the question.

What does the professor imply when she says this?

A) She thinks the student hates essay writing.
B) She thinks parts of the student's essay are scratched.
C) She thinks the student's essay lacks depth.
D) She thinks the student is on the wrong track.

➔ Answers: page 682.
➔ Scoring multi-answer questions: page 693.
➔ Audio script: page 731.

Office Hours: *Task Analysis*

In the sample office-hours prompt, the student has a problem and seeks help from a professor. The professor solves the student's problem by giving the student advice. This testing method is called *problem-solution.*

TOEFL uses the *problem-solution* testing method for speaking task #5. TOEFL recycles the same testing method for this task. The difference is the degree of formality. For speaking task #5, the two students speak informally (non academically). For this task, the student and the professor will speak formally (academically).

TOEFL's Testing Method

An understanding of TOEFL's testing method for this task begins with a rhetorical analysis of the sample office-hours conversation. This analysis will help you take effective notes and maximize scoring. Read as you listen to the sample conversation.

Sample: *Office-Hours Conversation*

Audio Track #41

Student
Professor Morgan? Hi. Do you have a minute?

Professor
Sure, Sue. Come in. What's up?

Student
I have a question about my essay you just gave back. Where should I start? I worked really hard on it and...Well, I thought I'd get a better grade. But...Yeah. Talk about a shock. Anyway, can you tell me why I got such a low grade?

Professor
Sure. Do you have the essay with you?

Student
Yes. Right here. It's on the question of legalizing marijuana. You asked us to pick a side and argue in favor of it. I took the pro side.

Professor
Yes. Now I remember. Let me take a look at it. Right. Right.

Student
Is it too short? Is that why I didn't get an A?

Professor
No. Length is really not an issue. Let me rephrase that. There's no connection between length and quality. Some might disagree, but frankly, some of the best essays I've graded have been short. Not one-page short, mind you, but, you know, a couple of really focused pages that address the subject with no extra verbiage. Some of the worst essays I've seen have been...Well, let's just leave it at that, shall we?

Student
Well, if length isn't a problem, then what is?

Professor
Well, it all starts with your opinion. Show me which sentence is your opinion?

Student
It's this one right...here.

Professor
Sorry, but that's not an opinion. You're simply telling me what you'll write about. Remember, your opinion must be arguable. Since you're arguing the pro side of the marijuana issue, you really need to state what you believe in no uncertain terms. By doing so, your audience will know from the start where you stand.

Student
That's exactly what I was having trouble with. My opinion.

Professor
Try this. Simply say, *Personally, I believe that...*, and then add what you believe. For example, *I believe that Americans should have the right to choose* or *I believe that marijuana should be legalized for medical purposes*. Got it?

Student
Yeah. Okay. I see.

Professor
Also, your opinion must be supportable. When I say supportable, I mean each sentence—sorry, I meant each body paragraph—must have one specific topic, then you must develop that topic in detail. Look at body paragraph one. You start off by saying *legalizing marijuana would be good for the economy* in the first sentence, then you suddenly switch to *it has many medical benefits* in the next sentence. This signals a clear lack of development of both topics.

Student
But that's what I believe.

Professor
Yes. But now we're talking the mechanics of developing and supporting your opinion. Do so by giving each supporting topic its own body paragraph. In this case, *legalizing marijuana would be good for the economy* is the topic of your first body paragraph, and *the medical benefits* is the topic of your second body paragraph.

Student
You mean, do what I did in paragraph three?

Professor
Exactly. In body paragraph three, you focus on how legalizing marijuana will decrease the crime rate. However, you still need to develop this topic in detail. Give an example. One with statistics. You know what I mean. Do the same for body paragraphs one and two. Remember: The more you develop your supporting examples, the more persuasive your argument will be. Right now, you're just scratching the surface. To be honest, this reads more like a first draft.

Student
I see what you mean. Can I rewrite it for a higher grade?

Professor
Sure. Can you have it on my desk by nine tomorrow morning?

Student
By nine? I'll try.

G+3TiC=C: *Mapping a Conversation*

An office-hours prompt combines two arguments: a fact-based argument and an opinion-based argument. The fact-based argument consists of general facts you can summarize. Those facts are not arguable. They are the premise, the topic of each body segment, and the conclusion. Inside the fact-based argument is an opinion-based argument. The opinion-based argument is the advice the professor gives the student. This *advice-giving process* occurs in the body of the conversation. Mapped out, the underlying structure of an office-hours prompt looks like this.

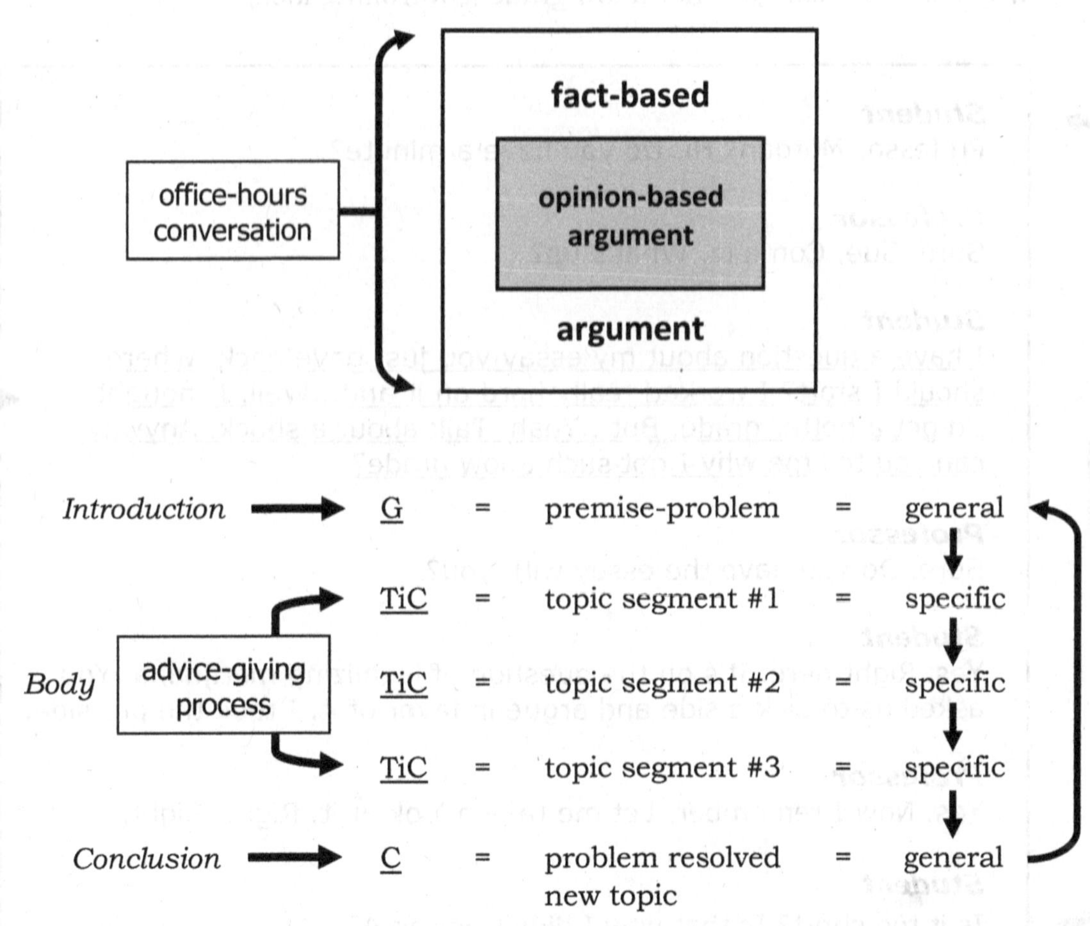

Note how the conclusion (C) in the sample conversation serves two rhetorical functions: 1) the student's problem is resolved; 2) a new topic is introduced.

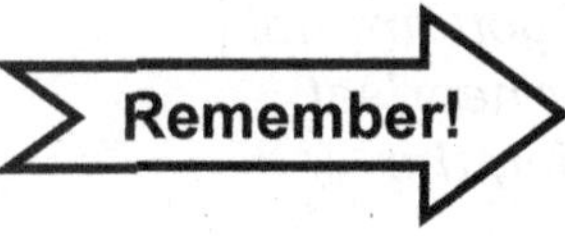

Note that there are no body paragraphs in the above map. Body paragraphs are specific to writing. Because this is a conversation, we will call each body paragraph a topic segment. A topic segment serves the same purpose as a body paragraph. Also, the number of topic segments will vary. There might be two topic segments (G+2TiC=C), three (G+3TiC=C), even four (G+4TiC=C). Be prepared for three.

Introduction

An office-hours prompt will start with a general introduction (G). It will introduce the premise. The premise will identify the main topic and the controlling idea. Combined, they are the problem. To identify the premise in the sample, ask, "What is the main topic?" Answer: *A student has a problem with her essay.* To find the controlling idea, ask, "What about it (the problem with her essay)?" Answer: *The student wants to know why her professor gave her a low grade.*

Premise: A student has a problem with her essay (main topic). She wants to know why her professor gave her a low grade (controlling idea).

G

Student
Professor Morgan? Hi. Do you have a minute?

Professor
Sure, Sue. Come in. What's up?

Student
I have a question about my essay you just gave back. Where should I start? I worked really hard on it and...Well, I thought I'd get a better grade. But...Yeah. Talk about a shock. Anyway, can you tell me why I got such a low grade?

Professor
Sure. Do you have the essay with you?

Student
Yes. Right here. It's on the question of legalizing marijuana. You asked us to pick a side and argue in favor of it. I took the pro side.

Professor
Yes. Now I remember. Let me take a look at it. Right. Right.

Student
Is it too short? Is that why I didn't get an A?

Sometimes the premise will be in the first line of dialogue. If you are not paying attention, if you are shuffling paper or adjusting your headset, you will miss it. If you miss, you will have difficulty answering the questions.

Remember!

Putting the premise in the first line of dialogue is a predictable TOEFL testing trick.

Topic Segments: *Advice-Giving Process*

In each topic segment (TiC), the professor will give the student advice. Giving advice means stating an opinion and supporting it with reasons. The professor's advice could be a course of action, a recommendation, a clarification, or all three. In topic segment one below from the sample, the advice starts with the professor analyzing the student's opinion. This is step one in the *advice-giving process*.

Professor
No. Length is really not an issue. Let me rephrase that. There's no connection between length and quality. Some might disagree, but frankly, some of the best essays I've graded have been short. Not one-page short, mind you, but, you know, a couple of really focused pages that address the subject with no extra verbiage. Some of the worst essays I've seen have been...Well, let's just leave it at that, shall we?

Student
Well, if length isn't a problem, then what is?

Professor
Well, it all starts with your opinion. Show me which sentence is your opinion?

start of the *advice-giving process*

Student
It's this one right...here.

Professor
Sorry, but that's not an opinion. You're simply telling me what you'll write about. Remember, your opinion must be arguable. Since you're arguing the pro side of the marijuana issue, you really need to state what you believe in no uncertain terms. By doing so, your audience will know from the start where you stand.

Student
That's exactly what I was having trouble with. My opinion.

Professor
Try this. Simply say, *Personally, I believe that...*, and then add what you believe. For example, *I believe that Americans should have the right to choose* or *I believe that marijuana should be legalized for medical purposes*. Got it?

Student
Yeah. Okay. I see.

In topic segment two below, the transition **Also** signals the next step in the advice-giving process: the topic of ***body paragraph development***. The professor develops this topic by giving the student advice about how to organize body paragraph topics and how to develop each topic. Combined, these form the illustration (i).

TiC

Professor
Also, your opinion must be supportable. When I say supportable, I mean each sentence—sorry, I meant ***each body paragraph—must have one specific topic, then you must develop that topic in detail***. Look at body paragraph one. You start off by saying *legalizing marijuana would be good for the economy* in the first sentence, then you suddenly switch to *it has many medical benefits* in the next sentence. This signals a clear lack of development of both topics.

Student
But that's what I believe.

Professor
Yes. But now we're talking the mechanics of developing and supporting your opinion. Do so by giving each supporting topic its own body paragraph. In this case, *legalizing marijuana would be good for the economy* is the topic of your first body paragraph and *the medical benefits* is the topic of your second body paragraph.

Student
You mean, do what I did in paragraph three?

Professor
Exactly. In body paragraph three, you focus on how legalizing marijuana will decrease the crime rate. However, you still need to develop this topic in detail. Give an example. One with statistics. You know what I mean. Do the same for body paragraphs one and two. Remember: The more you develop your supporting examples, the more persuasive your argument will be. **Right now, you're just scratching the surface. To be honest, this reads more like a first draft.**

Remember!

Note how the professor concludes this topic segment with an ***opinion****. Rhetorically, this is an opinion-insertion point. Make a note of opinion-insertion points. They are predictable testing points (see page 454 for more).*

Conclusion

The conversation will end with a short conclusion (C). In the conclusion, listen for a ***resolution to the problem*** and the introduction of a new topic. Often the new topic will contain an action that will be completed after the conversation ends.

Student
I see what you mean. ***Can I rewrite it for a higher grade?***

Professor
Sure. Can you have it on my desk by nine tomorrow morning?

Student
By nine? I'll try.

Rejoinders: *Identifying Transitions*

A conversation will not always have clear topic transitions. How can you identify topic transitions? By listening for rejoinders. For example, in the sample below, after the professor gives advice, the student says, *"I see" or "I understand."* These short sentences are called *rejoinders*. A rejoinder is a short reply of affirmation. They are part of language use (OPDU**L**=C). Rhetorically, rejoinders are transitional signal words telling you that *this is the conclusion of this topic segment and the start of the next.*

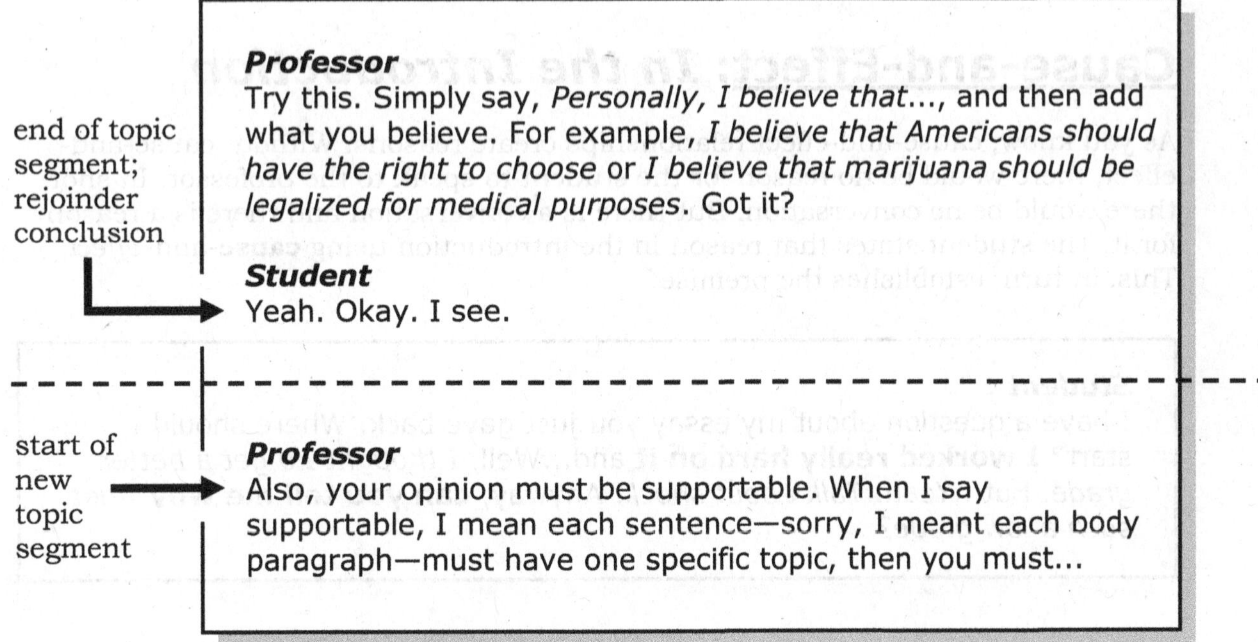

Professor
Try this. Simply say, *Personally, I believe that...*, and then add what you believe. For example, *I believe that Americans should have the right to choose* or *I believe that marijuana should be legalized for medical purposes*. Got it?

Student
Yeah. Okay. I see.

Professor
Also, your opinion must be supportable. When I say supportable, I mean each sentence—sorry, I meant each body paragraph—must have one specific topic, then you must...

Active-Passive Roles: *Rhetorical Functions*

Another way to identify topic segment transitions is by *active-passive roles*. Because the student is seeking advice, the student will listen to the professor. In other words, the student will play a *passive-listening role*. Because the professor will talk more, the professor will play an *active-advising role*. Because the professor is generally active and the student is generally passive, we can map out their rhetorical roles and the transitions based on their active-passive speech patterns.

G = premise

TiC = active professor gives first piece of advice
passive student rejoinder: "Wow, I never thought of that."

TiC = active professor gives second piece of advice
passive student rejoinder: "That's a good idea."

TiC = active professor gives third piece of advice
passive student rejoinder: "I understand."

C = problem solved + new topic introduced

Rhetorical Strategies

As you have seen, office-hours prompts consist of an outer, fact-based argument (general) and an inner, opinion-based argument (specific). This method of organization, general-specific-general, is predictable. The rhetorical strategies used are also predictable, the most important of which are cause-and-effect and process.

Cause-and-Effect: *In the Introduction*

As you know, cause-and-effect relationships create reasons. Without cause-and-effect, there would be no reason for the student to speak to the professor. In short, there would be no conversation. But there is a conversation and there is a reason for it. The student states that reason in the introduction using **cause**-and-*effect*. This, in turn, establishes the premise.

Student
I have a question about my essay you just gave back. Where should I start? **I worked really hard on it** and...Well, *I thought I'd get a better grade*. But...Yeah. *Talk about shock*. Anyway, **can you tell me why** *I got such a low grade*?

Cause-and-Effect: *In the Topic Segments*

Each topic segment will develop a specific topic. The professor will develop the topic by giving advice. That advice will be defined by **cause**-and-*effect*, for example.

1 This **cause**-and-*effect* relationship answers the student's question: Why did I get a low grade? Answer: A lack of development. Mapped out, the cause-and-effect relationship reads like this: **switch** (topics) (cause) = *lack of development* (effect) = *low grade* (effect).

2 Note how the professor uses **cause**-and-*effect* when advising how the student can get a higher grade. Mapped out, it reads like this: **give an example** (cause) = *more development* (effect) = *a more persuasive argument* (effect) = *a higher grade* (effect).

Professor
Also, your opinion must be supportable. When I say supportable, I mean each sentence—sorry, I meant each body paragraph—must have one specific topic, then you must develop that topic in detail. Look at body paragraph one.
1 **You start off by saying legalizing marijuana would be good for the economy in the first sentence, then you suddenly switch to it has many medical benefits in the next sentence.** *This signals a clear lack of development of both topics.*

Student
But that's what I believe.

Professor
Yes. But now we're talking the mechanics of developing and supporting your opinion. Do so by giving each supporting topic its own body paragraph. In this case, *legalizing marijuana would be good for the economy* is the topic of your first body paragraph and the medical benefits is the topic of your second body paragraph.

Student
You mean, do what I did in paragraph three?

Professor
Exactly. In body paragraph three, you focus on how legalizing marijuana will decrease the crime rate. However, you still need to develop this topic in detail.
2 **Give an example. One with statistics. You know what I mean. Do the same for body paragraphs one and two.** *Remember: the more you develop your supporting examples, the more persuasive your argument will be.* Right now, you're just scratching the surface. To be honest, this reads more like a first draft.

In each topic segment, information and attitudes will often be suggested by cause-and-effect. In the following example, the implied cause-and-effect relationship is in the student's rejoinder, "Yeah. Okay. I see."

Professor
Try this. Simply say, *Personally, I believe that...*, and then add what you believe. For example, *I believe that Americans should have the right to choose* or *I believe that marijuana should be legalized for medical purposes*. Got it?

rejoinder

Student
Yeah. Okay. I see.

In this context, "Yeah. Okay. I see" means, "Yes. I have heard your advice and I understand it." Mapped out using **cause**-and-*effect*, it reads like this:

The student has listened to the professor's advice (cause = "Yeah. Okay.") and now *the student understands how to improve her opinion* (effect = "I see.").

Cause-and-Effect: *In the Conclusion*

A cause-and-effect relationship will often appear in the conclusion. In the sample below, the student says, "I see what you mean." From this, we can infer that the student has listened to her professor's advice (cause) and now understands what she is doing wrong, and why she got a low grade (effect). Because the student understands (cause), her problem is solved (effect).

Student
I see what you mean. Can I rewrite it for a higher grade?

Professor
Sure. Can you have it on my desk by nine tomorrow morning?

Student
By nine? I'll try.

Note also how a new topic is introduced: "Can I rewrite it [my essay] for a higher grade?" The professor says, "Sure." From this, we can infer that the student will rewrite her essay and that—because she listened to her professor's advice—she will get a higher grade. Note how the future action is also a solution to the student's problem.

Process

In the sample, after the student states her problem, the professor gives her opinion and advice. It is a step-by-step, *advice-giving process.* The student, to solve her problem, and get a higher grade, will follow the professor's advice. Mapped out, the professor's *advice-giving process* reads like this.

Step #1: Rewrite the opinion.

Step #2: Support the opinion with examples.

Step #3: Develop the examples.

Step #4: Rewrite the essay

Step #5: Hand in the essay.

By combining process and cause-and-effect, you can see how these two rhetorical strategies develop the professor's opinion-based argument.

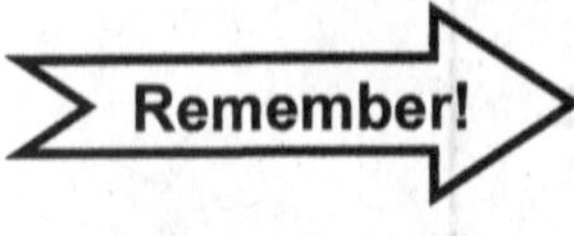

While listening, note the steps in the advice-giving process. Steps in the advice-giving process are often testing points for detail questions.

Cause-and-effect and process are not the only rhetorical strategies in a typical office-hours prompt. Within other office-hours prompts, there might be narration, compare-and-contrast, illustration, definition, classification, and/or description. Within the scope of this textbook, it is not possible to demonstrate how TOEFL uses each rhetorical strategy for testing purposes. However, the two rhetorical strategies you should focus on are cause-and-effect and process for the reasons described.

Now that you understand the rhetorical design of an office-hours prompt, let's integrate that knowledge with note-taking strategies. Accurate notes will help you answer questions more proficiently and maximize scoring on test day.

Note Taking: *Anticipating the Questions*

An important part of note taking is your ability to identify potential answers as you listen. From our analysis of an office-hours prompt, you know that an office-hours prompt will progress from general to specific to general (O**P**DUL=C). That means the questions will be in three predictable places: the introduction (premise), body (advice-giving process), conclusion (problem resolution + new topic). Using this three-part structure, divide a piece of note paper into the same three sections (see the next page).

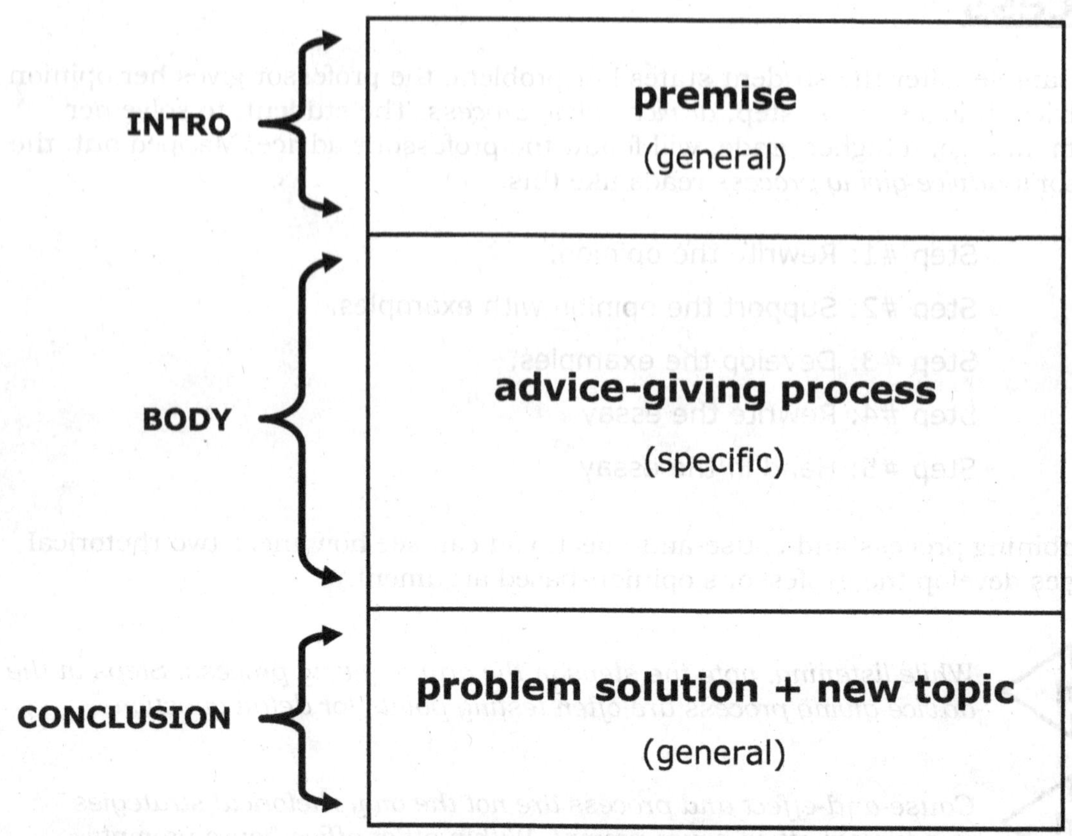

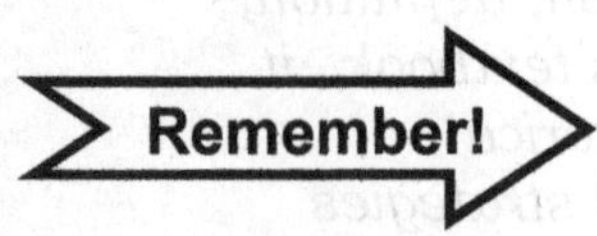

Some test-takers take a lot of notes. Some take only a few notes while others take no notes at all. There is no rule that says you must take notes. It is up to you. Only by practicing will you know whether you need to take notes or not. Your notes will not be rated.

Q *Are there any office-hours conversations in which two students are discussing a problem and solving it?*

A *According to ETS's official TOEFL iBT guidelines, no. Officially, there are are only student-professor office-hours conversations. If there were two students, it would not be an "office-hours" conversation (students do not have offices, not in America at least). However, if you come across a student-student office-hours prompt, apply the problem-solution strategies you have just learned for student-professor prompts. Remember: Even if the characters change, the strategies and the testing method will remain the same.*

Next, we will apply our rhetorical analysis of an office-hours prompt and note-taking strategies to an analysis of those questions you can expect on test day.

Questions

For office-hours prompts, there are two question types.

1. **Multiple-Choice One-Answer:** To answer, click on one of the four choices with the mouse, then click "Next," then "Okay." This is a one-point answer.

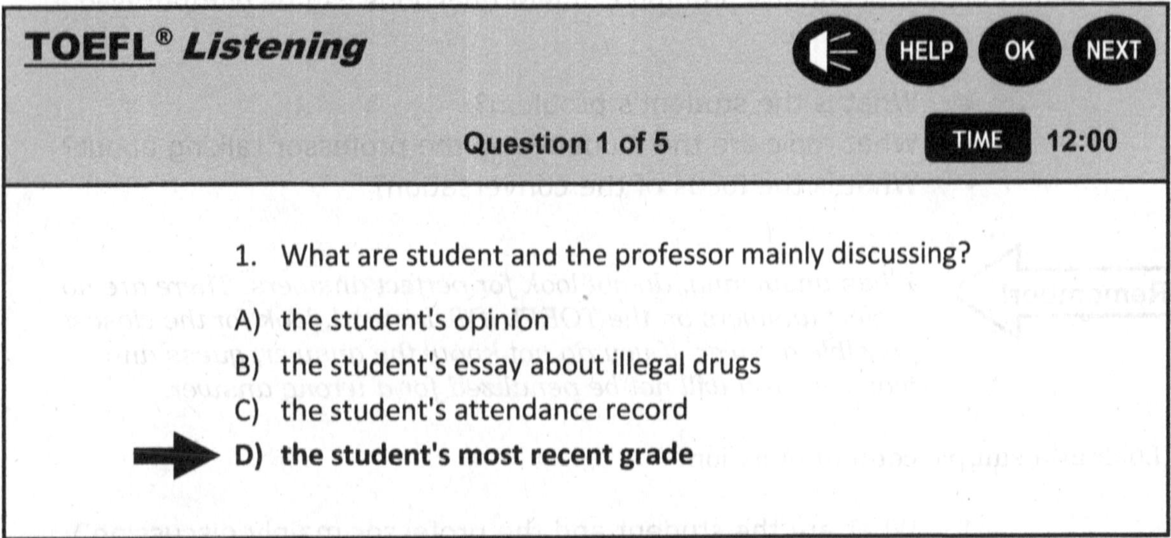

2. **Multiple-Choice Two-Answers:** To answer, click on two choices, then click "Next," then "Okay." Note: Some questions have three correct answers. Three correct equals two points. Two correct equals one point (see page 693 for scoring multi-answer questions).

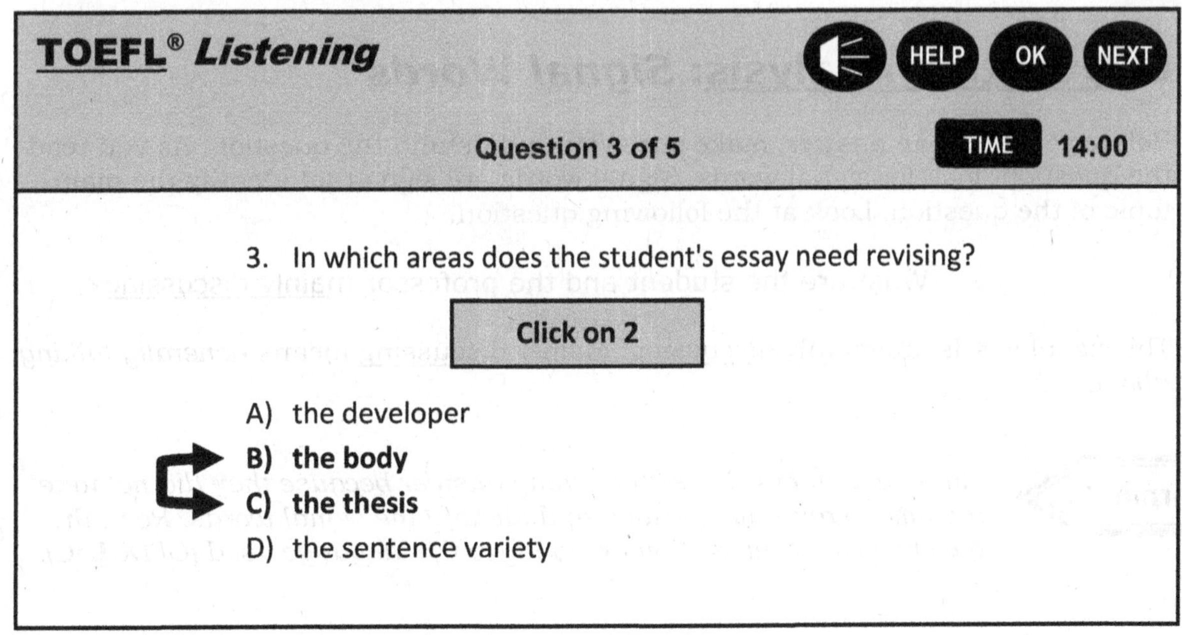

TOEFL® Listening
HELP
OK
NEXT
Question 3 of 5
TIME
14:00
3. In which areas does the student's essay need revising?
Click on 2
A) the developer
B) the body
C) the thesis
D) the sentence variety

Basic Comprehension Questions

1. Content Questions

Content questions measure your ability to synthesize and paraphrase the main information in an office-hours prompt. Content questions can be paraphrased a variety of ways, for example:

- What is the student's problem?
- What topic are the student and the professor talking about?
- What is the focus of the conversation?

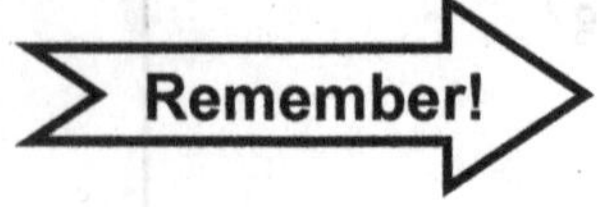

When answering, do not look for perfect answers. There are no perfect answers on the TOEFL iBT. Instead, look for the closest possible answer. If you do not know the answer, guess and move on. You will not be penalized for a wrong answer.

Look at a sample content question.

1. What are the student and the professor mainly discussing?

A) the student's opinion
B) the student's essay about illegal drugs
C) the student's attendance record
D) the student's most recent grade

a. Question Analysis: *Signal Words*

Before you select an answer, make sure you understand the question. As you read the question, look for signal words. Signal words are signs that identify the main topic of the question. Look at the following question.

1, What are the student and the professor mainly discussing?

The signal words are mainly discussing. Mainly discussing means *generally talking about.*

Many test-takers choose the wrong answer because they did not take the time to read the question and identify the signal words. Read the question carefully. As you do, analyze the language used (OPDUL=C).

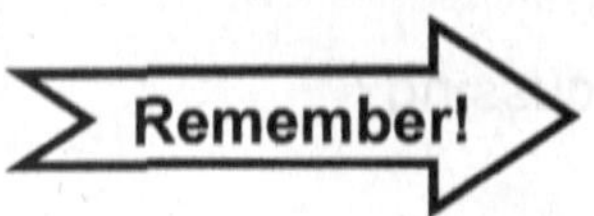
Remember!

Classroom experience proves that most test-takers understand the conversation; however, they fail to analyze and identify the signal words in the questions thus make incorrect answer choices.

b. Answer Location

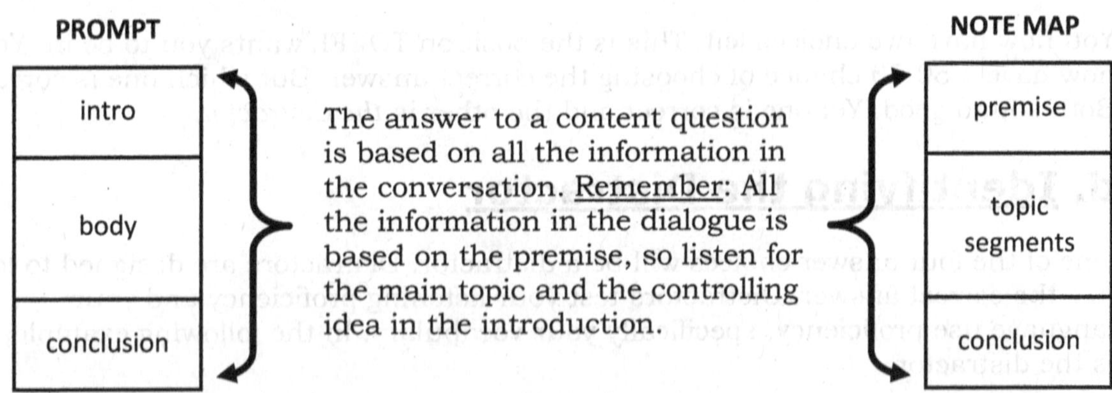
PROMPT
intro
body
conclusion
The answer to a content question is based on all the information in the conversation. Remember: All the information in the dialogue is based on the premise, so listen for the main topic and the controlling idea in the introduction.
NOTE MAP
premise
topic segments
conclusion

c. Choice Analysis: *Process of Elimination*

After you have analyzed the question, analyze the answer choices using the strategy called *process of elimination.* Look for choices that are:

1) off topic	3) too general	5) not known
2) too specific	4) not true	6) not accurate

Next, read each answer choice carefully. As you read, analyze the language used. In the following example, choice C is off topic. The student and the professor do not discuss this topic. Because C is off topic, eliminate it as a choice.

1. What are the student and the professor discussing?

A) the student's opinion
B) the student's essay about illegal drugs
off topic C) the student's attendance record
D) the student's most recent grade

Next, look at choice A. The student's opinion is a detail the student and the professor develop in a topic segment. A detail does not "mainly" (generally) describe the focus of the discussion. Because A is too specific, eliminate it as a choice.

1. What are the student and the professor mainly discussing?

too specific A) the student's opinion
B) the student's essay about illegal drugs
off topic C) the student's attendance record
D) the student's most recent grade

You now have two choices left. This is the position TOEFL wants you to be in. You now have a 50-50 chance of choosing the correct answer. But which one is correct? Both sound good. Yet one is correct and the other is *the distractor.*

d. Identifying the Distractor

One of the four answer choices will be a distractor. Distractors are designed to look like the correct answer. Distractors test your listening proficiency and your language use proficiency, specifically your vocabulary. In the following example, B is the distractor.

1. What are the student and the professor mainly discussing?

A) the student's opinion
distractor **B) the student's essay about illegal drugs**
C) the student's attendance record
D) the student's most recent grade

Why is B the distractor? Look at it closely. Yes, the student and the professor are talking about "the student's essay." But did the student write an essay about one illegal drug or about many "illegal drugs"? She wrote about one drug: marijuana. As you can see, B uses the plural "illegal drugs" to distract you into believing that illegal drugs = marijuana = the topic of the student's essay = the topic the student and the professor are mainly discussing. This is how a distractor will test your language use proficiency (OPDUL=C). That leaves D. D is correct because in the introduction, the student says, "I have a question about my essay you just gave back." In this context, "just gave back" means *most recent grade*, wherein *grade* is a synonym for essay. This, in turn, introduces the main topic, which the student and the professor discuss.

1. What are the student and the professor mainly discussing?

A) the student's opinion
B) the student's essay about illegal drugs
C) the student's attendance record
correct **D) the student's most recent grade**

Analyze each answer choice carefully. Classroom experience proves many test-takers select the distractor because they did not take the time to analyze the language used in each answer choice.

Practice: *Content Questions*

Directions: Listen to each prompt, then answer the question.

#1

Listen as a student talks to a professor.

What is the topic of discussion?

A) changing professors
B) changing classes
C) transferring majors
D) changing registrars

#2

Listen as a student talks to a professor.

What are the speakers mainly talking about?

A) The student's earthquake experience.
B) The student's academic record.
C) The student's new job.
D) The student's attendance record.

#3

Listen as a student talks to a professor.

What is the student's problem?

A) She always blows her presentation.
B) She always gets nervous in class.
C) She is nervous about her presentation.
D) She is too nervous to practice.

#4

Listen as a student talks to a professor.

What is the focus of the conversation?

A) the student's problem
B) illegal downloads
C) the student's need to save money
D) the course text

➔ Answers: page 682.
➔ Audio script: page 732.

2. Purpose Questions

Purpose questions measure your ability to identify the main reason or purpose for the conversation. A purpose question can be paraphrased a variety of ways, for example:

- Why is the student seeking the professor's help?
- Why does the student visit her professor?
- Why does the professor want to talk to the student?

Look at a sample purpose question.

1. Why does the student visit the professor?

A) to learn how to write better essays
B) to find out why she got a low grade on her essay
C) to discuss the pros and cons of the marijuana debate
D) to ask for an extension

a. Question Analysis: *Signal Words*

Before you select an answer, make sure you understand the question. As you read the question, look for signal words. Look at the following question.

1. Why does the student visit the professor?

The signals word are Why and visit. Why and visit suggest a reason. That reason is defined by the premise.

Premise: A student has a problem with her essay (main topic). She wants to know why her professor gave her a low grade (controlling idea).

b. Answer Location

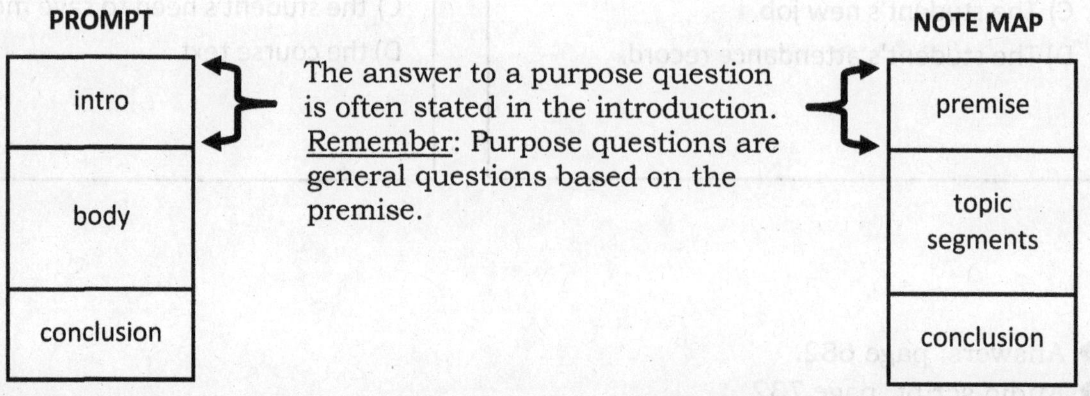
PROMPT
intro
body
conclusion
The answer to a purpose question is often stated in the introduction. Remember: Purpose questions are general questions based on the premise.
NOTE MAP
premise
topic segments
conclusion

c. <u>Choice Analysis</u>: *Process of Elimination*

After you have analyzed the question, analyze the answer choices using *process of elimination.* Look for choices that are:

1) off topic	3) too general	5) not known
2) too specific	4) not true	6) not accurate

As you read each choice, analyze the language used (OPDU**<u>L</u>**=C). Eliminate those choices you think fall into one of the above-six categories.

1. Why does the student visit the professor?

A) to learn how to write better essays
B) to find out why she got a low grade on her essay
not true C) to discuss the pros and cons of the marijuana debate
not true D) to ask for an extension

d. <u>Identifying the Distractor</u>

Next, identify the distractor. In this example, <u>A</u> is the distractor.

1. Why does the student visit the professor?

distractor A) to learn how to write better essays
correct B) to find out why she got a low essay grade
C) to discuss the pros and cons of the marijuana debate
D) to ask for an extension

The student was unhappy about her low essay grade, so she went to her professor to discuss it. The professor told her why she got a low grade, then advised her how to improve her essay. Thus <u>A</u> is a result of <u>B</u>. Did visiting her professor help her write "better essays"? We do not know. Therefore <u>B</u> is correct.

Practice: *Purpose Questions*

Directions: Listen to each prompt, then answer the question.

#1

Listen as a student talks to a professor.

Why does the student visit the professor?

A) to get permission to use the lab
B) to get a tech job in security
C) to get his signature to use the lab
D) to approve his lab work

#2

Listen as a student talks to a professor.

What is the student's purpose for talking to her professor?

A) to see if her friend is attending a lecture
B) to see if her friend likes the professor
C) to see if her friend can attend a lecture
D) to get permission for her friend

#3

Listen as a student talks to a professor.

What does the student need clarified?

A) the cause of the American Revolution
B) the causes of the Canadian compact
C) the difference between Canadians and Americans
D) how Canadians and Americans view government

#4

Listen as a student talks to a professor.

Why did the professor ask to see the student?

A) to argue a woman's right to choose
B) to encourage her to publish her argument
C) to encourage her to rewrite her essay
D) to talk about agents and publishing

➔ Answers: page 682.
➔ Audio script: page 734.

3. Detail Questions: *Single-Answer*

Single-answer detail questions measure your ability to identify facts that support and develop the student's concern and/or the professor's advice-giving process. A single-answer detail question can be paraphrased a variety of ways, for example:

- What does the student say about her opinion?
- Why does the professor mention statistics?
- Why does the professor like the student's topic?

Look at a sample detail question.

1. What does the student say about her opinion?

A) She worked on it a long time.
B) It gave her ideas for another essay.
C) She should make it shorter.
D) It gave her a lot of trouble.

a. Question Analysis: *Signal Words*

Before you select an answer, make sure you understand the question. As you read the question, look for signal words. The signal words in this question are student say about her opinion.

1. What does the student say about her opinion?

b. Answer Location

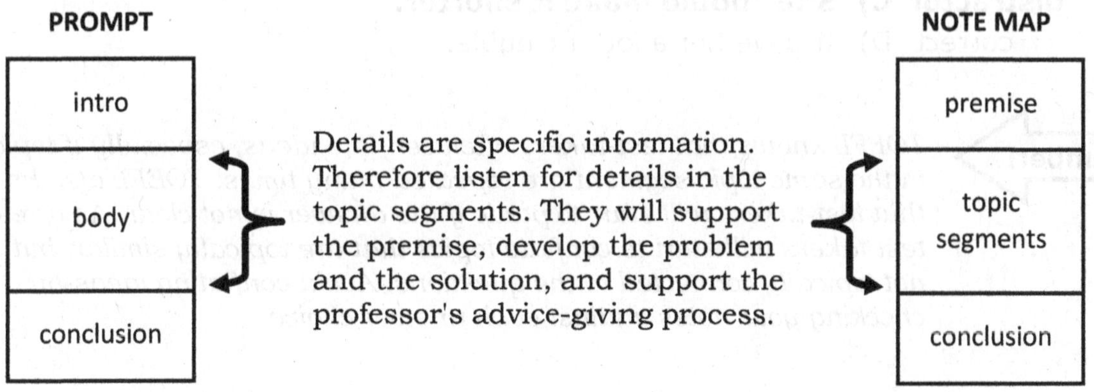
PROMPT
intro
body
conclusion
Details are specific information. Therefore listen for details in the topic segments. They will support the premise, develop the problem and the solution, and support the professor's advice-giving process.
NOTE MAP
premise
topic segments
conclusion

c. <u>Choice Analysis</u>: *Process of Elimination*

After you have analyzed the question, analyze the answer choices using process of elimination. Eliminate choices that are: 1) off topic; 2) too general; 3) not true; 4) not known; 5) not accurate; 6) too specific.

1. What does the student say about her opinion?

not known A) She worked on it a long time.
not known B) It gave her ideas for another essay.
C) She should make it shorter.
D) It gave her a lot of trouble.

d. <u>Identifying the Distractor</u>

Next, identify the distractor. In this example, <u>C</u> is the distractor. In the discussion, the professor talks about short *essays* not short opinions. Do not conflate short opinion and short essay.

<u>Conflating Ideas</u>

To conflate means to combine two or more ideas into one. For example, in the sample conversation, you hear the words "short essay" and "opinion" repeated. Because these words are topically related, and repeated, you might conflate them and infer that *a short essay should have a short opinion*. Therefore, the answer seems to be <u>C</u>. However, <u>C</u> is the distractor.

1. What does the student say about her opinion?

not known A) She worked on it a long time.
not known B) It gave her ideas for another essay.
distractor C) She should make it shorter.
correct D) It gave her a lot of trouble.

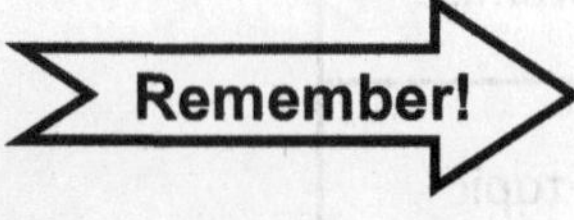

TOEFL knows that test-takers often conflate ideas, especially if topics in the same topic segment are repeated many times. TOEFL also knows that test-takers will start to panic if the answer is not clear. As a result, test-takers will start to conflate topics that are topically similar, but are not topically connected to the questions. Avoid conflating ideas by checking your notes against each answer choice.

Practice: *Single-Answer Detail Questions*

Directions: Listen as a student talks to a professor, then answer the questions.

#1

What can't the student do?

A) the presentation
B) biology
C) vivisection
D) the test

#2

What are the "objects of investigation?"

A) rats
B) mice
C) snakes
D) apes

#3

What can't be done virtually?

A) vivisection
B) the procedure
C) predicting the future
D) the course

#4

What percentage of the final grade is the assignment?

A) 4%
B) 14%
C) 30%
D) 40%

#5

What is the student dropping out of?

A) the program
B) school
C) the course
D) the experiment

#6

The professor says, "Life is full of..."

A) challenges
B) crossroads
C) assignments
D) choices

➔ Answers: page 682.
➔ Audio script: page 736.

4. Detail Questions: *Multi-Answer*

Multi-answer detail questions measure your ability to identify facts that support and develop the student's position and/or the professor's advice-giving process. A multi-answer detail question can be paraphrased a variety of ways, for example:

- What does the professor say about the length of an essay?
- The professor says that each body paragraph must have...
- In which areas does the student's essay need revising?

Look at a sample question. Note: Some questions have 3 answer choices (see page 693 for scoring multi-answer questions).

1. In which areas does the student's essay need revising?

Click on 2

A) the developer
B) the body
C) the thesis
D) the sentence variety

a. Question Analysis: *Signal Words*

Before you select an answer, make sure you understand the question. As you read the question, look for signal words. The signal words in this question are which areas, essay, and need revising.

1. In which areas does the student's essay need revising?

b. Answer Location

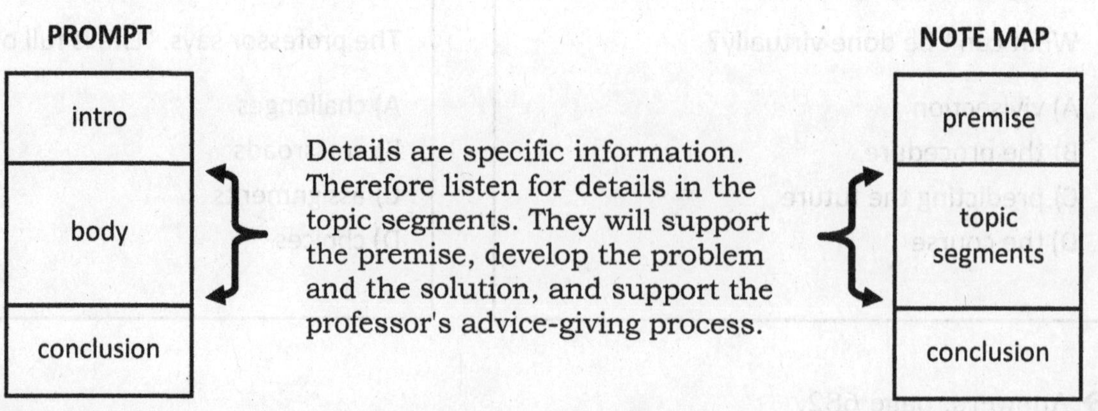
PROMPT
intro
body
conclusion
Details are specific information. Therefore listen for details in the topic segments. They will support the premise, develop the problem and the solution, and support the professor's advice-giving process.
NOTE MAP
premise
topic segments
conclusion

c. <u>Choice Analysis</u>: *Process of Elimination*

After you have analyzed the question, analyze the answer choices using *process of elimination.* Eliminate choices that are: 1) off topic; 2) too general; 3) not true; 4) not known; 5) not accurate; 6) too specific.

As you read each choice, analyze the language used. Eliminate those choices that fall into one of the above-five categories.

1. In which areas does the student's essay need revising?

Click on 2

A) the developer
B) the body
C) the thesis
not known D) the sentence variety

d. <u>Identifying the Distractor</u>

Next, identify the distractor. In this example, <u>A</u> is the distractor. <u>A</u> is a noun for a person, i.e., a software developer. If it were *development*—a noun describing the condition of being developed, as in *essay development*—it would be correct. If you choose <u>A</u>, you would be conflating developer and development. This is an example of how a noun with a similar spelling, but with a different meaning, is a distractor. Distinguishing between similar nouns and their meanings tests language use proficiency (OPDU**<u>L</u>**=C). <u>A</u> is also a homophone distractor (see page 435).

1. In which areas does the student's essay need revising?

Click on 2

distractor A) the developer
correct B) the body
correct C) the thesis
not known D) the sentence variety

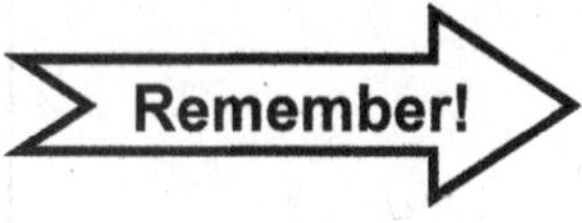

*Read each answer choice carefully. Focus on language use (OPDU**<u>L</u>**=C). Classroom experience proves that many test-takers select the distractor because they did not take the time to analyze the language used in each answer choice. TOEFL knows this. That is why TOEFL uses distractors.*

Practice: *Multi-Answer Detail Questions*

Directions: Listen to each prompt, then answer the question.

#1

Listen as a student talks to a professor. This is a 2-point question.

What must the student do to complete the assignment? Select three.

A) give a presentation
B) hand in a list of interviewers
C) write a summary
D) hand in a bibliography
E) hand in a list of interviewees

#2

Listen as a student talks to a professor. This is a 1-point question.

What does the student need from her professor? Select two.

A) an interview for a new job
B) letters recommending the position
C) signed letters of recommendation
D) to be interviewed by phone

#3

Listen as a student talks to a professor. This is a 2-point question.

What will the student take to the Amazon? Select three.

A) malaria pills
B) malaria spray
C) bug pills
D) bug spray
E) a charger

#4

Listen as a student talks to a professor. This is a 1-point question.

Which two graduate English degrees does the professor describe? Select two.

A) MBA
B) MFA
C) MA
D) PhD

➔ Answers: page 682.
➔ Scoring multi-answer questions: page 693.
➔ Audio script: page 737.

Pragmatic-Understanding Questions

1. Function Questions: *Authentic Language*

Function questions test your ability to judge how a speaker uses authentic language. Authentic language use includes hesitations, self-corrections, topic digressions, false starts, repetitions, restatements, idiom usage, and changes in tone. There are two types of function question: question-first and segment-first.

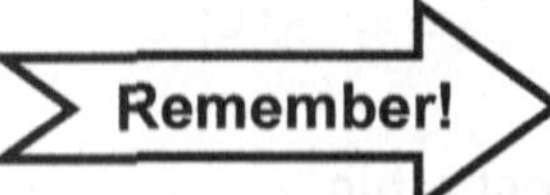

The headset symbol indicates a function question. 

1. Question-First

For this function question, you will hear instructions followed by a question. You will then hear a dialogue segment and answer a question. You will not see the replayed dialogue text on your screen. It is added here for demonstration purposes only.

Narrator: 6. Listen to part of a conversation, then answer the question. 

What does the student imply when she says this?

Student: "But...Yeah." 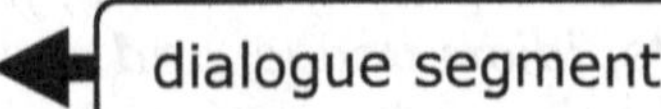

A) She forgot what she wanted to say.

correct **B) She is surprised by her low grade.**

C) She is disappointed by her poor performance.

D) She is not surprised she got a low grade.

Sometimes the segment comes before the question.

Narrator: 6. Listen to part of a conversation, then answer the question. 

Student: "But...Yeah."

Narrator: What does the student imply when she says this?

A) She forgot what she wanted to say.

B) She is surprised by her low grade.

C) She is disappointed by her poor performance.

D) She is not surprised she got a grade.

2. Segment-First

For this question, you will first hear instructions and an extended dialogue segment. You will then hear a question. The question will be based on a replayed part of the extended segment, for example:

Narrator: 5. Listen to part of a conversation, then answer the question.

Professor: "Remember: the more you develop your supporting examples, the more persuasive your argument will be. Right now, you're just scratching the surface. To be honest, this reads more like a first draft."

Narrator: What does the professor imply when she says this?

Professor: "Right now, you're just scratching the surface. To be honest, this reads more like a first draft."

A) She thinks the student hates essay writing.
B) She thinks parts of the student's essay are scratched.
correct C) She thinks the student's essay lacks depth.
D) She thinks the student is on the wrong track.

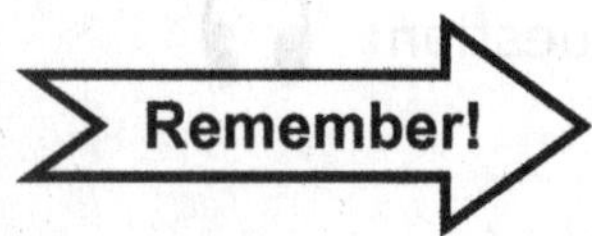

Function questions measure your ability to recognize authentic language. For the TOEFL iBT, authentic language is hesitations, self-corrections, topic digressions, false starts, repetitions, restatements, idiom usage, and changes in tone.

Hesitation

In the sample below, the student says But...Yeah. This is a hesitation. Hesitation is an example of authentic language use.

Student
I have a question about my essay you just gave back. Where should I start? I worked really hard on it and...Well, I thought I'd get a better grade. But...Yeah. Talk about a shock. Anyway, can you tell me why I got such a low grade?

Look at a sample question. Remember: You will not see the dialogue segment on your screen.

Narrator: 5. Listen to part of a conversation, then answer the question. 

What does the student imply when she says this?

Student: "But...Yeah."

A) She forgot what she wanted to say.
correct **B) She is surprised by her low grade.**
C) She is disappointed by her poor performance.
D) She is not surprised she got a low grade.

To answer this question correctly, you must infer the meaning of But...Yeah. From this hesitation, you can infer that the student thought she was going to get a higher grade. She was going to say so starting with *But...[I really thought I was going to get a higher grade]*, then stopped. "Yeah" infers *Wow, was I wrong and surprised.* Therefore, B is correct.

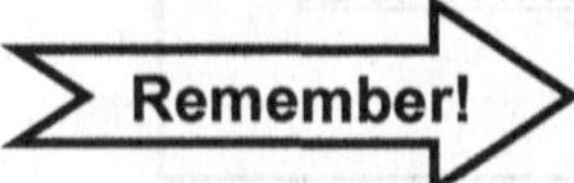

Make a note of hesitations. They are predictable testing points.

Self-Correction

In the sample below, the professor says Sorry, I meant... This is a self-correction. Self-correction is an example of authentic language use.

> ***Professor***
> Also, your opinion must be supportable. When I say supportable, I mean each sentence—sorry, I meant each body paragraph—must have one specific topic, then you must develop that topic in detail.

Look at a sample question.

Narrator: 4. Listen to part of a conversation, then answer the question. 

Why does the professor say this?

Professor: "Sorry, I meant each body paragraph.

correct **A) She made a mistake and is correcting it.**
B) She wants to change the topic to body paragraphs.
C) She feels the student doesn't know what she means.
D) She thinks the student should rethink her topic.

In English, "Sorry + I meant" signals a self-correction. In this case, the professor did not mean "each sentence." The professor meant "each body paragraph." The professor recognized her mistake and *self-corrected*. Therefore, A is correct.

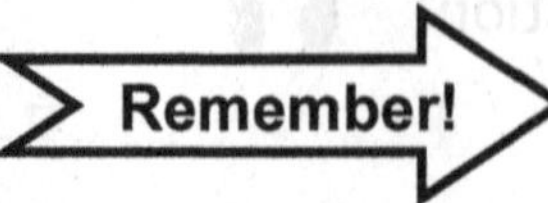

Make a note of self-corrections. They are possible testing points.

Topic Digression

In the sample below, the professor says Well, let's just leave it at that, shall we? This is the end of a topic digression. A topic digression is an example of authentic language use.

> ***Professor***
> Some might disagree, but frankly, some of the best essays I've graded have been short. Not one-page short, mind you, but, you know, a couple of really focused pages that address the subject with no extra verbiage. Some of the worst essays I've seen have been...Well, let's just leave it at that, shall we?

Look at a sample question.

Narrator: 8. Listen to part of a conversation, then answer the question. 

Why does the professor say this?

Professor: "Well, let's just leave it at that, shall we?

A) She must finish the conversation and leave.
B) She is finished giving the student advice.
correct C) She doesn't want to say anymore on the topic.
D) She feels the student doesn't understand the assignment.

In the above example, Well, let's just leave it at that, shall we? means *Enough about this subject It is off topic*. The professor realizes this. Therefore, C is correct.

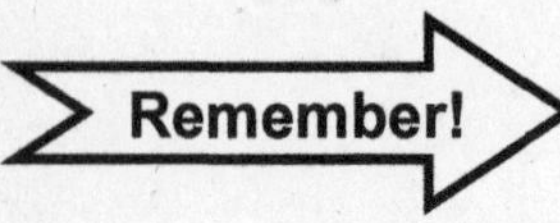

Make a note of topic digressions. They are predictable testing points.

False Start

In the sample below, the student says Where should I start? This is a false start. A false start is an example of authentic language use.

> ***Student***
> I have a question about my essay you just gave back. Where should I start? I worked really hard on it and...Well, I thought I'd get a better grade. But...Yeah. Talk about a shock. Anyway, can you tell me why I got such a low grade?

Look at a sample question.

Narrator: 9. Listen to part of a conversation, then answer the question. 

Why does the student say this?

Student: "Where should I start?"

A) because she knows what she wants to say

Correct **B) because she is not sure what to say**

C) because she doesn't know how to start her essay

D) because she wants the professor to tell her where to start

In this example, "Where should I start?" signals that the student is *having trouble explaining her purpose* for visiting the professor, and/or is nervous or embarrassed about her low grade. As a result, she uses a rhetorical question behind which she hesitates. This signals a false start. Therefore, B is correct.

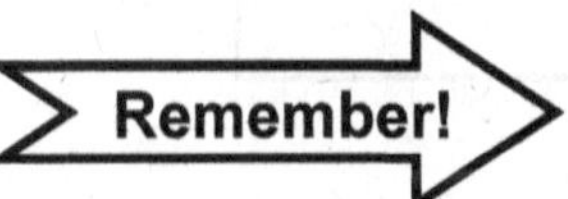

Make a note of false starts. They are predictable testing points.

Repetition

In the sample below, the professor says Right. Right. This is an example of repetition. Repetition is an example of authentic language use.

> ***Professor***
> Yes. Now I remember. Let me take a look at it. Right. Right.

On the next page, look at a function question based on this repetition.

Narrator: 5. Listen to part of a conversation, then answer the question. 

Why does the professor say this?

Professor: "Right. Right."

A) because by looking at the student, the professor remembers the student
B) because the professor believes the student did the right thing coming to see her
correct **C) because the professor is <u>confirming</u> that she remembers the student's essay**
D) because the professor is approving the student's revisions

In this example, "Right. Right" signals that the professor is reading the student's essay. As she reads the essay, she remembers and *<u>confirms</u>* it by repeating "Right. Right." In this context, "Right. Right" means, "Yes, now I remember this essay." Therefore, <u>C</u> is correct.

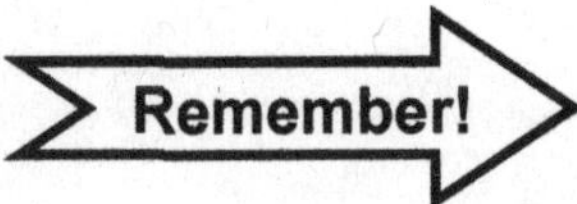

Make a note of repetitions. They are possible testing points.

Restatement

In the sample below, the professor says <u>In other words</u>. This is a restatement. A restatement is an example of authentic language use.

> ***Professor***
> Carcharodon carcharias is a rapacious killing machine. <u>In other words</u>, the great white shark will eat anything that enters the water.

Look at a sample question.

Narrator: 5. Listen to part of a conversation, then answer the question. 

Why does the professor say this?

Professor: "In other words, the great white shark will eat anything that enters the water.

A) to give examples of what great white sharks eat
B) to signal that the lecture topic is the great white shark
correct **C) to <u>rephrase</u> his main point in simpler terms**
D) to warn about the dangers of entering the water

In the previous example, "In other words" signals that the professor is restating or *rephrasing* a prior point. A restatement simplifies meaning for greater understanding. Therefore, C is correct.

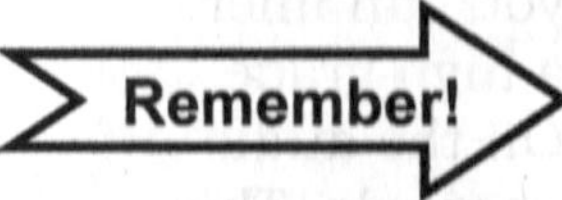

Make a note of restatements. They are possible testing points.

Idioms

To understand an idiom's function, you must infer its meaning specific to the context in which the idiom is used. This process is called contextualizing (see page 560). Look at the sample below. The professor says, Right now, you're just scratching the surface. This idiom is an example of authentic language use.

> **Professor**
> Right now, you're just scratching the surface.

Look at a question based on this idiom.

Narrator: 4. Listen to part of a conversation, then answer the question. What does the professor imply when she says this? 

Professor: "Right now, you're just scratching the surface."

A) She thinks the student hates essay writing.
B) She thinks parts of the student's essay are scratched.
correct **C) She thinks the student's essay lacks depth.**
D) She thinks the student is on the wrong track.

In the above example, note the word surface. Surface means shallow or not deep. Note that deep means a lack of depth. When talking about writing, depth means a lot of hard work. A lack of depth, however, means a lack of work. A lack of work = a lack of development. Instead of being deep into the topic (well developed because of hard work), the student's essay is still on the surface (not well developed because of a lack of work). As you can see, the idiom the professor uses functions both as a statement of fact and as an indirect warning (You need to work harder if you want higher grades). Therefore, C is correct.

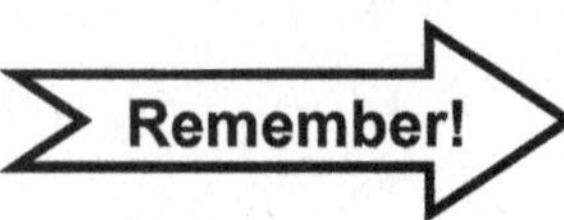

Make a note of idioms. They are predictable testing points.

Tone

Tone describes the feeling in a speaker's voice. For TOEFL, tone can include doubt, surprise, disbelief, excitement, anger, and relief. From a speaker's tone, you can infer meaning. Look at the sample below. The student thought she would get a high grade on her essay. We know because the student says, "Talk about a shock." On the audio track, the tone of surprise and disbelief in the student's voice matches her words. This is an example of inferring meaning from a speaker's tone.

> ***Student***
> I have a question about my essay you just gave back. Where should I start? I worked really hard on it and...Well, I thought I'd get a better grade. But...Yeah. Talk about a shock. Anyway, can you tell me why I got such a low grade?

Look at a sample question.

Narrator: 9. Listen to part of a conversation, then answer the question.

Why does the student say this?

Student: "Talk about a shock."

A) because she thinks the professor made a mistake

B) because she believes she deserves a better grade

correct **C) because her poor grade took her by surprise**

D) because the topic in her essay is quite shocking

The phrase *took her by surprise* means her low grade shocked and surprised her. Therefore, C is correct.

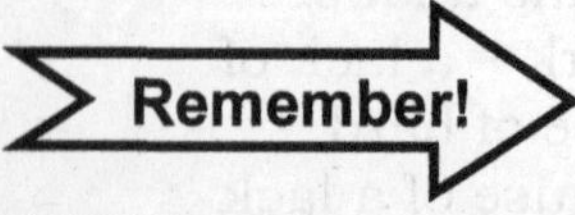

Make a note of tone. Tone often signals a predictable testing point.

Choice Analysis: *Process of Elimination*

After you have analyzed the question, analyze the answer choices using process of elimination. Eliminate those choices that are: 1) off topic; 2) too specific; 3) too general; 4) not true; 5) not known; 6) not accurate.

For a segment containing an idiom, choosing an answer can be a challenge. Look at the following example.

Narrator: 4. Listen to part of a conversation, then answer the question. 

What does the professor imply when she says this?

Professor: "Right now, you're just scratching the surface."

What does the professor imply when she says this?

not known A) She thinks the student hates essay writing.
B) She thinks parts of the student's essay are scratched.
C) She thinks the student's essay lacks depth.
not true D) She thinks the student is on the wrong track.

If you know the meaning of the idiom in question, select the appropriate answer. However, if you do not know the idiom, narrow your choices down to the distractor and the answer. In the example above, eliminate A. A is not known. The student does not state her opinion about essay writing nor can this be inferred. Next, eliminate D. D is not true. The student is *on the right track.* Seeking help from her professor proves it. You now have two choices left: the answer and a *homophone distractor.*

Homophone Distractor

Homophone is a Greek word: *homo* means the same, *phone* means voice or sound. In B below, the homophone distractor **scratched** sounds like, and has the same root as, **scratching** in the replayed segment. Therefore, B is a homophone distractor and C is correct.

Professor: "Right now, you're just **scratching** the surface. To be honest, this reads more like a first draft."

B) She thinks parts of the student's essay are **scratched**.
C) She thinks the student's essay lacks depth.

If you thought B was the answer because **scratched** and **scratching** share the same sound and root (same sound + same root = answer!), then you will have done what TOEFL expected you would do: selected the homophone distractor.

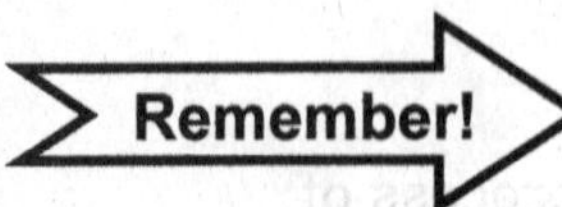

If an answer choice shares the same root and sound, and/or is spelled the same as a signal word in the question, it is a homophone distractor. Do not select it. Do not fall into the homophone distractor trap.

Homophone distractors are a predictable testing method used by TOEFL.

Answer Location

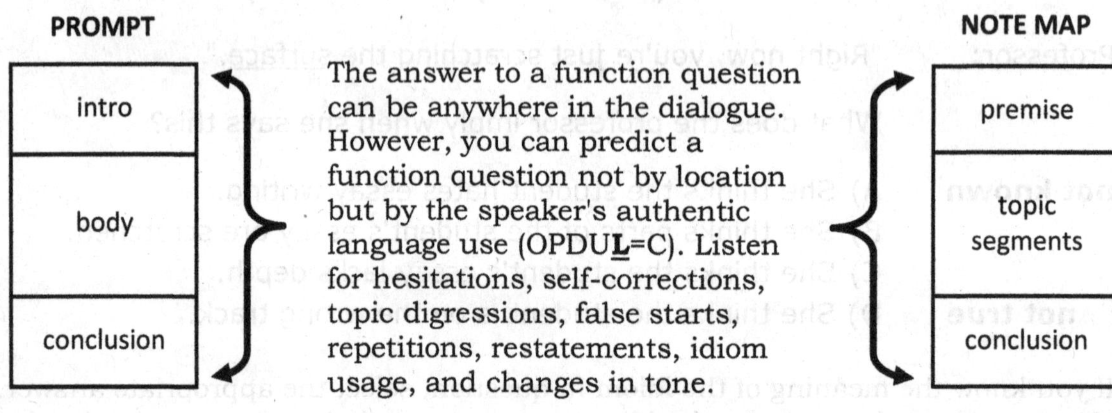

PROMPT
intro
body
conclusion
The answer to a function question can be anywhere in the dialogue. However, you can predict a function question not by location but by the speaker's authentic language use (OPDUL=C). Listen for hesitations, self-corrections, topic digressions, false starts, repetitions, restatements, idiom usage, and changes in tone.
NOTE MAP
premise
topic segments
conclusion

Practice: *Question-First Function Questions*

Directions: Answer each question based on what is stated or implied.

#1

Why does the professor say this? 

A) to help the student with late homework assignments
B) to warn the student that he is always late with work
C) to encourage the student to complete all the homework assignments
D) to warn the student that he is not following the homework policy

#2

Why does the professor say this? 

A) to bring the student up to date
B) to remind the student that he must research the topic of Rome and taxes
C) to summarize a point made in the lecture
D) to help the student make the connection between armies and populations

#3

Why does the professor say this? 

A) to avoid talking to the student
B) to suggest another time to meet
C) to invite the student to lunch
D) to remind the student that he can't meet because it is raining

#4

Why does the student say this? 

A) to explain the results of her research
B) to signal her excitement over the find
C) to explain the importance of research
D) to signal that she needs only a minute to explain her research topic

➔ Answers: page 682.
➔ Audio script: page 739.

Practice: *Segment-First Function Questions*

Directions: Answer each question based on what is stated or implied.

#1

Listen to part of a conversation, then answer the question.

Why does the professor say this? 

A) to repeat her point for accuracy
B) to signal that she will try to make her point clearer
C) to point out her mistake by rephrasing it
D) to teach the student about rephrasing

#2

Listen to part of a conversation, then answer the question.

Why does the professor say this? 

A) to explain how easy it is to steal music
B) to stress her point through repetition
C) to summarize an important point
D) to support her point with historical facts

#3

Listen to part of a conversation, then answer the question.

What does the professor mean when he says this?

A) computer modeling is important
B) computer modeling is out of date
C) computer modeling is dangerous
D) computer modeling is popular

#4

Listen to part of a conversation, then answer the question.

What does the professor mean when she says this? 

A) to acknowledge her mistake
B) to make the comparison clearer
C) to express her anger
D) to indicate a change in topic

➔ Answers: page 682.
➔ Audio script: page 740.

2. Attitude Questions

Attitude question measures your ability to identify a speaker's opinion (also called position or stance), degree of certainty, and feelings. Attitude questions are either direct or inferred (indirect).

Direct-Attitude Questions

Direct attitude means the speaker's opinion is stated as fact in the conversation. Direct attitude questions can be paraphrased a variety of ways, for example:

- What does the professor think about short essays?
- What is the professor's opinion of the student's essay?
- How does the student feel about her last essay grade?

Look at a sample question.

1. What does the professor think about short essays?

A) One focused page is best.
B) Short essays always get high grades.
C) A short, focused essay is best.
D) A short essay never has an opinion.

a. Question Analysis: *Signal Words*

As you analyze the question, identify signal words.

1. What does the professor think about short essays?

b. Answer Location

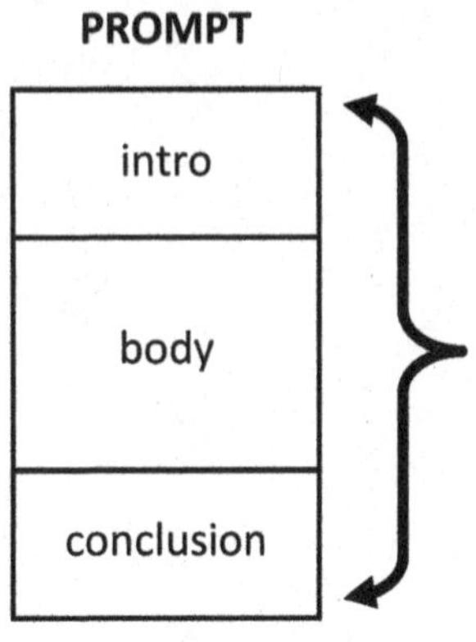

Because the advice-giving process is in the body of the conversation, listen for reactions (opinions) to the advice in the topic segments. Also, listen to how the student/ professor introduces the premise. Listen to each reaction to the premise and the resolution of the problem in the conclusion. The speakers' attitudes toward the problem are often different in the intro and the conclusion.

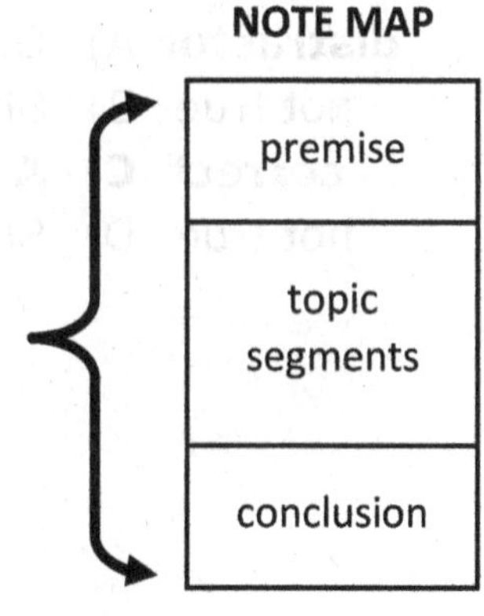

c. Choice Analysis: *Process of Elimination*

Use process of elimination to eliminate choices that are: 1) off topic; 2) too general; 3) not true; 4) not known; 5) not accurate; 6) too specific.

1. What does the professor think about short essays?

A) One focused page is best.
not true B) Short essays always get high grades.
C) A short, focused essay is best.
not true D) Short essays always get high grades.

d. Choice Distractors

In the example below, A and C contain the words "focused" and "best." This is an example of a choice distractor. Both A and C look good because the same words are in each. Also, the professor mentioned "focused" and "best." But in which context? Your choice will be based on the accuracy of your notes.

1. What does the professor think about short essays?

A) One **focused** page is **best.**
not true B) Short essays always get high grades.
C) A short, **focused** essay is **best.**
not true D) Short essays always get high grades.

In this example, A is the choice distractor. The professor directly states that some of the best essays she has read were only *"a couple of really focused pages that address the subject."* She does not directly (factually) state that *"one focused page is best."* She says the opposite: *"Some might disagree, but frankly, some of the best essays I've graded have been short. Not one-page short, mind you..."* Therefore, C is correct.

1. What does the professor think about short essays?

distractor A) One focused page is best.
not true B) Short essays always get high grades.
correct C) A short, focused essay is best.
not true D) Short essays always get high grades.

Practice: *Direct-Attitude Questions*

Directions: Listen to each prompt, then answer the questions.

#1

Listen as a student talks to a professor.

What does the professor believe?

A) The debating team will lose terribly.
B) The debating team will run out of time.
C) The debating team will win decisively.
D) The debating team will enjoy the challenge.

#2

Listen as a student talks to a professor.

What does the student believe?

A) Her presentation was great.
B) Her presentation was awful.
C) Her presentation needs more work.
D) Her presentation was a failure.

#3

Listen as a student talks to a professor.

What is the student's opinion of grades?

A) They are not part of the rewriting process.
B) They are necessary.
C) They are superfluous.
D) They really mean a lot.

#4

Listen as a student talks to a professor.

What is the professor's opinion of the student's thesis?

A) It is arguable therefore a thesis.
B) It needs more facts.
C) It is perfect for the topic.
D) It is not an opinion but a fact.

➔ Answers: page 683.
➔ Audio script: page 741.

Inferred-Attitude Questions

Inferred attitude means the speaker's opinion or position is not stated as fact in the conversation. Instead, it is suggested or implied. From the suggestion or implication, you must infer a conclusion based on the facts presented. Inferred-attitude questions can be paraphrased a variety of ways, for example:

- What does the professor imply about long essays?
- What can we infer about the student's essay?
- What can we infer about the professor's submission policy?

Look at a sample question.

1. What can we infer about the professor's submission policy?

A) Her assignments are based on controversial topics.
B) She permits a rewrite for an improved grade.
C) Her submission policy changes regularly.
D) She gives her students all the time they need to rewrite.

a. Question Analysis: *Signal Words*

As you analyze the question, identify signal words.

1. What can we infer about the professor's submission policy?

b. Answer Location

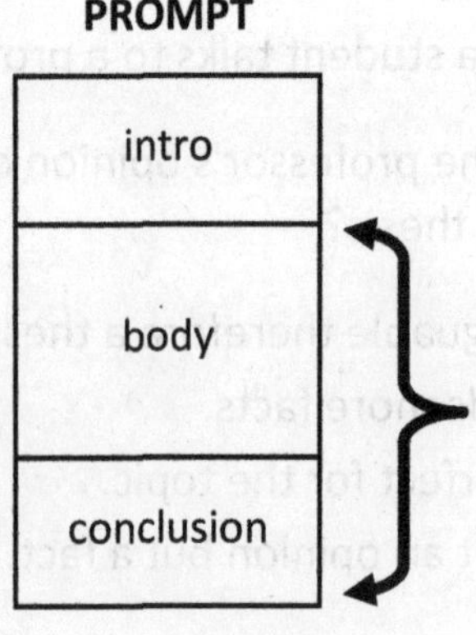

Listen to how the student reacts to the professor's advice in the topic segments. Listen for tone. Tone, especially a change in tone, often signals an inferred attitude either on the student's part or the professor's part.

Also, listen for a future action in the conclusion. Listen to how the student and the professor react to the future action. Their reactions will often infer an attitude toward the future action.

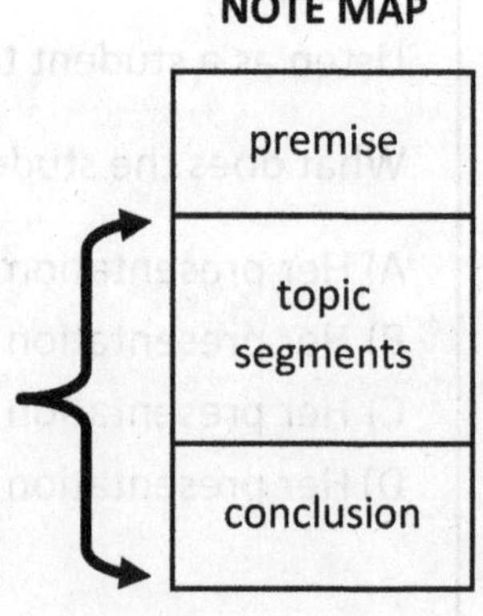

c. <u>Choice Analysis</u>: *Process of Elimination*

Listen to the conclusion ending the sample conversation, track #41, then analyze the question below. Use process of elimination to eliminate choices that are: 1) off topic; 2) too general; 3) not true; 4) not known; 5) not accurate; 6) too specific.

1. What can we infer about the professor's submission policy?

not known A) Her assignments are based on controversial topics.
B) She permits a rewrite for an improved grade.
not known C) Her submission policy changes regularly.
D) She gives her students all the time they need to rewrite.

d. <u>Identifying the Distractor</u>

In the question below, <u>D</u> is the distractor. From the sample conclusion, it is clear that the student can rewrite her essay for a better grade. Yes, the professor gives her more time, but not *"all the time [the student needs] to rewrite."* The student must hand in the rewrite the next morning. Therefore, <u>B</u> is correct.

1. What can we infer about the professor's submission policy?

not known A) Her assignments are based on controversial topics.
correct B) She permits a rewrite for an improved grade.
not known C) Her submission policy changes regularly.
distractor D) She gives her students all the time they need to rewrite.

Practice: ***Inferred-Attitude Questions***

Directions: Listen to each prompt, then answer the question.

#1

Listen as a student talks to a professor.

What can we infer about having the debate outside?

A) The professor approves of the idea.
B) The professor is against the idea.
C) The professor needs a change of pace.
D) The professor needs time to think it over.

#2

Listen as a student talks to a professor.

What can we infer from the conversation?

A) The student will rewrite her essay.
B) The student will ask for more time.
C) The student will change her opinion.
D) The student will avoid using clichés.

#3

Listen as a student talks to a professor.

What is the professor suggesting?

A) The student must not attend class with his cell phone.
B) The student must look for a new job.
C) The student must change phones.
D) The student is not following school policy regarding cell phones.

#4

Listen as a student talks to another student.

How does the man feel about having a chicken for a mascot?

A) He thinks it is a novel idea.
B) He would prefer the Earth instead.
C) He is far from persuaded.
D) He thinks it will be good for school spirit.

➔ Answers: page 683.
➔ Audio script: page 741.

Connecting-Information Questions

1. Inferred-Action Questions

Inferred-action questions measure your ability to identify what action a speaker will do next or in the future. To answer this question type, you must make an inference based on the facts presented in the conversation. Inferred-action question can be paraphrased a variety of ways, for example:

- What will the student do next?
- What will the student probably do tonight?
- What will the professor look for in the rewritten essay?

Look at a sample question.

1. What will the student probably do tonight?

A) She will do homework.
B) She will think about her professor's advice.
C) She will rewrite her opinion.
D) She will rewrite her essay.

a. Question Analysis: *Signal Words*

As you analyze the question, identify signal words.

1. What will the student probably do tonight?

b. Answer Location

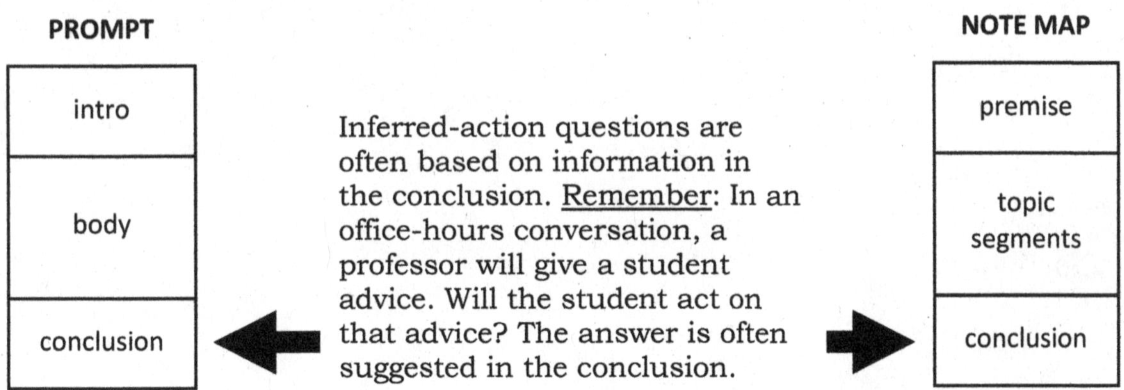

PROMPT
intro
body
conclusion
Inferred-action questions are often based on information in the conclusion. Remember: In an office-hours conversation, a professor will give a student advice. Will the student act on that advice? The answer is often suggested in the conclusion.
NOTE MAP
premise
topic segments
conclusion

c. <u>Choice Analysis</u>: *Process of Elimination*

Listen to the conclusion of the sample conversation, track #41, then analyze the question below. Eliminate choices that are: 1) off topic; 2) too general; 3) not true; 4) not known; 5) not accurate; 6) too specific.

1. What will the student probably do tonight?

not known A) She will do homework.
not known B) She will think about her professor's advice.
C) She will rewrite her opinion.
D) She will rewrite her essay.

d. <u>Identifying the Distractor</u>

In the example above, <u>C</u> is the distractor. Yes, the student will rewrite her opinion. We can infer this from the conclusion. However, her opinion is only one part of her essay. Therefore, <u>D</u> is correct. In the end, the student says, "I'll try." Try what? Try to rewrite her essay tonight so she can hand it in *"By nine tomorrow morning"* as the professor says.

1. What will the student probably do tonight?

not known A) She will do homework.
not known B) She will think about her professor's advice.
distractor C) She will rewrite her opinion.
correct D) She will rewrite her essay.

Practice: ***Inferred-Action Questions***

Directions: Listen to each prompt, then answer the question.

#1

Listen as a student talks to a professor.

What will the professor probably do?

A) give the student an A+
B) tell the student to rewrite his essay
C) suggest that the student try and publish his work
D) give the student an average grade

#2

Listen as a student talks to a professor.

We can infer from the conversation that the professor has not...

A) been to a mall
B) visited a high-tech recruitment center
C) listened to the student's comments
D) been in the military

#3

Listen as a student talks to a professor.

From the conversation, we can infer that the student will probably continue to...

A) disagree with her professor
B) support the right to privacy
C) disagree with the government
D) drop out of the class

#4

Listen as a student talks to a professor.

What will student probably do?

A) look for a job on Wall Street
B) look for a job in qualitative finance
C) ask the professor for a recommendation
D) expand her job search

➔ Answers: page 683.
➔ Audio script: page 743.

Service-Encounter Conversations

For this prompt type, a student will talk to a campus employee. The student and the employee will informally discuss a campus-related topic. An analysis of a service-encounter conversation begins by listening to a test sample.

Sample: *Service-Encounter Conversation* → **Audio Track #51**

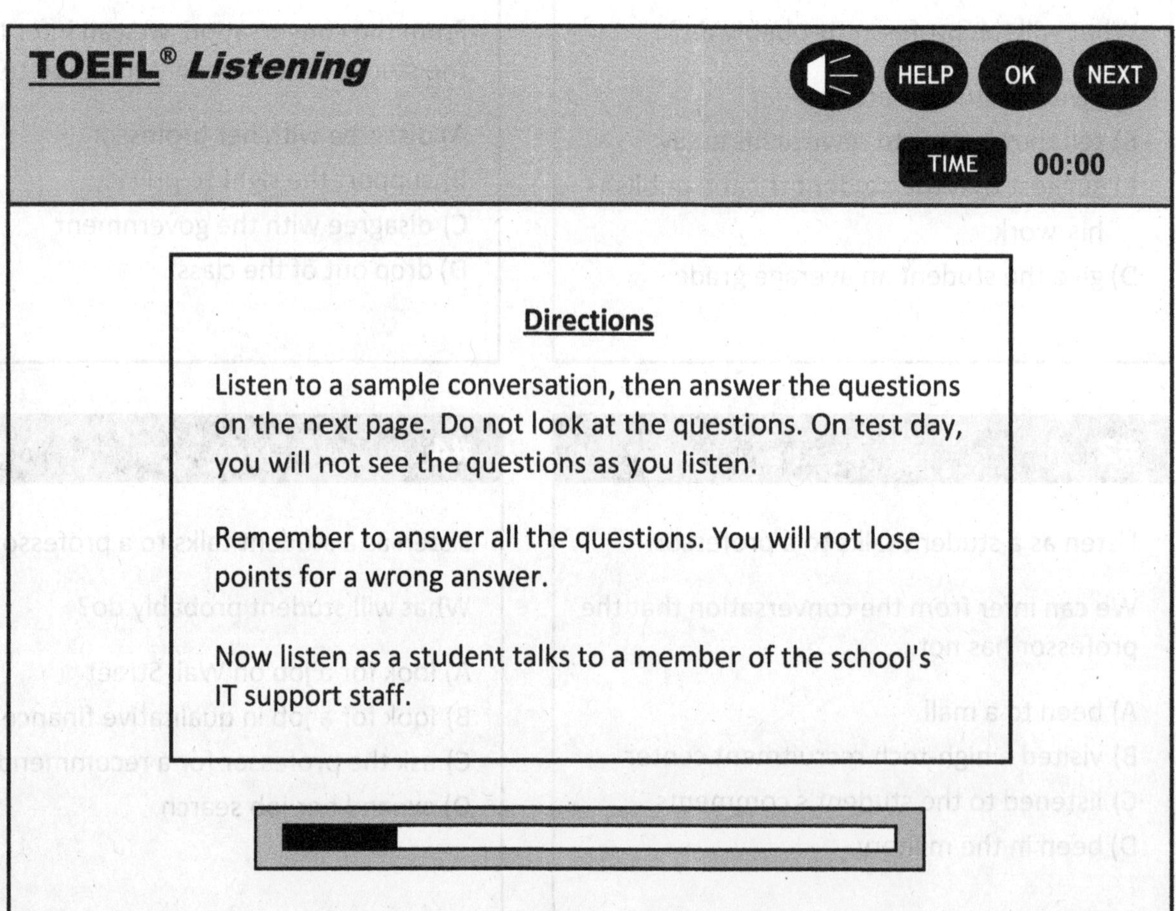
TOEFL® Listening
HELP
OK
NEXT
TIME
00:00
Directions
Listen to a sample conversation, then answer the questions on the next page. Do not look at the questions. On test day, you will not see the questions as you listen.
Remember to answer all the questions. You will not lose points for a wrong answer.
Now listen as a student talks to a member of the school's IT support staff.

Questions

Directions: Now get ready to answer the questions. Answer each question based on what is stated or implied in the conversation.

#1

What are the student and the IT staffer mainly discussing?

A) the student's new iPhone
B) the student's wi-fi issue
C) the school's security system
D) the latest virus going around

#2

What is the student's problem?

A) Her new iPod has a virus.
B) She needs a new wi-fi connection.
C) She can't connect to the school's wireless network.
D) She is having problems with the network.

#3

What are the wireless security settings? Select three. This is a 2-point question.

A) WPA
B) WEP2
C) WEP
D) WPA2
E) WPA-A

#4

Why does the student say this? 

A) because IT support fixed her iPod
B) because IT support was helpful
C) because IT support disconnected her
D) because IT support solved her issue

#5

Listen again to part of the conversation, then answer the question.

What does the student mean by this? 

A) She needs more information.
B) She is missing the point.
C) She understands completely.
D) She is apologizing for her mistake.

➔ Answers: page 683.
➔ Scoring multi-answer questions: page 693.
➔ Audio script: page 744.

Service Encounter: *Task Analysis*

In the sample service-encounter prompt, the student has a non academic problem. The problem is solved by the advice given by a non teaching, campus employee. This testing method is called *problem-solution.*

As you know, TOEFL uses the advice-giving, problem-solving testing method for office-hour prompts and for speaking task #5. That means you can apply office-hours strategies and speaking task #5 strategies to this task.

TOEFL's Testing Method

An understanding of TOEFL's testing method begins with an analysis of the sample service-encounter conversation. This analysis will help you take effective notes and maximize scoring. Read as you listen to the sample conversation.

Sample: *Service-Encounter Conversation*

Student
Hi. Is this IT support?

Staffer
Yes, it is. How can I help you? Let me guess. Your computer got hit by the email virus going round and you want to know how to restore your corrupted files, right?

Student
Actually, my computer didn't get hit.

Staffer
Oh, one of the lucky ones. So, what's up?

Student
I just bought an iPod Touch.

Staffer
Sweet. How much?

Student
A lot. Look, the reason I'm calling is because I can't connect my iPod to the internet.

Staffer
You mean the school's wireless network?

Student
Right.

Staffer
What exactly is the problem?

Student
When I open my email, a dialogue box asks me to log on to the school's wireless network. I log on with my school ID and my password, just like with my laptop, then another dialogue box pops up and says, "No wireless network." How can there be no wireless network when everybody around me is connected? I'm like totally confused. This never happens with my laptop. What am I doing wrong? It's something really simple, right?

Staffer
Probably security. What kind of encryption are you using?

Student
Excuse me?

Staffer
Encryption. The school's wireless network is encrypted.

Student
I'm sorry. I don't follow.

Staffer
Encryption basically means the wireless signal floating around the school here—well, not so much floating but, you know, covering—has been scrambled into a secret code that can only be opened by the right security setting on the device you're using. The old kind of wireless encryption is called WEP. That's short for wired-equivalent privacy. The school stopped using it two years ago because it had serious security issues. We now use WPA. That's short for wi-fi protected access. Your iPod is probably set for WEP.

Student
Ahhh...Right. Can you just tell me how to set it up? I'm kind of in a hurry here.

Staffer
Sure. Boot up your iPod. Go to your home screen. Open settings, then go to network. See it?

Student
Network. Network. Right.

Staffer
Open network, then open Wi-Fi.

Student
Okay. It's open.

Staffer
At the top of the screen, you should see security. Open it.

Student
Open security. Got it.

Staffer
You should see a menu that gives you a choice of encryption settings starting with WEP. See it?

Student
Got it. There's WEP followed by WPA and WPA2. Those are wireless security settings?

Staffer
Bingo. The school uses WPA, so select it and you should be good to go.

Student
Oh, my God. You're a genius!

Staffer
Sweet. Anything else I can help you with?

Student
Nope. That's it.

Staffer
Hey, would you mind filling out a survey? It's about how well I solved your problem. It would only take a sec.

Student
Sure. No problem.

G+3TiC=C: *Mapping a Conversation*

A service-encounter prompt is a fact-based argument in which a campus employee helps a student solve a non academic problem. The problem is resolved through an *advice-giving process*. This process occurs in the body of the conversation.

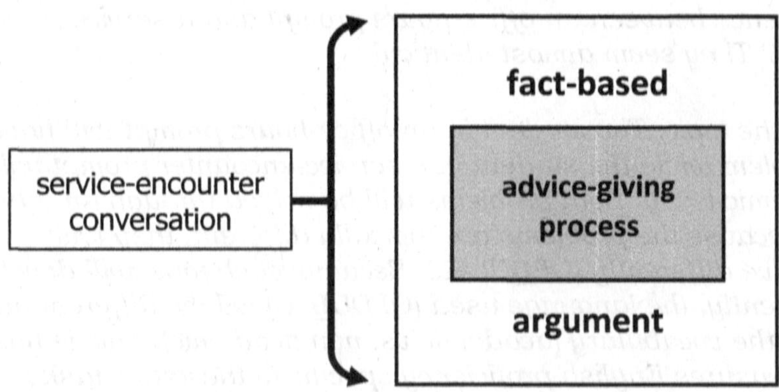

Mapped out, the sample service-encounter conversation looks like this.

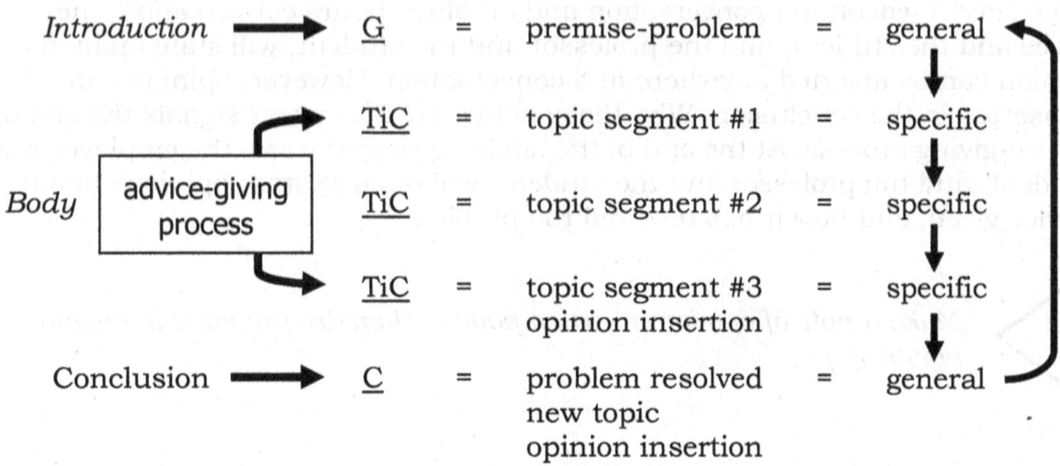

Note how the conclusion (C) in the sample conversation serves three purposes: 1) the student's problem is resolved; 2) a new topic is introduced (the evaluation form); 3) the student will state her opinion when filling out the evaluation form.

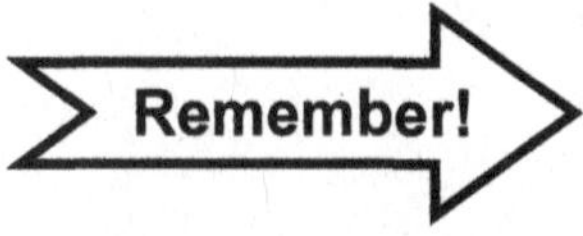

Note that there are no body paragraphs in the above map. Body paragraphs are specific to writing. Because this is a conversation, we will call each body paragraph a topic segment. A topic segment serves the same purpose as a body paragraph. Also, the number of topic segments will vary. There might be two topic segments (G+2TiC=C), three (G+3TiC=C), even four (G+4TiC=C). Be prepared for three.

Q *Does the conclusion always introduce a new topic?*

A *No. However, be prepared for a new topic in the conclusion. A new topic is a predictable way TOEFL tests your ability to infer future actions.*

Q *What is the difference between an office-hours prompt and a service-encounter prompt? They seem almost identical.*

A *The difference is the topic. The student in an office-hours prompt will have an academic problem while the student in a service-encounter prompt will have a non academic issue. Both problems will be solved through an advice-giving process. Because the problems are topically different, they will develop and resolve differently (OP**D**UL=C). Because each topic will develop and resolve differently, the language used (OPDU**L**=C) will be different as well, particularly the vocabulary (academic vs. non academic). This is how the TOEFL iBT measures English proficiency specific to these two tasks.*

Opinion-Insertion Points

During a service-encounter conversation and an office-hours conversation, the employee and the student, and the professor and the student, will state opinions. An opinion can be inserted anywhere in a conversation. However, opinions are often inserted in the conclusion. Why the conclusion? Because it signals the end of the advice-giving process. At the end of the advice-giving process, the employee and the student, and the professor and the student, will often express opinions about the advice given, and how it has resolved the problem.

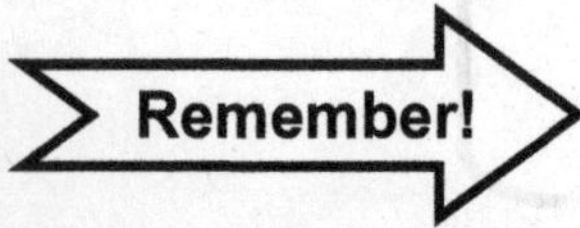

Make a note of opinion-insertion points. They are predictable testing points.

Introduction: *Rhetorical Functions*

An service-encounter prompt will start with a general introduction (G), which introduces the premise. The premise will define the main topic and the controlling idea. Combined, they are the problem. Look at the following premise. Note where it occurs in the sample introduction.

Premise: A student (main topic) wants to know why she can't connect her iPod to the school's wireless network (controlling idea).

G

Student
Hi. Is this IT support?

IT Support
Yes, it is. How can I help you? Let me guess. Your computer got hit by the email virus going round and you want to know how to restore your corrupted files, right?

Student
Actually, my computer didn't get hit.

IT Support
Oh, one of the lucky ones. So, what's up?

Student
I just bought an iPod Touch.

IT Support
Sweet. How much?

Student
A lot. Look, the reason I'm calling is because I can't connect my iPod to the internet.

IT Support
You mean the school's wireless network?

Student
Right.

IT Support
What exactly is the problem?

Note how a question signals the end of the introduction and signals the start of topic segment one.

Topic Segment One: *Rhetorical Functions*

In topic segment one below, the student defines and develops the problem: a lack of wi-fi connectivity. By doing so, the student teaches you about the topic. TOEFL uses this same *teaching-testing method* for the integrated writing task and for speaking tasks #3, #4, #5, and #6. Next, IT Support develops the topic with a description of encryption, using illustration (WEP and WPA), compare-and-contrast (WEP old vs. WPA new), and cause-and-effect (use WEP = no wi-fi connection).

Student
When I open my email, a dialogue box asks me to log on to the school's wireless network. I log on with my school ID and my password, just like with my laptop, then another dialogue box pops up and says, "No wireless network." How can there be no wireless network when everybody around me is connected? I'm like totally confused. This never happens with my laptop. What am I doing wrong? It's something really simple, right?

IT Support
Probably security. What kind of encryption are you using?

Student
Excuse me?

IT Support
Encryption. The school's wireless network is encrypted.

Student
I'm sorry. I don't follow.

IT Support
Encryption basically means the wireless signal floating around the school here—well, not so much floating but, you know, covering—has been scrambled into a secret code that can only be opened by the right security setting on the device you're using. The old kind of wireless encryption is called WEP. That's short for wired-equivalent privacy. The school stopped using it two years ago because it had serious security issues. We now use WPA. That's short for wi-fi protected access. Your iPod is probably set for WEP.

Student
Ahhh...Right. Can you just tell me how to set it up? I'm kind of in a hurry here.

Note how the student's request signals the conclusion of this segment. This request also signals the start of IT Support's step-by-step, *advice-giving solution* to the student's problem in the next topic segment.

Topic Segment Two: *Rhetorical Functions*

In topic segment two below, IT Support introduces a new topic: the step-by-step, advice-giving process aimed at solving the student's problem. Note the detailed steps. Note as well how the student inserts an opinion at the end of this segment.

IT Support
Sure. **1)** Boot up your iPod. **2)** Go to your home screen. **3)** Open settings, **4)** then go to network. See it?

Student
Network. Network. Right.

IT Support
5) Open network, **6)** then open Wi-Fi.

Student
Okay. It's open.

IT Support
At the top of the screen, you should see security. **7)** Open it.

Student
Open security. Got it.

IT Support
You should see a menu that gives you a choice of encryption settings starting with WEP. See it?

Student
Got it. There's WEP followed by WPA and WPA2. Those are wireless security settings?

IT Support
Bingo. **8)** The school uses WPA, so select it and you should be good to go.

Student
Oh, my God. You're a genius! ◀ **opinion insertion**

IT Support
Sweet. Anything else I can help you with?

Student
Nope. That's it.

Note how a rejoinder signals the conclusion of this topic segment.

Conclusion: *Rhetorical Functions*

In the conclusion, listen for a **new topic**. The new topic will often contain an action that will be completed after the conversation is finished. In this example, the future action is the student's inferred opinion regarding the service she received.

IT Support
Hey, would you mind **filling out a survey**? It's about how well I solved your problem. It would only take a sec.

Student
Sure. No problem. ◀ **inferred action + opinion**

Active-Passive Roles

The student in a service-encounter prompt, like the student in an office-hours prompt, will often play a *passive-listening role* while the campus employee will play an *active-advising role*. Because the campus employee is generally active and the student is generally passive, we can map out the underlying argument and the transitions based on their active-passive speech patterns.

G	=	student states premise-problem
TiC	=	active IT Support advice: "Boot up your iPod."
		passive student rejoinder: *"Done."*
TiC	=	active IT Support advice: "Anything else I can help you with?"
		passive student rejoinder: *"Nope. That's it."*
C	=	student problem solved + new topic introduced

Rhetorical Strategies

Service-encounter prompts, like office-hours prompts, are built on an underlying, fact-based argument with a predictable method of organization (**O**PDUL=C): general-specific-general. Another predictable feature is the rhetorical strategies used, the most important of which are cause-and-effect and process.

Cause-and-Effect: *In the Introduction*

In a service-encounter prompt, such as the sample, the student will state his/her problem (premise) in the introduction using cause-and-effect.

Premise: A student (main topic) wants to know why she can't connect her iPod to the school's wireless network (controlling idea).

Mapped out conversationally, the premise reads like this:

Premise: "I tried to connect my iPod to the school's wireless network (cause), but could not (effect)."

Note how the student is really saying, "I have a problem. I can't connect to the internet. What is the reason?" As you know, reasons are based on cause-and-effect relationships.

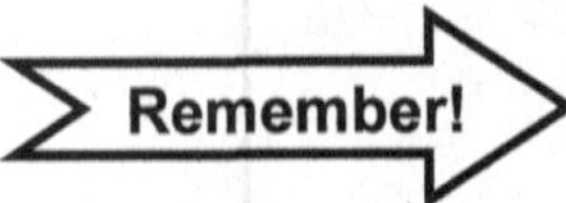

The student's problem signals the premise, which signals the start of the underlying fact-based argument upon which the employee's advice-giving process is built.

Cause-and-Effect: *In the Topic Segments*

Cause-and-effect is also used to identify the reason(s) for the student's problem. In topic segment two below, IT Support states the reason for the student's problem using **cause**-and-*effect*. Paraphrased, it reads like this:

Because you're using the old WEP system (cause), you can't connect your new iPod to the school's wireless network (effect).

> ***IT Support***
> Encryption basically means the wireless signal floating around the school here—well, not so much floating but, you know, covering—has been scrambled into a secret code that can only be opened by a student with the right school ID and password, and the right security setting. The old kind of wireless encryption was called WEP. That's short for wired equivalent privacy. **The school stopped using it [WEP] two years ago** *because it had serious security issues*. **We now use WPA.** That's short for wi-fi protected access. **Your iPod is probably set** *for WEP*.

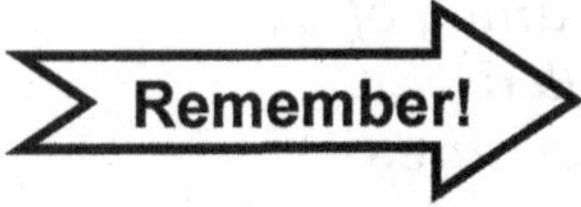

Once the reason for the problem is identified, the advice-giving process will begin. In the sample, the student follows IT Support's advice, tries using WPA (cause), and connects (effect). Result? Problem solved.

Cause-and-Effect: *In the Conclusion*

The new topic in the conclusion will often describe an implied cause-and-effect relationship. In the sample conclusion below, the student says, "Sure. No problem." This implies that the student will fill out the survey (action). When? We don't know. This fact is not stated. However, because IT Support solved the student's problem, we can infer that the student will say positive things (effect) about IT Support in the survey. This inferred approval process signals a continuation of the story after the conversation is finished. It also suggests that the student's opinion of the support process will be positive. These types of inferred future actions are predictable testing points. Make a note of them.

opinion insertion

IT Support
Hey, would you mind filling out a survey? It's about how well I solved your problem. It would only take a sec.

Student
Sure. No problem.

Process

As you know, the rhetorical strategy of process is an integral part of both service-encounter prompts and office-hours prompts, specifically in the body. In segment two of the sample service-encounter prompt below, IT Support uses process to solve the student's problem.

Step #1: Boot up your iPod.
Step #2: Go to your home screen.
Step #3: Open settings.
Step #4: Go to network.
Step #5: Open network.
Step #6: Open wi-fi.
Step #7: Open security.
Step #8: Select WPA. Problem solved.

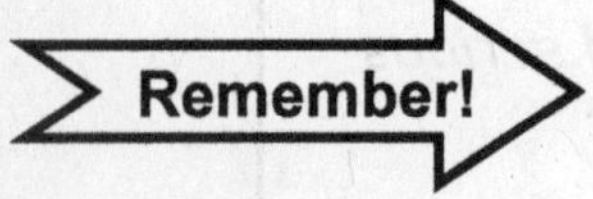

*The advice-giving process is not hard to identify. The challenge is understanding the language used to describe each step of the process. For example, in the sample, you know iPod, wi-fi, and network. They are part of your active English vocabulary. However, computer jargon like "boot up" and acronyms like WEP and WPA might not be part of your English vocabulary. In that case, you must learn the meaning of these new words by how they are used in context. This is called contextualizing (see page 560). This is how the TOEFL iBT measures language use proficiency (OPDU**L**=C) specific to listening.*

By combining cause-and-effect and process, you can see how these two rhetorical strategies support and develop the underlying fact-based argument in a service-hours prompt. You can also see how the TOEFL iBT recycles the same testing method in office-hours and in service-encounter prompts.

Question Types

The questions for a service-encounter prompt are the same as those for an office-hours prompt. Follow these steps when answering.

1. Make a Note Map

Anticipate the prompt's three-part structure by dividing your note map into the same three-part structure: introduction, body, conclusion. In the introduction, listen for the premise-problem; in the body, listen for the advice-giving process; in the conclusion, listen for the solution to the student's problem and a new topic. Listen for opinion insertions as well.

2. Authentic Language Use

While listening, note these authentic language use signals.

1) hesitation	3) topic digression	5) repetition	7) tone
2) self-correction	4) false start	6) restatement	8) idioms

3. Question Analysis: *Signal Words*

Read each question carefully. Make sure you understand it. Look for signal words in the question. Try and match the signals words in the question with words in your notes.

4. Choice Analysis: *Process of Elimination*

When analyzing the answer choices, eliminate choices that are:

1) off topic	3) too general	5) not known
2) too specific	4) not true	6) not accurate

5. Identify the Distractors

When analyzing the answer choices, look for the distractor. The distractor might be a homophone distractor (page 435) or an answer choice distractor (page 440).

Practice: ***Content Questions***

Directions: Listen to each prompt, then answer the question.

#1

Listen as a student talks to a security guard.

What is the main topic of discussion?

A) the student's parking ticket
B) the color of the parking lines
C) the lack of parking space
D) when the garage will close

#2

Listen as a student talks to an admin.

What is the focus of the conversation?

A) the student's ID card
B) the recent policy memo about tuition
C) the school's new policy
D) the government cutting back

#3

Listen as a student talks to a security guard.

What is the subject of discussion?

A) opening the lab
B) calling security
C) accessing the bio lab
D) completing an assignment

#4

Listen as a student talks to a librarian.

What is the subject of discussion?

A) a book the library has
B) a book the student has requested
C) a book the student wants to borrow
D) a book the library does not have

➔ Answers: page 683.
➔ Audio script: page 746.

Practice: *Purpose Questions*

Directions: Listen to each prompt, then answer the question.

#1

Listen as a student talks to an admin.

Why does the student visit financial aid?

A) to get course information
B) to learn about borrowing money
C) to pay back money borrowed
D) to find out about scholarships

#2

Listen as a student talks to maintenance.

Why does the student call maintenance?

A) to report a problem with her laptop
B) to report a wild animal problem
C) to report a problem with her room
D) to report a problem with her dorm

#3

Listen as a student talks to a security guard.

Why does the student visit security?

A) to get her stolen laptop back
B) to fill out a report
C) to request an investigation
D) to try and find her missing laptop

#4

Listen as a student talks to an admin.

Why does the student talk to the admin?

A) to buy tickets for her boyfriend and his family
B) to buy and sell game tickets on eBay
C) to purchase tickets for the big game
D) to purchase tickets for her boyfriend's family

➔ Answers: page 683.
➔ Audio script: page 748.

Practice: *Single-Answer Detail Questions*

Directions: Listen as a student talks to a campus employee.

#1

To whom does the student speak?

A) the manager of an art gallery
B) the manager of the school's gallery
C) the editor of Art House Magazine
D) her art professor

#2

What can't the student remember?

A) The last time she bought computer parts.
B) The last time she talked to her professor.
C) The last time she bought art material.
D) The last time she went to class.

#3

What is the student pushing with her art?

A) the envelope
B) her portfolio
C) her prices
D) her schedule

#4

How long will the student's exhibition last?

A) a month
B) two weeks
C) one week
D) a day

#5

How many days does the student have to prepare her exhibition?

A) three
B) two
C) seven
D) one

#6

Who is Karen Goldblatt?

A) a magazine publisher
B) the student's art professor
C) an art expert
D) a famous artist

➔ Answers: page 683.
➔ Audio script: page 750.

Practice: *Multi-Answer Detail Questions*

Directions: Listen to each prompt, then answer the question.

#1

Listen as a student talks to an admin. This is a 1-point question.

What information is required for the scholarship application? Select two.

A) a driver's license
B) high grades
C) letters of recommendation
D) volunteer experience

#2

Listen as a student talks to a librarian. This is a 1-point question.

Which books does the student put on reserve? Select two.

A) Howard's Human Prehistory
B) Mitchell's Methods of Archeology
C) Swift-Lee's Guide to Ancient Tools
D) Swift-Scott's Guide to Ancient Tools

#3

Listen as a student talks to an admin. This is a 1-point question.

How will the student pay for the tickets? Select two.

A) half Visa
B) half debit card
C) half cash
D) half MasterCard

#4

Listen as a student talks to a campus employee. This is a 1-point question.

What did the student order? Select two.

A) Pepsi
B) chicken wrap with onions, cheese, and jalapenos
C) turkey wrap with avocado and sprouts
D) Coke

➔ Answers: page 683.
➔ Scoring multi-answer questions: page 693.
➔ Audio script: page 751.

Practice: *Question-First Function Questions*

Directions: Answer each question based on what is stated or implied.

#1

Why does the student say this? 

A) to indicate that his Visa card is lost therefore he can't pay for the tickets
B) to explain that he has a lot of Visa cards
C) to indicate that he needs to use up the maximum amount available on his card
D) to indicate that he can't use his Visa because he has reached his limit

#2

Why does the admin say this? 

A) to stress that the student needs as many high grades as possible
B) to emphasize the fact that high grades are given to good students only
C) to remind the student that he must give his grades to the financial office
D) to stress that high grades are important when applying for a scholarship

#3

Why does the student say this? 

A) to suggest a growing interest
B) to suggest that she has no money
C) to suggest that it is time to leave
D) to suggest a lack of interest

#4

Why does the student say this? 

A) to express her joy and excitement
B) to express her shock and surprise
C) to express her doubt and confusion
D) to express her love and affection

➔ Answers: page 684.
➔ Audio script: page 752.

Practice: *Segment-First Function Questions*

Directions: Listen to each prompt, then answer the question.

#1

Listen to part of a conversation, then answer the question.

Why does the student say this? 

A) because she wants to reserve the book
B) because she does not want to reserve *Methods of Archeology*
C) because *Guide to Tools* is a better book
D) because she wants to reserve all three books

#2

Listen to part of a conversation, then answer the question.

What does security mean by this? 

A) the student must pay the fine
B) the student does not have to pay the fine
C) the student needs to move her car
D) security will report the student

#3

Listen to part of a conversation, then answer the question.

What does the student mean by this? 

A) You can say that again.
B) I can't believe it.
C) Of course.
D) Fantastic, isn't it?

#4

Listen to part of a conversation, then answer the question.

What does the student mean by this? 

A) I prefer Coke.
B) Pepsi is fine.
C) I want neither Coke nor Pepsi.
D) I want to cancel my order.

➔ Answers: page 684.
➔ Audio script: page 752.

Practice: ***Direct-Attitude Questions***

Directions: Listen to each prompt, then answer the question.

#1

Listen then answer the question.

How does the student feel about getting a scholarship?

A) amused
B) indifferent
C) relieved
D) worried

#2

Listen then answer the question.

What is the student's opinion of *Dummies* books?

A) You get a lot for a great price.
B) They are overpriced and lacking detail.
C) You never know what you will get.
D) They cover every subject.

#3

Listen then answer the question.

How does the student feel about putting titles on her work?

A) She loves to think up new titles.
B) She thinks it is a good idea for her show.
C) She thinks her titles are original.
D) She is against the idea.

#4

Listen then answer the question.

What does the admin think about buying so many tickets?

A) It is definitely not a wise idea.
B) It is definitely a risky decision.
C) It is definitely a great idea.
D) It is definitely worth considering.

➔ Answers: page 684.
➔ Audio script: page 753.

Practice: ***Inferred-Attitude Questions***

Directions: Listen to each prompt, then answer the question.

#1

Listen then answer the question.

How does the student feel about the new policy?

A) She can't support it.
B) She can't afford it.
C) She can't allow it.
D) She can't believe it.

#2

Listen then answer the question.

What does the student think about selling his used texts on eBay?

A) It's a great idea.
B) It's too complicated.
C) It's not an option.
D) It's fast and convenient.

#3

Listen then answer the question.

How does the admin react to the student's request?

A) mysteriously
B) sympathetically
C) skeptically
D) suspiciously

#4

Listen then answer the question.

How does the student feel about the staffer's help?

A) wonderful
B) excited
C) grateful
D) fruitful

➔ Answers: page 684.
➔ Audio script: page 754.

Practice: *Inferred-Action Questions*

Directions: Listen to each prompt, then answer the question.

#1

Listen then answer the question.

Where will the student probably go?

A) to pick up her reward
B) to financial aid
C) to the scholarship office
D) to the bank

#2

Listen then answer the question.

What will the student probably do?

A) go to the campus security office
B) buy a new cell phone
C) call campus security later
D) buy a silicone sleeve with red hearts

#3

Listen then answer the question.

What will the student probably do?

A) buy the book
B) reserve the book
C) pay the fine
D) contest the fine

#4

Listen then answer the question.

What will the student probably do?

A) reconsider taking the class
B) come back next week
C) make an appointment
D) get a medical release form

➔ Answers: page 684.
➔ Audio script: page 755.

Lecture Prompts

The listening section will include four academic lectures. Each lecture will last approximately 5 minutes. Each lecture will be followed by 6 questions. You cannot replay the lectures or the questions. You may takes notes.

Lecture Types

There are two lecture types: professor-only and professor-students. In a professor-only lecture, the professor will lecture with no student participation. In a professor-students discussion, a professor will discuss an academic topic with a group of students.

Lecture: *Professor-Only*

An analysis of a professor-only lecture begins by listening to a test sample. Start by making a note map based on the three-part structure of a fact-based argument.

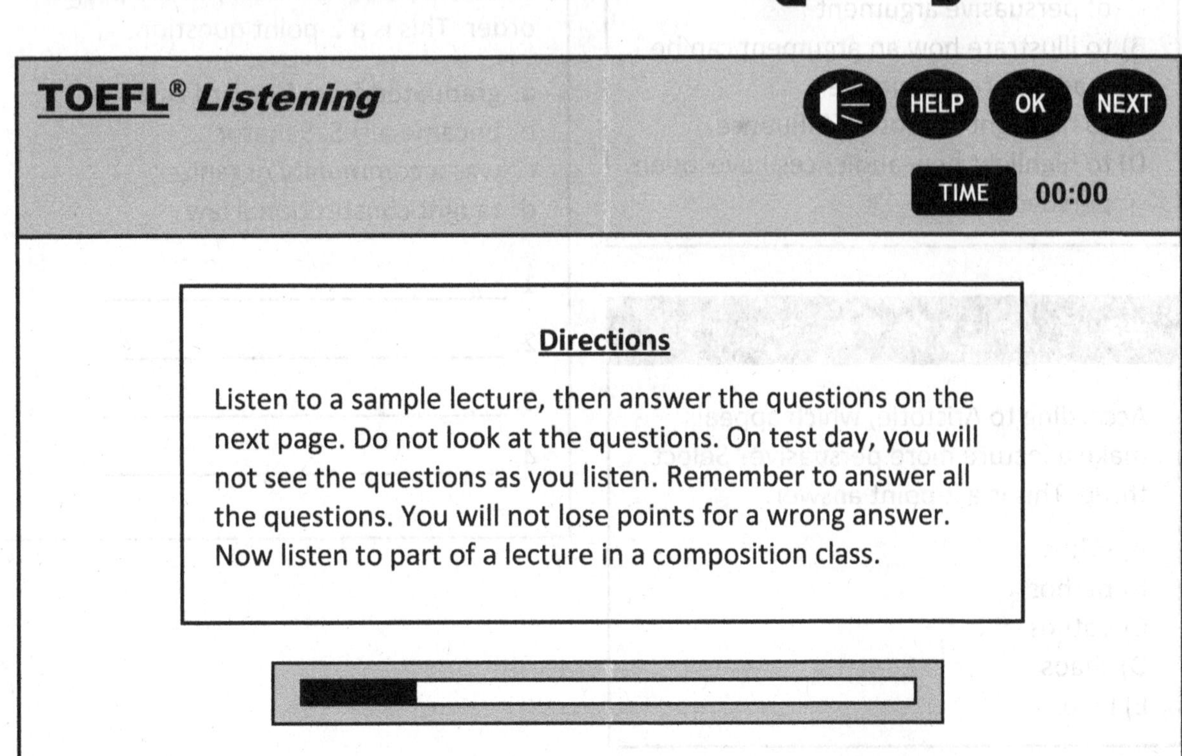

TOEFL® Listening
HELP
OK
NEXT
TIME
00:00
Directions
Listen to a sample lecture, then answer the questions on the next page. Do not look at the questions. On test day, you will not see the questions as you listen. Remember to answer all the questions. You will not lose points for a wrong answer. Now listen to part of a lecture in a composition class.

Questions

Directions: Now get ready to answer the questions. Answer each based on what is stated or implied in the lecture.

#1

What is the topic of the lecture?

A) Aristotle's philosophy
B) Aristotle's writing style
C) Aristotle's ancient lesson
D) Aristotle's modes of appeal

#2

What is the purpose of the lecture?

A) to demonstrate three different types of persuasive argument
B) to illustrate how an argument can be made more persuasive
C) to highlight Aristotle's influence
D) to highlight how audiences have been persuaded

#3

According to Aristotle, which appeals make a lecture more persuasive? Select three. This is a 2-point answer.

A) ethos
B) bathos
C) pathos
D) chaos
E) logos

#4

Why does the professor say this ? 

A) to warn that even the best arguments can fail to persuade an audience
B) to warn that persuaded people often change their minds during elections
C) to reinforce the idea that persuasive arguments guarantee results
D) to highlight the need for arguments

#5

The professor describes President Obama's personal history. Put President Obama's personal history in the proper order. This is a 2-point question.

a. graduated from Harvard Law
b. became a U.S. Senator
c. was a community organizer
d. taught constitutional law

1. ______________________
2. ______________________
3. ______________________
4. ______________________

#6

In the lecture, the professor describes Aristotle's three appeals and their functions in an argument. Indicate whether each of the following is a function of Aristotle's three appeals. This is a 3-point question.

	YES	NO
Logos appeals to reason using deduction or induction		
Ethos appeals to what is morally right.		
Pathos appeals to the emotions using both words and images.		
Logos combines both ethos and pathos.		
Ethos appeals to character.		

➔ Answers: page 684.
➔ Scoring multi-answer questions: page 693.
➔ Audio script: page 756.

Professor-Only: *Task Analysis*

TOEFL's Testing Method

An understanding of TOEFL's testing method for this task begins with a rhetorical analysis of the sample lecture. This analysis will help you take effective notes and maximize scoring. Read as you listen to the sample lecture.

Sample: *Professor-Only Lecture* → Audio Track #61

1 ➔ According to Aristotle, an argument can be made more persuasive by using three appeals: logos, pathos, and ethos.
2 ➔ Let's start with logos. Logos, or logic, appeals to reason. One way to appeal to reason is by using deduction. Deduction—and we'll come back to this later on—is a form of reasoning in which you make a conclusion based on a series of related facts or premises. Let's work through an example. First, you start with a major premise, such as...Oh, I don't know—*All English teachers are poor*. This general statement is followed by a specific statement or minor premise, in this case *Bob is an English teacher*. From these two premises, a conclusion logically follows: *Bob is poor*. Put it all together and it reads like this: *All English teachers are poor. Bob is an English teacher. Bob is poor*. As you can see, deduction can be pretty persuasive. Its closed or formal structure leaves no doubt as to Bob's financial situation relative to his profession. Induction is another form of logic that appeals to reason. When inducing, you combine a series of related facts, such as *Joan loves apples, Joan loves blueberries, Joan loves mangos.* From these facts, we can make a conclusion, in this case *Joan loves fruit*. Does she love all fruit? We don't know. She might abhor apricots. As you can see, induction is not as closed or conclusive as deduction. Still, add numbers to an inductive mix and the logic behind an argument whether to invest in a company can be quite appealing. For example, *ABC Company made a $20 billion profit last year; ABC made a $40 billion profit this year; ABC will make a $60 billion profit next year*. Conclusion? You do the math.
3 ➔ Pathos, in contrast, is an appeal to the emotions. By appealing to the emotions, the arguer can evoke sympathy from an audience. Sympathy, in turn, makes an argument more persuasive. Movies regularly employ pathos. Did you cry when E.T. finally went home? Were you terrified when Titanic sank or when Jaws rose out of the water, teeth flashing? If so, then the director persuaded you that two-dimensional images on a movie screen are so real, so life-like, you reacted to them emotionally. Pathos can also support logos. For example,

photographs often support news stories. What better way to evoke audience anger at an oil company than to place a photo of an oil-covered pelican next to an article about an oil spill.

4 ➔ Next we have ethos. Ethos is an appeal to character. For example, from whom would you buy a computer, a man in a business suit or a man in a T-shirt? Ethically, some might eschew the man in the T-shirt, a T-shirt being the antithesis of business attire therefore unethical, not trustworthy. However, such ethical conclusions have been turned on their heads, especially in America. Case in point: Whenever Apple introduces a new product, CEO Steve Jobs introduces the product wearing jeans and a T-Shirt. Does Jobs' choice of clothes diminish the quality of the product? No. If anything, Jobs' casual look enhances Apple's cool factor. As you can see, what was once ethically unacceptable—wearing jeans to work—is now perfectly acceptable.

5 ➔ Those, then, are Aristotle's three appeals. It's important to remember that a successful argument—a persuasive argument—combines all three appeals. Look at President Obama. As an argument for president, his life story was quite compelling. Why? Because it was defined by the three appeals. As a youth, he was a community organizer (ethos and pathos). He then studied law at Harvard (logos and ethos). After he graduated, he taught constitutional law at the University of Chicago (logos and ethos). He then became a U.S. senator (logos, pathos, and ethos). Combined, these three appeals made Barack Obama a persuasive argument to be president of the United States.

6 ➔ That said, keep in mind, however, that even when supported by all three appeals, there is no guarantee that a politician seeking office—or any other argument—will persuade an audience, for if any of the three appeals come under fire, the audience will fail to be persuaded.

Q *This lecture on Aristotle was task #6 on the speaking test. Does the TOEFL iBT recycle the same argument in different test sections?*

A *No. The TOEFL iBT does not recycle arguments across the four test sections. Each argument used for testing will be different and, according to ETS, used only once.*

R For demonstration purposes, the Aristotle lecture above has been recycled to illustrate that the structure of a fact-based argument does not change from task to task.

G+3TiC=C: *Mapping a Lecture*

A lecture is a verbal, fact-based argument in which a professor develops an academic topic. In the sample lecture, a professor in a composition class uses a fact-based argument to introduce and develop the topic of Aristotle's three appeals.

For testing purposes, TOEFL recycles fact-based arguments. That means you are already familiar with the structure of a fact-based lecture. That structure can be mapped out using G+3TiC=C.

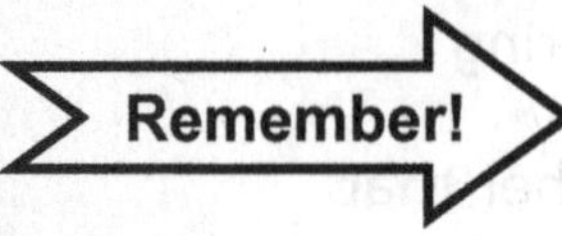

The number of body paragraphs depends on how ETS designs the lecture. The sample lecture has four body paragraphs (4TiC). On test day, expect three body paragraphs (3TiC).

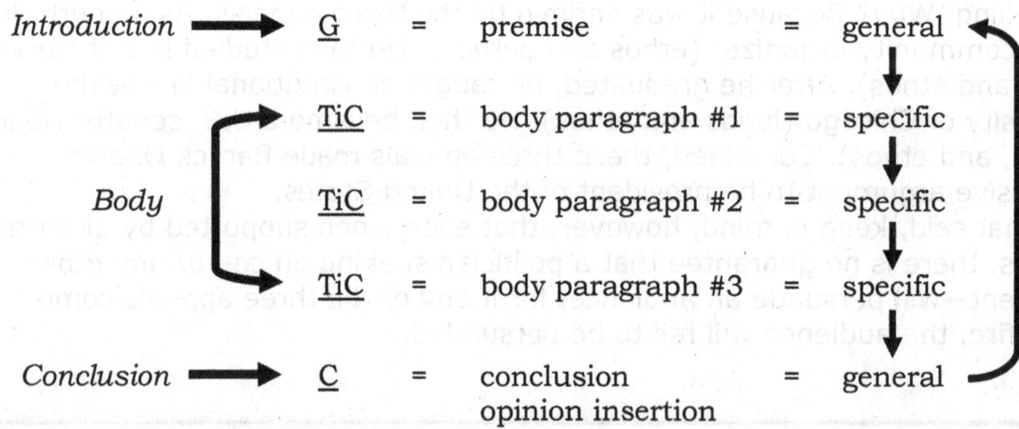

Opinion-Insertion Points

During a professor-only lecture, the professor will often insert an opinion. An opinion can be inserted anywhere in a lecture. However, for this task, a predictable insertion point is the conclusion. Why the conclusion? Because the conclusion signals the end of the lecture. In the conclusion, the professor will often summarize the argument in the lecture and the main topics. In that summary, the professor will often insert a comment. The inserted comment will be an opinion.

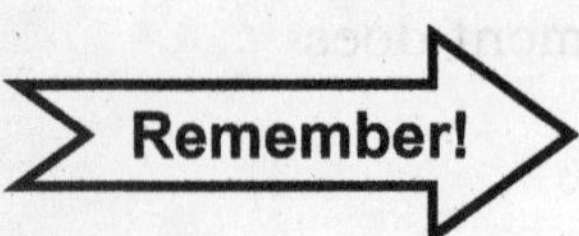

Make a note of opinion-insertion points. They are predictable testing points.

Introduction: *Rhetorical Functions*

A lecture will start with a general introduction (G). It will introduce the premise. To identify the premise in the sample, ask, "What is the main topic?" Answer: *Making an argument more persuasive.* In this example, to find the controlling idea, ask "How?" Answer: *By using Aristotle's three modes of appeal: logos, pathos, and ethos.*

Premise: Making an argument more persuasive (main topic) by using Aristotle's three modes of appeal: logos, pathos, and ethos (controlling idea).

Look at the sample introduction below. Note how short it is. Note also that it is the premise of the sample lecture, and that it tells you—in one sentence—what you will hear.

1 ➔ According to Aristotle, an argument can be made more persuasive by using three appeals: logos, pathos, and ethos.

Lecture introductions are predictably short. If you are not paying attention—if you are shuffling paper or adjusting your headset—you will miss the premise. If you miss the premise, you will miss the most important part of the lecture: the main topic and the controlling idea.

In the sample lecture introduction below, note the three **predictors**. Three predictors signal three body paragraphs. The predictors also signal the topic of each body paragraph: 1) logos = the topic body paragraph one; 2) pathos = the topic of body paragraph two; 3) ethos = the topic of body paragraph three (see page 104 to review predictors).

1 ➔ According to Aristotle, an argument can be made more persuasive by using three appeals: **logos**, **pathos**, and **ethos**.

Many of the lecture topics will be new to you. Therefore, TOEFL will teach you about them. TOEFL teaches you by starting with a premise, then developing it with supporting illustrations (body paragraphs). This way TOEFL is both a teaching and a testing tool. TOEFL employs the same teaching-testing method for the integrated writing task and for speaking task #3, #4, #5, #6, and for this task as well.

<u>Body Paragraphs</u>: *Rhetorical Functions*

Each body paragraph (TiC) will support and develop the lecture's premise. In body paragraph one below (paragraph <u>2</u> in the 6-paragraph lecture), note the standard, three-part paragraph structure: **Transition-topic**, *illustration(s)*, <u>Conclusion</u>. This three-part structure progresses from general (<u>T</u>ransition-topic) to specific (<u>i</u>llustration) to general (<u>C</u>onclusion). This structure, in turn, reflects the overall, three-part structure of the lecture itself.

TiC

2 → **Let's start with logos. Logos, or logic, appeals to reason.** *One way to appeal to reason is by using deduction. Deduction—and we'll come back to this later on—is a form of reasoning in which you make a conclusion based on a series of related facts or premises. Let's work through an example. First, you start with a major premise, such as...Oh, I don't know—All English teachers are poor. This general statement is followed by a specific statement or minor premise, in this case Bob is an English teacher. From these two premises, a conclusion logically follows: Bob is poor. Put it all together and it reads like this: All English teachers are poor. Bob is an English teacher. Bob is poor. As you can see, deduction can be pretty persuasive. Its closed or formal structure leaves no doubt as to Bob's financial situation relative to his profession. Induction is another form of logic that appeals to reason. When inducing, you combine a series of related facts, such as Joan loves apples, Joan loves blueberries, Joan loves mangos. From these facts, we can make a conclusion, in this case Joan loves fruit. Does she love all fruit? We don't know. She might abhor apricots. As you can see, induction is not as closed or conclusive as deduction. Still, add numbers to an inductive mix and the logic behind an argument whether to invest in a company can be quite appealing. For example, ABC Company made a $20 billion profit last year, ABC made a $40 billion profit this year, ABC will make a $60 billion profit next year.* <u>Conclusion? You do the math.</u>

The three-part paragraph structure (**T**ransition-topic, *illustration*, Conclusion) repeats in body paragraphs two and three (paragraphs 3 and 4 in the 6-paragraph lecture).

3 ➔ **Pathos, in contrast, is an appeal to the emotions.** *By appealing to the emotions, the arguer can evoke sympathy from an audience. Sympathy, in turn, makes an argument more persuasive. Movies regularly employ pathos. Did you cry when E.T. finally went home? Were you terrified when Titanic sank or when Jaws rose out of the water, teeth flashing? If so, then the director persuaded you that two-dimensional images on a movie screen are so real, so life-like, you reacted to them emotionally. Pathos can also support logos. For example, photographs often support news stories.* What better way to evoke audience anger at an oil company than to place the photo of an oil-covered pelican next to an article about an oil spill.

4 ➔ **Next we have ethos. Ethos is an appeal to character.** *For example, from whom would you buy a computer, a man in a business suit or a man in a T-shirt? Ethically, some might eschew the man in the T-shirt, a T-shirt being the antithesis of business attire therefore unethical, not trustworthy. However, such ethical conclusions have been turned on their heads, especially in America. Case in point: Whenever Apple introduces a new product, CEO Steve Jobs introduces the product wearing jeans and a T-Shirt. Does Jobs' choice of clothes diminish the quality of the product? No. If anything, Jobs' casual look enhances Apple's cool factor.* As you can see, what was once ethically unacceptable—wearing jeans to work—is now perfectly acceptable.

The three-part paragraph structure (**Transition-topic**, *illustration*, Conclusion) repeats in body paragraph four. Rhetorically, body paragraph four combines all three appeals and illustrates how, when combined, the three appeals support the argument that Barack Obama would make a good president. This, in turn, makes the Obama-for-president argument more persuasive.

5 ➔ **Those, then, are Aristotle's three appeals. It's important to remember that a successful argument—a persuasive argument—combines all three appeals**. *Look at President Obama. As an argument for president, his life story was quite compelling. Why? Because it was defined by the three appeals. As a youth, he was a community organizer (ethos and pathos). He then studied law at Harvard (logos and ethos). After he graduated, he taught constitutional law at the University of Chicago (logos and ethos). He then became a U.S. senator (logos, pathos and ethos).* Combined, these three appeals made Barack Obama a persuasive argument to be president of the United States.

Conclusion: *Rhetorical Functions*

The sample lecture ends with a conclusion (C). Note how this conclusion contains a warning. Note also how this warning is an opinion-insertion point.

6 ➔ That said, keep in mind, however, that even when supported by all three appeals, there is no guarantee that a politician seeking office—or any other argument—will persuade an audience, for if any of the three appeals come under fire, the audience will fail to be persuaded.

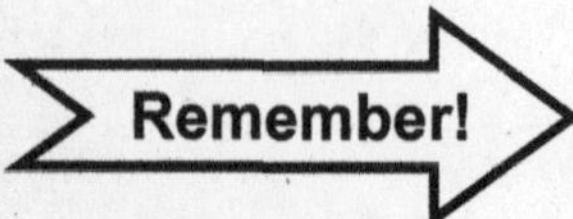

Make a note of all conclusion strategies. They are predictable testing points (see page 236 for conclusion strategies).

Rhetorical Strategies

In a fact-based lecture, the professor will use a rhetorical strategy to define the premise (main topic + controlling idea). For example, a date in the premise will signal...

The rhetorical strategy of narration.

On October 3, 1990, East and West Germany united after forty-five years of separation.

The premise might also use the rhetorical strategy of process...

Extracting oil from olives begins with perfectly ripened olives.

Or description...

At 29,029 feet, Mount Everest is the world's highest mountain.

Or cause-and-effect...

Many archeologists believe that climate change led to the extinction of the Neanderthals and the rise of Homo Sapiens, particularly in Europe.

Or compare-and-contrast...

Today, the Sahara Desert is a sun-baked sea of sand whereas in 7,000 BC, the Sahara was a fertile zone covered with lakes and savannah.

Or definition...

Simply put, the human genome is an organism's hereditary database encoded in the organism's DNA and RNA.

Or classification...

Pervasive development disorders include autism, Asperger syndrome, Rett syndrome, childhood disintegrative disorder (CDD), and pervasive developmental disorder not otherwise specified (PDD-NOS).

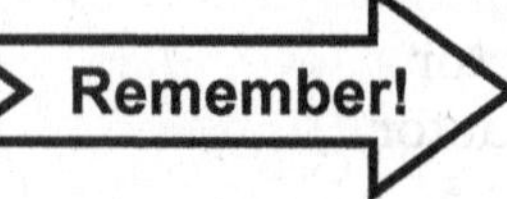

*The premise of the lecture will be defined by an applicable rhetorical strategy. However, as the lecture progresses, the premise will be developed by a variety of rhetorical strategies that, when combined, form a coherent argument (OPDUL=**C**).*

To review rhetorical strategies in the premise, see speaking task #4, pages 299-300.

Question Types

The questions for this task are the same as those used for office-hours and service-encounter prompts. For this task, three new question types are introduced. You will learn about them later on in this section. Those questions are:

- ordering questions
- yes-no questions
- connecting questions

Follow these steps when answering each question type.

1. Make a Note Map

Anticipate the lecture's three-part structure by dividing your note map into the same three-part structure: introduction, body, conclusion. In the introduction, listen for the premise; in the body, listen for supporting illustrations; in the conclusion, listen for a conclusion strategy and the professor's inserted opinion.

2. Authentic Language Use

While listening, note these authentic language use signals.

1) hesitation	3) topic digression	5) repetition	7) tone
2) self-correction	4) false start	6) restatement	8) idioms

3. Question Analysis: *Signal Words*

Read each question carefully. Make sure you understand it. Look for signal words in the question. Try and match the signal words in the question with words in your notes.

4. Choice Analysis: *Process of Elimination*

When analyzing the answer choices, eliminate choices that are:

1) off topic	3) too general	5) not known
2) too specific	4) not true	6) not accurate

5. Identify the Distractors

When analyzing the answer choices, look for the distractor. The distractor might be a homophone distractor (page 435) or an answer choice distractor (page 440).

Basic Comprehension Questions

Practice: *Content Questions*

Directions: Listen to each prompt, then answer the question.

#1

Listen to a professor, then answer the question.

What is the main topic of the lecture?

A) photoautotrophs
B) essential chemical processes
C) photosynthesis
D) classifying photosynthetic plants, algae and bacteria

#2

Listen to a professor, then answer the question.

What is the focus of the lecture?

A) computers
B) algorithms
C) brownies
D) software

#3

Listen to a professor, then answer the question.

What is the main topic of the lecture?

A) the evolution of early civilizations
B) the word civilization
C) the world's first spreadsheets
D) the importance of writing

#4

Listen to a professor, then answer the question.

What is the focus of the lecture?

A) translating Egyptian hieroglyphs
B) an important discovery
C) the Rosetta Stone
D) France's and Britain's historical claim

➔ Answers: page 684.
➔ Audio script: page 758.

Practice: *Purpose Questions*

Directions: Listen to each prompt, then answer the question.

#1

Listen to a professor, then answer the question.

Why does the professor introduce four more thinking tools?

A) to introduce more material
B) to indicate which tools are important
C) to develop and expand thinking styles
D) to expand and develop the topic

#2

Listen to a professor, then answer the question.

Why does the professor describe Frank Sinatra's breathing style?

A) to illustrate why Sinatra was talented
B) to illustrate how Sinatra could sing
C) to illustrate why Sinatra was original
D) to illustrate Sinatra's passion for words

#3

Listen to a professor, then answer the question.

Why does the professor stress fossil fuels?

A) to compare old and new societies
B) to contrast kings and despots
C) to contrast industrial and preindustrial societies
D) to illustrate one type of energy source

#4

Listen to a professor, then answer the question.

Why does the professor mention Europe in 2003?

A) as evidence of serious weather patterns
B) as evidence of how summer can kill
C) as evidence to support NOAA's claim
D) as evidence we need to drink more water

➔ Answers: page 684.
➔ Audio script: page 759.

Practice: *Single-Answer Detail Questions*

Directions: Listen to a lecture about education, then answer the questions.

#1

The first public schools in America were...

A) focused on teaching Protestant beliefs
B) free to all students, rich and poor
C) an alternative to Catholic schools
D) created for new immigrants

#2

In which year was the Boston Latin School founded?

A) 1735
B) 1837
C) 1600
D) 1635

#3

According to the lecture, the literacy rate for women in colonial America was...

A) very high
B) the same as for men
C) extremely low
D) improving

#4

What was the condition of the public school system in 1837?

A) growing rapidly as planned
B) a model of excellence around the world
C) in desperate need of reform
D) divided between Puritans and Catholics

#5

How did Horace Mann change the school year?

A) He added a six-week summer vacation.
B) He limited it to six years.
C) He added six days.
D) He increased it to six months.

#6

According to the lecture, what did Horace Mann believe?

A) Education decreased taxes.
B) Education was moral training.
C) Education was only for the rich.
D) Education was a religious duty.

➔ Answers: page 685.
➔ Audio script: page 760.

Practice: *Multi-Answer Detail Questions*

Directions: Listen to each prompt, then answer the question.

#1

Listen then answer the question. This is a 2-point question.

What three weapons did a Roman legionnaire carry? Select three.

A) gladius
B) gladiator
C) pugio
D) polio
E) pilum

#2

Listen then answer the question. This is a 2-point question.

What are the essential parts of a business plan? Select three.

A) a description of the profits
B) a statement describing the goals
C) the reason why the goals are attainable
D) a plan of action
E) how to maintain a competitive edge

#3

Listen then answer the question. This is a 2-point question.

According to the professor, the best ways to study marine life are... Select three.

A) in a laboratory
B) by submersibles
C) with specially designed cameras
D) by scuba diving
E) by computer simulation

#4

Listen then answer the question. This is a 1-point question.

What were the first major battles of the American Revolutionary War? Select two.

A) the Battle of White Plains
B) the Battle of Brooklyn
C) the Battle of the Heights
D) the Battle of Harlem Heights

➔ Answers: page 685.
➔ Scoring multi-answer questions: page 693.
➔ Audio script: page 761.

Pragmatic-Understanding Questions

Practice: *Question-First Function Questions*

Directions: Answer each question based on what is stated or implied.

#1

Why does the professor say this? 

A) to mention Sinatra's love of sports
B) to point out Sinatra's place in history
C) to detail Sinatra's many talents
D) to stress how original Sinatra was

#2

Why does the professor say this? 

A) to highlight the job of a marine biologist
B) to stress the need to respect nature
C) to reinforce the need for more research
D) to warn that the water should not be disturbed

#3

Why does the professor say this? 

A) to illustrate how different societies define civilization
B) to illustrate how taboos play a part in most societies
C) to warn against defining all societies the same way
D) to redefine the nature of society

#4

Why does the professor say this? 

A) to compare New York City today with New York City during the Revolutionary War
B) to contrast buildings now and buildings during the Revolutionary War
C) to illustrate two battles that took place on Manhattan island
D) to suggest that the students should go for an historical walk around New York

Turn the page for questions 5-8.

Practice: (cont'd)

#5

Why does the professor say this? 

A) to highlight a commonly known fact about weather-related deaths
B) to illustrate weather-related deaths in the United States
C) to classify hurricanes and tornadoes by how deadly they are
D) to state a little-known fact about hurricanes and tornadoes

#6

Why does the professor say this? 

A) to highlight Rome's need for an army
B) to illustrate how a census gave the Roman government accurate statistics
C) to define how ancient empires raised tax money by employing a census
D) to illustrate how a census was taken two-thousand years ago

#7

Why does the professor say this? 

A) to warn against global warming
B) to illustrate how an insect is destroying a local species in Asia
C) to show how global warming is affecting both bees and hornets in Europe
D) to illustrate the destructive power of the Asian hornet, an invasive species

#8

Why does the professor say this? 

A) to stress how astonished everyone was, then and now
B) to highlight how bad news affects people
C) to remind people what happened on December 11
D) to explain where she was on December 11, 2008

➔ Answers: page 685.
➔ Audio script: page 763.

Practice: *Segment-First Function Questions*

Directions: Answer each question based on what is stated or implied.

#1

Listen to part of a lecture, then answer the question.

Why does the professor say this? 

A) to stress that the battle is still going on
B) to suggest that France is the rightful owner of the Rosetta Stone
C) to suggest that the rightful owner of the Rosetta Stone is still in question
D) to suggest that Britain and France debate

#2

Listen to part of a lecture, then answer the question.

Why does the professor say this? 

A) to invite an argument
B) to invite debate
C) to invite a review
D) to invite questions

#3

Listen to part of a lecture, then answer the question.

Why does the professor say this? 

A) to introduce the next debate
B) to introduce the next question
C) to introduce the next topic
D) to introduce the next reason

#4

Listen to part of a lecture, then answer the question.

Why does the professor say this? 

A) to illustrate using a simple example
B) to classify using a simple recipe
C) to compare food to algorithms
D) to illustrate a simple exercise

➔ Answers: page 685.
➔ Audio script: page 764.

Practice: *Direct-Attitude Questions*

Directions: Listen to each prompt, then answer the question.

#1

Listen then answer the question.

The professor thinks corporate rehiring is...

A) a reliable economic indicator
B) one type of economic indicator
C) an unreliable economic indicator
D) a good indicator of sales

#2

Listen then answer the question.

What is the professor's position on drilling for oil offshore?

A) She is convinced it is a good idea.
B) She believes it needs more research.
C) She is not convinced it is a good idea.
D) She thinks a jury should decide the issue.

#3

Listen then answer the question.

What is the professor's view of Thomas Edison?

A) He thinks Edison had scruples.
B) He believes Edison was a divided man.
C) He thinks Edison coined great ideas.
D) He thinks Edison's quotes are memorable.

#4

Listen then answer the question.

The professor thinks that genetically modified food is...

A) affordable
B) dangerous
C) delicious
D) innocuous

→ Answers: page 685.
→ Audio script: page 765.

Practice: *Inferred-Attitude Questions*

Directions: Listen to each prompt, then answer the question.

#1

Listen then answer the question.

How does the professor feel about what happened off the Farallon Islands?

A) curious
B) confused
C) cautious
D) dumbfounded

#2

Listen then answer the question.

What is the professor's view of Microsoft?

A) It is no longer the industry leader.
B) It was founded by Bill Gates.
C) It competes directly with Apple.
D) It still controls the computer market.

#3

Listen then answer the question.

What is the professor's opinion of Cro-Magnon cave art?

A) Its purpose remains a mystery.
B) It needs to be preserved.
C) It is equal to the art of today.
D) It is best viewed on slides.

#4

Listen then answer the question.

The professor believes that...

A) It's possible that Cuban nationalists assassinated Kennedy.
B) The military complex probably killed Kennedy.
C) Kennedy was killed in Viet Nam.
D) Neither Cuban nationalists nor the military complex killed Kennedy.

➔ Answers: page 685.
➔ Audio script: page 766.

Connecting-Information Questions

Practice: *Inferred-Action Questions*

Directions: Listen to each prompt, then answer the question.

#1

Listen then answer the question.

What will the professor probably do next?

A) teach jargon using student examples
B) teach skateboarding jargon and slang
C) teach examples of skateboarding slang using student examples
D) teach the code of skateboarding

#3

Listen then answer the question.

What will the professor probably do next?

A) give another lecture
B) take a break
C) take a nap
D) take a vacation

#2

Listen then answer the question.

What will the professor talk about next?

A) Sinatra's early career
B) Sinatra's ethics
C) Sinatra's work habits
D) Sinatra's breathing techniques

#4

Listen then answer the question.

What will the professor demonstrate?

A) how to make an axe
B) how to make a primitive tool
C) how to make a hand axe
D) how to complete the assignment

➔ Answers: page 685.
➔ Audio script: page 767.

Ordering Questions

Ordering questions are detail questions. They measure your ability to identify the steps in a process or event, such as a moment in history or the stages in a person's or animal's life.

Practice: *Ordering Questions*

Directions: Listen to each prompt, then answer the question.

#1

Listen then answer the question.

The professor talks about the sockeye salmon. Put the life cycle of the sockeye in the correct order. This is a 2-point question.

a. return to the home river
b. alevin grow into fry
c. smolt head for the ocean
d. spawn in shallow water

1. ____________________
2. ____________________
3. ____________________
4. ____________________

#2

Listen then answer the question.

The professor talks about Jonathan James. Put James' computer hacking career in the proper order. This is a 2-point question.

a. accused of hacking major retailers
b. hacked the Defense Reduction Agency
c. hacked Bell-South
d. hacked the Miami-Dade school system

1. ____________________
2. ____________________
3. ____________________
4. ____________________

#3

Listen then answer the question.

The professor describes the life of F. Scott Fitzgerald. Put Fitzgerald's writing career in the proper order. This is a 2-point question.

a. screenplay contract with MGM
b. sold short stories to magazines
c. published *The Great Gatsby*
d. published *This Side of Paradise*

1. ______________________
2. ______________________
3. ______________________
4. ______________________

#4

Listen then answer the question.

The professor talks about the persistence hunt. Put the steps of the persistence hunt in order. This is a 2-point question.

a. move the herd
b. isolate and chase one kudu
c. find kudu
d. make a kill

1. ______________________
2. ______________________
3. ______________________
4. ______________________

➔ Answers: page 686.
➔ Scoring multi-answer questions: page 693.
➔ Audio script: page 768.

Yes-No Questions

Yes-No questions are detail questions. They measure your ability to identify correct and incorrect information in a passage.

Practice: *Yes-No Questions*

Directions: Listen to each prompt, then answer the question.

#1

The professor describes Black Friday. Indicate whether each of the following is true of Black Friday in the United States. This is a 3-point question.

	YES	NO
Black Friday is an official holiday.		
Black Friday is a bellwether for retailers and manufacturers.		
Black Friday prices are generally better than Cyber Monday prices.		
Black Friday marks the start of the Christmas shopping season.		
Black Friday is popular only on the east coast.		

#2

The professor talks about microcredit. Indicate whether each of the following is true of microcredit. This is a 3-point question.

	YES	NO
It is based on group financing called solidarity lending.		
It is a system of finance that extends credit to the very poor.		
The average size of the borrowing group is fifteen.		
It encourages relatives to borrow credit to start small businesses.		
It is popular around the world.		

#3

The professor talks about the Situationist International. Indicate whether each of the following is true of the Situationist International. This is a 3-point question.

	YES	NO
It combined Marxism and surrealism to fight consumerism.		
It was founded in 1957.		
They believed that the individual was a slave to advertising.		
Guy Debord believed in capitalism.		
The Situationist International is no longer active.		

#4

The professor talks about hybrid cars. According to the professor, which of the following are true of hybrid cars? This is a 3-point question.

	YES	NO
They are very popular.		
They are more expensive than conventional gas-powered cars.		
Their only source of energy is a large nickel battery.		
They average 50 miles per liter.		
They are environmentally friendly.		

➔ Answers: page 686.
➔ Scoring multi-answer questions: page 693.
➔ Audio script: page 769.

Connecting Questions

Connecting questions are detail questions. They measure your ability to identify specific topics and identify connections between those topics. Look at a sample question below.

Sample

The professor describes the three parts of an independent essay. Match each part of an independent essay in the top row with its corresponding part in the bottom row. This is a 2-point question.

a. thesis	b. body	c. conclusion

details	introduction	restated thesis

Using the mouse, *click and drag* each top row example under the corresponding space in the bottom row to make a topic match or connection.

Sample

The professor describes the three parts of an independent essay. Match each part of an independent essay in the top row with its corresponding part in the bottom row. This is a 2-point question.

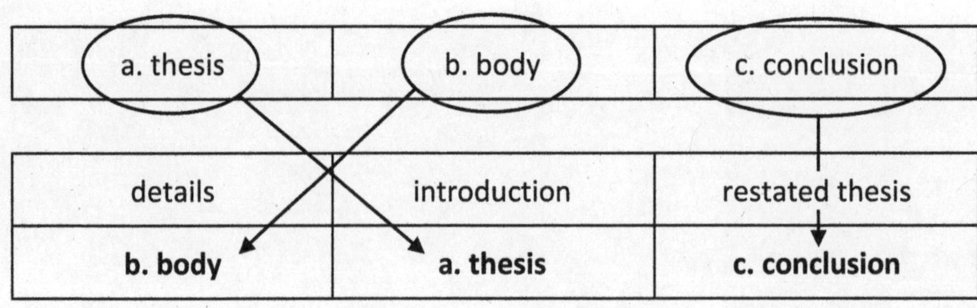

Practice: *Connecting Questions*

Directions: Listen to each prompt, then answer the question.

#1

The professor describes three military battles that changed history. Match each battle with each defeated military leader. This is a 2-point question.

a. Waterloo	b. Marathon	c. Teutoburg Forest

Varus	Darius	Napoleon

#2

The professor identifies three herbs used for plant-based medicine. Match each herb with its corresponding application. This is a 2-point question.

a. aloe vera	b. willow bark	c. milk thistle

aches and pains	liver health	burns and wounds

#3

The professor describes the parts of a prokaryote cell. Connect each part of a prokaryote cell with its corresponding function. This is a 2-point question.

a. cytoplasmic region	b. envelope	c. exterior

contains the genome	flagella for motion	protective filter

#4

The professor illustrates the life cycle of the sockeye salmon. Match each stage of the sockeye salmon's life cycle with a corresponding description of that stage. This is a 2-point question.

a. alevin	b. fry	c. smolt

a sockeye salmon approximately six months old	lives off the nutrient-rich yolk of the egg sack	will mature in the Pacific Ocean and return to the home river as an adult

➔ Answers: page 686.
➔ Scoring multi-answer questions: page 693.
➔ Audio script: page 771.

Professor-Students

An analysis of a professor-students discussion begins by listening to a test sample.

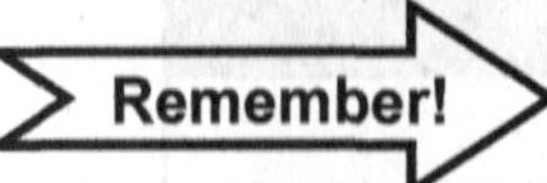

Remember to make a three-part note map before you begin.

Sample Discussion: *Professor-Students* → Audio Track #74

TOEFL® *Listening*

TIME 00:00

Directions

Listen to a sample discussion, then answer the questions on the next page. Do not look at the questions. On test day, you will not see the questions as you listen.

Remember to answer all the questions. You will not be penalized for a wrong answer.

Now listen to part of a discussion in an environmental class.

Questions

Directions: Now get ready to answer the questions. Answer each question based on what is stated or implied in the discussion.

#1

What is the discussion mainly about?

A) the North Pacific gyre
B) how plastic is polluting the Pacific
C) the North Pacific garbage patch
D) plastic and pelagic species

#2

What is the purpose of the discussion?

A) to highlight how pollution affects ocean currents
B) to illustrate how plastic garbage is polluting the North Pacific
C) to define an environmental disaster
D) to show the relationship between a gyre and plastic water bottles

#3

Why does the professor say this? 

A) to warn that plastic bottles are a growing problem
B) to stress his disbelief at the amount of plastic in daily use
C) to illustrate how much plastic he uses on a daily basis
D) to introduce the next topic

#4

Which pelagic species does the professor mention? Select three. This is a 2-point question.

A) whales
B) crabs
C) birds
D) sea turtles
E) fish

#5

The professor describes how plastic becomes part of the eco-system. Put those steps in order. This is a 2-point question.

a. plastic photodegrades into particles
b. plastic ends up in the Horse Latitudes
c. plastic enters the North Pacific
d. plastic is swept along by the gyre

1. ______________________
2. ______________________
3. ______________________
4. ______________________

#6

In the lecture, the professor describes the Horse Latitudes. Indicate whether each of the following is a characteristic of the Horse Latitudes. This is a 3-point question.

	YES	NO
They flow clockwise.		
Worldwide there are five.		
The center is a calm area that once trapped sailing ships.		
They are home to a variety of pelagic species.		
Plastic photodecomposes on the surface into toxic particulates.		

→ Answers: page 686.
→ Scoring multi-answer questions: page 693.
→ Audio script: page 773.

Discussion: *Task Analysis*

TOEFL's Testing Method

An understanding of TOEFL's testing method begins with a rhetorical analysis of the sample discussion. This analysis will help you take effective notes and maximize scoring. Read as you listen to the sample discussion once again.

Sample Discussion: *Professor-Students*

Audio Track #74

Professor
Today, we're going to discuss a man-made problem that's impacting oceans worldwide, a problem with no solution in sight. That problem is right in front of you. When you're finished with them, hopefully—as concerned and responsible citizens—you'll recycle so they won't end up on a Pacific island or a Cape Cod beach. Of course, you all know what I'm talking about: the ubiquitous polyethylene terephthalate. That said, let me begin by giving you a few eye-popping stats. Every year, Americans buy over 50 billion—yes, billion—bottles of water. That equates to 1,500 bottles consumed every second—every second. That number beggars the imagination. Of that number, eight out of ten end up in a landfill with the remaining twenty-percent recycled. And those numbers are only in America. What about the rest of the world? What about countries that can't afford to build expensive recycling plants? And what about all those bottles that are not recycled or dumped in landfills, in America and worldwide? Where does all that polyethylene terephthalate end up? Carol?

Carol
In the oceans.

Professor
Exactly. Can you elaborate on the homework?

Carol
Sure. According to the reading, there's this huge floating patch of garbage in the North Pacific. It's made up mostly of plastic bottles, but you can also find fish nets and micro pellets used for abrasive cleaning, plus all the stuff tossed off freighters and cruise ships. All this garbage is being swept along on what's called the North Pacific gyre.

Professor
Sorry, what exactly is that? A gyre?

Carol
It's the prevailing ocean current. In the North Pacific, the gyre moves west along the equator, then up past Japan to Alaska, then down the west coast of North America to the equator again. It's kind of like water spinning in a toilet bowl.

Professor
Good. So what's the connection between the North Pacific gyre and pelagic plastic?

Ann
Sorry, professor, what does pelagic mean again?

Professor
It means living or occurring at sea. The albatross, for example, is a pelagic bird. Carol?

Carol
Right, so where was I? Okay, so the stuff, I mean, you know, all that pelagic plastic, is swept along clockwise by the gyre. Eventually all that plastic junk finds its way into the center of the gyre and becomes stationary, you know, just sits there in an area called the Horse Latitudes, this area of calm in the center of the gyre. Years ago sailors would get trapped there due to a lack of wind and current. Today, it's basically one big, continuously-fed garbage dump in which pelagic plastic is the prevailing contaminant.

Professor
And it isn't going anywhere. In fact, it's spreading due to the decomposing nature of the contaminants themselves. Ann, can you jump in here and talk about the photodegradation process?

Ann
So when all this floating plastic is exposed to the sun, it begins to photodegrade until its reaches the molecular level. For example, take this book. Let's say it's floating in the center of the gyre, okay? The first thing to go are the covers, then the pages decompose freeing all the words. Next, the words break apart into letters. Finally, the ink in the letters photodecomposes into molecules. All that ends up in the gyre forming this thick, soupy liquid full of floating plastic particles that look like confetti.

Professor
A sea of confetti. That's a good way to put it. Beautiful, I'm sure, what with all that colored plastic floating around, but deadly. Very. All that particulate matter? It doesn't sink. Instead, it stays in the upper water column where it poses a significant threat to endemic wildlife. Pelagic birds, for example, consume the particulate matter mistaking it for food. They, in turn, feed it to their young who die of starvation or are poisoned by the toxic nature of polyethylene terephthalate. Other contaminants identified in the patch are PCB, DDT and PAH. When ingested, some of these toxins imitate estradiol which, as you know,

is a naturally occurring estrogenic hormone secreted mainly by the ovaries. You can imagine the effect these toxins have on the reproduction systems of endemic species, such as whales. Fish too ingest the decomposed plastic and become contaminated.

Carol
Professor, is it possible to clean it up?

Professor
So far? No. The particulate matter is so small, you need extremely fine nets—micronets basically—to scoop it up. But even if we had such nets, remember, the North Pacific is vast. It would take an armada constantly going back and forth to even put a dent in all that plastic while at the same time, new plastic—tons of it—is entering the gyre every day. How many bottles of water do Americans drink every year?

Carol
Fifty billion.

Professor
Precisely. And that statistic is already out of date.

Ann
That's a lot of garbage.

Professor
It is. And the thing is, we don't even know how big the patch is. Satellites can't pick up the particulate matter because it's too small. Not only that but when you're parked in the middle of it on a boat or a ship, you can't see it. The particulate matter is that small. So, how big is the great North Pacific garbage patch? Well, some say it's the size of Texas. Others claim it's twice the size of the U.S. Big no matter how you cut it. Okay, so that's the North Pacific. Worldwide how many gyres are there?

Carol
Five.

Professor
So if the center of the North Pacific gyre is one huge, floating garbage dump, what does that tell us about the other four gyres?

G+3TiC=C: *Mapping a Discussion*

A professor-students discussion is a verbal, fact-based argument in which a professor develops an academic topic with a group of students. In the sample discussion, a professor and two students develop the topic of the North Pacific garbage patch.

You know from previous tasks that the TOEFL iBT recycles fact-based arguments for testing purposes. That means you are already familiar with the structure of a fact-based discussion (argument). That structure can be mapped out using G+3TiC=C.

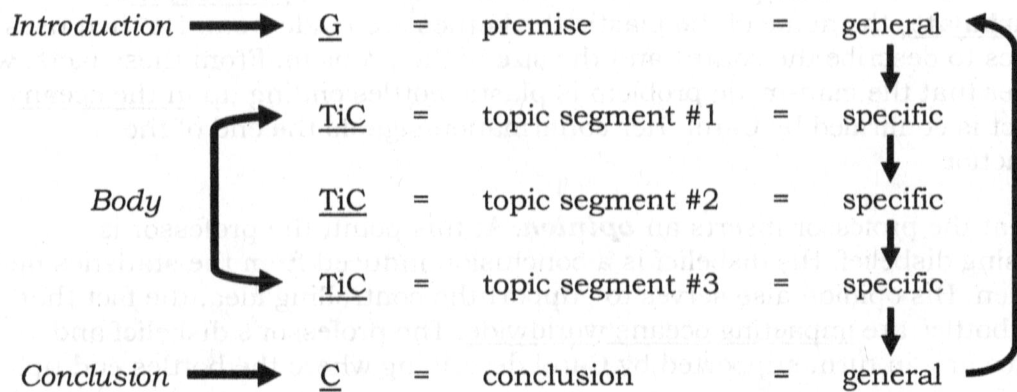

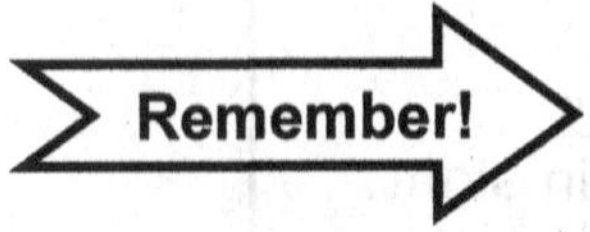

The body of a discussion is divided into topic segments. The number of topic segments will vary. There might be two (G+2TiC=C), three (G+3TiC=C). The sample discussion has four topic segments (G+4TiC=C).

Opinion-Insertion Points

During a professor-students discussion, the professor and the students will often insert opinions. Opinions can be inserted anywhere in a discussion. Predictable insertion points are the body and the conclusion. As the topic develops, the professor and students will often insert opinions about the topic in each segment. They will also insert opinions about the topic in the conclusion. At that point, the topic will be fully developed.

Introduction: *Rhetorical Functions*

The discussion will start with a general introduction (G), which introduces the premise. To identify the premise, ask, "What is the main topic?" Answer: *A man-made problem (plastic bottles).* To find the controlling idea, ask, "What about it?" Answer: *How the man-made problem (plastic bottles) is impacting oceans worldwide.*

> **Premise:** How plastic bottles (main topic) are impacting oceans worldwide (controlling idea).

In the introduction below, the professor introduces the main topic a man-made problem in the first sentence. Note that he does not say *plastic bottles*. Instead, he identifies the man-made problem (plastic bottles) by using **polyethylene terephthalate**, the name of the plastic the bottles are made from. He then uses statistics to describe the source and the size of the problem. From these facts, we can infer that the man-made problem is plastic bottles ending up in the oceans. This fact is confirmed by Carol. Her confirmation signals the end of the introduction.

Note that the professor inserts an ***opinion***. At this point, the professor is expressing disbelief. His disbelief is a conclusion induced from the statistics he has just given. His opinion also serves to support the controlling idea, the fact that plastic bottles are impacting oceans worldwide. The professor's disbelief and statistics are, in turn, supported by Carol describing where the bottles end up.

Professor

[premise] Today, we're going to discuss a man-made problem that's impacting oceans worldwide, a problem with no solution in sight. That problem is right in front of you. When you're finished with them, hopefully—as concerned and responsible citizens—you'll recycle so they won't end up on a Pacific island or a Cape Cod beach. Of course, you all know what I'm talking about: the ubiquitous **polyethylene terephthalate**. That said, let me begin by giving you a few eye-popping stats. Every year, Americans buy over 50 billion—yes, billion—bottles of water. That equates to 1,500 bottles consumed every second—every second. [opinion] ***That number beggars the imagination.*** Of that number, eight out of ten end up in a landfill with the remaining twenty-percent recycled. And those numbers are only in America. What about the rest of the world? What about countries that can't afford to build expensive recycling plants? And what about all those bottles that are not recycled or dumped in landfills, in America and worldwide? Where does all that **polyethylene terephthalate** end up? Carol?

Carol

In the oceans.

Active-Passive Roles: *Rhetorical Functions*

As the professor and the students develop the topic, they will alternate between active speaking and passive listening. The role each plays will serve a specific rhetorical function. For example, in the introduction, the professor plays an active speaking role, the function of which is to introduce the premise. This, in turn, starts the discussion.

Topic Segments: *Rhetorical Functions*

In topic segment one below (TiC), the speakers serve specific rhetorical functions.

Transition-and-Topic-Segment Introduction: The professor, using a question (1), transitions and introduces the topic of the first topic segment: ***homework***. Carol (2) answers and actively develops the homework topic with a specific example: *this huge floating patch of garbage in the North Pacific*. Carol develops the topic of the garbage patch by illustrating the different types of plastic found in the garbage patch.

Interjection: The professor (3) interjects with a question. To interject means to enter a conversation when another person is speaking. The professor interjects with a definition request (*Sorry, what exactly is that? A gyre?*). Carol (4) defines the meaning of gyre, then develops the topic segment. In short, she is actively delivering a well-developed, verbal topic segment (OP**D**UL=C). By doing so, she teaches you about gyres, and how they are being "impacted" by "a man-made problem": plastic bottles and other forms of plastic.

Professor
Exactly. Can you elaborate on the ***homework***?

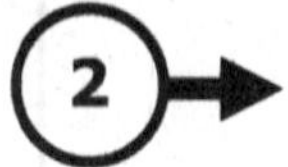

Carol
Sure. According to the reading, there's *this huge floating patch of garbage in the North Pacific*. It's made up mostly of plastic bottles, but you can also find fish nets and micro pellets used for abrasive cleaning, plus all the stuff tossed off freighters and cruise ships. All this garbage is being swept along on what's called the North Pacific gyre.

Professor
Sorry, what exactly is that? A gyre?

Carol
It's the prevailing ocean current. In the North Pacific, the gyre moves west along the equator, then up past Japan to Alaska, then down the west coast of North America to the equator again. It's kind of like water spinning in a toilet bowl.

In topic segment two (2TiC) below, the professor, using a question (1), introduces and transitions into the next topic segment: ***the connection between the North Pacific gyre and pelagic plastic***. Ann (2) interjects with a question (*Sorry, professor, what does pelagic mean again?*). Ann's interjection is a definition request. The professor (3) defines "pelagic" with an example (*the albatross*). Next, Carol (4) illustrates how "pelagic plastic" and the gyre are topically united. Once again, Carol actively delivers a well-developed, verbal topic segment (OP**D**UL=C). This teaching style (question-answer-question) is called *the Socratic Method*. The Socratic Method is the teaching method used in American classrooms. The TOEFL iBT employs the Socratic Method for testing purposes throughout the TOEFL iBT.

Professor
Good. So what's ***the connection between the North Pacific gyre and pelagic plastic?***

Ann
<u>Sorry, professor, what does pelagic mean again?</u>

Professor
It means living or occurring at sea. The albatross, for example, is a pelagic bird. Carol?

Carol
Right, so where was I? Okay, so the stuff, I mean, you know, all the pelagic plastic, is swept along clockwise by the gyre. Eventually all that plastic junk finds its way into the center of the gyre and becomes stationary, you know, just sits there in an area called the Horse Latitudes, this area of calm in the center of the gyre. Years ago sailors would get trapped there due to a lack of wind and current. Today, it's basically one big, continuously-fed garbage dump in which pelagic plastic is the prevailing contaminant.

Professor
And it isn't going anywhere. ***In fact, it's spreading due to the decomposing nature of the contaminants themselves***. <u>Ann, can you jump in here and talk about the photodegradation process?</u>

Note how the professor ends this topic segment with a ***concluding statement***. This signals the end of topic segment two. The professor's <u>question</u> signals a transition into the next topic segment.

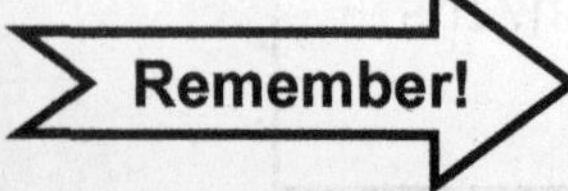

Questions and interjections are rhetorical signals. They signal that the topic is changing, developing, and/or that an important word or phrase is being defined or clarified. Note all questions and interjections. They are predictable testing points.

In topic segment three below (3TiC), the professor (1) introduces the next topic: the photodegradation process. Ann (2) develops this topic-process by comparing a decomposing book to a decomposing plastic bottle. By doing so, Ann is making an analogy. An analogy compares one thing to another. The purpose of this analogy is to define and simplify the steps in the photodegradation process. The professor (3) develops the process by describing the dangers of decomposed plastic to endemic wildlife. The professor (4) then gives a warning. This warning is an implied opinion that concludes this topic segment. What is the professor's **inferred opinion-warning**? Eating fish is a potential health risk.

Professor

And it isn't going anywhere. In fact, it's spreading due to the decomposing nature of the contaminants themselves. (1) Ann, can you jump in here and talk about the photodegradation process?

Ann

(2) So when all this floating plastic is exposed to the sun, it begins to photodegrade until it reaches the molecular level. For example, take this book. Let's say it's floating in the center of the gyre, (analogy) okay? The first thing to go are the covers, then the pages decompose freeing all the words. Next, the words break apart into letters. Finally, the ink in the letters photodecomposes into molecules. All that ends up in the gyre forming this thick, soupy liquid full of floating plastic particles that look like confetti.

Professor

(3) A sea of confetti. That's a good way to put it. Beautiful, I'm sure, what with all that colored plastic floating around, but deadly. Very. All that particulate matter? It doesn't sink. Instead, it stays in the upper water column where it poses a significant threat to endemic wildlife. Pelagic birds, for example, consume the particulate matter mistaking it for food. They, in turn, feed it to their young who die of starvation or are poisoned by the toxic nature of polyethylene terephthalate. Other contaminants identified in the patch are PCB, DDT and PAH. When ingested, some of these toxins imitate estradiol which, as you know, is a naturally occurring estrogenic hormone secreted mainly by the ovaries. You can imagine the effect these toxins have on the reproduction systems of endemic species, such as whales. (4) **Fish too ingest the decomposed plastic and become contaminated.**

An analogy is a rhetorical strategy and an example of authentic language use. It signals that the speaker is defining/ clarifying/ developing a point. A warning (4) is also an example of authentic language use. A warning signals the speaker's implied opinion. Make a note of all warnings and analogies. They are predictable testing points.

In topic segment four below (4TiC), the active-passive roles are reversed. Carol (1), using a question, transitions and introduces the next topic: *cleaning up pelagic plastic.* The professor (2) actively develops the topic. Note how Carol (3) repeats the statistic (fifty billion) the professor stated in the introduction. Ann (4) inserts her opinion about that statistic. The professor (5) continues to develop the topic. He concludes with **comparisons** illustrating the size of the garbage patch. He then asks a *question* (5) that signals a transition into the next topic segment.

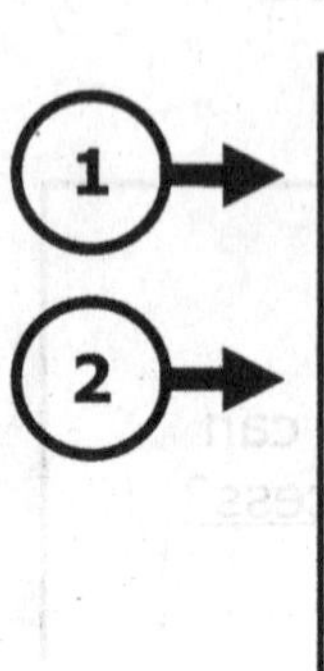

Carol
Professor, is it possible to clean it up?

Professor
So far? No. The particulate matter is so small, you need extremely fine nets—micronets basically—to scoop it up. But even if we had such nets, remember, the North Pacific is vast. It would take an armada constantly going back and forth to even put a dent in all that plastic while at the same time, new plastic—tons of it—is entering the gyre every day. How many bottles of water do Americans drink every year?

Carol
Fifty billion.

Professor
Precisely. And that statistic is already out of date.

Ann
That's a lot of garbage. [opinion]

Professor
It is. And the thing is, we don't even know how big the patch is. Satellites can't pick up the particulate matter because it's too small. Not only that but when you're parked in the middle of it on a boat or a ship, you can't see it. The particulate matter is that

small. **So, how big is the great North Pacific garbage patch? Well, some say it's the size of Texas. Others claim it's twice the size of the U.S. Big no matter how you cut it.** *Okay, so that's the North Pacific. Worldwide how many gyres are there?*

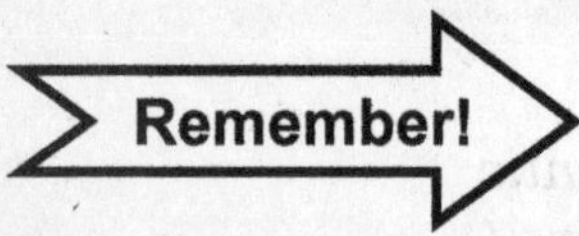

Repetition (3) is a rhetorical strategy and an example of authentic language use. Make a note of any repeated words or statistics. They are predictable testing points. Comparisons (5) are also rhetorical strategies. Note any. They too are predictable testing points.

Conclusion: *Rhetorical Functions*

The conclusion (C) will serve two rhetorical functions: to signal the end of the discussion and to introduce a new topic. Note how the professor (1) ***concludes*** the discussion with a question that signals a transition into the next topic. Carol (2) answers the question (*Five*). The professor then asks another question based on Carol's answer. From the professor's concluding question (3), we can infer that the next four topics will be the other four gyres, and how they are being impacted by plastic and other forms of pollution.

Professor
It is. And the thing is, we don't even know how big the patch is. Satellites can't pick up the particulate matter because it's too small. Not only that but even when you're parked in the middle of it on a boat or ship, you can't see it. The particulate matter is that small. So, how big is the Great Pacific Garbage Patch? Well, some say it's the size of Texas. Others claim it's twice the size of the U.S. Big no matter how you cut it. ***Okay, so that's the North Pacific. Worldwide how many gyres are there?*** (1)

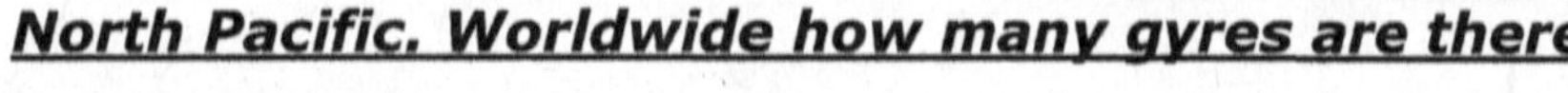

Carol
(2) Five.

Professor
(3) So if the center of the North Pacific gyre is one huge, floating garbage dump, what does that tell us about the other four gyres?

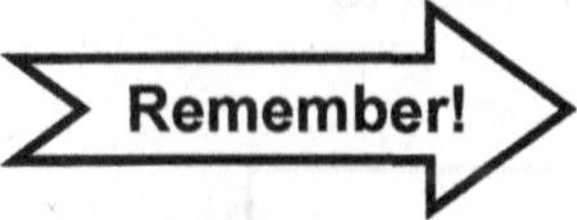

If the conclusion signals a new topic, make a note of it. A new topic is a predictable testing point.

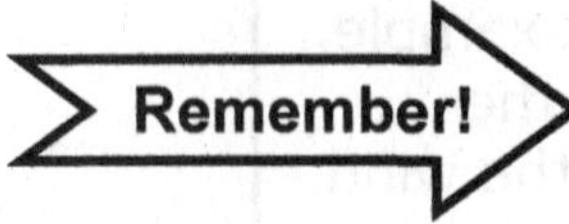

*A discussion is all about argument development using authentic language (OP**D**U**L**=C). The argument and the authentic language are delivered by the Socratic Method (question-answer-question).*

Rejoinders: *Identifying Transitions*

Rejoinders signal topic segment transitions. For example, the professor below expands the definition of pelagic with an illustration of a pelagic species (*the albatross*). Carol signals her understanding of the definition by saying, *"Yeah. Okay. I see."* This short sentence, or rejoinder, is an affirmation of understanding. Rhetorically, rejoinders are transitional signal words telling you that this is the conclusion of this topic segment and the professor (or student) is moving on to the next topic segment, such as below.

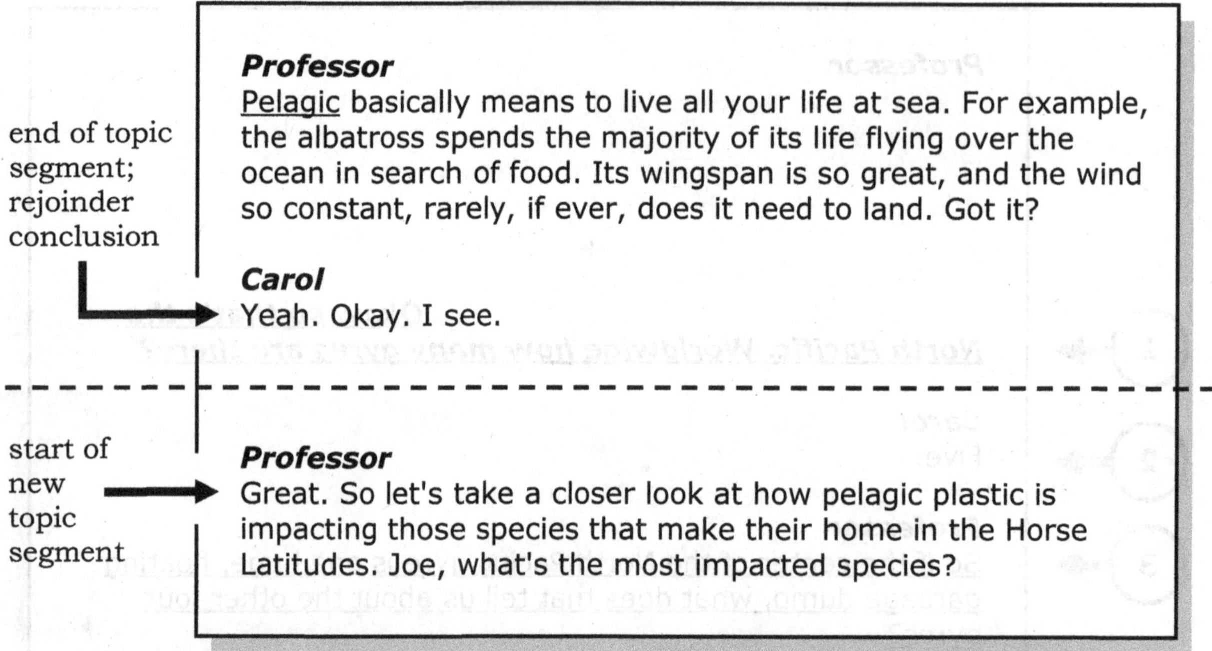

end of topic segment; rejoinder conclusion
Professor
Pelagic basically means to live all your life at sea. For example, the albatross spends the majority of its life flying over the ocean in search of food. Its wingspan is so great, and the wind so constant, rarely, if ever, does it need to land. Got it?
Carol
Yeah. Okay. I see.
start of new topic segment
Professor
Great. So let's take a closer look at how pelagic plastic is impacting those species that make their home in the Horse Latitudes. Joe, what's the most impacted species?

Not all rejoinders are topic segment transitions. For example, the rejoinder below is a confirmation of understanding in the middle of a topic segment. Note how the rejoinder splits the topic (*the albatross*). Note also how the professor continues to develop the topic after the student's rejoinder.

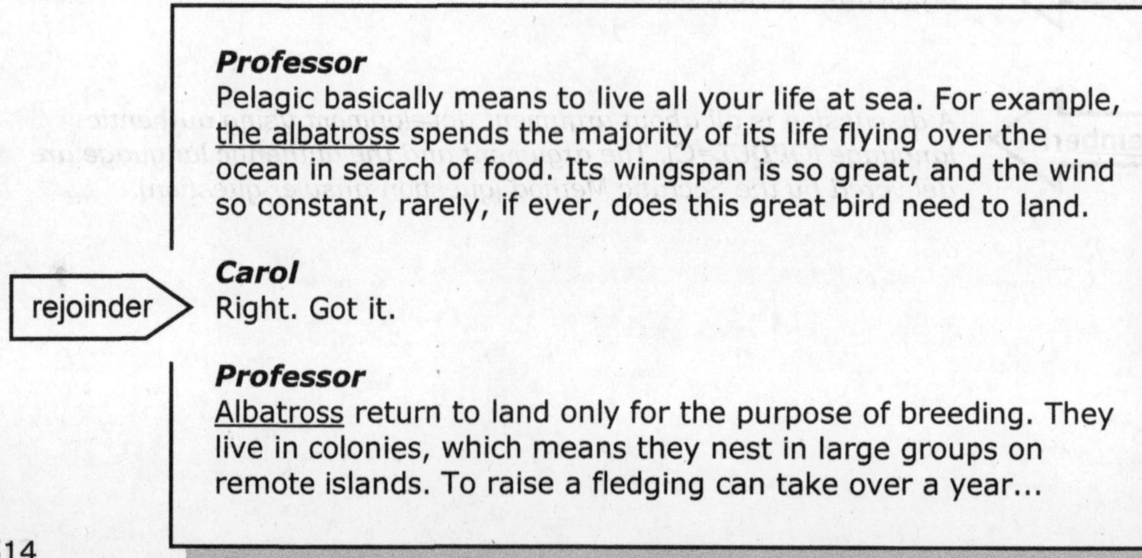

Professor
Pelagic basically means to live all your life at sea. For example, the albatross spends the majority of its life flying over the ocean in search of food. Its wingspan is so great, and the wind so constant, rarely, if ever, does this great bird need to land.
rejoinder
Carol
Right. Got it.
Professor
Albatross return to land only for the purpose of breeding. They live in colonies, which means they nest in large groups on remote islands. To raise a fledging can take over a year...

Question Types

The questions for this task are the same as those used for professor-only lecture prompts. Follow these steps when answering each question type.

1. Make a Note Map

Anticipate the discussion's three-part structure by dividing your note map into the same three-parts: introduction, body, conclusion. In the introduction, listen for the premise; in the body, listen for topic segments and supporting illustrations; in the conclusion, listen for the introduction of a new topic and the professor's and/or students' inserted opinions.

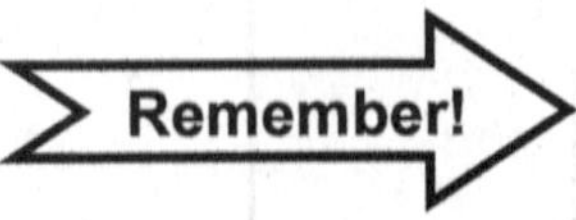

Some test-takers take a lot of notes. Some take a few notes while others takes no notes at all. There is no rule that says you must or must not take notes. It is up to you. Only by practicing will you know whether you need to take notes or not. Your notes will not be rated.

2. Authentic Language Use

While listening, note these authentic language use signals.

1) hesitation	3) topic digression	5) repetition	7) tone
2) self-correction	4) false start	6) restatement	8) idioms

3. Question Analysis: *Signal Words*

Read each question carefully. Make sure you understand it. Look for signal words in the question. Try and match the signals words in the question with words in your notes.

4. Choice Analysis: *Process of Elimination*

When analyzing the answer choices, eliminate choices that are:

1) off topic	3) too general	5) not known
2) too specific	4) not true	6) not accurate

5. Identify the Distractors

When analyzing the answer choices, look for the distractor. The distractor might be a homophone distractor (page 435) or an answer choice distractor (page 440).

Practice: *Discussion #1*

Audio
Track
#75

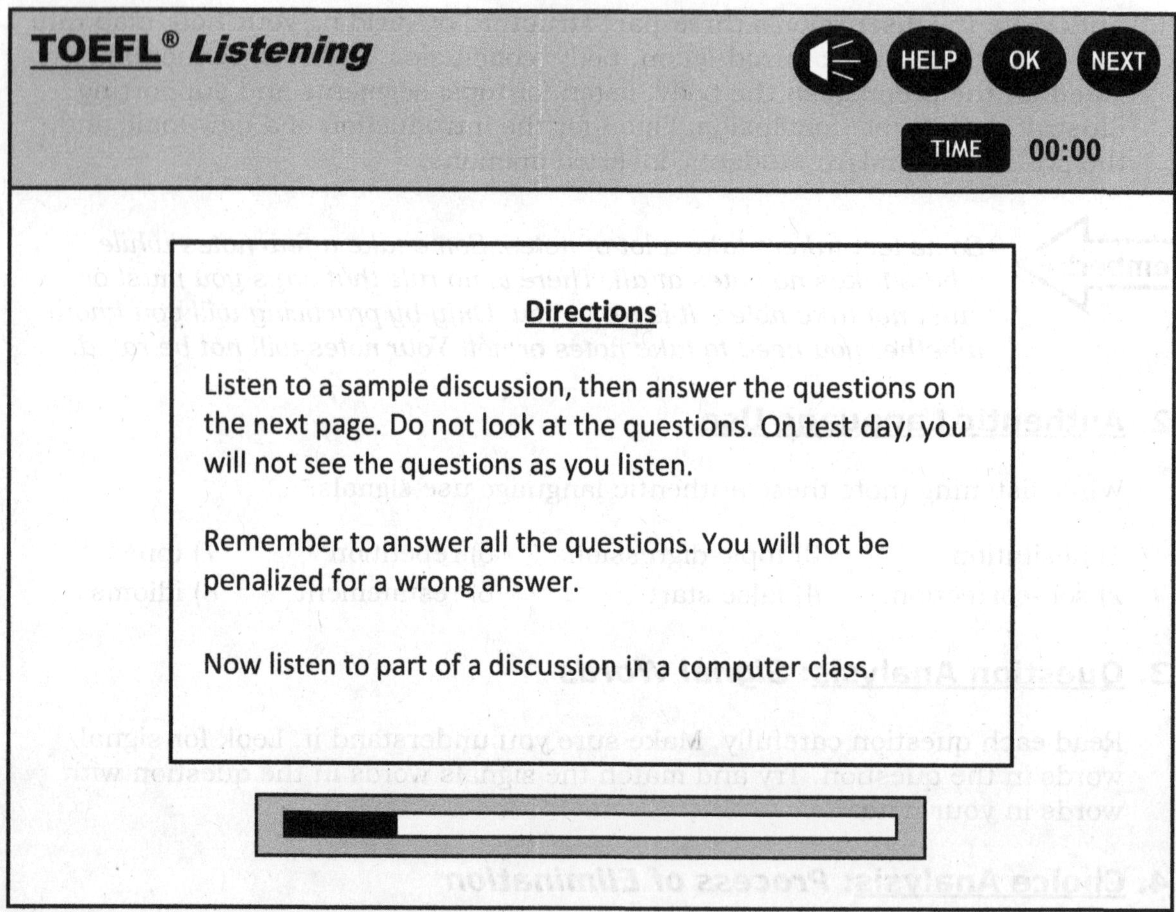
TOEFL® Listening
HELP
OK
NEXT
TIME
00:00
Directions
Listen to a sample discussion, then answer the questions on the next page. Do not look at the questions. On test day, you will not see the questions as you listen.
Remember to answer all the questions. You will not be penalized for a wrong answer.
Now listen to part of a discussion in a computer class.

Directions: Now get ready to answer the questions. Answer each question based on what is stated or implied in the discussion.

#1

What is the discussion mainly about?

A) malicious computers
B) Trojan horses
C) viruses
D) malware

#3

Why does the student say this? 

A) to compare the fate of the Trojans to users infected with Trojan horses
B) to illustrate where the name Trojan comes from
C) to develop the history of malware
D) to stress that Trojan horses are the most dangerous malware

#2

What is the purpose of the discussion?

A) to highlight various internet dangers
B) to identify types of malicious software and their effects
C) to describe the history of the internet in America
D) to classify methods of virus protection

#4

The student describes the history of computer viruses. Put that history in order. This is a 2-point question.

a. The Elk Clone virus attacks Apple computers.
b. The Brain appears to defend against software pirating.
c. The Creeper virus appears on ARPANET.
d. Computer scientists started writing about computer viruses.

1. ____________________
2. ____________________
3. ____________________
4. ____________________

Turn the page for questions #5 and #6.

#5

In the discussion, the student describes Trojan horses and computer viruses. Identify the characteristics of each. This is a 3-point question.

	Trojan horse	virus
Designed to disrupt or crash a host computer.		
Designed to secretly download a host computer's files.		
Spreads via portable media, such as flash drives.		
Often shows up as a legitimate link in an email message.		
First appeared on ARPANET as an innocuous experiment.		

#6

Listen to part of the discussion, then answer the question.

Why does the student say this? 

A) to express empathy
B) to express shock
C) to express disgust
D) to express anger

➔ Answers: page 686.
➔ Scoring multi-answer questions: page 693.
➔ Audio script: page 775.

Practice: *Discussion #2*

Audio
Track
#76

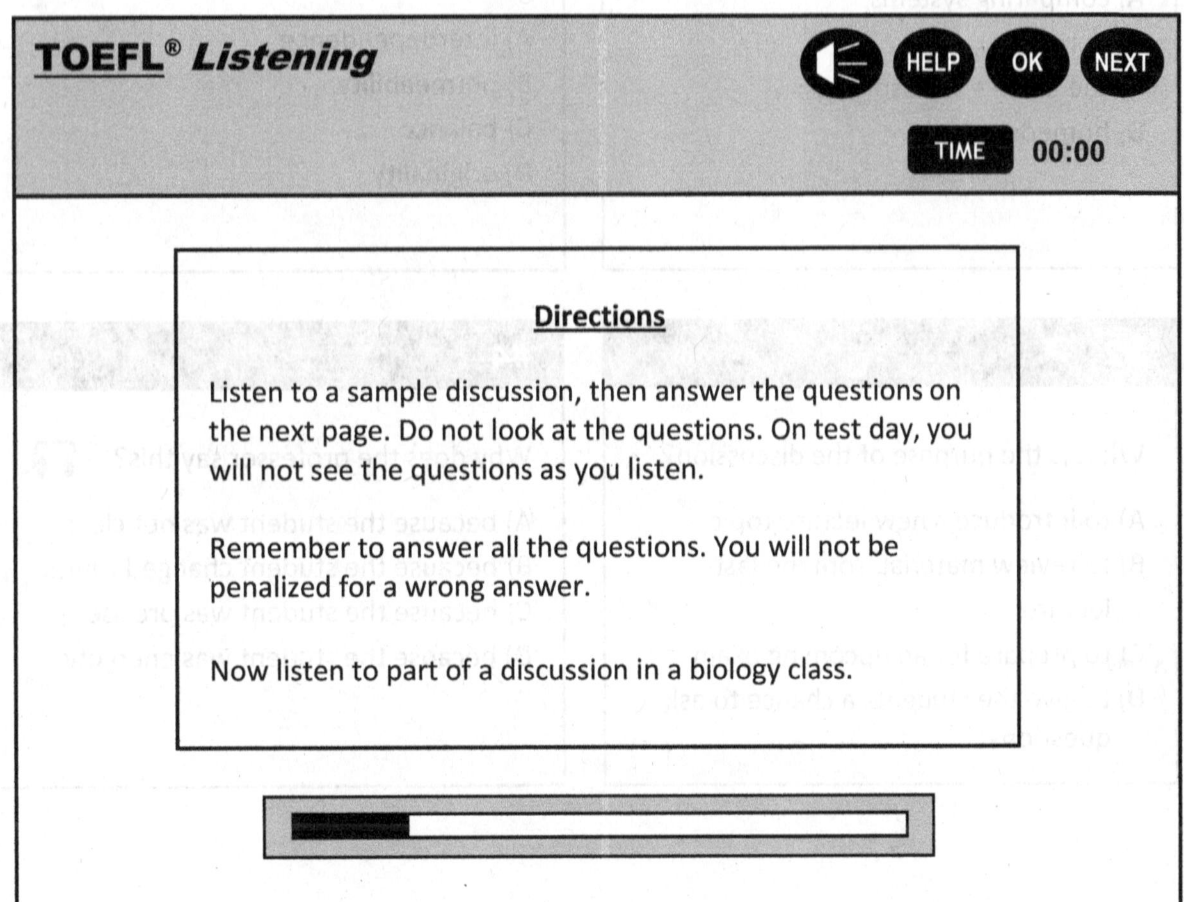
TOEFL® Listening
HELP
OK
NEXT
TIME
00:00
Directions
Listen to a sample discussion, then answer the questions on the next page. Do not look at the questions. On test day, you will not see the questions as you listen.
Remember to answer all the questions. You will not be penalized for a wrong answer.
Now listen to part of a discussion in a biology class.

Directions: Now get ready to answer the questions. Answer each question based on what is stated or implied in the discussion.

#1

What is the topic of the discussion?

A) comparing systems
B) borders
C) the Earth's atmosphere
D) homeostasis

#2

What is the purpose of the discussion?

A) to introduce a new lecture topic
B) to review material from the last lecture
C) to prepare for an upcoming exam
D) to give the students a chance to ask questions

#3

According to the discussion, all systems have what?

A) interdependence
B) permeability
C) balance
D) originality

#4

Why does the professor say this? 

A) because the student was not clear
B) because the student changed topics
C) because the student was precise
D) because the student was energetic

#5

In the discussion, the following topics are mentioned. Identify which are open systems and which are closed systems. This is a 3-point question.

	closed	open
The Earth		
The U.S. economy		
The human circulatory system		
The human body		
A computer network		

#6

Listen to part of the discussion, then answer the question.

Why does the student say this? 

A) to add to the definition of systems
B) to illustrate how open systems are like closed systems
C) to rephrase the definition of an open system
D) to describe how mass and energy cannot cross borders

➔ Answers: page 687.
➔ Scoring multi-answer questions: page 693.
➔ Audio script: page 777.

Listening Test

For this task, you will listen to two conversations, three lectures and one discussion. After each, total your score and add it to page 538. When you are finished the test, calculate your listening score.

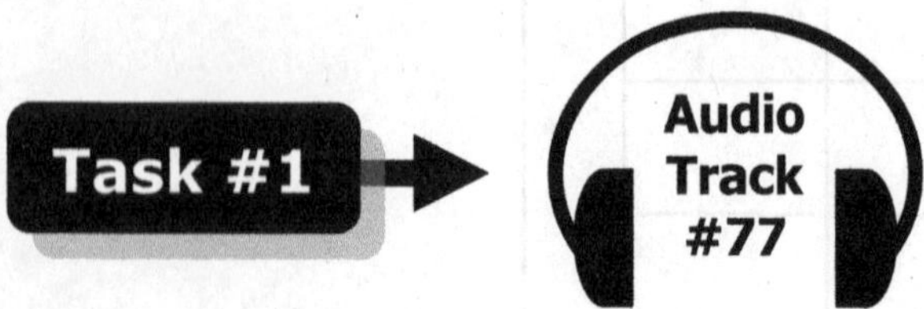

Directions: Listen to a discussion in a business class, then answer the questions on the next page.

Questions

Directions: Now get ready to answer the questions. Answer each question based on what is stated or implied in the discussion.

#1

What is the discussion mainly about?

A) counterfeit goods
B) counterfeit manufacturers
C) counterfeit currency
D) counterfeit laws

#2

What is the point of the discussion?

A) to illustrate the many ways knock-offs can enter a foreign market
B) to illustrate how consumers benefit from affordable products like fakes
C) to illustrate how counterfeit products threaten a company's bottomline
D) to illustrate unfair business practices

#3

Why does the professor say this? 

A) to illustrate that the problem of knock-offs is getting bigger
B) to signal a return to the main topic
C) to indicate that the problem of knock-offs is far bigger than most realize
D) to stress that accessories are the most knocked-off products

#4

How can knock-offs hurt a company? Select three. This is a 2-point question.

A) They can diminish brand equity.
B) They can hurt consumers.
C) They can reduce market share.
D) They can dramatically decrease costs.
E) They can force companies to spend a lot of money on legal fees.

#5

From the discussion, we can infer that "touts" on Fifth Avenue are...

a) tourists buying knock-offs
b) people selling knock-offs
c) people selling designer products
d) affordable products sold in summer

Turn the page for question #6

#6

According to the discussion, what is true about knock-offs? This is a 3-point question.

	YES	NO
They infringe upon American trademark law.		
They pose a serious threat to consumer health.		
They are always sold on internet sites.		
They are made in the U.S. and sold abroad.		
They can adversely affect a company's financial position.		

Total points = / 9

➔ **Add your score to page 538**

➔ Answers: page 687.
➔ Scoring multi-answer questions: page 693.
➔ Audio script: page 778.

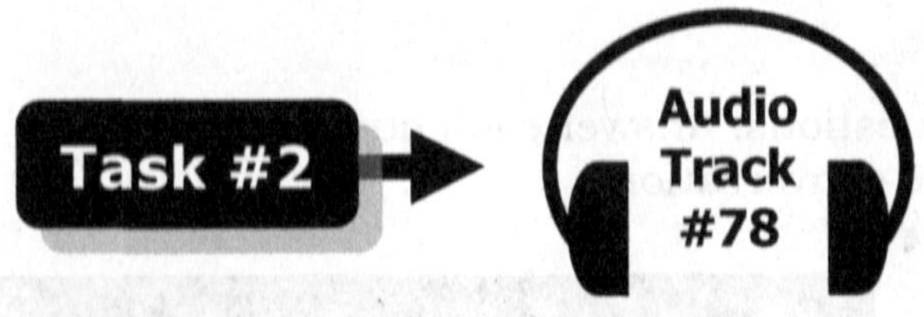

Directions: Listen as a student talks to a professor, then answer the questions on the next page.

Questions

Directions. Now get ready to answer the questions. Answer each question based on what is stated or implied in the conversation.

#1

What is the topic of the conversation?

A) the pros of PowerPoint
B) a recent presentation
C) essential strategies
D) the purpose of the presentation

#2

Why does the student visit the professor?

A) to find out more about the assignment
B) to change her presentation topic
C) to pick up handouts and get advice
D) to clarify the purpose of the assignment

#3

Why does the professor say this? 

A) to define how PowerPoint should be used in a presentation.
B) to remind the student to use tools such as PowerPoint
C) to state what he strongly believes
D) to illustrate how PowerPoint is a tool often used in presentations

#4

According to the professor, what will an audience do if the presenter loses control of a presentation? Select three. This is a 2-point question.

A) start to yawn
B) start to complain
C) ask for refunds
D) check their cell phones
E) walk out

#5

Listen again to part of the conversation, then answer the question.

What does the professor imply when he says this? 

A) to compare giving a presentation to walking
B) to stress the fact that the student must learn the basics first
C) to suggest that presentations move at different speeds
D) to repeat a point mentioned in the handout

➔ Answers: page 687.
➔ Scoring multi-answer questions: page 693.
➔ Audio script: page 780.

Total points = / 6

➔ Add your score to page 538

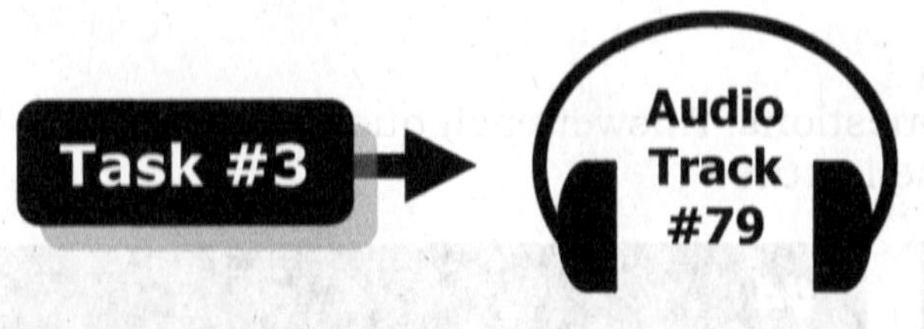

Directions: Listen to a lecture in an economics history class, then answer the questions.

Questions

Directions: Now get ready to answer the questions. Answer each question based on what is stated or implied in the lecture.

#1

What is the topic of the lecture?

A) Adam Smith and the influence of the European Enlightenment
B) Adam Smith and *The Wealth of Nations*
C) Adam Smith's life and history
D) The wisdom of Adam Smith

#2

What is the purpose of the lecture?

A) to classify Adam Smith's philosophy
B) to illustrate the important changes taking place in the mid 17th century
C) to define Adam Smith's influence
D) to illustrate how Adam Smith revolutionized economic thinking

#3

Why does the professor say this? 

A) to highlight that Thomas Edison was as smart as Adam Smith
B) to illustrate that Adam Smith was greatly influenced by Thomas Edison
C) to stress that Adam Smith, like Thomas Edison, was a great thinker
D) to classify great thinkers by their achievements

#4

From the lecture, we can infer that Smith considered mercantilism to be...

A) a successful economic system
B) an economic system lacking a rational and scientific approach
C) a system that benefitted all
D) a system upon which he based his economic theories

#5

The professor describes how Adam Smith's idea of "the invisible hand" works. Put these steps in order. This is a 2-point question.

a. trade expands
b. individual needs are met
c. systematic manufacturing
d. a nation acquires wealth

1. ______________________
2. ______________________
3. ______________________
4. ______________________

#6

The professor develops three topics. Match each topic with its corresponding description. This is a 2-point question.

a. European Enlightenment	b. The Wealth of Nations	c. Mercantilism

book written by Adam Smith describing how nations acquire wealth	economic nationalism aimed at acquiring gold by any means	18th century philosophy based on science and reason

Total points = / 8

➔ **Add your score to page 538**

➔ Answers: page 687.
➔ Scoring multi-answer questions: page 693.
➔ Audio script: page 782.

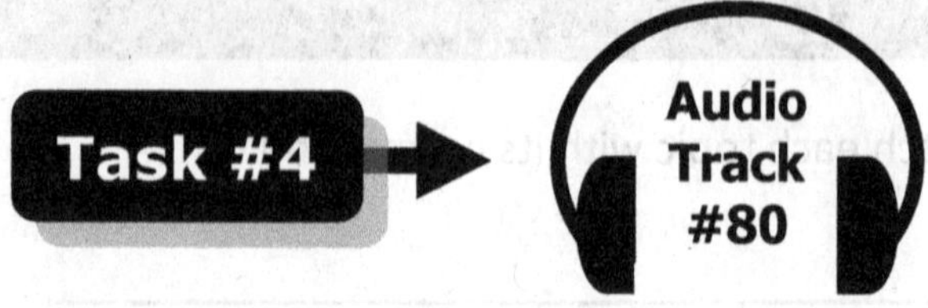

Directions: Listen to a lecture in an American literature class, then answer the questions on the next page.

Questions

Directions: Now get ready to answer the questions. Answer each question based on what is stated or implied in the lecture.

#1

What does the lecture mainly focus on?

A) a magazine called *The Black Mask*
B) the history of pulp fiction in America
C) the writers Carroll John Daly and Dashiell Hammett
D) great American detectives

#2

What is mentioned about *The Black Mask*? Select three. This is a 2-point question.

A) It was 128-pages long.
B) It started to sell in 1920.
C) It published formula writing.
D) It had no illustrations.
E) It was never popular.

#3

According to the lecture, what was Peter Collinson's real name?

A) Carroll John Daly
B) Dashiell Daly
C) Peter Hammett
D) Dashiell Hammett

#4

Why does the professor say this? 

A) to identify each writer's influences
B) to illustrate that Hammett had more life experience than Daly
C) to illustrate that Hammett lived a block from Daly's house
D) to describe what Hammett and Daly were doing in 1923

#5

The professor describes the life of Carroll John Daly. Put Daly's early life in the correct order. This is a 2-point question.

a. attended art school
b. published *Three-Gun Terry*
c. ran a movie theatre in Atlantic City
d. born in Yonkers, New York

1. ____________________
2. ____________________
3. ____________________
4. ____________________

Turn the page for question #6

#6

The professor mentions three dates. Match each date to the corresponding event. This is a 2-point question.

a. 1889	b. 1923	c. 1894

Three Gun Terry and *Arson Plus* were published in *The Black Mask.*	Carroll John Daly was born in Yonkers, New York.	Dashiell Hammett was born on a farm in Maryland.

Total points = / 9

➔ **Add your score to page 538**

➔ Answers: page 687.
➔ Scoring multi-answer questions: page 693.
➔ Audio script: page 783.

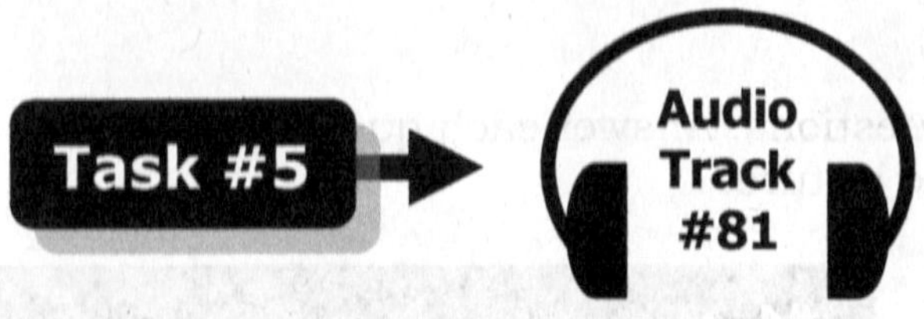

Directions: Listen to a lecture in a law class, then answer the questions on the next page.

Questions

Directions: Now get ready to answer the questions. Answer each question based on what is stated or implied in the lecture.

#1

What is the lecture mainly about?

A) a movie maker named Michael Moore
B) a politician named David Bossie
C) a U.S. Supreme Court ruling
D) a decision by the Elections Commission

#2

What does the professor say about *Hillary: The Movie*?

A) It won an Oscar for best documentary.
B) It is a 90-minute political attack ad.
C) It helped raise millions for Mrs. Clinton.
D) It was made by Michael Moore.

#3

Why does the professor say this? 

A) to indicate that something is wrong in the U.S. Supreme Court
B) to indicate how the Supreme Court's ruling has angered Hillary Clinton
C) to draw attention to how money can buy Supreme Court decisions
D) to illustrate how the Court's ruling is already creating controversy

#4

The professor mentions Ford. Why?

A) as an example of a corporation that could influence an election
B) as an example of a famous company
C) as an example of a supporter of a political candidate
D) as a reason why the Supreme Court made the right decision

#5

Listen again to part of the lecture, then answer the question.

What does the professor mean when she says this?

A) that *Hillary: The Movie* was a big hit during the '08 presidential primary
B) that *Hillary: The Movie* had little or no influence when it was released
C) that political movies are not popular during an election
D) that *Hillary: The Movie* was as popular as Michael Moore's film *911*

#6

According to the professor, how has the Supreme Court's decision changed the political landscape? This is a 3-point answer.

	YES	NO
Corporations can now buy and sell political candidates.		
Corporations can now run for elected office.		
Candidate funding can come from foreign companies in the U.S.		
Corporations can now influence voting through candidate funding.		
A U.S. corporation is considered an individual with voting rights.		

Total points = / 8

→ **Add your score to page 538**

→ Answers: page 687.
→ Scoring multi-answer questions: page 693.
→ Audio script: page 785.

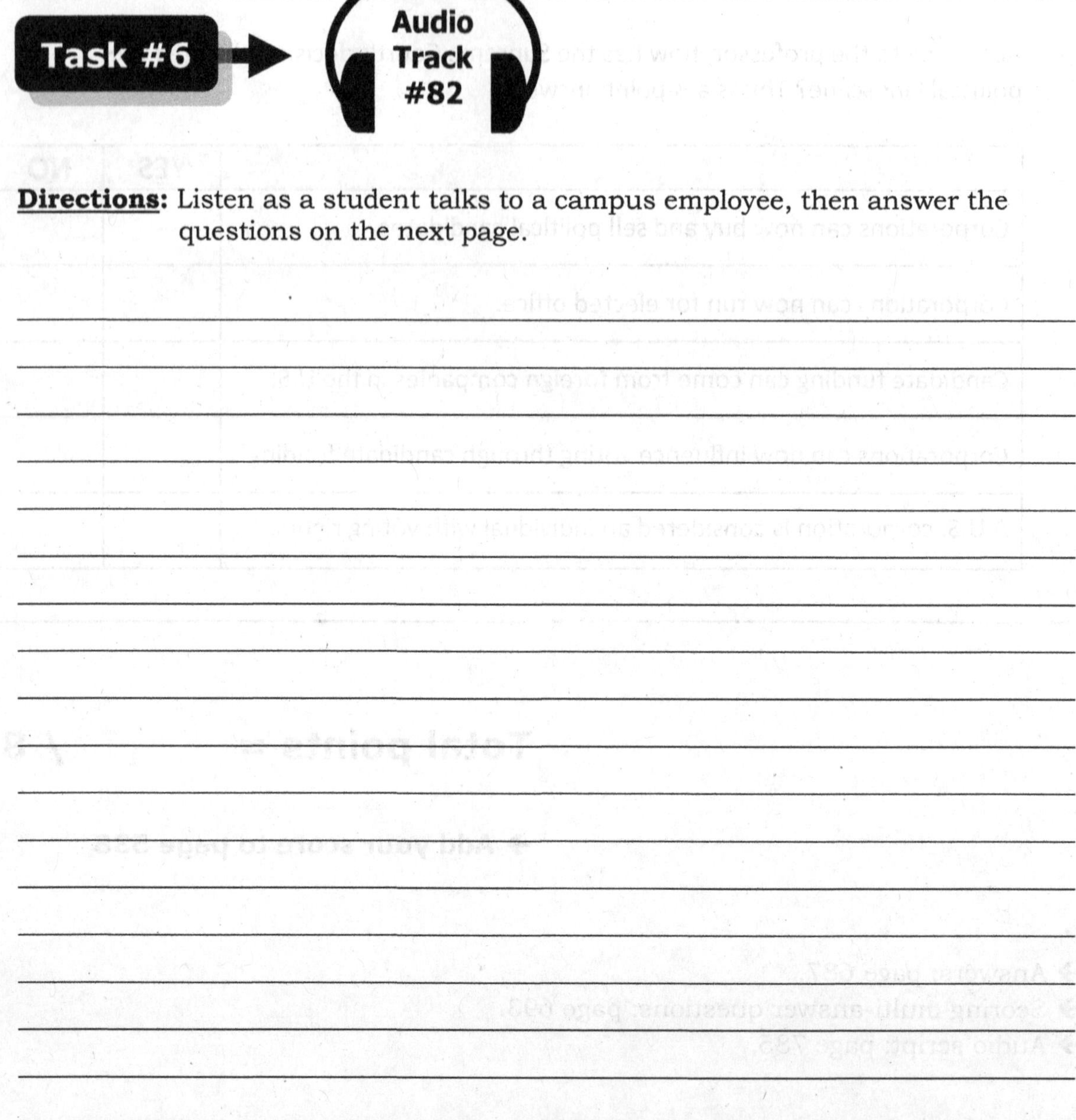

Directions: Listen as a student talks to a campus employee, then answer the questions on the next page.

Questions

Directions: Now get ready to answer the questions. Answer each question based on what was stated or implied in the conversation.

#1

What does the conversation focus on?

A) how easy e-book terminals are to use
B) problems with an e-book purchase
C) the need for secure passwords
D) fixing the kinks in the system

#2

From the conversation, we can infer that the student...

A) hates e-books
B) will never buy another e-book
C) will ask her professors for advice
D) will contact the e-book vendor

#3

What must the student's new e-book password be? Select three. This is a 2-point question.

A) at least six characters long
B) at least eight characters long
C) alphanumeric
D) alphabetical
E) case sensitive

#4

What can be inferred when the employee says this? 

A) Problems persist with the terminals.
B) The problems have been resolved.
C) There have been many complaints.
D) The store is not part of the e-book system.

#5

Listen again to part of the conversation, then answer the question.

Why does the student say this? 

A) She got the email.
B) She didn't get the email.
C) She forgot her email address.
D) She forgot to enter her email address.

➔ Answers: page 688.
➔ Scoring multi-answer questions: page 693.
➔ Audio script: page 786.

Total points = / 6

➔ Add your score to page 538

Calculate Your Listening Test Score

Enter the points for each task, total them, then convert your listening test score to a listening section score

Task #1	=	/ 9
Task #2	=	/ 6
Task #3	=	/ 8
Task #4	=	/ 9
Task #5	=	/ 8
Task #6	=	/ 6
total	=	/ 46 = listening test score

Convert your listening test score to a listening section score.

Test Score	Section Score	Test Score	Section Score
46	30	26	17
45	29	25	17
43	29	24	16
42	28	23	15
41	27	22	15
40	27	21	14
39	26	20	14
38	25	19	13
37	25	18	13
36	24	17	12
35	24	16	11
34	23	15	10
33	23	14	9
32	22	13	9
31	22	12	8
30	20	11	7
29	19	10	7
28	19	9	6
27	18	8	6

Listening Section Score = /30

➔ Record your score on page 707.

Reading

The reading section is the first section on the TOEFL iBT.

Reading | Listening | Speaking | Writing

The reading section is one hour. It measures your ability to read and understand academic passages. According to ETS, the passages "are excerpts from college-level textbooks that would be used in introductions to a discipline or topic." The task order is below.

TASK	WORDS	TIME	QUESTIONS
passage 1	650-750	20 minutes	12-14
passage 2	650-750	20 minutes	12-14
passage 3	650-750	20 minutes	12-14

On test day, you will read three passages. However, be prepared for five passages. Of the five passages, only three will be scored. The other two passages are "test" passages. ETS will use these passages on a future TOEFL test. You will not know which passages are scored. If you get five passages on test day, the time will increase to 90 minutes.

Topics

Expect a variety of academic topics in the reading section, topics such as history, literature, biology, economics, geology, astronomy, zoology, art, and sociology.

Q *Do I need to read about these topics before I take the TOEFL test?*

No. Remember: the TOEFL iBT is a learning test. That means each reading passage has been designed to teach you everything you need to know about the topic and answer the questions.

Directions

The reading section begins with the directions. Be familiar with them.

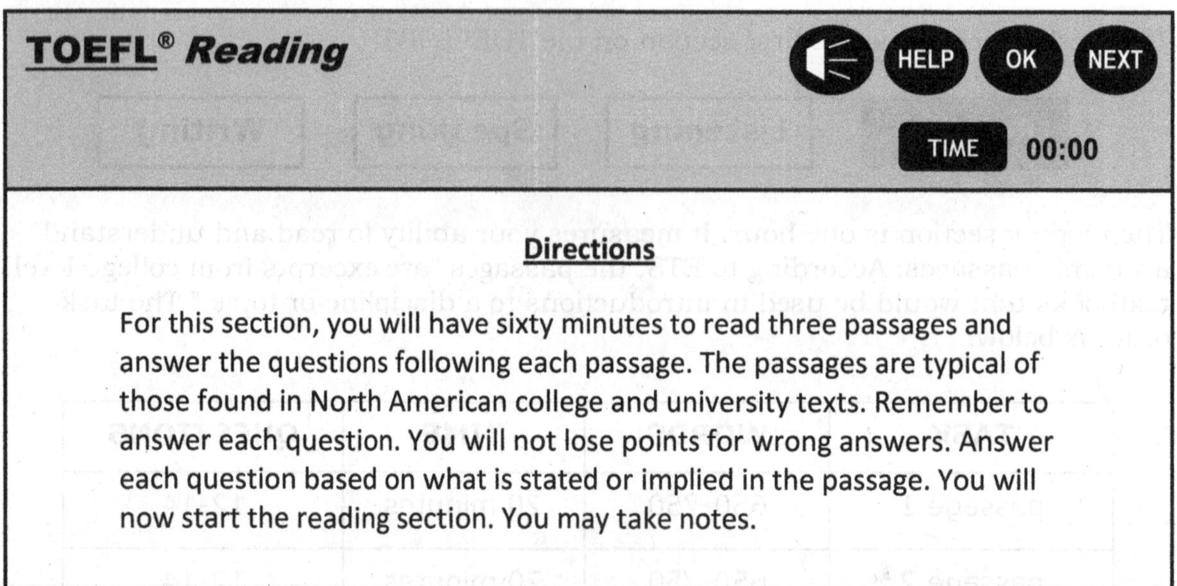

TOEFL® Reading
HELP
OK
NEXT
TIME
00:00
Directions
For this section, you will have sixty minutes to read three passages and answer the questions following each passage. The passages are typical of those found in North American college and university texts. Remember to answer each question. You will not lose points for wrong answers. Answer each question based on what is stated or implied in the passage. You will now start the reading section. You may take notes.

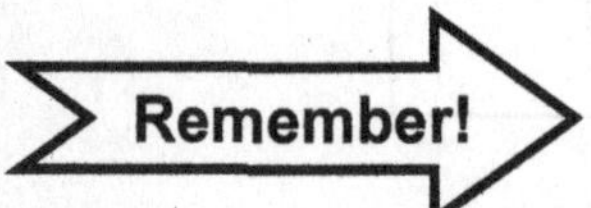

After the directions end, you will see the passage in the right pane (2). However, you will not see the questions in the left pane (1). To make the questions appear, scroll to the end of the passage, then scroll back to the start. The questions will appear in the left pane.

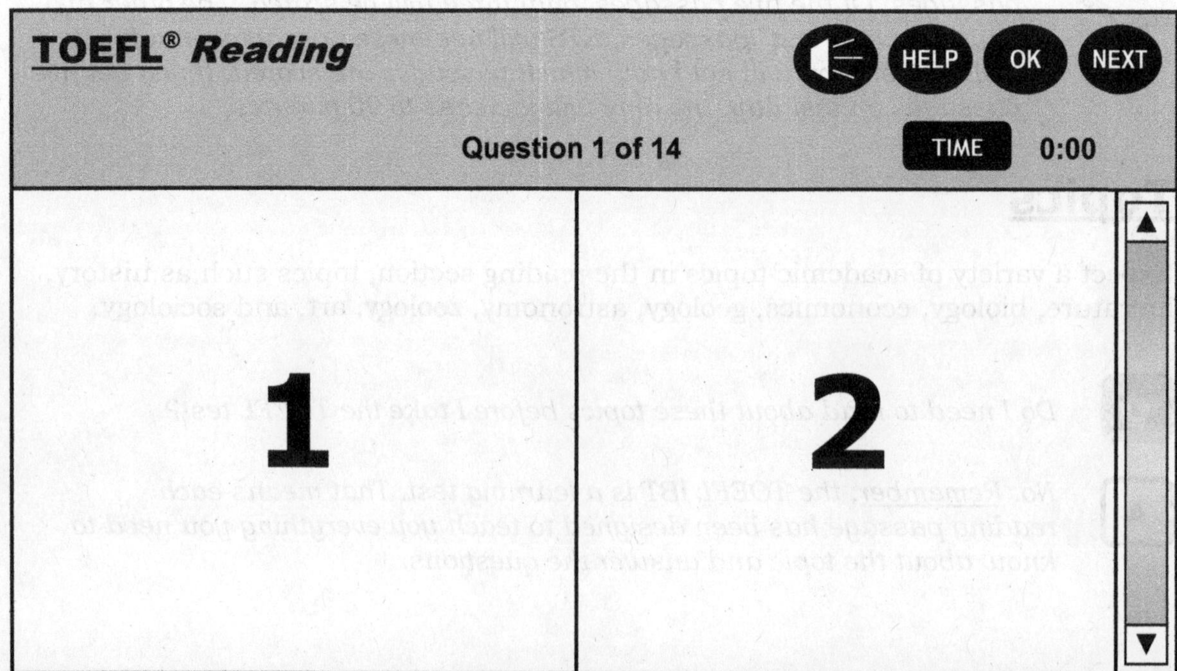

Sample: *Reading Passage*

You have 20 minutes to read and answer the questions that follow the passage.

Sample: *Adam Smith and The Wealth of Nations*

1 ➔ Adam Smith was born in Scotland in 1723. As a young man, he studied moral philosophy at the University of Glasgow and at Oxford. He eventually went on to tutor a nobleman's son. The position freed Smith from his daily work while affording him the opportunity to tutor while traveling throughout Europe. In France, Smith met Rousseau and Voltaire, leading proponents of the European Enlightenment. At its core, the European Enlightenment, guided by reason and science, questioned customs, morals, and traditional institutions, namely monarchies. Returning to Scotland, Smith set about writing his seminal *An Inquiry into the Nature and Causes of the Wealth of Nations*.

2 ➔ In *The Wealth of Nations*, Smith argues that building national economic wealth begins with a division of labor. Smith supports his argument by using a pin factory. In a typical pin factory of the day, each worker was responsible for making pins from start to finish. A worker would start by cutting the pin to size from a piece of wire, then straighten it, then sharpen the end, affix a head, polish it, then package it. In short, one man was responsible for each step of the pin-making process. Smith argued that such an approach was not only counter-productive but also time consuming inasmuch as once a worker finished one part of the task—say polishing a pin—he would pause before moving onto the next task. Such an approach, Smith argued, was inefficient, for workers were likely to "saunter" or pause between steps, which wasted time and substantially reduced productivity. Smith argued that the most efficient way to make pins was through a division of labor. Instead of ten men each separately making a pin from start to finish, each would be assigned one task, for example, one man would sharpen pins all day, another would polish them while a third would package them, and so on. By dividing labor this way, Smith theorized that the production of pins would dramatically increase. As a result, there would be more pins to sell and thus more money to be made. Smith's scientific approach to rationalizing the manufacturing process for greater productivity was indeed the product of Enlightenment thought.

3 ➔ A division of labor, however, was but one part of Smith's argument for creating wealth. An integral part of the wealth-making process, Smith claims, is the pin worker himself. He is performing his assigned task not for society's benefit nor for the benefit of the company, but for his own personal gain and security. The same follows with the owner of the pin factory. He too is out for personal gain, the health and the wealth of the nation the least of his, and his workers', worries. Yet by pursuing individual gain, Smith argues that the worker and the factory owner are in fact directly adding to the wealth of the nation by

utilizing a more efficient manufacturing process, one which stimulates trade, the buying and selling of goods, locally, nationally, and internationally. Smith coined this process "the invisible hand."

4 ➔ *The Wealth of Nations* is very much a reaction to the predominating economic theory of the day, that of Mercantilism. Mercantilists posited that the wealth of a nation depended on developing and maintaining national power thus it was a form of economic nationalism. Spain, at the time of Columbus, is a prime example of just such a nation. A nation like Spain preserved national power by accumulating as much gold as possible through strong exports, the limitation of imports, and a large population of poorly paid workers. ■ To develop exports, companies were subsidized by the government which also wrote laws to limit imports. ■ By limiting imports, the gold used to pay for imports would stay in the country and create a greater money supply and more credit. ■ Moreover, nations were geared toward acquiring and maintaining gold at all costs, including warring with each other. ■ Adam Smith, however, argued that trade benefitted all nations and that gold was not equal to wealth. Gold, Smith said, was like any other commodity, such as wheat or wool, and that it deserved no special treatment. More importantly, Smith says that the wealth of a nation is not based on the hoarding of gold, but on the free flow of goods manufactured in a systematic way, a way that serves the needs of the individual and, ultimately, the nation as a whole. With that, Adam Smith gave birth to what we now call economic theory. As Thomas Edison is to the light bulb, Adam Smith is to the science of economics.

Q *This reading passage was a lecture in the listening section test. Does the TOEFL iBT repeat the same task in different sections?*

A *No. The TOEFL iBT does not repeat tasks. Each task is new, as are the questions.*

R By recycling the Adam Smith lecture into a reading passage, you can see once again how an argument can be recycled from task to task. Because an argument can be recycled, the strategies you have learned to analyze arguments can also be recycled. That means all the test-taking strategies you have learned up to this point *can be applied to each reading section passage.* This process of recycling (integrating) strategies across all four test sections demonstrates that the TOEFL iBT is indeed a predictable (and integrated) game. It also illustrates how each test section uses arguments for testing purposes.

Questions

Directions: Answer each question based on what is stated or implied. If you do not know the answer, guess. You will not lose points for a wrong answer.

---

1. According to paragraph 1, when was Adam Smith born?

a) in the late sixteenth century
b) in the early eighteenth century
c) in the late eighteenth century
d) in the early seventeenth century

2. In paragraph 1, proponents is closest in meaning to...

a) associates
b) opponents
c) supporters
d) professionals

3. What is NOT true of the European Enlightenment?

a) It was based on reason.
b) It challenged customs and morals.
c) It was supported by kings and queens
d) It valued science.

4. In paragraph 1, what does seminal mean?

a) serious
b) interesting
c) controversial
d) original

5. In paragraph 2, to what does it refer?

a) worker
b) pin
c) wire
d) head

6. In paragraph 2, Adam Smith believes that economic wealth starts with what?

a) Mercantilism
b) a factory
c) an invisible hand
d) a division of labor

7. In paragraph 3, what does Smith mean by the "the invisible hand"?

   a) It is a rational and systematic manufacturing process creating wealth for a nation in a way that most do not notice or realize.
   b) It is a method of making pins over two hundred years ago that created wealth for Scotland.
   c) It is the government helping small businesses make money.
   d) It is an argument supporting the buying and selling of commodities, such as gold and silver.

8. In paragraph 3, why does Adam Smith mention the pin worker and the owner of the pin factory?

   a) to compare and contrast workers who benefitted the most from a new type of manufacturing process
   b) to classify the various types of workers in 1723 Scotland
   c) to define the process in which national wealth is created for both a pin worker and his employer
   d) to support his argument that a factory worker and a factory owner can both benefit financially from a systematic manufacturing process

9. Look at the four squares [■]. They indicate where the following sentence could be added to paragraph 4. Click on the square to insert the sentence into the passage.

   Witness England and Holland battling for control of present-day Manhattan in the early 1600's.

   A nation like Spain preserved national power by accumulating as much gold as possible through strong exports, the limitation of imports, and a large, population of poorly paid workers. ■ To develop exports, companies were subsided by the government which also wrote laws to limit imports. ■ By limiting imports, the gold used to pay for imports would stay in the country and create a greater money supply and more credit. ■ Moreover, nations were geared toward acquiring and maintaining gold at all costs, including warring with each other. ■ Adam Smith, however, argued that free trade benefitted all nations and that gold was not equal to wealth.

10. From the passage, it can be inferred that Adam Smith probably...

   a) owned a pin factory
   b) visited a pin factory
   c) worked in a pin factory
   d) studied workers

11. Which of the following sentences best restates the essential information in the highlighted sentence in paragraph 4? Incorrect choices will change the meaning and omit important information.

    a) Adam Smith adds that the wealth of a nation depends upon serving the needs of the individual first.
    b) Smith goes on to say that free trade is the best way to create wealth.
    c) Moreover, Smith says that nations become wealthy by accumulating gold and by systematically manufacturing goods, which are then freely traded.
    d) Smith believes that systematically manufactured goods freely traded create more national wealth than accumulating gold.

12. Directions: The sentence in bold is the first sentence of a brief summary of the passage. Complete the summary by selecting three answer choices. Your choices will express the most important ideas in the passage. Some choices are not in the passage or do not express important ideas. This is a 2-point question.

The passage discusses Adam Smith's book *The Wealth of Nations.*

-
-
-

Answer Choices

1. Smith's *The Wealth of Nations* represents the start of modern economic theory.
2. Smith illustrated how a factory worker wasted time when responsible for every step in the pin-making process.
3. Smith started to write *The Wealth of Nations* after he returned to Scotland from a long European trip.
4. Smith argued that to create national wealth, governments should subsidize companies.
5. Smith argued that Mercantilism was not a true wealth-building system.
6. Smith's theory of "the invisible hand" was influenced by the European Enlightenment.

13. In paragraph 4, the phrase subsidized by is closest in meaning to...
    a) supported by
    b) recorded by
    c) awarded by
    d) subsumed by

14. Directions: Complete the following table by indicating how Adam Smith's economic theories in *The Wealth of Nations* differed from what the Mercantilists believed. This is a 4-point question.

Mercantilists	Adam Smith
•	•
•	•
•	•
	•

1. Nations created wealth and power by amassing gold.
2. A satisfied work force will benefit a nation's economy as a whole.
3. Imports and exports should be manufactured by the government.
4. Exports made by poorly paid workers created national wealth.
5. National wealth starts with a rational approach to manufacturing.
6. Productivity will increase if the labor force is divided systematically.
7. War with other nations is part of national and economic policy.
8. Accumulating commodities does not create national wealth.
9. Free trade is an important part of military policy.

➔ Answers: page 688.
➔ Scoring multi-answer questions: page 693.

Scoring the Sample Reading Passage

The sample reading passage is a total of 18 points. Add up your score, then convert it to a reading section score using the guide below.

Sample Score	Section Score	Sample Score	Section Score
18 →	30	10	16
17	28	9	15
16	26	8	14
15	24	7	13
14	22	6	11
13	20	5	9
12	18	4	7
11	17	3	5

Reading Passage: *Task Analysis*

TOEFL's Testing Method

An understanding of TOEFL's testing method for this task begins with a rhetorical analysis of the reading sample. This analysis will help you take effective notes and maximize scoring.

G+3TiC=C: *Mapping out a Passage*

As you know, the TOEFL iBT recycles arguments as a means of testing English proficiency at the academic level. You also know that arguments can be mapped out. In the sample passage, the writer develops the topic of Adam Smith and *The Wealth of Nations* using a fact-based argument and deduction as the method of organization (**O**PDUL=C). That argument can be mapped out using G+3TiC=C.

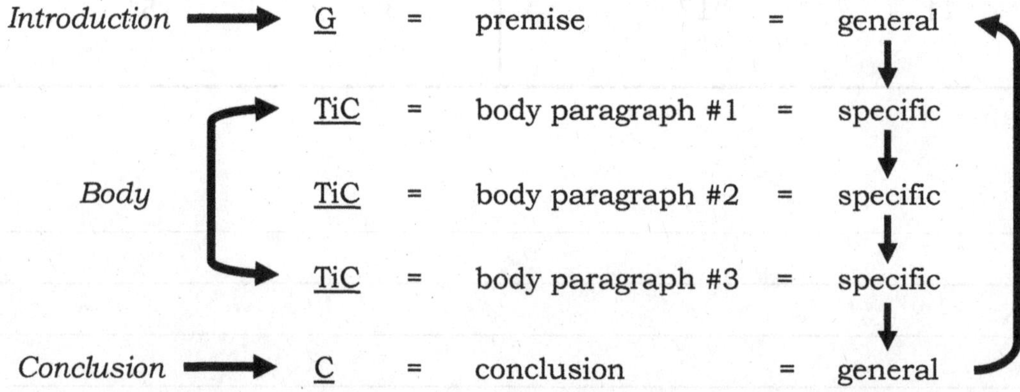

Some passages might have three body paragraphs (G+3TiC=C) or four (G+4TiC=C). The number of body paragraphs depends on how ETS designs the task.

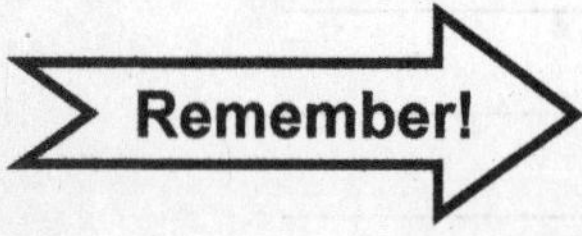

Because the reading passages are excerpts from actual books, there might not be a proper introduction. The passage might instead be a series of body paragraphs copied-and-pasted from a chapter in a book. In that case, the structure of the reading passage will map out as follows: all body paragraphs. No matter what the structure, the first sentence of the first paragraph will always introduce the main topic.

Body	TiC	=	body paragraph #1	=	specific ↓
	TiC	=	body paragraph #2	=	specific ↓
	TiC	=	body paragraph #3	=	specific

Introduction: *Rhetorical Functions*

Because the TOEFL iBT is a learning test, each passage (with or without a proper introduction) will start by introducing the main topic. By doing so, you will learn about the topic. The sample passage (see below) has a proper introduction. The main topic is Adam Smith. This fact is stated in the first sentence. The first sentence also identifies the context (Scotland in 1723). This information signals that the passage will describe an historical person and event, and will use the rhetorical strategy of narration to develop both. From these facts, we can also infer the premise. What is the main topic? Adam Smith. What about him (controlling idea)? His book *An Inquiry into the Nature and Causes of the Wealth of Nations.*

Premise: Adam Smith (main topic) and his book *An Inquiry into the Nature and Causes of the Wealth of Nations* (controlling idea).

1 ➔ Adam Smith was born in Scotland in 1723. As a young man, he studied moral philosophy at the University of Glasgow and at Oxford. He eventually went on to tutor a nobleman's son. The position freed Smith from his daily work while affording him the opportunity to tutor while traveling throughout Europe. In France, Smith met Rousseau and Voltaire, leading proponents of the European Enlightenment. At its core, the European Enlightenment, guided by reason and science, questioned customs, morals, and traditional institutions, namely monarchies. Returning to Scotland, Smith set about writing his seminal *An Inquiry into the Nature and Causes of the Wealth of Nations*.

Note how this introduction teaches you about the topic. ETS employs this same teaching-testing method for the integrated writing task, for speaking tasks #3, #4, #5 and #6, for all listening section tasks, and for each reading passage.

Can I use a dictionary?

No. TOEFL is testing your ability to understand new words, phrases and idioms in context. A dictionary negates this testing function. However, TOEFL does help you understand some new words. For example, if you see a word underlined in the text, such as aurox*, you can click on that word. The underline means the word is linked to a definition. Click on the word and a definition will pop up. Also, at the end of each passage, a few of the more challenging words in the passgage will be defined.*

Body Paragraphs: *Rhetorical Functions*

In body paragraph one below from the sample, note the three-part structure: **Transition-topic**, *illustration*(s), Conclusion. This structure, (TiC) reflects the overall, three-part structure of the passage itself. Note: On the test, each paragraph will be numbered. For example, the paragraph below is two of four paragraphs. Rhetorically, however, this is body paragraph one.

TiC

2 → **In *The Wealth of Nations*, Smith argues that building national economic wealth begins with a division of labor**. *Smith supports his argument by using a pin factory. In a typical pin factory of the day, each worker was responsible for making pins from start to finish. A worker would start by cutting the pin to size from a piece of wire, then straighten it, then sharpen the end, affix a head, polish it, then package it. In short, one man was responsible for each step of the pin-making process. Smith argued that such an approach was not only counter-productive but also time consuming inasmuch as once a worker finished one part of the task—say polishing a pin—he would pause before moving onto the next task. Such an approach, Smith argued, was inefficient, for workers were likely to "saunter" or pause between steps, which wasted time and substantially reduced productivity. Smith argued that the most efficient way to make pins was through a division of labor. Instead of 10 men each separately making a pin from start to finish, each would be assigned one task, for example, one man would sharpen pins all day, another would polish them while a third would package them, and so on.* By dividing labor this way, Smith theorized that the production of pins would dramatically increase. As a result, there would be more pins to sell and thus more money to be made. Smith's scientific approach to rationalizing the manufacturing process for greater productivity was indeed the product of Enlightenment thought.

Note above how the rhetorical strategy of description develops the *example* of the pin-making process. This descriptive, step-by-step process ends with a conclusion in which a **cause**-and-*effect* conclusion is made.

By dividing labor this way, Smith theorized *that the production of pins would dramatically increase. As a result, there would be more pins to sell and thus more money to be made.* **Smith's scientific approach to rationalizing the manufacturing process for greater productivity** *was indeed the product of Enlightenment thought.*

As you know, the rhetorical strategy of process is recycled throughout the TOEFL iBT. Why? Because process involves steps. Remembering and understanding those steps is a predictable way the TOEFL iBT tests your ability to organize ideas (**O**PDUL=C) while at the same time testing your ability to identify and remember the language used (OPDU**L**=C) in each step of the organizing process.

The repeating, three-part structure (**Transition-topic**, *illustration*, Conclusion) is repeated in body paragraph two below.

3 ➔ **A division of labor, however, was but one part of Smith's argument for creating wealth. An integral part of the wealth-making process, Smith claims, is the pin worker himself**. *He is performing his assigned task not for society's benefit nor for the benefit of the company, but for his own personal gain and security. The same follows with the owner of the pin factory. He too is out for personal gain, the health and the wealth of the nation the least of his, and his workers', worries. Yet by pursuing individual gain, Smith argues that the worker and the factory owner are in fact directly adding to the wealth of the nation by utilizing a more efficient manufacturing process, one which stimulates trade, the buying and selling of goods, locally, nationally, and internationally.* Smith coined this process "the invisible hand."

Note above how this body paragraph ends with a conclusion stating a cause-and-effect relationship. That relationship can be inferred from the phrase "the invisible hand." The invisible hand is: 1) the pin worker and the factory owner working (cause) for personal gain (effect), which, in turn, adds to the nation's wealth (effect). In this relationship, you can see how compare-and-contrast and cause-and-effect work together to create a process, one that Adam Smith argues builds national wealth.

Note also how the first supporting illustration (the pin worker) develops to include a second example (the factory owner). These two supporting illustrations result in the rhetorical strategy of compare-and-contrast (the pin worker compared to the factory owner).

As you know, the rhetorical strategy of compare-and-contrast is recycled throughout the TOEFL iBT. Why? Because compare-and-contrast describes the similarities and differences between two topics, in this case the pin worker and the factory owner. Remembering and understanding similarities and differences between topics is a predictable way the TOEFL iBT tests your ability to organize ideas (**O**PDUL=C) and your ability to identify the language used (OPDU**L**=C) to describe the similiarities and the differences between those ideas.

The repeating, three-part paragraph structure (**Transition-topic**, *illustration*, Conclusion) is repeated in body paragraph three below. Note how in developing the example of Mercantilism, the writer uses: 1) **cause**-and-*effect* (Mercantilists posited that *the wealth of a nation depended on* **developing and maintaining national power** *thus it was a form of economic nationalism*); 2) illustration (Spain, Holland, England); 3) process (acquire gold = limit imports, subsidize exports, go to war).

TiC

4 ➔ ***The Wealth of Nations* is very much a reaction to the predominating economic theory of the day, that of Mercantilism**. *Mercantilists posited that the wealth of a nation depended on developing and maintaining national power thus it was a form of economic nationalism. Spain, at the time of Columbus, is a prime example of just such a nation. A nation like Spain preserved national power by accumulating as much gold as possible through strong exports, the limitation of imports, and a large population of poorly paid workers. To develop exports, companies were subsidized by the government which also wrote laws to limit imports. By limiting imports, the gold used to pay for imports would stay in the country and create a greater money supply and more credit. Moreover, nations were geared toward acquiring and maintaining gold at all costs, including warring with each other. Adam Smith,* ***however****, argued that trade benefitted all nations and that gold was not equal to wealth. Gold, Smith said, was like any other commodity, such as wheat or wool, and that it deserved no special treatment. More importantly, Smith says that the wealth of a nation is not based on the hoarding of gold, but on the free flow of goods manufactured in a systematic way, a way that serves the needs of the individual and, ultimately, the nation as a whole.* With that, Adam Smith gave birth to what we now call economic theory. As Thomas Edison is to the light bulb, Adam Smith is to the science of economics.

Note how ***however*** signals Smith's *refutation of the gold theory*. This signals the beginning of Smith's thesis arguing against Mercantilism, the anti-thesis.

Adam Smith, ***however****, argued that trade benefitted all nations and that gold was not equal to wealth. Gold, Smith said, was like any other commodity, such as wheat or wool, and that it deserved no special treatment.* More importantly, Smith says that the wealth of a nation is not based on the hoarding of gold, but on the free flow of goods manufactured in a systematic way, a way that serves the needs of the individual and, ultimately, the nation as a whole.

thesis

The rhetorical strategy of *thesis anti-thesis* is recycled throughout the TOEFL iBT (see the argument counter-argument integrated essay and speaking task #3). Why? Because *thesis anti-thesis* is a common way to compare and contrast two opposing arguments. Understanding the similarities and differences between two opposing arguments is a predictable way the TOEFL iBT tests your ability to organize ideas (**O**PDUL=C) while at the same time testing your ability to identify the language used (OPDU**L**=C) to describe the similarities and the differences between the two arguments in question.

Q *Will every reading passage contain a thesis and an anti-thesis?*

A *No. It all depends on how ETS designs the task. If a passage does contain a thesis and an anti-thesis, make a note of it. It will signal a predictable testing point.*

Conclusion: *Rhetorical Functions*

Some passages will have a separate paragraph for a conclusion and some will not. The sample does not have a separate paragraph for the conclusion. Instead, the conclusion is the last sentence of body paragraph four. The conclusion restates the premise: With that, Adam Smith gave birth to what we now call economic theory. How did Smith do that? With his seminal book *The Wealth of Nations*.

> ...and that it deserved no special treatment. More importantly, Smith says that the wealth of a nation is not based on the hoarding of gold, but on the free flow of goods manufactured in a systematic way, a way that serves the needs of the individual and, ultimately, the nation as a whole. With that, Adam Smith gave birth to what we now call economic theory. **As Thomas Edison is to the light bulb, Adam Smith is to the science of economics.**

Note also that the last sentence is the author's **inserted opinion**. By comparing Adam Smith's *The Wealth of Nations* to Thomas Edison's light bulb, the author believes that Smith, like Edison, was a man of great influence.

As you know, opinion insertions in fact-based essays are recycled throughout the TOEFL iBT. Opinion insertions are a common way to identify a writer's or a speaker's position regarding the topic in a fact-based argument. Recognizing opinion insertions is a predictable way the TOEFL iBT tests your ability to comprehend opinions and your ability to identify the language that signals an opinion.

Rhetorical Strategies

The sample passage demonstrates all eight rhetorical strategies (see page 26).

narration	The story of Adam Smith and the development of his text, *An Inquiry into the Nature and Causes of the Wealth of Nations.*
illustration	The pin factory; the pin worker; the pin factory owner; Mercantilist economic theory; mercantilist nations (Spain, England, Holland).
process	making pins; mercantilists fighting for gold; mercantilists limiting imports while expanding exports; a division of labor; the invisible hand; how a nation acquires wealth.
definition	of the European Enlightenment; of Mercantilism; of the division of labor; of the invisible hand; how a nation acquires wealth.
description	of the pin making process; of the pin worker's needs; of the factory owner's needs; of the invisible hand; of mercantilist economic theory; of the division of labor; of the invisible hand.
cause-effect	Smith: a division of labor (cause) = the invisible hand (effect) = a nation acquires wealth (effect). Mercantilists: hoard gold + limit imports + increase exports (cause) = economic power + national power (effect) = a nation acquires wealth (effect).
classification	Mercantilist nations: Spain, England, Holland.
compare-contrast	Adam Smith's economic theories vs. Mercantilism. Adam Smith and Thomas Edison.

The TOEFL iBT measures English-language proficiency at the academic level by recycling and testing your ability to apply the above-eight rhetorical strategies.

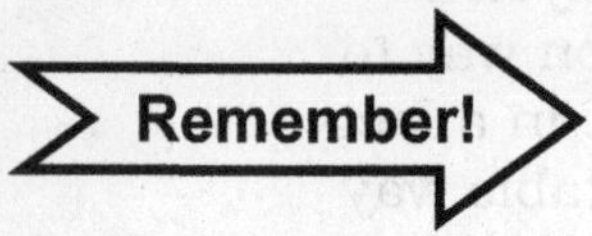

To get the highest possible TOEFL iBT score, you must be able to recognize and proficiently apply the above-eight rhetorical strategies in combination with fact-based and opinion-based arguments when reading, speaking, listening, and writing.

Questions: *Four Ways to Answer*

For each reading passage, there are four question types.

multiple-choice	sentence-insertion
summary-completion	complete-a-table

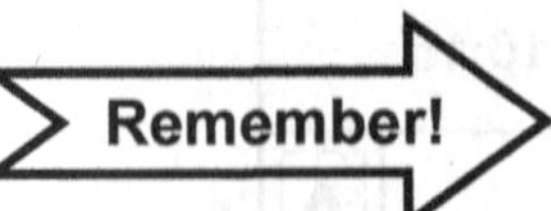

You can answer the questions in any order. For example, you can answer question nine first, then scroll back to question one, etc.

1. Multiple-Choice Questions

This question type has four answer choices. Click on one of the four choices with the mouse, click "Next," then "Okay." This is a 1-point answer.

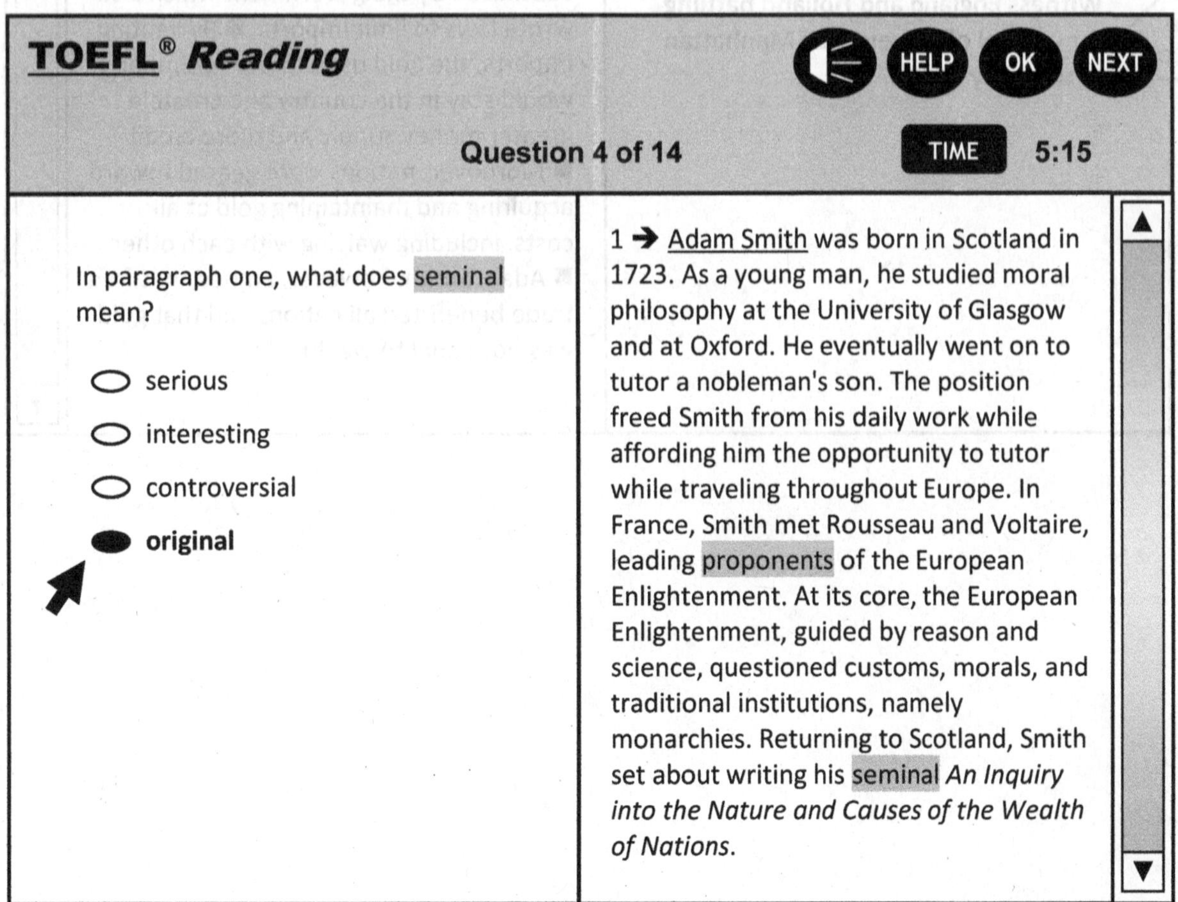

2. Sentence-Insertion Questions

This question type has four answer choices. Each choice is indicated by a black square in the passage in the right pane. Each black square is a possible insertion point for the insertion sentence in the left pane. In the right pane, answer by clicking on the black square where you think the insertion sentence should be inserted into the passage. This is a 1-point question.

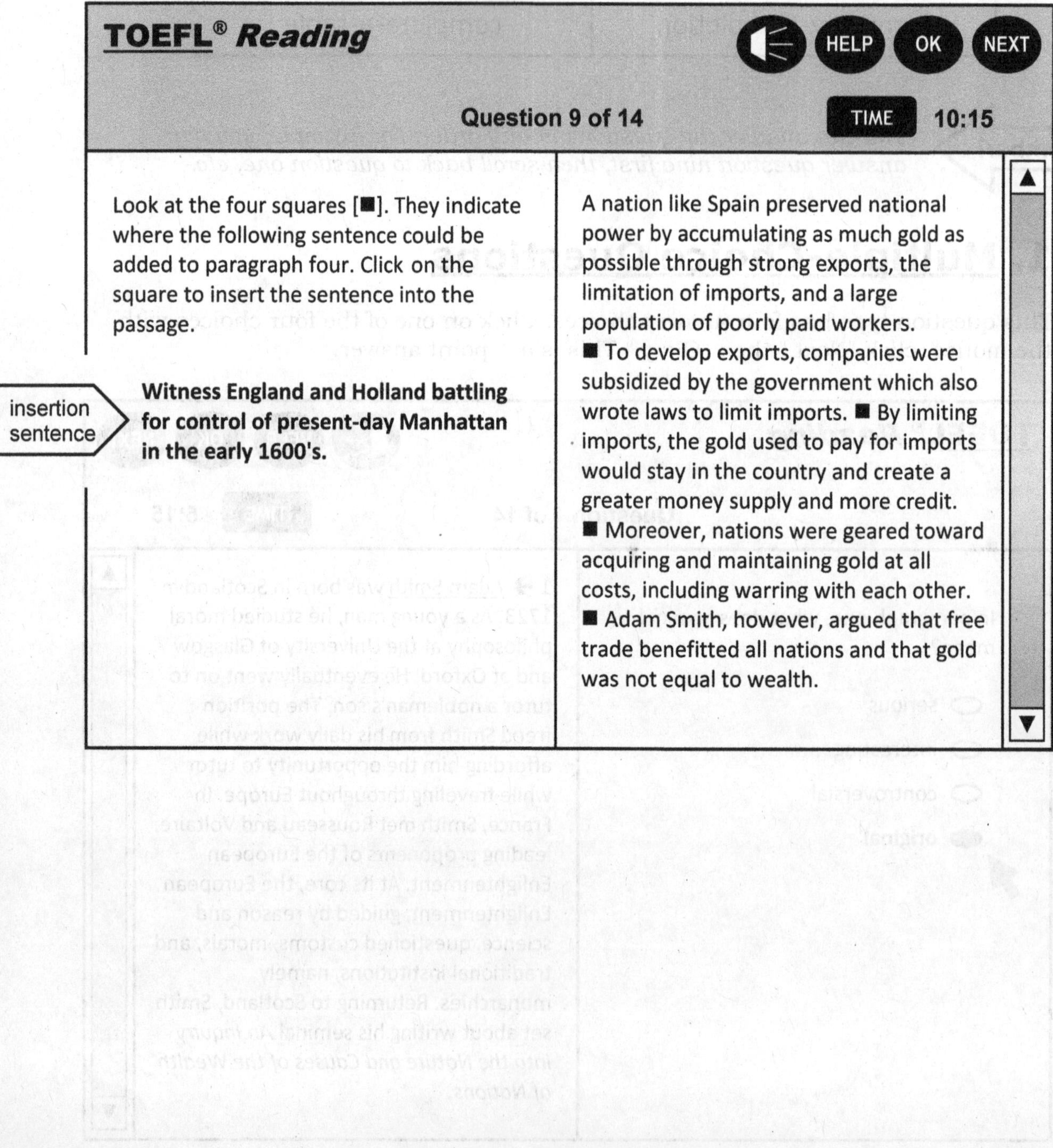
TOEFL® Reading
HELP
OK
NEXT
Question 9 of 14
TIME
10:15
Look at the four squares [■]. They indicate where the following sentence could be added to paragraph four. Click on the square to insert the sentence into the passage.
insertion sentence
Witness England and Holland battling for control of present-day Manhattan in the early 1600's.
A nation like Spain preserved national power by accumulating as much gold as possible through strong exports, the limitation of imports, and a large population of poorly paid workers.
■ To develop exports, companies were subsidized by the government which also wrote laws to limit imports. ■ By limiting imports, the gold used to pay for imports would stay in the country and create a greater money supply and more credit.
■ Moreover, nations were geared toward acquiring and maintaining gold at all costs, including warring with each other.
■ Adam Smith, however, argued that free trade benefitted all nations and that gold was not equal to wealth.

This is how the insertion sentence will look when inserted.

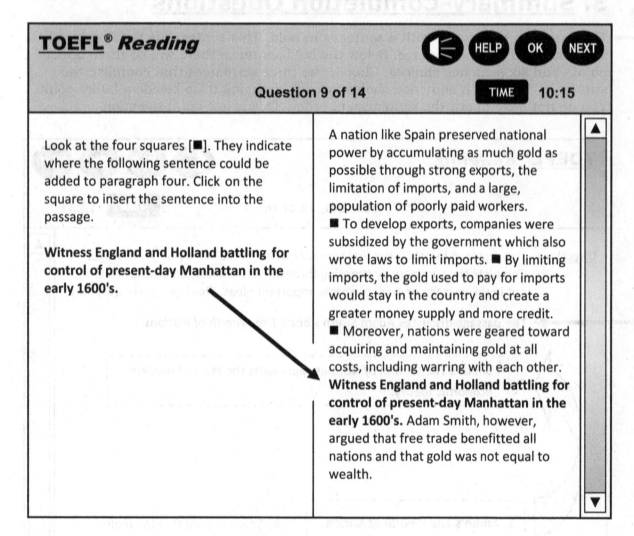

TOEFL® *Reading*

HELP OK NEXT

Question 9 of 14 TIME 10:15

Look at the four squares [■]. They indicate where the following sentence could be added to paragraph four. Click on the square to insert the sentence into the passage.

Witness England and Holland battling for control of present-day Manhattan in the early 1600's.

A nation like Spain preserved national power by accumulating as much gold as possible through strong exports, the limitation of imports, and a large, population of poorly paid workers. ■ To develop exports, companies were subsidized by the government which also wrote laws to limit imports. ■ By limiting imports, the gold used to pay for imports would stay in the country and create a greater money supply and more credit. ■ Moreover, nations were geared toward acquiring and maintaining gold at all costs, including warring with each other. **Witness England and Holland battling for control of present-day Manhattan in the early 1600's.** Adam Smith, however, argued that free trade benefitted all nations and that gold was not equal to wealth.

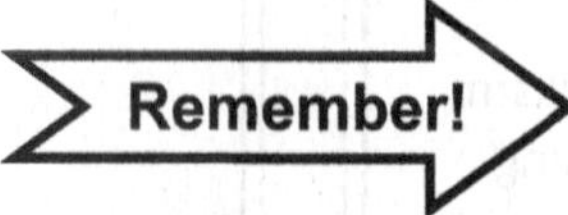

On test day, when you click on a black square, the insertion sentence will <u>not</u> insert. The above-example is for demonstration purposes only.

3. Summary-Completion Questions

This question type starts with a sentence in bold. This sentence is the first in a short summary of the passage. Below the bold sentence there will be three bullet points and six sentence choices. Choose the three sentences that complete the summary. Move each sentence choice by click-dragging it up beside a bullet point. You do not have to put the sentences in order. This is a 2-point question.

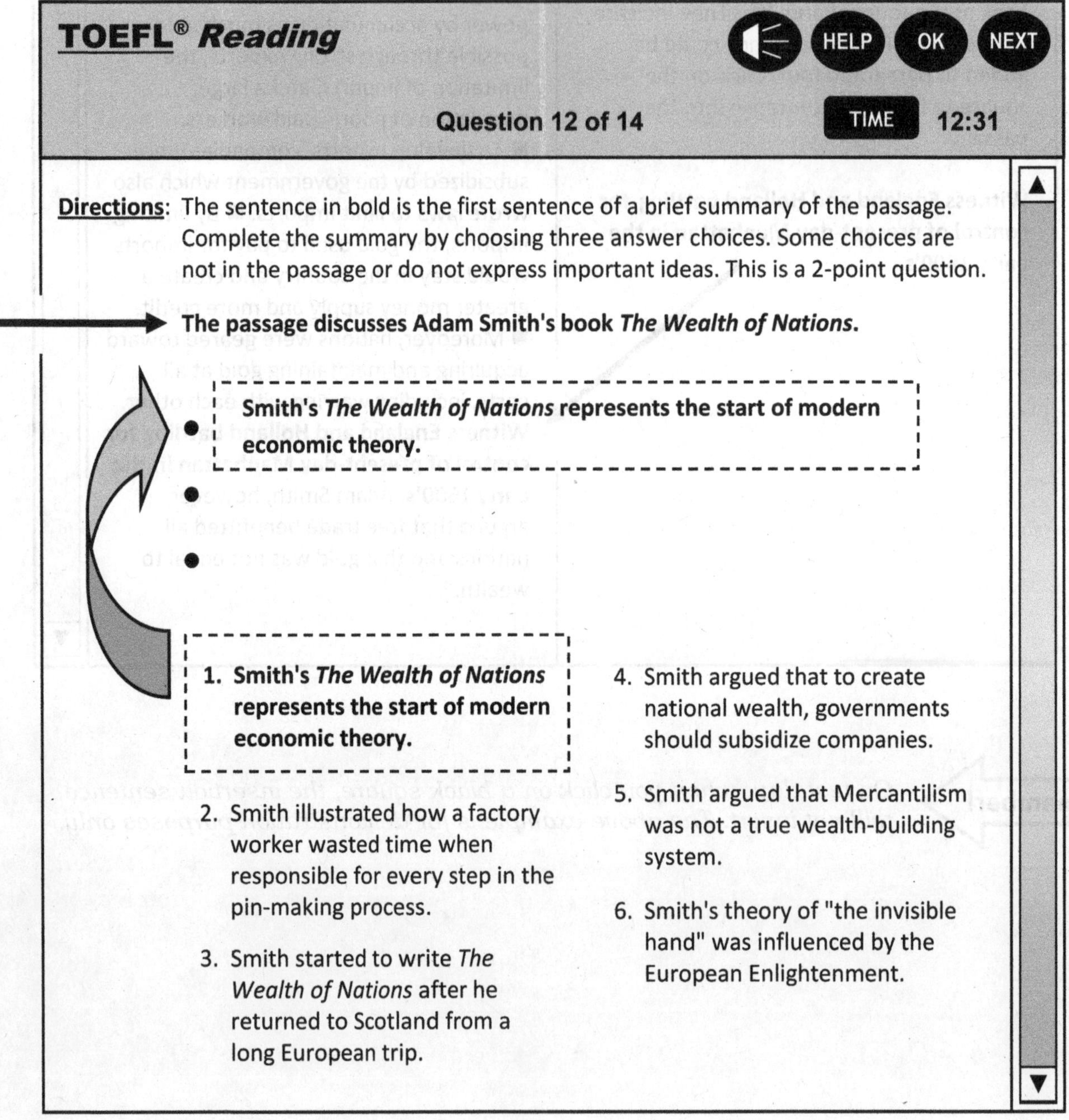
TOEFL® Reading
HELP
OK
NEXT
Question 12 of 14
TIME
12:31
Directions: The sentence in bold is the first sentence of a brief summary of the passage. Complete the summary by choosing three answer choices. Some choices are not in the passage or do not express important ideas. This is a 2-point question.
The passage discusses Adam Smith's book The Wealth of Nations.
Smith's The Wealth of Nations represents the start of modern economic theory.
1. Smith's The Wealth of Nations represents the start of modern economic theory.
2. Smith illustrated how a factory worker wasted time when responsible for every step in the pin-making process.
3. Smith started to write The Wealth of Nations after he returned to Scotland from a long European trip.
4. Smith argued that to create national wealth, governments should subsidize companies.
5. Smith argued that Mercantilism was not a true wealth-building system.
6. Smith's theory of "the invisible hand" was influenced by the European Enlightenment.

➔ see page 693 for scoring multi-answer questions

Complete-a-Table Questions

For this question type, you must complete a table. From the nine answer choices, choose seven by click-dragging each under the corresponding topic heading. This is a 3-point question. Note: The answers do not have to be in order.

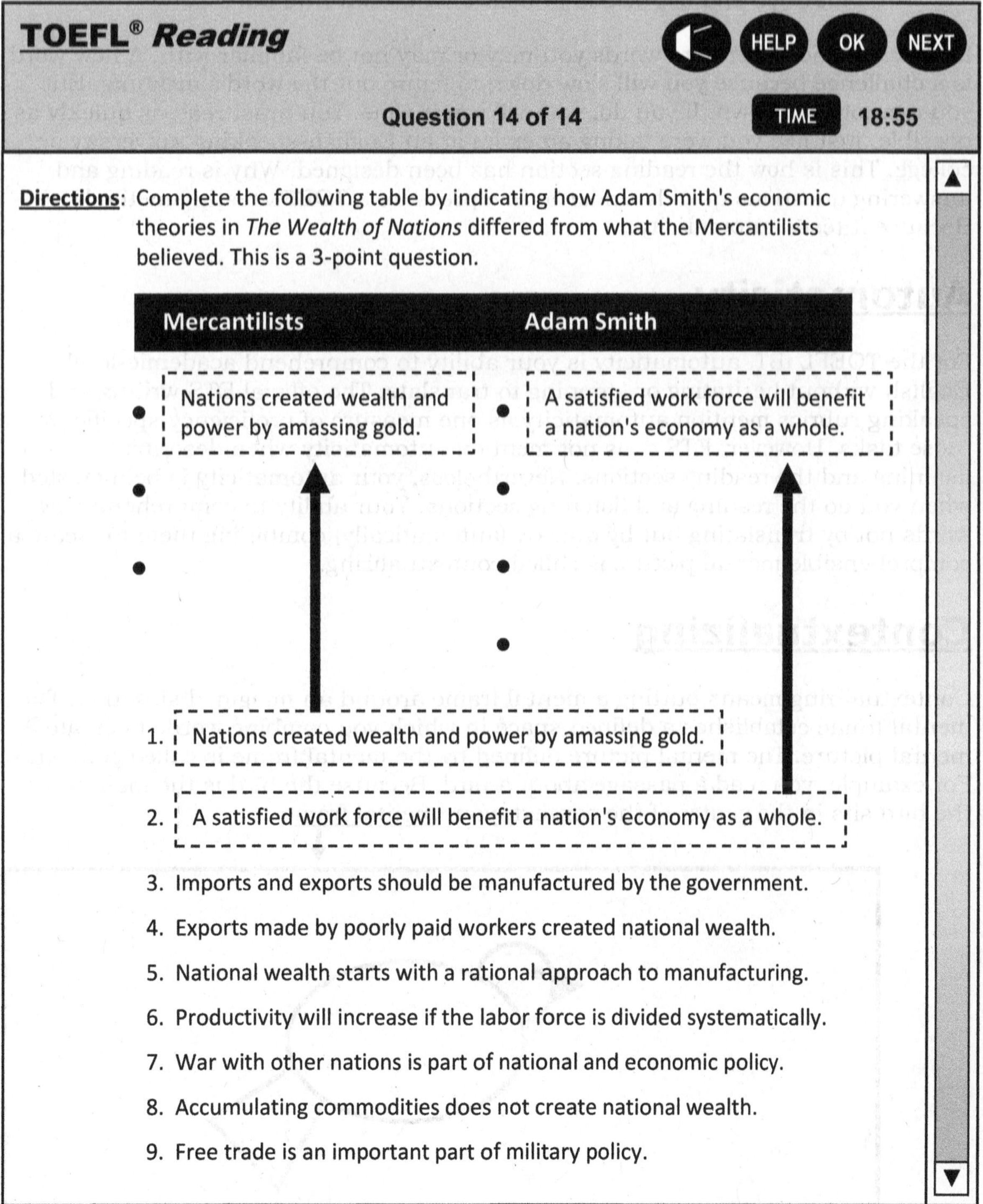
TOEFL® Reading
HELP
OK
NEXT
Question 14 of 14
TIME 18:55
Directions: Complete the following table by indicating how Adam Smith's economic theories in The Wealth of Nations differed from what the Mercantilists believed. This is a 3-point question.
Mercantilists
Adam Smith
Nations created wealth and power by amassing gold.
A satisfied work force will benefit a nation's economy as a whole.
1. Nations created wealth and power by amassing gold.
2. A satisfied work force will benefit a nation's economy as a whole.
3. Imports and exports should be manufactured by the government.
4. Exports made by poorly paid workers created national wealth.
5. National wealth starts with a rational approach to manufacturing.
6. Productivity will increase if the labor force is divided systematically.
7. War with other nations is part of national and economic policy.
8. Accumulating commodities does not create national wealth.
9. Free trade is an important part of military policy.

Reading Strategies

The reading passages are long and challenging, and contain many new words. For example, a sentence from a passage might read like this.

> The incumbent president, famous for being a martinet, is both mendacious and capricious in moments of extreme duress.

In this sentence, there are words you may or may not be familiar with. A new word is a challenge because you will slow down to figure out the word's meaning. But you cannot slow down. If you do, you will waste time. You must read as quickly as possible, just like you were taking an exam at an English-speaking university or college. This is how the reading section has been designed. Why is reading and answering questions quickly under a time pressure a TOEFL testing method? Because it tests automaticity.

Automaticity

For the TOEFL iBT, automaticity is your ability to comprehend academic-level English without hesitating or stopping to translate. The official ETS writing and speaking rubrics mention automaticity as one measure of proficiency specific to those tasks. However, ETS does not mention automaticity when describing the listening and the reading sections. Nevertheless, your automaticity is being tested when you do the reading and listening sections. Your ability to comprehend new words not by translating but by quickly (automatically) combining them to create a comprehensible mental picture is called contextualizing.

Contextualizing

Contextualizing means putting a mental frame around an imagined situation. The mental frame establishes a defined space in which you combine words to create a mental picture. The mental picture defined by the mental frame is called context. For example, you read a passage about a bird. Because the bird is the main topic, the bird sits in the center of the context, your mental frame.

Where is the bird? You do not know. You need to read on to create more context. By doing so, you fill in your mental frame. As you read on, you learn that the bird is sitting on a nest on a branch in a tree. You can infer that the bird is probably female because the nest infers eggs and eggs infer female. Note how inferring (combining images to make a conclusion) is part of the contextualizing process.

As you read on, you learn that the nesting bird is watching another bird. Is the second bird the nesting bird's mate or a threat? You do not know. You can only infer. To complete the context, you must continue to read.

As you can see, contextualizing is an additive process, one in which inferring is an integral part. The more you read, the more your mental frame fills up with context (information). The faster you read, the faster you complete the context. However, if you pause to translate or reread for understanding, you will not complete the context. This lack of automaticity will waste time and limit your ability to answer the questions correctly and completely.

"I Need More Time!"

Many test-takers feel that the reading section should be longer. One hour, they say, is not enough. Worse, they feel they are not reading but speed reading. And they are right. This is one way the reading section tests you: by forcing you to read like a native speaker under a time pressure. Remember that the TOEFL iBT was designed by psychometricians (psychometric = mind + measure). Psychometricians study how test-takers perform under a time pressure while doing standardized tests, such as the TOEFL iBT. The psychometricians who designed the TOEFL iBT believe that one hour is the right amount of time for test-takers to read and learn three reading passages and answer the questions. If you had more time, another twenty minutes let's say, you would have more time to translate and contextualize. That, the psychometricians would argue, would not be an accurate way of measuring English-language proficiency specific to reading at the academic level.

Q *What is the best way to prepare for the reading section?*

A *Read, read, read. The more you read, the more you learn how to contextualize. The more you contextualize, the more you develop your vocabulary. A larger vocabulary means a higher TOEFL score.*

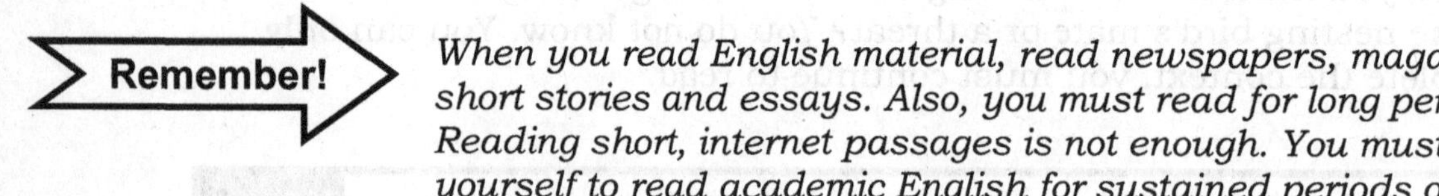

When you read English material, read newspapers, magazines, novels, short stories and essays. Also, you must read for long periods of time. Reading short, internet passages is not enough. You must train yourself to read academic English for sustained periods of time, one or two hours at least.

Q *What about memorizing word lists? Is that a good way to prepare for the reading section?*

A *No. Why not? Because word lists have no context. Remember: At the TOEFL level, the best way to learn and remember new words is from context. Word lists are helpful only if the words come from a specific context. For example, you are reading an essay about Abraham Lincoln. As you read, make a list of new words. By doing so, you will be killing two birds with one stone: you will be learning how to contextualize while expanding your vocabulary. That is how advanced language learners learn, not by memorizing word lists but by contextualizing. This is especially true for idioms.*

Warning! *In order to use an idiom proficiently, you must know the context in which to use it. Simply memorizing the definition of an idiom is not recommended. If you are unsure of the context, do not use the idiom or translate it from your language into English. More often than not an idiom in your language does not translate into English. An idiom used incorrectly will demonstrate a lack of language-use proficiency (OPDU**L**=C).*

How to Read a Passage

Because there is not enough time to read each passage closely, you must manage your time so that you can read each passage and answer all questions within the time limit. There are three ways to do so.

1. Read the question first. Identify signal words in the question, then skim and scan for those same signal words in the corresponding body paragraph.

2. Read the paragraph first, then answer the question.

3. Read the entire passage first, then go back and answer the questions sequentially. Warning: This strategy is time-consuming. Watch the clock.

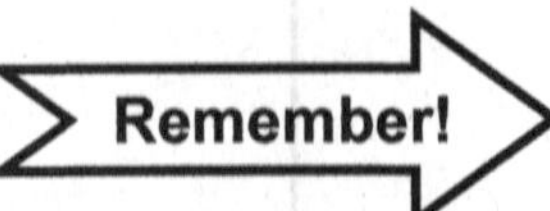

Everybody reads differently. Only by practicing will you learn which reading strategy is best for you.

How to Locate Answers

Because you are under a time pressure, you will need to find answers quickly. There are two ways to do so: by skimming and by scanning.

Skimming: *Locating General Information*

Each passage will be presented paragraph by paragraph on your screen. The first thing you must do is identify the topic of each paragraph. Do so by skimming. When you skim, you read for general information. That information is in the topic sentence. Read the topic sentence, then jump (skim) over the example and read the conclusion. Often the conclusion will restate the topic introduced in the topic (first) sentence. When you are finished, apply what you have learned to the question.

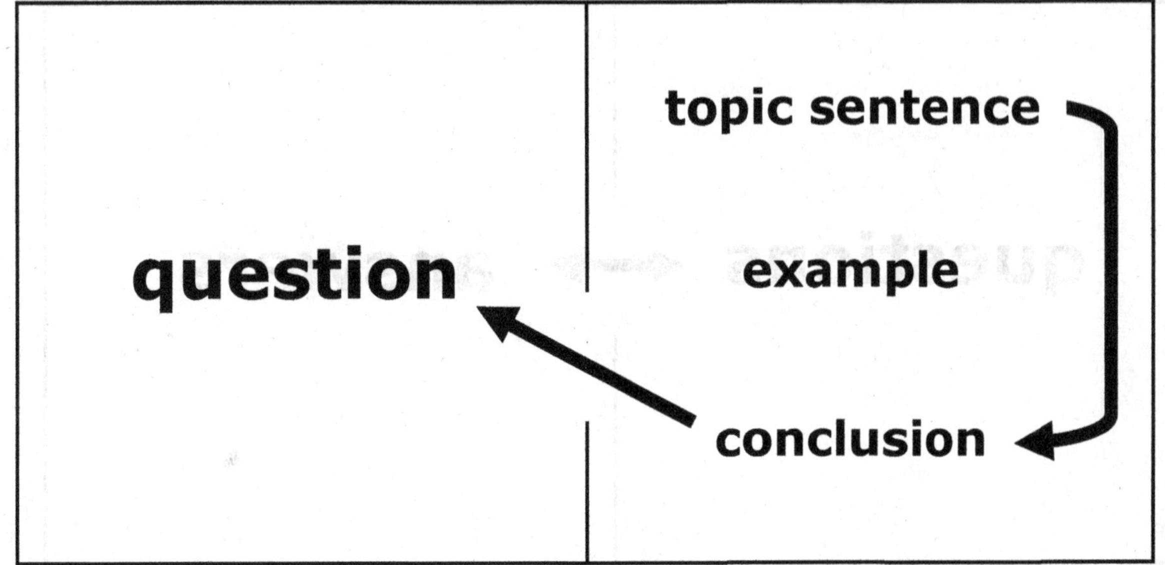

<u>Scanning</u>: *Locating Specific Information*

When you scan a passage, you are looking for details. Start by reading the question. Identify signal words in the question, then quickly move your eyes back and forth along each line in the passage. As you do, look for words that match the signal words in the question. Quickly scan the paragraph from start to finish, then return to the question to confirm the details you have located. Do not read each sentence. You will waste time.

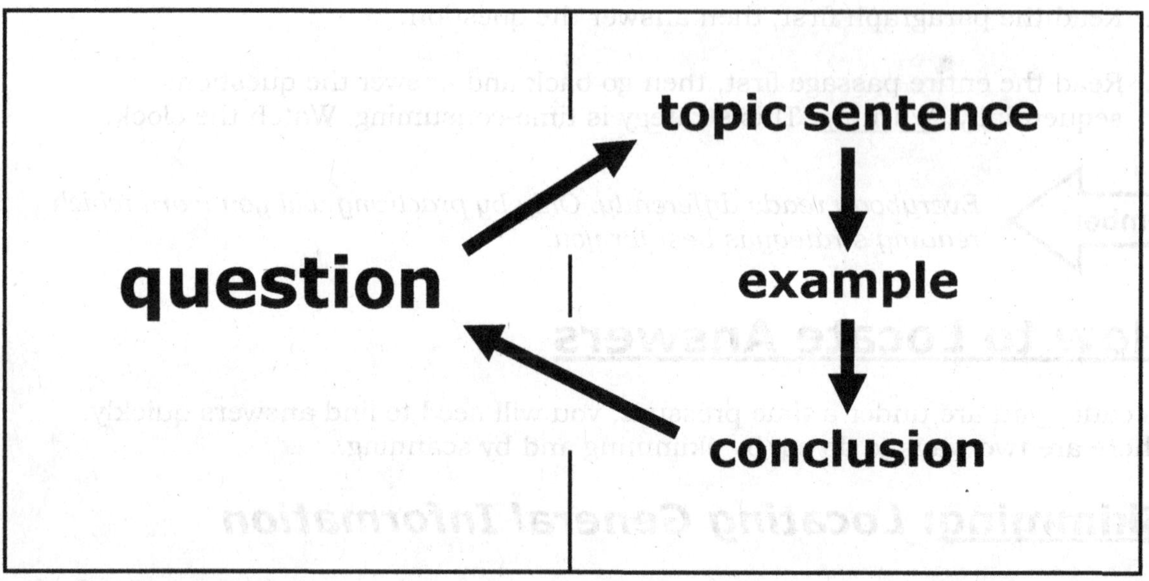

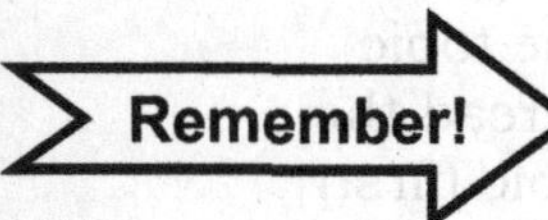

The answers for multiple-choice and sentence insertion questions will be in the right pane opposite the question. Complete-a-table questions and summary-completion questions, however, will test your knowledge of the entire passage.

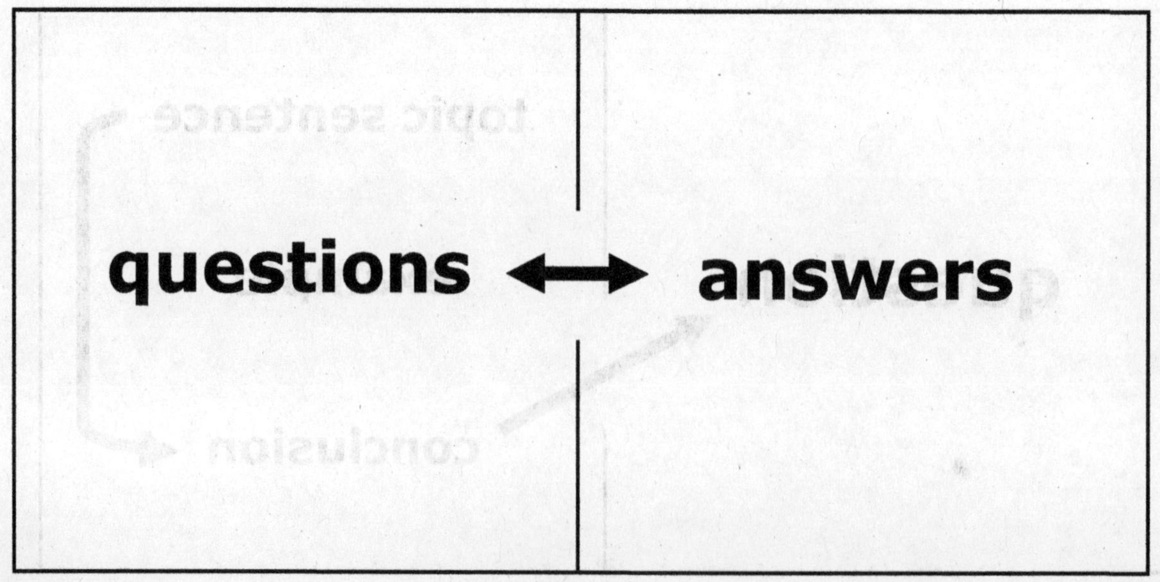

Basic Information and Inference Questions

1. Factual Information Questions

Each passage will have between 3-6 factual information questions. These questions are W-questions (who, what, where, when, why, and how). They measure your ability to identify details that support and develop the main topic in a body paragraph and/or passage. Factual information questions can be paraphrased a variety of ways, for example:

- According to paragraph 1, when was Adam Smith born?
- In paragraph 2, Adam Smith believes that economic wealth begins with what?
- In paragraph 3, why does Adam Smith mention the pin worker and the owner of the pin factory?

Look at a sample factual information question.

6. In paragraph 2, Adam Smith believes that economic wealth starts with what?

a) Mercantilism
b) a factory
c) an invisible hand
d) a division of labor

a. Question Analysis: *Signal Words*

Before you select an answer, make sure you understand the question. As you read the question, look for signal words. Signal words identify the words you must scan or skim for in the corresponding paragraph or in the passage as a whole. Look at the following question. The signal words are paragraph 2 and economic wealth starts with what. Scan paragraph 2 for these signal words.

6. In paragraph 2, Adam Smith believes that economic wealth starts with what?

b. Choice Analysis: *Process of Elimination*

When you find a possible answer, compare it to the four answer choices. Using *process of elimination,* eliminate choices that are: 1) off topic; 2) too general; 3) too specific; 4) not known; 5) not true; 6) not accurate.

In the following example, A is not true. Adam Smith argues against Mercantilism. Eliminate A as a choice. C is also not true. Adam Smith uses this metaphor (an invisible hand) to describe what happens when all steps of a rationalized manufacturing process are working as one. Also, creating wealth cannot begin with a metaphor (a comparison).

6. In paragraph 2, Adam Smith believes that economic wealth starts with what?

not true a) Mercantilism
b) a factory
not true c) an invisible hand
d) a division of labor

You now have two choices left. This is the position TOEFL wants you to be in. You now have a 50-50 chance of choosing the correct answer. But which one is it? Both sound good. Yet one is correct and the other is the distractor.

You learned about distractors in the listening section (page 435 and page 440). You can recycle those same strategies when analyzing reading section answer choices for distractors.

c. Identifying the Distractor

Distractors are designed to look like the correct answer. Distractors test your reading comprehension and language use proficiency. In this example, B is the distractor.

6. In paragraph 2, Adam Smith believes that economic wealth starts with what?

not true a) Mercantilism
distractor b) a factory
not true c) an invisible hand
d) a division of labor

Why is B the distractor? A factory is indeed an essential part of the wealth making process. However, Smith does not talk about any factory. He talks about a "pin factory." Thus B is too general as well. Also, what happens inside the pin factory is the more important point. According to Smith, the labor force inside a pin factory should be divided. This will result in greater productivity, which will result in a nation acquiring wealth. Therefore, D is correct.

Analyze each question and each answer choice carefully. Classroom experience proves that many test-takers select the distractor because they did not take the time to analyze the language used in the question and in the answer choices.

Practice #1: *Factual Information Questions*

Directions: You have ten minutes to read the passage and answer the questions.

Penicillin

1 ➔ *Penicillium chrysogenum* is a common mold, a mold being a fungus that has multi-cellular arms or filaments called hyphae. Also known as *Penicillium notatum, Penicillium chrysogenum* can be found living indoors on food. Its spores, units of asexual reproduction that can evolve into a new organism, are carried by the air and are a major cause of allergens in humans. In 1928, Scottish scientist Alexander Fleming discovered that *Penicillium notatum* contained a bacteria-killing antibiotic, an antibiotic Fleming named penicillin.

2 ➔ Alexander Fleming was born in 1881 in Scotland. At the age of twenty, he entered St. Mary's Hospital in London and studied medicine, then went on to become the assistant bacteriologist to Sir Almroth Wright, a pioneer in immunology and vaccine therapy. During World War One, Fleming served as a captain in the Royal Army Medical Corps and worked on the frontlines where he witnessed firsthand soldiers dying of sepsis. Sepsis, or systematic inflammatory response (SIRS), is blood poisoning due to the presence of bacteria in the blood. To fight off the bacteria, the body enters an inflammatory state accompanied by a high fever. Fleming witnessed widespread sepsis, most of which was caused by infected wounds. Antiseptics were widely available yet Fleming believed they killed only surface bacteria while failing to eradicate deeper bacteria. After the war, Fleming was determined to find a cure for sepsis. He discovered lysozyme, an enzyme found in tears. It was a natural anti-bacterial yet was ineffective against more powerful infections. In 1928, while researching the properties of staphylococci, a genus of gram-positive bacteria, he stumbled upon *Penicillium notatum.*

1. According to paragraph 1, what are capable of reproducing asexually?

a) filaments
b) hypha
c) spores
d) penicillin

2. According to paragraph 2, where did Fleming see evidence of widespread SIRS?

a) in the Royal Medical Corp
b) in St. Mary's Hospital
c) in1881 in Ayrshire, Scotland
d) in frontline soldiers

3. What did Fleming come to believe about antiseptics?

a) They were ineffective.
b) They killed deeper bacteria.
c) Lysozyme was effective.
d) They were too expensive.

4. What did Alexander Fleming find by chance in 1928?

a) Penicillium notatum
b) gram-positive bacteria
c) lysozyme
d) sepsis

5. According to paragraph 3, what did the blue-green mold do?

a) It contaminated a fungus.
b) It destroyed the staphylococci.
c) It built colonies of staphylococci.
d) It turned into staphylococci cultures.

6. To what did Fleming eventually change the name mold juice?

a) staphylococci
b) penicillin
c) paratyphoid fever
d) penicillium genus

7. According to paragraph 4, by 1939 what had Fleming concluded?

a) that penicillin was a wonder drug all would benefit from
b) that he had wasted his time researching penicillin
c) that Sir William Dunn should read his 1929 research paper
d) that penicillin was not economically viable

3 ➔ By 1928, Fleming was regarded as a brilliant researcher whose laboratory was, more often than not, a mess. That same year, returning to his lab after an August holiday, Fleming discovered that his staphylococci cultures had been contaminated by a fungus. Fleming was intent on throwing the cultures out when he noticed that the staphylococci colonies had been surrounded by an invading blue-green mold. Much to Fleming's surprise, the invading mold had eradicated the staphylococci it had surrounded whereas those colonies of staphylococci that had not been touched by the mold were still thriving. Fleming set about isolating and growing the mold which produced a substance that killed not only staphylococci, but also a number of other disease-causing bacteria, such as pneumonia, scarlet fever, meningitis and diphtheria while having no effect on typhoid fever or paratyphoid fever. Fleming called the bacteria-killing substance "mold juice." Once he'd established that the mold was in fact part of the genus penicillium, he called it penicillin.

4 ➔ In 1929, Fleming published the results of his experiments in the British Journal of Experimental Pathology. Yet despite such initial promise, his work garnered little attention, for growing penicillium was difficult while extracting the antibiotic agent, the bacteria-killing penicillin itself, was even harder. These results, combined with tests proving that penicillin worked slowly, convinced Fleming that penicillin had no commercial appeal. By 1939, Fleming, having labored long and hard over penicillin, finally turned his attention to other matters. Penicillin, in his mind, had no future beyond his lab. Then, in that same year, the Australian scientist Howard Walter Florey, director of the Sir William Dunn School of Pathology at Oxford University, read Fleming's paper in which he described the anti-bacterial effects of penicillium. Florey immediately saw the potential of penicillium and, with the help of Ernst Chain, immediately went to work.

8. According to paragraph 5, what percentage of the one-hundred milligrams of penicillin that Florey and Chain made was unusable?

a) ten
b) ninety
c) one
d) one-hundred

5 ➔ With grants from the Medical Research Council in England and from the Rockefeller Foundation in the United States, Florey and Chain were able to produce one hundred milligrams of penicillin that was only ten percent pure. Then, in one the most famous experiments in medical history, Florey injected eight mice with a lethal dose of the streptococci bacteria. He then treated four of the eight mice with the penicillin. The four non-injected mice died. Tests were then done on humans suffering from the same bacterial infections as the mice. The humans recovered at remarkable rates. However, because England was at war, there was not enough money to expand production, so Florey and Chain flew to the United States where the government became involved in large-scale production. By 1943, frontline soldiers with infections were being treated with a new wonder drug called penicillin.

pioneer: an innovator; a discoverer

staphylococci: a common type of bacteria generally harmless.

➔ Answers: page 688.

Practice #2: *Factual Information Questions*

Directions: You have ten minutes to read the passage and answer the questions.

Biological Classification

1 ➔ In biological classification, the eight major classifications are ranked hierarchically starting with Life and ending with the Common name. Life is the label given to those objects that have self-sustaining biological processes. Objects that do not signal a self-sustaining biological process are either inanimate, such as rocks, or dead. For an organism to be a self-sustaining biological process, it must have a metabolism, a metabolism being a series of integrated chemical processes that enable the organism to maintain an input-output balance called homeostasis. Homeostasis, in turn, allows a living organism to maintain its structure, to grow, and to reproduce. All living organisms on Earth, including humans, are carbon and water-based cellular structures.

2 ➔ In order to understand the vast complexities of Life, scientists have divided it into Domains. According to the three-Domain system developed by Carl Woese in 1990, Life is comprised of three Domains: Archaea, Bacteria, and Eukarya. Archaea are a large group of prokaryotes, prokaryotes being single-celled microorganisms with no nucleus. Woese discovered and named Archaea in the late 1970's. Archaea live in extreme environments, such as hot springs and deep petroleum deposits. Bacteria are also prokaryotes, yet they are genetically and biochemically distinct from Archaea. At over five nonillion (5×10^{30}), bacteria form much of the Earth's biomass. Finally, there are Eukarya. Cells within this group are called eukaryotes. These cells have a wall or membrane inside of which there is a nucleus that contains genetic material. Humans cells are eukaryotic.

1. According to paragraph 1, a self-sustaining biological process must have what?

a) homeostasis
b) a balance
c) chemical processes
d) a metabolism

2. According to paragraph 2, what have scientists divided into Domains?

a) Bacteria
b) Archaea
c) Life
d) complexities

3. Why are human cells eukaryotic?

a) because they contain a membrane that holds eukaryotic cells
b) because they contain genes that contain walls and membranes
c) because they are biochemically distinct from Archaea
d) because they contain a nucleus that contains genetic material

4. According to paragraph 3, who is Carl Linnaeus?

a) the man who first identified two Kingdoms
b) the man who first created binomial Kingdoms
c) the man who first identified six Kingdoms
d) the first Swiss scientist

5. Into which three Phylum is the Kingdom Plantae divided?

a) Magnoliopsida, Amphia, Bryophyta
b) Magnoliopsida, Bryophyta, Animalia
c) Magnoliopsida, Chordata, Pinophyta
d) Magnoliopsida, Pinophyta, Bryophyta

6. What are macaques?

a) hominids
b) Cercopithecidae
c) baboons
d) Hominidae

7. To what does 97% refer?

a) humans
b) criterion
c) Hominidae
d) DNA

3 ➔ Following Life and Domain is Kingdom. In 1735, Carl Linnaeus, a Swedish botanist and zoologist credited with establishing binomial nomenclature (the naming of species), believed there were two kingdoms: Vegetabilia and Animalia. Today that list has grown to six: Bacteria (prokaryotes), Protozoa (eukaryotes), Chromista (a eukaryotic supergroup), Fungi (eukaryotic organisms, such as yeasts molds and mushrooms), Plantae (trees, herbs, bushes, grasses), and Animalia (multicellular eukaryotic organisms). The Kingdom Plantae is subdivided into three divisions or Phylum: Magnoliopsida, Pinophyta, Bryophyta while the Kingdom Animalia is divided into two Phylum: Chordata (vertebrates, such as humans) and Arthropoda (invertebrates, such as insects). Each Phylum is further divided into a Class. For example, Chordata is divided into two Classes: Amphibia and Mammalia. Amphibians, such as frogs and salamanders, are ectothermic or cold-blooded. However, not all Amphibia are the same thus they are divided into Orders based on the similarities they share. The same holds true for homeothermic Mammalians. One Order of Mammalians is Primates.

4 ➔ Primates are mammals that have large brains, walk on two or four limbs and rely on stereoscopic vision. In Order Primates, there are two distinct classifications called Families: Hominidae (hominids) and Cercopithecidae. Cercopithecidae are Old World monkeys native to Asia and Africa, monkeys such as baboons and macaques while Family Hominidae represents the great apes (gorillas, chimpanzees, orangutans) and humans. One criterion for classifying humans and apes in the same Family is that humans and apes share 97% of the same DNA.

5 ➔ Next, Family Hominidae is divided by genus. Genus is Latin meaning type. The genus Homo includes extinct early humans species. Species, the lowest order of classification, describes a group of organisms that can be classified based on similar physical characteristics and, more importantly, the ability to reproduce their

8. According to paragraph 5, what classification follows genus?

a) Homo sapiens
b) species
c) neanderthalis
d) Latin

9. How many biological classifications are there?

a) 7
b) 6
c) 9
d) 8

kind. Early human species are Homo neanderthalis, who lived between 130,000 to 30,000 years ago, and Homo habilis, who lived approximately 2.5 million years ago. These early species of the genus Homo had large brains, lived in social groups, and walked upright. The only living species of the Homo genus is the species Homo sapiens or, the Common name for which is humans.

6 ➔ Working backwards, human is the Common name for the species Homo sapiens. Homo Sapiens, in turn, belong to the Genus Homo which belongs to the Hominidae Family in the Order Primates, Primates being a part of the Class Mammalia, which is one of two sub groups in the Phylum Chordata belonging to the Kingdom Animalia, which, along with Kingdom Plantae, comprises Life as we know it.

<u>biomass</u>: biological material from living or non living organisms

<u>homeothermic</u>: warm-blooded

➔ Answers: page 688.

2. Vocabulary Questions

Each passage will have between 3-5 vocabulary questions. These questions measure your ability to understand new words, phrases and idioms by inferring their meaning from the context in which they are used. The word, phrase or idiom being tested will be highlighted in the passage. Vocabulary questions can be paraphrased a variety of ways, for example:

- What does the idiom a piece of cake mean?
- In paragraph 2, what does discombobulated mean?
- Hypothesis means what?

Look at a sample vocabulary question.

2. In paragraph 1, proponents is closest in meaning to...

a) associates
b) opponents
c) supporters
d) professionals

a. <u>Question Analysis</u>: *Signal Words*

Before you select an answer, make sure you understand the question. As you read the question, look for signal words. Signal words identify the words you must scan or skim for in the corresponding paragraph or in the passage as a whole. The signal words in this question are <u>in paragraph 1</u> and the highlighted word proponents.

2. In paragraph 1, proponents is closest in meaning to...

Next, scan for the signal word proponents in paragraph 1.

1 ➔ Adam Smith was born in Scotland in 1723. As a young man, he studied moral philosophy at the University of Glasgow and at Oxford. He eventually went on to tutor a nobleman's son. The position freed Smith from his daily work while affording him the opportunity to tutor while traveling throughout Europe. **In France, Smith met Rousseau and Voltaire, leading proponents of the European Enlightenment.** At its core, the European Enlightenment, guided by reason and science, questioned customs, morals, and traditional institutions, namely monarchies. Returning to Scotland, Smith set about writing his seminal *An Inquiry into the Nature and Causes of the Wealth of Nations*.

b. Answer-Choice Analysis

Use the following strategies when selecting an answer.

1. Active Vocabulary

If the highlighted word is part of your active vocabulary, make a selection and move on.

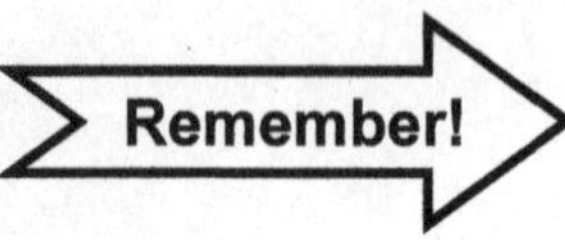

If you have "a feeling" you know the right answer, trust your feeling. Your "feeling" is your passive vocabulary talking to you. Classroom experience proves that test-takers often trust their feelings, but then go back and change their answers only to realize that they had made the right choice all along. This strategy applies to all TOEFL tasks.

If you do not know the highlighted word, use these strategies when selecting.

2. Identifying the Distractor Using Prefixes

One of the four answer choices will be a distractor. In this example, D is a homophone distractor. Note how *proponents* and *professionals* both start with the prefix *pro.* This gives each word the same first syllable sound. However, do not conclude that *professionals* is the correct answer simply because it sounds like *proponents.* It is not. It is a homophone distractor.

2. In paragraph 1, proponents is closest in meaning to...

a) associates
b) opponents
c) supporters
distractor d) professionals

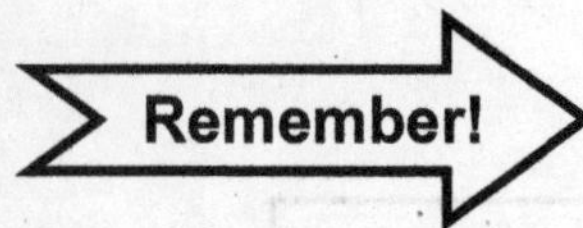

Do not infer meaning from sound. For example, night *and* knight *sound exactly the same but have completely different meanings.*

3. Identifying the Distractor Using Suffixes

A distractor can also be identified by its suffix. A suffix is a word ending, such as *ment.* The suffix *ment* means *condition of.* For example, *excitement* means the condition of being excited. If the highlighted word has the same suffix as one of the four choices (see below), that choice is a homophone distractor.

2. What does irascible mean?

answer a) quick-tempered
b) fearless
distractor c) susceptible
d) friendly

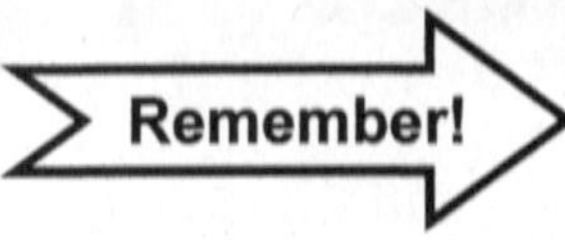

You can expect at least one distractor in each vocabulary question. However, the ability to identify the distractor is only one step in identifying the answer. You must also be able to infer the meaning of each answer choice by analyzing the context in which it is used.

4. Process of Elimination: *Antonyms*

After you identify the distractor, use process of elimination to narrow down your choices. Start by identifying antonyms. An antonym is a word with the opposite meaning, for example B, *opponents*. The prefix *op* means *opposite*. Therefore B is not correct. The context supports this conclusion. *Rousseau and Voltaire* were not against (opponents of) the European Enlightenment. Instead, they *questioned... traditional institutions* and *monarchies*. If they questioned the king, they challenged his political ideas. This infers that they opposed the king's political authority. Therefore B is an antonym of proponents.

2. In paragraph 1, proponents is closest in meaning to...

	a) associates
antonym	b) opponents
	c) supporters
distractor	d) professionals

You now have two choices left. A is off topic. Because *Rousseau and Voltaire* were part of the European Enlightenment, they were indeed associates. However, their association is not the topic. The topic is *Rousseau and Voltaire* and *the European Enlightenment* versus *traditional institutions and monarchies*. If *Rousseau and Voltaire* were opposed to *traditional institutions and monarchies*, then we can infer that they were *supporters* of *the European Enlightenment*. Therefore, C is correct.

2. In paragraph 1, proponents is closest in meaning to...

off topic	a) associates
antonym	b) opponents
correct	c) supporters
distractor	d) professionals

Is there always an antonym in the four choices?

It depends on how ETS designs the question. However, an antonym among the answer choices is a common method of testing language use (OPDUL=C). That said, be prepared for antonyms.

5. Inferring Meaning Using Rhetorical Strategies

You can also infer the meaning of a word, phrase or idiom by identifying how rhetorical strategies place it in context. First, identify the context. The context for *proponents* is sentence 5 and sentence 6 of paragraph 1.

> 1 ➔ Adam Smith was born in Scotland in 1723. As a young man, he studied moral philosophy at the University of Glasgow and at Oxford. He eventually went on to tutor a nobleman's son. The position freed Smith from his daily work while affording him the opportunity to tutor while traveling throughout Europe. **5) In France, Smith met Rousseau and Voltaire, leading proponents of the European Enlightenment. 6) At its core, the European Enlightenment, guided by reason and science, questioned customs, morals, and traditional institutions, namely monarchies.** Returning to Scotland, Smith set about writing his seminal *An Inquiry into the Nature and Causes of the Wealth of Nations*.

Next, identify the rhetorical strategies within the context. In this example, note the cause-and-effect relationship: *the European Enlightenment* questioning (cause) *customs, morals, and traditional institutions, namely monarchies*. The inferred effect suggests a conflict of ideas. Groups in conflict have leaders. This fact is inferred by the participle adjective leading. The leaders of the European Enlightenment were *Rousseau and Voltaire*. Because *Rousseau and Voltaire* were leaders and in conflict with *monarchies*, we can infer that they were pro Enlightenment. Therefore, *proponents* infers *supporters*, or C.

Look at the next example. The highlighted phrase is the idiom in dire straits. The context is the first two sentences.

> 2 ➔ **1) By the early nineteenth century, the "common" or public school system was in dire straits. 2) The schools were poorly equipped, one-room buildings with poorly paid, poorly trained teachers.** Students, if they attended classes, attended in winter, and for only a few weeks...

Note how sentence 2 uses the rhetorical strategies of illustration (*schools*) plus description (*poorly equipped; one-room buildings; poorly paid, poorly trained teachers*). These rhetorical strategies refer back to the topic of the *public school system* in sentence 1. Thus we can infer that if the conditions of *the schools* (specific) were extremely bad, then the conditions of the *public school system* (general) were equally bad. Therefore, in the answer choices (see next page), look for a synonym meaning *extremely bad conditions*. In this context, *in a desperate state* means extremely bad conditions. Therefore, D is correct. C is too general. Yes, the schools were *ageing* (getting old), but ageing does not always mean in bad condition.

2. In paragraph 2, in dire straits is closest in meaning to...

distractor a) poor
antonym b) in good state
too general c) ageing
correct d) in a desperate state

In the question above, note how the homophone distractor *poor* does not sound like the highlighted idiom in dire straits. Instead, it sounds like the adverb *poorly*, which is repeated three times in sentence two (see text box 2 previous page).

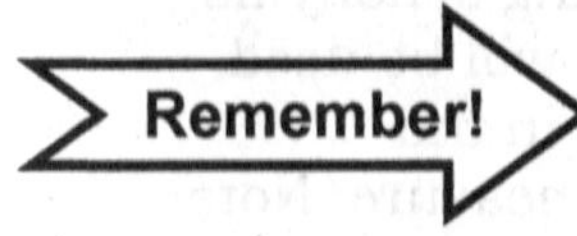

Do not infer meaning from repetition. Just because a word is repeated for emphasis in the passage, such as "poorly," does not mean that it is the correct answer simply because it has changed form (adverb poorly *to adjective* poor*). It is a homophone distractor.*

In the question above, note the difference between *poor* (A) and *in a desperate state* (D). *Poor* infers no money while *in a desperate state* infers a crisis situation due to many factors including no money. Thus D is the best answer because it defines a broader context of problems: *poorly equipped schools; one-room buildings; poorly paid, poorly trained teachers.*

Look at another example. The highlighted phrase is the idiom went bust. The context is the first four sentences.

5 ➔ 1) The railroad boom, however, went bust in 1893. 2) Like the internet bubble of 2000 and the real estate bubble of 2008, the railroad boom was a result of companies over-extending. 3) Simply put, by 1893 there were too many railroads and too many bad loans and too much market speculation. 4) This led to the collapse of over five hundred banks while dozens of railroads, including the Union Pacific Railroad, declared bankruptcy. Confidence in the economy was restored when gold was found in Canada's Klondike, leading to the Klondike Gold Rush of 1897.

Note in sentence 1 how however is between *boom* and *went bust*. However signals a contrast between *boom* and *went bust*. From the passage, we know that *boom* means a time of great economic development. Therefore, we can infer that *went bust* is the opposite of *boom*. In other words, the end of the boom. Therefore, A is correct. A is a synonym that describes what happens to an economic boom: it will eventually crash, as did the railroad boom.

9. What does the phrase went bust mean?

correct a) crashed
distractor b) burst
not accurate c) slowed
not true d) expanded

Sentence 3 confirms that A is the best choice. Note in sentence 3 how *too* is repeated for emphasis: *too many railroads; too many bad loans; too much market speculation.* This infers that the boom had ended. If something has crashed, it has come to an end. Sentence 4 also confirms that A is the best choice. Note in sentence 4 the effects of the crash: *the collapse of over five hundred banks; the Union Pacific declared...bankruptcy.* A crash, in this context, is synonymous with collapse.

6. Synonyms in Context

You can also infer the meaning of a word, phrase or idiom by identifying synonyms in context. A synonym in context means that a word and its synonym will be used within the same context. For example, read the highlighted sentences in the following paragraph. Note the highlighted word *gauge*. Gauge means measure. Note that a synonym of *gauge* is Measuring. This is an example of synonyms in context.

> 2 ➔ Also, one will argue that forecasting climate change on a computer is not always accurate. However, what the article fails to mention is that computer modeling accurately predicts broader trends in climate change, and that these trends all indicate increased warming trends. **Measuring the GMST is indeed a critical part in measuring climate change. However, such a detailed analysis is not the only way to gauge future climate change.** Remember: 85% of the world's energy needs come from the burning of fossil fuels...

Look at a sample question.

3. In paragraph 2, what does gauge mean?

	a) evaluate
correct	b) measure
	c) weigh
distractor	d) gouge

7. Understanding the Entire Passage

Often the meaning of a word can only be inferred by an understanding of the entire passage. For example, the word seminal in the following example.

4. In paragraph 1, what does seminal mean?

a) serious
b) interesting
c) controversial
d) original

Now read the paragraph in which seminal is located.

1 ➔ Adam Smith was born in Scotland in 1723. As a young man, he studied moral philosophy at the University of Glasgow and at Oxford. He eventually went on to tutor a nobleman's son. The position freed Smith from his daily work while affording him the opportunity to tutor while traveling throughout Europe. In France, Smith met Rousseau and Voltaire, leading proponents of the European Enlightenment. At its core, the European Enlightenment, guided by reason and science, questioned customs, morals, and traditional institutions, namely monarchies. Returning to Scotland, Smith set about writing his seminal *An Inquiry into the Nature and Causes of the Wealth of Nations*.

As you can see, the meaning of *seminal* cannot be inferred from paragraph one. There is not enough information. To infer the meaning of *seminal*, you must read the entire passage. As you do, look for context clues. The context clues are in the last sentence in **bold** in paragraph four. Thomas Edison was a genius-inventor. His light bulb was an original idea. Because that is a comparative sentence, we can infer the same about Adam Smith: his book *The Wealth of Nations* was also an original idea. Therefore, *seminal* is closest in meaning to D. A is the distractor.

4 ➔ *The Wealth of Nations* is very much a reaction to the predominating economic theory of the day, that of Mercantilism. Mercantilists posited that the wealth of a nation depended on developing and maintaining national power thus it was a form of economic nationalism. Spain, at the time of Columbus, is a prime example of just such a nation. A nation like Spain preserved national power by accumulating as much gold as possible through strong exports, the limitation of imports, and a large, population of poorly paid workers. ■ To develop exports, companies were subsidized by the government which also wrote laws to limit imports. ■ By limiting imports, the gold used to pay for imports would stay in the country and create a greater money supply and more credit. ■ Moreover, nations were geared toward acquiring and maintaining gold at all costs, including warring with each other. ■ Adam Smith, however, argued that trade benefitted all nations and that gold was not equal to wealth. Gold, Smith said, was like any other commodity, such as wheat or wool, and that it deserved no special treatment. More importantly, Smith says that the wealth of a nation is not based on the hoarding of gold, but on the free flow of goods manufactured in a systematic way, a way that serves the needs of the individual and, ultimately, the nation as a whole. With that, Adam Smith gave birth to what we now call economic theory. **As Thomas Edison is to the light bulb, Adam Smith is to the science of economics.**

Practice #1: *Vocabulary Questions*

Directions: You have ten minutes to read the passage and answer the questions.

Flooding

1 ➔ Water. We take it for granted. Yet without it, life, as we know it, would perish. We use water in myriad ways. We use it for cooking, for cleaning, for generating electricity, and for relaxation. We use it in religious ceremonies, in agriculture, and for transportation. Suffice it to say, water's value is inestimable. And there is a lot of it. Seventy percent of the Earth is covered in water while three-quarters of the human body is water. Some theorize that human blood tastes salty because eons ago, our ancestors lived in the oceans, the salty taste of human blood evidence proving our ancestors did indeed have aquatic origins. Whatever the case maybe, water is the source of life, not only for humans but for all organisms on Earth.

2 ➔ However, much like the Roman god Janus, water has two faces. One is that of life while the other is of death. Water's dual nature as savior and destroyer is evidenced in the natural phenomenon known as flooding. In a nutshell, flooding occurs when a body of water escapes its natural boundaries and temporarily submerges the surrounding landscape. Historically, flooding has caused untold human misery and destruction. Witness the Central China floods of 1931, the greatest natural disaster ever recorded. Three rivers flooded and left over three million people dead. Yet without flooding, we might not be where we are today.

3 ➔ As a naturally occurring phenomenon, floods have been, since the dawn of time, an integral part of human evolution. A prime example is the Nile River in Egypt. For ancient Egyptians, the flooding of the Nile was an auspicious event. The Egyptians believed that the flooding was caused by the tears of the God Isis as she cried for her dead husband,

1. What does take it for granted mean?

a) assume it will always change
b) assume it will always be there
c) assume it will always be granted
d) assume it will always have value

2. Myriad is closest in meaning to...

a) valuable
b) miraculous
c) many
d) wasteful

3. In a nutshell means what?

a) more importantly
b) not to mention
c) in brief
d) for example

4. Untold is closest in meaning to...

a) cannot be mentioned
b) cannot be counted
c) cannot be expressed
d) cannot be changed

5. In paragraph 3, what does auspicious mean?

a) suggesting future success
b) suggesting renewed authority
c) suggesting a weather change
d) suggesting an evolutionary event

6. Mundane means what?

a) seasonal
b) special
c) arcane
d) ordinary

7. Silt is closest in meaning to...

a) damage left by flood water
b) mud deposited by flood water
c) man-made fertilizer in flood water
d) crops benefiting from flood water

8. What does the phrase holds true for mean?

a) refers to
b) applies to
c) compares to
d) holds on to

9. What does endemic mean?

a) renewing
b) beneficial
c) native
d) endangered

10. In paragraph 4, double-edged sword is closest in meaning to...

a) sharp and dangerous
b) negative and positive
c) twice as dangerous
d) double the reward

Osiris. However, a more mundane reason can be found, one that occurred then and today, two thousand miles south of Egypt in equatorial Africa. There, in the hills and mountains of present-day Rwanda, Tanzania and Ethiopia, torrential rains fell from June to September. The rain filled the lakes and rivers that fed the Nile, forcing the Nile to flood its banks as it raced north to Egypt and the Mediterranean. For the Egyptians, the annual flood symbolized rebirth. The flooding waters recharged the depleted groundwater while leaving behind a layer of silt in the fields. The silt added much needed nutrients to the heavily farmed soil. This, in turn, fertilized crops, such as flax and wheat, a valuable food source the Egyptians exported. By doing so, the early Egyptians developed wealth and became a major power in the Middle East. In short, without the annual flooding of the Nile, Egyptian civilization, as we now know it, would not exist. The same holds true for the Tigris and Euphrates Rivers flowing south through Iraq and into the Persian Gulf. Flood water caused by rain and snow melt in Syria and Turkey forced the Tigris and Euphrates to flood their banks and replenish crop fields with much needed silt. This cycle of rebirth through flooding is as old as the Earth itself, for even if man does not stand to benefit, endemic biomass does, the flooding of the Amazon is a good example of how flood water has sustained endemic biodiversity for millennia.

4 ➔ Yet flooding is indeed a double-edged sword, the aforementioned China floods of 1931 the most salient example of the destructive power of flooding water. Another, more recent example, was the 2010 Pakistan flood. Unusually heavy monsoon rains, the worst in almost a century, caused flash flooding, an unexpected and unforeseen rise in flood water, often with catastrophic effects. At one point, one-fifth of Pakistan—an area the size of England—was under water. All told, some twenty million people were affected while over two thousand died. Worse, Pakistan's infrastructure was severely disrupted with the total economic cost estimated at forty billion

dollars. And there's a new threat on the horizon. With Arctic and Antarctica ice melting at precipitous rates, scientists predict that before the end of the century, Manhattan will be under water.

11. Precipitous is closest in meaning to...

a) precarious
b) expected
c) slow
d) extreme

➔ Answers: page 689.

Practice #2: *Vocabulary Questions*

Directions: You have ten minutes to read the passage and answer the questions.

---

1. In paragraph 1, what does preeminent mean?

a) precious
b) richest
c) oldest
d) greatest

2. In paragraph 2, pioneer means...

a) pilot
b) leader
c) follower
d) worker

3. The idiom put his nose to the grind stone is closest in meaning to...

a) studied harder
b) studied regularly
c) studied less
d) studied with Oberth

4. What does banned mean?

a) outlawed
b) destroyed
c) authorized
d) supported

Wernher Von Braun

1 ➔ Everyone knows that America put the first man on the moon. What most don't realize, however, is that the Saturn V, the launch rocket that sent Apollo 11 astronauts Neil Armstrong, Buzz Aldrin and Michael Collins to the moon, was designed by Germans, in particular the rocket scientist and space architect Wernher Von Braun. In 1975, Von Braun was awarded America's highest science award, the National Medal of Science. Many consider Von Braun to be the preeminent rocket scientist of the twentieth century.

2 ➔ Wernher Von Braun was born into an aristocratic family on March 23, 1912 in Wirsitz, Germany, now present-day Poland. As a boy, Von Braun did not do well in school. Mathematics and physics gave him particular trouble. Then he read *Die Rakete zu den Planetenräumen* (The Rocket into Interplanetary Space) by rocket pioneer Hermann Oberth. It was a turning point. Inspired by Oberth's book, Von Braun put his nose to the grind stone and finished at the top of his class. Von Braun, envisioning that one day man would fly to the moon, went on to receive various technical degrees and became a member of the German Society for Space Travel, where he worked on liquid-fueled rocket engines with Oberth. However, the Nationalist Socialist German Workers Party, which took power in 1932, banned all work on rockets that was not government related. Braun, not wanting to give up his dream of putting a man in space, found work with the German army, designing and testing rockets. By 1934, one of his rockets had flown to a height of 3.5 kilometers. With the German army on the move, rocket development became a top priority of the German military. As a result, a large rocket facility was built at

5. Instrumental is closest in meaning to...

a) essential
b) industrious
c) determined
d) instructive

6. Orchestrated means what?

a) exacerbated
b) originated
c) ameliorated
d) organized

7. What does expunged mean?

a) preserved
b) reorganized
c) deleted
d) hidden

8. What does the cutting edge mean?

a) the most dangerous
b) the most typical
c) the sharpest
d) the most advanced

9. Containing means...?

a) limiting
b) destroying
c) challenging
d) imitating

Peenemünde. There Von Braun became the leader of "the rocket team" and was instrumental in developing the V-2, a liquid-propelled, 46-foot long ballistic missile that could hit London five-hundred miles away. The V-2, built by slave labor in underground factories, represents the birth of the rocket age, a lineage that extends through both the American and Russian post-war missile and space programs to this day.

3 ➔ In the spring of 1945, with World War Two rapidly drawing to a close, Von Braun orchestrated the surrender of himself and five hundred of his top scientists to the rapidly advancing American army. By then, the Americans were well aware of Von Braun, so much so that he had topped America's Black List, a secret list of German scientists and engineers the Americans were intent on capturing for the knowledge they possessed. Under a plan called Operation Paperclip, Von Braun and many of his colleagues secretly went to work for the American government in Fort Bliss, Texas. There, they continued to design and build rockets, their association with the Nazi party secretly expunged from their public record. Throughout the 1950's, Von Braun and his Peenemünde team represented the cutting edge of rocket technology. They built the Jupiter missile, the first missile to carry a nuclear warhead. Von Braun and his team also built the Jupiter-C, which carried the first American satellite into Earth orbit, thus signaling the start of the space race. In 1955, Von Braun became a naturalized American citizen. Meanwhile, he continued to champion the idea of building rockets that would explore space. As early as 1952, his plans for space exploration included space stations and trips to Mars. He even wrote a science fiction novel exploring the possibilities. The American government, however, was more interested in containing the Russian threat than in exploring space. In 1958, the American government formed NASA (National Aeronautic and Space Program). Two years later, NASA opened the Marshall Space Flight Center and Von Braun was chosen to be the director. Von Braun agreed on one condition: that he could develop the Saturn

rocket, the launch rocket that would send Apollo 11 to the moon. The American government relented. And the rest is history. On July 16, 1969, Von Braun's boyhood dream of sending a man to the moon was realized when Apollo 11 commander Neil Armstrong was the first man to walk on the moon.

4 ➔ By 1970, interest in space travel began to wane. The moon had been reached and the U.S. government was cutting back on the costly Apollo program. Von Braun, however, wanted the Saturn V program to continue. His next goal was to build a rocket that would carry men to Mars. Yet it was not to be. In 1970, Von Braun was reassigned to an administrative position in Washington, DC, a position from which he soon resigned to become vice president of an aerospace company. On June 16, 1997, Wernher Von Braun died. He is buried in Alexandria, Virginia. Despite Von Braun's achievements, many continue to question his past affiliation with the Nazi party and to what extent he condoned slave labor to build Nazi Germany's rocket program. However history judges Wernher Von Braun, one thing cannot be denied: He put America on the moon.

10. In paragraph 4, what does wane mean?

a) increase
b) pause
c) diminish
d) expand

11. What does affiliation with mean?

a) knowledge of
b) association with
c) affinity for
d) disinterest in

➔ Answers: page 689.

3. Negative Factual Information Questions

Each passage will have 2 or fewer negative factual information questions. This question type is a detail question. It measures your ability to identify and verify information that is not true or not stated in the passage. Negative factual questions can be paraphrased a variety of ways, for example:

- According to paragraph 1, all of the following are true EXCEPT?
- The author describes each step of the building process EXCEPT?
- In paragraph 3, what is NOT mentioned about Mercantilism?

Look at a negative factual information question from the sample passage on page 541.

3. What is NOT true of the European Enlightenment?

a) It was based on reason.
b) It challenged customs and morals.
c) It was supported by kings and queens
d) It valued science.

a. Question Analysis: *Signal Words*

Before you select an answer, make sure you understand the question. As you read the question, look for signal words. Signal words identify the words you must scan or skim for in the corresponding paragraph or in the passage as a whole. Look at the following question. The signal words are NOT true and European Enlightenment.

3. What is NOT true of the European Enlightenment?

Next, scan the passage for European Enlightenment.

b. Choice Analysis: *Process of Elimination*

Once you have identified the topic of the European Enlightenment in the passage, go to choice A and identify the signal words. In choice A, the signal words are based on reason.

3. What is NOT true of the European Enlightenment?

a) It was based on reason.
b) It challenged customs and morals.
c) It was supported by kings and queens
d) It valued science.

Next, go back to the topic of the European Enlightenment in the passage and check (verify) if the European Enlightenment was or was not based on reason. In the sample passage, it says that the European Enlightenment was based on reason. Therefore, A is true. Repeat this check-and-verify process for the remaining three choices.

The process of checking and verifying four answer choices is time consuming. Watch the clock. If this question type is giving you trouble and/or taking too much time, guess and move on. You will not be penalized for a wrong answer.

c. Identifying the Distractor

For this question type there are no distractors. The answer choices are either true or false, included in the passage or not, etc. In the following sample, C is correct because it is not true. It is the exception.

3. What is NOT true of the European Enlightenment?

true a) It was based on reason.
true b) It challenged customs and morals.
not true c) It was supported by kings and queens
true d) It valued science.

Analyze the question and each answer choice carefully. Classroom experience proves that many test-takers select the wrong answer because they did not take the time to check and verify each answer choice.

Practice #1: *Negative Factual Questions*

Directions: You have ten minutes to read the passage and answer the questions.

---

1. All of the following are true of the Bennett sisters EXCEPT?

a) There are five.
b) Their father is patient.
c) They are nobility.
d) Their mother is moody.

2. In paragraph 1, all of the following are true of Mr. Darcy EXCEPT?

a) He is kind.
b) He has a strong intellect.
c) He is Elizabeth's social equal.
d) He first met Elizabeth when visiting the Bennett's house.

Women of Influence

1 ➔ Jane Austen's novel *Pride and Prejudice*, voted Best British novel in a 2005 BBC poll, was originally titled *First Impressions*. Austen wrote it between October 1796 and August 1797. The story centers on the Bennett family, particularly the five sisters whose mother, Mrs. Bennett—a mercurial soul always on the verge of nervous collapse—is determined to marry them off to rich husbands thus ensuring their financial futures while securing for them positions of high social status in early nineteenth century England. Mr. Bennett, a patient and level-headed man with a modest income, puts up with his wife's machinations while displaying a particular fondness for his second oldest daughter, Elizabeth. Elizabeth, with her keen intellect and independent character, watches with a critic's eye as her sisters find varying degrees of success while searching for husbands. When Mr. Darcy, a rich land owner of noble birth, visits the Bennett household, Mrs. Bennett sees another marrying opportunity for her daughters. Elizabeth, however, sees only the snobbish arrogance typical of Mr. Darcy's privileged class, one that is far and above the Bennett's station. In time, however, Elizabeth realizes that her pride has blinded her and, as a result, prejudiced her toward Mr. Darcy, a kind man whose intellect and independence mirror Elizabeth's. In short, Elizabeth and Mr. Darcy are cut from the same cloth. In this light, they are a perfect match and find happiness in wedlock.

3. In paragraph 2, what is NOT mentioned about *Pride and Prejudice*?

a) It is a comedy.
b) It is told from Elizabeth's perspective.
c) It continues to sell well.
d) It is a snapshot of English society in the early 1800's.

2 ➔ *Pride and Prejudice*, a title that aptly defines the conflict Elizabeth and Mr. Darcy must face and overcome to find love, was published in 1813. The story, told from Elizabeth's point-of-view, is a window on early nineteenth century English moral values, particularly in regard to the rights of women, or the lack thereof, a condition Jane Austen observes with no small amount of satire. To date, *Pride and Prejudice* has sold over 20 million copies confirming Jane Austen as one of the most influential writers of the English language.

4. According to paragraph 3, all of the following are true of Dian Fossey EXCEPT?

a) She studied gorillas in Rwanda.
b) She was accepted into a group of gorillas.
c) She studied gorillas for twenty-five years.
d) She proved that gorillas were not Hollywood stereotypes.

5. What is NOT true of Dian Fossey?

a) National Geographic made her and Peanuts famous.
b) She found work in TV.
c) Her work ended in 1985.
d) She believed gorillas and humans shared the same traits.

3 ➔ Another woman whose influence is still felt today is Dian Fossey. These days it is commonplace to see biologists on TV studying animals in the wild close up, so close it is as if the human observer were part of the animal group being studied. One of the scientists to first the bridge the gap between wild animals and a human observer was Dian Fossey. Fossey did so with the mountain gorillas of Rwanda. She studied them from 1967 up to her death in 1985. Fossey's ability to study and observe wild mountain gorillas while actually being among them revolutionized not only the study of gorillas, and wildlife in general, but also changed our view of gorillas. No longer were they "King Kongs" but, as Fossey herself said, they were "dignified, highly social, gentle giants, with individual personalities, and strong family relationships." The moment Fossey was accepted into the gorilla's world occurred in 1970 when an adult male Fossey had named Peanuts, touched her hand. The moment was immortalized in a National Geographic photograph seen around the world.

6. In paragraph 4, what is NOT mentioned?

a) Where Dian Fossey studied.
b) The name of the director of the Fossey Fund.
c) The name of Fossey's publisher.
d) The impact her death had on the mountain gorillas in Parc National des Volcans.

4 ➔ Fossey's reputation grew with the publication of her book *Gorillas in the Mist.* By then she'd received her PhD from Cambridge and was teaching at Cornell University. Fame brought Fossey the money she needed to support her research and to establish sanctuaries for the mountain gorillas whose habitat was being destroyed by social unrest and whose numbers were being decimated by poachers. Fossey, determined to stop the unlawful killing of gorillas for meat, waged war

on the poachers, so much so that many believe that it was poachers who murdered Fossey in her cabin at Karisoke, the name of her research camp in the Parc National des Volcans in Rwanda. Despite Fossey's death, her influence lives on. Thanks to the Atlanta-based Fossey Fund, directed by Sigourney Weaver, who starred as Fossey in *Gorillas in the Mist*, the mountain gorilla population has been slowly increasing from a low of 250 in the early 1980's to an estimated 480 today. Such success is attributable to Fossey's pioneering work and to ecotourism, which brings tourists to the Parc National des Volcans so that they too might experience mountain gorillas as Dian Fossey had.

➔ Answers: page 689.

Practice #2: *Negative Factual Questions*

Directions: You have ten minutes to read the passage and answer the questions.

Methods of Research

1 ➔ There are two methods of research: qualitative and quantitative. Qualitative research is based on events observed by the researcher while quantitative researched is based on numerical data gathered by the researcher. A rainbow analogy exemplifies the two approaches. A researcher applying the qualitative approach would conclude, after personal observation, that a rainbow is an arc of colors with red on the outer edge of the arc and violet on the inner edge, with orange, yellow, blue and indigo in between. A researcher applying the quantitative approach would, in contrast, measure the varying intensities of color and the angle of refraction causing those colors, then compare those numbers to a broader statistical survey of rainbows. As you can see, quantitative research is scientific while qualitative research is holistic, a methodology based on observation and interpretation. Yet despite the differences, researchers use both with the intent of compiling information that is both reliable and credible.

1. In paragraph 1, all of the following are true EXCEPT?

a) quantitative research employs statistical surveys
b) quantitative research is scientific
c) qualitative research is based on personal observation
d) quantitative research is holistic

2 ➔ To produce reliable and credible research, a researcher using the qualitative approach focuses on the why and how of decision making, specifically in regard to human behavior, such as why a child will sit in front of a computer for hours at a time or how a tribe of Amazonian Indians deals with a threat to its territory from a neighboring tribe. By observing events as they unfold—by actually being in the field—the researcher has a front row seat on trying to answer why a child is addicted to the computer or how a tribe of Amazon Indians secures its territory from incursions. The researcher does this by focusing on language, signs, and meaning. Historically, researchers in the social sciences, such as anthropologists, sociologists and

2. In paragraph 2, all of the following are true EXCEPT?

a) qualitative research targets focus groups
b) qualitative research is deductive
c) qualitative research can be biased
d) qualitative research tries to answer the why and how

3. In paragraph 2, the following are mentioned EXCEPT?

a) focus group
b) anthropologist
c) neighborhood
d) computer modeling

psychologists, have employed the qualitative approach, one that, by its very nature, is inductive, induction being a form of logic in which a conclusion is based on a series of observable facts. To obtain information, however, the researcher must limit the focus of his or her study. For example, if you are a researcher trying to answer the question why some children are addicted to the computer, it would not be possible for you to observe all the children in a particular city, state or country. Instead, you would establish a context or a focus group—a group of computer-using children in a neighborhood say—a group which, by its limited size, would be accessible and easily observed. Yet by limiting the size of the study group, less data will be obtained which, in turn, might raise questions about the reliability of your research. Also, you might come under scrutiny, for readers and other researchers might ask how neutral you were when compiling data, especially if you were observing your own children using a computer.

4. In paragraph 3, the following are mentioned EXCEPT?

a) quantitative research is non biased
b) quantitative research uses mathematical models
c) quantitative research is used by politicians
d) quantitative research compiles observed data.

3 ➔ In contrast, quantitative research focuses on the gathering of large amounts of <u>empirical</u> data, then feeding that data into mathematical models that, in turn, provide the researcher with statistics. From these statistics, a researcher can make conclusions based not on his own personal involvement with the subject but on what the numbers are telling him. This impersonal approach removes any researcher bias from the research process and, more importantly, increases the reliability of the research and any conclusions based on that research. Politicians often employ quantitative research. For example, the president wants to raise taxes but first he wants to know if the public is for or against the idea. To find out, he conducts a national opinion survey that asks the question: Are you in favor of raising taxes? The more people answer the survey, the more accurate the results. The more accurate the results, the more informed the president will be when finally deciding whether to raise taxes or not. This, then, is another difference between qualitative and quantitative research:

quantitative research compiles data from much larger research groups while qualitative research is limited to what the researcher can, as an individual, practically observe.

4 ➔ Despite their differences, the two methods of research, when used in tandem, can produce reliable and credible results. For example, a researcher has concluded through observation that Hispanics make up the majority of students in a local English-as-a-second language program. By surveying other schools in her city or state—by using quantitative research—the researcher could then compile statistical data to prove if her initial hypothesis about Hispanics and English language programs is indeed accurate.

5. Which of the following is NOT mentioned in paragraph 4?

a) when combined, quantitative and qualitative research are effective
b) qualitative research is a good way to prove a hypothesis based on research done quantitatively
c) a hypothesis based on qualitative research can be confirmed using quantitative research
b) quantitative research can compare the results of qualitative research over a much larger surveyed area

empirical: based on observation or experience

compiling: collecting then editing data in a document

➔ Answers: page 689.

4. Inference Questions

Each passage will have 2 or fewer inference questions. These questions measure your ability to make conclusions based on facts stated directly in a paragraph or in the passage as a whole. Inference questions can be paraphrased a variety of ways, for example:

- What can be inferred about the internet in paragraph 1?
- In paragraph 2, what does the author imply about Bill Gates?
- Which of the following can be inferred about Columbus?

Look at an inference question from the sample passage on page 541.

10. From the passage, it can be inferred that Adam Smith probably...

a) owned a pin factory
b) visited a pin factory
c) worked in a pin factory
d) studied workers

a. Question Analysis: *Signal Words*

Before you select an answer, make sure you understand the question. As you read the question, look for signal words. Signal words identify the words you must scan or skim for in the corresponding paragraph or in the passage as a whole. Look at the following question. The signal words are Adam Smith probably.

10. From the passage, it can be inferred that Adam Smith probably...

Probably means the information is not directly stated in that passage. Therefore, you must infer it based on the answer choices. Do so by first scanning each answer choice for signal words. The signal words are the verbs and the noun *factory*. Scan the passage for the noun *factory* and the verbs associated with *factory*.

a) owned a pin *factory*
b) visited a pin *factory*
c) worked in a pin *factory*
d) studied workers

Use process of elimination when selecting an answer.

b. <u>Choice Analysis</u>: *Process of Elimination*

Using *process of elimination*, eliminate choices that are: 1) off topic; 2) too specific; 3) too general; 4) not known; 5) not true; 6) not implied; 7) not accurate.

In the following question, <u>A</u> and <u>C</u> are not correct. There is not enough factual information in the passage to suggest that either of these two choices is probably true.

10. From the passage, it can be inferred that Adam Smith probably...

not implied a) owned a pin factory
b) visited a pin factory
not implied c) worked in a pin factory
d) studied workers

You now have two choices left. One is the distractor.

c. <u>Identifying the Distractor</u>

Distractors are designed to look like the correct answer. In this example, <u>D</u> is the distractor. Adam Smith did not study "workers." That description is too general. Smith, instead, studied specific workers, specifically "pin workers." When did Adam Smith study pin workers? When he visited a pin factory. Why did he visit a pin factory? To do research for his book *The Wealth of Nations*. Therefore, <u>B</u> is correct.

10. From the passage, it can be inferred that Adam Smith probably...

not implied a) owned a pin factory
correct b) visited a pin factory
not implied c) worked in a pin factory
distractor d) studied workers

Practice #1: *Inference Questions*

Directions: You have ten minutes to read the passage and answer the questions.

Crypsis

1. What can be inferred about the tawny frogmouth?

a) It is an frog.
b) It is a monkey.
c) It is a bird.
d) It is a snake.

1 ➔ Crypsis, the ability of an organism to avoid being seen by another organism, can be achieved through camouflage and mimicry. Camouflage means hiding by blending in with the environment. An organism that employs camouflage is the tawny frogmouth of Australia. When seen, the tawny frogmouth is often confused with an owl; however, the tawny frogmouth is not an owl but a nightjar. The tawny frogmouth gets its name from its large, wide beak. It is nocturnal and feeds primarily on insects. When sleeping during the day, or when threatened, the tawny frogmouth perches on a branch of a tree that is the same color as the tawny frogmouth's plumage. Camouflaged during the day this way, the tawny frogmouth is virtually invisible to the observer. Blending in with the native environment in such a manner is called cryptic coloration. This is the most common form of crypsis.

2. What can be inferred about the flounder?

a) Predators can easily see it.
b) It preys on a variety of fish.
c) Predators mistake it for sand.
d) It has the same camouflage as the tawny frogmouth.

2 ➔ Another organism that benefits from cryptic coloration is the flounder. Flounders spend the majority of their time on the ocean floor thus evolution has provided the flounder with a speckled coloration that matches the color of the ocean floor. The flounder's ability to camouflage itself by appearing to look like the ocean floor makes it invisible to predators hoping to make a meal out of the flounder while at the same time allowing the flounder to ambush its prey, animals such as shrimp and crabs. In the aforementioned tawny frogmouth, camouflage served only one purpose: to protect. With the flounder, however, camouflage serves a dual purpose: to help it survive by avoiding being detected and possibly eaten while at the same time allowing it to ambush its prey. Tigers too rely on cryptic coloration for survival and for hunting. The tiger's vertical black and orange stripes

allow it to blend in with the environment. Deer and other prey that confuse the tiger's stripes for light and shade more often than not end up on the dinner plate.

3 ➔ Disruptive camouflage is the opposite of cryptic coloration. With disruptive camouflage, an organism tries to confuse the observer by changing shape and color or, as in the octopus's case, by ejecting a cloud of black ink, which disrupts the predator's sense of smell. This allows the octopus to escape. The pufferfish, a small, slow moving fish, employs another type of disruptive camouflage. If threatened, the pufferfish balloons into a ball by filling its stomach with water. At the same time, spikes protrude from its body making the otherwise small pufferfish look like a much larger and more dangerous fish. A predator, looking for a small fish, and not wanting to risk a confrontation with a ballooned pufferfish, would move on to easier prey. However, if a predator were to attack, it would run into the pufferfish's second line of defense, the poison tetrodotoxin, a neurotoxin with no known antidote. The only vertebrate whose toxin is more lethal than the pufferfish's is the golden dart frog's.

4 ➔ A second form of crypsis is mimicry. An example is the lo moth. In the center of each wing is a large black dot called an eyespot. When observed, these eyespots look like the eyes of a large predator, such as an owl. In this equation, the mimic, the lo moth, is sharing the characteristics of a different species called the model. By modeling itself after a larger animal, the lo moth sends a signal to the observer that it is a potential threat and should not be eaten. This relationship, one in which a species shares similarities with another species while pretending to be a threat, is called a Batesian mimic. Named after Henry Walter Bates, the English scientist who first observed mimicry in the wild, a Batesian mimic is a sheep in wolf's clothing. Another example is *Malpolon moilensis* or false cobra. This cobra looks and moves like its more lethal cousin, the hooded cobra, but is innocuous.

3. In paragraph 3, it is suggested that one way a predator locates an octopus is by...

a) shape
b) sound
c) taste
d) smell

4. What does the author suggest about the pufferfish?

a) It uses poison to kill its prey.
b) It is deadlier than the golden dart frog.
c) It is the second deadliest vertebrate in the world.
d) Its toxin has a known antidote.

5. In paragraph 4, we can infer that a sheep in wolf's clothing...

a) is a threat
b) is toxic
c) is harmless
d) is a snake

➔ Answers: page 689.

Practice #2: *Inference Questions*

Directions: You have ten minutes to read the passage and answer the questions.

A Landmark Ruling

1. In paragraph 1, what can we infer about the Supreme Court's decision?

a) It has changed the Supreme Court.
b) It has limited the rights of the individual in the United States.
c) It has dramatically changed the definition of a U.S. corporation.
d) It has changed the constitution in a way that benefits corporations.

2. In paragraph 2, what does the author imply when he says that *Hillary: The Movie* "barely appeared on the radar"?

a) That *Hillary: The Movie* was widely seen by many Americans then.
b) That *Hillary: The Movie* was seen by very few Americans at the time.
c) That *Hillary: The Movie* was not on TV during the 2008 presidential primary.
d) That *Hillary: The Movie* was banned.

1 ➔ In January, 2010, the Supreme Court of the United States ruled on the case the US Supreme Court vs. the Federal Elections Commission. In this landmark ruling, the bitterly-divided Court ruled 5-4 that corporations enjoy the same First Amendment rights as do individuals. In other words, a corporation, no matter what the size, is considered a citizen. Microsoft. General Electric. Exxon. In the eyes of the Supreme Court, they are all citizens—individuals—thus legally entitled to protection under the Constitution. That protection includes the right to free speech. Suffice it to say, the ruling set off a firestorm of protest. But before we get to that, let's map out how this landmark ruling came about.

2 ➔ In 2004, Oscar-winning documentary filmmaker Michael Moore released *Fahrenheit 911*, a scathing indictment of how then Republican President George W. Bush failed to act during the 9/11 crisis. In Moore's film, Bush comes off looking like a man entirely unsuited to be president. In short, Moore argues that President Bush failed in a time of national crisis. The Republicans were furious. Not to be outdone, David Bossie, a veteran Republican strategist, made a film attacking Democrat Hillary Clinton, who was then starting her run for president. But the movie, titled *Hillary: The Movie*, barely appeared on the radar during the 2008 presidential primary season. Why? Because the Federal Elections Commission restricted Bossie's film from being shown. The decision to restrict the film was based on the fact that the film was made not by David Bossie himself, as an individual, but by a corporation. That corporation was Citizens United. A lower court ruled that *Hillary: The Movie* wasn't a movie at all, but instead a 90-minute attack ad telling

3. In paragraph 2, we can infer that David Bossie...

a) used his own money to make *Hillary: The Movie.*
b) used corporate money to make a film attacking Hillary Clinton.
c) is really a filmmaker and not a political strategist.
d) believes the Federal Elections Commission made the right decision.

4. What can we infer about the lower court's decision?

a) The Supreme Court agreed with it.
b) The Supreme Court banned it.
c) The Supreme Court voted for it.
d) The Supreme Court rejected it.

5. In paragraph 3, what does the author suggest when he says "And smoke is already on the horizon"?

a) That the Court's ruling is already having positive effects.
b) That the Court's ruling is already causing controversy.
c) That the Court's ruling was not clear.
d) That the Court's ruling is already out of date.

voters not to vote for Hillary Clinton. In that light, the lower court ruled that under the current campaign rules established by the Federal Elections Commission, Citizens United—being a legal corporate entity—was prohibited from financing political commercials. Basically, the Federal Elections Commission said corporate money has no place in American politics. What did Dave Bossie do? He turned around and sued the Federal Elections Commission, the argument being that Citizens United was being denied the right to free speech. In January, 2010, the Supreme Court agreed with Bossie's argument and overruled the lower court's decision. In delivering its ruling, the Supreme Court said, and I quote, "Political spending is a form of protected speech under the First Amendment, and the government may not keep corporations or unions from spending money to support or denounce individual candidates in elections." It doesn't get much clearer than that.

3 ➔ Now, you may wonder, why is this such a big deal? Why has this decision sent shock waves through the American political system? Think of it this way: the Supreme Court says that if the Ford Motor Company wants to donate a billion dollars to help elect a candidate—a candidate who will help Ford move its factories overseas—then Ford, as an individual, has every right to do so. Those opposed to the decision say that this is patently unfair. Corporate money, they argue, will go directly into political advertising which, in turn, will give an unfair advantage to corporate-sponsored candidate. For example, imagine you are a school teacher and you decide to run for Congress and your opponent is funded by IBM or Google. In short, those who oppose corporate political funding fear that the American political system is no longer based on the one person, one vote proposition. Instead, elections will simply be bought by the candidate who has the most money, namely, corporate money. And smoke is already on the horizon. Recently it has been revealed that the American Chamber of Commerce—the largest association of businesses in America,

6. What will the essay develop next?

a) Examples to support the Court's ruling.
b) Examples to support the argument that the Court's ruling is negatively impacting corporations.
c) Evidence proving that foreign money is already entering the American political system.
d) An argument in support of ruling against the Chamber of Commerce.

representing every type of business from Microsoft down to your local gas station owner—has been soliciting money from foreign corporations with U.S. operations, money which is finding its way into the American political system regardless of what members of the Chamber of Commerce might think. Let's examine the evidence.

<u>landmark</u>: a turning point

<u>scathing</u>: bitter and severe

<u>indictment</u>: document served to one accused of fault or offense

➔ Answers: page 690.

5. Rhetorical-Purpose Questions

Each passage will have 2 or fewer rhetorical-purpose questions. These questions measure your ability to identify how the writer uses rhetorical strategies to develop an opinion-based or a fact-based argument. The rhetorical strategies used for testing are narration, description, illustration, definition, compare-contrast, classification, process, and cause-and-effect (see page 26 for more on rhetorical strategies).

Rhetorical-purpose questions can be paraphrased a variety of ways, for example:

- In paragraph 1, what was the effect of the tsunami?
- In paragraph 4, how are computers classified?
- How does the author define the concept of quality control?

Look at a sample rhetorical-purpose question.

8. In paragraph 3, why does Adam Smith mention the pin worker and the owner of the pin factory?

a) to compare and contrast workers who benefitted the most from a new type of manufacturing process
b) to classify the various types of workers in 1723 Scotland
c) to define the process in which national wealth is created for both a pin worker and his employer
d) to support his argument that a factory worker and a factory owner can both benefit financially from a systematic manufacturing process

a. Question Analysis: *Signal Words*

As you read the question, look for signal words. Signal words identify those words you must scan or skim for in the corresponding paragraph or in the passage as a whole. The signal words in the sample question are in paragraph 3. That is where the answer is. Mention is also a signal word. Rhetorically, mention means *use as an example.* Those examples are the pin worker and the owner of the pin factory.

8. In paragraph 3, why does Adam Smith mention the pin worker and the owner of the pin factory?

paraphrased, the question reads like this...

8. In paragraph 3, why does Adam Smith *use the examples of* the pin worker and the owner of the pin factory?

Next, scan the answer choices for signal words. Note how in the sample below the signal words are rhetorical strategies followed by **cause**-and-*effect*.

a) to compare and contrast workers who *benefitted the most from* **a new type of manufacturing process**
b) to classify the various types of workers in 1723 Scotland
c) to define the process in which **national wealth is created** *for both a pin worker and his employer*
d) to support his argument that a *factory worker and a factory owner can both benefit financially from* **a systematic manufacturing process**

Next, scan paragraph 3. Locate the signal words the pin worker and the owner of the pin factory. When you locate them, note how they are used rhetorically in the passage, then compare that usage to A, B, C, and D above.

b. Choice Analysis: *Process of Elimination*

Using process of elimination, eliminate answer choices that are not rhetorically accurate. Some answer choices will not be rhetorically accurate because they are: 1) off topic; 2) too specific; 3) too general; 4) not known; 5) not true; 6) not implied; 7) not accurate.

8. In paragraph 3, why does Adam Smith mention the pin worker and the owner of the pin factory?

a) to compare and contrast workers who benefitted the most from a new type of manufacturing process
b) to classify the various types of workers in 1723 Scotland
c) to define the process in which national wealth is created for both a pin worker and his employer
d) to support his argument that a factory worker and a factory owner can both benefit financially from a systematic manufacturing process

A is not correct because it is not true. Neither the pin worker nor the factory owner benefitted "the most". This effect suggests inequality whereas Smith argued that national wealth benefitted all equally. Also, in A note the phrase "a new type of manufacturing process." Which "new type of manufacturing process"? It does not say thus this phrase is too general. This, combined with a rhetorical strategy based on a superlative (the most), eliminates A. B is also incorrect because it is not accurate. Adam Smith was born in 1723.

not true-too general a) to compare and contrast workers who benefitted the most from a new type of manufacturing process
not accurate b) to classify the various types of workers in 1723 Scotland
c) to define the process in which national wealth is created for both a pin worker and his employer
d) to support his argument that a factory worker and a factory owner can both benefit financially from a systematic manufacturing process

You now have two choices left. One is the distractor.

c. Identifying the Distractor

In this example, C is the distractor.

8. In paragraph 3, why does Adam Smith mention the pin worker and the owner of the pin factory?

not true-too general a) to compare and contrast workers who benefitted the from a new type of manufacturing process

not accurate b) to classify the various types of workers in 1723 Scotland

distractor c) to define the process in which **national wealth is created** *for both a pin worker and his employer*

d) to support his argument that a factory worker and a factory owner can both benefit financially from a systematic manufacturing process

Note the inferred **cause**-and-*effect* relationship in C. It seems correct however it is not true. "National wealth" is not created for "both a pin worker and his employer". It is for everyone's benefit. Also, Smith defines a "process" but what process? In the passage, Smith specifically mentions the pin-making process, but this topic (process) is not defined in C thus C is also too general. Therefore, by process of elimination, D is correct. The systematic manufacturing process Smith mentions is the pin-making process, a process a factory worker (a pin worker) and a factory owner (the owner of a pin factory) "can both benefit from" financially. These two illustrations (factory worker + factory owner) define the correct **cause**-and-*effect* relationship that develops and supports Smith's "argument" paraphrased in D.

8. In paragraph 3, why does Adam Smith mention the pin worker and the owner of the pin factory?

not true-too general a) to compare and contrast workers who benefitted the most from a new type of manufacturing process

not accurate b) to classify the various types of workers in 1723 Scotland

distractor c) to define the process in which national wealth is created for both a pin worker and his employer

correct d) to support his argument that *a factory worker and a factory owner can both benefit financially from* **a systematic manufacturing process**

As you know from previous tasks, TOEFL recycles eight rhetorical strategies for testing purposes. Those eight rhetorical strategies are narration, description, illustration, definition, compare-contrast, classification, process, and cause-and-effect. That means you can recycle what you have learned about each rhetorical strategy and apply it when answering reading section questions.

Practice #1: *Rhetorical-Purpose Questions*

Directions: You have ten minutes to read the passage and answer the questions.

Cognitive Bias

1 ➔ Passing judgment is human nature. Some of our judgments are accurate while others are flawed. Often a judgment is flawed because we have not taken the time to think an issue through and instead make a snap decision based on experience. A snap decision resulting in an error of judgment is called a cognitive bias. Some of the more common cognitive biases are the bandwagon effect, stereotyping, and the halo effect. Let's start with the bandwagon effect.

2 ➔ Have you ever bought something because all your friends had bought it, or tried a new restaurant simply because all your friends had? If so, then you have demonstrated the cognitive bias called the bandwagon effect. Historically, the word bandwagon describes a wagon pulled by a horse. On the wagon, a band is playing music. If you like the music, then you will follow the bandwagon, maybe even jump on. Either way, you have literally joined the group. Years ago, politicians used bandwagons to spread their messages. If many voters were following a politician's bandwagon, and you concluded that so many people must mean the politician deserves your vote, then you would have joined the bandwagon. How you came to that conclusion is known as an information cascade. An information cascade is an integral part of the bandwagon effect. It occurs when you conclude, without evidence, that if everybody is doing it, then they must be right and you must be wrong. Because you are wrong, you follow those who are right: the group or bandwagon.

1. How is the author of this passage using classification?

a) to identify and develop three common forms of cognitive bias
b) to identify and define the process of decision making
c) to illustrate how people make snap decisions
d) to contrast opposing views on the theory of cognitive bias

2. In paragraph 2, why does the author use the example of a political bandwagon?

a) to illustrate how bandwagons are used in politics, past and present
b) to compare and contrast how voters can be easily influenced
c) to classify various types of political campaign strategies
d) to illustrate the historical origin of the term bandwagon and its effect

3. What happens as a result of a cascade of information?

a) The individual concludes that he/she is right and the group is wrong.
b) The individual joins the group believing there must be truth in numbers.
c) The individual makes the correct choice based on the evidence.
d) The individual literally jumps on the bandwagon.

4. Why does the author mention teenagers?

a) to explain why teenagers do the things they do
b) to expand the topic of politics
c) to provide another example of a decision making process
d) to give another example of the bandwagon effect

5. What does the bandwagon effect often produce?

a) stereotypes
b) shopaholics
c) individuals
d) bargains

6. Why does the author introduce the topic of hamburgers?

a) to classify different stereotypes and how they originate
b) to contrast bargain shoppers and hamburger lovers
c) to add another step in the process of stereotyping
d) to illustrate how stereotypes are generalizations that do more harm than good

7. In paragraph 5, how does the author introduce the topic of the halo effect?

a) by using an illustration
b) by using a classification
c) by using a process
d) by using a definition

3 ➔ The bandwagon effect is not limited to politics. It also describes why some teenagers get into trouble. Not wanting to be left out of the group, a teenager will join in even if he or she knows that what they are doing is wrong. This is one way teenagers start drinking and smoking, by jumping on the bandwagon figuratively.

4 ➔ Another example of the bandwagon effect is Black Friday. Black Friday is a national day of sales in which millions jump on the bandwagon and flock to stores looking for pre-Christmas bargains. Do these people really need to wait in front of Wal-Mart at four a.m. in order to be first in line for the best bargains, or are they all just shopaholics? If you assume that all Black Friday shoppers are shopaholics, then you would be stereotyping. Stereotyping is another common cognitive bias. When you stereotype someone, you are concluding, without evidence, that the character traits of one individual are consistent throughout the group. For example, your friend Bill eats nothing but hamburgers. Because Bill is American, you conclude that all Americans eat hamburgers, which of course is not true, much like the fallacy that all Black Friday shoppers are shopaholics is not true. Just because you go shopping on Black Friday does not mean you are a shopaholic. True, many Black Friday shoppers are shopaholics; however, many simply want to save money or are with friends or family. Whatever the case, stereotyping can lead to offense, so be careful when making sweeping generalities based on experience rather than on sound evidence.

5 ➔ But let's say you jump on the bandwagon anyway and join the four a.m. stampede into Wal-Mart. You want a Samsung big-screen TV so you race for the electronics department. The only problem is everybody else wanted a Samsung TV, and now they are all gone. Then a man says, "Wal-Mart TVs are just as good as Samsungs. In fact, Samsung makes Wal-Mart TVs." Is that true? You don't know. Meanwhile, the man grabs a Wal-Mart TV and everyone else jumps on the bandwagon until

8. According to paragraph 5, what can the halo effect result in?

a) a snap decision that often results in consumer satisfaction
b) a snap decision that often ends in customer disappointment
c) a snap decision that is a bargain
d) a snap decision based on research

there is only one Wal-Mart TV left. What do you do? You grab it. Why? Because you like Wal-Mart TVs? No. The fact is you have never heard of a Wal-Mart TV before. But you have heard of Samsung, and you know that Samsung is high quality. So what do you do? You make a snap decision based on experience: If Samsung makes Wal-Mart TVs, like the man said—and you know that Samsung is good—then Wal-Mart TVs must be good. Right? Right. Only later when you get it home do you realize that your Wal-Mart TV was made by the Cheap-O TV Company. This then is an example of the halo effect. The halo effect is a cognitive bias in which you believe that the value or quality of one thing (Samsung TV) spills over and increases the value of another thing (Wal-Mart TV).

9. What does the Apple iPad tell us about the halo effect?

a) Apple products benefit from the halo effect.
b) Apple products are always cutting edge.
c) Apple products need no advertising.
d) Apple products are the best.

6 ➔ Another example is the Apple iPad. When it first came out, many questioned whether it would fly. Considering Apple's track record for delivering cutting edge products, such as the wildly successful iPod, was there any doubt? No. When the iPad arrived in stores, people lined up to buy it. Had they ever seen or used an iPad before? No. But that didn't stop sales from going through the roof. Why was the iPad such a hit? Because of the halo effect.

<u>stampede</u>: a mass movement based on impulse

➔ Answers: page 690.

Practice #2: *Rhetorical-Purpose Questions*

Directions: You have ten minutes to read the passage and answer the questions.

The Gilded Age

1 ➔ The verb *to gild* means to apply a layer of gold to an object. Mark Twain used the adjectival form of this verb when he coined the phrase the Gilded Age. The Gilded Age, from 1869 to 1893, represents American economic prosperity at its height. And for good reason. The Gilded Age created many firsts, such as a new class of super-rich, men like John D. Rockefeller, J. P. Morgan, Andrew Mellon, Cornelius Vanderbilt, and Andrew Carnegie. It also witnessed the birth of the first corporations, such as General Electric and Standard Oil. Yet it was the railroad companies that were the engine that drove the Gilded Age, companies like Union Pacific and the Central Pacific Railroad. In 1869, four years after the Civil War, these two railroads linked up at Promontory Summit in Utah thereby establishing the first continental railroad in North America. Now, instead of sailing south around South America to go from New York City to San Francisco—a trip that could take three weeks, if the weather were good—the trip could now be made in six-days by train. The impact was immediate. With the east now linked with the west, thousands seeking free land and a new future headed west. When the railroad arrived in Denver in 1870, it had a population of 5,000. Ten years later it was 36,000.

2 ➔ To accommodate the movement of people and material, hundreds of new railroads were built. And they needed steel. Lots of it. Yet steel making was, and still is, a capital-intensive business. It took money to build steel factories and to mine the ore necessary for smelting in coke ovens fueled by coal. Investment capital was needed. Banks, jumping on the bandwagon, met the demand and Wall Street, as we know it, came into its own. The boom in steel making created a

1. In paragraph 1, what was the effect of the transcontinental railroad's completion in 1869?

a) It made a new class of people.
b) It put ships out of business
c) It signaled the start of the Gilded Age.
d) It helped end the Civil War.

2. Why does the author mention Denver, Colorado?

a) to illustrate the development of a western town in the 1870's
b) to illustrate the rate at which people were moving west in 1870
c) to demonstrate how the west was linked to the east in 1869
d) to describe how the railroad was important in the Gilded Age

3. In paragraph 2, what was the direct effect of the need for steel?

a) increased spending
b) the birth of Wall Street
c) a great migration west
d) more railroads

4. Why does the author mention ATT, Western Union and farming?

a) because they all wanted to make a profit
b) because they all benefitted from the building of the railroad
c) because they were all American
d) because each needed steel

5. According to paragraph 3, what created company loyalty?

a) defining goals
b) increased productivity
c) a chain of command
d) a well-run railroad

6. Why does the author use the example of the Singer sewing machine?

a) to demonstrate how women in the Gilded Age worked
b) to classify women's work in the late nineteenth century
c) to illustrate how the Gilded Age was a time of technological progress
d) to show how American politics and the railroads were connected

demand not only for investment capital but for factory workers as well. Most of those workers were newly-arrived immigrants. The steel they made in east coast factories built rails and rail cars, all of it heading west to serve the farmers who needed to ship their beef and wheat back east by rail. In this way, the railroad spawned the farming industry and helped to expand the telegraph industry, for the fastest and easiest way to build new telegraph lines was to follow the railroads into the newly created towns dotting the west. They did, and American Telephone and Telegraph (ATT) and Western Union took their place beside Union Pacific Railroad, Carnegie Steel, Standard Oil, and Mellon Bank as being America's most profitable companies.

3 ➔ Railroad companies are also credited with developing what today is known as the modern management system. With so much building, the railroads needed a clear chain of command to keep things running smoothly. This they did by creating clear managerial roles while establishing career goals that employees at all levels could pursue. This, combined with internal promotions, led to greater employee loyalty and productivity. Other companies soon followed suit. This gave rise to the American middle class, especially in big east coast cities.

4 ➔ Manufacturing too benefited from the railroad boom. One consumer item that changed millions of women's lives was the Singer sewing machine. By 1880, over three million homes had a Singer. Why was this invention so revolutionary? Prior to the Singer sewing machine, women had to stay home and make clothes for their families, a time-consuming task that left women with little or no free time for anything else. Yet the Singer sewing machine changed all that. It not only sped up the clothes-making process, but also led to the development of textile factories where clothes, such as those for railroad workers, were mass produced. The result was that clothes were cheaper and women no longer had to hand-stitch clothes for their families. With the advent of the Singer sewing

machine, women now had more free time, time they could devote to women's rights, such as the right to vote, which they won in 1920.

5 ➔ The railroad boom, however, went bust in 1893. Like the internet bubble of 2000 and the real estate bubble of 2008, the railroad boom was a result of companies over-extending. Simply put, by 1893 there were too many railroads and too many bad loans and too much market speculation. This led to the collapse of over five hundred banks while dozens of railroads, including the Union Pacific Railroad, declared bankruptcy. Confidence in the economy was restored when gold was found in Canada's Klondike, leading to the Klondike Gold Rush of 1897.

7. Why does the author compare the railroad boom to the internet and real estate bubbles of the early twenty-first century?

a) to highlight the repeating nature of economic bubbles
b) to stress that economic bubbles are bad for the economy
c) to illustrate how the railroad boom was different from later internet and real estate booms
d) to emphasize the need for more government control

➔ Answers: page 690.

6. Reference Questions

Each passage will have 2 or fewer reference questions. A reference question is a grammar question. This question type measures your ability to connect words grammatically using referents and their antecedents. The referent will be highlighted in the passage. The referents will be either a *pronoun* or a *pronoun + noun*. Reference questions can be phrased a variety of ways, for example:

- What does the phrase these bacteria refer to in paragraph 5?
- In paragraph 3, them refers to what?
- What does theirs refer to in paragraph 6?

Look at a sample reference question.

5. In paragraph 2, to what does it refer?

a) worker
b) pin
c) wire
d) head

a. Question Analysis

Make sure you understand the question before you answer. Do so by identifying the grammatical function of the highlighted referent. In this example, the referent it is a third-person pronoun (*he, she, it*).

5. In paragraph 2, to what does it refer?

a) worker
b) pin
c) wire
d) head

Next, locate the highlighted referent in the passage.

2 ➔ In *The Wealth of Nations*, Smith argues that building national economic wealth begins with a division of labor. Smith supports his argument by using a pin factory. In a typical pin factory of the day, each worker was responsible for making pins from start to finish. A worker would start by cutting the pin to size from a piece of wire, then straighten it, then sharpen the end, affix a head, polish it, then package it. In short, one man was responsible for each step of the pin-making process...

Remember: A referent pronoun will always come after its noun antecedent. For example, in the sentence below, the pronoun it is the referent. It refers to (connects back to) the noun antecedent **pin**.

> A worker would start by cutting the **pin** to size from a piece of wire, then straighten it, then sharpen the end, affix a head, polish it, then package it.

b. Choice Analysis: *Process of Elimination*

If the highlighted referent is a pronoun (see below), the correct answer will be a noun. Therefore, eliminate choices that are not nouns, for example:

2. In paragraph 1, it refers to...

adverb	a) already
correct	b) book
verb	c) borrow
adjective	d) interesting

By process of elimination, B is correct.

Look at the question from the sample passage. Note that the highlighted referent in the question is the pronoun it, and that the four choices are all nouns. In this example, B is correct.

5. In paragraph 2, to what does it refer?

	a) worker
correct	b) pin
	c) wire
	d) head

> A worker would start by cutting the **pin** to size from a piece of wire, then straighten it, then sharpen the end, affix a head, polish it, then package it.

To confirm that B is correct, first identify which part of speech it is. In the sentence above, it is the object of the verb package. Next, using process of elimination, ask yourself: Package what? A, a worker? No. You cannot package a worker. Topically, that does not make sense. C, package a piece of wire? No. The topic is making pins not wire. Also, wire is the object of a preposition not a verb. D, package the head (of a pin)? Head is the object of the verb affix. Topically, the head of a pin becomes part of the **pin** when it is affixed (connected) to the wire. Because the context is the process of making a pin (head + wire = pin), the topical and grammatical answer is **pin**. This confirms that B is correct. Package what? The **pin** (the finished product).

Look at the next example.

> 1 ➔ We Americans assume that all business cultures are like ours. Nothing could be further from the truth. Many **Middle Eastern and Asian cultures** prefer to do business face-to-face. Discussing business over tea or while having dinner is an integral part of the business process in these cultures. Such traditions help develop mutual respect and trust...

If the referent is a *pronoun + noun*, such as these cultures above, the four answer choices will also be noun phrases. In this example, A is the correct answer.

7. In paragraph 1, what does these cultures refer to?

a) Middle Eastern and Asian cultures
b) old and new cultures
c) traditional and non traditional cultures
d) American cultures

Confirm your choice by asking: What cultures? B, *old and new cultures*? No. They are not mentioned in this context. C, *traditional and non traditional cultures*? No. They are not mentioned in this context either. D, *American cultures*? The word *Americans* appears is this context; however, *Americans* means people not cultures thus is not topically correct. Therefore, A is correct.

Pronoun Types

On test day, expect reference questions based on the following pronoun types.

Subjective Pronouns: *she, he, it, we, they*

Teleconferencing might be fast and easy but it's certainly not cheap, especially when companies need to upgrade their computer systems continually if they want to stay competitive.

In the example above, the referent they refers to the antecedent companies. To confirm it, ask: Who are they? Answer: companies. Note also that topically, companies, not systems, stay competitive. This confirms that companies is the topical and grammatical antecedent of they.

Objective Pronouns: *her, him, it, us, them*

Sue was surprised to find her car keys. She thought she had lost them.

In the example above, the referent them refers to the antecedent keys. To confirm it, ask: Sally lost what? Answer: Keys.

Possessive Pronouns: *hers, his, its, ours, theirs*

The American park system was created for the benefit of all Americans. The parks are theirs to enjoy.

In the example above, the referent theirs refers to the antecedent Americans. To confirm it, ask: Who is theirs? Answer: Americans.

Demonstrative Pronouns: *this, that, these, those*

The problem is not a lack of development. The issue is a lack of coherence. That is the problem.

In the example above, the referent That refers to the antecedent a lack of coherence. To confirm it, ask: What is the problem? Answer: A lack of coherence.

Relative Pronouns: *who, whoever, whom, whomever, that, which, in which, of which, by which*

Nobody would disagree that violent video games are designed with killing in mind, just like no would disagree that problem-solution scenarios in which an anti-hero blasts his way to freedom reinforce detrimental behavior in adolescents.

In the example above, the referent in which refers to the antecedent problem-solution scenarios. To confirm it, ask: In which? Answer: In problem-solution scenarios.

Reflexive Pronouns: *herself, himself, itself, ourselves*

These days, doctors are prescribing fewer antibiotics for the common cold. Instead, doctors prefer that the body heal itself.

In the example above, the referent itself refers to the antecedent body. To confirm it, ask: Heal what? Answer: The body.

Note: In the sample above, the modal should has been dropped from the second sentence. Note how the verb heal remains plural in the example above and below.

These days, doctors are prescribing fewer antibiotics for the common cold. Instead, doctors prefer that the body should heal itself.

British and Canadian English often drop the modal.

British and Canadian English: Ann's parents insist that she go to McGill.
American English: Ann's parents insist that she must go to Yale.

Indefinitive Pronouns: *all, some, somebody, someone, many, few, fewer, one, none*

In the paragraph below, the referent one refers to the antecedent word. To confirm it, ask: One what? Answer: Word.

> The comparative *fewer* is rapidly disappearing from the English canon, replaced by the ubiquitous—and grammatically incorrect—*less*. For example, it's quite common to see ads that read, "Eat Mary's Ice Cream. It has less calories." Politicians also commit this grammatical faux pas. Not a day goes by in which a politician is not screaming, "Americans need to pay less taxes!" As you know, fewer takes a plural countable noun, such as, "Joe has *fewer problems* than Al," or "The effect of colony collapse disorder has resulted in *fewer honey bees*." Note that we can count calories (one calorie, two calories) and problems (one problem, two problems), and honey bees (one honey bee, two honey bees). *Less*, in contrast, takes a non countable noun, such as "English teachers make far *less money* than corporate lawyers." Can we count money (one money, two monies?) No. Sadly, the word fewer will soon be one for the history books.

Q *Are there any other grammar-type questions, such as fill-in-the-blanks-with-the-correct-word or identify-the-mistake-in-the-sentence?*

A *No. Reference questions are the only pure grammar questions on the TOEFL iBT.*

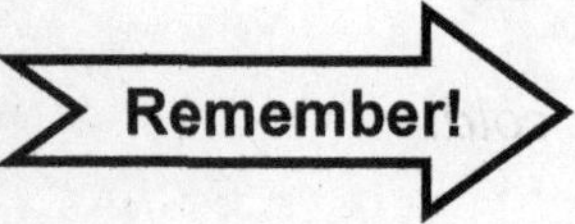

Grammar proficiency is tested throughout the TOEFL iBT. Grammar proficiency is part of language use (OPDUL=C).

Practice: *Reference Questions*

Directions: You have ten minutes to complete questions 1 to 11.

---

1. What does it refer to?

a) army
b) tax money
c) Roman government
d) census

2. To what does their refer?

a) manpower
b) demographers
c) heads
d) civilizations

Census taking, however, is nothing new. Many ancient civilizations regularly took a census of population, for example Rome. Because Rome had a large standing army, it needed money and men. By periodically taking a census, the Roman government knew how much tax money it could raise for the army and the available manpower it could draw from. It wasn't until the second half of the nineteenth century that the process of census taking changed. Instead of just counting heads and money, demographers started to broaden their statistic gathering to include age, occupation, marital status, and education.

---

3. He refers to...

a) white man
b) Rowlandson
c) God
d) Sully

4. To what does in which refer?

a) Eden
b) environment
c) message
d) Na'vi

Rowlandson's influence is still felt today. A prime example of Rowlandson's influence is the movie *Avatar*. *Avatar*, however, is very much a post-modern captivity narrative. What do I mean by that? Take a look at the story. What happens? The Na'vi—which are nothing more than Native Americans—capture Sully, a white man. Sully lives with the Na'vi yet instead of escaping with the message that faith in God will save you, he returns with the message that the white man is destroying the environment, the environment being the Na'vi and the Eden in which they live.

---

5. They refers to...

a) buffalo
b) cowbirds
c) family
d) nomad

6. To what does this problem refer?

a) lose their food source
b) raising a family
c) were nomadic
d) was very much an opportunist

As mentioned, the cowbird was originally a nomad, travelling with the buffalo and eating whatever the buffalo kicked up, insects, seeds, whatever. In this light, the cowbird was very much an opportunist. Yet the cowbird had a problem. Because cowbirds were nomadic, raising a family was a problem. If they stopped to raise a brood, they'd lose their food source for the buffalo were always on the move. The cowbird, ever the opportunist, resolved this problem in a unique way, one that characterizes the species to this day.

7. Of which refers to what?

a) water
b) seamount
c) variety
d) fish

Seamounts are of great interest not only to biologists but to the commercial fishing industry as well. And for good reason. The nutrient-rich water around a seamount is home to an immense variety of fish, many of which have commercial value. One such fish is the orange roughy.

---

8. To what does These organisms refer?

a) plants, algae, and photoautotrophs
b) plants, algae, and many species of bacteria
c) photosynthesis, photoautotrophs, and many species of plants
d) organisms, plants, and many species of bacteria

For plants to survive, they must convert carbon dioxide into sugar using energy from the sun. This conversion process is called photosynthesis. Organisms that depend on photosynthesis for survival are called photoautotrophs. Plants, as well as algae and many species of bacteria, fall under this classification. These organisms are unique in that they are the only ones to produce their own food by photosynthesis, a chemically complex process in which oxygen is a waste byproduct. Suffice it to say, without photosynthesis, life on Earth would cease to exist.

---

9. Of which refers to...

a) literate, urbanized, state-level societies
b) archeologists
c) civilization
d) state-level societies

Before we proceed, we really need to define the term civilization. Within the word itself lies the root "civil" meaning to display the appropriate behavior. Yet this definition of civilization is far too broad, for what might be considered appropriate behavior in one society might be taboo in another. Simply put, archeologists apply the term civilization when describing literate, urbanized, state-level societies, the earliest of which were city-states in southwest Asia and along the Nile River.

---

10. To what does it refer?

a) hot air
b) heat
c) moisture
d) hot day

➔ Answers: page 690.

According to the National Oceanographic and Atmospheric Administration (NOAA), extreme heat is "one of the most underrated and least understood of the deadly weather phenomena." Why is this the case? First off, the danger is less obvious. Think about it. A mass of hot air settles over us and we think, okay, it's just another hot day. To cool off, our bodies perspire. This moisture evaporates. By doing so, it draws excess heat from our bodies.

7. Sentence-Simplification Questions

Each passage will have either one or no sentence-simplification question. This question type measures your ability to analyze how the highlighted sentence in the passage has been paraphrased into a shorter sentence. The correct answer will restate the main ideas in the highlighted sentence. Sentence-simplification questions are stated one way, for example:

11. Which of the following sentences best restates the essential information in the highlighted sentence in paragraph 4? Incorrect choices will change the meaning and omit important information.

    a) Adam Smith adds that the wealth of a nation depends upon serving the needs of the individual first.
    b) Smith goes on to say that free trade is the best way to create wealth.
    c) Moreover, Smith says that nations become wealthy by accumulating gold and by systematically manufacturing goods, which are then freely traded.
    d) Smith believes that systematically manufactured goods freely traded create more national wealth than gold.

4 ➔ *The Wealth of Nations* is very much a reaction to the predominating economic theory of the day, that of Mercantilism. Mercantilists posited that the wealth of a nation depended on developing and maintaining national power thus it was a form of economic nationalism. Spain, at the time of Columbus, is a prime example of just such a nation. A nation like Spain preserved national power by accumulating as much gold as possible through strong exports, the limitation of imports, and a large population of poorly paid workers. ■ To develop exports, companies were subsidized by the government which also wrote laws to limit imports. ■ By limiting imports, the gold used to pay for imports would stay in the country and create a greater money supply and more credit. ■ Moreover, nations were geared toward acquiring and maintaining gold at all costs, including warring with each other. ■ Adam Smith, however, argued that trade benefitted all nations and that gold was not equal to wealth. Gold, Smith said, was like any other commodity, such as wheat or wool, and that it deserved no special treatment. More importantly, Smith says that the wealth of a nation is not based on the hoarding of gold, but on the free flow of goods manufactured in a systematic way, a way that serves the needs of the individual and, ultimately, the nation as a whole. With that, Adam Smith gave birth to what we now call economic theory. As Thomas Edison is to the light bulb, Adam Smith is to the science of economics.

a. Question Analysis

Before you select an answer, make sure you understand the question. Next, analyze the highlighted sentence in the passage. All the information you need to know will be in the highlighted sentence. Next, identify the rhetorical strategies in the highlighted sentence. In the highlighted sentence below, the writer uses the rhetorical strategies of cause-and-effect, compare-and-contrast, and illustration.

> More importantly, Smith says that the wealth of a nation is not based on the hoarding of gold, but on the free flow of goods manufactured in a systematic way, a way that serves the needs of the individual and, ultimately, the nation as a whole.

Note also how the writer uses the rhetorical strategy of argument counter-argument. Before but, the writer paraphrases how Smith refutes the Mercantilist economic theory argument. After but, the writer paraphrases Smith's counter argument in support of systematic manufacturing to create national wealth.

b. Choice Analysis: *Process of Elimination*

After you have identified the rhetorical strategies in the highlighted sentence, identify the rhetorical strategies in each answer choice.

Choice A uses **cause**-and-*effect* and illustration.

a) Adam Smith adds that *the wealth of a nation depends upon* **serving the needs of the individual first.**

Choice B uses **cause**-and-*effect*.

b) Smith goes on to say that **free trade** *is the best way to create wealth*.

Choice C uses **cause**-and-*effect* and illustration.

c) Moreover, Smith says that *nations become wealthy* **by accumulating gold** and **by systematically manufacturing goods, which are then freely traded.**

Choice D uses illustration, **cause**-and-*effect*, ***compare-and-contrast***, and (1) argument (2) counter-argument.

d) Smith believes that (1) systematically manufactured goods **freely traded** *create* ***more*** *national wealth* than (2) gold.

Based on rhetorical strategies alone, D is the best choice so far.

To confirm that D is correct, compare the topic in each answer choice to the topic in the highlighted sentence. In the four answer choices below, look for topics that: 1) are off topic; 2) lack development; 3) are contradictory; 4) are factually wrong; 5) are grammatically different; 6) are not accurate rhetorically.

> More importantly, Smith says that the wealth of a nation is not based on the hoarding of gold, but on the free flow of goods manufactured in a systematic way, a way that serves the needs of the individual and, ultimately, the nation as a whole.

a) Adam Smith adds that the wealth of a nation depends upon serving the needs of the individual first.

This choice is not correct because it lacks topic development (OP**D**UL=C). It does not include the topics of "gold" or "the free flow of goods manufactured in a systematic way", both of which are in the highlighted sentence. Also, the "wealth of a nation" does not depend on "serving the needs of the individual first." This point is factually and rhetorically wrong. Smith, instead, believes that the wealth of a nation depends on "the free flow of goods manufactured in a systematic way." The end result is that all ("the nation as a whole") benefit.

b) Smith goes on to say that free trade is the best way to create wealth.

This choice is not correct because it lacks topic development (OP**D**UL=C). Yes, Smith believes that "free trade" creates wealth. But what kind of "wealth"? The highlighted sentence says "the wealth of a nation." This choice only says "wealth" thus it is too general. Also, this sentence uses the superlative "the best way." The highlighted sentence does not use this grammatical form.

c) Moreover, Smith says that nations become wealthy by accumulating gold and by systematically manufacturing goods, which are then freely traded.

This choice is not correct because it is factually wrong. Smith does not say that nations become wealthy by "accumulating gold." Rhetorically, this is a contradiction. In this choice, Smith is a Mercantilist. Also, the transitions "Moreover" and "More importantly" are not grammatically synonymous. Combined, these demonstrate a lack of topical unity and language-use (OPD**UL**=C).

d) Smith believes that systematically manufactured goods freely traded create more national wealth than gold.

This choice is correct because it correctly paraphrases the topics in the highlighted sentence, grammatically and rhetorically. This demonstrates organization, progression, development, unity, and language-use paraphrasing. The result is a coherent choice (OPDUL=**C**) that correctly restates the highlighted sentence.

c. Language-Use Distractors

When analyzing the answer choices, look for language-use distractors (OPDU**L**=C). Look at the highlighted sentence below. Note the word abolitionist, then note the **language-use distractor** in choices A, B, and C. Each distractor has the same prefix *ab* as abolitionist thus is a homophone distractor with a different meaning.

> Prior to the Civil War, John Brown, a deeply religious man born in Torrington, Connecticut, was an abolitionist who fought against the south's slave-based economy.

a) John Brown, a deeply religious man born in Torrington, Connecticut, fought and **abolished** slavery in the south before the Civil War.

b) By the time the Civil War had started, John Brown, a deeply religious New England Yankee, had promised to rid the south of slavery **absolutely**.

c) Before the Civil War, John Brown, a religious man originally from Connecticut, **abhorred** the southern slave system.

d) John Brown, a New England Yankee with strong religious convictions, struggled hard to end slavery in the southern states before the Civil War.

Answer-Choice Analysis

a) John Brown, a deeply religious man born in Torrington, Connecticut, fought and abolished slavery in the south before the Civil War.

This choice is not correct. Abolitionist in the highlighted sentence is a noun while abolished in this choice is a verb. An abolitionist is a person who wants to end slavery while abolished means that John Brown, in this context, abolished (ended) slavery in the south. This fact in not stated in the highlighted sentence. This example tests language-use proficiency (OPDU**L**=C), specifically your ability to distinguish between a verb distractor (abolished) and a noun (abolitionist) with the same *ab* prefix, and how the meaning of each differs in this context.

b) By the time the Civil War had started, John Brown, a deeply religious New England Yankee, had promised to rid the south of slavery absolutely.

This choice is not correct. Absolutely is an adverb of degree meaning *completely*. The highlighted sentence does not contain an adverb that describes the degree to which John Brown will rid the south of slavery. This example tests language-use proficiency (OPDU**L**=C), specifically your ability to distinguish between an adverb distractor (absolutely) and a noun (abolitionist) with the same *ab* prefix, and how the meaning of each differs in this context.

c) Before the Civil War, John Brown, a religious man originally from Connecticut, abhorred the southern slave system.

This choice is not correct. The adjective abhorred means *to hate with extreme prejudice*. We can infer that because John Brown was an abolitionist, he abhorred slavery. However, because abhorred and abolitionist are not synonymous, they are topically different. That means that the highlighted sentence and this choice are also topically different. This example tests language-use proficiency (OPDU**L**=C), specifically your ability to distinguish between an adjective distractor (abhorred) and a noun (abolitionist) with the same *ab* prefix, and how the meaning of each differs in this context.

d) John Brown, a New England Yankee with strong religious convictions, struggled hard to end slavery in the southern states before the Civil War.

This choice is correct. Note that this choice contains no words with the prefix *ab*. Instead, the phrase "struggled hard to end slavery" infers abolitionist. What was John Brown? An abolitionist. What was an abolitionist? A person who "struggled hard to end slavery in the southern states before the Civil War." Therefore, this choice and the highlighted sentence are topically and grammatically united.

Practice #1: *Sentence-Simplification*

Directions: Read each numbered sentence and the restatement below it. If the restatement is correct, put a C in the blank. If it is not correct, put an I in the blank.

1. Scientists have determined that large bodies of liquid water do not exist on Mars thus there is very little water vapor in the Martian atmosphere.

   ____ Because liquid water, like lakes and oceans, is not present on Mars, the air contains few water molecules.

2. Post-impressionism is distinct from impressionism in that the post-impressionists placed more emphasis on geometric shapes and bold, arbitrary colors whereas the impressionists were concerned with capturing a general impression of a scene with less emphasis on line and form.

   ____ The impressionists believed that the post-impressionists, with their focus on shapes and natural colors, were less concerned with capturing the general feeling of a landscape when painting.

3. Semiotics, the study of signs and symbols and signification, can be divided into the study of semantics, syntactics, and pragmatics.

   ____ The study of semiotics, signs and symbols can be subdivided into three groups: semantics, syntactics and pragmatics.

4. Issue framing is a form of rhetoric in which the issue you present is delivered in a such a way as to guarantee that most of your audience will agree with you.

____ Issue framing is a form of rhetoric that can persuade an entire audience.

5. One of the earliest forms of clock was the water clock, a device that measured time by the flow of water, a method that lacks the precision of today's timepieces.

____ Water clocks lacked precision therefore were unable to measure time.

6. Although many theories suggest that Greek fire was a form of petroleum, there is still no clear evidence proving the original chemical nature of the substance though its use as an early weapon of terror is well documented.

____ Greek fire is a well-documented early weapon of terror which was made from gasoline.

7. In anthropology, a fossil is distinct from an artifact in that a fossil is a bone turned to stone whereas an artifact is a product, such as a knife or a bracelet, made by an individual living in a society.

____ Fossils and artifacts are different because the former is a bone that has become stone while the latter is a man-made product.

8. Historically, a letter of marque granted the bearer the right to seize goods or property in the name of the government, a process which, essentially, made piracy legal.

____ Many years ago, if a person carried a letter of marque, it meant that he could steal things with the permission of his government.

9. PEM, protein-energy malnutrition, is responsible for fifty percent of the deaths of children under five in developing nations worldwide.

____ PEN is responsible for fifty percent of the deaths of children worldwide in nations that are developing.

10. Encomienda, a system in which indigenous peoples formed the basis of Spain's colonial labor force, one that supplied the Spanish with gold and supplies, was first introduced by Columbus on the island of Hispaniola, now present-day Haiti and the Dominican Republic.

____ On the island of Hispaniola, Christopher Columbus introduced an economic system that turned the native inhabitants into a colonial labor force.

11. While some see Gilded Age industrialists, such as John D. Rockefeller and Andrew Carnegie, as charitable individuals whose fortunes built some of Manhattan's most famous buildings, like Carnegie Hall and the Rockefeller Center, others view them as robber barons whose charitable donations were simply a way to avoid paying taxes.

_____ Some consider men like Rockefeller and Carnegie to be great philanthropists while others consider them to be nothing more than tax dodgers.

12. In 1215, the Magna Carta—a legal document that said that the king was not above the law—was signed by King John, who promptly abandoned it; it was reissued by his son, Henry the Third, albeit in a revised form, when he took the throne in 1216.

_____ King Henry of England supported then rejected the Magna Carta unlike his son, John the Third, who brought it back in 1216 even though it had been modified.

➔ Answers: page 690.

Practice #2: *Sentence Simplification*

Directions: You have ten minutes to read the following paragraphs and answer the questions.

1 ➔ The literary theory that predominated in the middle decades of the twentieth century, and is still prevalent today, is called New Criticism. Named after the 1941 book *The New Criticism* by John Crowe Ransom, New Criticism espoused an objective approach to literary analysis. Moreover, new critics argued that a literary work, be it a poem, a play, or a novel, had to be closely read in order to determine how the piece worked as a self-referential object free of external bias. By that, proponents of New Criticism meant that the aesthetic value of a work came from its inherent structure and the words therein supported by literary devices, such as analogy, metaphor, allusion, rhyme and meter, and plot. In short, the aesthetic value of a literary work rests on an objective evaluation of what lies between the covers. Prior to the New Criticism movement, literary critics judged the merits of a literary work by the author's intent, how readers reacted to the work, and by the cultural context in which the work was written. The new critics, however, argued that such an approach had little or nothing to do with the work itself as an aesthetic object. Rather, the new critics asserted that the meaning of a text could be determined only by a close reading in which the literary devices therein combined to create a theme which, in turn, helped to identify the best way to interpret the work free of external influence and bias.

1. **Which of the following sentences best restates the essential information in the highlighted sentence in paragraph 1? Incorrect choices will change the meaning and omit important information.**

a) In short, the new critics argued that a literary work had to be free of external influence and bias in order to be worth reading.

b) On the contrary, critics supported the idea that reading a book was the best way to judge its value.

c) Instead, the new critics believed that a piece of literature could best be understood by an objective, unbiased reading of the text's literary devices.

d) In addition, the new critics argued that a close reading of a literary work was the only way to determine if the work had a theme.

2 → The Socratic method, named after the Greek philosopher Socrates, is a method of debate in which critical thinking is developed by asking and answering questions in order to establish and clarify opposing viewpoints. The Socratic method is, essentially, a process that eliminates negative hypotheses by identifying contradictions in logic. This, in turn, helps to shape opinions and to identify general truths. The Socratic method is an integral part of western education, particularly in law school. A law professor, wanting to test his students' knowledge of a case, will start by asking a student to summarize the court's ruling specific to the case. The professor will then question the student to see if the student agrees or disagrees with the court's ruling. Often the professor will turn devil's advocate and challenge the student's opinion of the court's ruling. This, in turn, will help the student to clarify his or her understanding of the case and their position regarding it. The professor can then offer his or her opinion, or ask another student to challenge the first student's opinion. **[A]** The purpose of such an exercise is not to embarrass a student by forcing him or her to defend his or her ideas in public discourse, but to explore all sides of an issue in order to test the logic of an argument and, more importantly, how to apply the law. This approach to teaching, one in which both the teacher and the students engage in ongoing debates about a particular topic, is one of the foundations of the western educational tradition. **[B]** In fact, it can be argued that a successful class is one in which free and active debate is encouraged by the teacher while a class in which a teacher simply lectures with little or no discourse is of far less benefit to the student body.

2. Which of the following sentences best restates the essential information in highlighted sentence A in paragraph 2? Incorrect choices will change the meaning and omit important information.

a) This particular teaching method teaches students about public speaking and the law.

b) This exercise is good practice because law students need to be able to express opinions in court.

c) The purpose of the exercise is to help students speak more proficiently when arguing.

d) This teaching method helps law students understand the complexities of legal issues while helping them apply the law.

3. Which of the following sentences best restates the essential information in highlighted sentence B in paragraph 2? Incorrect choices will change the meaning and omit important information.

a) By definition, a successful class is one which benefits both the students and the teacher.

b) A class in which the teacher does all the talking is far less beneficial for the students than one in which the teacher employs the Socratic method.

c) Students who understand the Socratic method are much smarter than those who don't.

d) It can be argued that a successful class starts with good students and a good teacher.

3 ➔ Marsupials are a distinct class of mammals in that they have a very short gestation period, between four to five weeks. As a result, they give birth prematurely. A joey, the name for a marsupial infant, is thus born in the fetal state. Once free of the womb, the joey crawls or wiggles helpless and blind, its long forearms designed to help it progress across its mother's fur until it finds its ways into the pouch. Because a joey cannot regulate its own body heat, it must rely on the heat inside its mother's pouch, a temperature that must remain between 30-32 Celsius in order for the joey to survive. Once inside the pouch, the joey finds a teat to which it attaches itself. Several months later, the joey will emerge from the pouch and begin the process of learning how to survive. Because female marsupials have such short gestation periods, they are at less risk of environmental dangers, such as being vulnerable to predators, plus in times of drought, their chances of survival increase inasmuch as they do not need to carry a still-growing fetus to term, as do placental mammals, such as humans.

4. Which of the following sentences best restates the essential information in highlighted sentence in paragraph 3? Incorrect choices will change the meaning and omit important information.

a) Owing to the fact that female marsupials have short gestation periods, they are more vulnerable to predator attack.

b) Because of a short gestation periods, a female marsupial has a better chance of survival unlike other placental mammals.

c) Since marsupials are vulnerable to attack and are at greater environmental risk from droughts, they must give birth quickly.

d) Environment factors have forced marsupials to develop ways of survival that put them at less risk.

4 ➔ What sets the aboriginal peoples of the Pacific Northwest apart from the rest of the indigenous peoples of North America is the totem pole. The making of a totem pole starts with a cedar tree, the height of which can range anywhere from ten to two-hundred feet. The branches of the tree are removed as is the bark. A carver, a highly respected member of the tribe, then sculpts faces into the pole. The faces are those animals the native people encounter on a daily basis, animals such as ravens, killer whales, eagles, bears, and salmon. Early Christian missionaries had assumed that totem poles were shamanistic symbols and were worshipped as such. However, anthropologists now know that totem poles carry no religious significance. Instead, each totem pole tells the story of the clan that erected it. Those stories might be the recounting of a great battle or a great hunt. Another misconception about the totem pole was that the stories were once thought to ascend in a vertical order with the most important character crowning the pole. **A** This, in turn, gave rise to the popular idiom, "The low man on the totem pole," namely, the person residing at the bottom of the hierarchy, such as a junior worker in an office who has little or no authority compared to those above. Research however, now indicates that the indigenous people place no value on how the brightly colored faces are arranged. The origin of the totem pole was once a mystery too. Some have hypothesized that the scarcity of old totem poles, those going back two or three centuries, suggested that the tradition of carving of totem poles started when the indigenous tribes of the Pacific Northwest acquired iron tools from Europeans. This notion too has been rejected. Anthropologists now believe that ancient totem poles are rare due to the climate of the Pacific Northwest. **B** This area, stretching from Vancouver, Canada north to Alaska, gets so much rain, the Pacific coast forest is considered a rainforest on par with the Amazon. With so much rain and snow, and because they are made of wood, most of the really old totem poles have simply rotted away. One particular kind of totem pole is the shame pole. These poles are erected as reminders to those who neglected to pay debts. The most famous shame pole depicts former Exxon CEO Lee Raymond. On this pole, Raymond's face is upside down, a constant reminder that Exxon never fully paid the debt the court says it still owes to clean up the oil spill caused by the super tanker, the Exxon Valdez, a catastrophic oil spill that destroyed the pristine Alaskan shoreline near the town of Valdez, Alaska.

5. Which of the following sentences best restates the essential information in highlighted sentence A in paragraph 4? Incorrect choices will change the meaning and omit important information.

a) An idiom that describes a low position in the social hierarchy had its origin with the totem pole.

b) A person of little or no authority will often be compared idiomatically to a junior office worker carved on the bottom of a totem pole.

c) The idiom "the low man on the totem pole" originated with the indigenous tribes of the Pacific Northwest as a means of describing a position of no authority in the social hierarchy.

d) A person with no authority will often think of totem poles when he or she uses the idiom "the low man on the totem pole."

6. Which of the following sentences best restates the essential information in highlighted sentence B in paragraph 4? Incorrect choices will change the meaning and omit important information.

a) The Pacific coast rainforest gets as much rain as the Amazon.

b) The Pacific coast is as big as the Amazon rainforest.

c) The Pacific coast rainforest, extending from Canada to Alaska, gets almost as much rainfall as does the Amazon.

d) The Amazon and the Pacific coast rainforest are the same size and get as much rain.

5 ➔ Nobody would disagree that violent video games are designed with killing in mind, just like no would disagree that problem-solution scenarios in which an anti-hero blasts his way to freedom reinforce detrimental behavior in adolescents. But wait just a minute here. Where are the parents is this equation? If such games are so perilous to the youth of our nation, then turn the darn things off and tell the kids to go bounce a ball. Blaming a video game for poisoning a kid's behavior is like saying guns kill people. Wrong. Guns don't kill people. People kill people. Likewise, video games don't make bad kids. Parents make bad kids. Period.

7. Which of the following sentences best restates the essential information in the highlighted sentence in paragraph 5? Incorrect choices will change the meaning and omit important information.

a) Everybody would agree that video games are about killing and that the actions of the anti-hero have a negative influence on young viewers.

b) Nobody would disagree that video games are about death and destruction and that children love to watch the behavior of heroes.

c) Adolescents prefer to watch violent video games, a fact nobody would disagree with.

d) Some would disagree that violent video games are designed with killing in mind and that heroes are a bad influence on adolescent viewers.

6 ➔ In AD 476, the Western Roman Empire, its territories controlled by corrupt and ineffective governors, fell to an invading army of Goths. This event was a turning point in world history, for it marks the end of classical antiquity and the beginning of the Early Middle Ages in Europe. The Early Middle Ages (circa 500 to 1000 AD) was a time of social and economic chaos. With the collapse of the Western Roman Empire, long distance trade was abandoned, for the trade routes built by Rome and secured by its once-powerful army were now under the control of varying Germanic tribes constantly at war with each other. The precipitous decline in trade directly affected manufacturing. Pottery, for example, was an industry that vanished almost overnight, as did the trade in luxury goods, such as silk and spices from the Far East and salt from Africa. With them went the merchant class, men whose money was the tax base upon which Rome had survived. The Early Middle Ages was in such turmoil that it is often referred to as the Dark Ages. The Roman Empire, which had been a stabilizing economic and cultural force for over five hundred years, had given way to a Europe in which anarchy reined supreme. Out of the chaos rose various Germanic tribes, one of which was the Franks, the ruler of which was Charles Martel, or Charles "The Hammer." Martel is credited with devising what today is known as the feudal system. In order to wage war and protect his ever-expanding empire, Martel needed to maintain a large standing army. That army was made up of heavily armored horseman called vassals. The vassals, who would later on be known as knights, swore allegiance to Martel. In return, Martel granted them large tracts of land called fiefs. The vassals then leased their land to peasant farmers. The peasants, little more than slaves, were heavily taxed for their work, the money going to Martel for the purpose of expanding the Frankish empire which, by the 800's, included most of western Europe and was under the control of Martel's grandson, Charlemagne. Charlemagne had by then established a central court in Aachen in present-day Germany. For protecting the Pope Leo III, he was crowned the Holy Roman Emperor, for Charlemagne's empire did indeed mirror that of ancient Rome's. With Charlemagne creating a stable social order, there was a renewed interest in writing, art, architecture, and the study of scripture. This period is known as the Carolingian Renaissance, a period many historians believe was the precursor to the European Renaissance, circa 1300 to 1600. When Charlemagne died in 814, he was succeeded by his son, Louis the Pius. Upon his death, his three sons divided the empire into three kingdoms, territories which would eventually evolve into present-day France, Germany and Italy.

A

B

C

8. Which of the following sentences best restates the essential information in highlighted sentence <u>A</u> in paragraph 6? Incorrect choices will change the meaning and omit important information.

a) In AD 476, the Western Roman Empire was invaded by an army of Goths, which supported Rome's corrupt and ineffective governors.

b) The territories of the Western Roman Empire had been, by AD 476, invaded and destroyed by an invading army of Goths, who replaced corrupt and ineffective governors.

c) In AD 476, the Western Roman Empire fell because its territories had no government.

d) The Western Roman Empire, unable to control its territories, was destroyed by an army of invaders in AD 476.

9. Which of the following sentences best restates the essential information in highlighted sentence <u>B</u> in paragraph 6? Incorrect choices will change the meaning and omit important information.

a) Europe, no longer under the Rome's supreme control, was finally stable both politically and culturally.

b) Europe fell into political lawlessness once Rome's influence was gone.

c) The collapse of the Roman Empire gave Europe supreme power.

d) In Europe, disorder and political unrest reined supreme for five hundred years under Roman economic and cultural control.

10. Which of the following sentences best restates the essential information in highlighted sentence <u>C</u> in paragraph 6? Incorrect choices will change the meaning and omit important information.

a) The taxes Martel forced from peasants helped him conquer western Europe, an empire eventually ruled by his son, Charlemagne.

b) By 800, most of the peasants of western Europe were under the control of Charlemagne and Martel.

c) For the purpose of expanding his empire, Martel forced peasants to pay taxes, money that eventually went to Martel's son, Charlemagne.

d) Martel taxed peasants in order to expand the Frankish Empire which, by 800, was ruled by Charlemagne, Martel's grandson.

➔ Answers: page 691.

8. Sentence-Insertion Questions

Each passage will have either one or no sentence-insertion question. For this question, you will insert a sentence into a paragraph. By doing so, you are developing the paragraph grammatically, topically and rhetorically. When the sentence is inserted in the right place, the paragraph will demonstrate coherence (OPDUL=**<u>C</u>**). Sentence-insertion questions are stated one way, for example:

9. Look at the four squares [■]. They indicate where the following sentence could be added to paragraph 4. Click on the square to insert the sentence into the passage.

insertion sentence

Witness England and Holland battling for control of present-day Manhattan in the early 1600's.

A nation like Spain preserved national power by accumulating as much gold as possible through strong exports, the limitation of imports, and a large, population of poorly paid workers. ■ To develop exports, companies were subsidized by the government which also wrote laws to limit imports. ■ By limiting imports, the gold used to pay for imports would stay in the country and create a greater money supply and more credit. ■ Moreover, nations were geared toward acquiring and maintaining gold at all costs, including warring with each other. ■ Adam Smith, however, argued that free trade benefitted all nations and that gold was not equal to wealth.

When you are ready to make a choice, click on <u>one</u> black square. For this example, square four is the correct insertion point, so you would click on it.

A nation like Spain preserved national power by accumulating as much gold as possible through strong exports, the limitation of imports, and a large, population of poorly paid workers. ■ To develop exports, companies were subsidized by the government which also wrote laws to limit imports. ■ By limiting imports, the gold used to pay for imports would stay in the country and create a greater money supply and more credit. ■ Moreover, nations were geared toward acquiring and maintaining gold at all costs, including warring with each other. ■ **Witness England and Holland battling for control of present-day Manhattan in the early 1600's.** Adam Smith, however, argued that free trade benefitted all nations and that gold was not equal to wealth.

On test day, when you click on a black square, the insertion sentence will not insert. The insertion sentence has been inserted above for demonstration purposes only.

a. Question Analysis

Begin by analyzing the insertion sentence. The insertion sentence is like a piece of a puzzle. The puzzle is the paragraph. You must figure out where the insertion sentence (the piece) fits into the paragraph (the puzzle). Start by dividing the insertion sentence into three sections: head / middle / end.

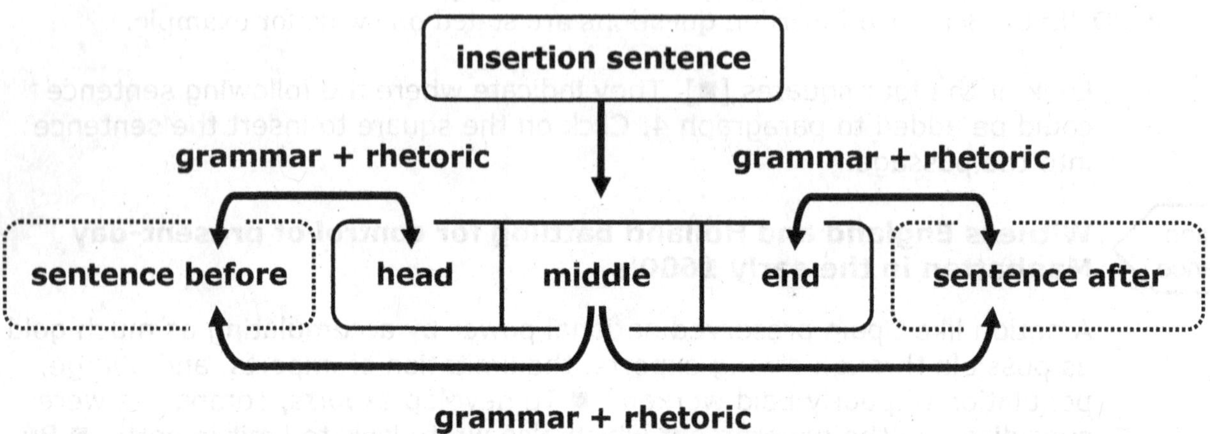

Each section of the insertion sentence will connect to the sentence before it and to the sentence after it, grammatically, topically and rhetorically. This task measures your ability to identify these integrated connections.

Analyzing the Insertion Sentence

When analyzing the insertion sentence, start at the head. The head will often contain a transitional signal word or phrase, such as Witness in the sample.

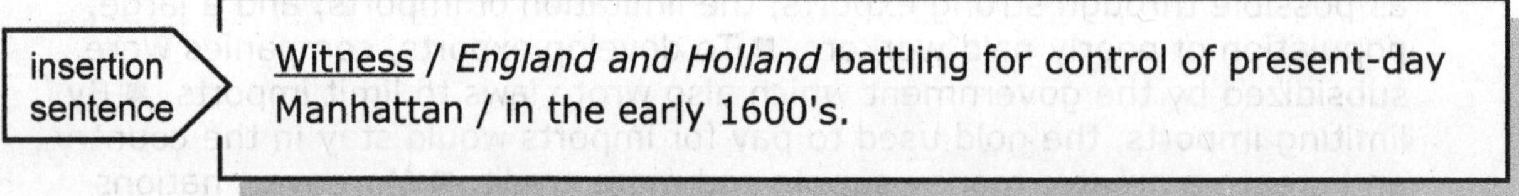

Witness, in this context, is a verb. It is also a synonym for the transitional phrase *for example*. Witness, therefore, grammatically signals the rhetorical purpose of the insertion sentence: to provide illustrations that will develop the general topic introduced *in the sentence before*. Those examples are *England and Holland*. They are the noun objects of the verb Witness. *England and Holland* refer back to the plural noun nations and to the pronoun phrase each other in the sentence before (see next page). Therefore, insertion point four is correct grammatically, topically and rhetorically. Because the insertion point is correct, the paragraph with the insertion points demonstrates coherence (OPDUL=**C**).

> A nation like Spain preserved national power by accumulating as much gold as possible through strong exports, the limitation of imports, and a large, population of poorly paid workers. ■ To develop exports, companies were subsidized by the government which also wrote laws to limit imports. ■ By limiting imports, the gold used to pay for imports would stay in the country and create a greater money supply and more credit. ■ Moreover, nations were geared toward acquiring and maintaining gold at all costs, including warring with each other. **Witness *England and Holland* battling for control of present-day Manhattan in the early 1600's.** Adam Smith, however, argued that free trade benefitted all nations and that gold was not equal to wealth.

Note that the prepositional end phrase, in the early 1600's, signals the end of the Mercantilist argument. The topic then changes in the last sentence. In the last sentence, the writer states Adam Smith's argument against Mercantilism. However grammatically signals the topical and rhetorical contrast between the Mercantilist argument and Smith's counter argument.

b. Choice Analysis: *Process of Elimination*

To confirm your choice, use process of elimination. Doing so will eliminate those insertion points that do not grammatically, topically and rhetorically connect to the insertion sentence.

The first insertion point (A) is not correct (see below. Note: For demonstration purposes, the black squares have been replaced by a corresponding letter).

If you insert the insertion sentence at (A), the paragraph will lack coherence. Why? Because the insertion sentence is developing the topics of *England and Holland*. However, *England and Holland* are not mentioned in sentence one. The topics of sentence one are Spain, exports and imports. Note in sentence two how the infinitive phrase To develop continues the topics of exports and imports. Therefore, sentence one and two cannot be separated because they are topically, grammatically and rhetorically connected, with sentence two giving an example of how exports were developed: they *were subsidized by the government*.

> 1) A nation like Spain preserved national power by accumulating as much gold as possible through strong exports, the limitation of imports, and a large population of poorly paid workers. **(A)** 2) To develop exports, companies *were subsidized by the government* which also wrote laws to limit imports.

The second insertion point (B) is also not correct. In sentence two, the topics of **exports** and **imports** are continued. Note at the head of sentence three the transitional phrase *By limiting imports*. This phrases refers to the topics of exports and imports in sentence one and two. It also signals a continuation of these topics in sentence three. In sentence two, note the **cause**-and-*effect* relationship: **To develop exports, companies were subsidized by the government which also wrote laws** *to limit imports*. The cause-and-effect result of import-limiting laws is described in sentence three: **By limiting imports, the gold used to pay for imports** *would stay in the country and create a greater money supply and more credit*. Therefore, sentences one, two and three cannot be separated because they are grammatically, topically and rhetorically connected.

> 1) A nation like Spain preserved national power by accumulating as much gold as possible through strong **exports**, the limitation of **imports**, and a large population of poorly paid workers. (A) 2) To develop **exports**, companies were subsidized by the government which also wrote laws to limit **imports**. **(B)** 3) By limiting **imports**, the gold used to pay for **imports** would stay in the country and create a greater money supply and more credit.

The third insertion point (C) is also not correct. The topic of gold in sentence three is continued in sentence four. Sentence four uses the rhetorical strategies of description and illustration to describe how the gold in sentence three was acquired: through warring. At the head of sentence four, note the transitional signal word Moreover. Moreover is a synonym for *In addition*. In this context, sentence four is adding more information to develop the topic of gold in sentence three. Therefore, grammatically, topically and rhetorically sentence three and four cannot be separated.

> 1) A nation like Spain preserved national power by accumulating as much gold as possible through strong exports, the limitation of imports, and a large, population of poorly paid workers. (A) 2) To develop exports, companies were subsidized by the government which also wrote laws to limit imports. (B) 3) By limiting imports, the **gold** used to pay for imports would stay in the country and create a greater money supply and more credit. **(C)** 4) Moreover, nations were geared toward acquiring and maintaining gold at all costs, including warring with each other. (D) **Witness *England and Holland* battling for control of present-day Manhattan in the early 1600's.** Adam Smith, however, argued that free trade benefitted all nations and that gold was not equal to wealth.

By process of elimination, the fourth insertion point (D) is correct.

c. Signal Words

When analyzing the insertion sentence, look for signal words at the head of the insertion sentence. Signal words at the head of the insertion sentence provide a good indication of where the insertion sentence can be inserted into the paragraph.

The following are transitional signal words often found at the head of the insertion sentence.

Addition	**Sequence**	**Restatement**	**Consequence**
Also,	After...	In other words,	As a result,
Additionally,	As soon as...	To clarify,	Accordingly,
Moreover,	At first,	In essence,	For this reason,
Furthermore,	At last...	Essentially,	For those reasons,
Further,	Finally,	To paraphrase,	Consequently,
For example,	Before long,	In brief,	Subsequently,
For instance,	In the first place,	In a nutshell,	Therefore,
To illustrate,	Meanwhile,	In other words,	Thereupon,
Besides that,	Next,	Basically,	Thus,
Likewise,	Soon after,	Simply put,	Hence,

Emphasis	**Contrast**	**Similarity**	**Conclusion**
Truly,	Yet,	Likewise,	In conclusion,
Indeed,	But,	Together with...	To conclude,
In fact,	However,	Coupled with...	In sum,
Again,	In contrast,	In the same way...	To sum up,
Of course,	Conversely,	In the same manner,	In the end,
Suffice it to say,	On the contrary,	In a like manner,	All in all,
In the same fashion,	On the one hand,	In the same fashion,	Finally,
Equally important...	Despite...	Similarly...	Lastly,
To repeat,	Even so,	Correspondingly,	In closing,
With this in mind,	Nevertheless,	Much like...	Naturally,

d. Signal Words: *Pronouns*

If the head of the insertion sentence has no signal words, look for pronoun signal words. In the following highlighted insertion sentence, It is a pronoun signal word at the head of the sentence. Note how It is followed by *is a process*.

> It *is a process* that begins with a set of initial conditions, called input, then provides an output, a result, based on a fixed set of rules or instructions.

The clause It *is a process* refers to a specific topic in the sentence before. But which topic and which sentence? Look at the paragraph below. Insertion point (A) looks correct. The word process in sentence one is topically connected to process in the insertion sentence. However, *do not be distracted by one word.* If you insert the insertion sentence at (A), the paragraph will lack coherence. Why? Because rhetorically, sentence one is a general definition that is defined and developed in sentence two. In other words, sentence one is a general statement and sentence two is a specific statement supporting sentence one. This topic progression is indicated by the transitional signal phrase More specifically at the head of sentence two. Therefore, sentence one and two cannot be separated because they are connected grammatically, topically and rhetorically.

> 1) An algorithm is a process that performs a series of operations aimed at solving a problem. **(A)** 2) More specifically, an algorithm has a starting point followed by a sequence of well-defined instructions terminating at an end point. **(B)** 3) Algorithms lie at the heart of computer software. **(C)** 4) Software, as you know, is basically a sequence of instructions aimed at carrying out a task. 5) That task is called a computation. **(D)** 6) A more common form of algorithm is a recipe for, oh, I don't know—let's say brownies. 7) The recipe tells you where to start, the steps to follow, and what the outcome will be. 8) An algorithm, however, cannot stop you from eating them all.

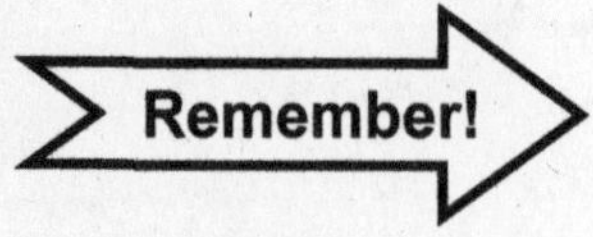

The rhetorical relationship between the insertion sentence and the sentence before often moves from general (sentence before) to specific (insertion sentence). Look for this relationship when identifying rhetorical and grammatical connections.

sentence before = general → **insertion sentence = specific**

The correct insertion point is (D). It, in the insertion sentence, refers to the noun computation. What is a computation? Answer: It *is a process*. Rhetorically, the insertion sentence defines computation (*It is a process...*), then describes that process (...*that begins with a set of initial conditions, called input, then provides an output, a result, based on a fixed set of rules or instructions*).

5) That task is called a computation. **(D) It *is a process* that begins with a set of initial conditions called input, then provides an output, a result, based on a fixed set of rules or instructions. 7)** A more common form of algorithm is a recipe for, oh, I don't know—let's say brownies. 8) The recipe tells you where to start, the steps to follow, and what the outcome will be. 9) An algorithm, however, cannot stop you from eating them all.

Note the adjective phrase based on a fixed set of rules or instructions at the end of the insertion sentence. Grammatically and topically, this adjective phrase refers to the noun recipe in the sentence after, sentence seven. A recipe is an algorithm. The example of "brownies" in sentence seven develops the general statement in the insertion sentence. This confirms that insertion point (D) is correct

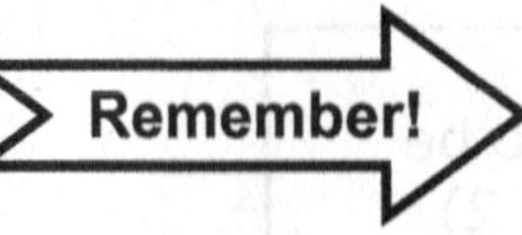

An example will not always begin with a signal phrase, such as "For example" or "Witness." To identify an example, you must first analyze the grammatical, topical and rhetorical function of the insertion sentence and the sentence before and the sentence after each insertion point.

e. Insertion Sentences: *No Signal Words*

Often the insertion sentence will have no signal words at the head, in the middle, or at the end, such as the example below. If the insertion sentence has no signal words, identify the rhetorical strategy. In this example, the rhetorical strategy is classification.

> Animal behavior can be classified according to the time of day an animal is active.

Next, determine if the insertion sentence is a general statement or a specific statement. The example above is a general statement. That suggests that this insertion sentence is either a topic sentence or a concluding sentence.

The insertion point for the insertion sentence is (A).

> **Animal behavior can be classified according to the time of day an animal is active.** Animals, such as horses, elephants and most birds, are said to be diurnal because they are active during the day and rest at night. ■ Those animals active at dawn and dusk are said to be crepuscular. ■ Beetles, skunks and rabbits fall into this category. ■ The third group are those animals that sleep during the day and are active at night. They are called nocturnal. A good example is the bat...

To confirm that (A) is the correct insertion point, analyze the first four sentences in the paragraph. Rhetorically and topically, the first four sentences are examples that support the general topic (animal classification) in the insertion sentence. The three supporting examples (diurnal, crepuscular, nocturnal) are explained and described. The result is a definition of each animal type. Combined, the first four sentences grammatically, topically and rhetorically support the general statement in the insertion sentence thus will come after it. Therefore, (A) is correct.

> **(A)** 1) Animals, such as horses, elephants and most birds, are said to be diurnal because they are active during the day and rest at night. **(B)** 2) Those animals active at dawn and dusk are said to be crepuscular. **(C)** 3) Beetles, skunks and rabbits fall into this category. **(D)** 4) The third group are those animals that sleep during the day and are active at night. 5) They are called nocturnal. 6) A good example is the bat. Bats have highly developed eyesight, hearing and smell. 7) This helps them avoid predators and locate food. 8) Being nocturnal also helps them avoid high temperatures during the day, especially in deserts where temperatures can reach well over one hundred degrees Fahrenheit. 9) There are two types of bat: micro bats, or true bats, and mega bats, also called fruit bats. 10) Let's start with mega bats.

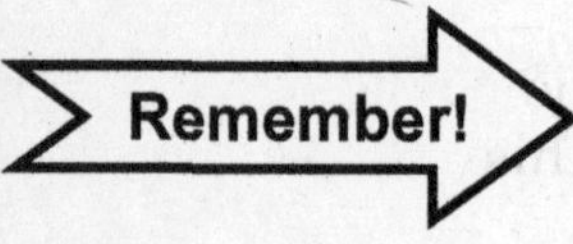

A topic sentence will not always begin with a transitional word or phrase, such as "First" or "Next" or "In addition." To identify a topic sentence, first analyze the grammatical, topical and rhetorical function of the insertion sentence and the sentence before and the sentence after each insertion point.

If, by your analysis, the insertion sentence is a general statement, but not the topic sentence, it might be a concluding sentence, such as the next example. Note that this highlighted insertion sentence has no signal words at the head, in the middle, or at the end.

> Darwin's theory revolutionized scientific thought, for according to Darwin, natural selection proved that divine creation played no part in the creation and evolution of organisms.

The insertion point for this insertion sentence is (D).

> **(A)** 1) Charles Darwin is famous for his groundbreaking book *On the Origin of Species* published in 1851. **(B)** 2) In it, *Darwin theorized that all organisms evolved through natural selection*. **(C)** 3) Natural selection, as defined by Darwin, is the process in which an organism inherits traits that make it more likely to survive and successfully reproduce, and thus become more common. 4) **(D)**

In the insertion sentence, the phrase Darwin's theory revolutionized scientific thought sounds like a general topic sentence. However, in sentence two, note how the prepositional phrase In it refers to *On the Origin of Species* in sentence one. Note also in sentence two how the book's theory is summarized (...*Darwin theorized that all organisms evolved through natural selection*). The topic of natural selection at the end of sentence two is the main topic in sentence three. Therefore, sentence one, two and three are grammatically, topically and rhetorically connected. By process of elimination, the correct insertion point is D or insertion point 4.

> ■ Charles Darwin is famous for his groundbreaking book *On the Origin of Species* published in 1851. ■ In it, *Darwin theorized that all organisms evolved through natural selection*. ■ Natural selection, as defined by Darwin, is the process in which an organism inherits traits that make it more likely to survive and successfully reproduce, and thus become more common. **Darwin's theory revolutionized scientific thought, for according to Darwin, natural selection proved that divine creation played no part in the creation and evolution of organisms.**

Practice: *Sentence-Insertion Questions*

Directions: You have ten minutes to read all the passages and answer the questions.

---

1. Look at the four squares [■]. They indicate where the sentence in bold could be added to the following paragraph. Click on the square to insert the sentence into the passage.

   The most common of these are aspirin and ibuprofen while capsaicin, the main capsaicinoid in chili peppers, is applied topically.

   Costal cartilage is the cartilage that connects the ribs to the sternum. The condition in which the costal cartilage between the ribs becomes inflamed is known as costochondritis. Strenuous exercise can bring it on and the pain can be quite intense. ■ However, even in the most extreme cases, costochondritis is considered benign. ■ Treatment usually consists of rest and analgesics. ■ If the pain is too great, then steroid injections, even surgery, are options. ■ Symptoms of costochondritis are quite similar to those indicative of heart attack. Therefore, medical attention should be sought if the pain persists.

2. Look at the four squares [■]. They indicate where the sentence in bold could be added to the following paragraph. Click on the square to insert the sentence into the passage.

   One of the most influential post-war art movements was that of pop art.

   ■ Flowering in mid 1950's Britain and late 1950's America, pop art was a reaction to the elitism of abstract expressionism. ■ Instead of employing paint on canvas, artists, such as Andy Warhol, instead found inspiration in popular images found in advertising, comic books and commercials products hence the name pop art. ■ In this way, pop art was a direct reflection of post-war America, one in which the mass production of consumer products and television advertising were dominant culture forces. ■

3. Look at the four squares [■]. They indicate where the sentence in bold could be added to the following paragraph. Click on the square to insert the sentence into the passage.

   The Iranian calendar today is based on Khayyám's measurements.

   Omar Khayyám, born in Persia in 1048 AD, was a polymath, a man whose genius ranged from astronomy to philosophy to poetry. Recognized as one of the greatest medieval mathematicians, Khayyám authored the *Treatise on Demonstration of Problems of Algebra.* ■ In it, Khayyám provides a geometric method for solving cubic equations. ■ Khayyám's contributions to algebra eventually found their way to Europe, as did the work of many other influential Persian mathematicians. ■ In astronomy, Khayyám measured a solar year and concluded that it was 365.2421 days. ■ Yet despite his scientific achievements, Omar Khayyám is most famous for his poetry, in particular his book of poems *The Rubáiyát of Omar Khayyám*. *The Rubáiyát* consists of about one thousand quatrains, a quatrain being a poem consisting of four lines or rubaais.

4. Look at the four squares [■]. They indicate where the sentence in bold could be added to the following paragraph. Click on the square to insert the sentence into the passage.

   Another striking feature of the electric eel is that, unlike other fish, it breathes air directly, surfacing every ten minutes or so to gulp down air, air which accounts for eighty percent of its oxygen requirement.

   The electric eel is an apex predator found in the Amazon and Orinoco Rivers of South America. Like its name says, it is indeed electric, dangerously so. The charge it produces can reach up to one amp at 800 volts, enough to incapacitate half a dozen people. Such a lethal evolutionary attribute is produced in body-length organs filled with cells called electroplaques. When the eel is resting, proteins force positively charged ions out of these cell. The electroplaque cells are then negatively charged. ■ When the eel needs to create an electric shock, it opens the cell walls and lets the positive ions rush back in thus creating a charge. ■ The electric eel, which is not a true eel but a knifefish—a species of fish with long thin bodies and no fins—employs the charge when hunting, for protection, and to attract a mate. ■ Why an electric eel doesn't shock itself remains a mystery. ■

5. Look at the four squares [■]. They indicate where the sentence in bold could be added to the following paragraph. Click on the square to insert the sentence into the passage.

Nowadays commercial producers rely on centrifugation to facilitate the separation process.

The process of making olive oil has changed little since olives were first used as a food source over six thousand years ago in the eastern Mediterranean. The process starts with picking the fruit, either by hand or by machine. To preserve freshness, the fruit is taken immediately to the processing facility. There, the fruit is cleaned with water while any remaining leaves and debris are removed. Next, the fruit is put into a mill which crushes the fruit into a paste. This is a critical step for it tears the flesh cells thus releasing the oil from the vacuoles. Malaxing, or mixing the paste, is next. This can last for up to forty-five minutes. This is another critical step, for it allows droplets of oil to form into larger ones. Heating can expedite the process however heating can reduce the quality of the oil. ■ Finally, the paste is pressed, a process in which the oil itself is separated from the pulp. ■ Traditionally, the paste was ground between two mill stones, a process that is commonly called the "first pressing" or "cold pressing." ■ These terms, however, are somewhat obsolete. ■

6. Look at the four squares [■]. They indicate where the sentence in bold could be added to the following paragraph. Click on the square to insert the sentence into the passage.

This process, one that gives the comet an atmosphere, is called sublimation.

A comet—a loose mixture of dust, ice, and rock particles—is distinct from a meteorite in that a comet is a small solar system body (neither a dwarf star nor a planet) whereas a meteorite is a piece of space debris that survives an impact with Earth. While falling to Earth, a meteorite will begin to heat up as it meets resistance from the atmosphere. That resistance is in the form of friction. The heat is so intense the meteorite turns into a fireball. When appearing in the night sky, meteors trail a long glowing trail thus they are called "falling stars" or "shooting stars." A comet also has a tail. Like a meteorite, a comet's tail is also due to heating. ■ When a comet passes close to the Sun, the area enveloping the comet, the coma, heats up. ■ Within the coma, solids turn to gas. ■ As the comet orbits the Sun, the sublimated particles trail behind the comet for a great distance. ■ Such a sight has, over the years, instilled fear, so much so that comets are traditionally seen as bad omens whereas the tradition is to make a wish when seeing a shooting star.

➔ Answers: page 691.

Read-to-Learn Questions

9. Prose-Summary Questions

Each passage will have one prose-summary question. This question type measures your ability to understand the passage as a whole and complete a summary of it. The summary will be a general outline of the passage's main ideas. The six answer choices will be a mix of main ideas, minor ideas, off-topic ideas, and ideas that are not accurate. To complete this task, you must identify the three correct main ideas. The other three choices are distractors. Prose-summary questions are stated one way, for example:

12. Directions: The sentence in bold is the first sentence of a brief summary of the passage. Complete the summary by selecting three answer choices. Your choices will express the most important ideas in the passage. Some choices are not in the passage or do not express important ideas. This is a 2-point question.

The passage discusses Adam Smith's book *The Wealth of Nations.*

•
•
•

Answer Choices

1. Smith's *The Wealth of Nations* represents the start of modern economic theory.
2. Smith illustrated how a factory worker wasted time when responsible for every step in the pin-making process.
3. Smith started to write *The Wealth of Nations* after he returned to Scotland from a long European trip.
4. Smith argued that to create national wealth, governments should subsidize companies.
5. Smith argued that Mercantilism was not a true wealth-building system.
6. Smith's theory of "the invisible hand" was influenced by the European Enlightenment.

a. Question Analysis

Before you begin, make sure you understand the question and the directions. In the directions below, the phrase brief summary means *general summary.* The phrase the most important ideas means *general statements*. The phrase not in the passage means *off topic* or *not accurate.* The phrase do not express important ideas means the phrases are *too specific.*

12. Directions: The sentence in bold is the first sentence of a brief summary of the passage. Complete the summary by selecting three answer choices. Your choices will express the most important ideas in the passage. Some choices are not in the passage or do not express important ideas. This is a 2-point question.

    Paraphrased, the directions read like this...

12. Directions: The sentence in bold is the first sentence of a general summary of the passage. Complete the summary by selecting three answer choices. The correct three choices will be general statements expressing the main ideas in the passage. Wrong choices will be off topic, not accurate or too specific.

For this task, the TOEFL iBT is once again recycling and testing your understanding of general vs. specific ideas. As you know from previous tasks, general statements are opinions, premises, topic sentences, and conclusions while specific statements are supporting illustrations. Apply your understanding of these rhetorical strategies when selecting answers for this task.

b. Main Topic and Controlling Idea

Next, analyze the bold sentence that follows the directions. The bold sentence is the first sentence of the brief summary. In the following sample, note that it is a general statement describing *the premise of the passage.*

The passage discusses Adam Smith's *book The Wealth of Nations.*

When analyzing the bold sentence, identify the main topic and the controlling idea. In the example above, the main topic is Adam Smith. To find the controlling idea, ask: What about him? Answer: His book *The Wealth of Nations.*

c. Answer-Choice Analysis

After you identify the main topic and the controlling idea in the bold sentence, analyze the six answer choices. To make a selection, move the cursor over the choice, click and hold the cursor over the text to select it, slide the selected text up beside a bullet point, then release it (see page 558 for more).

Q *Do I have to put the answers in the correct order, or any order?*

A *No. This is not an ordering question. You simply have to select three general statements that are topically related to the bold sentence.*

When analyzing each answer choice, ask two questions.

1) Is this choice a general statement or a specific statement? In the question below, choices 1, 5 and 6 are all general statements. Choices 2 and 3, in contrast, are specific statements.

2) Is this statement off-topic and/or inaccurate? In the question below, choice 4 is not accurate. It contradicts what is stated in the passage.

The passage discusses Adam Smith's book *The Wealth of Nations.*

- 1. Smith's *The Wealth of Nations* represents the start of modern economic theory.
- 5. Smith argued that Mercantilism was not a true wealth-building system.
- 6. Smith's theory of "the invisible hand" was influenced by the European Enlightenment.

Answer Choices

1. Smith's *The Wealth of Nations* represents the start of modern economic theory.

2. Smith illustrated how a factory worker wasted time when responsible for every step in the pin-making process.

3. Smith started to write *The Wealth of Nations* after he returned to Scotland from a long European trip.

4. Smith argued that to create national wealth, governments should subsidize companies.

5. Smith argued that Mercantilism was not a true wealth-building system.

6. Smith's theory of "the invisible hand" was influenced by the European Enlightenment.

The passage discusses Adam Smith's book *The Wealth of Nations.*

Answer Choices

general — 1. Smith's *The Wealth of Nations* represents the start of modern economic theory.

specific — 2. Smith illustrated how a factory worker wasted time when responsible for every step in the pin-making process.

specific — 3. Smith started to write *The Wealth of Nations* after he returned to Scotland from a long European trip.

4. Smith argued that to create national wealth, governments should subsidize companies. — not true

5. Smith argued that Mercantilism was not a true wealth-building system. — general

6. Smith's theory of "the invisible hand" was influenced by the European Enlightenment. — general

For this question, choices 1, 5 and 6 are correct.

Some choices will be very close. The difference is in the details. Also, you are not looking for perfect answers. You are looking for the best answers.

e. Process of Elimination

To confirm your choices, use process of elimination. Choices 2 and 3 above are too specific. Choice 2 describes a problem related to the pin-making process, a problem Smith identified. Choice 3 is a narrative detail describing when Smith started to write *The Wealth of Nations*. These choices are too specific thus not correct.

Choices 2 and 3 are distractors. The information is true according to the passage. However, that does not mean choices 2 and 3 are correct for this task. For this task, correct choices are true general statements. Do not be distracted by details even if they are true.

Choice 4 is not true. Adam Smith does not argue in favor of governments subsidizing companies. That is the Mercantilist argument. Choice 4 is not accurate because it is a contradiction therefore not correct.

f. Time-Saving Strategy

This question type is often the last question in each passage. At that point, you might be running out of time. If you are running out of time, use this strategy.

1. Do not reread the passage looking for general statements. By this point, you should already be familiar with the general topic of the passage.

2. Focus on the answer choices. Look for details in each choice. If you think a choice contains details, such as dates, names, or a step in a process, do not choose it. It is too specific. This will leave choices that are off topic and/or not accurate. Eliminate those choices. By doing so, you will end up with choices that are general statements. Select them.

3. Eliminate choices that are not topically related to each other or to the main topic and the controlling idea in the bold sentence. In the graphic below, choices 3, 5 and 6 are correct because they are true general statements, they are topically related to the bold sentence, and they are factually correct.

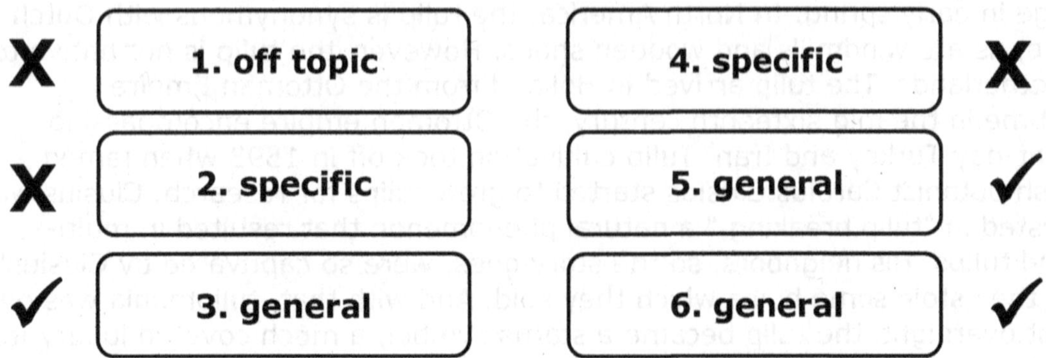

Practice: *Prose-Summary Questions*

Directions: You have ten minutes to read the passages and answer the questions.

Passage One: The Tulip Bubble

1 ➔ The seventeenth century is known as the Dutch Golden Age. During this period, the Dutch empire, centered in the port city of Amsterdam, stretched from Manhattan Island in North America to the spice islands in Southeast Asia. The engine that drove the Dutch empire was the Dutch East India Company, a company considered to be the world's first multi-national corporation. Funded by shareholders and the Bank of Amsterdam, the Dutch East India Company was, by 1640, the dominant force in the world economy. Ships arriving in Amsterdam were filled with exotic cargo, such as nutmeg, cinnamon, and pepper from the islands of Indonesia. They also carried silk, tea, and porcelain from China and beaver fur from Manhattan. Dutch merchants became fabulously wealthy. They had their portraits painted by Rembrandt and Vermeer, and sought ways to reinvest their money. One investment opportunity was in tulips.

2 ➔ The tulip is a flowering plant that grows from a bulb similar in appearance to an onion. In North America, tulips are one of the first flowering plants to emerge in early spring. In North America, the tulip is synonymous with Dutch culture, as are windmills and wooden shoes. However, the tulip is not native to the Netherlands. The tulip arrived in Holland from the Ottoman Empire sometime in the mid sixteenth century, the Ottoman empire encompassing present-day Turkey and Iran. Tulip cultivation took off in 1593 when famed Flemish botanist Carolus Clusius started to grow tulips for research. Clusius was interested in "tulip breaking," a natural phenomenon that resulted in multi-colored tulips. His neighbors, so the story goes, were so captivated by Clusius's tulips they stole some bulbs which they sold. And with that, tulipmania was on. Almost overnight, the tulip became a status symbol, a much coveted luxury item sought by rich and poor alike.

3 ➔ Dutch tulips were classified according to color. Solid reds, yellows, and white were called Couleren while multi-colored, striped tulips were called Rosen (red or pink vertical stripes on a white background), Violetten, (purple or lilac stripes on a white background), and Bizarden (red or purple stripes on a yellow background). Today, botanists know that tulip striping, the thing that made them so valuable in the early seventeenth century, is caused by a virus known as the tulip breaking virus. At the time, however, this fact was not known. What is known is that world's first economic bubble was created by the buying and selling of tulip bulbs.

4 ➔ Much like stocks on Wall Street today, tulips were traded with buyers hoping to turn around and sell their bulbs at much higher prices, prices that had nothing to do with reality. For example, for one tulip bulb, a man traded

twelve acres of land while another bought forty bulbs for 100,000 florins. At the time, a skilled laborer earned less than one-hundred-and-fifty florins a year. Perhaps the most outrageous trade was the man who traded for one bulb "a silver drinking cup, a suit of clothes, a complete bed, 1,000 pounds of cheese, two tons of butter, four tons of beer, two barrels of wine, twelve fat sheep, eight fat swine, four fat oxen, four lasts of rye, [and] four lasts of wheat." When the mania reached its peek in the winter of 1636, buyers were no longer willing to plant their bulbs come spring. They deemed it too risky. Instead, the trend was to have parties in which people viewed unplanted tulip bulbs arranged on tables.

5 ➔ In the winter of 1636, every Dutchman it seemed was trying to cash in on the tulip craze. The government could do nothing to stop it. Money kept pouring into the tulip market and prices kept going up with no one actually taking possession of the bulbs they had purchased. Moreover, the Dutch, like Americans and the 1929 stock market, were convinced that the good times were here to stay. By the winter of 1637, however, Dutch tulip traders could no longer find buyers willing to pay such exorbitant prices for their bulbs. Panic erupted when one buyer failed to show up to claim his purchase. Within days, prices plummeted. The tulip bubble had finally burst.

1. Directions: The sentence in bold is the first sentence of a brief summary of the passage. Complete the summary by selecting three answer choices. Your choices will express the most important ideas in the passage. Some choices are not in the passage or do not express important ideas. This is a 2-point question.

The passage discusses the Dutch tulip bubble.

-
-
-

Answer Choices

1. In the sixteenth century, tulips were classified by color: red, white, and yellow.
2. The Dutch mania for tulips started when bulbs from a botanist's garden were stolen then sold.
3. During the Dutch Golden Age, many exotic products were imported into Amsterdam, including spices and tulips.
4. The price for one tulip bulb was often more than a common man made in one year.
5. Speculators drove the price of tulip bulbs so high, the market finally collapsed due to a lack of buyers.
6. The Dutch East India company was a major investor in tulip bulbs.

➔ Answers: page 691. Scoring multi-answers: page 693.

Passage Two: ***The Women of Liberia Mass Action for Peace***

1 ➔ Of all the peace movements in recent years, one in particular stands out: *The Women of Liberia Mass Action for Peace*. In 2003, the movement, through non violent protest, ended the second Liberian civil war and ousted president Charles Taylor. Taylor, a warlord who had overthrown his predecessor, was accused of a plethora of crimes including crimes against humanity for the brutal repression of his fellow Liberians. Rebel groups, supported by neighboring Guinea and Côte d'Ivoire, attempted to overthrow Taylor. In early 2003, the rebels controlled most of the countryside and were laying siege to the capital of Monrovia. Taylor fought back with paramilitary units he called Small Boy Units. These units marked a new type of warfare. Instead of regular soldiers, Small Boy Units consisted of war-orphaned boys as young as eight. To entice boys to join his army, Taylor promised gifts and assault weapons. Taylor ordered his Small Boy Units to terrorize the civilian population using any means possible, including rape and torture. Small Boy Units were particularly savage. Because of their lack of maturity, the boys believed that they were invincible thus feared nothing as they terrorized the populace and battled the invading rebels. Peace conferences were held, but the fighting continued with civilians caught in the middle. By 2003, Liberia had been in a state of constant civil war for thirteen years. Finally, one woman said enough. That woman was Leymah Gbowee.

2 ➔ At the age of seventeen, Leymah Gbowee moved from central Liberia where she was born to the capital Monrovia. Trained as a trauma counselor, she helped child soldiers who had fought in Taylor's Small Boy Units. By doing so, Gbowee witnessed firsthand the physical and psychological damage Taylor had visited upon the people of Liberia. Determined to stop the war, Gbowee brought Christian and Muslims mothers together and formed *The Women of Liberia Mass Action for Peace*. United, the mothers of Liberia believed that "Regardless of whom you pray to, during war our experience as a community and as mothers [is] the same."

3 ➔ Dressed in white, the Christian and Muslim mothers staged daily, non violent protests in the fish market of the capital. With their numbers growing, the WLMAP forced Taylor to attend peace talks in neighboring Ghana. The talks were held in the presidential palace with Gbowee and a delegation from the WLMAP there to monitor the talks. The talks, however, broke down when the warring parties refused to negotiate. With the delegates threatening to leave, Gbowee and her delegation took action. They blocked the doors and windows of the presidential palace and would not let the delegates leave without a resolution. In the end, Taylor resigned as president of Liberia and found refuge in Nigeria. With Taylor's exit, Liberia's second civil war came to an end. Elections were held and Ellen Johnson Sirleaf was elected president thus making her the first female head of an African state. These changes would not have been possible if it were not for Leymah Gbowee and her determination to bring peace to Liberia.

4 ➔ The achievements of Leymah Gbowee and the WLMAP are documented in the movie *Pray the Devil Back to Hell* by Gini Reticker and Abigail E. Disney. To date, the film has won many awards while Leymah Gbowee herself has received many prestigious honors including the John F. Kennedy Profile in Courage Award. Leymah Gbowee continues to fight for peace and women's rights as the executive director of the Women Peace and Security Network, Africa (WIPSEN), an organization devoted to building relationships to support and promote women and youth throughout West Africa.

1. Directions: The sentence in bold is the first sentence of a brief summary of the passage. Complete the summary by selecting three answer choices. Your choices will express the most important ideas in the passage. Some choices are not in the passage or do not express important ideas. This is a 2-point question.

   The passage discusses the achievements Leymah Gbowee.

   •

   •

   •

Answer Choices

1. Leymah Gbowee protested against Liberia's second civil war by organizing peaceful demonstrations in which Christian and Muslim mothers united.
2. Leymah Gbowee helped child soldiers become responsible members of society once again.
3. She was trained a trauma counselor.
4. As a result of Leymah Gbowee's peace efforts, Liberia elected Africa's first female president.
5. Leymah Gbowee has received many awards including the Nobel Peace Prize.
6. Leymah Gbowee's actions at the Ghana peace conference helped end Liberia's second civil war.

➔ Answers: page 691.
➔ Scoring multi-answers: page 693.

Passage Three: *Knock-offs*

1 ➔ Today, we're going to look at another factor that can severely impact a company's bottomline. That issue is knock-offs. Essentially, a knock-off is a copy of an original, trademarked product or design illegally manufactured for sale and distribution. More importantly, in the U.S., a trademarked product is a government registered mark, a mark that gives a brand its unique identity. Copy that trademark—knock off some Nike Air-Maxs with the Nike symbol on them—and you're breaking the law.

2 ➔ A good place to find knock-offs is on Fifth Avenue. Why Fifth Avenue? Tourists. Many of them would love to buy something on Fifth Avenue but, let's face it, Fifth Avenue is not exactly Wal-Mart. Your average tourist is not about to shell out five-hundred bucks for a Dolce-and-Gabanna belt when just down the street, there's a tout selling a knock-off from a suitcase. The tourist, wanting a Dolce-and-Gabanna belt, sees the knock-off, and hey, the tourist isn't stupid. Who cares if it's fake? That belt looks real enough, especially the logo, you know, the brand mark. How much is the knock-off? Twenty bucks, if that? And the original? Five hundred? A thousand? And accessories are just the tip of the iceberg. Knock-offs are having the greatest impact on pharmaceuticals. In fact, today's Wall Street Journal has a front page story on it. According to the article, the U.S. population age 65 and older stands at 40 million or 2.9 percent of the current population. That's about one in every eight Americans. By 2030, that number will double to 80 million.

3 ➔ Why are these numbers significant? Because people over 65 need medication for everything from arthritis to cholesterol to cancer. A woman in the article is taking twenty different pills every day. So let's say you are that woman. You have a fixed monthly income of one-thousand dollars. Out of that thousand, you must pay for rent, bills and food. You're also taking a variety of medications, some of which cost a hundred bucks a pill. When you add it up, you can't afford such expensive medication. So what do you do? You look for cheaper alternatives and end up buying a knock-off. And what, you might ask, is the big deal, especially if those bogus pills are saving you—and thousands like you—money? The problem is there's no government oversight or quality control on the manufacturing side. As a result, a knock-off manufacturer can simply fill capsules with sugar, put a name like Pfizer on it, and customers think they're getting the real deal when in fact they're not.

4 ➔ So let's bring it full circle, shall we? How does all this impact the bottomline? First off, companies can lose the incentive to innovate. If I'm a drug company, let's say, and my products are continually being ripped off, what is the point in developing new products if I know that I will lose money in the long run? Also, the more my products are knocked off, the more consumers will begin to suspect my products. In other words, one bad apple can hurt the whole bunch. This, in turn, will result in a significant loss of brand equity. Also, if I manufacture drugs, I can lose significant market share to knock-offs that are chemically the same as the drugs I'm producing. The consumer is not stupid. Word gets around. They know what works and what doesn't. If a knock-off sells

for fifty bucks, and the original sells for two hundred—and it works, stops the pain—it's pretty obvious which one you're going to buy.

5 ➔ Are companies fighting back? Indeed, they are. A famous case is Tiffany versus eBay. Tiffany claimed that eBay was infringing upon Tiffany's trademark, the Tiffany name itself, by publishing advertising on eBay, advertising in which people were selling counterfeit Tiffany products via eBay. According to Tiffany, more than thirty percent of the so-called Tiffany jewelry on eBay is fake. The court, however, ruled against Tiffany saying that Tiffany, quote, "has the sole burden to police the improper use of its trademark." In other words, if someone is counterfeiting your products, it is your job to stop them.

1. Directions: The sentence in bold is the first sentence of a brief summary of the passage. Complete the summary by selecting three answer choices. Your choices will express the most important ideas in the passage. Some choices are not in the passage or do not express important ideas. This is a 2-point question.

   The passage discusses the effect knock-offs have on a company.

   •

   •

   •

Answer Choices

1. The incentive to innovate can be impacted severely.
2. Belts and other accessories are some of the most common knock-offs on eBay.
3. Market share can be greatly reduced.
4. A company's brands can lose their equity.
5. Americans over 65 will be forced to spend more money on cheaper drugs.
6. Pharmaceutical companies, such as Tiffany and Pfizer, are directly affected by counterfeit products.

➔ Answers: page 691.
➔ Scoring multi-answer questions: page 693.

10. Complete-a-Table Questions

Each passage will have one complete-a-table question. This question type measures your ability to identify details in the passage and connect them topically to a main topic heading.

Graphically, this task maps out as follows. You will be given two or three main topic headings. In this example, there are two main topic headings. Note that they are general topics.

The main topic headings will be followed by a list of topically-related choices. Note that the choices below are all *specific examples*.

apple
tomato
spinach
carrot
orange
kale
dill

From the choices, you will select those which are topically related to each main topic heading. Doing so completes the task.

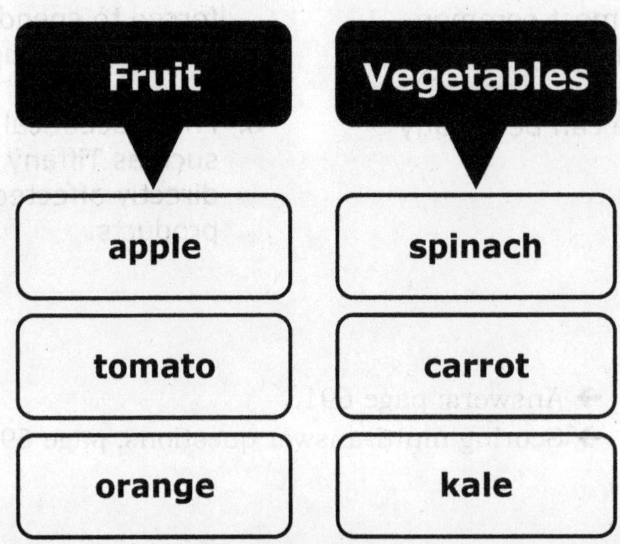

This question type is the opposite of a prose-summary question (page 643). For a prose-summary question, you must connect *general statements to general topic headings*. For this task, complete-a-table, you must topically connect *specific details to general topic headings*.

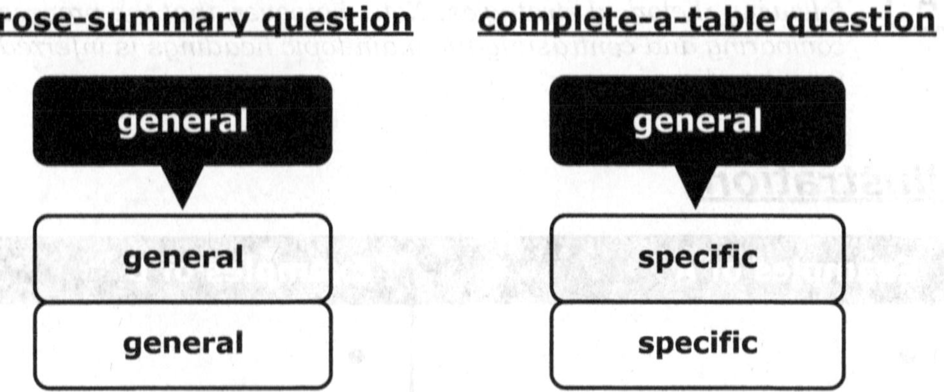

For this task, the TOEFL iBT is once again recycling and testing your understanding of general vs. specific ideas.

a. Question Analysis

Make sure you understand the question before you answer. Next, identify the rhetorical strategy in the question. In the sample below, the question is asking you to **compare-and-contrast** the details in Adam Smith's economic theories (argument) to the details in the Mercantilist argument.

14. Directions: Complete the following table by indicating **how** Adam Smith's economic theories in *The Wealth of Nations* **differed from** what the Mercantilists believed. This is a 4-point question.

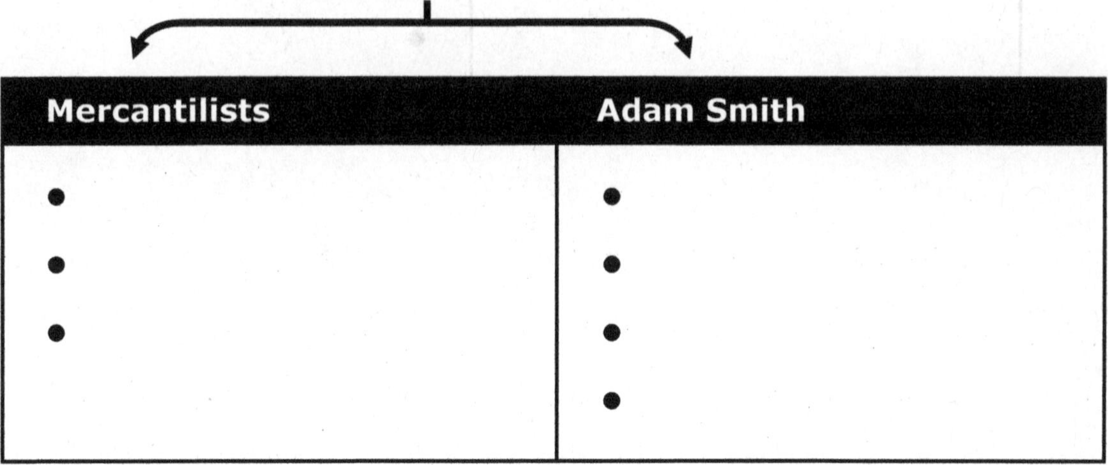

Q *Are all complete-a-table questions about comparing and contrasting the the main topic headings?*

A *The rhetorical strategy in the topic heading could be any of the following rhetorical strategies. Note, however, that the process of comparing and contrasting the main topic headings is inferred in all topic headings.*

Illustration

Examples of A	Examples of B
• • •	• • • •

Cause-and-Effect

Causes	Effects
• • •	• • • •

Pros and Cons

Pros	Cons
•	•
•	•
•	•
	•

Compare-and-Contrast

Topic A	Topic B	Topic C
•	•	•
•	•	•
	•	

Definition

Definition of A	Definition of B
•	•
•	•
•	•
	•

Process

Process A	Process B
• • •	• • • •

Description

Description of A	Description of B	Description of C
• •	• • •	• •

Q *Do I have to put the answers in the correct order, or any order?*

A *No. This is not an ordering question.*

b. Main Topic and Controlling Idea

In the sample question below, the main topic headings, the *Mercantilists* and *Adam Smith* are stated in the question and at the top of the answer box. To find the controlling idea, ask: What about them (the Mercantilists and Adam Smith)? Answer: How their economic theories differed (controlling idea).

14. Directions: Complete the following table by indicating how Adam Smith's economic *theories* in *The Wealth of Nations* differed from what the Mercantilists believed. This is a 4-point question.

Mercantilists	Adam Smith
•	•
•	•
•	•
	•

c. Answer Location

As you know, details are located in the body paragraphs. To locate details, first identify the signal words in the answer choice you are focusing on. For example, in sentence one, the signal word is gold. Next, scan the passage for the word gold and confirm whether sentence one is factually correct or not specific to each argument (Mercantilists vs. Smith). Repeat this process for all the choices. Note: Two answers will not be used.

1. Nations created wealth and power by amassing gold.
2. A satisfied work force will benefit a nation's economy as a whole.
3. Imports and exports should be manufactured by the government.
4. Exports made by poorly paid workers created national wealth.
5. National wealth starts with a rational approach to manufacturing.
6. Productivity will increase if the labor force is divided systematically.
7. War with other nations is part of national and economic policy.
8. Accumulating commodities does not create national wealth.
9. Free trade is an important part of military policy.

Because this is a detail question, you must spend more time locating specific answers. As you do, watch the clock. This question can eat up a lot of time. If you are running out of time, guess and move on. Never leave an answer blank.

d. Answer-Choice Analysis

For this question type, many test-takers choose the wrong answers because they did not spend enough time analyzing the answer choices. For example, sentence three is not a choice because it is not mentioned in the passage and because it is not accurate (neither Smith nor the Mercantilists supported this idea). Sentence nine sounds correct but it is factually wrong. Yes, according to the passage, military policy was part of Mercantilist economic theory however free trade was not.

1. Nations created wealth and power by amassing gold.
2. A satisfied work force will benefit a nation's economy as a whole.
3. *Imports and exports should be manufactured by the government.*
4. Exports made by poorly paid workers created national wealth.
5. National wealth starts with a rational approach to manufacturing.
6. Productivity will increase if the labor force is divided systematically.
7. War with other nations is part of national and economic policy.
8. Accumulating commodities does not create national wealth.
9. *Free trade is an important part of military policy.*

The correct answers are below.

Mercantilists	Adam Smith
• 1	• 2
• 4	• 5
• 7	• 6
	• 8

Because this is a detail question, you must spend more time locating specific answers. As you do, watch the clock. This question can eat up a lot of time. If you are running out of time, guess and move on. Never leave an answer blank.

Practice: *Complete-a-Table Questions*

Directions: You have twenty minutes to read the following passages and answer the questions.

Passage One: *Impressionists and Pre-Raphaelites*

1 ➔ The nineteenth century witnessed many art movements. However, one in particular tends to overshadow all the rest. That art movement is Impressionism, a school of painting that originated in France in the late 1860's.

2 ➔ The Impressionists were a radical group of painters who broke all the rules of academic painting. In Europe at the time, academic painters were traditionalists who gave the public what they wanted: great canvases that depicted heroic figures and ancient scenes painted with brushwork so fine some paintings looked more like photographs. The Impressionists, however, refuted such a conservative approach to painting. Instead of painting indoors, as did the academics, the Impressionists took their easels outside and painted "en plein air," in the open air. Instead of painting classical scenes which glorified a heroic past, the Impressionists painted scenes of every day life, such as sailboats on a river and bustling city streets. Instead of spending hours on one painting, the Impressionists strove to capture the moment with broken brush strokes using mixed and unmixed paint as a means of recreating the physical properties of light. Critics were outraged. This new style of painting was not painting in the formal, classical sense but were sketches and impressions. Hence the term impressionists.

3 ➔ Initially, the Impressionists and their revolutionary approach to painting was rejected by the French art world, a closed and cliquish world that was dictated by the tastes of the Académie des Beaux-Arts. The academy gave its stamp of approval to those artists it favored while rejecting those it deemed too radical. Those radicals were the Impressionists, men like Edouard Manet and his painting *Dejeuner sur l'herbe* (Luncheon on the Grass), a painting many critics believe represents the start of modernist painting yet at the time outraged the conventional art world. Undaunted, Manet and the Impressionists charted their own course and soon the art world realized that the work of Manet, Renoir, Monet and Degas, among others, was indeed making an impact, one that persists to this day. In fact, impressionist paintings are so ubiquitous, it would be easy to assume that it was the only art movement of any significance during the nineteenth century. Nothing could be further from the truth. Twenty miles across the English Channel, some twenty years before the Impressionists shook the French art world, the school of painting known as the Pre-Raphaelite Brotherhood was shaking the foundations of the British art world.

4 ➔ The Pre-Raphaelite Brotherhood was formed in 1848 by John Everett Millais, Dante Gabriel Rossetti, and William Holman Hunt. Like all great art movements, it rejected the old in favor of the new. In this light, the Pre-Raphaelite Brotherhood was similar to the Impressionists some twenty years later. However, where the Impressionists captured impressions outside in natural light, the Pre-Raphaelite Brotherhood drew inspiration from romantic poetry and medieval themes, and conveyed them on large canvases painted in studios. The subjects were bathed in a realistic light and were rendered with great attention to detail. This radical new approach to painting, one in which romanticism and naturalism merged, rejected the predominating Mannerist school in which the human form was exaggerated in settings that were both unreal and filled with hard, unnatural light.

5 ➔ Like the Impressionists, the Pre-Raphaelite Brotherhood outraged the art establishment with their radical new approach to painting. One painting in particular, *Christ in the House of His Parents* by John Millais, caused a firestorm of criticism. Critics, including Charles Dickens, claimed the painting was blasphemous. Worse, Dickens said Mary, the mother of Christ, was ugly when in fact Millais had based her on his sister-in-law, Mary Hodgkinson. The Pre-Raphaelite Brotherhood's love of medieval themes and details also drew sharp rebukes. Yet, like the Impressionists, the Pre-Raphaelite Brotherhood refused to be swayed by popular opinion. Today, paintings, such as Millais's *Ophelia*, Rossetti's *Beata Beatrix*, and Hunt's *Scapegoat* are acknowledged masterpieces. Moreover, the influence of the Pre-Raphaelite Brotherhood can be seen in the protean work of William Morris, a prolific artist and textile designer who founded the decorative art firm William, Marshall and Faulkner, a commercial art house that, in 1860, signaled the beginning of the decorative arts, a movement that spawned the Arts and Crafts movement and Art Nouveau, of which Louis Comfort Tiffany was a central figure.

1. Directions: Complete the table by indicating how the Impressionists' theory of art differed from the Pre-Raphaelite Brotherhood's theory of art. This is a 4-point question.

Impressionists	Pre-Raphaelite Brotherhood
•	•
•	•
•	•
•	

1. Painting outdoors was preferred to painting in a studio.
2. They found inspiration in romantic poetry and medieval themes.
3. They were influenced by Mannerism.
4. They captured the feeling of a scene rather than every detail.
5. They rejected the academic school of painting with its heroic themes.
6. They utilized big canvases.
7. They captured the physical properties of light in paint.
8. Naturalism was important even though they worked inside.
9. It was founded in 1838.

➔ Answers: page 692.
➔ Scoring multi-answer questions: page 693.

Passage Two: *Housing in the Middle Ages*

1 ➔ During the Middle Ages, peasant families lived in rural houses close to the fields in which they worked, land which was controlled by a lord in a castle. A typical peasant house, usually built by the family themselves, was a primitive shelter that provided little more than a place to eat and sleep. Construction materials included earth and wood for the walls and thatching for the roof. The most common rural structure was the longhouse or house-barn. Rectangular in shape, this dwelling had doors on opposite ends and on the sides thus ensuring cross ventilation. Inside, the floor plan was divided in half with one end forming the hearth, the place where the family prepared and ate their meals and slept. The opposite half was occupied by livestock, typically a cow for milk, chickens for meat and eggs, and a horse that pulled the plow. In winter, the heat rising off the animals kept the structure warm. Because there was no chimney, the interior was often smoky. The exit for the smoke was through holes at either end of the roof. Fire was a constant threat as was the risk of contracting diseases from living in such close proximity to animals.

2 ➔ Those with more money and social status, namely land-owning families, lived in houses separate from the livestock. The house consisted of two floors. The first floor was the hall, the place where the family ate and entertained around a central fireplace. For the landowner, the hall was of central importance for it was there that the landowner fed his family and his servants, the meals themselves a measure of the landowner's wealth and hospitality. Above the hall was a private family room called the solar. It consisted of beds and a fireplace for heating and was reached by a private staircase. On the ground floor off the hall were the buttery and the pantry. The pantry, a name still in use today, was a storage room for dry foodstuffs, such as flour and spices, while the buttery was cold storage for perishables, such as butter, cheese, and eggs.

3 ➔ Houses built in cities and towns, unlike rural houses, were built in rows and often shared the same walls. As a result, they occupied less horizontal space while raising vertically several floors. On the ground floor facing the street there was often a shop behind which were the living quarters. The kitchen too was located on the ground floor with a small light court separating it from the house.

This transitional space prevented odors and fire from spreading from the kitchen to the rest of the house. Because houses were built so close, and made of wood and thatch, they were highly combustible. During the Middle Ages, cities were often engulfed in flames, the source of which was often traceable to a kitchen fire. The city of London experienced two such conflagrations, the Great Fire of 1135 and the Great Fire of 1212.

4 ➔ At the top of the social ladder were the nobility. They resided in fortified residences called castles. Early castles were built of wood and earth, and evolved into massive stone edifices, many of which were surrounded by a water barrier called a moat. Castles were built in places of strategic importance, such as on a trade route or at the mouth of a harbor. Militarily, they provided protection from invaders and offered a base from which raids could be launched. Inside their high stone walls were stables, granaries, and workshops, all of which served the noble, his family, and his staff. The land surrounding the castle was farmed by peasants who, in times of trouble, sought the protection of the lord. In return, the peasants served as soldiers under the lord and paid for the use of his land through taxes and by sharing part of the harvest. Thus the castle also served as a center of administration.

2. Directions: Complete the table by matching the construction type to the house type. This is a 4-point question.

Peasant House	Land-Owner House
•	•
•	•
•	•
•	

1. shaped like a rectangle
2. had a storage room for dairy products
3. had a private second floor accessible by stairs
4. had granaries and workshops
5. humans and animals shared the one main room
6. four doors on the ground floor
7. had a great hall for eating and entertaining
8. no chimney
9. surrounded by a moat

➔ Answers: page 692.

➔ Scoring multi-answer questions: page 693.

Passage Three: ***The Panama Canal***

1 ➔ The Panama Canal is one the great engineering feats of the modern era. Stretching forty miles across the Isthmus of Panama, the canal connects the Atlantic Ocean to the east with the Pacific Ocean to the west. Before the canal opened in 1914, a ship sailing from New York to San Francisco south around South America had to travel fourteen-thousand miles. The Panama Canal cut that distance in half.

2 ➔ Connecting the Atlantic and the Pacific had been envisioned as early 1513. In September of that year, Spanish explorer and conquistador Vasco Núñez de Balboa was the first European to lay eyes on the Pacific Ocean after having crossed the Isthmus of Panama, home to one of the most inhospitable jungles on Earth. However, it wasn't until 1888 that the French, led by Ferdinand de Lesseps, began construction on the canal. By then, de Lesseps was famous the world over for building the Suez Canal, a waterway that connects the Mediterranean Ocean and the Red Sea. In 1856, de Lesseps, a diplomat by trade, was awarded the concession to build the Suez Canal from Said Pasha, the viceroy of Egypt. With that concession, de Lesseps started the Suez Canal Company. The indefatigable de Lesseps gathered a team of international engineers and employed thousands of workers. After ten years of digging, much of it done by forced labor, the Suez Canal opened on November 17, 1869 to much fanfare. With the completion of the Suez Canal, and the completion of the American transcontinental railroad six months earlier, the world could now be traversed without stopping. As for de Lesseps, the man who dug a canal through the desert, his popularity soared. In May 1879, when the Geographical Society in Paris voted to build a canal across the Isthmus of Panama, de Lesseps was chosen to lead the project.

3 ➔ From the outset, construction of the Panama Canal was plagued with problems. Malaria and yellow fever decimated the workers while landslides from torrential rains buried dredges and filled in land that had been excavated. To raise money for the failing project, de Lesseps encouraged the average Frenchman to do his patriotic duty and buy shares in the Panama Canal Company. Banking on his reputation as the man who had built the Suez Canal, de Lesseps raised the necessary capital. Yet scandal soon broke out. De Lesseps and a number of others had bribed journalists and politicians to lie about the failing canal. The value of the company's stock plummeted. Millions of people lost everything overnight. The Panama Canal Scandal, as it was called, marked the end of French construction on the canal, and the end for de Lesseps as a free-wheeling entrepreneur and canal builder. All told, with the canal unfinished, some 20,000 canal workers, the majority of whom had been recruited from islands in the Caribbean, had succumbed to disease and work-related accidents.

4 ➔ In 1904, the United States government under President Theodore Roosevelt, bought the Panama Canal Company from the French. At the time, Panama was Colombian territory. The Americans offered to buy Panama from Colombia but the government of Colombia steadfastly refused. Soon after,

Panamanian separatists revolted against Colombia. With the support of the American military, the Panamanians won their independence and the nation of Panama was formed. In return, Panama granted America the right to build a canal and administer it indefinitely. In August, 1914 the canal was finished two years ahead of schedule. Yet the world paid scant attention for all heads were turned toward Europe where World War One had started that very same month and year.

5 ➔ Despite the political controversy surrounding the Panama Canal even to this day, its construction is notable for many milestones. One was the eradication of yellow fever, a disease that had decimated the French workforce. Scientists identified the mosquito as the carrier of the disease thus living and working quarters were regularly fumigated. The result was a dramatic reduction in yellow fever and malaria deaths. Another milestone lies in the construction of the canal itself. It is the world's first all-electric installation. The raising and the lowering of the locks, and the trains that move ships into position, are all powered by electric motors designed and built by General Electric, a company started by Thomas Edison.

3. <u>Directions</u>: Complete the table by contrasting de Lesseps' building of the Suez Canal and the Panama Canal. This is a 4-point question.

Suez Canal	Panama Canal
•	•
•	•
•	•
•	

1. finished in 1914
2. took ten years to build
3. was unfinished
4. was started before Panama was independent
5. used forced labor
6. 20,000 workers died building it
7. connected the Mediterranean Ocean and the Red Sea
8. made de Lesseps famous
9. was designed by Thomas Edison

➔ Answers: page 692.

➔ Scoring multi-answer questions: page 693.

Reading Test

For this task, you will read three passages. After each, total your score and add it to page 681. When you are finished the test, calculate your reading test score. You have sixty minutes to read passage and answer the questions.

Passage One: *The American Bison*

1 ➔ The American bison or buffalo is the largest terrestrial animal in North America. They are endemic to the western Great Plains, a corridor of grassland stretching from the Canadian provinces of Manitoba, Saskatchewan and Alberta south through the American states of North Dakota and Montana down to Texas. Bison are herbivores with long shaggy coats. Cows are smaller than bulls, which can weigh up to 2,500 pounds. When the first white explorers came in contact with the bison, they reported herds so vast they stretched from one horizon to the next. Despite such numbers, the white man decimated the great bison herds, so much so that by the late nineteenth century, the American bison was almost extinct. The building of the railroad was a big reason for the slaughter. Hunters no longer had to ride horses to hunt buffalo. Instead, they shot buffalo by the thousands from train cars. The skins and meat were sold while the rest of the body was left to rot. Later the bones would be gathered and sent back east for fertilizer. The killing of the buffalo opened up land for settlers flooding in from the east. A photo taken in 1870 illustrates the destruction visited upon the buffalo. In the photo, a man stands on top of a mountain of buffalo skulls rising over fifty feet.

2 ➔ The near total slaughter of the American bison had the greatest impact on the indigenous tribes of the Great Plains. For millennia, these Native Americans depended upon the bison for literally everything. To say that the bison was a walking supermarket is no exaggeration. Tribes such as the Sioux, the Cheyenne and the Arikara hunted buffalo for meat which they ate raw, cooked, and preserved in a dried form called pemmican. The skin they turned into clothing and the sides of dwellings while the thick dense fur made ideal blankets for cold winter nights. The horns were used for drinking and for mixing paint, the hooves for glue, and the bones for tools and weapons. In short, the culture and survival of the plains Indian was based entirely upon the buffalo. One of the iconic figures of the American west is the plains Indian hunting buffalo from horseback.

3 ➔ ■ However, the horse was late in arriving on the North American continent. ■ Historically, the horse arrived with Spanish explorers, circa 1500. ■ The horse they brought was the barb horse, a native of North Africa and long domesticated by Berber tribesmen. ■ The name barb is a contraction of Barbary Coast, a term Europeans gave the northern coast of Africa which, at the time, was a haven for Barbary Pirates. It was this horse, the barb horse, which the Spanish explorers brought to North America. Over time, the barb horse escaped from the Spanish and was captured and tamed by the Indians. By doing so, the plains Indian

gained a new mode of transportation and an ideal platform from which to hunt the fast-moving buffalo.

4 ➔ Prior to 1500, the Indians of the Great Plains hunted buffalo on foot, a perilous endeavor that often resulted in the death of more than one hunter. The process began with the entire village heading out for the hunt. With a buffalo herd fast approaching—and here we are talking a million or more animals—the villagers would line up beside cairns, piles of rocks that had been erected by previous hunters going back to prehistoric times. The cairns acted as driving lanes that funneled the buffalo towards a cliff. The villagers lined up on both sides of the herd and, by waving blankets and skins, they would force the buffalo into a stampede. Unable to stop, the buffalo would be forced to jump off the cliff. This form of mass hunting is called a buffalo jump. Thousands of buffalo would die. Yet they would not go to waste, for the Indians made use of everything. The largest buffalo jump in North America is Ulm Pishkun Buffalo Jump, a national park near Great Falls, Montana. The cliff there is over a mile in length with bones at the base of the cliff compacted some thirteen feet deep. That is a lot of buffalo. But remember, at that time, between 900 and 1500 CE, buffalo herds were so large, it took days for them to pass one point. Those days are long gone; however, thanks to conservation efforts, the American bison has made a strong comeback and remains to this day an enduring symbol of the American west.

1. In paragraph 1, to what does they refer?

   a) bison
   b) first white explorers
   c) herbivores
   d) cow and bulls

2. The word extinct in paragraph 1 is closest in meaning to...

   a) ancient
   b) missing
   c) endangered
   d) gone

3. In paragraph 1, why does the author mention "a mountain of buffalo skulls"?

   a) to describe what life was like in America in 1870
   b) to illustrate how many buffalo had been killed by 1870
   c) to support the view that buffalo hunting was popular
   d) to explain how buffalo bones were turned into fertilizer

4. In paragraph 2, the word iconic is closest in meaning to...

   a) symbolic
   b) historic
   c) ironic
   d) specific

5. What is NOT TRUE about the American bison in paragraph 2?

   a) Indigenous tribes of the Great Plains hunted it for thousands of years.
   b) It was central to Indian culture and survival on the Great Plains.
   c) It supplied the plains Indian with almost all their needs.
   d) Cowboys are often pictured hunting it on horseback.

6. Look at the four squares [■]. They indicate where the following sentence could be added to paragraph 3. Click on the square to insert the sentence into the passage.

   The horse was indeed an integral part of plains Indian culture.

   ■ However, the horse was late in arriving on the North American continent. ■ Historically, the horse arrived with Spanish explorers, circa 1500. ■ The horse they brought was the barb horse, a native of North Africa and long domesticated by Berber tribesmen. ■ The name barb is a contraction of Barbary Coast, a term Europeans gave the northern coast of Africa which, at the time, was a haven for Barbary Pirates.

7. In paragraph 3, the word haven is closest in meaning to...

   a) place
   b) shelter
   c) state
   d) maven

8. In paragraph 3, what can we infer about the barb horse?

   a) It was used by pirates.
   b) The Spanish sold it to the plains Indians around 1500.
   c) The Spanish had domesticated it before 1500.
   d) The barb horse was fast.

9. In paragraph 4, what does the phrase perilous endeavor mean?

   a) necessary job
   b) dangerous task
   c) group effort
   d) ancient method

10. In paragraph 4, why does the author mention the buffalo jump?

    a) to illustrate how Indians hunted buffalo in the nineteenth century
    b) to classify hunting methods prior to 1870
    c) to illustrate how the plains Indians hunted buffalo prior to the horse
    d) to develop the topic of hunting on the Great Plains

11. In paragraph 4, why does the author mention cairns?

    a) to illustrate that a buffalo jump was a dangerous form of hunting
    b) to compare how different Indians hunted buffalo on the Great Plains
    c) to demonstrate the process of building a buffalo jump circa 1500
    d) to illustrate that the same hunting site was used for thousands of years

12. Which of the following sentences best restates the essential information in the highlighted sentence in paragraph 4? Incorrect choices will change the meaning and omit important information.

    a) Rock markers lined roads on which the buffalo traveled to a cliff.
    b) Rock markers acted as guides between which the buffalo were directed toward a cliff.
    c) Piles of rock marked the edge of the cliff where the buffalo jumped.
    d) Rock piles shaped like funnels were positioned on the edge of a cliff.

13. Directions: The sentence in bold is the first sentence of a brief summary of the passage. Complete the summary by selecting three answer choices. Your choices will express the most important ideas in the passage. Some choices are not in the passage or do not express important ideas. This is a 2-point question.

The passage discusses the American bison.

-
-
-

Answer Choices

1. It is native to the western Great Plains of North America.
2. It was hunted to extinction.
3. It played a central role in plains Indian culture.
4. It has thick hair, weighs almost a ton, and can run very fast.
5. It was nearly wiped out by hunters in the nineteenth century.
6. The Spanish used its bones for fertilizer.

➔ Answers: page 692. ➔ Scoring multi-answer questions: page 693.

Passage Two - *Charles and Ray Eames*

1 ➔ The motto of the husband and wife design team of Charles and Ray Eames was "the most of the best for the greatest number of people for the least." This philosophy is best represented in their form-fitting chairs.

2 ➔ Prior to World War II, the Eames were rethinking furniture design with the aim of building furniture that was affordable, comfortable, and could be mass produced. The fruition of that idea was the Eames Lounge Chair Wood. It was made of plywood, thin layers of wood that are glued together against the grain for extra strength. The Eames molded the plywood using techniques they themselves developed. The chair won the Museum of Modern Art's Organic Furniture Competition in 1940. However, production difficulties and the start of World War II delayed production. The delay was fortuitous for the Eames for it turned their attention to making molded wooden leg splints for the military, an idea they applied to the lounge chair. The result was a stylish, simple-to-make, form-fitting chair with complex curves that formed around the back and under the knees with the seat and back joined by a flexible lumbar support making the chair one of the first with a flexible backrest. In the world of furniture and industrial design, the Eames Lounge Chair Wood was a revolution, so much so that it was called "the chair of the century." Its simplicity of design and construction stood in stark contrast to furniture of the day, which was heavy and complex to make.

3 ➔ Today, the Eames Lounge Chair Wood is highly prized by collectors and remains an icon of modern design, as are many other Eames designs, such as the 1956 Lounge Chair and Ottoman, another example of the Eames belief in form and function. The Eames also designed one-piece plastic chairs, fiberglass chairs, and wire-mesh chairs, as well as space-saving storage units that could be assembled quickly at home. The Eames' creations were mass produced thus in the Eames' furniture, we witness the merging of artistic design and mass production, a hallmark of post-war America consumerism. In fact, what you are sitting on now—be it a computer chair, a fiberglass seat in a McDonald's, or a metal-framed fabric chair in an airport—is a direct descendant of the Eames Lounge Chair Wood. Walk around stores like IKEA and the Pottery Barn, and you will experience firsthand the enduring influence of the Eames' pioneering furniture designs.

4 ➔ Furniture design, however, was but one facet of the Eames' genius. They also designed textiles, buildings, toys, and made over one hundred short films on topics ranging from Franklin and Jefferson to explaining mathematical concepts, such as how computers work. ■ They are also credited with creating one of the first multi-screen films, *Glimpses of the USA*. ■ The film was commissioned by the U.S. Information agency for a 1959 exhibition in Moscow, an exhibition that showcased American progress at the height of the Cold War. ■ The film, employing seven screens, is a day-in-the-life of America with an emphasis on the power and scope of American capitalism. ■

5 → The Eames are also renowned for designing groundbreaking exhibitions, the most important of which was *Mathematica: A World of Numbers and beyond...* In 1961, The California Museum of Science and Industry in Los Angeles opened and invited companies to present exhibitions. One company was IBM. At the time, IBM was on the cutting edge of computer science, a science based on mathematics. IBM commissioned the Eames to design an interactive exhibition that would explain the history and the science of mathematics in a way that the layman would understand. Like all the Eames' work, the exhibition was infused with a whimsy and a playfulness that transformed the complex into something accessible to all. *Mathematica: A World of Numbers and beyond...* is considered a work of art in its own right, one that remains the model upon which all interactive science exhibitions are based.

6 → Later in life when Charles Eames was asked to explain his design philosophy, he used what he called the banana leaf parable. In southern India, the broad flat banana leaf is used as a base for food, much like a plate or dish. According to Charles Eames, the banana leaf is the foundation from which ideas grow. In other words, when designing, the Eames always imagined the banana leaf, a natural design that is simple, functional and affordable. Any ideas that developed from the banana leaf, the original basic idea, had to reflect the simplicity, the functionality, and the affordability of the banana leaf itself. The genius of Charles and Ray Eames' work is a testament to the banana leaf parable.

fortuitous: lucky
splint: a brace or support

1. In paragraph 1, the word motto is closest in meaning to...

a) main topic
b) guiding principle
c) basic rule
d) important message

2. In paragraph 2, fruition is closest in meaning to...

a) realization
b) frustration
c) disappointment
d) conclusion

3. In paragraph 2, why was the Eames Lounge Chair Wood called "the chair of the century"?

a) because it was the best chair at the time
b) because it was the first chair designed by a husband and wife team
c) because it sold the most at the time
d) because it was the most influential furniture design at the time

4. In paragraph 3, all of the following are true EXCEPT...

   a) The Eames designed space-saving storage units.
   b) The Eames designed wire-mesh chairs.
   c) The Eames often worked alone.
   d) The Eames' influence can been seen in IKEA, McDonalds, and airports.

5. In paragraph 4, why does the author introduce the topic of the Cold War?

   a) to establish the political context in which the Eames' film *Glimpses of America* was shown to a Russian audience
   b) to remind us that America and Russia were quite different at the time
   c) to illustrate how art was not influenced by the politics of the time
   d) to describe the effects the Eames' film had on audiences

6. Look at the four squares [■]. They indicate where the following sentence could be added to paragraph 4. Click on the square to insert the sentence into the passage.

   People in Moscow, it was reported, lined up for blocks and were brought to tears by what they saw flashing by on the screens.

   They also designed textiles, buildings, toys, and made over one hundred short films with topics ranging from Franklin and Jefferson to explaining mathematical concepts, such as how computers work. ■ They are also credited with creating one the first multi-screen films, *Glimpses of the USA*. ■ The film was commissioned by the U.S. Information agency for a 1959 exhibition in Moscow, an exhibition that showcased American progress at the height of the Cold War. ■ The film, employing seven screens, is a day-in-the-life of America with an emphasis on the power and scope of American capitalism. ■

7. In paragraph 5, what does the phrase groundbreaking mean?

   a) innovative
   b) exciting
   c) dangerous
   d) affordable

8. In paragraph 5, upon which refers to...

   a) a work of art
   b) one
   c) *Mathematica: A World of Numbers and beyond...*
   d) the model

9. Which of the following sentences best restates the essential information in the highlighted sentence in paragraph 5? Incorrect choices will change the meaning and omit important information.

   a) The exhibition was easy to understand because the Eames used fantasy and humor in order to teach difficult subjects in a simple way.
   b) The exhibition combined complex science and humor to explain how to use the latest technology.
   c) The exhibition was easy to comprehend because the Eames simplified complex information so that people could play with computers.
   d) The Eames understood the importance of complex information and how to play with it.

10. In paragraph 5, layman is closest in meaning to...

   a) audience
   b) scientists
   c) average man
   d) families

11. In paragraph 6, what does parable mean?

   a) a personal philosophy
   b) a belief shared by many
   c) a brief story with a lesson
   d) a religious book

12. What can we infer from the passage?

   a) Everyone bought the Eames' designs.
   b) The Eames were the most important artists in post-war America.
   c) The Eames' design influence is still widely felt today.
   d) Charles and Ray Eames were happily married.

13. Directions: Complete the following table by illustrating Charles and Ray Eames' achievements in furniture design and other media. This is a 4-point question.

Furniture Design	Other Media
•	•
•	•
•	•
•	

1. toys
2. molded plywood chairs
3. short films
4. fiberglass chairs
5. one-piece plastic chairs
6. computer games
7. plywood lounge chairs
8. exhibitions
9. painting

➔ Answers: page 692.

➔ Scoring multi-answer questions: page 693.

Passage Three: *Plant Defense Mechanisms*

1 ➔ During the Ordovician Period some four-hundred-and-fifty million years ago, land plants evolved from aquatic plants. Once on land, plants had to adapt or die. One adaptation was a protective coating to reduce the damage to tissues due to evaporation. Another was seeds that could survive dry conditions. Such defense mechanisms ensured plant survival and diversification. With such adaptation, plants were able to flourish. Yet with the proliferation of plants came a sudden increase in plant-eating insects. As a result, plants had to develop defense mechanisms against herbivory while insects, in order to survive, had to develop ways to defeat plant defense mechanisms. This process of reciprocal evolutionary change, in which life forms influence each other's development, is called co-evolution. Co-evolution is generally regarded as having led to the creation of much of the Earth's biomass.

2 ➔ The defense mechanisms plants employ against herbivores and other potential threats, such as fungus and bacteria, are either constitutive or induced. Constitutive defense mechanisms are those defenses which a plant has developed over time. For example, to prevent deer from eating it, the raspberry plant has long stems which are covered with sharp thorns while fruit trees produce gummosis, a sticky, sap-like material that traps insects. One plant, the voodoo lily, protects itself by smelling like rotting flesh. This unusual defense mechanism keeps herbivores away while attracting carrion-eating insects that pollinate the lily thus ensuring its survival.

3 ➔ Another form of constitutive defense occurs at the molecular level. These are toxins which the plant produces. If ingested, the results can be fatal. One of the more famous examples is the Greek philosopher Socrates. Accused of corrupting the youth of Athens, Socrates was condemned to death by drinking poison hemlock. Its cousin, water hemlock, is considered the most toxic plant in North America. Many common vegetables and fruits are also poisonous. The potato, for example, is a member of the deadly nightshade family. The stems and leaves of the potato plant contain a glycoalkaloid poison, a toxin that manifests itself as a green color in old potatoes or potatoes exposed to prolonged periods of light.

4 ➔ In contrast, induced defense mechanisms are those which a plant develops and sends to the part of it which has been injured. Such mechanisms occur at the molecular level and are produced by the plant only when needed. For example, in an article by T. R. Green and C. A. Ryan, when a potato plant is attacked by the Colorado potato beetle, the action will induce in the potato plant the production of a proteinase inhibitor which targets those parts of the potato plant that are exposed to air due to wounding. Proteinase inhibitors are enzymes that break down protein left behind at the wound by the potato beetle thus preventing infection. Another induced defense mechanism occurs when an herbivore eats part of a plant. ■ This, in turn, induces the release and activation of a cyanogenic glycoside, a poison common in the leaves of many popular fruit and nut trees, such as the cherry, the almond, the peach, and the apple. ■ In an

herbivore, these can cause extreme salivation, gastroenteritis, and diarrhea. ■ An herbivore, having been afflicted this way, will think twice the next time it approaches a tree or plant with such a defense mechanism. ■

5 ➔ Plants can also defend themselves from herbivores by changing shape. This induced mechanism is called thigmonasty. Mimos pudica, commonly known as the shy plant, is a salient example of such behavior. When touched or shaken, the leaves of the shy plant fold inward and the plant itself droops. Scientists speculate that this induced movement can shake off harmful insects or frighten away other herbivores. Another explanation is that by folding up and drooping, the shy plant is pretending to be dead thus presenting itself as unappetizing.

<u>reciprocal</u>: mutual exchange

1. In paragraph 1, flourish is closest in meaning to...

   a) thrive
   b) reproduce
   c) flounder
   d) vanish

2. In paragraph 1, what does herbivory mean?

   a) feeding on seeds
   b) feeding on biomass
   c) feeding on insects
   d) feeding on plants

3. What constitutive defense mechanisms does the author compare and contrast in paragraph 2?

   a) raspberry gummosis, fruit tree thorns, voodoo lily smell
   b) raspberry stems, fruit tree fungus, voodoo lily bacteria
   c) voodoo lily smell, raspberry thorns, fruit tree traps
   d) raspberry thorns, fruit tree gummosis, voodoo lily smell

4. In paragraph 3, why does the author use the example of Socrates?

   a) to show how the early Greeks used plant medicine
   b) to illustrate the effects of poison hemlock
   c) to add to the classification of dangerous plants
   d) to warn that hemlock can be fatal if ingested

5. In paragraph 3, manifests is closest in meaning to...

   a) manipulates
   b) multiplies
   c) reveals
   d) reviles

6. In paragraph 4, to what does which refer?

   a) potato plant
   b) proteinase inhibitor
   c) production
   d) Colorado potato beetle

7. In paragraph 4, all of the following are true EXCEPT...

   a) proteinase inhibitors are enzymes
   b) the potato plant uses proteinase inhibitors as a defense mechanism
   c) proteinase inhibitors target exposed areas resulting from herbivory
   d) proteinase inhibitors are constitutive defense mechanisms

8. Look at the four squares [■]. They indicate where the following sentence could be added to paragraph 4. Click on the square to insert the sentence into the passage.

   By chewing a leaf, for example, enzymes in the herbivore's saliva break down the cell membranes.

   Another induced defense mechanism occurs when an herbivore eats part of a plant. ■ This, in turn, releases and induces the activation of cyanogenic glycosides, a poison common in the leaves of many popular fruit and nut trees, such as the cherry, the almond, the peach, and the apple. ■ In the herbivore, these can cause extreme salivation, gastroenteritis, and diarrhea. ■ An herbivore, having been afflicted this way, will think twice next time it approaches a tree or plant with such a defense mechanism. ■

9. In paragraph 4, afflicted is closest in meaning to...

   a) harmed
   b) depicted
   c) warned
   d) taught

10. In paragraph 4, why does the author mention gastroenteritis?

    a) to give an example of an effect resulting from consuming leaves containing cyanogenic glycoside
    b) to give an example of an effect resulting from consuming leaves containing proteinase inhibitors
    c) to provide another a reason for supporting the argument that cyanogenic glycosides are the most effective form of induced plant defense mechanism
    d) to illustrate an effect resulting from consuming leaves containing toxins

11. From the passage, it can be inferred that...
    a) Through co-evolution, plants have developed many ways to defend themselves against herbivory.
    b) Scientists have been able to identify how plants defend themselves from environmental factors.
    c) By successfully defending against herbivory, plants one day will no longer be threatened by herbivores, such as deer and insects.
    d) The evolutionary process of plants is little understood by scientists.

12. Which of the following sentences best restates the essential information in the highlighted sentence in paragraph 5? Incorrect choices will change the meaning and omit important information.
    a) The shy plant protects itself by convincing herbivores that it is not alive thus probably wouldn't taste very good.
    b) By drooping over and folding up, the shy plant dies thus herbivores will have no appetite for it.
    c) Herbivores are less interested in eating dead plants than living plants.
    d) The reason why the shy plant pretends to be dead is because it cannot protect itself from herbivores.

13. Directions: The sentence in bold is the first sentence of a brief summary of the passage. Complete the summary by selecting three answer choices. Your choices will express the most important ideas in the passage. Some choices are not in the passage or do not express important ideas. This is a 2-point question.

The passage discusses plant defenses.

-
-
-

Answer Choices

1. Plant defenses are a result of co-evolution.
2. Plant defenses are either constitutive or induced.
3. Thigmonasty is an induced plant defense characteristic of the potato plant.
4. Toxic defense mechanisms in plants are always fatal.
5. Herbivory is the science of plant defense mechanisms.
6. Plant defense mechanisms evolved when land plants evolved from water plants.

14. Directions: Complete the following table by indicating which plant defense mechanisms are induced and which are constitutive. This is a 4-point question.

Induced	Constitutive
•	•
•	•
•	•
	•

1. cyanogenic glycoside
2. gummosis
3. glycoalkaloid poison
4. thigmonasty
5. foul odor
6. thorns
7. nightshade
8. proteinase inhibitors
9. glucose enzymes

➔ Answers: page 693.

➔ Scoring multi-answer questions: page 693.

Calculate Your Reading Test Score

Passage #1 = / 14

Passage #2 = / 16

Passage #3 = / 18

Total = / 48

Convert your test score to a section score below. Record your section score on page 707.

Test Score	Section Score	Test Score	Section Score
48 →	30	28	18
47	29	27	17
46	28	26	17
45	28	25	16
44	27	24	15
43	27	23	14
42	26	22	14
41	26	21	13
40	25	20	12
39	25	19	12
38	24	18	11
37	24	17	11
36	23	16	10
35	22	15	10
34	21	14	9
33	21	13	8
32	20	12	7
31	20	11	6
30	19	10	6
29	19		

Answer Key

Page	Task	?#	Answer	Distractor
399	Office-Hours	1	D	B
	Sample	2	B	A
		3	B,C	A
		4	C	A
		5	C	B
417	Content Questions	1	B	C
		2	D	A
		3	C	A
		4	D	B
420	Purpose Questions	1	C	A
		2	C	D
		3	D	C
		4	B	D
423	Single-Answer	1	C	D
	Detail Questions	2	B	A
		3	A	B
		4	D	B
		5	C	B
		6	B	D
426	Multi-Answer	1	A,D,E	B
	Detail Questions	2	C,D	A
		3	A,D,E	C
		4	B,C	D
437	Question-First	1	D	B
	Function Questions	2	C	D
		3	B	D
		4	B	D
438	Segment-First	1	B	A
	Function Questions	2	B	C
		3	D	A
		4	A	C

Page	Task	?#	Answer	Distractor
441	Direct-Attitude	1	C	B
	Questions	2	A	D
		3	C	D
		4	D	B
444	Inferred-Attitude	1	B	C
	Questions	2	D	C
		3	D	A
		4	C	B
447	Inferred-Action	1	A	C
	Questions	2	B	A
		3	B	C
		4	D	A
449	**Service-Encounter**	1	B	A
	Sample	2	C	D
		3	A,C,D	B
		4	D	B
		5	B	A
462	Content Questions	1	A	B
		2	A	C
		3	C	A
		4	C	D
463	Purpose Questions	1	D	B
		2	B	C
		3	D	A
		4	D	A
464	Single-Answer	1	B	A
	Detail Questions	2	C	A
		3	A	C
		4	C	B
		5	D	A
		6	C	A
465	Multi-Answer	1	B,C	D
	Detail Questions	2	A,D	B
		3	C,D	A
		4	A,C	D

Page	Task	?#	Answer	Distractor
466	Question-First	1	D	C
	Function Questions	2	D	A
		3	D	A
		4	B	C
467	Segment-First	1	B	A
	Function Questions	2	B	C
		3	A	B
		4	B	A
468	Direct-Attitude	1	C	A
	Questions	2	A	D
		3	D	C
		4	C	D
469	Inferred-Attitude	1	D	B
	Questions	2	C	A
		3	C	D
		4	C	B
470	Inferred-Action	1	B	C
	Questions	2	A	C
		3	C	B
		4	D	A
472	**Professor-Lecture**	1	D	A
	Sample	2	B	A
		3	A,C,E	B
		4	A	B
		5	1.C 2.A 3.D 4.B	
		6	Y,N,Y,N,Y	
483	Content Questions	1	C	D
		2	B	D
		3	A	D
		4	C	D
484	Purpose Questions	1	D	A
		2	C	A
		3	C	A
		4	C	B

Page	Task	?#	Answer	Distractor
485	Single-Answer	1	A	C
	Detail Questions	2	D	A
		3	C	B
		4	C	D
		5	D	A
		6	B	D
486	Multi-Answer	1	A,C,E	B
	Detail Questions	2	B,C,D	E
		3	B,C,D	A
		4	B,D	C
487	Question-First	1	D	B
	Function Question	2	B	D
		3	C	B
		4	A	B
		5	D	A
		6	B	D
		7	D	B
		8	A	C
489	Segment-First	1	C	A
	Function Question	2	D	C
		3	C	B
		4	A	C
490	Direct-Attitude	1	B	C
	Questions	2	C	D
		3	D	C
		4	B	D
491	Inferred-Attitude	1	D	B
	Questions	2	A	C
		3	A	D
		4	D	B
492	Inferred-Action	1	C	B
	Questions	2	C	B
		3	C	B
		4	C	B

Page	Task	?#	Answer	Distractor
493	Ordering Questions	1	1.A 2.D 3.B 4.C	
		2	1.C 2.D 3.B 4.A	
		3	1.D 2.B 3.C 4.A	
		4	1.C 2.A 3.B 4.D	
495	Yes-No Questions	1	N,Y,N,Y,N	
		2	Y,Y,N,N,Y	
		3	Y,Y,Y,N,Y	
		4	Y,Y,N,N,N	
499	Connecting Questions	1	C. Teutoburg Forest = Varus	
			B. Marathon = Darius	
			A. Waterloo = Napoleon	
		2	B. willow bark = aches-pains	
			C. milk thistle = liver health	
			A. aloe vera = burns-wounds	
		3	A. cytoplasmic... = contains genome	
			C. exterior = flagella for motion	
			B. envelope = protective filter	
		4	B. fry = six months old	
			A. alevin = lives off yolk sack	
			C. smolt = mature in Pacific	
502	**Professor-Students**	1	C	A
		2	B	A
		3	B	A
		4	A,C,E	D
		5	1.C 2.D 3.B 4.A	
		6	N,N,Y,Y,Y	
517	Practice #1: Discussion	1	D	A
		2	B	A
		3	A	B
		4	1.D 2.C 3.A 4.B	
		5	V,TH,V,TH,V	
		6	A	C

Page	Task	?#	Answer	Distractor
520	Practice #2: Discussion	1	D	C
		2	B	A
		3	C	A
		4	C	D
		5	C,O,C,O,C	
		6	C	A
522	**Listening Test**			
523	Task #1	1	A	B
		2	C	D
		3	C	A
		4	A,C,E	B
		5	B	C
		6	Y,Y,N,N,Y	
526	Task #2	1	D	C
		2	D	A
		3	C	A
		4	A,D,E	B
		5	B	D
528	Task #3	1	B	D
		2	D	C
		3	C	D
		4	B	A
		5	1.C 2.B 3.A 4.D	
		6	B,C,A	
531	Task #4	1	C	A
		2	A,B,C	D
		3	D	C
		4	B	A
		5	1.D 2.A 3.C 4.B	
		6	B,A,C	
534	Task #5	1	C	D
		2	B	D
		3	D	A
		4	A	C
		5	B	C
		6	N,N,Y,Y,Y	

Page	Task	?#	Answer	Distractor
537	Task #6	1	B	D
		2	D	B
		3	B,C,E	D
		4	A	D
		5	B	D
539	**READING SECTION**			
543	Sample	1	B	D
	Adam Smith and The	2	C	D
	Wealth of Nations	3	C	
		4	D	A
		5	B	C
		6	D	B
		7	A	B
		8	D	C
		9	square 4	
		10	B	D
		11	D	C
		12	1, 5, 6	
		13	A	D
		14	Mercantilists = 1,4,7	
			Adam Smith = 2,5,6,8	
567	Practice #1	1	C	D
	Factual Information	2	D	A
	Questions	3	A	B
	Penicillin	4	A	B
		5	B	D
		6	B	D
		7	D	B
		8	B	A
570	Practice #2	1	D	A
	Factual Information	2	C	D
	Questions	3	D	B
	Biological Classification	4	A	B
		5	D	B
		6	B	C
		7	D	B
		8	B	A
		9	D	A

Page	Task	?#	Answer	Distractor
580	Practice #1	1	B	C
	Vocabulary Questions	2	C	A
	Flooding	3	C	D
		4	B	C
		5	A	C
		6	D	C
		7	B	A
		8	B	D
		9	C	D
		10	B	D
		11	D	A
583	Practice #2	1	D	A
	Vocabulary Questions	2	B	A
	Wernher Von Braun	3	A	B
		4	A	B
		5	A	D
		6	D	C
		7	C	D
		8	D	C
		9	A	C
		10	C	B
		11	B	C
588	Practice #1	1	C	
	Negative Factual Info	2	C	
	Questions	3	A	
	Women of Influence	4	C	
		5	B	
		6	C	
591	Practice #2	1	D	
	Negative Factual Info	2	B	
	Questions	3	D	
	Methods of Research	4	D	
		5	B	
596	Practice #1	1	C	A
	Inference Questions	2	C	B
	Crypsis	3	D	A
		4	C	A
		5	C	A

Page	Task	?#	Answer	Distractor
598	Practice #2	1	C	D
	Inference Questions	2	B	C
	A Landmark Ruling	3	B	A
		4	D	B
		5	B	C
		6	C	D
604	Practice #1	1	A	B
	Rhetorical Purpose	2	D	A
	Cognitive Bias	3	B	C
		4	D	A
		5	A	B
		6	D	A
		7	A	C
		8	B	C
		9	A	D
607	Practice #2	1	C	A
	Rhetorical Purpose	2	B	A
	The Gilded Age	3	B	D
		4	B	A
		5	D	C
		6	C	A
		7	A	B
615	Practice	1	C	B
	Reference Questions	2	B	C
		3	D	C
		4	A	B
		5	B	C
		6	A	B
		7	D	B
		8	B	C
		9	A	D
		10	C	A
621	Practice #1	1	C	
	Sentence Simplification	2	I	
	Fill-in-the-blank	3	I	
		4	I	
		5	I	
		6	I	

Page	Task	?#	Answer	Distractor
	Sentence Simplification	7	C	
	Fill-in-the-blank	8	C	
		9	I	
		10	C	
		11	C	
		12	I	
624	Practice #2	1	C	A
	Sentence Simplification	2	D	C
		3	B	A
		4	B	C
		5	A	C
		6	A	D
		7	A	B
		8	D	C
		9	B	C
		10	D	A
640	Practice	1	3	
	Sentence-Insertion	2	1	
	Questions	3	4	
		4	4	
		5	4	
		6	3	
649	Practice: Passage One	1	2,4,5	1 specific
	Prose-Summary			3 not true
	The Tulip Bubble			6 unknown
651	Passage Two	1	1,4,6	2 specific
	Women of Liberia...			3 specific
				5 not true
653	Passage Three	1	1,3,4	2 unknown
	Knock-Offs			5 unknown
				6 not true

Page	Task	?#	Answer	Distractor
662	Practice: Passage One	1	Impressionists 1,4,5,7	3 not true
	Complete-a-Table		Pre-Raphaelites 2,6,8	9 not true
	Impressionists...			
664	Passage Two	1	Peasant House 1,5,6,8	4 = castle
	Housing...		Land-Owner House 2,3,7	9 = castle
666	Passage Three	1	Suez Canal 2,5,7,8	1 not true
	Panama Canal		Panama Canal 3,4,6	9 not true
667	**READING TEST**			
668	Passage 1	1	B	A
	The American Bison	2	D	C
		3	B	C
		4	A	C
		5	D	
		6	1	
		7	B	D
		8	C	B
		9	B	C
		10	C	D
		11	D	C
		12	B	C
		13	1,3,5	2 not true
				4 specific
				6 unknown
672	Passage 2	1	B	D
	Charles and Ray Eames	2	A	B
		3	D	A
		4	C	
		5	A	C
		6	4	
		7	A	B
		8	D	A
		9	A	B
		10	C	A
		11	C	A
		12	C	B
		13	Furniture Design 2,4,5,7	6 unknown
			Other Media 1,3,8	9 unknown

Page	Task	?#	Answer	Distractor
677	Passage 3	1	A	B
	Plant Defenses...	2	D	C
		3	D	C
		4	B	D
		5	C	A
		6	B	A
		7	D	
		8	1	
		9	A	B
		10	A	D
		11	A	C
		12	A	C
		13	1,2,6	3,4,5 not true
		14	Induced 1,4,8	7 plant type
			Constitutive 2,3,5,6	9 unknown

Scoring Multi-Answer Questions

Using the following guide when scoring multi-answer questions.

<u>1-point question</u> = 2 ✓ = 1 point
1 ✓ = 0 points

<u>2-point question</u> = 3 ✓ = 2 points
2 ✓ = 1 point
1 ✓ = 0 points

<u>2-point question</u> = 4 ✓ = 2 points
3 ✓ = 1 point
2 ✓ = 0 points
1 ✓ = 0 points

<u>3-point question</u> = 5 ✓ = 3 points
4 ✓ = 2 points
3 ✓ = 1 point
2 ✓ = 0 points
1 ✓ = 0 points

<u>4-point question</u> = 7 ✓ = 4 points
6 ✓ = 3 points
5 ✓ = 2 points
4 ✓ = 1 points
3 ✓ = 0 point
2 ✓ = 0 points
1 ✓ = 0 points

Independent Essay Proficiency Checklist

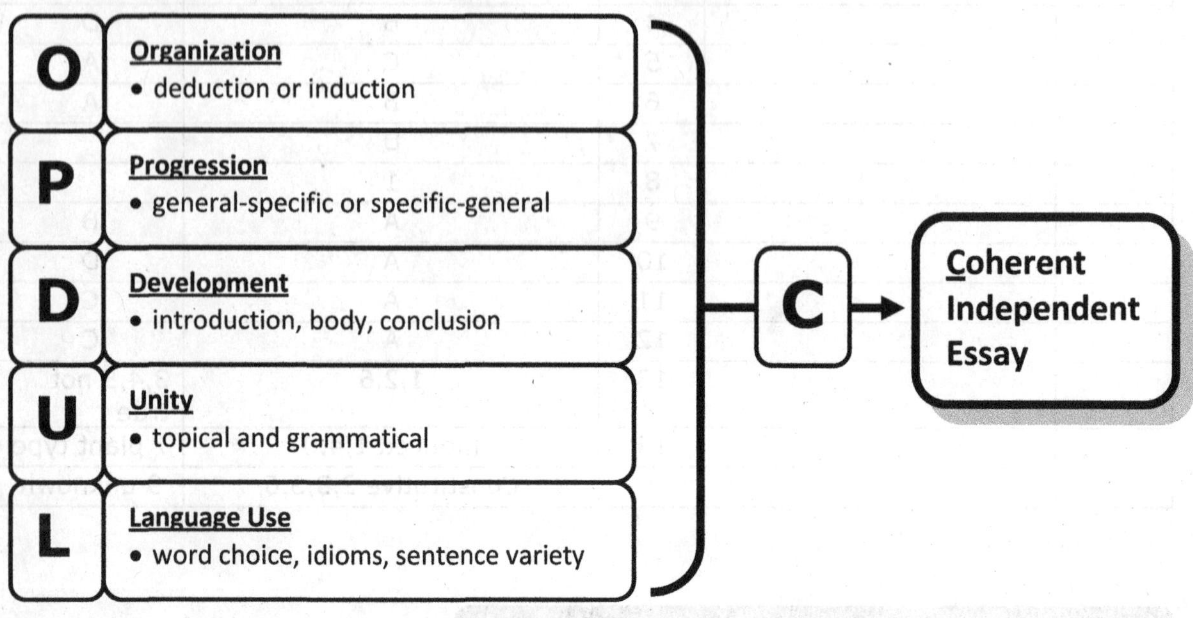

Checklist

1. Does my essay demonstrate organization?
   - Deduction Yes __ No __
   - Induction Yes __ No __
2. Does my essay demonstrate progression?
   - General-specific Yes __ No __
   - Specific-general Yes __ No __
3. Does my essay demonstrate development?
   - Introduction Yes __ No __
   - Body Yes __ No __
   - Conclusion Yes __ No __
4. Does my essay demonstrate unity?
   - Topical Yes __ No __
   - Grammatical Yes __ No __
5. Does my essay demonstrate proficient language use?
   - Word choice Yes __ No __
   - Idioms Yes __ No __
   - Sentence variety Yes __ No __
6. Does my essay demonstrate coherence?

   Yes __ No __

Independent Essay Rating Guide

Task Rating: 4.0 - 5.0

An essay in this range is Coherent because it generally demonstrates proficiency in **all** of the following areas.

O The essay demonstrates a clear and consistent method of organization.

P The essay demonstrates a clear and consistent progression of ideas.

D The essay demonstrates development of the introduction, body and conclusion; the supporting illustrations are clear and well developed; some areas might lack development and/or an idea might not be completely explained.

U The essay demonstrates topical and grammatical unity; some topical and/or grammatical connections might not be clear or accurate. These errors are minor and do not affect meaning or coherence.

L The essay demonstrates consistent language use; some word choice and/or idiom usage might not be clear or accurate, and/or there might be syntax errors. These errors are minor and do not affect meaning or coherence.

Task Rating: 2.5 - 3.5

An essay in this range demonstrates a lack of proficiency in **one or more** of the following areas.

O The essay demonstrates organization; however, it might not always be clear or consistent.

P The essay demonstrates a progression of ideas; however, it might not always be clear or consistent.

D The essay demonstrates development; however, the introduction, body and/or conclusion might lack development, and/or might not provide enough supporting examples or be sufficiently explained.

U The essay demonstrates topical and grammatical unity; however, there might be topical digressions and/or connections that are not always clear or accurate.

L The essay demonstrates basic but accurate language use with limited sentence variety; inaccurate word choice and/or idiom usage, and/or syntax errors might make the meaning of some sentences unclear.

Task Rating: 1.0 - 2.0

An essay in this range demonstrates a serious lack of proficiency in **one or more** areas:

O The essay demonstrates a serious lack of organization.

P The essay demonstrates a serious lack of progression.

D The essay demonstrates a serious lack of development in all areas.

U The essay demonstrates a serious lack of topical and grammatical unity.

L The essay demonstrates a serious lack of language use in all areas.

Notes

Integrated Essay Proficiency Checklist

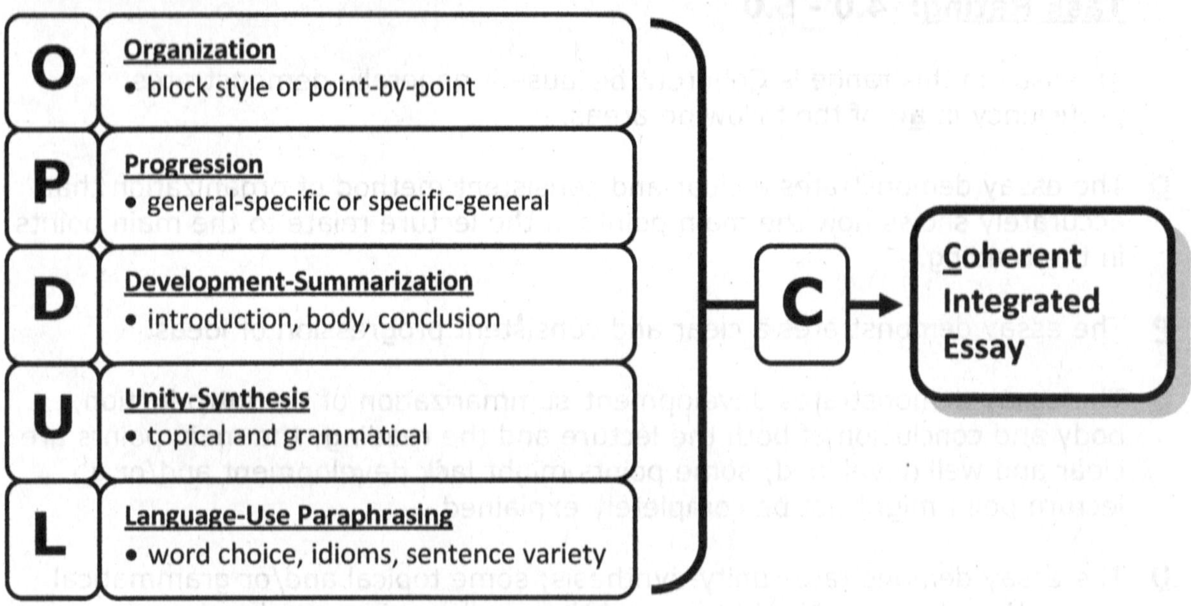

Checklist

1. Does my essay demonstrate organization?

- Block style Yes __ No __
- Point-by-point Yes __ No __

2. Does my essay demonstrate progression?

- General-specific Yes __ No __
- Specific-general Yes __ No __

3. Does my essay demonstrate development-summarization?

- Introduction Yes __ No __
- Body Yes __ No __
- Conclusion Yes __ No __

4. Does my essay demonstrate unity-synthesis?

- Topical Yes __ No __
- Grammatical Yes __ No __

5. Does my essay demonstrate proficient language-use paraphrasing?

- Word choice Yes __ No __
- Idioms Yes __ No __
- Sentence variety Yes __ No __

6. Does my essay demonstrate coherence?

Yes __ No __

Integrated Essay Rating Guide

Task Rating: 4.0 - 5.0

An essay in this range is Coherent because it generally demonstrates proficiency in **all** of the following areas.

O The essay demonstrates a clear and consistent method of organization that accurately shows how the main points in the lecture relate to the main points in the reading.

P The essay demonstrates a clear and consistent progression of ideas.

D The essay demonstrates development-summarization of the introduction, body and conclusion of both the lecture and the reading; the main points are clear and well developed; some points might lack development and/or a lecture point might not be completely explained.

U The essay demonstrates unity-synthesis; some topical and/or grammatical connections between the lecture and the reading might not be clear or accurate. These errors are minor and do not affect meaning or coherence.

L The essay demonstrates consistent and accurate language-use paraphrasing; some word choice and/or idiom usage might not be accurate or clear, and/or there might be syntax errors. These errors are minor and do not affect meaning or the connection of the main points.

Task Rating: 2.5 - 3.5

An essay in this range demonstrates a lack of proficiency in **one or more** of the following areas.

O The essay demonstrates organization; however, the connection between the main points in the lecture and the main points in the reading is not always clear or consistent.

P The essay demonstrates a progression of ideas; however, it might not always be clear or consistent.

D The essay demonstrates development-summarization; however, the main points in the introduction, body and/or conclusion of the lecture and/or the reading might lack development, and/or a main point in the lecture might be missing.

U The essay demonstrates topical and grammatical unity; however, the connection between the main lecture and reading points is not always clear or accurate.

L The essay demonstrates basic language-use paraphrasing with limited sentence variety; frequent and inaccurate word choice and/or idiom usage, and/or errors in syntax make the meaning of some sentences and connections unclear.

Task Rating: 1.0 - 2.0

An essay in this range demonstrates a serious lack of proficiency in **one or more** of the following areas.

O The essay demonstrates a serious lack of organization; the connection between the main points in the lecture and the main points in the reading is not clear or accurate.

P The essay demonstrates a serious lack of progression.

D The essay demonstrates a serious lack of development-summarization in the introduction, body and conclusion of the lecture and the reading; some points have been summarized; however, most lecture points are missing, and/or the summarization of the lecture and/or the reading is not clear or accurate.

U The essay demonstrates a serious lack of topical and grammatical unity; the main points in the lecture and the reading are not topically related and/or the connections between points is not accurate or clear.

L The essay demonstrates a serious lack of language-use paraphrasing; frequent errors in basic word choice and/or syntax make the meaning of sentences unclear.

Notes

Independent Speaking Proficiency Checklist

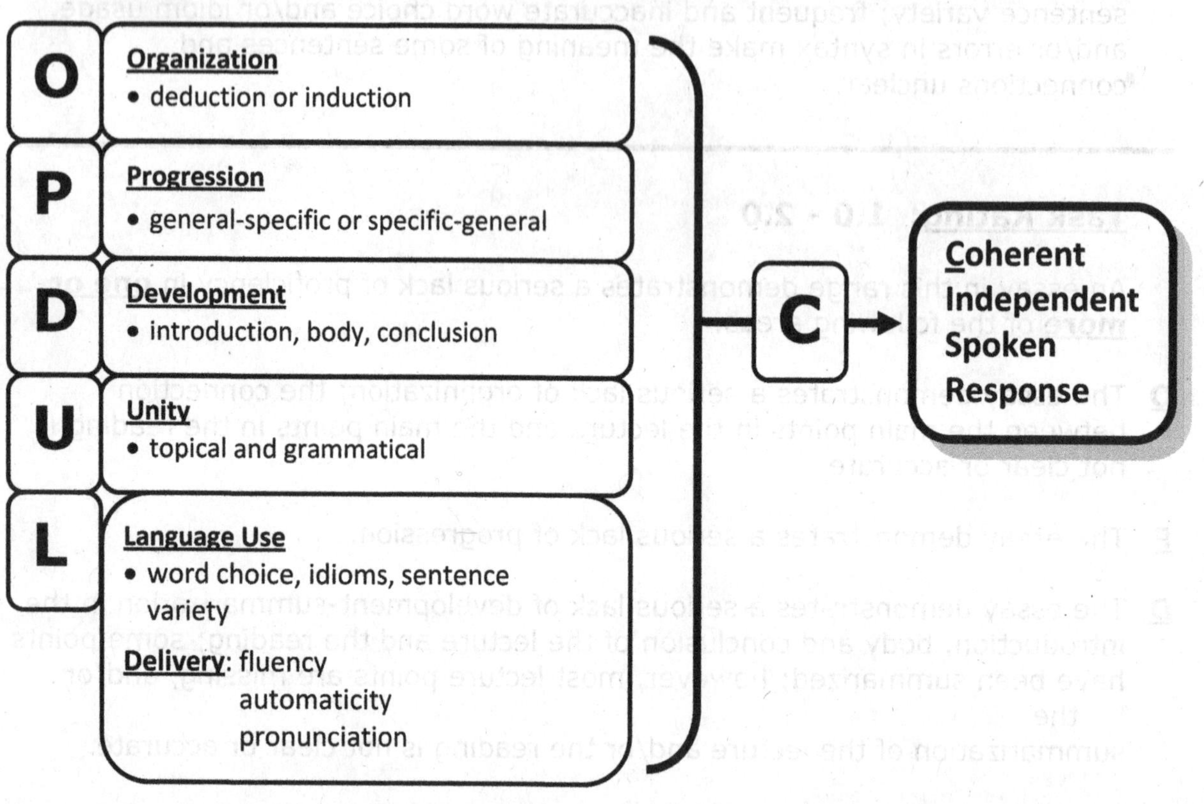

Checklist

1. Does my response demonstrate organization?

- Deduction Yes __ No __
- Induction Yes __ No __

2. Does my response demonstrate progression?

- General-specific Yes __ No __
- Specific-general Yes __ No __

3. Does my response demonstrate development?

- Introduction Yes __ No __
- Body Yes __ No __
- Conclusion Yes __ No __

4. Does my response demonstrate unity?

- Topical Yes __ No __
- Grammatical Yes __ No __

5. Does my response demonstrate proficient language use?

- Word Choice Yes __ No __
- Idioms Yes __ No __
- Sentence variety Yes __ No __

Is my delivery proficient?

- Fluency Yes __ No __
- Automaticity Yes __ No __
- Pronunciation Yes __ No __

6. Does my response demonstrate coherence?

Yes __ No __

Independent Speaking Rating Guide

Task Rating: 3.5 - 4.0

A response in this range is Coherent because it generally demonstrates proficiency in **all** of the following areas.

O The response demonstrates a clear and consistent method of organization.

P The response demonstrates a clear and consistent progression of ideas.

D The response demonstrates development of the introduction, body and conclusion; the supporting illustrations are clear and well developed; minor omissions do not effect meaning or coherence.

U The response demonstrates topical and grammatical unity; the relationship between ideas is clear and accurate both topically and grammatically.

L The response demonstrates clear and accurate language use; minor errors in word choice and/or idiom usage and/or syntax do not affect meaning or coherence.

The delivery demonstrates consistent and accurate fluency, pronunciation and automaticity; minor difficulties in each area do not affect meaning and/or coherence, or require listener effort to understand.

Task Rating: 2.5 - 3.0

A response in this range demonstrates proficiency in at least **two** of the following areas.

O The response demonstrates organization.

P The response demonstrates a progression of ideas.

D The response demonstrates limited development; the introduction, body and/or conclusion might lack development, particularly in the body.

U The response demonstrates topical and grammatical unity; however, the relationship between ideas might not always be clear or accurate.

L The response demonstrates a limited range of word choice and/or idiom usage, and/or sentence variety; inaccurate word choice and/or idiom usage, and/or syntax errors might make the meaning of some words and sentences unclear.

The delivery demonstrates fluency, pronunciation and automaticity; however, difficulties in one or more areas requires listener effort to understand.

Task Rating: 1.5 - 2.0

A response in this range demonstrates a lack of proficiency in at least **two** of the following areas.

O The response demonstrates a serious lack of organization.

P The response demonstrates a serious lack of progression.

D The response demonstrates limited development; the examples lack details and repeat.

U The response demonstrates a lack of topical and grammatical unity; the connection of ideas is not clear or accurate.

L The response demonstrates a limited range of word choice and/or idiom usage and/or sentence variety; however, inaccurate word choice and/or idiom usage, and/or syntax errors makes the meaning of words and sentences unclear. The delivery demonstrates difficulties in fluency and/or pronunciation, and/or automaticity; these difficulties make the meaning of words and sentences unclear and require listener effort to understand.

Task Rating: 0.0 - 1.0

A response in this range demonstrates a serious lack of proficiency in at least **two** of the following areas.

O The response demonstrates a serious lack of organization.

P The response demonstrates a serious lack of progression.

D The response demonstrates a serious lack of development in all areas.

U The response demonstrates a serious lack of topical and grammatical unity.

L The response demonstrates a serious lack of language use in all areas.

Integrated Speaking Proficiency Checklist

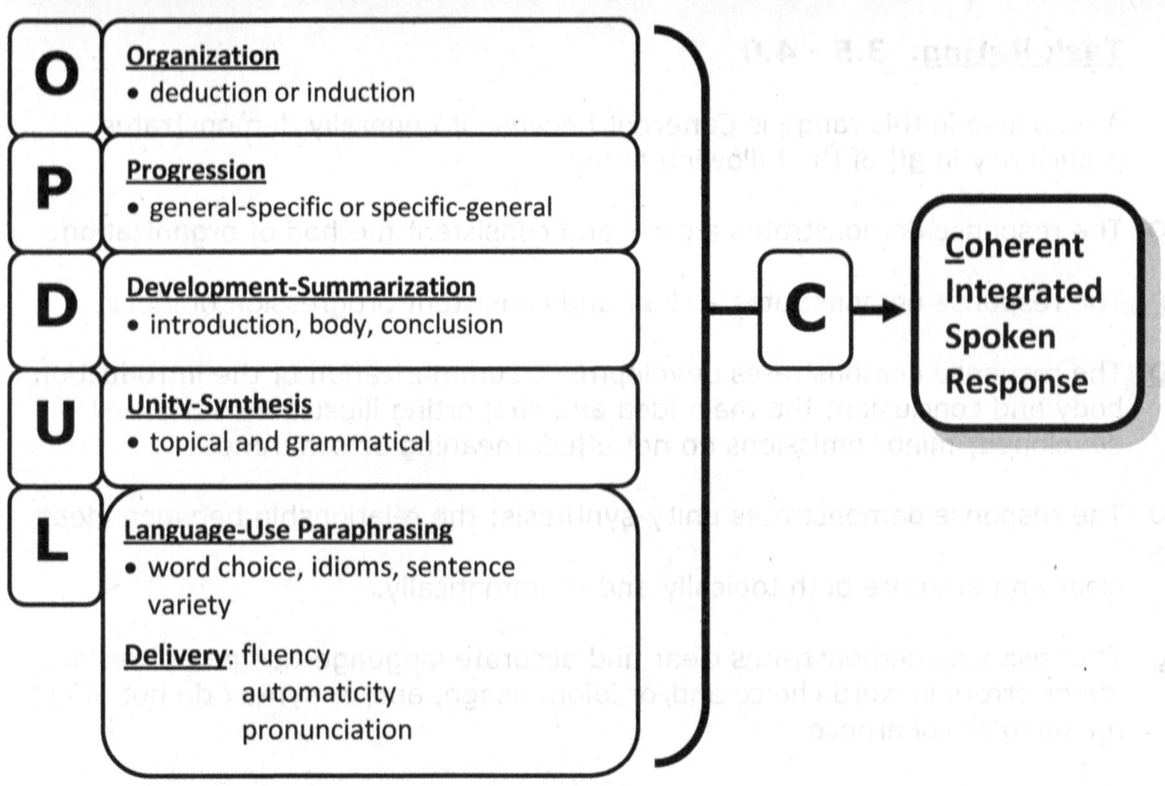

Checklist

1. Does my response demonstrate organization?

- Deduction Yes __ No __
- Induction Yes __ No __

2. Does my response demonstrate progression?

- General-specific Yes __ No __
- Specific-general Yes __ No __

3. Does my response demonstrate development-summarization?

- Introduction Yes __ No __
- Body Yes __ No __
- Conclusion Yes __ No __

4. Does my response demonstrate unity-synthesis?

- Topical Yes __ No __
- Grammatical Yes __ No __

5. Does my response demonstrate proficient language-use paraphrasing?

- Word choice Yes __ No __
- Idioms Yes __ No __
- Sentence variety Yes __ No __

Is my delivery proficient?

- Fluency Yes __ No __
- Automaticity Yes __ No __
- Pronunciation Yes __ No __

6. Does my response demonstrate coherence?

Yes __ No __

Integrated Speaking Rating Guide

Task Rating: 3.5 - 4.0

A response in this range is Coherent because it generally demonstrates proficiency in **all** of the following areas.

O The response demonstrates a clear and consistent method of organization.

P The response demonstrates a clear and consistent progression of ideas.

D The response demonstrates development-summarization of the introduction, body and conclusion; the main idea and supporting illustrations are well developed; minor omissions do not affect meaning or coherence.

U The response demonstrates unity-synthesis; the relationship between ideas is clear and accurate both topically and grammatically.

L The response demonstrates clear and accurate language-use paraphrasing; minor errors in word choice and/or idiom usage, and/or syntax do not affect meaning or coherence.

The delivery demonstrates consistent and accurate fluency, pronunciation and automaticity; minor difficulties in each area do not affect meaning and/or coherence.

Task Rating: 2.5 - 3.0

A response in this range demonstrates proficiency in at least **two** of the following areas.

O The response demonstrates organization.

P The response demonstrates a progression of ideas; however, it might not always be accurate or clear.

D The response demonstrates development-summarization; however, the introduction, body and/or conclusion might be incomplete due to a lack of details and/or a point not being sufficiently explained.

U The response demonstrates unity-synthesis; however, the relationship between ideas might not always be clear, accurate or consistent due to a lack of topical and/or grammatical unity.

L The response demonstrates limited language-use paraphrasing; word choice and/or idiom usage, and/or syntax might be inaccurate or incomplete making the meaning of words and sentences unclear.

Minor difficulties in fluency and/or pronunciation and/or automaticity require listener effort to understand.

Task Rating: 1.5 - 2.0

A response in this range demonstrates a serious lack of proficiency in at least **two** of the following areas.

O The response demonstrates a serious lack of organization.

P The response demonstrates a serious lack of progression.

D The response demonstrates limited and incomplete development-summarization.

U The response demonstrates a lack of unity-synthesis; the connection of ideas is not clear, accurate or consistent; the response is often off topic because the test-taker does not understand the requirements of the task.

L The response demonstrates limited language use with little or no paraphrasing; inaccurate word choice and/or syntax errors makes the meaning of words and sentences consistently unclear.

The delivery demonstrates frequent difficulties in fluency and/or pronunciation and/or automaticity; these difficulties make the meaning of words and sentences unclear and require listener effort to understand.

Task Rating: 0.0 - 1.0

A response in this range demonstrates a serious lack of proficiency in **two or more** of the following areas.

O The response demonstrates a serious lack of organization.

P The response demonstrates a serious lack of progression.

D The response demonstrates a serious lack of development-summarization in all areas.

U The response demonstrates a serious lack of unity-synthesis in all areas.

L The response demonstrates a serious lack of language-use paraphrasing in all areas.

Notes

Your TOEFL iBT® Range Score

To calculate your TOEFL iBT range score, add up your section test scores.

Writing Test Score	**=**	**/ 30**
Speaking Test Score	**=**	**/ 30**
Listening Test Score	**=**	**/ 30**
Reading Test Score	**=**	**/ 30**
Total Tests Score	**=**	**/ 120**
TOEFL iBT Range Score	**=**	**/ 120**

Your TOEFL iBT Range Score

Your range score is an approximate score. It estimates your test-day score within a ten-point range. For example, you scored 85/120 on the tests above. That means you will score between 80 and 90 on test day with an estimated mid-range score of 85/120. Use the chart below to estimate your TOEFL iBT range score.

TOEFL iBT Scores →

120	100	80 ←
119	99	79
118	98	78
117	97	76
116	96	75
115	95	74
114	94	73
113	93	72
112	92	71
111	91	70
110	90	69
109	89	68
108	88	67
107	87	66
106	86	65
105	85	64
104	84	63
103	83	62
102	82	61
101	81	60

In 2010, the average worldwide TOEFL iBT score was 80/120.*

*Data courtesy of ETS.

Audio Scripts

Argument Counter-Argument Integrated Essay

Sample Dialogue: Big Oil - Track #1 - Page 135

Prof: 1 ➔ On the contrary, oil companies do more harm than good.
2 ➔ For starters, big oil eliminates jobs to increase profits. Last year, oil companies reduced their work force by 25% while profits were up 50% percent. This trend does not appear to be changing.
3 ➔ Also, oil companies avoid paying taxes by moving overseas. One company, Hamilton, moved to Dubai to reduce its U.S. corporate tax rate. How does this help our roads and bridges?
4 ➔ Worse, petroleum products are the number one cause of global warming. Every day cars pour billions of tons of CO_2 into the atmosphere. CO_2 has been directly linked to the greenhouse effect.
5 ➔ The evidence is clear. Oil companies do more harm than good.

Sample Dialogue: Internet Piracy - Track #2 - Page 146

Prof: 1 ➔ It happens every second of every day all over the world. One click and that new song—the one you didn't pay for—is on your iPod. You may think it's legal. After all, downloading music is fast and easy, right? Think again. It goes without saying that downloading music off the web without paying for it is a crime.
2 ➔ I know. I know. Some will argue that "It's my democratic right to download music without paying for it." Nonsense. The internet might have started out with the intention of being a democracy but believe me, those days are long gone. The internet these days is about two things: information and money. Big money. One of the biggest money makers on the web is music, and music is protected by law. If you download U2's latest album, let's say, and you don't pay for it, then you are breaking the copyright law that says U2 owns that music. It is their property and you just stole it. If you want to listen to U2, you've got to buy it, no ifs, ands or buts.
3 ➔ Also, the artist has a legal right to get paid for his or her work no matter how or where it is downloaded. How would you like it if somebody were stealing your music? This is exactly what Napster was doing. Napster was the first peer-to-peer music sharing site. Musicians, however, took Napster to court for not paying royalties, money owed each time a song was downloaded via Napster. Napster argued that it was just helping friends share music. The courts disagreed. Napster paid a big fine and is now a pay site.
4 ➔ Moreover, illegally downloading music off the web is not a privacy issue. If you break the law by illegally downloading music, you are a criminal. I'm sorry, but you can't have it both ways. You can't break the law and hide behind the privacy issue. The law is clear. Criminals have no right to privacy. Period.
5 ➔ It bears repeating that downloading music without paying for it is a crime no matter what anyone says about "the freedom of cyberspace." Just because downloading music is fast and easy doesn't mean you have the right to steal it.

Teleconferencing - Track #3 - Page 164

Prof: 1 ➔ We Americans assume that all business cultures are like ours. Nothing could be further from the truth. Many Middle Eastern and Asian cultures prefer to do business face-to-face. Discussing business over tea or while having dinner is an integral part of the business process in these cultures. Such traditions help develop mutual respect and trust not only between business partners but between international employees working for the same company. Unfortunately, in the rush for convenience and cost saving, Americans fail to appreciate that not all business cultures view teleconferencing as the ultimate business solution.

2 ➔ The article goes on to say that blue chip companies saved an average of $40 million last year by cutting travel costs. What the article doesn't tell you is that for every dollar saved by cutting travel costs, these same companies paid two dollars to upgrade their intranet systems. Teleconferencing might be fast and easy but it's certainly not cheap, especially when companies need to continually upgrade their computer systems if they want to stay competitive.

3 ➔ Some would argue that teleconferencing is the perfect tool for problem solving, especially when operating under a deadline. Yet how do you know if the information you are receiving is timely and accurate? A good example is the American who called up a colleague in Japan. Because the Japanese colleague was new and did not want to lose face, and because the American was his boss, he told the American exactly what he wanted to hear. The American believed he had the solution to his problem only to realize later that the information was not accurate.

Task #1 - Track #4 - Global Warming - Page 171

Narrator: Directions. Now listen to a lecture on the same topic.

Prof: 1 ➔ It's amazing how some scientists bend the facts to serve their own agendas. That said, let me shed some light on the carbon sink issue. The CO2 released from carbon sinks has a different isotopic ratio than the CO2 produced by our burning of fossils fuels. In other words, carbon sink CO2 and fossil fuel CO2 have different fingerprints. This fact, ignored by the article, proves that the rise of CO2 in the atmosphere during the 20th century is indeed man-made, and that global warming will only increase.

2 ➔ Also, one will argue that forecasting climate change on a computer is not always accurate. However, what the article fails to mention is that computer modeling accurately predicts broader trends in climate change, and that these trends all indicate increased warming trends. Measuring the GMST is indeed a critical part of measuring climate change. However, such a detailed analysis is not the only way to gauge future climate change. Remember: 85% of the world's energy needs come from the burning of fossil fuels. Where does all that C02 go? Into the atmosphere as greenhouse gases. You don't need a computer model to conclude that all that CO2 poses a serious problem.

3 ➔ Global warming is a natural phenomena we are just beginning to understand? What is this guy smoking? Researchers at Texas A&M have proven that increased water vapor serves to amplify the warming process. In other words, water vapor is like gasoline poured onto an already raging fire. That fire is those greenhouse gases already present in the atmosphere. How do we stop that fire? By substantially reducing our dependence on fossil fuels.

Narrator: Now get ready to write your response. Summarize the points made in the lecture and show how they cast doubt on the points made in the reading. You have 20 minutes to complete this task.

Task #2 - Track #5 - America and Oil - Page 173

Narrator: Directions. Now listen to a lecture on the same topic.

Prof: 1 ➔ The oil debate refuses to die, and for good reason: we are addicted to oil. Like a junkie, we just can't live without it. However, like a drug addict, if we don't stop, our addiction will eventually kill us despite what the so-called oil experts think.

2 ➔ Yes, it's true that millions work in the U.S. petroleum industry. It is also true that U.S. oil companies are moving overseas in record numbers. Why? Because big oil is about one thing: making money for their shareholders. They do so by reducing their tax burden as much as possible. This is achieved by moving to countries with low corporate tax rates. These same countries have few regulations regarding environmental safety thus oil companies can avoid investing in environmental protection technologies required in the U.S.

3 ➔ As for convenience? Let's face it. Convenience kills. Go to the remotest islands in the Pacific Ocean, and what do you find? Plastic water bottles and disposable razors piled up on the shores. Even more depressing is the fact in the North Pacific there is a floating garbage dump the size of Texas. This garbage dump is comprised mainly of plastic bottles. My esteemed colleague is all for convenience, just as long as he doesn't have to look at its effects. In other words, out of sight, out of mind.

4 ➔ The fact that we are being held hostage by oil-rich countries who hate us is our own fault. Since World War II, the U.S. has supported dozens of dictators in order secure a steady source of cheap oil at any price. As for offshore oil freeing us from foreign oil, nothing could be further from the truth. Statistics indicate that our offshore reserves represent only eight percent of our total oil needs. Who are the hostages in this debate? The American people being fed the lie that our future energy needs lie just offshore.

5 ➔ Statistics are very persuasive. Here are a few of my own. That 8,000 barrels mentioned in the article? Most of it comes from countries like Nigeria. Since 1958, over 13 million barrels of oil have spilled in the Niger Delta, Nigeria's main oil producing area. That's one *Exxon Valdez* supertanker every year. Worse, little, if any, of that oil has been cleaned up. If that isn't an argument for freeing our addiction to oil, I don't know what is.

Narrator: Now get ready to write your response. Summarize the points made in the lecture and show how they cast doubt on the points made in the reading. You have 20 minutes to complete this task.

Task #3 - Track #6 - Computer Games - Page 175

Narrator: Directions. Now listen to a lecture on the same topic.

Prof: 1 ➔ When parents or educators want to blame something for all the ills of our youth, they immediately point the figure at video games and brand them as being anti-social destroyers of youth and all that we hold sacred and dear. Well, excuse me if I disagree.

2 ➔ Nobody would disagree that violent video games are designed with killing in mind, just like no would disagree that problem-solution scenarios in which an anti-hero blasts his way to freedom reinforces detrimental behavior in adolescents. But wait just a minute here. Where are the parents in this equation? If such games are so perilous to the youth of our nation, then turn the darn things off and tell the kids to go bounce a ball. Blaming a video game for poisoning a kid's behavior is like saying guns kill people. Wrong. Guns don't kill

people. People kill people. Likewise, video games don't make bad kids. Parents make bad kids. Period.

3 ➔ Let's move on to the idea that video games create a "false sense of reality." Look around you. What do you see? Surprise. Surprise. The world is built on false realities. Movies, internet social networks, music videos, even rock concerts. I mean, come on, who hasn't walked away from a rock concert thinking, "Man, I wanna be a rock star!" I sure did. I still do! Talk about delusions. So let's put the hyperbole aside and call a spade a spade, shall we? False realities have always been here, and they always will.

4 ➔ Finally, the woman issue. Seriously, if you're looking for feminine role models in a violent video game—any video game—then you're the one who needs to take a good hard look in the mirror. Video games are not repositories of virtue nor are they purveyors of moral rectitude. Far from it. They are what they are: entertainment vehicles, pure, plain and simple. To think otherwise is to miss the point completely, that point being that, like it or not, violent video games are symbols of free speech. That's right. Democracy in action. If you don't like what you're hearing, turn them off. The choice is yours.

Narrator: Now get ready to write your response. Summarize the points made in the lecture and show how they cast doubt on the points made in the reading. You have 20 minutes to complete this task.

Task #4 - Track #7 - Standardized Testing - Page 177

Narrator: Directions. Now listen to a lecture on the same topic.

Prof: 1 ➔ Proponents of standardized testing are quick to wave the flag of comparative statistics as being the best way to measure academic performance. Yet what supporters of standardized testing fail to realize is that, in their rush for statistics, they have boiled education down to a game, a game in which there are winners and losers. I'm sorry, but education is not about dividing students into winners and losers. It's about uniting with a focus on equality, the very thing standardized testing destroys by pointing the finger at those schools with lower-than-average scores.

2 ➔ The article goes on to describe how teachers benefit from standardized testing. By using statistics, teachers know which subjects to focus on to increase scores, the example being math. Okay, so math is a problem. But why does it suddenly become a teaching priority? Why should English or history suffer? The reason is clear: this is not about providing students with a balanced education. It's about satisfying administrators and their constant demand for higher scores, for higher scores suggest that all is well when, more often than not, statistics lie, for if too much emphasis is placed on one subject, other subjects will suffer in turn. And who is to blame for that? Teachers trying to please administrators while ignoring the needs of their students.

3 ➔ My biggest complaint with standardized testing is that someone is always to blame. If it's not the student's fault for getting a low score, then it must be the teacher's. If only it were so simple. What if on test day, a student were tired, or sick, or had family problems, or wasn't getting enough to eat? Are teachers to blame for all these variables? If you believe in low-scoring test results, then you have to say yes: bad teaching is to blame for poor student scores. Unfortunately, many excellent teachers have been fired because standardized testing has provided such leaps of logic.

4 ➔ Let's be honest. Standardized testing is a numbers game played by administrators and teachers with the students left out in the cold. The sooner we get rid of standardized testing the better.

Narrator: Now get ready to write your response. Summarize the points made in the lecture and show how they cast doubt on the points made in the reading. You have 20 minutes to complete this task.

Task #5 - Track #8 - Organic Food - Page 179

Narrator: Directions. Now listen to a lecture on the same topic.

Prof: 1 ➔ A major trend in the food industry is the increasing popularity of organic food. Yes, organic is more expensive. There's no denying that, just as there's no denying the health risks associated with eating non organic strawberries. Most are unaware that non organic strawberries are one of the most chemically contaminated fruits you can buy. Why? Because farmers apply two chemicals to every crop: a pesticide to protect the fruit from insects and a fungicide to protect the roots from fungus. Both the pesticide and the fungicide contain chemicals that have been linked to breast cancer in woman and to a 50% reduction in sperm count in men. By eating organic strawberries, you can substantially reduce your exposure to these risks.

2 ➔ The author goes on to say that organic food is hard to find. This is simply not true. All you have to do is go to your local grocery store and you will find organic food. Many of the bigger stores, for example, even have organic sections. Not only that but Wal-Mart now offers a wide variety of organic produce. In fact, I buy a lot of organic products at Wal-Mart, such as milk and cottage cheese and, yes, even organic rice.

3 ➔ As for non organic versus organic milk, of course, there's no difference in taste. Why should there be? The whole point of organic milk is not to change the taste but to eliminate pesticides and other man-made chemicals from the milk production process. A big part of that process is the genetically engineered growth hormone rBGH. Farmers give their cows rBGH which, in turn, makes the cows produce far more milk than is naturally possible. Worse, rBGH stays in the milk and enters your body when you drink it. Moreover, research has linked rBGH to colon, breast and prostate cancer.

4 ➔ In the end, buying organic is an investment in your health. Personally, I don't mind paying a little extra. At least I know what I'm eating.

Narrator: Now get ready to write your response. Summarize the points made in the lecture and show how they cast doubt on the points made in the reading. You have 20 minutes to complete this task.

Show-Support Integrated Essay

Sample Lecture: Animal Behavior - Track #9 - Page 182

Prof: 1 ➔ Good afternoon. In this lecture, we'll focus on a common nocturnal animal, the bat. There are two types of bat: micro bats, or true bats, and mega bats, also called fruit bats. Let's start with mega bats.

2 ➔ Size wise, mega bats are from two to sixteen inches in length. Mega bats have extremely sensitive sight and smell. This helps them locate the flowers and fruit upon which they feed. It is while eating that mega bats play an important role in the distribution of plants. Like bees, mega bats serve as pollinators. When they lick nectar or eat flowers, their bodies become covered in pollen which they, in turn, carry to other trees and plants thereby acting as pollinators. In fact, many of the fruits and vegetables on our tables, such as bananas and peaches, would not be there if mega bats did not pollinate plants and trees.

3 ➔ Next are micro bats. As the name implies, micro bats are quite small, about the size of a mouse. To find food, micro bats use echolocation, high frequency sounds they bounce off insects. The most common micro bat is the vesper or evening bat. Like mega bats, micro bats play an important role in the environment. The average vesper bat, for example, can eat one thousand mosquitoes in one night. By doing so, they control the mosquito population.

Task #1 - Track #10 - Brown-Headed Cowbird - Page 190

Narrator: Directions. Now listen to a lecture on the same topic.

Prof: 1 ➔ In this lecture, we'll take a closer look at the breeding habits of the brown-headed cowbird. The cowbird is what's called a brood parasite. Let me explain. As mentioned, the cowbird was originally a nomad, travelling with the buffalo and eating whatever the buffalo kicked up, insects, seeds, whatever. In this light, the cowbird was very much an opportunist. Yet the cowbird had a problem. Because they were nomadic, raising a family was a problem. If they stopped to raise a brood, they'd lose their food source, for the buffalo were always on the move. The cowbird, ever the opportunist, resolved this problem in a unique way, one that characterizes the species to this day.

2 ➔ When it comes time to lay her eggs, the female cowbird, instead of building a nest, deposits her eggs in the nest of another, much smaller host bird. The cowbird eggs then hatch. Because the cowbird chicks are much bigger than the host chicks, the host brood dies while the mother bird—unable to tell the difference between her own brood and the cowbird brood—is forced to feed the baby cowbirds till they fly off. This parasitic process—one in which one animal takes advantage of another—makes the brown-headed cowbird a true brood parasite. Cowbird eggs have been found in the nests of over 220 species, all the way from hummingbirds to raptors. The result is that many bird species are threatened with extinction due to the cowbird's parasitic breeding habits.

Narrator: Now get ready to write your response. Summarize the points made in the lecture and show how they add to and support the information in the reading. You have 20 minutes to complete this task.

Task #2 - Track #11 - Demography - Page 192

Narrator: Directions. Now listen to a lecture on the same topic.

Prof: 1 ➔ Before demographers can study a population, they have to know how many people comprise that population. To determine the size of a population, the population must be counted. The process of counting people is called a census of population, or simply a census. The United Nations broadens the definition of a census by stating that a census of population is "the total process of collecting, compiling and publishing demographic, economic and social data pertaining, at a specified time or times, to all persons in a country or delimited territory."

2 ➔ In the United States, a census is taken every ten years. This information is essential for a variety of reasons, in particular the establishment of political districts. By determining the size of a population in a given state, the federal government can then apportion the state into Congressional districts based not on geography but on population. This ensures equal representation in Congress wherein populous states, such as California, are awarded more Congressional representatives while states with fewer people, such as Montana, are awarded fewer Congressional representatives. This system of representation based on a census of population is the foundation of the American electoral system.

3 ➔ Census taking, however, is nothing new. Many ancient civilizations regularly took a census of population, for example Rome. Because Rome had a large standing army, it needed money and men. By periodically taking a census, the Roman government knew how much tax money it could raise for the army and the available manpower it could draw from. It wasn't until the second half of the nineteenth century that the process of census taking changed. Instead of just counting heads and money, demographers started to broaden their statistic gathering to include age, occupation, marital status, and education.
4 ➔ Recently, however, census taking has come under attack in Europe and the United States. Many believe that the compiling of an individual's statistical data is an invasion of privacy and should be stopped.

Narrator: Now get ready to write your response. Summarize the points made in the lecture and show how they add to and support the information in the reading. You have 20 minutes to complete this task.

Writing Test

Integrated Essay: Cell Phones - Track #12 - Page 198

Narrator: Directions. Now listen to a lecture on the same topic.

Prof: 1 ➔ According to the article you read for homework, cell phones are a silent killer threatening us all. If you believe that, then you also believe in the tooth fairy. Let me set the record straight.
2 ➔ Cell phones do not cause cancer. Period. Why not? Because cell phone radiation is non ionizing. What does that mean? It means that cell phone radiation has too few electrons thus cannot cause cancer unlike ionizing radiation produced by X-rays. Moreover, cell phone RF levels are tested and retested by the manufacturers to ensure that radiation levels meet the strict standards set by the Federal Communications Commissions. That said, put to rest any notion that you might be harming yourself whenever you make a call.
3 ➔ And, yes, cell phones can be a distraction, but they are not the only distraction on the roads today. Drive along any interstate and you'll be distracted by any number of things, from billboards to speeding transport trucks to construction crews, not to mention little Jilly and Billy screaming for attention in the back seat. Suffice it to say, the world is full of distractions.
4 ➔ As for colony collapse disorder, cell-phone usage is only one of many factors that must be taken into account. Other factors include the bacterial infection called foulbrood, and the varroa mite, an infectious insect that preys on bee larvae. Climate change too is suspected. Global warming has brought new and invasive species. One such species, the Asian hornet, has spread across Europe and into Britain. The Asian hornet raids hives for bee larvae and the bees are powerless to stop this invader. To say that the cell phone threatens honey bees with extinction is like saying hamburgers are responsible for childhood obesity without considering chocolate and high-fructose breakfast cereals.

Narrator: Now get ready to write your response. Summarize the points made in the lecture and show how they cast doubt on the points made in the reading. You have 20 minutes to complete this task.

Speaking Section

Task #3 - Integrated Speaking

Sample Dialogue: Organic-Food Policy - Track #13 - Page 271

Narrator: Now listen as two students discuss the announcement.

Man: Hi, Wendy.
Woman: Hey, Tom. Have you heard about the new organic food policy?
Man: Yeah. What a great idea. It's about time the school did something to improve the food around here.
Woman: If you ask me, I think the new policy is all wrong.
Man: Why?
Woman: Because organic food is way more expensive. In some cases, at least fifty percent more. Add that to labor costs, you know, money to pay the cafeteria staff, and I'm going to be paying a lot more for my coffee and the milk I put in it. I hate to think what a salad will cost. Organic may be cheaper in the future, but right now it's for people with money not poor students like me.
Man: But think of all the health benefits. You'll be eating food that doesn't have any chemicals or antibiotics in it. Not only that but all that good organic food will be lower in fat and calories. I mean, that's got to be good, right?
Woman: Don't be fooled. A hamburger is a hamburger whether the meat is organic or not. Both will have the same amount of fat and calories. The only difference is the organic hamburger has no pesticides or antibiotics in it.
Man: Well, I still think it's a good idea. By offering organic food, we'll be eating a lot better. Even the snacks in the vending machines will be organic. It's definitely the wave of the future. Best of all, we'll be helping local farmers.
Woman: What I don't like is the university telling us what we can and can't eat. Not everybody wants to eat organic, you know. If I want to eat non organic, that's my choice. Sorry, but the school should not be in the health care business.

Task #1 - Track #14 - Digital Text Book Policy - Page 285

Narrator: Directions. Now listen as two students discuss the announcement.

Woman: Hey, Steve. Have you heard about the campus bookstore going digital? What a great idea. Digital texts are definitely the wave of the future. Now, instead of lining up to buy texts, we can just download them at home.
Man: I don't know. Whenever I read a computer screen for a long time, I get wicked headaches. I prefer paper, really. With a regular book, I can study for hours and not feel like my brain is melting. Believe me, I'm not looking forward to studying organic chemistry off a computer screen.
Woman: You should upgrade. Get a computer with a better screen, like my iPad. It's amazing. The screen resolution is so good, I no longer buy regular books. Upgrade, definitely. Your brain will thank you for it.
Man: I'm sorry but upgrading my computer is a luxury I can't afford, what with my car and rent. But with this new policy, I'll have to buy one. Obviously, the school thinks students are made of money.
Woman: Think of it this way: going digital is good for the environment. Think of all the trees you'll be saving. Mother Nature will thank you for it.
Man: What I don't like is there's longer a buy-back. It was great, the book store buying back all our old texts at the end of the semester. But now, with this new policy,

I'm out a couple hundred bucks easy. With that money, I could've bought a new computer.

Woman: Try selling your old texts on eBay.
Man: You just read my mind.

Narrator: Now get ready to answer the prompt. The man gives his opinion about the new policy. State his position and explain the reasons he gives for holding that opinion. You have 30 seconds to develop your response and 60 seconds to speak.

Task #2 - Track #15 - Dress-Code Policy - Page 287

Narrator: Directions. Now listen as two students discuss the announcement.

Woman: A dress code? Give me a break.
Man: That's the new policy. Starting next semester.
Woman: Where does the school get off telling us what we can or can't wear? Hel-lo. This is the United States. Last I heard it was a democracy. What I wear is none of the school's business. I'm paying them to educate me not to deny me the right to wear shorts.
Man: I can understand the policy. Some students really push the envelope when it comes to fashion. I mean, c'mon, school is not the place to be flashing skin or walking around dressed like a rock star. It's distracting. Seriously. This is a university not a club.
Woman: Where does it stop? That's what I want to know. First clothes, then what? Are they going to tell us what to read? What to eat? What to think? Give them an inch and they'll take a mile, believe me.
Man: When I went to high school, we all wore the same uniform and nobody complained. Uniforms created greater equality. Also, I didn't have to worry about what I was going to wear every day.
Woman: Sorry, but that analogy doesn't cut it. High school uniforms are simply a way to control adolescents with way too much energy. This is a university. We're supposed to be responsible adults, remember? By taking away our right to dress as we please, the school no longer trusts us. They're treating us like kids, and I don't like it.

Narrator: Now get ready to answer the prompt. The woman expresses her opinion about the announcement. State her opinion and explain the reasons she gives for holding that opinion. You have 30 seconds to develop your response and 60 seconds to speak.

Task #3 - Track #16 - School Mascot - Page 289

Narrator: Directions. Now listen as two students discuss the announcement.

Woman: So, Phil, what's your pick for the new school mascot?
Man: What are the choices again?
Woman: A bear and a chicken. I'm voting for the chicken.
Man: You want the symbol of our school to be a chicken? You can't be serious.
Woman: I am. Think about it. What other school has a chicken mascot?
Man: Alice....
Woman: Every other school has an eagle, a bear...
Man: I like bears.
Woman Or some kind of dog. Bor-ing. But a chicken? That would make our school unique.

Man: It'll make everybody laugh at us. The Greenwich College Chickens? No way. No way.
Woman: But that's the point. Why does a mascot have to be serious? Why can't a mascot be fun, like a chicken, or a goat, or a giraffe even? Education is way too serious.
Man: Alice...
Woman: What?
Man: Earth to Alice.
Woman: What!
Man: We eat chickens.
Woman: Go on.
Man: Read the announcement. A chicken does not "symbolize the strength and traditions of our three-hundred-year-old institution." A bear, however, represents strength and determination, the school motto, remember? Seriously. Vote for the bear. It's going to win hands down.
Woman: Yeah, well, don't count your chickens before they're hatched.

Narrator: Now get ready to answer the prompt. The woman expresses her opinion about the announcement. State her opinion and explain the reasons she gives for holding that opinion. You have 30 seconds to develop your response and 60 seconds to speak.

Task #4 - Track #17 - No-Pets Policy - Page 291

Narrator: Directions. Now listen as two students discuss the announcement.

Man: It's about time the school did something. My dormitory is like a zoo.
Woman: I take it you don't like animals.
Man: No. Actually, I love animals. It's my allergies that don't like animals. Cats are the worst—there're six on my floor alone. Six! I can hardly sleep I sneeze so much. It's so bad, I'm falling behind.
Woman: Yeah. I can see where you're coming from. Still, before this new policy, there was no law against having a pet in a dorm, so you can't really blame someone for having a pet.
Man: If you'd heard the noise at night, you'd be singing another tune. The dogs in the next dorm just bark and bark. One starts and they all start. It's driving me crazy. What I wouldn't give for a good night's sleep.
Woman: The school really should have a dorm that allows pets. I know a school in Vermont that does that. Supposedly having a pet at school increases your grade-point average.
Man: I fail to see how a snake can improve my grade-point average.
Woman A snake? Who's got a snake?
Man: My roommate. You ever tried to studying for a physics exam with a six-foot snake crawling across your desk? Fun. And my physics professor wonders why I got a B- on the last test.
Woman: A snake is definitely pushing it. But to tell you the truth, I'm not sure if this new policy will really change things. People love their pets. And if they want one, they'll have one, policy or not.

Narrator: Now get ready to answer the prompt. The man gives his opinion about the new policy. State his position and explain the reasons he gives for holding that opinion. You have 30 seconds to develop your response and 60 seconds to speak.

Task #5 - Track #18 - New School President - Page 293

Narrator: Directions. Now listen as two students discuss the announcement.

Man: Did you say William Alfred Liddell?
Woman: That's right. Haven't you heard? He's our new president. His business record is impressive. Why the face?
Man: Because Wild Bill Liddell is famous for tearing schools apart.
Woman: Just what Old Lovell needs. The buildings are ancient, enrollment is at an all-time low, and our teams are a joke. It's about time we had a money man running the show. Let's face it, education is all about money. And if Wild Bill means business, if he can shake this place up, he's got my vote.
Man: The last school Liddell ran, Saint Lionel's prep, he ran into the ground.
Woman: What do you mean?
Man: Saint Lionel's brought Wild Bill in to turn things around. He fired half the teaching staff and closed half the buildings. Not only that but he sold off a big chunk of school property, this beautiful old forest, to a golf course developer to raise money. In less than a year Saint Lionel's closed. Wild Bill was obviously more interested in the bottomline than in education.
Woman: So what do suggest? That Old Lovell stay the course? If we do, we hit the iceberg. If this school needs a boss like William Liddell, I say go for it. It's about time this place had a wake up call.
Man: Here's another reason why I'm leaving. Tuition just went up.
Woman: What?
Man: This place is too rich for me.
Woman: Wait. Wait. Why did tuition go up?
Man: Ask Wild Bill.

Narrator: Now get ready to answer the prompt. The woman expresses her opinion about the announcement. State her opinion and explain the reasons she gives for holding that opinion. You have 30 seconds to develop your response and 60 seconds to speak.

Task #4 - Integrated Speaking

Sample Lecture: Animal Behavior - Track #9 - Page 296 + 302

Narrator: Directions. Now listen to a lecture on animal behavior.

Prof: 1 ➔ Good afternoon. In this lecture, we'll focus on a common nocturnal animal, the bat. There are two types of bat: micro bats, or true bats, and mega bats, also called fruit bats. Let's start with mega bats.
2 ➔ Size wise, mega bats are from two to sixteen inches in length. Mega bats have extremely sensitive sight and smell. This helps them locate the flowers and fruit upon which they feed. It is while eating that mega bats play an important role in the distribution of plants. Like bees, mega bats serve as pollinators. When they lick nectar or eat flowers, their bodies become covered in pollen which they, in turn, carry to other trees and plants thereby acting as pollinators. In fact, many of the fruits and vegetables on our tables, such as bananas and peaches, would not be there if mega bats did not pollinate plants and trees.
3 ➔ Next are micro bats. As the name implies, micro bats are quite small, about the size of a mouse. To find food, micro bats use echolocation, high frequency sounds they bounce off insects. The most common micro bat is the vesper or evening bat. Like mega bats, micro bats play an important role in the

environment. The average vesper bat, for example, can eat one thousand mosquitoes in one night. By doing so, they control the mosquito population.

Task #1 - Track #19 - Bestsellers - Page 313

Narrator: Directions. Now listen to a lecture on the same topic.

Prof: In early America, circa 1650, the center of publishing was in the Massachusetts Bay Colony. Leaders of the colony printed religious pamphlets as a means of keeping up settler morale, for the early settlers were on the edge of a savage new frontier. One such settler was Mary Rowlandson. In 1657, Rowlandson was captured by Indians. After eleven weeks, a ransom was paid and Rowlandson was freed. She went on to write about her experience in a book titled *The Sovereignty and Goodness of God: Being a Narrative of the Captivity and Restoration of Mrs. Mary Rowlandson.* In her book, Rowlandson describes the ordeal of being captured by Indians. By doing so, Rowlandson created the genre of writing known as the captivity narrative. Simply put, the captivity narrative describes how a god-fearing person is captured by godless devils called Indians. In the end, the god-fearing person, backed by an undying faith in God, is freed thus proving that good always conquers evil. Rowlandson's book was so popular it went through four editions and became America's first bestseller.

Narrator: Now get ready to answer the prompt. How do the reading and the lecture add to our understanding of the term bestseller in a contemporary and in an historical sense? You have 30 seconds to develop your response and 60 seconds to speak.

Task #2 - Track #20 - Refining - Page 315

Narrator: Directions. Now listen to a lecture on the same topic.

Prof: 1 ➔ A barrel of crude oil is the oil industry's standard unit of measurement. One barrel contains 42 gallons or 159 liters. Within that barrel of crude is a complex mixture of molecules called hydrocarbons. Hydrocarbons are what's left of plants and animals that lived billions of years ago. This organic matter, deep within the Earth, is heated by the Earth which, over time, turns it into crude oil hence the term fossil fuel. To make consumer petroleum products from a barrel of crude oil, products such as gasoline and diesel fuel, the hydrocarbons must be separated. That separation process is done at a refinery through a process called fractional distillation.

2 ➔ Fractional distillation starts by boiling raw, unprocessed crude oil. The hydrocarbons in the oil all have different boiling points. This means they can be separated through distillation, a process in which the raw crude oil is changed into its gaseous form through boiling. When a particular hydrocarbon reaches its boiling point, it changes from a solid to a vapor. This vapor is then drained off into a separate holding tank where it is cooled and condensed into liquid form. The lightest products, those which have the lowest boiling point, such as gasoline, exit from the top of the boiler while the heaviest products—those with the highest boiling points, such as lubricating oil—exit from the bottom.

Narrator: Now get ready to answer the prompt. Refining is a complex and dangerous process. Using information from the reading and lecture, describe this process. You have 30 seconds to develop your response and 60 seconds to speak.

Task #3 - Track #21 - Brown-Headed Cowbird - Page 317

Narrator: Directions. Now listen to a lecture on the same topic.

Prof: 1 ➔ In this lecture, we'll take a closer look at the breeding habits of the brown-headed cowbird.
2 ➔ The cowbird is what's called a brood parasite. Let me explain. As mentioned, the cowbird was originally a nomad, travelling with the buffalo and eating whatever the buffalo kicked up, insects, seeds, whatever. In this light, the cowbird was very much an opportunist. Yet the cowbird had a problem. Because they were nomadic, raising a family was a problem. If they stopped to raise a brood, they'd lose their food source, for the buffalo were always on the move. The cowbird, ever the opportunist, resolved this problem in a unique way, one that characterizes the species to this day.
3 ➔ When it comes time to lay her eggs, the female cowbird, instead of building a nest, deposits her eggs in the nest of another, much smaller host bird. The cowbird eggs then hatch. Because the cowbird chicks are much bigger than the host chicks, the host brood dies while the mother bird—unable to tell the difference between her own brood and the cowbird brood—is forced to feed the baby cowbirds till they fly off. This parasitic process—one in which one animal takes advantage of another—makes the brown-headed cowbird a true brood parasite.

Narrator: Now get ready to answer the prompt. The brown-headed cowbird is a brood parasite. How do the reading and lecture define and develop this classification? You have 30 seconds to develop your response and 60 seconds to speak.

Task #4 - Track #22 - Seamounts - Page 319

Narrator: Directions. Now listen to a lecture on the same topic.

Prof: 1 ➔ Seamounts are of great interest not only to biologists but to the commercial fishing industry as well. And for good reason. The nutrient-rich water around a seamount is home to an immense variety of fish, many of which have commercial value. One such fish is the orange roughy.
2 ➔ In the mid 1970's, orange roughy was found in great numbers around seamounts near New Zealand. The greatest concentrations were found one kilometer down, a depth once thought impossible to fish. But this did not stop the fishing industry. No longer did depth protect the fish. Helped by new GPS technology, bottom trawling was born. Bottom trawling involves dragging a net across the ocean floor. This is a very destructive form of fishing for not only does the net catch orange roughy, but it also destroys the ocean floor and catches other species that are not commercially valuable. This method of fishing was so effective, and the demand for orange roughy so great, that they were practically wiped out.
3 ➔ Another fish directly impacted by bottom trawling is the armorhead. In the 1960's, huge numbers of armorheads were discovered around seamounts northwest of Hawaii. In no time at all, Russian and Japanese fishing fleets virtually wiped out the armorhead. Like orange roughy, armorhead stocks have yet to recover.

Narrator: Now get ready to answer the prompt. Seamounts are under threat. Why? Using information from the reading and the lecture, illustrate the threat and the reason for it. You have 30 seconds to develop your response and 60 seconds to speak.

Task #5 - Track #23 - Robert E. Lee - Page 321

Narrator: Directions. Now listen to a lecture on the same topic.

Prof: 1 ➔ Like most great military generals, Lee was a gambler. Two battles illustrate this tendency. The first is the battle of Chancellorsville in May, 1863. There, Lee broke all the rules of military engagement. Faced by a Union army twice the size of his own, Lee divided his much smaller army not once, not twice, but three times. In the process, Lee defeated the Union army and established his reputation as a general equal to Napoleon. Time and again, Lee defeated the much larger Union Army.
2 ➔ While Chancellorsville was Lee's greatest victory, the battle of Gettysburg, in July, 1863 was Lee's greatest defeat. On the third day of battle, Lee, convinced that one final blow would break the Union line, sent the Army of Northern Virginia marching across a mile-wide field. The waiting Union army annihilated Lee's men. The South never recovered.
3 ➔ At war's end, many in the North wanted Lee hung for treason. However, Lee never stood trial. Lincoln wanted reconciliation not revenge.

Narrator: Now get ready to answer the prompt. Using information from the reading and the lecture, illustrate the historical significance of Robert E. Lee. You have 30 seconds to develop your response and 60 seconds to speak.

Task #5 - Integrated Speaking

Sample Dialogue: Harvard Law - Track #24 - Page 324

Narrator: Listen to a sample dialogue.

Man: Hi, Betty. What's wrong?
Woman: Well, there's good news and bad.
Man: Okay, so what's the good news?
Woman: I got accepted into Harvard law.
Man: Congratulations! That's fantastic.
Woman: Thanks. Now for the bad news. Harvard is not cheap. I nearly died when I saw the tuition.
Man: Yeah, but it's Harvard. Ivy League.
Woman: I know. I want to go, but I can't afford it. I already have four years worth of undergrad loans at this school. If I do three years of Harvard law, I'll be even more in debt. I'm not sure what to do.
Man: What about applying for a scholarship? How are your grades?
Woman: I'm at the top of my class.
Man: There you go. You'd have a really good chance of getting a scholarship. Some scholarships pay all your tuition. If you don't get a full scholarship, you should at least get something for books. I got a scholarship here, and boy did I save a bundle.
Woman: Applying for a scholarship is definitely an option. I'll have to check it out.
Man: You could also take time off and work for a year or two, you know, postpone admittance. That way you could save money for tuition. You might not be able to pay off the full cost, but you could at least pay off some of it. That way you'd owe less in the long run.
Woman: Yeah. Obviously, I have a decision to make.

Sample Dialogue: Professor Forgets - Track #25 - Page 328

Narrator: Listen to a sample dialogue.

Student: Professor Morrison?
Professor: Hi, Sue. Come in. What's up?
Student: I just wanted to remind you of the meeting tonight in Anderson Hall.
Professor: Meeting? What meeting?
Student: The Environmental Club meeting. You said you'd come and give a talk about winning the National Science Prize.
Professor: Tonight? Oh, no. I promised the Biology Club I'd speak to them tonight in Farnell Hall.
Student: I see. But we're expecting a big crowd. We've been advertising it all month. We even sold tickets to raise money. I guess I'll just have to refund them.
Professor: Look, maybe we can work something out. You know, I could always record my talk to the Biology Club, then email you the file. That way you could present my talk to your group at your convenience.
Student: Yeah. That would work.
Professor: Also, I'm part of a lecture tomorrow night over at Gethin-Jones Hall. The topic is ethics and nano engineering. You have to buy tickets, but since I'm speaking, I'm sure I can get you and your group in free. I'd be willing to stay after and answer questions about the prize. What do you think?
Student: That's a possibility too. Let me talk to my group first and see what they say.

Task #1 - Track 26 - Pet Policy - Page 344

Narrator: Directions. Listen to a conversation between two students.

Man: Hey, Mary. You look upset. What's wrong?
Woman: Hi, Steve. Oh, it's nothing, really.
Man: C'mon...
Woman: Well, there's this new school policy.
Man: The one about pets?
Woman: Yeah. I don't know what to do. It's breaking my heart. I can't give Pete up. I just can't. It'd be like giving away my, you know, child.
Man: You're going to have to do something. The school is really cracking down on pets. Have you considered putting Pete up for adoption? You could get him a good home and you'd feel better knowing he was okay. You could probably arrange to see him on weekends.
Woman: I thought about that. But I've had Pete for so long. Oh, who thought up this stupid policy? Do you know how many pets there are? Practically everyone's got one. Julie. Sylvia. Jason. He just got a new puppy.
Man: Doesn't matter. Rules are rules.
Woman: I hate rules.
Man: Why don't you donate Pete to a zoo?
Woman: A zoo? I never thought of that.
Man: You should give it a try. Pete would have a nice, safe home with all the mice he could eat. And he wouldn't get lonely. People would be stopping by to see him all the time. Talk about living.
Woman: Do you know anyone who would take Pete? Your parents maybe?
Man: My parents? Are you kidding. My mother hates snakes.

Narrator: Now get ready to answer the prompt. The students discuss two solutions to the woman's problem. Identify the problem and the solutions, then state which solution you think is best and why. You have 20 seconds to develop your response and 60 seconds to speak.

Task #2 - Track 27 - Euthanasia Debate - Page 346

Narrator: Directions. Listen to a conversation between two students.

Man: Hey, Sue. You got a minute?
Woman: Sure, Brian. What's up?
Man: I'm taking Political Science. Part of my course requirement is to debate some hot-button issue, you know, like amnesty for illegals or gay marriage.
Woman: So what's the problem? Why so wound up?
Man: The topic is euthanasia. I'm supposed to argue against it, but I'm pro euthanasia. I believe people have the right to die whenever and however they please. Call it freedom of choice. Call it whatever. No way am I arguing against a person's right to choose.
Woman: Know what I think? I think you're blowing this thing way out of proportion. I also think Professor Smith gave you the con side as a way of teaching you.
Man: Teaching me? Teaching me what?
Woman: Think about it. By arguing the opposite of what you believe, maybe Professor Smith wants you to see both sides of the argument. Maybe this is really an exercise in understanding. In that case, I think you should do it. I mean, life is not always about getting your own way, you know.
Man: True.
Woman: Another option is to tell Professor Smith you refuse to debate on moral grounds. You'd be true to your beliefs, and I'm sure he'd understand. But he might also fail you, so you're definitely taking a risk if you back out. Look. There's Professor Smith now. So, what're you going to do?
Man: I don't know. I'm still debating.

Narrator: Now get ready to answer the prompt. The students discuss two solutions to the man's problem. Identify the problem and the solutions, then state which solution you think is best and why. You have 20 seconds to develop your response and 60 seconds to speak.

Task #3 - Track #28 - Job Offer - Page 348

Narrator: Directions. Listen to a conversation between two students.

Man: Hey, Sylvia. Did you get the job?
Woman: I did.
Man: Congratulations. You don't look so thrilled.
Woman: I am. Very. But I've got a choice to make. I applied for a part-time position, right?
Man: Right.
Woman: So I go for the interview and before you know it, they're offering me a full-time position with benefits.
Man: Whoa. So what're you going to do?
Woman: That's the $64,000.00 question.
Man: Why don't you tell them you'll work part-time, then do full-time when you graduate? That way you could finish your education and have a job when you graduate. They might even pay for the rest of your education that way.
Woman: Oh, I don't know. Asking them to pay for my education when they've already offered so much seems a bit, you know, greedy.

Man: Okay. So quit school. Serious. You've got a once-in-a-lifetime job offer. With the economy the way it is, you'd be crazy not to take it. Best of all, the pressure of finding a job would be gone just like that.

Woman: But what about my master's degree?

Man: Work for a few years, then finish it part-time in the evening. People do it all the time, work and go to school at the same time. By working, you could pay for your master's if your company won't pay. What was that job again?

Woman: Entertainment director on a cruise ship. It goes all over the world. Miami. Rio. Greece.

Man: Sweet.

Narrator: Now get ready to answer the prompt. The students discuss two solutions to the woman's problem. Identify the problem and the solutions, then state which solution you think is best and why. You have 20 seconds to develop your response and 60 seconds to speak.

Task #4 - Track #29 - Roommate Problems - Page 350

Narrator: Directions. Listen to a conversation between two students.

Woman: Hey, Jack. How's your new roommate?

Man: Don't ask. The guy is a disaster.

Woman: Worse than Frank?

Man: You have no idea. And exams are coming up.

Woman: So what're you going to do?

Man: Short of dropping out? I have no idea.

Woman: Move out. Serious. That would be the simplest solution. Just tell the guy, "Sorry, dude, I can't live this way." Why waste energy on something you don't need? Go for it. Be free. Just leave. Focus on what matters: exams.

Man: But I like my dorm. The top floor has the best view of the lake and the breeze in summer is great. Also, I don't know where I'd go. Apartments in town aren't exactly cheap, you know.

Woman: Okay, then go to the housing office. Write out a complaint detailing why you want a new roommate and then let them take care of it. That's their job. Remember: You're paying a lot for this education. You have the right to be satisfied.

Man: But then it would get around that I complain about people. I'm not sure if that's the way I want to go. Maybe as a last resort.

Narrator: Now get ready to answer the prompt. The students discuss two solutions to the man's problem. Identify the problem and the solutions, then state which solution you think is best and why. You have 20 seconds to develop your response and 60 seconds to speak

Task #5 - Track #30 - Professor Plagiarizes - Page 352

Narrator: Directions. Listen to a conversation between two students.

Man: Are you sure?

Woman: Yes. My professor plagiarized my essay, not just a few words, but an entire page verbatim in his last research paper.

Man: This happened once before. A student accused her professor of plagiarism.

Woman: And?

Man: The professor was fired.

Woman: Great. Maybe I should just forget the whole thing. Maybe I should be flattered that a professor borrowed my work, and just shut up about it.

Man: Marilynn, the man did not borrow your work. He stole it. If you'd done this, stolen his work, you would've been kicked out of school in two seconds. No. There's no way you can back down. You've got to confront the man. You need to take your essay and his paper to his office, and tell him in no uncertain terms that what he did was wrong.

Woman: But he's one of the most popular professors.

Man: He's a thief.

Woman: He gave me an A+ —for the essay he plagiarized!

Man: Look, if you don't want to confront him, then you've got to go to the Dean. This is a serious breech of academic ethics. The sooner you confront the man, the better. Who knows how many other student essays he's plagiarized?

Woman: But if I go to the Dean, it'll be all over the school in no time.

Man: Yeah, well, I know what I'd do.

Narrator: Now get ready to answer the prompt. The students discuss two solutions to the woman's problem. Identify the problem and the solutions, then state which solution you think is best and why. You have 20 seconds to develop your response and 60 seconds to speak.

Task #6 - Integrated Speaking

Sample Lecture: Animal Behavior - Track #31 - Page 357

Narrator: Listen to a lecture in a zoology class.

Prof: 1 ➔ Animal behavior can be classified according to the time of day an animal is active. Animals, such as horses, elephants and most birds, are said to be diurnal because they are active during the day and rest at night. Those animals active at dawn and dusk are said to be crepuscular. Beetles, skunks and rabbits fall into this category. The third group are those animals that sleep during the day and are active at night. They are called nocturnal. A good example is the bat. Bats have highly developed eyesight, hearing and smell. This helps them avoid predators and locate food. Being nocturnal also helps them avoid high temperatures during the day, especially in deserts where temperatures can reach well over one hundred degrees Fahrenheit. There are two types of bat: micro bats, or true bats, and mega bats, also called fruit bats. Let's start with mega bats.

2 ➔ Size wise, mega bats range from two to sixteen inches in length. Mega bats have extremely sensitive sight and smell. This helps them locate the flowers and fruit upon which they feed. It is while eating that mega bats play an important role in the distribution of plants. Like bees, mega bats serve as pollinators. When they lick nectar or eat flowers, their bodies become covered in pollen which they, in turn, carry to other trees and plants thereby acting as pollinators. In fact, many of the fruits and vegetables on our tables, such as bananas and peaches, would not be there if mega bats did not pollinate plants and trees.

3 ➔ Next are micro bats. As the name implies, micro bats are quite small, about the size of a mouse. To find food, micro bats use echolocation, high frequency sounds they bounce off insects. The most common micro bat is the vesper or evening bat. Like mega bats, micro bats play an important role in the environment. The average vesper bat, for example, can eat one thousand mosquitoes in one night. By doing so, they control the mosquito population.

Task #1 - Track #32 - Charles Darwin - Page 371

Narrator: Directions. Listen to a lecture in a biology class.

Prof: 1 ➔ In Darwin's lifetime, *On the Origin of Species* sold well; however, it did not sell as well as another popular Darwin book. That book, published in 1881, is titled *The Formation of Vegetable Mould Through the Action of Worms, With Observations on Their Habits*. With the publication of this book, Darwin revolutionized soil and agricultural science. Let's take a look at how he did it.
2 ➔ While most people saw earthworms as an ugly, useless nuisance, Darwin realized their value through a series of experiments. However, his research was overtaken by the writing of *On the Origin of Species*. Later in life, Darwin returned to his study of earthworms and proved that earthworms were not useless pests but in fact played a crucial role in maintaining healthy soil. Darwin observed that earthworms were busy at work turning over the soil by eating it and excreting it. The turning of soil allowed water to penetrate more deeply and allowed more oxygen to enter the ground while the fertilizing added nutrients.
3 ➔ Darwin proved the earthworm's value by doing a simple experiment. In a field near his house, Darwin scattered small pieces of coal. In time, the earthworms had moved so much soil that the pieces of coal had settled deep in the soil proving that the worms were indeed at work turning the soil. With this discovery, Darwin proved that the common earthworm was not a pest but an essential part of the agricultural process.

Narrator: Now get ready to answer the prompt. According to the lecture, how did Charles Darwin revolutionize agricultural science? You have 20 seconds to develop your response and 60 seconds to speak.

Task #2 - Track #33 - Estrogen (HRT) - Page 373

Narrator: Directions. Listen to a lecture in a women's studies class.

Prof: 1 ➔ In women, estrogen regulates the development of female sexual characteristics and reproduction. As a woman reaches middle age, around age 45, the estrogen level decreases. Indications of decreased estrogen are hot flashes, mood swings, and weak or broken bones due to a loss of bone mass. It wasn't until the early 1960's that author Robert Wilson in his book *Feminine Forever* recommended that women could stop the aging process by taking estrogen pills. Suddenly, women started taking estrogen and were feeling much better for it. However, in the early 1970's, a rise in uterine cancer was connected to an increase in estrogen usage, so women stopped taking estrogen almost overnight. In the late 1970's, doctors did an about face and said that it was okay to take estrogen combined with another hormone, progestin. By the 1990's, doctors were so enthusiastic about the estrogen-progestin combination that they were telling women that hormone replacement therapy (HRT for short) was the solution to stopping heart attacks. In short, HRT was a life-saver. By 2000, almost six million women in the United States were taking some form of HRT. That, then, is a brief history of estrogen use in America. But is the news all good? No.
2 ➔ A lot of research has been done on estrogen, the most striking of which was a report by the Women's Health Initiative. Of the 16,000 women they were studying, HRT had increased the risk of heart attack by 29%, breast cancer by 24%, blood clots by 100%, and stroke by 41%. The evidence was clear: hormone-replacement therapy was life-threatening.

Narrator: Now get ready to answer the prompt. The lecture talks about hormone replacement therapy (HRT). Summarize the recent history of HRT usage in the United States and its impact on women's health. You have 20 seconds to develop your response and 60 seconds to speak.

Task #3 - Track #34 - White-Collar Crime - Page 375

Narrator: Directions. Listen to a lecture in a sociology class.

Prof: 1 ➔ Most have never heard of Professor Edwin Sutherland yet we've all heard the phrase white collar crime. Sutherland came to define white collar crime as a "crime committed by a person of respectability and high social status in the course of his occupation," a perfect example of which is Bernard L. Madoff.

2 ➔ On December 11, 2008, the business world was rocked by news no one could believe. Even now, people are still shaking their heads. On that December day, Bernard L. Madoff was arrested for securities fraud. Madoff freely confessed that his private investment fund was in fact a Ponzi scheme, a criminal enterprise in which Madoff took money from one party and, instead of investing it as promised, gave it to another party while taking a cut in the process.

3 ➔ How did Madoff get away with it and for so long? The answer is simple. Madoff was one of the most respected men on Wall Street. He'd served as chairman of the Board of Directors of the National Association of Securities Dealers and was one of the first to champion electronic trading. He was active in high society as well, serving on the boards of prestigious universities and charities. In short, Bernie Madoff commanded so much business and social respect that no one ever suspected that he was running a criminal enterprise. And why would people suspect him? After all, his private investment fund was making people rich, even in bad times. Yet when the stock market crashed in the fall of 2008, Madoff's house of cards crashed with it. With stock prices falling, Madoff investors suddenly wanted their money back. The only problem was Madoff could not return their investments. The money had simply vanished.

Narrator: Now get ready to answer the prompt. How does the lecture define and develop the concept of white-collar crime? You have 20 seconds to develop your response and 60 seconds to speak.

Task #4 - Track #35 - Space Junk - Page 377

Narrator: Directions. Listen to a lecture in an astronomy class.

Prof: 1 ➔ The space race ended when America landed men on the moon on July 16, 1969. Today, the exploration of space continues with the Space Shuttle making regular trips to the International Space Station where scientists are developing new technologies that might one day take us to Mars.

2 ➔ Now, let's change gears and talk about the side of the space race you rarely hear about. In man's race to conquer space, we've created a huge problem with no apparent solution. That problem is space junk. At last count, there were over ten thousand man-made objects in low Earth orbit. What worries scientists most is the larger pieces of space junk, such as satellites. When big pieces of space junk collide, they literally explode. This, in turn, creates thousands of smaller pieces of junk, all of which are orbiting the Earth at more than 17,000 miles per hour. Combined, these smaller pieces of space junk create a corrosive effect when they hit other objects, much like sandblasting a building. This rain of space junk can seriously damage not only operating satellites but it's also a threat to all space flights, manned or otherwise.

3 ➔ The ever-increasing problem of space junk has become known as the Kessler Syndrome. Donald Kessler, a NASA scientist, describes a scenario in which there is so much space junk colliding and dividing that one day it will be too dangerous for man to travel into space. In other words, the garbage orbiting the Earth will destroy anyone and anything that tries to enter it.

Narrator: Now get ready to answer the prompt. According to the lecture, what are the origins of space junk and why is it a problem? You have 20 seconds to develop your response and 60 seconds to speak.

Task #5 - Track #36 - Sharks - Page 379

Narrator: Directions. Listen to a lecture in a marine biology class.

Prof: 1 ➔ All sharks are carnivorous. Some sharks, like the tiger shark, will eat just about anything. However, most sharks are more selective, such as the whale shark, which feeds only on plankton, microscopic organisms on the bottom of the ocean food chain. The most feared shark is the great white. However, despite Hollywood's best efforts, experts do not consider the great white to be the most dangerous. That label goes to the bull shark.

2 ➔ The bull shark, also known as the whaler shark, gets its name from its stocky body, flat nose, and aggressive behavior. Bull sharks can reach a length of six-and-a-half feet and are commonly found patrolling shorelines near populated areas. They will eat anything that comes their way, including garbage and other sharks. What makes the bull shark so aggressive is that their bodies contain more testosterone than any other animal. This makes them arguably the most aggressive predator on the planet. But it doesn't stop there. Bull sharks thrive in any kind of water, including fresh water. Scientists have found bull sharks thousands of miles up the Amazon and as far up the Mississippi River as Illinois. In Nicaragua, bull sharks have even been seen jumping rapids like salmon to get upstream. In Australia, a bull shark travelled eighty miles up an inland waterway system and killed a swimmer.

Narrator: Now get ready to answer the prompt. What does the lecture teach us about sharks? You have 20 seconds to develop your response and 60 seconds to speak.

Speaking Test

Task #3 - Track #37 - Computer Policy - Page 383

Narrator: Directions. Now listen as two students discuss the announcement.

Woman: You've got to be kidding. No laptops in class? Where did you hear this?

Man: I read it on the school web site. Starting Monday, you can't use a laptop in class. If you do, you'll be asked to leave or turn it off. Actually, I think it's a good idea. In my psychology class, everybody's taking notes on their laptops. That's forty people all typing away. You can't believe the noise.

Woman: But my laptop is my life. I always take notes with it. And now they expect me to use a pen? Forget it. Writing by hand is too slow. Not only that but I'll have to rewrite my notes when I get home. Talk about a waste of time. This new policy is definitely going to make a lot of people angry.

Man: I don't think so. The school is just trying to improve classroom conditions. Imagine trying to teach when everybody is looking at their computers and not at you. Laptops are definitely coming between the teacher and the students.

Woman: What angers me is the school said I had to buy a laptop. It was a requirement. So I bought one even though I couldn't afford it. And now the school is telling me not to use the laptop they told me I had to buy? Ridiculous. If I can't use my laptop in class, then the school should refund the cost of buying it. It's only fair.

Narrator: Now get ready to answer the prompt. The woman expresses her opinion about the new policy. State her opinion and explain the reasons she gives for maintaining that position. You have 30 seconds to develop your response and 60 seconds to speak.

Task #4 - Track #38 - The Green Revolution - Page 385

Narrator: Directions. Now listen to a lecture on the same topic.

Prof: 1 ➔ The benefits of the Green Revolution cannot be denied. Yet, as with all revolutions, it takes time to measure the full impact of change both in the short and the long term.

2 ➔ During the Green Revolution, only a select few crops were grown. Those crops, such as wheat, were grown on a massive scale. As a result, soil quality decreased dramatically as the wheat drained nutrients from the soil. Instead of letting the land regenerate by letting it go fallow, or rest, for a year—as was the traditional practice—farmers instead added synthetic fertilizers to boast crop yields. The result was the complete exhaustion of soil quality, so much so that today many large expanses of land are simply dead.

3 ➔ At the same time that a wheat crop was being fed a diet of synthetic fertilizer, it was also being protected against insects with pesticides, such as DDT. DDT, along with many other synthetic pesticides, has since proven to be carcinogenic. DDT was so dangerous, in fact, it was banned because it was wiping out the American bald eagle. And where did all that fertilizer and pesticide end up? In the water system. This caused an explosion of water plants such as algae that thrives on nitrogen-rich fertilizers. This, in turn, reduced the oxygen level to the point where today many once-healthy bodies of water are now dead zones.

Narrator: Now get ready to answer the prompt. What is the Green Revolution and what are its short and long term effects? You have 30 seconds to develop your response and 60 seconds to speak.

Task #5 - Track #39 - Job Options - Page 387

Narrator: Directions. Listen to a conversation between a student and a professor.

Student: So you see, Professor Selznick, I'm not really sure if I need a PhD. I mean, is a PhD really worth it what with all the extra time and money?

Prof: Well, Tiffany, it all depends. Where do you see yourself in ten years?

Student: Good question. To be perfectly honest, I have no idea. That's why I'm here.

Prof: Well, if you plan to teach, a PhD is essential. Colleges and universities won't even look at you if you don't have a PhD. The competition is that stiff. And with the job market the way it is, colleges and universities can pick and choose as they please. Even many high schools these days require a PhD.

Student: So for a teaching job, a PhD will definitely improve my chances of getting hired?

Prof: There's no guarantee, but yes. You have an MBA, right?

Student: Yes. In finance.

Prof: Well, there's always Wall Street. You don't need a PhD to trade stocks and bonds. Surprisingly, though, a lot of business research is done by those with

PhD's in quantitative finance. They use computer modeling. It's all the rage. You could write your ticket with a background like that.

Student: My friend suggested Wall Street as well. I'm just not sure about living in Manhattan. It's really expensive. Not only that but you practically have to inherit a place to park.

Prof: True. Look, I've got to run. Let me know what you decide, okay?

Student: I will. Thanks professor.

Narrator: Now get ready to respond. The professor offers two solutions to the student's problem. Identify the problem and the solutions, then state which solution you think is best and why. You have 20 seconds to develop your response and 60 seconds to speak.

Task #6 - Track #40 - Aristotle's Appeals - Page 389

Narrator: Directions. Listen to a lecture in a composition class.

Prof: 1 ➔ According to Aristotle, there are three modes of appeal: logos, pathos, and ethos. Let's start with logos. Logos, or logic, appeals to reason. One way to appeal to reason is by using deduction. Deduction—and we'll come back to this later on—is a form of reasoning in which you make a conclusion based on a series of related facts or premises. When deducing, you start with a major premise, such as...Oh, I don't know *All English teachers are poor.* This general statement is followed by a specific statement or minor premise, such as *Bob is an English teacher.* From these two premises, a conclusion logically follows: *Bob is poor.* Induction is another form of logic that appeals to reason. When inducing, you combine a series of related facts, such as *Joan loves apples*; *Joan loves blueberries*; *Joan loves mangos.* From these facts, we can make a conclusion: *Joan loves fruit.*

2 ➔ Pathos, in contrast, is an appeal to the emotions. By appealing to the emotions, the arguer can evoke sympathy from an audience. Sympathy, in turn, makes an argument more persuasive.

3 ➔ Next we have ethos. Ethos is an appeal to character. For example, from whom would you buy a laptop computer, a man in a business suit or a man in a T-shirt? Ethically, some might eschew the man in a T-shirt, a T-shirt being the antithesis of business attire therefore unethical, not trustworthy.

4 ➔ Those, then, are Aristotle's three appeals. It's important to remember that a successful argument—a persuasive argument—combines all three appeals.

Narrator: Now get ready to respond. According to the lecture, what are Aristotle's three appeals? Use examples to support your summary. You have 20 seconds to develop your response and 60 seconds to speak.

Listening Section

Office-Hours Conversations

Track #41 - Sample: Office-Hours Conversation - Page 398

Narrator: Sample. Office-hours conversation. Directions. Listen to a sample conversation, then answer the questions on the next page. Do not look at the questions. On test day, you will not see the questions as you listen. Remember to answer all the questions. You will not lose points for a wrong answer. Now listen as a student talks to a professor.

Student: Professor Morgan? Hi. Do you have a minute?
Prof: Sure, Sue. Come in. What's up?
Student: I have a question about my essay you just gave back. Where should I start? I worked really hard on it and...Well, I thought I'd get a better grade. But...Yeah. Talk about a shock. Anyway, can you tell me why I got such a low grade?
Prof: Sure. Do you have the essay with you?
Student: Yes. Right here. It's on the question of legalizing marijuana. You asked us to pick a side and argue in favor of it. I took the pro side.
Prof: Yes. Now I remember. Let me take a look at it. Right. Right.
Student: Is it too short? Is that why I didn't get an A?
Prof: No. Length is really not an issue. Let me rephrase that. There's no connection between length and quality. Some might disagree, but frankly, some of the best essays I've graded have been short. Not one-page short, mind you, but, you know, a couple of really focused pages that address the subject with no extra verbiage. Some of the worst essays I've seen have been...Well, let's just leave it at that, shall we?
Student: Well, if length isn't a problem, then what is?
Prof: Well, it all starts with your opinion. Show me which sentence is your opinion?
Student: It's this one right...here.
Prof: Sorry, but that's not an opinion. You're simply telling me what you'll write about. Remember, your opinion must be arguable. Since you're arguing the pro side of the marijuana issue, you really need to state what you believe in no uncertain terms. By doing do so, your audience will know from the start where you stand.
Student: That's exactly what I was having trouble with. My opinion.
Prof: Try this. Simply say, *Personally, I believe that...*, and then add what you believe. For example, *I believe that Americans should have the right to choose* or *I believe that marijuana should be legalized for medical purposes.* Got it?
Student: Yeah. Okay. I see.
Prof: Also, your opinion must be supportable. When I say supportable, I mean each sentence—sorry, I meant each body paragraph—must have one specific topic, then you must develop that topic in detail. Look at body paragraph one. You start off by saying *legalizing marijuana would be good for the economy* in the first sentence, then you suddenly switch to *it has many medical benefits* in the next sentence. This signals a clear lack of development of both topics.
Student: But that's what I believe.
Prof: Yes. But now we're talking the mechanics of developing and supporting your opinion. Do so by giving each supporting topic its own body paragraph. In this case, *legalizing marijuana would be good for the economy* is the topic of your first body paragraph, and the medical benefits is the topic of your second body paragraph.
Student: You mean, do what I did in paragraph three?

Prof: Exactly. In body paragraph three, you focus on how legalizing marijuana will decrease the crime rate. However, you still need to develop this topic in detail. Give an example. One with statistics. You know what I mean. Do the same for body paragraphs one and two. Remember: The more you develop your supporting examples, the more persuasive your argument will be. Right now, you're just scratching the surface. To be honest, this reads more like a first draft.

Student: I see what you mean. Can I rewrite it for a higher grade?

Prof: Sure. Can you have it on my desk by nine tomorrow morning?

Student: By nine? I'll try.

Narrator: Now get ready to answer the questions. Answer each question based on what is stated or implied in the conversation.

1. What are the student and the professor mainly discussing?
2. Why does the student visit the professor?
3. In which areas does the student's essay need revising? Select two. This is a 1-point question.
4. What does the professor think about short essays?

5. Listen again to part of the conversation, then answer the question.

Prof: Remember: The more you develop your supporting examples, the more persuasive your argument will be. Right now, you're just scratching the surface. To be honest, this reads more like a first draft.

Narrator: What does the professor imply when she says this?

Prof: Right now, you're just scratching the surface.

Track #42 - Practice: Content Questions - Page 417

Narrator: Practice. Content questions. Directions. Listen to each prompt, then answer the question.

Narrator: 1. Listen as a student talks to a professor.

Student: Professor Peters?

Prof: Hi, Phyllis. Thanks for dropping by. Were you able to transfer?

Student: Not yet. The registrar said I had to wait a week.

Prof: That class is always full. Professor Cameron is really popular. You sure you don't want to take my class?

Student: No offense, professor, but chemistry is not what I'm aiming for.

Prof: What happened to pre-med?

Student: It's history. Back to square one, I guess.

Prof: Don't worry. Finding your major is all part of the process. Let me know if you need any more help.

Student: Thanks, professor.

Narrator: Now get ready to answer the question. What is topic of discussion?

Narrator: 2. Listen as a student talks to a professor.

Prof: Hi, Gina.

Student: You wanted to see me, professor Austin?

Prof: I do. You've been missing in action, lately. So far you've missed six classes.
Student: Really? Are you sure?
Prof: That's what my records show. Your homework is all up to date and you completed your presentation. It's just your attendance.
Student: How many classes can I miss?
Prof: The limit is five. How's your attendance in other classes?
Student: About the same. This new job I have really eats up a lot of my time.
Prof: Just to let you know, if you miss anymore classes, I will have no choice but to lower you a grade overall.
Student: Can you show me the last day I was absent?
Prof: Sure. It's on my spreadsheet here. You missed, let's see...You missed last Friday. That makes six absences.
Student: But I was here last Friday.
Prof: Are you sure?
Student: Yes. You asked me to summarize the different types of earthquakes and...
Prof: Ah, you said you were in an earthquake last year in San Francisco. Right. Now I remember. How did that work out, anyway? You didn't really say.
Student: I was terrified. The windows fell out of the hotel I was in and the building shook for about three seconds, but nobody was hurt. The weird thing was it's like I had absolutely no control. I just had to ride it out.
Prof: I was in Thailand back when that big earthquake hit in 2004. I thought the world was coming to an end. It hit 9.1 on the Richter scale.
Student: Whoa.
Prof: You know what? I'm confusing you with the other Gina. Gina...?
Student: Jones.
Prof: Right.
Student: It happens a lot, actually.
Prof: I can imagine. So you've only missed five classes. My apologies.

Narrator: Now get ready to answer the question. What are the speakers mainly talking about?

Narrator: 3. Listen as a student talks to a professor.

Student: You know, professor, it's not as easy as I thought.
Prof: Like most things it takes practice.
Student: The worst part is I'm so nervous. What should I do?
Prof: Before you give your presentation tomorrow, do some breathing exercises, you know, breathe in, breathe out. That's what I always do. It works for me.
Student: I hope I don't blow it.
Prof: Don't worry. You'll be fine.

Narrator: Now get ready to answer the question. What is the student's problem?

Narrator: 4. Listen as a student talks to a professor.

Student: Professor Morrison?
Prof: Hi, Bill. Come in. We need to talk. Were you answering questions with your iPhone last class?
Student: Ah...Yeah. I was. Why?
Prof: And the class text is on your iPhone, I take it?
Student: Oh, yeah. That's right.
Prof: All one thousand pages?
Student: Ah, yeah. The quality's amazing. Want to see?

Prof: Ah, no. I didn't know that the assigned text was downloadable. Where did you get it from, if you don't mind my asking?
Student: I downloaded it from this site in, you know...Europe. Why?
Prof: I assume it's legal, this site in Europe?
Student: Actually, over there they have different laws about downloading material. They're not as uptight about it as we are.
Prof: That's not the point. The point is you are supposed to buy a hard copy of the course text.
Student: What if I don't have the money?
Prof: Then try the library. They always have copies on reserve.
Student: What if all the copies have been checked out?
Prof: Have you checked?
Student: I have. Every day. All out.
Prof: Look, I'm not trying to play cop, okay? It's just that when you enroll in a course, you have to buy a hard copy of the text. Those are the rules. The nature of the game. What about a used one?
Student: Used or new it's all the same. When added up, my average text book cost is over $700.00. That might not be a lot of money to you, but it is to me. I have two part-time jobs and I still can't make ends meet. I mean, can you blame me for trying to save some money?
Prof: Okay, so where does that leave us?

Narrator: Now get ready to answer the question. What is the focus of the conversation?

Track #43 - Practice: Purpose Questions - Page 420

Narrator: Practice. Purpose questions. Directions. Listen to each prompt, then answer the question.

Narrator: 1. Listen as a student talks to a professor.

Prof: Hi, Raquel. I got your email. Tell me again why you need my signature?
Student: The lab tech won't let me work at night without it.
Prof: That's strange. I've never had to approve anything before.
Student: It's for security. That's what the lab tech said. She's so persnickety.
Prof: Just my signature? Anything else?
Student: Nope. If you could sign this permission form, that would be great.
Prof: Sure. No problem.

Narrator: Now get ready to answer the question. Why does the student visit the professor?

Narrator: 2. Listen as a student talks to a professor.

Prof: Hi, Lilian. What's up?
Student: I was wondering, professor, if my friend could sit in on one of your lectures. She's thinking of taking your course, but would like to know a little bit more about it first. You know, kind of like test the waters first.
Prof: Generally, it's not the school's policy to allow non registered students to attend lectures.
Student: I understand.
Prof: Here's what I suggest. Tell your friend to email me and I can talk to her privately. That's probably the best option.
Student: Actually, I have two friends who want to talk to you.

Narrator: Now get ready to answer the question. What is the student's purpose for talking to her professor?

Narrator: 3. Listen as a student talks to a professor.

Student: Could you explain that again, professor?
Prof: Sure. As I said in class, one essential difference between Canada and the United States is the individual's view of government. Americans have a long distrust of government going back to the Revolution. As a result, they hate paying taxes and generally view the government as a threat to individual rights.
Student: And Canadians?
Prof: Canadians are more willing to trust their government. The relationship is more a social compact with universal health care playing a big part. Rarely, if ever, will you hear a Canadian complaining about health care or claiming that his or her *rights* are being denied.
Student: In class, you said something about Canadians having an inferiority complex. What's that all about?
Prof: Right. Many Canadians are stuck on the idea that if you're really want to make it big, you have to go south to Harvard and Hollywood, the reason being that making it in America is the true measure of success. I'm sure this attitude is changing, what with globalization, but think about it: What was the last Canadian movie you saw?
Student: Ah...
Prof: Exactly. But you know all the Canadian actors, right? Jim Carey, the guy who plays Austin Powers, Kim Catrall in *Sex and the City,* Keifer Sutherland in *24,* Michael J. Fox, you know, *Back to the Future,* and James Cameron, director of *Avatar.*
Student: Really? James Cameron is Canadian?
Prof: Born and raised. And that's just film. Now, as all that talent flows south, American culture floods north, so much so that American culture threatens to eliminate any sense of Canadian identity. To combat this, the Canadian government must, you know, step up to the plate and financially support indigenous industries, like publishing and film, with tax money. In short, Canadian tax money is a way of preserving the Canadian identity against American cultural hegemony. Once again, the social compact is in play here. Most Canadians think that's a good thing. Here in America, that would never happen. Washington investing in Hollywood? Forget it.
Student: So what would happen if the Canadian government withdrew its tax support of indigenous industries like film and publishing?
Prof: What would happen? You do the math.

Narrator: Now get ready to answer the question. What does the student need clarified?

Narrator: 4. Listen as a student talks to a professor.

Prof: Hey, Jane.
Student: You wanted to see me, professor?
Prof: Right. Come in. Close the door.
Student: Is this about what I said in class? I apologize if I came off sounding too strong. But I really believe what I said about a woman's right to choose.
Prof: No need to apologize. Your argument was bang on. It blew me away. In fact, I think you should put it in writing.
Student: You mean, an essay?

Prof: Exactly. It stands a good chance of being published.
Student: Really? No way.
Prof: Sure.
Student: That's great. Really. But I have no clue how to go about it.
Prof: You mean getting it out there?
Student: Yeah. I mean, where do I start?
Prof: Start by putting it down on paper, of course. I'll help you with the editing and formatting.
Students: Thanks.
Prof: At the same time google academic journals, you know, Yale, Princeton, Harvard.
Student: Harvard? Really?
Prof: Why not? Start at the top. That's what I always say.
Student: Why academic journals?
Prof: Often they're theme-related. The trick is to find a journal related to what you're writing about. Women's issues are very topical, so you stand a good chance of getting published.
Student: What about getting an agent?
Prof: You can try. But the thing about agents is that they're in the business of making money. That means they want a commercial product. Your essay, while good, is not what I would call commercial.
Student: Right. I understand. No money. Just bragging rights.

Narrator: Now get ready to answer the question. Why did the professor ask to see the student?

Track #44 - Practice : Single-Answer Detail Questions - Pg. 423

Narrator: Practice. Single-answer detail questions. Directions. Listen as a student talks to a professor, then answer the questions.

Student: Professor Dirk? Is this a good time?
Prof: Cindy. It's always a good time. Come in. Come in.
Student: I've been reviewing my notes and what you said last time we met.
Prof: Good. Good. And? What's wrong? Cold feet?
Student: Frozen, actually. I know that it's all part of the scientific process, but I'm not sure if I can go through with it, you know, vivisection. I know all the arguments—that it's for science, and it's how progress is made, and to fight disease we have no other choice—but I just can't do it. I can't hurt a living animal.
Prof: Keep in mind, Cindy, that we breed these mice especially for this purpose. They are not pets; they have no names, have very little human contact. They are simply objects of investigation, an essential link—a critical link—in medical research. Did you know that in the twentieth century almost every medical achievement was based on animal testing? Even today, right now, schools and labs all over the country are doing the same thing: using animals to advance the cause mankind.
Student: Right. Is it possible to do it digitally?
Prof: Vivisection? I'm afraid not. True, we have some pretty amazing software, but a computer can't extract DNA. And that's what this assignment is all about: cells extracted to process DNA. One day I'm sure it'll all be done virtually, but that is then and this is now. Like it or not, vivisection is the only way to get the target DNA—and to complete the assignment.
Student: Would it be all right if I just watched?

Prof: I'm afraid not. This is a hands-on assignment. It constitutes 40% of your final grade. I really need to see the extraction process from start to finish. That said, class starts in ten minutes. So, what've you decided?
Student I've decided that I'm not cut out for this.
Prof: But you want to be a vet, yes?
Student: I did. I'm great at chemistry and biology. I am. I even thought I could work with animals in a lab, but obviously I can't. The thing is I never would have known that if I hadn't taken this course. The thought of experimenting on a living animal no matter what the reason is...Well, I think you know where I stand.
Prof: Then you're dropping the course. Is that what I'm hearing?
Student: I am. That's why I came by. I wanted to thank you for all your help, and for listening to me, strange as it must seem.
Prof: It's not strange at all. Life is full of crossroads. What about your other courses?
Student: I'll finish them and take a break for awhile. Maybe work for a year of two. I need to rethink just what it is I want to do. Being a vet obviously isn't in the cards.

Narrator: Now get ready to answer the questions.

1. What can't the student do?
2. What are the "objects of investigation?"
3. What can't be done virtually?
4. What percentage of the final grade is the assignment?
5. What is the student dropping out of?
6. The professor says, "Life is full of..."

Track #45 - Practice: Multi-Answer Detail Questions - Page 426

Narrator: Practice. Multi-answer detail questions. Directions. Listen to each prompt, then answer the question.

Narrator: 1. Listen as a student talks to a professor. This is a two-point question.

Student: So, ah, professor, let me get this straight. To complete this assignment, I need to give a ten-minute presentation and hand in a written summary of my presentation. Correct?
Prof: No. A summary is not necessary. Just a bibliography.
Student: Properly annotated, right?
Prof: No. Just give me the author, publisher, and date of publication.
Student: What about when the author was born?
Prof: Not necessary.
Student: Okay. Ah, one more thing. What about the interviews I did?
Prof: Really? You did interviews? Great. Who did you talk to?
Student: I talked to Professor William Foster.
Prof: Bill Foster? The Bill Foster? From Oxford?
Student: Yes. I ran into him by chance at a bookstore downtown. I just walked up to him and said, "Are you Professor Foster, the one who wrote *Metaphysical Moments in the New Millennium*? And he said yes. I asked him if I could talk to him about it and he said sure. We actually talked for about two hours in a Starbucks. It was amazing. He is so smart. And funny. He had me in stitches. I thought he was so serious. I mean, you look at his photos and you'd think he was this grumpy old curmudgeon, what with that beard and all the crazy hair. Boy, was I wrong. Talk about judging a book by its cover.
Prof: You're very lucky. Normally William Wellington Foster doesn't give interviews or travel. I can't remember the last time he left the UK. Did you get his autograph?
Student: I did.
Prof: He didn't mind?

Student: Not at all. I also interviewed Karen Scott, you know, the famous feminist writer who wrote *Listening to the Apple of Your Eye*. I'm not sure if I'll use her, but it was pretty interesting. She disagrees with pretty much everything Foster says, so it was a great counterpoint.
Prof: You've been working hard. Excellent.
Student: So what should I do?
Prof: Hand in a list of all those you interviewed.
Student: Okay. When's it all due?
Prof: A week from Monday.

Narrator: Now get ready to answer the question. What must the student do to complete the assignment? Select three.

Narrator: 2. Listen as a student talks to a professor. This is a one-point question.

Prof: Hi, Liz. I got your email. You said you needed some help?
Student: Yes. I'm applying for a summer internship at Amnesty International.
Prof: Great. The experience will keep you in good stead.
Student: I need a letter recommendation. I was wondering if you could...
Prof: Sure. How many do you need?
Student: Two, actually. With your signature on each.
Prof: Consider it done. Anything else?
Student: Yes. They might call and interview you. Would you mind?
Prof: Not at all. Ah, any idea when they might call?
Student: No. But I can find out.
Prof: Great. That'd be a big help. So, are you going to work stateside or abroad?
Student: I'm not sure. There's an opening in their Rome office. I speak Italian so I'd definitely go if they'd ask me. But it's not paid, so that's a problem.
Prof: You know, I have a friend working for Amnesty International, an old classmate from NYU. She's pretty high-ranking. I could talk to her, see if she could hire you on. The pay wouldn't be much, mind you, but at least you'd get your foot in the door.
Student: Thanks, professor. That's very generous. Really. But let me sleep on it. Okay?

Narrator: Now get ready to answer the question. What does the student need from her professor? Select two.

Narrator: 3. Listen as a student talks to a professor. This is a two-point question.

Student: Professor Salander?
Prof: Oh, hi, Liz. Did you get my message?
Student: I did. Thanks. By the way, thanks to you I got the job.
Prof: Job?
Student: Helping Professor Larson.
Prof: Right. Congrats. Isn't Professor Larson a kick?
Student: Totally. He's got me doing tons of research. And get this. He wants me to go to the Amazon over Christmas and help him tag jaguars!
Prof: Fantastic. Just remember to take a lot of bug spray and malaria pills.
Student: Really?
Prof: Forewarned is forearmed, right?
Student: Right. I'm taking my laptop too, but I'm not sure how I'll get power. I mean, it's the Amazon, right? Not a lot of outlets in a jungle.
Prof: Try solar.
Student: Really? You mean like a solar-powered laptop?

Prof: No. A charger. I took one to the Peru on my last dig. I set it out on a rock every morning. It's basically a small sheet of photovoltaic cells. They capture sunlight and turn it into electricity. It sure is handy. Believe me.

Student: That's exactly what I need.

Prof: As a matter of fact, it's right here in my drawer. A few hours in the sun and this thing will charge anything. You want to borrow it?

Student: Really?

Prof: It's not doing anything sitting here in the drawer.

Narrator: Now get ready to answer the question. What will the student take to the Amazon? Select three.

Narrator: 4. Listen as a student talks to a professor. This is a one-point question.

Prof: There are two graduate English degrees, Norma. An MA, a master of arts, and a doctorate, a PhD.

Student: What's the difference between an MA and an MFA?

Prof: The focus of an MA is research. For example, you choose an area you want to study, like—oh, I don't know, let's say early Greek tragedies—and you study it with the aim of one day teaching it.

Student: And an MFA?

Prof: The focus of an MFA is on writing. It's geared more toward those who want to write fiction or non fiction. In that sense, it's more an art course, like, you know, music or graphic design.

Student: So which do you recommend?

Narrator: Now get ready to answer the question. Which two graduate English degrees does the professor describe? Select two.

Track #46 - Practice: Question-First Function Questions - Pg. 437

Narrator: Practice. Question-first function questions. Directions. Answer each question based on what is stated or implied.

Narrator: 1. Why does the professor say this?

Prof: Toni, you know that each homework assignment is due at the end of the every week. I would love to bend the rules for you, but that would not be fair to other students. That said, you have till Friday to put things right.

Narrator: 2. Why does the professor say this?

Prof: As I mentioned in class, Carlos—last class—because Rome had a large standing army—this huge, massive army—it constantly needed money and men. By periodically taking a census of population—you know, counting heads basically—the Roman government knew how much tax money it could raise for the army and the available manpower it could draw from.

Narrator: 3. Why does the professor say this?

Prof: Look, Bill, I can't meet today. I have a faculty meeting in five minutes. Take a rain check? How about we aim for...ah, noon tomorrow?

Narrator: 4. Why does the student say this?

Student: I did the research as you suggested and discovered something amazing. I mean, I don't know how to put this. It's...Well, you'll see. It'll totally blow you away. You got a minute, professor?

Track #47 - Practice: Segment-First Function Questions - Pg. 438

Narrator: Practice. Segment-first function questions. Directions. Answer each question based on what is stated or implied.

Narrator: 1. Listen to part of a conversation, then answer the question.

Prof: No. Length is really not an issue. Let me rephrase that. There is no connection between length and quality. Some might disagree, but frankly, some of the best essays I've graded have been short.

Narrator: Why does the professor say this?

Prof: Let me rephrase that.

Narrator: 2. Listen to part of a conversation, then answer the question.

Prof: The thing to remember about internet piracy is this: It's plague, a plague costing consumers and businesses billions, a plague that is only getting worse.

Narrator: Why does the professor say this?

Prof: It's plague, a plague costing consumers and businesses billions, a plague that is only getting worse.

Narrator: 3. Listen to part of a conversation, then answer the question.

Woman: So for a teaching job, a PhD will definitely improve my chances of getting hired?
Prof: There's no guarantee, but yes. You have an MBA, right?
Woman: Yes. In finance.
Prof: Well, there's always Wall Street. You don't need a PhD to trade stocks and bonds. Surprisingly, though, a lot of business research is done by those with PhD's in quantitative finance. They use computer modeling. It's all the rage. You could write your ticket with a background like that.

Narrator: What does the professor mean when he says this?

Prof: It's all the rage.

Narrator: 4. Listen to part of a conversation, then answer the question.

Student: Professor Page, what exactly is rock and roll? I missed it in class.
Prof: Good question, Jimmy. Rock and roll is basically blues with an attitude. Let me try that again. Rock and roll is a salad, a big musical salad with the heart of a rebel. Ah, now I'm mixing metaphors.

Narrator: What does the professor mean when she says this?

Prof: Ah, now I'm mixing metaphors.

Track #48 - Practice: Direct-Attitude Questions - Page 441

Narrator: Practice. Direct-attitude questions. Directions. Listen to each prompt, then answer the questions.

Narrator: 1. Listen as a student talks to a professor.

Student: Professor Pickett, do you have a minute?
Prof: Hi, Justine. Sure. What's up?
Student: I just wanted to get your opinion on something.
Prof: Shoot.
Student: Do you think I stand a chance in the debate tomorrow?
Prof: Not only do I think you've got a chance—you and the rest of the debating team—but I think we are going to clean Harvard's clock.

Narrator: What does the professor believe?

Narrator: 2. Listen as a student talks to a professor.

Prof: Hey, Tina. Thanks for dropping by. So what did you think of your presentation? I didn't get the chance to ask you in class.
Student: Personally? To be honest? I think I nailed it.

Narrator: What does the student believe?

Narrator: 3. Listen as a student talks to a professor.

Student: Rewrite, professor? You mean, my essay? Again?
Prof: Yes. I'm giving you the chance to improve your grade.
Student: But I like what I wrote. It's how I feel, what I believe. Besides, grades really don't mean that much to me.

Narrator: What is the student's opinion of grades?

Narrator: 4. Listen as a student talks to a professor.

Student: What did you think of my thesis, Professor?
Prof: Let's see. You say, and I quote, "Videos games are a popular form of entertainment." That's not a thesis, Charleen. It's a fact and thus not arguable.
Student: But it's true.
Prof: Right. True because it's a fact.
Student: Oh. Right. I get it.

Narrator: What is the professor's opinion of the student's thesis?

Track #49 - Practice: Inferred-Attitude Questions - Page 444

Narrator: Practice. Inferred-attitude questions. Directions. Listen to each prompt, then answer the question.

Narrator: 1. Listen as a student talks to a professor.

Student: Professor Bergman? Hi. Got a minute?
Prof: Sure Peggy. What's up?
Student: It's about the debate tomorrow.
Prof: You're arguing for more government, correct?
Student: Less.
Prof: Right. So, all prepared?
Student: I think so. Anyway, the reason I stopped you is because, well, tomorrow's supposed to be a really nice day, and I thought it'd be kind of cool to do the debate outside on the quad. It'd be a nice change of pace, don't you think? You know, on the grass under a tree. We could get some food too. Maybe some pizza or something.
Prof: Or something.
Student: Well, what do think?
Prof: I don't.

Narrator: What can we infer about having the debate outside?

Narrator: 2. Listen as a student talks to a professor.

Prof: "Computer games are the best thing since sliced bread." Really, Lilian? That's your thesis?
Student: Ah, yeah. Why? It's an opinion, right?
Prof: It is.
Student: So what's the matter?
Prof: Don't get me wrong. I'm all for analogies as a way to start an essay. But this one? It seems, how should I put it—like a fish out of water. Do you catch my drift?
Student: Right. Lose the cliché.

Narrator: What can we infer from the conversation?

Narrator: 3. Listen as a student talks to a professor.

Prof: Hi, Peter. Thanks for dropping by.
Student: Sure. What's wrong? I know. It's my cell phone, right?
Prof: It is rather annoying. Right in the middle of class. Can't you turn it off?
Student: I can. But I'm expecting an important call. It's about a job. I interviewed and everything. If I turn my phone off, I might miss it.
Prof: What about vibrating mode?
Student: Yeah. I can do that. But I might miss the call, and I really need this job. Serious. The job market has really gone south. I've been looking for ages. What's this?
Prof: It's the school policy regarding cell phone use in classrooms.
Student: I got one, thanks. You handed them out on the first day of class.
Prof: Maybe you should review it. Point number one in particular. Read it carefully so we can avoid having this conversation again.

Narrator: What is the professor suggesting?

Narrator: 4. Listen as a student talks to another student.

Woman: But that's the point. Why does a mascot have to be serious? Why can't a mascot be fun, like a chicken or a goat, or a giraffe even? Education is way too serious.
Man: Alice...
Woman: What?
Man: Earth to Alice.
Woman: What!

Narrator: How does the man feel about having a chicken for a mascot?

Track #50 - Practice: Inferred-Action Questions - Page 447

Narrator: Practice. Inferred-action questions. Directions. Listen to each prompt, then answer the question.

Narrator: 1. Listen as a student talks to a professor.

Prof: "Proponents of standardized testing are quick to wave the flag of comparative statistics as being the best way to measure academic performance." I like that. I do. Very good. Drives the point home. "Yet what supporters of standardized testing fail to realize is that, in their rush for statistics, they have boiled education down to a game, a game in which there are winners and losers. I'm sorry, but education is not about winners and losers." And that is your point, Josh. And it's a good one. Excellent essay. Bravo. Well done.
Student: Really, professor? You're joking, right?
Prof: No. That's why I wanted to see you. This is an excellent piece of writing. Well researched, well developed. You've hit the nail right on the head. Not only that but you've worked hard. You should be proud.
Student: Thanks.

Narrator: What will the professor probably do?

Narrator: 2. Listen as a student talks to a professor.

Student: Professor Keaton, that was a great point you made in a class, you know, the one about how video games teach a false sense of reality. I was at the mall yesterday and there was this new military recruiting center. I couldn't believe it. It was like walking into a video game store.
Prof: I've heard about these new high-tech recruiting centers.
Student: You should see the stuff they've got. You can climb into an Apache or an F-16, and suddenly you're flying over a desert, or an ocean—like it's the real thing. Not only that, but you get shot at. It's like you're in a...in a...
Prof: A war?
Student: Yeah. I mean, it was real—but it wasn't—just like what you were talking about in class, you know, creating a false sense of reality using virtual images.
Prof: Right. So, Henry, did you sign up?

Narrator: We can infer from the conversation that the professor has not...

Narrator: 3. Listen as a student talks to a professor.

Prof: Really, Claudia? But, in the end, don't we have to sacrifice some freedom to be safe?

Student: It depends, professor, on how you define safe?
Prof: Okay, fair enough. So how do you define it?
Student: Simple. What I do in the privacy of my home is nobody's business but my own. Period. I don't need the government telling me what I can or can't do with my computer or anything else. The United States is a democracy not a dictatorship.

Narrator: From the conversation, we can infer that the student will probably continue to...

Narrator: 4. Listen as a student talks to a professor.

Student: As you can see, I'm still not sure what direction I should take after graduating. You'd think with a PhD I could write my ticket.
Prof: There's always Wall Street, you know. You don't need a PhD to trade stocks and bonds. Surprisingly, though, a lot of business research is done by those with PhD's, particularly in quantitative finance. They use computer modeling. It's all the rage. The money's not too bad either.
Student: I like the idea of Wall Street. I do. And thanks for the advice, professor, but I think I need to broaden my horizons.

Narrator: What will the student probably do?

Track #51 - Sample: Service-Encounter Conversation - Pg. 448

Narrator: Sample. Service-Encounter Conversation. Directions. Listen to a sample conversation, then answer the questions on the next page. Do not look at the questions. On test day, you will not see the questions as you listen. Remember to answer all the questions. You will not lose points for a wrong answer. Now listen as a student talks to a member of the school's IT support staff.

Student: Hi. Is this IT support?
Support: Yes, it is. How can I help you? Let me guess. Your computer got hit by the email virus going round and you want to know how to restore your corrupted files, right?
Student: Actually, my computer didn't get hit.
Support: Oh, one of the lucky ones. So, what's up?
Student: I just bought an iPod Touch.
Support: Sweet. How much?
Student: A lot. Look, the reason I'm calling is because I can't connect my iPod to the internet.
Support: You mean the school's wireless network?
Student: Right.
Support: What exactly is the problem?
Student: When I open my email, a dialogue box asks me to log on to the school's wireless network. I log on with my school ID and my password, just like with my laptop, then another dialogue box pops up and says, "No wireless network." How can there be no wireless network when everybody around me is connected? I'm like totally confused. This never happens with my laptop. What am I doing wrong? It's something really simple, right?
Support: Probably security. What kind of encryption are you using?
Student: Excuse me?
Support: Encryption. The school's wireless network is encrypted.
Student: I'm sorry. I don't follow.
Support: Encryption basically means the wireless signal floating around the school here—well, not so much floating but, you know, covering—has been scrambled into a secret code that can only be opened by the right security setting on the device

you're using. The old kind of wireless encryption is called WEP. That's short for wired-equivalent privacy. The school stopped using it two years ago because it had serious security issues. We now use WPA. That's short for wi-fi protected access. Your iPod is probably set for WEP.

Student: Ahhh..,Right. Can you just tell me how to set it up? I'm kind of in a hurry here.
Support: Sure. Boot up your iPod. Go to your home screen. Open settings, then go to network. See it?
Student: Network. Network. Right.
Support: Open network, then open Wi-Fi.
Student: Okay. It's open.
Support: At the top of the screen, you should see security. Open it.
Student: Open security. Got it.
Support: You should see a menu that gives you a choice of encryption settings starting with WEP. See it?
Student: Got it. There's WEP followed by WPA and WPA2. Those are wireless security settings?
Support: Bingo. The school uses WPA, so select it and you should be good to go.
Student: Oh, my God. You're a genius!
Support: Sweet. Anything else I can help you with?
Student: Nope. That's it.
Support: Hey, would you mind filling out a survey? It's about how well I solved your problem. It would only take a sec.
Student: Sure. No, problem.

Narrator: Now get ready to answer the questions. Answer each question based on what is stated or implied in the conversation.

1. What are the student and the IT staffer mainly discussing?
2. What is the student's problem?
3. What are the wireless security settings? Select three.
4. Why does the student say this?

Student: Oh, my God. You're a genius!

5. Listen again to part of the conversation, then answer the question.

Support: What exactly is the problem?
Student: When I open my email, a dialogue box asks me to log on to the school's wireless network. I log on with my school ID and my password, just like with my laptop, then another dialogue box pops up and says, "No wireless network." How can there be no wireless network when everybody around me is connected? I'm like totally confused. This never happens with my laptop. What am I doing wrong? It's something really simple, right?
Support: Probably security. What kind of encryption are you using?
Student: Excuse me?
Support: Encryption. The school's wireless network is encrypted.
Student: I'm sorry. I don't follow.

Narrator: What does the student mean by this?

Student: I'm sorry. I don't follow.

Track #52 - Practice: Content Questions - Page 462

Narrator: Practice. Content questions. Directions. Listen to each prompt, then answer the question.

Narrator: 1. Listen as a student talks to a security guard.

Student: Really? I got a ticket for parking in the wrong spot? But I thought student parking was red.
Security: Staff is red. Students yellow. Visitors blue.
Student: You know, somebody should repaint the lines. They're really hard to see.
Security: Here. Give me your ticket. We'll let it slide this time.
Student: Thanks.
Security: And remember.
Student: Yes?
Security: The garage closes at eleven.

Narrator: What is main topic of discussion?

Narrator: 2, Listen as a student talks to an admin.

Student: Hi. Can you tell me if my student ID ready?
Admin: Sure. Name?
Student: Jane Smitts. I had my picture taken yesterday.
Admin: Let me check. Smart. Smith. Smitts. Here you go. That'll be ten dollars.
Student: Ten dollars? I have to shell out ten bucks for an ID? Excuse me? Since when do I have to pay for my student ID?
Admin: Since the new policy. Cash or charge?
Student: Wa...Wait. I don't get it. New policy? What new policy? I thought getting a student ID was part of my tuition.
Admin: It was. But because of government cutbacks, the school now has to charge extra for IDs. It was announced in a school-wide memo.
Student: Memo? What memo?
Admin: An email memo. It was sent out to all students and faculty two months ago. Cash or charge?
Student: I didn't get a memo.
Admin: It's posted right here.
Student: What if I don't want to pay?
Admin: All students are required to carry a digital photo ID. If security stops you, or you need access a lab or to use the library, you'll need to identify yourself.
Student: What if I just hold up my tuition receipt? That would prove I'm a student here, right?
Admin: It would. But the new policy says you must carry a digital photo ID.
Student: Okay. So if you were me, what would you do?
Admin: I'm really not the person to ask.
Student: Who is?
Admin: The registrar. Cynthia Nichols. Second floor. Room 310. Next.

Narrator: What is the focus of the conversation?

Narrator: 3. Listen as a student talks to a security guard.

Security: Are you the student who called security?
Student: Yes. The bio lab is supposed to be open but the door's locked. Can you unlock it for me? I really have to complete an assignment by tomorrow morning. If I don't, my head's going to be on the chopping block.
Security: No problem. And you are?
Student: Kenichi. Kenichi Mori. Just call me George.
Security: Right. There you go, George. The door's open.
Student: Thanks. What happens if I have to step out for a minute?
Security: The door will lock. Are you alone?
Student: Yes.
Security: Then give security a ring. I'll scoot on by and open it for you. Also, I'll need to see some ID.
Student: Sure. There you go.
Security: Thanks.

Narrator: What is subject of discussion?

Narrator: 4. Listen as a student talks to a librarian.

Admin: What's the title of that book again?
Student: *PowerPoint for Dummies.*
Admin: *PowerPoint for Dummies*? I'm afraid not. The school library doesn't carry those titles.
Student: Really? Why not?
Admin: I can't say for sure. Probably because they send the wrong message.
Student: Really? But I use them all the time. They're fast and easy. And cheap.
Admin: Hey, if it works? Anything else?
Student: Ah, yeah. I'm also looking for another book. Just let check my notes. It's for my philosophy class.
Admin: With Professor Reamer?
Student: Yeah.
Admin: I had her. Isn't she great?
Student: Yeah—and tough. She's got us burning the midnight oil.
Admin: She does make you hit the books. So you're probably looking for Kant, right?
Student: No. Not Kant.
Admin: Kierkegaard?
Student: No. Oh, what is it? It's right on the tip of my tongue.
Admin: Schopenhauer?
Student: We've done all those guys. Here it is. *The Birth of Tragedy.*
Admin: Nietzsche. Right. *The Birth of Tragedy.* Let me see if it's available. Napster. Negotiating. Neologisms. Nietzsche. You're in luck. It's on the shelf. Number N789.PH34. Here I'll right down.
Student: Thanks. Which floor?
Admin: Fourth.

Narrator: What is the subject of discussion?

Track #53 - Practice: Purpose Questions - Page 463

Narrator: Practice. Purpose questions. Directions. Listen to each prompt, then answer the question.

Narrator: 1. Listen as a student talks to an admin.

Admin: So which scholarship did you have in mind?
Student: One with full tuition. You know, for the whole year.
Admin: There's a lot of competition for those. Suffice it to say, they go fast.
Student: So I'm too late?
Admin: For this year? Yes. Would like to apply for next year?
Student: Actually, I need the money now. Are there any scholarships I can apply for?
Admin: Let me take a look. What's your major?
Student: Philology.
Admin: Philology. A philosopher, huh?
Student: Yeah. Sorta.
Admin: Okay. Philology. There's no scholarship specific to that discipline.
Student: What is there?
Admin: There's the Scott-Shackleton Scholarship for Polar Research. It's five-thousand dollars.
Student: I don't think so. Anything else?
Admin There's the Pierce-Val Scholarship for Economics. It's one thousand, and...Let's see. What else? How about this? The Parker-Bowles Research Scholarship for the Enrichment of the Humanities.
Student: Humanities? That's a pretty broad area.
Admin: It's a ten-thousand dollar research grant. Are you researching anything related to the humanities?
Student: No. I'm still in first year. Looks like I'm out of luck then.
Admin: Can I suggest something?
Student: Sure.
Admin: Philology is a definitely humanity.
Student: I know. But, like I said, I'm not researching anything.
Admin: There's no harm in applying. Hey, you never know?

Narrator: Why does the student visit financial aid?

Narrator: 2. Listen as a student talks to maintenance.

Staffer: Hello? Campus Maintenance.
Student: Hi. I'm a student over in Noble Hall. Dorm Eight.
Staffer: Let me guess. The toilet, right?
Student: Ah, no. Not this time. The raccoon. He's back.
Staffer: In the garbage?
Student: Actually, he's parked under my bed. Can you come over and, you know, talk to him?
Staffer: Don't try and touch him.
Student: I wasn't planning to. Actually, I was planning to study calculus. I have an exam tomorrow, but my guest is a bit of a...What should I say? Distraction?
Staffer: Understood. I'm on my way.

Narrator: Why does the student call maintenance?

Narrator: 3. Listen as a student talks to a security guard.

Student: Hi. I'd like to report a stolen laptop.
Security: Are you sure it was stolen?
Student: Definitely.
Security: Ah, where and when?
Student: I forgot it in the library this morning. When I went back to look, it was gone. Man, my life was on that thing.
Security: What kind of laptop is it?
Student: A MacBook Air. I just bought it.
Security: Drag.
Student: Tell me about it. Has it turned up? Probably not, huh?
Security: As a matter of fact...
Student: Oh, man. Awright! Thank you so much!
Security: Don't thank me. Thank the library. One of the staff saw it and dropped it off about an hour ago.

Narrator: Why does the student visit security?

Narrator: 4. Listen as a student talks to an admin.

Student: Hi. I'd like to buy some tickets, please.
Admin: Sure. Which sport? Football? Soccer? Lacrosse? Field hockey?
Student" Lacrosse, please. Can I get twenty?
Admin: Twenty?
Student: Yeah. My boyfriend's team is playing and he asked me to get tickets for his family.
Admin: Big family.
Student: Tell me about it.
Admin: You know, if you purchase twenty-five tickets, I can give you a twenty-percent discount, with a student ID, of course.
Student: I only need twenty. Besides, what would I do with the other five?
Admin: Keep them for the next game.
Student: So they're transferable? The tickets?
Admin: That's right. Only for faculty and students though.
Student: For lacrosse or any sport?
Admin: Any sport.
Student: Basketball too?
Admin: That's right. Basketball tickets sold out ages ago.
Student: What if I don't use them? The other five. Can I get a refund?
Admin: No. You have to use them. So, what's it going to be?
Student: Oh, man. Decisions. Decisions.
Admin: You know, since our ladies basketball team became number one in the country, people have been scrambling to buy tickets. You can't believe the demand. In fact, I just heard a pair sold on eBay for five-hundred bucks for tomorrow night's game—and we're not even playing a ranked team. You buy twenty-five tickets with a twenty-percent student discount and you'll be sitting in the catbird seat, believe me.
Student: All right. I'm sold. Give me twenty-five with the discount.

Narrator: Why does the student talk to the admin?

Track #54 - Practice: Single-Answer Detail Questions - Pg. 464

Pg. 464

Narrator: Practice. Single-answer detail questions. Directions. Listen as a student talks to a campus employee.

Student: Hello?
Admin: Yes? Oh, come in. Can I help you?
Student: Are you Bill Jenkins? The gallery manager?
Admin: I am.
Student: Professor Gainsborough said I should talk to you about having a show here in the gallery.
Admin: Oh, right. You must Sylvia. So nice to meet you. Professor Gainsborough speaks very very highly of you.
Student: Really?
Admin: He does. So tell me. What did you have in mind?
Student: I'd like to exhibit my graduate portfolio.
Admin: Great. What medium?
Student: I'm not sure how to classify it. Lately, I've been combining photographs and old computer parts.
Admin: Oh, really?
Student: I found them, actually. The computer parts. In a dumpster. In fact, I find all my material. I can't remember the last time I bought something.
Admin: Found art. I see. Sounds intriguing. Do you have anything I can look at?
Student: Yes. I brought some examples. It's not exactly mainstream. Most of the time I'm pushing the envelope.
Admin: Oh, I like this. Does it have a title?
Student: No. I just number them.
Admin: Why's that?
Student: Well, I can never think of a good title. They all sound, you know, lame. So how is the schedule? You must be really booked.
Admin: Let me check. Ah, next month...Let's see. Gloria Samuels will show for the first two weeks. She works in oil. Landscapes. Very traditional. Ah, after Gloria, for the last two weeks of the month, it's David Hopkins.
Student: Really? David Hopkins the sculptor?
Admin: The one and only. Straight from a show in London. Have you heard?
Student: No. What?
Admin: The Queen bought one of his pieces. Ah, will you price your work?
Student: You mean sell it?
Admin: That's right. How about next Monday? Emily Lopez was slated to show, but she had to cancel. She called just before you walked in. Mind you, it would only be for a week. That's the best I can do, I'm afraid. It's short notice, I know but...
Student: No. No. Next Monday would be great. What should I do?
Admin: Well, today's Thursday. I suggest we meet here tomorrow morning. Let's say, ah, nine? Bring whatever work you want to show and we'll go from there. The current show, Joseph Sands—have you seen it?
Student: Yes. I'm not a big fan of expressionism. Not that it's bad. It's just not my cup of tea.
Admin: To each his own. Anyway, Joseph will be out of here Saturday night. That gives us all day Sunday to get your show up and running.
Student: What about pricing? I'd really like to try and sell a few pieces.
Admin: Pricing is up to you. That said, I wouldn't go crazy. For example, this piece here...
Student: Number nine?
Admin: Easily five hundred.
Student: Five hundred?

Admin: Maybe more. You know, I think I'll call Karen Goldblatt. She's the editor of Art House Magazine. She really should see these. She'll know how to price them.

Narrator: Now get ready to answer the questions.

1. To whom does the student speak?
2. What can't the student remember?
3. What is the student pushing with her art?
4. How long will the student's exhibition last?
5. How many days does the student have to prepare her exhibition?
6. Who is Karen Goldblatt?

Track #55 - Practice: Multi-Answer Detail Questions - Page 465

Narrator: Practice. Multi-answer detail questions. Directions. Listen to each prompt, then answer the question.

Narrator: 1. Listen as a student talks to an admin. This is a 1-point question.

Admin: High grades are essential. That's a given for a scholarship. And letters.
Student: You mean letters of recommendation?
Admin: Yes.
Student: What about volunteering?
Admin: Not essential, but it doesn't hurt to put it down. Here's the application form.

Narrator: What information is required for the scholarship application? Select two.

Narrator: 2. Listen as a student talks to a librarian. This is a 1-point question.

Student: Hi, I'd like to put three books on reserve.
Admin: Okay. Which ones?
Student: I'd like to reserve *Howard's Human Prehistory*, *Mitchell's Methods of Archeology*, and *Swift-Lee's*—sorry, *Swift-Scott's Guide to Ancient Tools.*
Admin: That's it?
Student: Yes. Thanks. When will they be available?
Admin: Let me check. *Prehistory and Tools* should be available next week. *Methods of Archeology*? Could be a while. It's very popular.
Student: Then scratch it.

Narrator: Which books does the student put on reserve? Select two.

Narrator: 3. Listen as a student talks to an admin. This is a 1-point question.

Student: Right. So how much are the tickets?
Admin: For twenty-five?
Student: Yes.
Admin: That will be...Just a second. Five hundred dollars.
Student: Whoa. Is that the student rate with the discount?
Admin: Yes. How would you like to pay?
Student: Just a sec. How about Visa? Half cash, half Visa?
Admin: Whatever works.
Student: Sorry. It'll have to be MasterCard. My Visa's maxxed out.

Narrator: How will the student pay for the tickets? Select two.

Narrator: 4. Listen as a student talks to a campus employee. This is a 1-point question.

Student: Excuse me? Excuse me?
Worker: Yo.
Student: I got the wrong order. I wanted a turkey wrap with avocado and sprouts.
Worker: Avocado and sprouts? Not chicken with onions, cheese and jalapenos?
Student: No.
Worker: Sure?
Student: Positive.
Worker: Who ordered the chicken wrap with onions, cheese and jalapenos?
Student: Not me. Can I get a Coke too?
Worker: Pepsi okay?
Student: Whatever.

Narrator: What did the student order? Select two.

Track #56 - Practice: Question-First Function Questions - Pg. 466

Narrator: Practice. Question-first function questions. Directions. Answer each question based on what is stated or implied.

Narrator: 1. Why does the student say this?

Student: My Visa's maxxed out.

Narrator: 2. Why does the admin say this?

Staffer: High grades are essential. That's a given for a scholarship.

Narrator: 3. Why does the student say this?

Student: It's just not my cup of tea.

Narrator: 4. Why does the student say this?

Student: I have to shell out ten bucks for an ID?

Track #57 - Practice: Segment-First Function Questions - Pg. 467

Narrator: Practice. Segment-first function questions. Directions. Listen to each prompt, then answer the question.

Narrator: 1. Listen to part of a conversation, then answer the question.

Admin: Let me check. *Prehistory and Tools* should be available next week. *Methods of Archeology*? Could be a while. It's very popular.
Student: Then scratch it.

Narrator: Why does the student say this?

Student: Then scratch it.

Narrator: 2. Listen to part of a conversation, then answer the question.

Student: Really? I got a ticket for parking in the wrong spot? But I thought student parking was red.
Security: Staff is red. Students yellow. Visitors blue.
Student: You know, somebody should repaint the lines. They're really hard to see.
Security: Here. Give me your ticket. We'll let it slide this time.

Narrator: What does security mean by this?

Security: We'll let it slide this time.

Narrator: 3. Listen to part of a conversation, then answer the question.

Student: Hi. I like to buy some tickets, please.
Admin: Sure. Which sport? Football? Soccer? Lacrosse? Field hockey?
Student: Lacrosse, please. Can I get twenty?
Admin: Twenty?
Student: Yeah. My boyfriend's team is playing and he asked me to get tickets for his family.
Admin: Big family.
Student: Tell me about it.

Narrator: What does the student mean by this?

Student: Tell me about it.

Narrator: 4. Listen to part of a conversation, then answer the question.

Worker: Who ordered the chicken wrap with onions, cheese and jalapenos?
Student: Not me. Can I get a Coke too?
Worker: Pepsi okay?
Student: Whatever.

Narrator: What does the student mean by this?

Student: Whatever.

Track #58 - Practice: Direct-Attitude Questions - Page 468

Narrator: Practice. Direct-attitude questions. Directions. Listen to each prompt, then answer the question.

Narrator: 1. Listen then answer the question.

Admin: Congratulations. You got a scholarship.
Student: I did? Great. It's really a load off my mind.

Narrator: How does the student feel about getting a scholarship?

Narrator: 2. Listen then answer the question.

Admin: Do you often read *Dummies* books?
Student: Sure. All the time. They cover practically every subject. Web design. Photoshop. How to play the piano. Pets. You name it. I buy them because you get more bang for your buck.

Narrator: What is the student's opinion of *Dummies* books?

Narrator: 3. Listen then answer the question.

Admin: Found art. I see. Sounds intriguing. Do you have anything I can look at?
Student: Yes. I brought some examples. It's not exactly mainstream. Most of the time I'm pushing the envelope.
Admin: Oh, I like this. Does it have a title?
Student: No. I just number them.
Admin: Why's that?
Student: Well, I can never think of a good title. They all sound, you know, lame. So how is the schedule?

Narrator: How does the student feel about putting titles on her work?

Narrator: 4. Listen then answer the question.

Student: Oh, man. Decisions. Decisions.
Admin: You know, since our ladies basketball team became number one in the country, people have been scrambling to buy tickets. You can't believe the demand. In fact, I just heard a pair sold on eBay for five-hundred bucks for tomorrow night's game—and we're not even playing a ranked team. You buy twenty-five tickets with a twenty-percent student discount and you'll be sitting in the catbird seat, believe me.

Narrator: What does the admin think about buying so many tickets?

Track #59 - Practice: Inferred-Attitude Questions - Page 469

Narrator: Practice. Inferred-attitude questions. Directions. Listen to each prompt, then answer the question.

Narrator: 1. Listen then answer the question.

Student: Ten dollars? I have to shell out ten bucks for an ID?

Narrator: How does the student feel about the new policy?

Narrator: 2. Listen then answer the question.

Student: Hi, I'd like to return this book for resale.
Admin: Sorry, we're not reselling used texts anymore.
Student: Really? Since when?
Admin: Since last month when the bookstore started selling ebooks.
Student: So what should I do?

Admin: Try selling them on eBay.
Student: eBay? Yeah, right. Me and a million other guys.

Narrator: What does the student think about selling his used texts on eBay?

Narrator: 3. Listen then answer the question.

Student: Hi, I'd like to apply for grad school.
Admin: Great. Which program are you interested in?
Student: One that'll help me make the most money in the shortest time possible.
Admin: O-kay.

Narrator: How does the admin react to the student's request?

Narrator: 4. Listen then answer the question.

Security: Hey, you can't park there. Hey!
Student: Ah, sorry. I'm a new student here.
Security: Student parking's on the third floor. You need to get a tag.
Student: How do I do that?
Security Police office. Fourth floor. FitzGerald Building. Here. Use this temporary tag till you get a new one.
Student: Dude. All right. You are the man.

Narrator: How does the student feel about the staffer's help?

Track #60 - Practice: Inferred-Action Questions - Page 470

Narrator: Practice. Inferred-action questions. Directions. Listen to each prompt, then answer the question.

Narrator: 1. Listen then answer the question.

Student: Hi. I've come to pick up my scholarship money.
Admin: For that you'll need to go to financial aid. They'll take care of you.

Narrator: Where will the student probably go?

Narrator: 2. Listen then answer the question.

Staffer: Campus Security. Briana speaking.
Student: Hi. I lost my cell phone this morning. Has anyone turned one in?
Staffer: A few.
Student: Any iPhones? One with a pink silicon sleeve with little red hearts on it?
Staffer: Red hearts? Just a sec...You're in luck.

Narrator: What will the student probably do?

Narrator: 3. Listen then answer the question.

Student: Hi, my name is Lisa Jones. I have a couple of books on reserve. Have they come in yet?
Admin: Let me check. Yes, they have.
Student: Great.
Admin: I see you have an outstanding late fee on *Fundamentals of Physics*. A dollar to be exact. You'll need to pay that first before you sign out anymore books.

Narrator: What will the student probably do?

Narrator: 4. Listen then answer the question.

Admin: Hi, can I help you?
Student: I'd like to sign up for the total workout fitness class starting next week.
Admin: Great. Fill out this form.
Student: How much is it?
Admin: Twenty dollars. You'll need a medical release form too.

Narrator: What will the student probably do?

Professor-Only

Track #61 - Sample: Professor-Only Lecture - Page 471

Narrator: Sample. Professor-only lecture. Directions. Listen to a sample lecture, then answer the questions on the next page. Do not look at the questions. On test day, you will not see the questions as you listen. Remember to answer all the questions. You will not lose points for a wrong answer. Now listen to part of a lecture in a composition class.

Prof: 1 ➔ According to Aristotle, an argument can be made more persuasive by using three appeals: logos, pathos, and ethos.
2 ➔ Let's start with logos. Logos, or logic, appeals to reason. One way to appeal to reason is by using deduction. Deduction—and we'll come back to this later on—is a form of reasoning in which you make a conclusion based on a series of related facts or premises. Let's work through an example. First, you start with a major premise, such as...Oh, I don't know—*All English teachers are poor.* This general statement is followed by a specific statement or minor premise, in this case *Bob is an English teacher.* From these two premises, a conclusion logically follows: *Bob is poor.* Put it all together and it reads like this: *All English teachers are poor. Bob is an English teacher. Bob is poor.* As you can see, deduction can be pretty persuasive. Its closed or formal structure leaves no doubt as to Bob's financial situation relative to his profession. Induction is another form of logic that appeals to reason. When inducing, you combine a series of related facts, such as *Joan loves apples, Joan loves blueberries, Joan loves mangos.* From these facts, we can make a conclusion, in this case *Joan loves fruit.* Does she love all fruit? We don't know. She might abhor apricots. As you can see, induction is not as closed or conclusive as deduction. Still, add numbers to an inductive mix and the logic behind an argument whether to invest in a company can be quite appealing. For example, *ABC Company made a $20 billion profit last year, ABC made a $40 billion profit this year, ABC will make a $60 billion profit next year.* Conclusion? You do the math.
3 ➔ Pathos, in contrast, is an appeal to the emotions. By appealing to the emotions, the arguer can evoke sympathy from an audience. Sympathy, in turn, makes an argument more persuasive. Movies regularly employ pathos. Did you cry when E.T.

finally went home? Were you terrified when Titanic sank or when Jaws rose out of the water, teeth flashing? If so, then the director persuaded you that two-dimensional images on a movie screen are so real, so life-like, you reacted to them emotionally. Pathos can also support logos. For example, photographs often support news stories. What better way to evoke audience anger at an oil company than to place a photo of an oil-covered pelican next to an article about an oil spill.
4 ➔ Next we have ethos. Ethos is an appeal to character. For example, from whom would you buy a computer, a man in a business suit or a man in a T-shirt? Ethically, some might eschew the man in the T-shirt, a T-shirt being the antithesis of business attire therefore unethical, not trustworthy. However, such ethical conclusions have been turned on their heads, especially in America. Case in point: Whenever Apple introduces a new product, CEO Steve Jobs introduces the product wearing jeans and a T-Shirt. Does Jobs' choice of clothes diminish the quality of the product? No. If anything, Jobs' casual look enhances Apple's cool factor. As you can see, what was once ethically unacceptable—wearing jeans to work—is now perfectly acceptable.
5 ➔ Those, then, are Aristotle's three appeals. It's important to remember that a successful argument—a persuasive argument—combines all three appeals. Look at President Obama. As an argument for president, his life story was quite compelling. Why? Because it was defined by the three appeals. As a youth, he was a community organizer (ethos and pathos). He then studied law at Harvard (logos and ethos). After he graduated, he taught constitutional law at the University of Chicago (logos and ethos). He then became a U.S. senator (logos, pathos and ethos). Combined, these three appeals made Barack Obama a persuasive argument to be president of the United States.
6 ➔ That said, keep in mind, however, that even when supported by all three appeals, there is no guarantee that a politician seeking office—or any other argument—will persuade an audience, for if any of the three appeals come under the fire, the audience will fail to be persuaded.

<u>Narrator</u>: Now get ready to answer the questions. Answer each based on what is stated or implied in the lecture.

1. What is the topic of the lecture?
2. What is the purpose of the lecture?
3. According to Aristotle, which appeals make a lecture more persuasive? Select three. This is a 2-point question.

4. Why does the professor say this? 

<u>Prof</u>: That said, keep in mind, however, that even when supported by all three appeals, there is no guarantee that a politician seeking office—or any other argument—will persuade an audience, for if any of the three appeals come under the fire, the audience will fail to be persuaded.

5. The professor describes President Obama's personal history. Put President Obama's personal history in the proper order. This is a 2-point question.

6. In the lecture, the professor describes Aristotle's three appeals and their functions in an argument. Indicate whether each of the following is a function of Aristotle's three appeals. This is a 3-point question.

Track #62 - Practice: Content Questions - Page 483

Narrator: Practice. Content questions. Directions. Listen to each prompt, then answer the question.

Narrator: 1. Listen to a professor, then answer the question.

Prof: For plants to survive, they must convert carbon dioxide into sugar using energy from the sun. This conversion process is called photosynthesis. Organisms that depend on photosynthesis for survival are called photoautotrophs. Plants, as well as algae and many species of bacteria, fall under this classification. These organisms are unique in that they are the only ones to produce their own food by photosynthesis, a chemically complex process in which oxygen is a waste byproduct. Suffice it to say, without photosynthesis, life on Earth would cease to exist.

Narrator: What is the main topic of the lecture?

Narrator: 2. Listen to a professor, then answer the question.

Prof: An algorithm is a process that performs a series of operations aimed at solving a problem. More specifically, an algorithm has a starting point followed by a sequence of well-defined instructions terminating at an end point. Algorithms lie at the heart of computer software. Software, as you know, is basically a sequence of instructions aimed at carrying out a task. That task is called a computation. It is a process that begins with a set of initial conditions, called input, then provides an output, a result, based on a fixed set of rules or instructions. A more common form of algorithm is a recipe for, oh, I don't know—let's say brownies. The recipe tells you where to start, the steps to follow, and what the outcome will be. An algorithm, however, cannot stop you from eating them all.

Narrator: What is the focus of the lecture?

Narrator: 3. Listen to a professor, then answer the question.

Prof: Archeologists agree that a major turning point in world history was the appearance of literate civilizations in southwest Asia and along the Nile River. This period dates from about the fourth millennium BCE to around 1,200 BCE. Yet before we proceed, we really need to define the term civilization. Within the word itself lies the root "civil" meaning to display the appropriate behavior. Yet this definition of civilization is far too broad, for what might be considered appropriate behavior in one society might be taboo in another. Simply put, archeologists apply the term civilization when describing literate, urbanized, state-level societies, the earliest of which were city-states in southwest Asia and along the Nile River. The wealth of these city-states was derived from many sources, a major one of which was agriculture. To record the buying and selling of a grain like wheat, a system of record keeping was developed, one in which marks and symbols were carved into tablets or pressed into clay. Primitive, indeed, but arguably the world's first spreadsheets. To understand them, one had to read thus with writing came reading. Soon taxes were being recorded and laws written. This, in turn, created a system of government officials to collect the tax and a military to enforce the laws. This was indeed a turning point. Suddenly, everyone knew their position in society based on what was written.

Thus it can be said that the earliest civilizations were built on the written word, as is ours today.

Narrator: What is the main topic of the lecture?

Narrator: 4. Listen to a professor, then answer the question.

Prof: Ancient Egyptians used a formal writing system called hieroglyphs. Hieroglyphs combine logographic as well as alphabetic elements. For years, scholars were unable to decipher the meaning of hieroglyphs. The Rosetta Stone changed all that. In 1799, a French soldier, part of Napoleon's expedition to Egypt, discovered it in a temple. On it was a decree by King Ptolemy V in engraved text. The decree is in three languages: Egyptian hieroglyphs, Egyptian demotic script, and ancient Greek. Scholars who knew ancient Greek suddenly had a means by which they could finally translate hieroglyphs. In 1801, the British defeated the French in Egypt and the Rosetta Stone fell into British hands, where it has remained ever since. This, then, has led to the debate about who actually owns the Rosetta Stone, a debate that persists to this day.

Narrator: What is the focus of the lecture?

Track #63 - Practice: Purpose Questions - Page 484

Narrator: Practice. Purpose questions. Directions. Listen to each prompt, then answer the question.

Narrator: 1. Listen to a professor, then answer the question.

Prof: Okay. A quick review. The goal of thinking. What is it? To make sense of the world. How do we do that? By acquiring knowledge. Okay, so how do we acquire knowledge? Good question. With the brain, obviously. But seriously. We acquire knowledge with tools—thinking tools. Last time we identified four of those tools: memory, association, reason, and pattern discernment and recognition. To that list add experience, invention, experimentation, and intuition. Right. So before we begin, jump in with any questions you might have.

Narrator: Why does the professor introduce four more thinking tools?

Narrator: 2. Listen to a professor, then answer the question.

Prof: It goes without saying that Frank Sinatra was in a league of his own. Who can deny his artistry and influence? Yet besides his dazzling blue eyes and self-effacing smile, what made teenage girls—bobby soxers as they were called back in the 1940's—crazy about Frank Sinatra? One thing was his breathing technique. While singing, instead of taking a breath in the middle of a long phrase like singers of the day always did, Sinatra would sing through to the end without taking a breath. The bobby soxers loved it. They felt as if Sinatra really knew the words and was talking directly to them. In other words, Sinatra's breathing technique was pure passion. That is one reason why a young Francis Albert Sinatra set the world on fire back in the 1940's. Another reason was his work ethic.

Narrator: Why does the professor describe Frank Sinatra's breathing style?

Narrator: 3. Listen to a professor, then answer the question.

Prof: So far, we've been talking about preindustrial societies, societies which were essentially agrarian-based with political and economic power concentrated in the hands of a king or despot. An industrial society, quite the contrary, is one in which power and economic influence are dispersed throughout society and, more importantly—and this is the point that needs stressing—industrial societies are based on fossil fuels whereas preindustrial societies are not.

Narrator: Why does the professor stress fossil fuels?

Narrator: 4. Listen to a professor, then answer the question.

Prof: This may come as a surprise, but hurricanes and tornadoes do not account for the most weather-related deaths in the United States. Heat and drought do. According to NOAA—the National Oceanographic and Atmospheric Administration—extreme heat is "one of the most underrated and least understood of the deadly weather phenomena." Why is this the case? First off, the danger is less obvious. Think about it. A mass of hot air settles over us and we think, okay, it's just another hot day. To cool off, our bodies perspire. The moisture evaporates. By doing so, it draws excess heat from our bodies. If we don't drink enough water, we perspire less and the excess heat stays in the body. As a result, our core body temperature rises dramatically and we risk death from heat stroke. This is what happened in Europe in 2003 when over 26,000 people died in the hottest summer on record.

Narrator: Why does the professor mention Europe in 2003?

TRACK #64 - Practice: Single-Answer Detail Questions - Pg. 485

Narrator: Practice. Single-answer detail questions. Directions. Listen to a lecture about education, then answer the questions.

Prof: 1 ➔ In America, public education had its genesis in the New England Colonies of Massachusetts, Connecticut and New Hampshire. At the time, circa 1600, these colonies were settled by two main religious groups: the Puritans and the Congregationalists; both were Protestant, both were fiercely independent, both rejected the centralized power of Catholicism, and both shared the belief that educating children was critical to the survival of their beliefs; thus the earliest form of public education in America was funded by the Protestant church with the tenets of Protestantism the core curriculum.

2 ➔ The first publicly supported high school in America, the Boston Latin School, was founded in 1635. Now, I need to be clear here. Publicly supported doesn't mean what it means today: a public school system funded by tax dollars. Quite the contrary, back in 1635, public education meant that church money paid for books and teachers' salaries while students had to pay tuition. These so-called public schools, of which the Boston Latin School was the first, educated an elite, all-male student body in Latin and Greek, the humanities and philosophy with an emphasis on religious studies, for it was assumed that the students would become teachers or ministers espousing the Protestant faith.

3 ➔ At the same time, immigrants were arriving in the New England colonies. These immigrants, many of whom were Catholic, soon came into conflict with the Puritans and the Congregationalists over the issue of public education. The Catholics viewed the English-dominated public education system as simply a way in which the English Protestants could impose their religious views. As a

result, the Catholics rejected the Protestant-based, public-school system and created a system of private Catholic schools, a system which survives to this day.

4 ➔ As you can see, the educational system in colonial America was very much a religious conflict. Keep in mind, however, that these schools, for Catholics and Protestants alike, were for the sons of the rich and politically powerful. For those boys on the lower end of the social scale, charity or "common schools" were set up. While public money paid for books and teachers, students still had to pay tuition, money most simply did not have. Instead, most school-age boys became apprentices learning a trade. As for girls, they were educated at home by mothers and grandmothers. Girls learned how to cook and sew with the aim of being a good housewife thus the literacy rate among women was very low.

5 ➔ By the early nineteenth century, the common or public school system was in dire straits. The schools were poorly equipped, one-room buildings with poorly paid, poorly trained teachers. Students, if they attended classes, attended in winter and only for a few weeks. The rest of the time they worked in agriculture or in the growing number of factories, for the industrial revolution was picking up steam, particularly in big east coast cities like Boston, New York and Philadelphia.

6 ➔ In 1837, with the public school system hitting rock bottom, Horace Mann, a social reformer and a powerful Massachusetts politician, decided enough was enough. Mann—a leader in the temperance movement and a builder of insane asylums—was appointed secretary of Massachusetts' newly created Board of Education, the first of its kind in America. Mann, believing that all children should learn in common schools, set about reforming the public school system. He established institutes to train teachers. He increased teacher salaries, increased the school year to six months, and raised money for books and school construction. Mann pursued these reforms because he believed that public education would result in greater economic prosperity for the individual, the state and the country while teaching respect for private property. This, Mann argued, would decrease the crime rate, for the industrial revolution had created a rising class of urban poor. By providing public money for public schools, Mann viewed education as a means of controlling the crime rate. Thus "moral training", as Mann called it, was part of the curriculum along with standardized lessons and classroom drills. This, Mann also argued, would create greater equality for the masses and greater economic prosperity for all.

Narrator: Now get ready to answer the questions.

1. The first public schools in America were...
2. In which year was the Boston Latin School founded?
3. According to the lecture, the literacy rate for women in colonial America was...
4. What was the condition of the public school system in 1837?
5. How did Horace Mann change the school year?
6. According to the lecture, what did Horace Mann believe?

Track #65 - Practice: Multi-Answer Detail Questions - Page 486

Narrator: Practice. Multi-answer detail questions. Directions. Listen to each prompt, then answer the question.

Narrator: 1. Listen then answer the question. This is a 2-point question.

Prof: The Roman Army was a highly disciplined and highly feared military force that, by 300 BCE, had made the Republic of Rome an unrivalled empire controlling eastern Europe and much of the Mediterranean. The basic unit of the Roman

Army was the legion. A legion was comprised of approximately 4,200 legionnaires. These men, both professional and conscript, were each equipped with three weapons: a pugio, a long dagger or knife, a gladius, a short thrusting sword (from which the word "gladiator" is derived), and a pilum, a two-meter javelin. With a shield for protection, and dressed in body armor, the legionnaire was a killing machine. Imagine the terror the tribes of Europe felt when the Roman army came marching over the hill.

Narrator: What three weapons did a Roman legionnaire carry? Select three.

Narrator: 2. Listen then answer the question. This is a 2-point question.

Prof: A business plan has three essential parts starting with a formal statement that outlines a set of specific goals. Those goals will be either for profit or not-for profit. A for-profit business plan will describe goals aimed at the creation of wealth whereas a not-for profit business plan will focus on a mission statement in order to receive tax exempt status from the government. Next, the business plan will describe the reason why the stated goals are attainable. Depending on the plan, those reasons will be supported by a market analysis and a competitor analysis, and whatever research is necessary to attain the stated goal. Finally, a business plan will state how the business will go about achieving those goals. In other words, a plan of action. Let's begin by defining the first part of a business plan: defining the goals.

Narrator: What are the essential parts of a business plan? Select three.

Narrator: 3. Listen then answer the question. This is a 2-point question.

Prof: A critical part of a marine biologist's research is to compile data by observing events and by collecting samples. However, because the oceans are so vast, and because most of what is going on is happening below the waves, marine biologists must devise ways to observe and collect samples. Some use nets and dredges for gathering samples while others use computers for compiling data. Still others perform experiments in labs designed to recreate specific ocean environments. However, the best way, and frankly the only way, to observe and collect data is to get your feet wet. In other words, you've got to enter the ocean itself and see things with the naked eye. One way is to dive in scuba gear or in specially equipped research submersibles. The other is to employ specially designed video equipment with bait to attract the animal in question. No matter what the method of research, the goal of the marine biologist—it goes without saying—is to collect data in a manner that leaves the marine environment undisturbed.

Narrator: According to the professor, the best ways to study marine life are... Select three.

Narrator: 4. Listen then answer the question. This is a 1-point question.

Prof: If you walk around New York City today, with its skyscrapers and densely packed districts, it's hard to imagine that during the American Revolutionary War, two battles took place there in the fall of 1776. The first was the Battle of Long Island, also known as the Battle of Brooklyn or the Battle of Brooklyn Heights. This battle was the first major battle of the American Revolutionary War, coming soon after the United States declared Independence from Britain.

At the Battle of Brooklyn Heights, a superior British force attacked and forced the Continental Army, led by George Washington, to retreat to present-day Harlem on Manhattan Island. There, the Americans and the British fought again with the British withdrawing to regroup. Historians call this engagement the Battle of Harlem Heights. Washington, fearing a British trap at Harlem, retreated north to present-day White Plains.

Narrator: What were the first major battles of the American Revolutionary War? Select two.

Track #66 - Practice: Question-First Function Questions - Pg. 487

Narrator: Practice. Question-first function questions. Directions. Answer each question based on what is stated or implied.

Narrator: 1. Why does the professor say this?

Prof: It goes without saying that Frank Sinatra was in a league of his own.

Narrator: 2. Why does the professor say this?

Prof: No matter what the method of research, the goal of the marine biologist—it goes without saying—is to collect data in a manner that leaves the marine environment undisturbed.

Narrator: 3. Why does the professor say this?

Prof: Yet this definition of civilization is far too broad, for what might be considered appropriate behavior in one society might be taboo in another.

Narrator: 4. Why does the professor say this?

Prof: If you walk around New York City today, with its skyscrapers and densely packed districts, it's hard to imagine that during the American Revolutionary War, two battles took place there in the fall of 1776.

Narrator: 5. Why does the professor say this?

Prof: This may come as a surprise, but hurricanes and tornadoes do not account for the most weather-related deaths in the United States.

Narrator: 6. Why does the professor say this?

Prof: Census taking, however, is nothing new. Many ancient civilizations regularly took a census of population, for example Rome. Because Rome had a large standing army, it needed money and men. By periodically taking a census, the Roman government knew how much tax money it could raise for the army and the available manpower it could draw from.

Narrator: 7. Why does the professor say this?

Prof: Global warming has brought new and invasive species. One such species, the Asian hornet, has spread across Europe and into Britain. The Asian hornet raids hives for bee larvae and the bees are powerless to stop this invader.

Narrator: 8. Why does the professor say this?

Prof: On December 11, 2008, the business world was rocked by news no one could believe. Even now, people are still shaking their heads.

Track #67 - Practice: Segment-First Function Questions - Pg. 489

Narrator: Practice. Segment-first function questions. Directions. Answer each question based on what is stated or implied.

Narrator: 1. Listen to part of a lecture, then answer the question.

Prof: In 1801, the British defeated the French in Egypt and the Rosetta Stone fell into British hands, where it has remained ever since. This, then, has led to the debate about who actually owns the Rosetta Stone, a debate that persists to this day.

Narrator: Why does the professor say this?

Prof: This, then, has led to the debate about who actually owns the Rosetta Stone, a debate that persists to this day.

Narrator: 2. Listen to part of a lecture, then answer the question.

Prof Last time we identified four of those tools: memory, association, reason, and pattern discernment and recognition. To that list add experience, invention, experimentation, and intuition. Right. So before we begin, jump in with any questions you might have.

Narrator: Why does the professor say this?

Prof: Right. So before we begin, jump in with any questions you might have.

Narrator: 3. Listen to part of a lecture, then answer the question.

Prof: It goes without saying that Frank Sinatra was in a league of his own. Who can deny his artistry and influence? Yet besides his dazzling blue eyes and self-effacing smile, what made teenage girls—bobby soxers as they were called back in the 1940's—crazy about Frank Sinatra?

Narrator: Why does the professor say this?

Prof: Yet besides his dazzling blue eyes and self-effacing smile, what made teenage girls—bobby soxers as they were called back in the 1940's—crazy about Frank Sinatra?

Narrator: 4. Listen to part of a lecture, then answer the question. 

Prof: A more common form of algorithm is a recipe for, oh, I don't know—let's say brownies. The recipe tells you where to start, the steps to follow, and what the outcome will be. An algorithm, however, cannot stop you from eating them all.

Narrator: Why does the professor say this?

Prof: Oh, I don't know—let's say brownies.

Track #68 - Practice: Direct-Attitude Questions - Pg. 490

Narrator: Practice. Direct-attitude questions. Directions. Listen to each prompt, then answer the question.

Narrator: 1. Listen then answer the question.

Prof: Many buy into the argument that corporate rehiring is an indication that the economy is finally turning around. However, corporate hiring figures are only one way of gauging economic health. In my estimation, a better indicator of a market turn around is home sales. Why home sales? Because the American economy is based on the construction of houses. Think about it. Manufacturing is linked to the home. You buy a home, you need a car—and a washing machine, and a lawnmower, and a computer, and a flat-screen TV. And on and on. Once homes start selling, only then will I believe that the economy has turned the corner.

Narrator: The professor thinks corporate rehiring is...

Narrator: 2. Listen then answer the question.

Prof: Offshore drilling? To meet our energy needs and free us from foreign oil? Sorry, but the jury is still out on that one.

Narrator: What is the professor's position on drilling for oil offshore?

Narrator: 3. Listen then answer the question.

Prof: Thomas Edison falls into two camps. You either love him for his achievements or hate him for his complete lack of scruples. All that aside, no one can argue with the fact that he coined some pretty memorable lines, such as this one: "Genius is one percent inspiration and ninety-nine percent perspiration."

Narrator: What is the professor's view of Thomas Edison?

Narrator: 4. Listen then answer the question.

Prof: To risk beating a dead horse, I will say it again. Despite what the lobbyists say, genetically modified food is not fit for human consumption. Period.

Narrator: The professor thinks that genetically modified food is...

Track #69 - Practice: Inferred-Attitude Questions - Page 491

Narrator: Practice. Inferred-attitude questions. Directions. Listen to each prompt, then answer the question.

Narrator: 1. Listen then answer the question.

Prof: Put a killer whale and a great white shark together, and which one will come out the winner? That answer was made clear off the Farallon Islands in October, 1997. The Farallons are home to thousands of elephant seals, a rich food source for great whites. On that October day, a great white was hunting when it was attacked and eaten by a killer whale. This incident, captured on video, turned conventional wisdom on its head: the great white does not rule the waves after all. Even more shocking was the fact that on that very same day, the one hundred-or-so great whites that had been hunting off the Farallons at the time of the killer whale attack suddenly disappeared. Vanished like scared rats. Even now I'm shaking my head.

Narrator: How does the professor feel about what happened off the Farallon Islands?

Narrator: 2. Listen then answer the question.

Prof: As a computer company, Apple, with its cutting-edge products, is the envy of its rivals, a position once held by Microsoft, a company founded by Bill Gates, a Harvard drop-out and the focus of today's lecture.

Narrator: What is the professor's view of Microsoft?

Narrator: 3. Listen then answer the question.

Prof: Perhaps the greatest mystery concerning Cro-Magnon man is why did he paint on the walls of caves? Not just sketches but enormous murals of wild horses and deer, painted with such masterly detail they practically come alive even after 20,000 years. Were these paintings part of a shamanistic ritual? Was Cro-Magnon man simply bored and looking for distraction, or do we see in all the bison and aurox, man's first attempt at asking the question we still ask to this day: Who am I? Of course, seeing the paintings in person is best; however, their power is not diminished even in these slides.

Narrator: What is the professor's opinion of Cro-Magnon cave art?

Narrator: 4. Listen then answer the question.

Prof: I know. I know. Some say President John F. Kennedy was assassinated by Cuban Nationalists for failing to invade communist Cuba while others claim Kennedy was assassinated by the military-industrial complex seeking to profit from the Viet Nam conflict, a conflict Kennedy was, at the time of his death, determined to end. I also know that if I had a dime for every time I heard those two theories, I'd be rich by now.

Narrator: The professor believes that...

Track #70 - Practice: Inferred-Action Questions - Page 492

Narrator: Practice. Inferred-action questions. Directions. Listen to each prompt, then answer the question.

Narrator: 1. Listen then answer the question.

Prof: 1 ➔ There seems to be some confusion as to the difference between slang and jargon. Remember that jargon is a type slang. The difference is that I can learn jargon—for example computer jargon—and I can become a systems engineer or an app designer. Moreover—and this is key—jargon is inclusive. That means I can learn computer jargon, invented words like virus and mouse, and computer professionals will accept me. In other words, learn the code, join the group. Thus jargon is inclusive
2 ➔ Slang, in its purest sense, however, is an excluding code. I can learn, for example, all the rap slang I want, such as "Yo, s'up homey? Dawg, bust a move!" or "Crib cost beaucoup Benjamins," but will Fifty Cent or Lil Wayne or Snoop Dog accept me into their group, their gang? After all, I know the language, the code, right? Not likely. In this light, slang is like a wall, a wall of invented words designed for two purposes: to exclude me from the group and to keep outsiders—other gangs and the police—from figuring out what we, our gang, are saying. Of course, rap slang is only one kind of slang. Teenagers use slang all the time, skateboarders in particular. Any skateboarders out there? Ah, yes. Quite a few.

Narrator: What will the professor probably do next?

Narrator: 2. Listen then answer the question.

Prof: While singing, instead of taking a breath in the middle of a long phrase like singers of the day always did, Sinatra would sing through to the end without taking a breath. The bobby soxers loved it. They felt as if Sinatra really knew the words and was talking directly to them. In other words, Sinatra's breathing technique was pure passion. That is one reason why a young Francis Albert Sinatra set the world on fire back in the 1940's. Another reason was his work ethic.

Narrator: What will the professor talk about next?

Narrator: 3. Listen then answer the question.

Prof: That brings us to the end of the lecture. Just to recap, napping for twenty-minutes each day restores energy, increases productivity, and boosts memory. In Greece, researchers found that men who napped three times a week had a thirty-seven percent lower risk of heart-related deaths. The benefits of napping speak for themselves. Personally, I do it all the time. That said, you know where I'll be. If you have a question, email me.

Narrator: What will the professor probably do next?

Narrator: 4. Listen then answer the question.

Prof: The process of making a hand axe, you might think, is no big deal. After all, what's so hard about knocking the sides off a round rock to make a razor-sharp cutting edge, right? I mean, if some Cro-Magnon guy could do it way back when, I can do it too. Easier said than done. Watch.

Narrator: What will the professor demonstrate?

Track #71 - Practice: Ordering Questions - Page 493

Narrator: Practice. Ordering questions. Directions. Listen to each prompt, then answer the question.

Narrator: 1. Listen then answer the question.

Prof: In the fall, when a sockeye salmon is approximately five-years old, it leaves the Pacific Ocean, where it has grown to maturity, and returns to the home river where it was born. Once in the home river—how sockeye return to the river of their birth remains a mystery—the sockeye navigates upstream and spawns in shallow water, then dies. In a few months, between January and April, the eggs turn into alevin, a tiny fish with the yolk sack still attached. The alevin live off the yolk and grow into fry. After a period of growth, they will head downstream in late spring, making the transition from the fresh water of the home river to the salt water of the ocean as smolt. Once in the ocean, the smolt will grow into adults, then return to the home river in five years to begin the cycle all over again.

Narrator: The professor talks about the sockeye salmon. Put the life cycle of the sockeye in the correct order. This is a 2-point question.

Narrator: 2. Listen then answer the question.

Prof: In the world of computer hackers, one name stands out: Jonathan James, aka c0mrade. Between August and October of 1999, James, aged 16, hacked into the computers of BellSouth. Next, he hacked the Miami-Dade school system. Soon after, he hit the computers of the Defense Reduction Agency, a division of the United States Department of Defense. James installed a sniffer, a piece of hidden software that intercepted thousands of passwords giving him almost complete access to Department of Defense computers, including the computer's of NASA. From the NASA computers, James downloaded the software that controlled the temperature and the humidity on the Space Station. On January 26, 2000, James was arrested and incarcerated, making him the first juvenile to be jailed for computer hacking. Why did he do it? As James himself said, "I was just looking around, playing around. What was fun for me was a challenge to see what I could pull off." James committed suicide in May, 2008 after federal authorities accused him of being part of a conspiracy that had committed the largest computer identify theft in American history, the hacking into of the computers of retailers TJ Maxx, Marshalls, Boston Market, Barnes and Noble, and many others.

Narrator: The professor talks about Jonathan James. Put James' computer hacking career in the proper order. This is a 2-point question.

Narrator: 3. Listen then answer the question.

Prof: One of the more tragic figures in American literary history is F. Scott Fitzgerald. Fitzgerald died in Hollywood on December 21, 1940, at the age of 44. He'd been trying to revive his career by writing screenplays which he despised. Yet, always desperate for money, Fitzgerald had no choice but to serve Hollywood. No longer was he the golden boy whose short stories of rebellious young men and women defined the Jazz Age, a name Fitzgerald himself had coined to describe the 1920's. In 1920, at age 25, Fitzgerald rocketed to the top of the literary world with his first novel, *This Side of Paradise.* Soon after, the Saturday Evening Post was paying him $4,000.00 for his short stories, an incredible sum even by today's standards. In 1925, Fitzgerald published *The Great Gatsby.* Fitzgerald went on to write *Tender is the Night* in 1934, but it failed to sell. With the Depression eclipsing the Jazz Age, with his short stories no longer in demand, and burdened by a mentally unstable wife, Fitzgerald hit rock bottom. In 1937, he settled in Los Angeles where he landed a six-month writing contract with MGM yet he continued to drink heavily while producing nothing of substance. Fitzgerald died believing he was a failure while *The Great Gatsby* lives on, a novel many critics consider the greatest American novel ever written.

Narrator: The professor describes the life of F. Scott Fitzgerald. Put Fitzgerald's writing career in the proper order. This is a 2-point question.

Narrator: 4. Listen then answer the question.

Prof: The sand people of the Kalahari Desert are the only tribe left on Earth who use what many scientists consider to be the oldest method of hunting known to man: the persistence hunt. On foot, under a scorching African sun and armed only with spears, the hunters locate a herd of kudu, kudu being a species of large antelope. The hunters then move the herd using only hand signals to communicate. By continually moving the herd, the hunters tire their prey. Hours later, the hunters will isolate one animal, usually a male whose heavy horns have caused him to tire faster than the females. At this point, with the sun pounding down, and a kudu separated from the herd, one hunter, the fastest of the group, continues the hunt alone. This hunter, called "the runner," chases the lone kudu for hours until, exhausted from the heat, it stops to rest. It is then that the runner moves in for the kill.

Narrator: The professor talks about the persistence hunt. Put the steps of the persistence hunt in order. This is a 2-point question.

Track #72 - Practice: Yes-No Questions - Page 495

Narrator: Practice. Yes-no Questions. Directions. Listen to each prompt, then answer the question.

Narrator: 1. Listen then answer the question.

Prof: Despite its ominous sounding name, Black Friday is not the day the world ends. Instead, it is the traditional beginning of the Christmas shopping season in the United States. An east coast term dating back to 1966, Black Friday is now a nationwide event. It is not an official holiday, per se; however, because it falls on the Friday between Thanksgiving Day and the weekend after Thanksgiving, many workers take Friday off. For retailers, Black Friday is a bellwether. If consumer spending is up on Black Friday, it generally means that consumer spending over the Christmas period will also be up. This will be good news for retailers and manufacturers alike. Following hot on the heels of Black Friday is Cyber Monday, the official start of the online Christmas shopping season. Smart consumers have learned to wait for Cyber Monday to buy big ticket items like TVs and computers, for Cyber Monday bargains are generally better than anything offered by traditional Black Friday brick-and-mortar retailers.

Narrator: The professor describes Black Friday. Indicate whether each of the following is true of Black Friday in the United States. This is a 3-point question.

Narrator: 2. Listen then answer the question.

Prof: 1 ➔ Microcredit is a system of finance wherein banks lend very small amounts of money to the extremely poor, people who would have no access to credit otherwise. The idea originated with Muhammad Yunus, a Bangladeshi economist. The result was the Grameen Bank of Bangladesh. The bank extends microloans, or grameencredit, to the impoverished without collateral. The poor, in turn, use these loans to generate income through self-employment. A key point to remember is that the loans are for groups only, the average size of which is five. The members can choose who will participate in the group but they cannot be related. This form of group financing is called solidarity lending. This approach spreads the cost of repaying the loan across a group of borrowers. It also discourages free riders while encouraging group decision-making and financial responsibility. As a result, the group builds up wealth and exits poverty. It is a radical approach to financing that has proven successful in Bangladesh and in India. In fact, microcredit is now so popular that many banks worldwide offer microloans. For his work, Muhammad Yunus and Grameen Bank were jointly awarded the Nobel Peace Prize for economics in 2006.
2 ➔ Recently, however, microcredit has come under a cloud due to unscrupulous lending practices whereby banks—without questioning the borrower's ability to repay—lend borrowers huge, high-interest rate loans they cannot possibly repay. As a result, an alarming number of borrowers have simply walked away from their loans. The same thing happened in America in 2007 when mortgage lenders extended huge, high-interest loans to borrowers who could not possibly repay them. The result was the near collapse of the global economy.

Narrator: The professor talks about microcredit. Indicate whether each of the following is true of microcredit. This is a 3-point question.

Narrator: 3. Listen then answer the question.

Prof: As a political movement, the Situationist International combined Marxist ideology and surrealism to wage war against consumerism. The Situationists, founded in 1957, argued that mainstream capitalism, through the mass media, was destroying the experience of daily life through false images, the worst offender being consumer advertising. The result, the Situationists believed, was that the individual was no longer a participant in life but a slave controlled by false images created by capitalist interests. The group's main proponent was Guy Debord. Debord argued that authentic social life had been replaced with false representations. Debord wanted to wake up the spectator drugged by advertising. The Situationists did so by creating "situations," mass events in which people turned their backs on the mass media and came together as one. Only through situations, Debord argued, could individuals free themselves from capitalism and thereby reclaim the freedom of experiencing life in its original sense, namely as an individual free of the capitalist influence. The largest and most famous situation was the General Strike in France in 1968. Today, the Situationist International, having long since dissolved, has found new voice in various anarchist movements.

Narrator: The professor talks about the Situationist International. Indicate whether each of the following is true of the Situationist International. This is a 3-point question.

Narrator: 4. Listen then answer the question.

Prof: 1 ➔ Hybrid cars are all the rage these days. Yet are they all that fuel-efficient? Will they actually save you money in the long run? And are they really environmentally friendly? Let's take a closer look under the hood.
2 ➔ A hybrid car is basically two engines: one gas, one electric. A hybrid is engineered this way to be fuel efficient, averaging 50 miles to the gallon. However, those two engines, plus the huge battery in the back, mean that the cost of buying a hybrid is substantially higher than a good old gas car. A regular gas car will cost on average $4,000.00 less than a hybrid. If the hybrid costs $18,000.00, let's say, then the owner—to justify the hybrid as a fuel-saver—must somehow make up the $4,000.00 difference in fuel costs. What's happening in the news, even as we speak? That's right. The price of gas is once again going up. If gas prices go up, it's going to be virtually impossible for the hybrid owner to make up the $4000.00 cost difference. So why buy a hybrid? That's the $64,000.00 question.
3 ➔ And, of course, there's always the hybrid's dirty little secret: the nickel it takes to make a hybrid's battery. Where does that nickel—all one-hundred-and-seventeen pounds of it—come from? Canada. How is it extracted? By digging massive holes in the Earth. Not very environmentally-friendly, I'm afraid.

Narrator: The professor talks about hybrid cars. According to the professor, which of the following are true of hybrid cars? This is a 3-point question.

Track #73 - Practice: Connecting Questions - Page 499

Narrator: Practice. Connecting questions. Listen to each prompt, then answer the question.

Narrator: 1. Listen then answer the question.

Prof: 1 ➔ Today, we'll begin our look at three major battles that changed the course of history. After a brief intro of each, we'll analyze each in depth and identify how that military event determined the social landscape as we now know it. The battles we'll focus on are Marathon, Teutoburg Forest, and Waterloo.
2 ➔ First Marathon. The Battle of Marathon took place in 490 BCE. Persian King Darius, attempting to conquer Greece, landed on Greek soil near the town of Marathon with a massive army. The much smaller Greek army, using hoplites or citizen soldiers, pushed the invader back into the sea. This victory preserved Greece and gave us classical Greece as we know it.
3 ➔ Next we'll explore the Battle of Teutoburg Forest. This engagement occurred in 9 CE. By that date, Rome had successfully conquered western Europe and was turning east with the aim of conquering what is today's Germany east of the Rhine River. Determined to subdue the Germanic tribes once and for all, three Legions under Varus marched east of the Rhine and right into a trap. The

Germanic tribes, led by Arminius, an ex Roman cavalry officer, annihilated the Roman army to a man. Historians believe that as many as 20,000 Roman soldiers died. Historians also believe that this—the complete destruction of an elite Roman army—marked the start of the decline of the Roman Empire
4 ➔ Finally, we'll travel to Waterloo, a small town in Belgium. There, on June 18, 1815, Napoleon Bonaparte, back from exile—and determined to rule as Emperor once again—was defeated by a combined British and Prussian force. It was a close battle. As the British commander the Duke of Wellington said, it was "A near miss thing."

Narrator: The professor describes three military battles that changed history. Match each battle with each defeated military leader. This is a 2-point question.

Narrator: 2. Listen then answer the question.

Prof: 1 ➔ Herbalism is a traditional plant-based medicine. It is also known as botanical medicine, herbology, and phytotherapy. Herbalism has a long history stretching back to the dawn of time. Today, over 122 compounds used in modern medicine have been derived from plant sources. Some of the more common herbal medicines in use today are milk thistle, a thistle extract used for centuries to maintain liver health, aloe vera, a traditional remedy for burns and wounds, and willow bark, a tree bark extract the Greeks used for aches and pains, the main ingredient of which has been synthesized into today's aspirin.
2 ➔ Despite herbalism's long tradition, doubt remains as to the efficacy of plant-based medicines. Moreover, the dangers are all too real. For example, comfrey can cause liver damage and ginseng can cause insomnia and schizophrenia. Moreover, unscrupulous manufacturers can vary the quality and quantity of the herb in question which, in turn, poses another danger. What should you do? Consult your physician and proceed with caution.

Narrator: The professor identifies three herbs used for plant-based medicine. Match each herb with its corresponding application. This is a 2-point question.

Narrator: 3. Listen then answer the question.

Prof: There are two types of cells: eukaryotic and prokaryotic. Prokaryote cells are simpler and smaller. They have three architectural regions: the exterior, consisting of projecting flagella and pili used for motion; the cell envelope, a plasma membrane giving the cell rigidity and serving as a protective filter, and the cytoplasmic region, a region that contains the genome condensed in a nucleoid. Eukaryotic cells are much larger than prokaryotic cells yet retain a similar structure. The major difference between the two cell types is that the interior of a eukaryotic cell is divided into membrane-bound compartments in which specific metabolic processes occur.

Narrator: The professor describes the parts of a prokaryote cell. Connect each part of a prokaryote cell with its corresponding function. This is a 2-point question.

Narrator: 4. Listen then answer the question.

Prof: In the fall, when a sockeye salmon is approximately five-years old, it leaves the Pacific Ocean, where it has grown to maturity, and returns to the home river where it was born. Once in the home river—how sockeye return to the river of their birth remains a mystery—the sockeye navigates upstream and spawns in shallow water, then dies. In a few months, between January and April, the eggs turn into alevin, a tiny fish with the yolk sack still attached. The alevin live off the yolk and grow into fry. After a period of growth, they will head downstream in late spring, making the transition from the fresh water of the home river to the salt water of the ocean as smolt. Once in the ocean, the smolt will grow into adults, then return to the home river in five years to begin the cycle all over again.

Narrator: The professor illustrates the life cycle of the sockeye salmon. Match each stage of the sockeye salmon's life cycle with a corresponding description of that stage. This is a 2-point question.

Professor-Students

Track #74 - Sample Discussion - Page 501

Narrator: Sample discussion. Professor-Students. Directions. Listen to a sample discussion, then answer the questions on the next page. Do not look at the questions. On test day, you will not see the questions as you listen. Remember to answer all the questions. You will not be penalized for a wrong answer. Now listen to part of a discussion in an environmental class.

Prof: Today, we're going to discuss a man-made problem that's impacting oceans worldwide, a problem with no solution in sight. That problem is right in front you. When you're finished with them, hopefully—as concerned and responsible citizens—you'll recycle so they won't end up on a Pacific island or a Cape Cod beach. Of course, you all know what I'm talking about: the ubiquitous polyethylene terephthalate. That said, let me begin by giving you a few eye-popping stats. Every year, Americans buy over 50 billion—yes, billion—bottles of water. That equates to 1,500 bottles consumed every second—every second. That number beggars the imagination. Of that number, eight out of ten end up in a landfill with the remaining twenty-percent recycled. And those numbers are only in America. What about the rest of the world? What about countries that can't afford to build expensive recycling plants? And what about all those bottles that are not recycled or dumped in landfills, in America and worldwide? Where does all that polyethylene terephthalate end up? Carol?

Carol: In the oceans.

Prof: Exactly. Can you elaborate on the homework?

Carol: Sure. According to the reading, there's this huge floating patch of garbage in the North Pacific. It's made up mostly of plastic bottles, but you can also find fish nets and micro pellets used for abrasive cleaning, plus all the stuff tossed off freighters and cruise ships. All this garbage is being swept along on what's called the North Pacific gyre.

Prof: Sorry, what exactly is that? A gyre?

Carol: It's the prevailing ocean current. In the North Pacific, the gyre moves west along the equator, then up past Japan to Alaska, then down the west coast of North America to the equator again. It's kind of like water spinning in a toilet bowl.

Prof: Good. So what's the connection between the North Pacific gyre and pelagic plastic?

Ann: Sorry, professor, what does pelagic mean again?

Prof: It means living or occurring at sea. The albatross, for example, is a pelagic bird. Carol?

Carol: Right, so where was I? Okay, so the stuff, I mean, you know, all that pelagic plastic, is swept along clockwise by the gyre. Eventually all that plastic junk finds its way into the center of the gyre and becomes stationary, you know, just sits there in an area called the Horse Latitudes, this area of calm in the center of the gyre. Years ago sailors would get trapped there due to a lack of wind and current. Today, it's basically one big, continuously-fed garbage dump in which pelagic plastic is the prevailing contaminant.

Prof: And it isn't going anywhere. In fact, it's spreading due to the decomposing nature of the contaminants themselves. Ann, can you jump in here and talk about the photodegradation process?

Ann: So when all this floating plastic is exposed to the sun, it begins to photodegrade until it reaches the molecular level. For example, take this book. Let's say it's floating in the center of the gyre, okay? The first thing to go are the covers, then the pages decompose freeing all the words. Next, the words break apart into letters. Finally, the ink in the letters photodecomposes into molecules. All that ends up in the gyre forming this thick, soupy liquid full of floating plastic particles that look like confetti.

Prof: A sea of confetti. That's a good way to put it. Beautiful, I'm sure, what with all that colored plastic floating around, but deadly. Very. All that particulate matter? It doesn't sink. Instead, it stays in the upper water column where it poses a significant threat to endemic wildlife. Pelagic birds, for example, consume the particulate matter mistaking it for food. They, in turn, feed it to their young who die of starvation or are poisoned by the toxic nature of polyethylene terephthalate. Other contaminants identified in the patch are PCB, DDT and PAH. When ingested, some of these toxins imitate estradiol which, as you know, is a naturally occurring estrogenic hormone secreted mainly by the ovaries. You can imagine the effect these toxins have on the reproduction systems of endemic species, such as whales. Fish too ingest the decomposed plastic and become contaminated.

Carol: Professor, is it possible to clean it up?

Prof: So far? No. The particulate matter is so small, you need extremely fine nets—micronets basically—to scoop it up. But even if we had such nets, remember, the North Pacific is vast. It would take an armada constantly going back and forth to even put a dent in all that plastic while at the same time, new plastic—tons of it—is entering the gyre every day. How many bottles of water do Americans drink every year?

Carol: Fifty billion.

Prof: Precisely. And that statistic is already out of date.

Ann: That's a lot of garbage.

Prof: It is. And the thing is, we don't even know how big the patch is. Satellites can't pick up the particulate matter because it's too small. Not only that but when you're parked in the middle of it on a boat or a ship, you can't see it. The particulate matter is that small. So, how big is the great North Pacific garbage patch? Well, some say it's the size of Texas. Others claim it's twice the size of the U.S. Big no matter how you cut it. Okay, so that's the North Pacific. Worldwide how many gyres are there?

Carol: Five.

Prof: So if the center of the North Pacific gyre is one huge, floating garbage dump, what does that tell us about the other four gyres?

Narrator: Now get ready to answer the questions. Answer each question based on what is stated or implied in the discussion.

1. What is the discussion mainly about?
2. What is the purpose of the discussion?

3. Why does the professor say this? 

Prof: That number beggars the imagination.

Narrator: 4. Which pelagic species does the professor mention? Select three. This is a 2-point question.

Narrator: 5. The professor describes how plastic becomes part of the eco-system. Put those steps in order. This is a 2-point question.

Narrator: 6. In the lecture, the professor describes the Horse Latitudes. Indicate whether each of the following is a characteristic of the Horse Latitudes. This is a 3-point question.

Track #75 - Practice: Discussion #1 - Page 516

Narrator: Practice. Discussion one. Directions. Listen to a sample discussion, then answer the questions on the next page. Do not look at the questions. On test day, you will not see the questions as you listen. Remember to answer all the questions. You will not be penalized for a wrong answer. Now listen to part of a discussion in a computer class.

Prof: Welcome everybody. Hope you had a good weekend. Today, we're going to start with Ann. Ann was assigned the task of researching malware. Ann? What did you come up with?

Ann: A lot, actually. I'm sure you all know what malware means, but just in case, malware is short for malicious software. It's software designed with the purpose of entering your computer without your permission. It's like somebody suddenly enters your house or apartment and starts checking the place out. By the way, if you have any questions, just stop me. Okay? Great. So where was I? Ah, right. Malware. Malware comes in all shapes and sizes. There are viruses, Trojan horses, spyware, adware, scareware. Most of it is spread by the internet. Here's a great fact I found. According to Symantec, there's more malware being released every year than legitimate software.

Prof: Ann, where did it all start?

Ann: You mean, what was the first piece of malware?

Prof: Yes. Were you able to find out?

Ann: I was. It was a virus, actually. Starting around 1949, computer scientists began writing about computer viruses and how they could reproduce like human viruses. The first computer virus, you know, the first real piece of code, didn't appear until 1972. That was the Creeper Virus.

Betty: 1972? Was the internet even around then?

Ann: No, it wasn't. Not as we know it. Back then they had something called ARPANET. That's short for Advanced Research Projects Agency Network. It all started during the Cold War in the 1950's. The U.S. military needed a way to make sure that its military computers stayed connected if attacked, so the government got all these guys from Harvard and MIT to design an interconnected information system. They did and called it ARPANET. ARPANET is basically the start of the internet as we know it. Anyway, a guy named Bob Thomas was working on ARPANET when he created the Creeper virus. He did it as an experiment to see if it would work, and it did. He sent it to computers on ARPANET and it started reproducing. However, it never left ARPANET and was harmless. Like I said, it was just an experiment. The first computer virus to appear outside a lab was the Elk Clone. It was created by Richard Skrenta in 1981. The Elk Clone attacked Apple computers.

Prof: Ann, how did it get on Apple computers in the first place?

Ann: By floppy disk. Back then, people shared them and that's how the Elk Clone spread. When it infected a computer, it would display a poem. Pretty tame, really. In1986, the first PC virus, the Brain, was created by the Farooq Alvi Brothers. And get this. They created it as a way of preventing the medical software they'd developed from being pirated. If you copied their software off the internet, or wherever, you'd get a warning saying something like, "Warning! You've just been infected. Call us for the vaccination."

Prof: So what's the difference between a virus and a Trojan horse?

Ann: A computer virus can reproduce just like, say, the flu virus. You know the flu virus is invading your body when you feel really sick. That's because the virus is overwhelming your body's defense system. It's the same with computer viruses. They reproduce and overwhelm the host computer. That's what happened to me once. I got a virus that made all the words on my screen melt.

Betty: How did you get it?

Ann: Probably on a flash drive. That's how a lot of viruses travel, by portable media.

Betty: So what did you do?

Ann: I had to reformat my hard drive and reload all my programs.

Betty: Drag.

Ann: Tell me about it. A Trojan horse, on the other hand, is a piece of malware designed not just to mess up your computer but to control it without your knowing it. Trojan horses often show up as legitimate links in emails. This tricks the user into opening the link just like the Trojan horse the Greeks used to trick the Trojans into opening Troy. And we all know what happened to the Trojans, don't we?

Prof: And once in a host computer, then what?

Ann: It can do any number of things, like start sending spam to everyone on your email list or downloading bank files and passwords.

Betty: So let me see if I've got this straight. A Trojan horse seeks to control or steal from a host computer whereas a virus simply disrupts or crashes a computer. Correct?

Ann: You got it.

Narrator: Now get ready to answer the questions. Answer each question based on what is stated or implied in the discussion.

1. What is the discussion mainly about?
2. What is the purpose of the discussion?
3. Why does the student say this? 

   Student: And we all know what happened to the Trojans, don't we?

4. The student describes the history of computer viruses. Put that history in order. This is a 2-point question.
5. In the discussion, the student describes Trojan horses and computer viruses. Identify the characteristics of each. This is a 3-point question.
6. Listen to part of the discussion, then answer the question. 

   Betty: So what did you do?
   Tom: I had to reformat my hard drive and reload all my programs.
   Betty: Drag.

Narrator: Why does the student say this?

Betty: Drag.

Track #76 - Practice: Discussion #2 - Page 519

Narrator: Practice. Discussion two. Directions. Listen to a sample discussion, then answer the questions on the next page. Do not look at the questions. On test day, you will not see the questions as you listen. Remember to answer all the questions. You will not be penalized for a wrong answer. Now listen to part of a discussion in a biology class.

Prof: Homeostasis. We talked about it last class. Before we push on, however, let's revisit what we know. Who wants to start us off? Linda?

Linda: In a nutshell, homeostasis is a process—a system-regulating process—that helps an organism maintain a stable internal environment or balance. That system can be either open or closed.

Prof: Good. Very succinct. Can you give us an example of a closed system?

Linda: A closed system? Ah, let's see. A computer network. And the Earth.

Prof: And what exactly is a system? Harold?

Harold: A system—all systems actually—is a series of interdependent parts forming an integrated whole with a common purpose.

Prof: So how is the Earth a closed system? How does that work? Linda?

Linda: Because, like you said, a system is closed if it has a definable border. For Earth, that definable border is the atmosphere dividing us from whatever's out there.

Prof: And what can pass through our atmosphere, the Earth's border, so to speak?

Linda: Only the sun's energy, you know, heat, which the Earth absorbs. As the Earth cools, it gives off heat. By doing so, the temperature of the Earth is maintained. It's just like the human body. To maintain a balance, we sweat to keep cool and shiver to keep warm. Also, with the Earth, mass cannot pass through the Earth's atmospheric border.

Prof: What do you mean by mass?

Linda: I mean, large objects. Solids. You also mentioned last class that a closed system is an isolated system, which is exactly what the Earth is. We're just floating around in space like a self-contained bubble protected by a border—the atmosphere—through which heat energy enters and leaves. This creates a balance which is what homeostasis is all about.

Prof: And within that balance, life, as we know it, exists. Excellent. As Linda said, homeostasis is all about a system maintaining a balance. The word homeostasis itself actually means *staying the same* or *in one place*, just like the Earth circling the sun, year in, year out, absorbing heat, losing heat. That, then, is what homeostasis is all about: balance. And there are—as I said last lecture—two ways a system can maintain homeostasis, by being either closed or open. Okay, so we've identified a closed system. What about an open one? Harold? You want to take the wheel?

Harold: Sure. An open system is one in which mass and energy can both cross a border. In doing so, they cross from one environment into the next, and back again. In other words, an open system, to be homeostatic, must be permeable. Countries, for example, are open systems. Well, most, anyway. Take us, for example, you know, the U.S. People and products—mass and energy—flow back and forth across our borders every day. The result is a stable, system-regulating process or society. Economists call this a steady-state economy.

Prof: Great. Can you give us a biological example?

Harold: The human body. To survive, to maintain homeostasis, we must constantly take in energy in the form of mass, you know, food. And when we're finished processing that food, that mass, we get rid of it to maintain the balance.

Prof: And the human body is also a closed system, right?

Harold Parts of it, yes.

Prof: For example?
Harold: The circulatory system. Blood is pumped from the heart through a series of veins and arteries, and back again. Objects with mass, like food, cannot permeate this system; however, energy, such as oxygen and carbon dioxide, come and go, as well nutrient-based energy that comes from digested food.
Linda: Professor, can we circle back to the Earth for a sec?
Prof: Sure.
Linda: What about meteors? Aren't they a kind of mass penetrating the Earth's atmospheric border? And wouldn't that then make the Earth an open system?
Prof: Good point. But no. Meteors burn up in the Earth's atmosphere long before they reach the Earth's surface. Of course, there is always the possibility that an asteroid will hit the Earth, such as the one that wiped out the dinosaurs 65 million years. It was so big, it failed to burn up. But those are few and far between. Also, it's important to remember that a system demonstrates homeostasis only when there is a balance. The asteroid that wiped out the dinosaurs is an excellent of how a mass penetrated the Earth's atmospheric border and destroyed that balance.

Narrator: Now get ready to answer the questions. Answer each question based on what is stated or implied in the discussion.

1. What is the topic of the discussion?
2. What is the purpose of the discussion?
3. According to the discussion, all systems have what?
4. Why does the professor say this? 

Prof: Good. Very succinct.

5. In the discussion, the following topics are mentioned. Identify which are open systems and which are closed systems. This is a 3-point question.
6. Listen to part of the discussion, then answer the question. 

Student: An open system is one in which mass and energy can both cross a border. In doing so, they cross from one environment into the next, and back again. In other words, an open system, to be homeostatic, must be permeable.

Narrator: Why does the student say this?

Student: In other words, an open system, to be homeostatic, must be permeable.

Listening Test

Task #1 - Track #77 - Page 522

Narrator: Listening test. Task one. Directions. Listen to a discussion in a business class, then answer the questions on the next page.

Prof: We recently talked about factors that can reduce a company's bottomline such as lawsuits, increased taxation, and loss due to natural events, such as hurricanes and earthquakes. Today we're going to look at another factor that can severely impact a company's bottomline. That issue is knock-offs. Now what do I mean by knock-off? Essentially a knock-off is a counterfeit product.

Joe: Professor, you mean like a fake?

Prof: Fake. Knock-off. Bogus. Counterfeit. Call it what you will. At the end of the day, it's all the same thing: a copy of an original, trademarked product or design illegally manufactured for sale and distribution. More importantly, a trademark is a government registered mark that gives a brand its unique identity. A couple of more famous trademarks are, Jill?

Jill: Nike's swoosh and, you know, what's that one? The two letters locked together? You see it on bags and belts. Dino...?

Prof: Dolce and Gabbana, the fashion designers. Very appealing. And very knocked off. Good. Ah, let's push on. Remember: a trademark is a unique mark or symbol that is protected by law. That means the full weight and protection of American law stands behind it. Copy that trademark, knock off some Nikes with the Nike symbol on them, and you're breaking the law. The country worst hit by knock-offs is the United States. Annually, the U.S. loses more than $200 billion dollars to foreign-made knock-offs. Now, what we commonly think of as knock-offs are watches and sunglasses, you know, the stuff you see on street, Fifth Avenue being a prime example of what I'm talking about.

Joe: Professor, why Fifth Avenue? Why sell knock-offs in such a pricey retail district? I could never figure that out.

Prof: That's a good question. Jill? What do you surmise?

Jill: My guess is that Fifth Avenue attracts a lot of tourists.

Prof: Right. So?

Jill: So a lot of them would love to buy something on Fifth Avenue, but things are not exactly cheap. Your average tourist is not about to shell out five hundred bucks for a Dolce-and-Gabbana belt when just down the street, a tout is selling a knock-off of the same thing for peanuts. The tourist isn't stupid. Who cares if that belt is fake? It looks real. And the price is definitely right.

Prof: So by being in the right place at the right time, the tout steps in to meet a need.

Jill: Right. Supply and demand, or in this case, demand and supply.

Prof: Sounds plausible. I like how you've inverted demand and supply. Of course, the touts could be there simply because there's less competition from other touts or fewer police. Whatever the reason, D-and-G takes a hit. How much is that knocked-off belt? Twenty bucks? And the original? Five hundred? A thousand? And accessories are just the tip of the iceberg. Knock-offs are having the greatest impact on which sector?

Jill: Pharmaceuticals.

Prof: Exactly. In fact, today's Wall Street Journal has a front page story on it. Did anyone read it?

Joe: Yeah. I did. Online.

Prof: Can you give us the gist?

Joe: Sure. According to the article, the U.S. population, ah, age 65 and older stands at 40 million or 2.9 percent of the current population. That's about one in every eight Americans. By 2030, that number will double to 80 million.

Prof: Why are these numbers significant?

Joe: Why? Because people over 65 need medication for everything from arthritis to cholesterol to cancer. The woman in the article is taking twenty different pills every day. Twenty!

Prof: So how does this connect with counterfeiting?

Joe: The problem is the cost. Let's say you're retired, like the woman in the article. You have a fixed monthly income of one thousand dollars. Out of that one thousand you must pay for rent and bills and food. You're also taking a variety of medications, some of which cost a hundred bucks a pop. When you add it up, many retired people can't pay for such expensive medication, especially if you're taking twenty pills a day. So what do you do? They end up buying knock-offs.

Jill: Which is good. So why is fake pharma so bad? If those pills are saving retired people money, what's the harm in that?

Joe: The problem is there's no government oversight or quality control on the manufacturing side. As a result, a knock-off manufacturer can simply fill capsules with sugar, put a name like Pfizer or Bayer on them, and the customer thinks they're getting the real deal when they're not.

Prof: That's exactly it. So let's bring it full circle. How does all this impact the bottomline? Jill?

Jill: Knock-offs hurt the bottomline for myriad reasons. First off, companies can lose the incentive to innovate.

Prof: How so? Joe?

Joe: Well, if I'm a drug company, and my products are continually being ripped off, then what's the point in developing new products if I know I'll lose money in the long run? Also, the more my products are knocked off, the more people will begin to suspect my products, particularly the quality. This, in turn, will result in a significant loss of brand equity.

Prof: Anything else?

Jill: If I manufacture drugs, I can lose significant market share to knock-offs that are chemically the same as the drugs I'm producing. The consumer is not stupid. Word gets around. They know what works and what doesn't. If a knock-off sells for fifty bucks, and the original sells for two hundred, it's pretty obviously which one I'm going to buy.

Prof: Even at the risk of your health?

Jill: What value is my health when expensive brand-name drugs are putting me in the poor house?

Prof: Good way to put it. Now let's be clear. Companies are indeed willing to protect their brand equity by taking their cases to court. One such case was Tiffany vs. eBay. Keith, summarize the Tiffany case for us, will you?

Narrator: Now get ready to answer the questions. Answer each question based on what is stated or implied in the discussion.

1. What is the discussion mainly about?
2. What is the point of the discussion?

3. Why does the professor say this? 

Prof: And accessories are just the tip of the iceberg.

4. How can knock-offs hurt a company? Select three. This is a 2-point question.

5. From the discussion, we can infer that "touts" on Fifth Avenue are...

6. According to the discussion, what is true about knock-offs? This is a 3-point question.

Task Two - Track #78 - Page 525

Narrator: Listening test. Task two. Directions. Listen as a student talks to a professor, then answer the questions on the next page.

Student: Professor Huston?

Prof: Jill, hi. Come in. I got your email. Thanks. Your presentation is on...

Student: Havaiannas.
Prof: Right. Those famous Brazilian flip flops.
Student: Do you have a pair?
Prof: No. But my daughter has three. She practically lives in them. Right, so how can I help you? In your email, you mentioned you needed help with your presentation. Let me just pull it up here so I can jog my memory.
Student: I don't need help so much as clarification. I understand we have to pick a product and do a ten-minute presentation on it.
Prof: Correct.
Student: But I'm not sure why we can't use PowerPoint. Isn't PowerPoint, you know...
Prof: An integral part of a business presentation? You would think. I mean, how can you give a presentation these days and not use PowerPoint, right?
Student: That's pretty much my thinking.
Prof: Well, since this is your first presentation—I'm assuming it is—I want you to focus on the basics of speaking before an audience and not just flip through a bunch of PowerPoint slides. That's what presenters often do, so much so that PowerPoint takes over. It becomes the presentation while the presenter fades into the background. Not a good thing. As a result, the presentation turns into a slide show with the presenter simply reading bullet points off a screen. At that point, you lose control of your audience. If you lose control, you're no longer in a position to persuade your audience to buy whatever it is you're selling.
Student: And it could get pretty boring, just reading slides.
Prof: Very. Your audience will start checking their cell phones, start yawning, even walk out. Remember: you are pitching your product with the purpose of persuading your audience that your product will change their lives.
Student: I see. So it's all about me being up front and center persuading an audience.
Prof: Bingo. And the way to persuade an audience is to be continually in contact with them. That means making constant eye contact. Body language is critical too. Were you in class when I handed out the guidelines for the presentation?
Student: Yes, I got them. Thanks. In the hand out, you said we could bring a product sample. Now, I don't want to beat a dead horse, but wouldn't it be easier to just take a photo of the product and make a PowerPoint slide?
Prof: Like I said, you've got to walk before you can run. Walking means learning the basics of a good presentation, and a good presentation is all about using personality to persuade. Believe me, some of the best presentations I've seen have not used PowerPoint. That said, I will allow a product sample. Just one.
Student: Got it. Product sample. No PowerPoint.
Prof: Good. Anything else?
Student: What if I get nervous? What if I just, you know, blank out.
Prof: Don't worry. There are ways to handle nerves. Take a look at this other handout.
Student: Thanks. We will eventually use PowerPoint?
Prof: Ah, yeah. Next semester. But even then, the point to remember is this: PowerPoint is not the presentation. It is simply a support tool.

Narrator: Now get ready to answer the questions. Answer each question based on what is stated or implied in the conversation.

1. What is the topic of the conversation?
2. Why does the student visit the professor?

3. Why does the professor say this? 🎧

Prof: PowerPoint is not the presentation. It is simply a support tool.

4. According to the professor, what will an audience do if the presenter loses control of a presentation? Select three. This is a 2-point question.

5. Listen again to part of the conversation, then answer the question. 

Prof: Like I said, you've got to walk before you can run. Walking means learning the basics of a good presentation, and a good presentation is all about using personality to persuade. Believe me, some of the best presentations I've seen have not used PowerPoint. That said, I will allow a product sample. Just one.

Narrator: What does the professor imply when he says this?

Prof: Like I said, you've got to walk before you can run.

Task Three - Track #79 - Page 527

Narrator: Listening test. Task three. Directions. Listen to a lecture in an economics history class, then answer the questions.

Prof: 1 ➔ Adam Smith was born in Scotland in 1723. As a young man, he studied moral philosophy at the University of Glasgow and at Oxford. He eventually went on to tutor a nobleman's son. The position freed Smith from his daily work while affording him the opportunity to tutor while traveling throughout Europe. In France, Smith met Rousseau and Voltaire, leading proponents of the European Enlightenment. At its core, the European Enlightenment, guided by reason and science, questioned customs, morals, and traditional institutions, namely monarchies.

2 ➔ Returning to Scotland, Smith set about writing his seminal *An Inquiry into the Nature and Causes of the Wealth of Nations.* In it, Smith argues that building national economic wealth begins with a division of labor. Smith supports his argument by using a pin factory. In a typical pin factory of the day, each worker was responsible for making pins from start to finish. A worker would start by cutting the pin to size from a piece of wire, then straighten it, then sharpen the end, affix a head, polish it, then package it. In short, one man was responsible for each step of the pin-making process. Smith argued that such an approach was not only counter-productive but also time consuming inasmuch as once a worker finished one part of the task—say polishing a pin—he would pause before moving onto the next task. Such an approach, Smith argued, was inefficient, for workers were likely to "saunter" or pause between steps, which wasted time and substantially reduced productivity. Smith argued that the most efficient way to make pins was through a division of labor. Instead of ten men each separately making a pin from start to finish, each would be assigned one task, for example, one man would sharpen pins all day, another would polish them while a third would package them, and so on. By dividing labor this way, Smith theorized that the production of pins would dramatically increase. As a result, there would be more pins to sell and thus more money to be made. Smith's scientific approach to rationalizing the manufacturing process for greater productivity was indeed the product of Enlightenment thought.

3 ➔ A division of labor, however, was but one part of Smith's argument for creating wealth. An integral part of the wealth-making process, Smith claims, is the pin worker himself. He is performing a task not for society's benefit nor for the benefit of the company, but for his own personal gain and security. The same follows with the owner of the pin factory. He too is out for personal gain, the health and wealth of the nation the least of his, and his workers', worries.

Yet by pursuing individual gain, Smith argues that the worker and the factory owner are, in fact, directly adding to the wealth of the nation by utilizing a more efficient manufacturing process, one which stimulates trade, the buying and selling of goods, locally, nationally, and internationally. Smith coined this process "the invisible hand."

4 ➔ *The Wealth of Nations* is very much a reaction to the predominating economic theory of the day, that of Mercantilism. Mercantilists posited that the wealth of a nation depended on developing and maintaining national power thus it was a form of economic nationalism. Spain, at the time of Columbus, is a prime example of just such a nation. A nation like Spain preserved national power by accumulating as much gold as possible through strong exports, the limitation of imports, and a large population of poorly paid workers. To develop exports, companies were subsided by the government, which also wrote laws to limit imports. By limiting imports, the gold used to pay for imports would stay in the country and create a greater money supply and more credit. Nations, such as Spain, England and Holland were geared toward acquiring and maintaining gold at all costs, including warring with each other. Witness England and Holland battling for control of today's Manhattan in the early 1600's. Adam Smith, however, argued that free trade benefitted all nations and that gold was not equal to wealth. Gold, Smith said, was like any other commodity, such as wheat or wool, and that it deserved no special treatment. More importantly, Smith says that the wealth of a nation is not based on the hoarding of gold, but on the free flow of goods manufactured in a systematic way, a way that serves the needs of the individual and, ultimately, the nation as a whole. With that, Adam Smith gave birth to what we now call economic theory. As Thomas Edison is to the light bulb, Adam Smith is to the science of economics.

<u>Narrator</u>: Now get ready to answer the questions. Answer each question based on what is stated or implied in the lecture.

1. What is the topic of the lecture?
2. What is the purpose of the lecture?
3. Why does the professor say this? 

<u>Prof</u>: As Thomas Edison is to the light bulb, Adam Smith is to the science of economics.

4. From the lecture, we can infer that Smith considered mercantilism to be...
5. The professor describes how Adam Smith's idea of "the invisible hand" works. Put these steps in order. This is a 2-point question.
6. The professor develops three topics. Match each topic with its corresponding description. This is a 2-point question.

Task Four - Track #80 - Page 530

<u>Narrator</u>: Listening test. Task four. Directions. Listen to a lecture in an American literature class, then answer the questions on the next page.

<u>Prof</u>: 1 ➔ *The Black Mask*, a 128-page illustrated pulp fiction magazine, first hit the newsstands in 1920. Like all pulp magazines, *The Black Mask* was formula writing at its very best or, more often than not, its very worst. But then in May of 1923, a story appeared in *The Black Mask* that would forever change pulp

fiction and American culture as a whole. That story was Carroll John Daly's crime novelette *Three Gun Terry*. In the annals of detective fiction, *Three Gun Terry* is indeed a first. Why? Because Terry Mack, the hero of the story, is "the world's first hard-boiled private detective."

2 ➔ With the publication of *Three Gun Terry*, subscriptions to *The Black Mask* soared. Terry Mack was a hit. Then, in October, 1923, six months after the publication of *Three Gun Terry, The Black Mask* published a crime story by an aspiring writer named Peter Collinson. The title was *Arson Plus*. The hero was a nameless private-eye who worked for the Continental Detective Agency. In time, the hero of *Arson Plus* would come to be known as the Continental Operative or simply "the Op." *Arson Plus* was so popular Collinson decided to put his real name on subsequent *Black Mask* stories. That name was Dashiell Hammett, a name that would, over time, relegate Carroll John Daly and his seminal *Three Gun Terry* to literary obscurity. Therein lies the question: Whatever happened to *Three Gun Terry*? Moreover, why has Carroll John Daly, a writer whom critics acknowledge as being the originator of an American literary icon—the hard-boiled private-eye—why has his name fallen off the map while Dashiell Hammett went on to receive most of the credit for creating the genre of writing called hard-boiled crime fiction? That is the question we will try to answer in this lecture.

3 ➔ Carroll John Daly was born in Yonkers, New York in 1889. After high school, he attended the American Academy of Dramatic Arts. He went on to run a movie theater in Atlantic City. In May, 1923, when *The Black Mask* published *Three Gun Terry*, Daly was thirty-three and living as a recluse in White Plains, a suburb of New York City. Why was Daly a recluse? Nobody knows. But we do know this: rarely, if ever, did he venture into Manhattan, the setting for *Three Gun Terry*. Once Daly did make the trip into the city. When he returned home, so the story goes, he couldn't find his house. A neighbor had to point it out to him. Once, for the sake of research, Daly decided maybe he should get to know what it was like to handle a gun. Daly bought a gun only to be arrested for carrying a concealed weapon. As one friend observed, "That was the end of Carroll John Daly's research."

4 ➔ Samuel Dashiell Hammett was born in 1894 on a farm in Maryland. At fourteen, guided by "a rebellious temperament," he dropped out of school and went to work for the railroad. In 1915, at the age of twenty-one, he joined the Pinkerton Detective Agency. As a Pinkerton operative, or "Op," Hammett saw everything from "petty theft to murder." In 1918, Hammett left Pinkerton's, joined the army and contracted influenza. Soon after he developed tuberculosis. He left the army and went back to Pinkerton's but poor health forced him to resign. In 1922, weakened by disease and in need of work, Hammett, encouraged by a friend, turned to writing.

5 ➔ As aspiring crime writers, Daly and Hammett couldn't have been more different. By 1923, Hammett had been around the block and then some, whereas Daly never left his house. Yet it was Daly who wrote *Three Gun Terry*, a shocking crime novelette that introduced Terry Mack, the world's first hard-boiled private-eye.

Narrator: Now get ready to answer the questions. Answer each question based on what is stated or implied in the lecture.

1. What does the lecture mainly focus on?
2. What is mentioned about *The Black Mask*? Select three. This is a 2-point question.
3. According to the lecture, what was Peter Collinson's real name?
4. Why does the professor say this? 

Prof: By 1923, Hammett had been around the block and then some whereas Daly never left his house.

5. The professor describes the life of Carroll John Daly. Put Daly's early life in the correct order. This is a 2-point question.

6. The professor mentions three dates. Match each date to the corresponding event. This is a 2-point question.

Task Five - Track #81 - Page 533

Narrator: Listening test. Task five. Directions. Listen to a lecture in a law class, then answer the questions on the next page.

Prof: 1 ➔ In January, 2010, the Supreme Court of the United States ruled on the case the U.S. Supreme Court vs. the Federal Elections Commission. In this landmark ruling, the bitterly-divided Court ruled 5-4 that corporations enjoy the same First Amendment rights as do individuals. In other words, a corporation, no matter what the size, is considered a citizen. Microsoft. General Electric. Exxon. In the eyes of the Supreme Court, they are all citizens—individuals—thus legally entitled to protection under the Constitution. That protection includes the right to free speech. Suffice it to say, the ruling set off a firestorm of protest. But before we get to that, let's map out how this landmark ruling came about.

2 ➔ In 2004, Oscar-winning documentary filmmaker Michael Moore released *Fahrenheit 911*, a scathing indictment of how then Republican President George W. Bush failed to act during the 9/11 crisis. In Moore's film, Bush comes off looking like a man entirely unsuited to be president. In short, Moore argues that President Bush failed in a time of national crisis. The Republicans were furious. Not to be outdone, David Bossie, a veteran Republican strategist, made a film attacking Democrat Hillary Clinton, who was then starting her run for president. But the movie, titled *Hillary: The Movie*, barely appeared on the radar during the 2008 presidential primary season. Why? Because the Federal Elections Commission restricted Bossie's film from being shown. The decision to restrict the film was based on the fact that the film was made not by David Bossie himself, as an individual, but by a corporation. That corporation was Citizens United. A lower court ruled that *Hillary: The Movie* wasn't a movie at all, but instead a 90-minute attack ad telling voters not to vote for Hillary Clinton. In that light, the lower court ruled that under the current campaign rules established by the Federal Elections Commission, Citizens United—being a legal corporate entity—was prohibited from financing political commercials. Basically, the Federal Elections Commission said corporate money has no place in American politics. What did David Bossie do? He turned around and sued the Federal Elections Commission, the argument being that Citizens United was being denied the right to free speech. In January, 2010, the Supreme Court agreed with Bossie's argument and overruled the lower court's decision. In delivering its ruling, the Supreme Court said, and I quote, *"Political spending is a form of protected speech under the First Amendment, and the government may not keep corporations or unions from spending money to support or denounce individual candidates in elections."* It doesn't get much clearer than that.

3 ➔ Now, you may wonder, why is this such a big deal? Why has this decision sent shock waves through the American political system? Think of it this way: the Supreme Court says that if the Ford Motor Company wants to donate a billion dollars to help elect a candidate—a candidate who will help Ford move its factories overseas—then Ford, as an individual, has every right to do so. Those

opposed to the decision say that this is patently unfair. Corporate money, they argue, will go directly into political advertising which, in turn, will give an unfair advantage to corporate-sponsored candidates. For example, imagine you are a school teacher and you decide to run for Congress and your opponent is funded by IBM, or Google even. In short, those who oppose corporate political funding fear that the American political system is no longer based on the one person, one vote proposition. Instead, elections will simply be bought by the candidate who has the most money, namely, corporate money. And smoke is already on the horizon.

4 ➔ Recently it has been revealed that the American Chamber of Commerce—the largest association of businesses in America, representing every type of business from Microsoft down to your local gas station owner—has been soliciting money from foreign corporations with U.S. operations, money which is finding its way into the American political system regardless of what members of the Chamber of Commerce might think. Let's examine the evidence.

<u>Narrator</u>: Now get ready to answer the questions. Answer each question based on what is stated or implied in the lecture.

1. What is the lecture mainly about?
2. What does the professor say about *Hillary: The Movie*?
3. Why does the professor say this? 

<u>Prof</u>: And smoke is already on the horizon.

4. The professor mentions Ford. Why?
5. Listen again to part of the lecture, then answer the question.

<u>Prof</u>: The Republicans were furious. Not to be outdone, David Bossie, a veteran Republican strategist, made a film attacking Democrat Hillary Clinton, who was then starting her run for president. But the movie, titled *Hillary: The Movie*, barely appeared on the radar during the 2008 presidential primary season.

<u>Narrator</u>: What does the professor mean when she says this?

<u>Prof</u>: But the movie, titled *Hillary: The Movie*, barely appeared on the radar during the 2008 presidential primary season.

6. According to the professor, how has the Supreme Court's decision changed the political landscape? This is a 3-point answer.

Task Six - Track #82 - Page 536

<u>Narrator</u>: Listening test. Task six. Directions. Listen as a student talks to a campus employee, then answer the questions on the next page.

<u>Student</u>: Hi. Can you help me?
<u>Admin</u>: Sure. What's up?
<u>Student</u>: I'm having trouble downloading my e-text on this terminal here. I keep entering my information, you know, student ID, password, and the thing keeps denying me access.

Admin: We're still working the kinks out of the system, I'm afraid. They just installed these terminals last week.
Student: Do the other campus bookstores have e-book terminals?
Admin: No. We're the first. Let's try this again. You got your credit card?
Student: Yes.
Admin: Okay, insert it and let's see what happens. Ah, so there's the home screen. Enter your name and password.
Student: Okay. See? It always denies my password and it spits out my card.
Admin: Which one are you using?
Student: Which one what?
Admin: Which password are you using?
Student: The one I always use when I log onto the school's system.
Admin: That's the problem. This system does not recognize Campus Net passwords.
Student: Why not?
Admin: For security.
Student: So I have to create a new password? Is that it?
Admin: Didn't you get the email outlining all this?
Student: There was an email?
Admin: Like I said, we're still working the kinks out of the system. Let's try it again. We'll go to the home screen. Now enter your new password in this box here. Make sure it's case sensitive and alphanumeric, at least eight characters.
Student: Okay.
Admin: Now hit enter. There you go. There's the course page. The required texts are listed by title in the sidebar here. Choose the one you need.
Student: Done.
Admin: Now enter your credit card and hit enter.
Student: Can I pay cash instead?
Admin: Sure. Just slip the bills into the slot here and you should be good to go.
Student: Thanks. Ah...Excuse me?
Admin: Ah, yes?
Student: Why isn't it giving me change? I put in four twenties. I should get $5.73 back.
Admin: That's strange. It was working fine this morning.
Student: Look, I got a class. I really need to get going. Can you just give me my change from the cash register?
Admin: Sorry.
Student: Why not?
Admin: Like I said, these terminals are not on the school's network. They're hooked up to the vendor's system till we get the kinks worked out. I'm going to have to call the vendor and have someone come look at it.
Student: What about my change?
Admin: You'll have to settle that with the vendor.
Student: Great. I prefer the old system. All I had to do was grab a book off a shelf and pay for it.
Admin: You'd be surprised how many say that.

Narrator: Now get ready to answer the questions. Answer each question based on what was stated or implied in the conversation.

1. What does the conversation focus on?
2. From the conversation, we can infer that the student...
3. What must the student's new e-book password be? Select three. This is a 2-point question.

4. What can be inferred when the employee says this? 

<u>Prof</u>: Like I said, we're still working the kinks out of the system. Let's try that again.

5. Listen again to part of the lecture, then answer the question.

<u>Student</u>: So I have to create a new password? Is that it?
<u>Admin</u>: Didn't you get the email outlining all this?
<u>Student</u>: There was an email?

<u>Narrator</u>: Why does the student say this?

<u>Student</u>: There was an email?

Independent Essay Ratings

Agree-Disagree Prompts

Zoo Essay - range score: 4.0-5.0

TV Essay - range score: 4.0-5.0

Preference Prompt

Laptop vs. Desktop Essay - range score: 4.0-5.0

Organization	deduction	√
	induction	
Progression	general-specific	√
	specific-general	
Development	introduction	X
	body	√
	conclusion	X
Unity	topical	√
	grammatical	√
Language Use	word choice	√
	idioms	X
	sentence variety	√

Note: The check sign (√) means *proficient*; the **X** means *lacks proficiency*.

Compare-Contrast Prompt

1. New Delhi Essay - range score: 4.0-5.0

Organization	deduction	√
	induction	
Progression	general-specific	√
	specific-general	
Development	introduction	X
	body	√
	conclusion	X
Unity	topical	√
	grammatical	√
Language Use	word choice	√
	idioms	X
	sentence variety	√

2. Eating-Out Essay - range score: 4.0-5.0

Organization	deduction	√
	induction	
Progression	general-specific	√
	specific-general	
Development	introduction	**X**
	body	√
	conclusion	**X**
Unity	topical	√
	grammatical	√
Language Use	word choice	√
	idioms	**X**
	sentence variety	√

Advantage-Disadvantage Prompt

Owning-a-Car Essay - range score: 2.5-3.0

Organization	deduction	√
	induction	
Progression	general-specific	√
	specific-general	
Development	introduction	**X**
	body	**X**
	conclusion	**X**
Unity	topical	**X**
	grammatical	**X**
Language Use	word choice	**X**
	idioms	**X**
	sentence variety	**X**

Advantage Prompt

Telecommuting Essay - range score: 4.0-5.0

Organization	deduction	√
	induction	
Progression	general-specific	√
	specific-general	
Development	introduction	X
	body	√
	conclusion	X
Unity	topical	√
	grammatical	√
Language Use	word choice	√
	idioms	√
	sentence variety	√

Disadvantage Prompt

Online Education Essay - range score: 2.5-3.5

Organization	deduction	√
	induction	
Progression	general-specific	√
	specific-general	
Development	introduction	X
	body	X
	conclusion	X
Unity	topical	√
	grammatical	√
Language Use	word choice	√
	idioms	X
	sentence variety	√

Reason Prompts

1. Technology Essay (internet) - range score: 4.0-5.0

Organization	deduction	√
	induction	
Progression	general-specific	√
	specific-general	
Development	introduction	X
	body	√
	conclusion	X
Unity	topical	√
	grammatical	√
Language Use	word choice	√
	idioms	√
	sentence variety	√

2. Travel Essay - range score: 2-5-3.5

Organization	deduction	√
	induction	
Progression	general-specific	√
	specific-general	
Development	introduction	X
	body	X
	conclusion	X
Unity	topical	X
	grammatical	X
Language Use	word choice	X
	idioms	X
	sentence variety	X

3. Change-the-World Essay - range score: 1.0-2.0

Organization	deduction	X
	induction	X
Progression	general-specific	X
	specific-general	X
Development	introduction	X
	body	X
	conclusion	X
Unity	topical	X
	grammatical	X
Language Use	word choice	X
	idioms	X
	sentence variety	X

4. Technology Essay - range score: 4.0-5.0

Organization	deduction	
	induction	√
Progression	general-specific	
	specific-general	√
Development	introduction	X
	body	√
	conclusion	X
Unity	topical	√
	grammatical	√
Language Use	word choice	√
	idioms	√
	sentence variety	√

Quality Prompt

Shelton University Essay - range score: 4.0-5.0

Organization	deduction	√
	induction	
Progression	general-specific	√
	specific-general	
Development	introduction	**X**
	body	√
	conclusion	**X**
Unity	topical	√
	grammatical	√
Language Use	word choice	√
	idioms	√
	sentence variety	√

Advanced Independent Essays

1. Agree-Disagree Prompt
   - range score: 4.0-5.0
2. Preference Prompt
   - range score: 4.0-5.0
3. Compare-Contrast Prompt
   - range score: 4.0-5.0
4. Advantage-Disadvantage Prompt
   - range score: 4.0-5.0
5. Advantage Prompt
   - range score: 4.0-5.0
6. Disadvantage Prompt
   - range score: 4.0-5.0
7. Reason Prompt
   - range score: 4.0-5.0
8. Quality Prompt
   - range score: 4.0-5.0

Integrated Essay Ratings

Argument-Counter Argument Essay

1. Zoo Essay - range score: 4.0-5.0

Organization	point-by-point	√
	block	
Progression	general-specific	√
	specific-general	
Development-Summarization	introduction	√
	body	√
	conclusion	√
Unity-Synthesis	topical	√
	grammatical	√
Language Use-Paraphrasing	word choice	√
	idioms	X
	sentence variety	√

Show-Support Essay

Animal Behavior Essay - range score: 4.0-5.0

Organization	point-by-point	
	block	√
Progression	general-specific	√
	specific-general	
Development-Summarization	introduction	√
	body	√
	conclusion	√
Unity-Synthesis	topical	√
	grammatical	√
Language Use-Paraphrasing	word choice	√
	idioms	X
	sentence variety	√

Speaking Task Ratings

Speaking Task #1

1. Travel-and-Learning Prompt
   - range score: 3.5-4.0

2. Work-and-High-School Prompt
   - range score: 3.5-4.0

3. People-Living-Longer Prompt: range score: 3.5-4.0

Organization	deduction	√
	induction	
Progression	general-specific	√
	specific-general	
Development	introduction	√
	body	√
	conclusion	√
Unity	topical	√
	grammatical	√
Language Use	word choice	√
	idioms	X
	sentence variety	√
Delivery	fluency	√
	automaticity	√
	pronunciation	√

1. Technology Prompt (car) - range score: 3.5-4.0

Organization	deduction	√
	induction	
Progression	general-specific	√
	specific-general	
Development	introduction	√
	body	√
	conclusion	√
Unity	topical	√
	grammatical	√
Language Use	word choice	√
	idioms	X
	sentence variety	√
Delivery	fluency	√
	automaticity	√
	pronunciation	√

Speaking Task Two

1. Exercising Prompt
   - range score: 3.5-4.0

2. Airport Prompt
   - range score: 3.5-4.0

3. Cook-or-Ready-to-Eat-Meals Prompt
   - range score: 3.5-4.0

4. Shopping Prompt
   - range score: 3.5-4.0

4. Homeschooling Prompt
   - range score: 3.5-4.0

Speaking Task Three

1. Organic-Food-Policy Prompt
   - range score: 3.5-4.0

Speaking Task Four

1. Animal Behavior Prompt
   - range score: 3.5-4.0

Speaking Task Five

1. Professor-Forgets Prompt
   - range score: 3.5-4.0

Speaking Task Six

1. Animal Behavior
   - range score: 3.5-4.0

Also by *Bruce Stirling*

Speaking and Writing Strategies for the TOEFL® iBT
Nova Press, Los Angeles, USA

Speaking and Writing Strategies for the TOEFL® iBT
Chinese version published by
Foreign Language Teaching and Research Press
Beijing, China

Speaking and Writing Strategies for the TOEFL® iBT
published by Prakash Books, New Delhi, India
available at uRead.com

500 Words, Phrases and Idioms for the TOEFL® iBT
plus Typing Strategies
Nova Press, Los Angeles, USA

Practice Tests for the TOEFL® iBT
Nova Press, Los Angeles, USA

Got a TOEFL® question? Ask Bruce Stirling

Visit TOEFL® Pro on facebook

and at

www.toeflpro.blogspot.com

Acknowledgements

For their editorial insights and suggestions, the author would like to thank Patricia Stirling, Kateryna Kucher, Cora Van Laer, Martina Sulakova, Gretchen Anderson, Yosra Ben Chikh Brahim, and Jeff Kolby at Nova Press.

For their contributions to the audio CD, the author would like to thank Patricia Stirling, Gretchen Anderson, Jennie Farnell, Bill and Liz Foster, Ami Kothari, and Jon Conine.